AME ENGAGE™

Welcome to the fully integrated and interactive online learning hub for
Introduction to Accounting: Concepts and Applications, V1.0

Online & Interactive

AME Learning's integrated and interactive online learning hub, AME Engage™, contextualizes the study of accounting in a practical, hands-on online learning environment. Designed to personalize the learning experience and engage students *before* class, our multi-sensory online tutorials guide students through the key accounting concepts for each chapter. These tutorials help students to *learn by doing,* using a variety of effective learning tools ranging from gaming to interactive problem solving.

In order to encourage students to truly understand the concepts rather than simply rely on memorization, AME Engage™ features randomized algorithmic homework questions, allowing students to practice the same concept repeatedly at their own leisure. The "Take me to the text" online homework feature links each question to the relevant examples in the digital textbook, immediately providing students the help they need at any time and from anywhere. Instructors have full control over all resources in AME Engage™, and can therefore effectively tailor their online environment according to their own teaching style.

Unique PIN Code

If you purchased this book brand-new, the PIN Card (image to the right) is attached to the front cover. Open this to get your unique **PIN Code**, then follow the instructions to log in to AME Engage™.

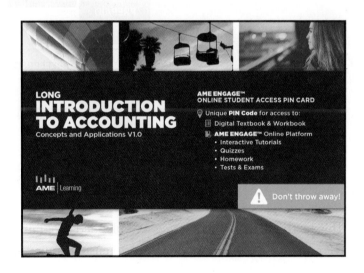

Don't have a PIN Card?

If you **did not** purchase this book brand-new, you will need to purchase your unique PIN Code at www.amelearning.com/store or contact your campus bookstore.

Instructor looking for access?

Please contact your AME Learning or Paradigm Education Solutions representative.

The AME Approach to Learning Accounting

AME utilizes a unique method to simplify accounting concepts, using step-by-step logic to ensure that the subject is extremely easy to understand. Accounting concepts are communicated using straightforward language and AME Accounting Maps™ that make potentially complex transactions simpler and easier to follow.

The AME Accounting Map™ is used throughout the textbook to show the impact of transactions on the financial statements. It is a visual representation of the balance sheet and income statement. The Accounting Map™ is also used in our interactive tutorials. Increases and decreases in values of specific items are clearly shown on the Map without needing to resort to technical accounting terminology.

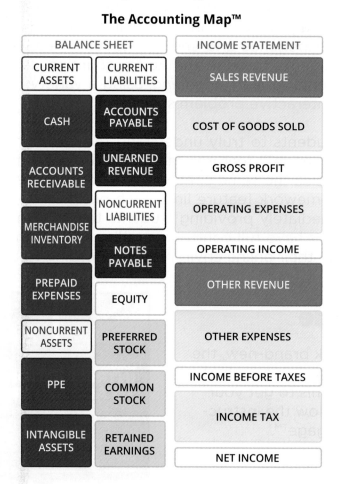

The Accounting Map™

This textbook is part of a larger and blended program that is being used to teach the course. As an instructor, it is recommended to follow these steps to ensure your students get the most out of the program.

1. Encourage students to use the interactive online tutorials before attending each class.

2. Use the PowerPoint™ presentations to provide visuals to assist with teaching the material.

3. Online quizzes are available to test student's comprehension of the material. Quizzes can be used either before or after class.

4. Online post-class homework questions are available to test student's ability to complete accounting problems. These should be used after class.

INTRODUCTION TO ACCOUNTING
CONCEPTS AND APPLICATIONS
V1.0

Lead Authors
Suzanne K. Long, CPA, MBA, MAED
Neville Joffe
Penny Parker, CPA, CGA, MBA

Contributors and Reviewers

Ronnie Carter, CPA
Patrick Henry Community College

Suryakant Desai, Ed.D., CPA, CFP
Dallas County Community College District

Cathy Duffy, Ed.D., M.Sc., B.Sc.
Champlain College

Dr. Regan Garey, D.B.A., M.B.A., B.S., B.A.
Lock Haven University

Sharon O'Reilly, M.B.A., B.A.
Gateway Technical College

Textbook ISBN: 978-1-926751-86-3
Workbook ISBN: 978-1-926751-87-0

Introduction to Accounting: Concepts and Principles, V1.0
Authors: Suzanne K. Long/Neville Joffe/Penny Parker
Publisher: AME Learning Inc.
Content Contributors and Developmental Editors:
        Graeme Gomes/Kobboon Chotruangprasert/Vicki Austin
Production Editors: Graeme Gomes/Lisa McManus/Melody Yousefian
Copy Editor: Lisa McManus
Indexer: Elizabeth Walker
Typesetter: Paragon Prepress Inc.
Vice President and Publishing Manager: Linda Zhang
Cover Design: Pixon Design
Online Course Design & Production: AME Multimedia Team

2 3 4 MCRL 20 19 18

Printed in China

This book is written to provide accurate information on the covered topics.
It is not meant to take the place of professional advice.

For more information contact:

AME Learning Inc.
410-1220 Sheppard Avenue East
Toronto, ON, Canada M2K 2S5
Phone: 416.479.0200
Toll-free: 1.888.401.3881
E-mail: info@amelearning.com
Visit our website at: www.amelearning.com

About the Author

Suzanne K. Long has been teaching at Jackson (Community) College since 2001. Additional teaching assignments include Hillsdale College, Western Michigan University, Davenport University and Kellogg Community College.

She is a licensed CPA in the State of Michigan with past professional experience at Plante Moran CPA's.

Suzanne started her education at Hillsdale College in southern Michigan, earning a bachelor's degree in accounting. After working and teaching for several years, she completed an MBA from Western Michigan University.

Years of teaching led to a desire to understand students and the learning process, and she completed an MAED from Michigan State University with a focus on higher education.

Suzanne is an NISOD (National Institute for Staff and Organizational Development) Teaching Award recipient and a member of the MICPA (Michigan Association of CPAs) and TACTYC (Teachers of Accounting at Two Year Colleges).

Suzanne is also an active white belt Nia dance instructor, life enthusiast, loving mother and wife.

A Note from the Author

Consider what brings you to this point in life. You are pursuing academic goals that tie to your career goals. All of this translates to a better life for you.

Develop Yourself

By learning accounting, you are developing your professional skills. Imagine three legs of a barstool. All three are needed for the stool to be of any use. Similarly, you need an array of business skills to be successful in your career. You need people skills. Think communication, relationships and leadership training. You need technical skills. Think of those skills specific to your field and your area of expertise. You need accounting and business skills. Think accounting, management and finance training. Throughout your career, you will grow and develop. Your accounting skills will be one critical element in your array of business skills as you self-actualize and become your best self.

Add Value

One of the true keys to understanding business is to understand accounting. As you master what the business really does, you also master how the business works and how it can be profitable. This is golden. Your true business knowledge leads to the ability to forecast, protect, leverage and promote. Consider business examples such as IBM vs. Microsoft and Blockbuster vs. Netflix. A strong grasp of accounting and business also contributes to your understanding of business sustainability and long-term viability. Consider the issue of customer pricing as opposed to the cost of goods sold for the business. Reviewing and balancing these categories of revenues and costs is critical for profitability and overall business success. In short, when you understand accounting, you become valuable to your organization.

Make a Difference

By applying your accounting skills, you can make a difference in the world. You may become a key member of a leadership team with a company providing an in-demand product or service. You truly believe in your product and that the world is a better place due to the innovation and leadership of your company. Be a part of that leadership team. You may go your own way and start your own business. Perhaps you have an idea or a way of going about things that is not happening now in business. Your new business can be a symbol of positive change. You may believe in a specific cause or humanitarian mission. For some, there can be no greater purpose in life than to support, strengthen and enhance an exceptional nonprofit organization. Your accounting knowledge can lead to your reputation as a top-level business manager making a profound difference in the world with your organization.

We are delighted to have you with us for this brief period of time. Our goal at AME is for you to have a positive learning experience as you explore new topics and new ways of thinking.

All my best to you in your professional journey,

Suzanne

The AME Learning System™

It started 20 years ago when company founder Neville Joffe developed an innovative game-based methodology to help his employees understand basic financial concepts. Today, the AME Learning System™ is an award-winning teaching strategy. It's unique, patented and most importantly, it works. Designed initially to teach the principles of accounting and financial literacy to people with no previous financial education, the AME Learning System™ has now accelerated learning for hundreds of thousands of students and professionals across North America.

The system incorporates the best of cognitive science, technology and learning principles into an active learning approach that emphasizes constant decision-making, real-world examples and process over memorization.

The patented Accounting Map™ Tutorials are the foundation of the system. Using a logical, visually based approach that translates accounting concepts into common experiences and terminology, the interactive, online tutorials employ the "flipped classroom" strategy that is revolutionizing contemporary learning. Students complete tutorials *before* their in-class instruction consolidates their understanding of the material. Then, plain-language, real-world style exercises help students practice and explore key lessons. When this system meets AME Engage – our distinctive online learning experience – it creates an unmatched connection between learners and content.

Our blended-learning packages offer print and digital resources that can support each other or stand alone to provide the learning experience that best fits everyone's needs. Our system is completely modular, allowing students, learners and clients to customize their learning goals and experiences, even as we continuously update our content and technology.

Full-Cycle Support

The heart of the AME Learning System™ is our connection to you. We customize your experience, your content and your support because we know our customers personally. We ensure our technology is portable and interoperable with your platforms and we organize our materials to match your needs and processes. Behind it all, the AME Assistant Team – our in-house accounting and learning specialists – work as your virtual teaching assistants, helping you build the learning experience, develop tests and exams and refine your curriculum.

Who's It For?

The AME Learning System™ can support everyone looking to enhance their understanding of the financial world, including school-age and higher-education students, people starting their own businesses, employees preparing for their first management roles and people looking for new jobs or retraining in mid-career.

Virtual schools, online universities and traditional colleges are customizing the AME Learning System™ to train accounting-majors, entrepreneurs, paralegals, human resources professionals and people working in agriculture, hospitality and sports management. Our system is for anyone who wants to learn more, retain more and understand more about accounting and finance.

Textbook and Workbook Features

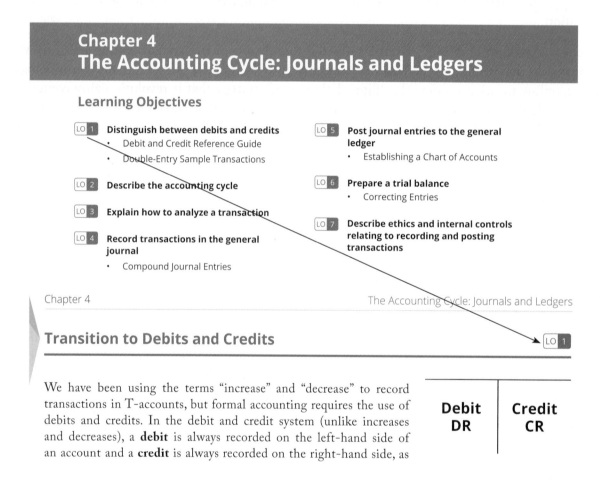

Access **ameengage.com** for integrated resources including tutorials, practice exercises, the digital textbook and more.

Every chapter has reminders for students to check their online course for additional resources to help explain the accounting topics.

The learning outcomes in each chapter are prepared using Bloom's taxonomy. In the textbook, each heading in the chapters is linked to at least one learning outcome. The learning outcomes are also linked to all the questions in the workbook.

Chapter 4
The Accounting Cycle: Journals and Ledgers

Learning Objectives

LO 1 **Distinguish between debits and credits**
   •   Debit and Credit Reference Guide
   •   Double-Entry Sample Transactions

LO 2 **Describe the accounting cycle**

LO 3 **Explain how to analyze a transaction**

LO 4 **Record transactions in the general journal**
   •   Compound Journal Entries

LO 5 **Post journal entries to the general ledger**
   •   Establishing a Chart of Accounts

LO 6 **Prepare a trial balance**
   •   Correcting Entries

LO 7 **Describe ethics and internal controls relating to recording and posting transactions**

Chapter 4   The Accounting Cycle: Journals and Ledgers

Transition to Debits and Credits   LO 1

We have been using the terms "increase" and "decrease" to record transactions in T-accounts, but formal accounting requires the use of debits and credits. In the debit and credit system (unlike increases and decreases), a **debit** is always recorded on the left-hand side of an account and a **credit** is always recorded on the right-hand side, as

Debit DR	Credit CR

Making it Real to You is a new feature that highlights how the chapter topic relates to students' personal and professional lives. It turns accounting concepts into situational contexts to help students understand the importance of what they are about to learn.

At the end of the chapter is a summary, highlighting key points for each learning objective.

In Summary

LO 1   Distinguish between debits and credits

▶ Debits are recorded on the left side of an account and credits are recorded on the right side. For the accounting equation to stay in balance, the total value of the debits must equal the total value of the credits.

▶ Assets, expenses and owner's withdrawals increase with debits and decrease with credits. Liabilities, revenues and owner's capital increase with credits and decrease with debits.

LO 2   Describe the accounting cycle

▶ The accounting cycle consists of the steps required to prepare financial statements. The cycle repeats every period.

Within each chapter are several Pause & Reflect exercises for students to complete. These break down large chapters into smaller manageable parts to help enforce the concepts learned. Solutions to the Pause & Reflect exercises are in Appendix I of the textbook.

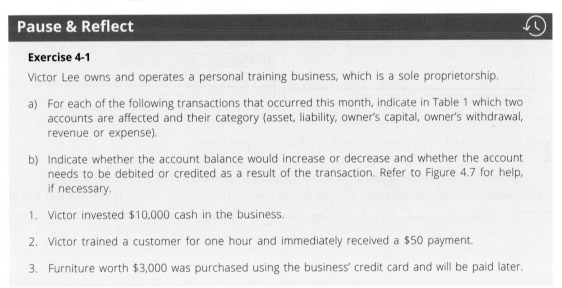

Pause & Reflect

Exercise 4-1

Victor Lee owns and operates a personal training business, which is a sole proprietorship.

a) For each of the following transactions that occurred this month, indicate in Table 1 which two accounts are affected and their category (asset, liability, owner's capital, owner's withdrawal, revenue or expense).

b) Indicate whether the account balance would increase or decrease and whether the account needs to be debited or credited as a result of the transaction. Refer to Figure 4.7 for help, if necessary.

1. Victor invested $10,000 cash in the business.

2. Victor trained a customer for one hour and immediately received a $50 payment.

3. Furniture worth $3,000 was purchased using the business' credit card and will be paid later.

Each chapter has a Review Exercise covering the major topics of the chapter. The Review Exercises are prepared so students can complete them and then compare their answers to the solutions. Solutions to the Review Exercises are in Appendix I of the textbook.

Review Exercise 4-1

Catherine Gordon is running her own sole proprietary business called CG Accounting. CG Accounting provides bookkeeping services to small and mid-sized companies. The company prepares financial statements on a monthly basis and had the following closing balances at the end of May 2018.

CG Accounting Balance Sheet As at May 31, 2018			
Assets		**Liabilities**	
Cash	$4,200	Accounts Payable	$2,300
Accounts Receivable	3,100	Unearned Revenue	600
Equipment	6,000	Notes Payable	4,000
		Total Liabilities	6,900
		Owner's Equity	
		Gordon, Capital	6,400
Total Assets	$13,300	**Total Liabilities + Owner's Equity**	$13,300

CG Accounting uses a variety of accounts and account numbers in its accounting records.

Account Description	Account #
ASSETS	
Cash	101
Accounts Receivable	105
Prepaid Insurance	110
Equipment	120
Accumulated Depreciation—Equipment	125

Account Description	Account #
REVENUE	
Service Revenue	400
EXPENSES	
Advertising Expense	500
Bad Debt Expense	505
Insurance Expense	510

The workbook is comprised of assessment and application questions.

* Assessment questions (AS) are designed to test theory and comprehension of topics.
* Application questions (AP) are split into Group A and Group B problems. These questions test the ability to perform the accounting functions, such as creating journal entries and financial statements.

Chapter 4

THE ACCOUNTING CYCLE: JOURNALS AND LEDGERS

LEARNING OBJECTIVES

LO 1   Distinguish between debits and credits

LO 2   Describe the accounting cycle

LO 3   Explain how to analyze a transaction

LO 4   Record transactions in the general journal

LO 5   Post journal entries to the general ledger

LO 6   Prepare a trial balance

LO 7   Describe ethics and internal controls relating to recording and posting transactions

AMEENGAGE   *Access **ameengage.com** for integrated resources including tutorials, practice exercises, the digital textbook and more.*

Assessment Questions

AS-1 LO 1

What

A de

Application Questions Group A

AP-1A LO 1 3

Esteem Fitness provides fitness services for its customers. During June 2018, Esteem Fitness had the following

Application Questions Group B

AP-1B LO 1 3

Perfect Party is owned by Candace Rodriguez and provides party planning services. During April 2018, Perfect Party had the following transactions.

Apr 1	The owner invested $5,800 cash into the business
Apr 4	Planned a party for a customer for $740; the customer will pay later
Apr 6	Paid $600 cash for rent for the month

Some additional segments

This textbook was designed to make your learning experience productive and engaging. To that end, we have added some segments to each chapter that highlight learning objectives.

A CLOSER LOOK

The *A Closer Look* segments are meant to closely examine a part of the chapter to broaden your understanding of an underlying concept. They may also include an example that applies the concepts being learned, in a way that is easy to understand and follow.

WORTH REPEATING

The *Worth Repeating* segments are meant to remind students of concepts in accounting already learned, and to highlight current concepts being taught that are "worth repeating."

IN THE REAL WORLD

The *In The Real World* segments are meant to provide applied examples of elements being learned. They are meant to put some of the concepts being learned in context and to drive home the point that eventually, accounting has to be done outside the classroom. We hope that these segments give you a sense of what "the real world" can be like for the accountant or business professional.

GAAP vs IFRS

The *GAAP vs IFRS* segments are meant to discuss differences in the treatment of the topic being covered in the chapter based on the two different *sets* of accounting standards. Not all topics will have a difference between the two.

AME ENGAGE™

Welcome to the fully integrated and interactive online learning hub for *Introduction to Accounting: Concepts and Applications, V1.0.*

The AME Learning™ Cycle for Students

The AME Learning Cycle is a unique learning method that integrates the textbook seamlessly with the online platform to achieve a fun and interactive learning experience. The online learning hub, AME Engage, guides students every step along the way to achieve successful knowledge retention. The pre-class interactive tutorials allow students to not only better prepare for in-class work but also engage with difficult concepts whenever and wherever. The post-class algorithmic homework provides a platform for students to practice workbook questions online and receive instant feedback.

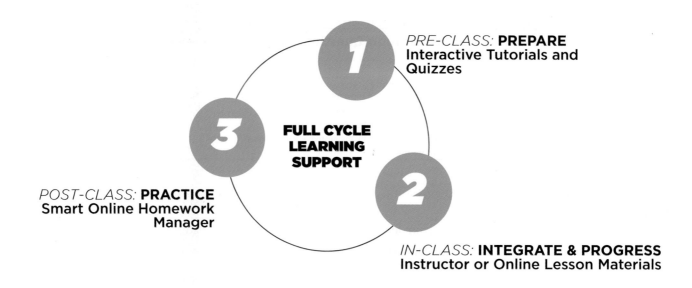

1 PRE-CLASS: **PREPARE** Interactive Tutorials and Quizzes

FULL CYCLE LEARNING SUPPORT

2 IN-CLASS: **INTEGRATE & PROGRESS** Instructor or Online Lesson Materials

3 POST-CLASS: **PRACTICE** Smart Online Homework Manager

AME Engage: Features

Interactive Online Tutorials
Interactive multi-sensory video clips featuring hands on practice with our innovative Accounting Map™.

Online Homework Manager
Algorithmic homework questions, assignments, projects, cases, tests and quizzes.

Resource Library
Focus-in on key lesson objectives with Microsoft Excel™ worksheet templates and our vast PowerPoint™ library.

Digital Textbook
Practical explanations and examples seamlessly integrated with workbook and online homework.

Digital Workbook
Hundreds of questions and cases perfectly integrated with textbook lessons and online homework.

Student Tech Support
Call 1 (888) 401-3881 x 2 from 9am to 5pm EST Monday to Friday or email support@amelearning. com 24 hours a day and 7 days a week.

AME ENGAGE™

Welcome to the fully integrated and interactive online learning hub for
Introduction to Accounting: Concepts and Applications, V1.0.

Full Cycle Instructor Support

At AME Learning, we proudly provide full cycle instructor support for teaching a stimulating and rewarding class. Our AME Assistant™ Team consists of highly qualified content experts, technical support specialists and resource managers, who can provide you with personalized assistance from custom content development to on-demand training and technical support. Our AME Engage online learning hub offers you a resource center that combines the best content with powerful teaching tools to achieve the desired flexibility and control.

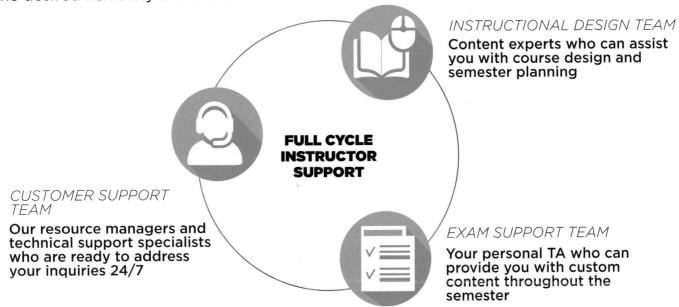

INSTRUCTIONAL DESIGN TEAM
Content experts who can assist you with course design and semester planning

FULL CYCLE INSTRUCTOR SUPPORT

CUSTOMER SUPPORT TEAM
Our resource managers and technical support specialists who are ready to address your inquiries 24/7

EXAM SUPPORT TEAM
Your personal TA who can provide you with custom content throughout the semester

Instructor Support: Features

⊕ Personalized Instructional Design
A unique and personalized service tailors to the needs of each curriculum and each instructor.

⊞ Personalized Exam Support
Custom content creation throughout the semester for both paper based and online exams.

ⓘ Online Question Bank
Over 1,500 questions organized by chapter and include multiple choice, matching, and computational problems.

⚲ Workbook Solution Manual
Step-by-step solutions to all workbook questions available in print or in digital format.

⊞ Online Resource Library
Powerful online resource center with additional teaching tools such as online cases, Microsoft PowerPoint© and Microsoft Excel© templates.

⊘ Instructor Training & Technical Support
On-demand support to integrate our products, technology and services into your course for optimum teaching and results.

Brief Table of Contents

Introduction

Detailed Table of Contents

Chapter 3: The Accounting Framework

Chapter 4: The Accounting Cycle: Journals and Ledgers

Chapter 5: The Accounting Cycle: Adjustments

Chapter 6: The Accounting Cycle: Statements and Closing Entries

Chapter 7: Accounting for Cash: Internal Controls and Fraud Prevention

Chapter 8: Accounting For Receivables

Chapter 11: Accounting for Noncurrent Assets

Chapter 14: Analyzing Accounting Information

Chapter 1
Personal Accounting

Learning Objectives

LO 1   **Describe the purpose of accounting**

LO 2   **Describe the balance sheet**

LO 3   **Describe the income statement**

LO 4   **Define an accounting period**

LO 5   **Explain how the accounting equation works**

- Introduction to T-Accounts

LO 6   **Explain accrual-based accounting**

- Cash Flow vs. Accruals
- Cash-Based vs. Accrual-Based Accounting

LO 7   **Explain how to account for debt**

LO 8   **Explain how to account for assets**

LO 9   **Explain how to account for prepaid expenses**

LO 10   **Demonstrate how double entries are recorded in T-accounts**

LO 11   **Describe ethics and internal controls related to personal accounting**

- Personal Ethics
- Internal Controls

AMEENGAGE™   *Access **ameengage.com** for integrated resources including tutorials, practice exercises, the digital textbook and more.*

MAKING IT REAL TO YOU

You may not realize it, but everywhere you go, just about everything you do has something to do with accounting. From that beverage you buy on the way to work or school, to the cost of the cellular service you rely on for your smartphone, to the college courses you enroll in and the textbooks you buy—these are all transactions, and they all involve accounting. Perhaps you have a part-time job and receive a printed paycheck from your employer—or maybe your pay is electronically deposited to your bank account. Consider how you pay for food, transportation and personal needs, as well as saving for your short-term and long-term financial goals. Whether you pay for all of your personal needs with cash, by credit card, or by an electronic payment system, this involves accounting for both you and the businesses that provide these goods and services. It is all accounting. Let us start with something personal first.

The Purpose of Accounting

Accounting is a system to identify, measure and communicate all the financial activities of an individual or a business. Personal accounting tracks how much an individual is worth. Whether you live a simple or luxurious lifestyle, you need money to sustain your personal life. Most people want to save enough money to allow them to retire comfortably. The better you can manage your finances and bring in more money than you spend, the more wealth you have.

It is important to maintain records of the activities that increase or decrease your net worth (i.e. how much you earn, how much you invest and how much you spend). The key concepts that drive your personal economic life are very similar to those used in business. In fact, learning basic accounting is a crucial life skill for everyone.

Most people associate accounting with calculators, computers and long lists of numbers. That may be true to some degree when you are a practicing bookkeeper or accountant; however, understanding accounting involves not only numbers but also a logical way of thinking.

Here is an example of the logic behind one of the concepts you will learn in this course, net worth. Which scenario in Figure 1.1 would you prefer?

Scenario 1

Assets (what you own)

Cash	$3,000
Contents of Home	6,000
Automobile	15,000
House	80,000
Total Assets	$104,000

Scenario 2

Assets (what you own)

Cash	$5,000
Contents of Home	8,000
Automobile	20,000
House	100,000
Total Assets	$133,000

FIGURE 1.1

Scenario 2 appears to be preferable. However, some crucial information is missing. You must not only look at how much you own (assets) but also consider how much you owe (liabilities), as shown in Figure 1.2.

Assets = all that you OWN

Value of Assets = $75,000

Liabilities = all that you OWE

Value of Liabilities = $50,000

FIGURE 1.2

In examining the scenarios in Figure 1.3, which one would you now prefer?

Scenario 1

Assets (what you own)

Cash	$3,000
Contents of Home	6,000
Automobile	15,000
House	80,000
Total Assets	**$104,000**

Liabilities (what you owe)

Bank Loan	$0
Credit Card Account	2,000
Mortgage	60,000
Automobile Loan	5,000
Student Loan	5,000
Total Liabilities	**$72,000**
Net Worth*	**$32,000**

Scenario 2

Assets (what you own)

Cash	$5,000
Contents of Home	8,000
Automobile	20,000
House	100,000
Total Assets	**$133,000**

Liabilities (what you owe)

Bank Loan	$8,000
Credit Card Account	4,000
Mortgage	80,000
Automobile Loan	5,000
Student Loan	10,000
Total Liabilities	**$107,000**
Net Worth*	**$26,000**

*Net Worth = Assets (amount you own) LESS Liabilities (amount you owe)

FIGURE 1.3

Even though you may own more in Scenario 2, you also owe a lot more. Overall, we seek to maximize net worth. The end result is that Scenario 2 is worth less than Scenario 1.

The Balance Sheet

The **balance sheet** is a permanent document used to record what you own (assets), what you owe (liabilities) and what you are worth (net worth) on a specific date. An **asset** is something you own that benefits you now and in the future. This includes items such as the cash you have, the house and car you own, the furniture and electronics in your home, and investments you have made. Cash is listed first since it is the asset that can be most conveniently used to exchange for other things.

On the other hand, **liabilities** are obligations. Usually, these obligations mean you owe cash to someone else. One example of a liability is unpaid accounts. Unpaid accounts include amounts owing on credit cards, and bills for items like utilities or cell phones that you have not yet paid. Other longer term liabilities include items such as bank loans and mortgages. Unpaid accounts is listed first on the balance sheet since this is the debt you have to pay first.

Net worth is what is left if you cash out (i.e. successfully sell all your assets and get the value equivalent to the recorded amount) and pay everything you owe (your liabilities). Tracking the amount you are worth is a fundamental component of accounting in both your personal life and your business life.

The balance sheet provides a *snapshot* of your financial position. The difference between the value of what you own and what you owe is your net worth. The date of the balance sheet is presented as "As at..." because it represents a snapshot of your finances at a particular point in time. For example, a balance sheet prepared on December 31, 2018 would have the date "As at December 31, 2018." The next four figures will show different scenarios to illustrate how net worth is determined by both assets and liabilities.

In Figure 1.4, note that you have $7,000 in cash. At this point, if you needed to pay everything that you owe ($105,500), you would need to sell some of your assets (i.e. convert the value of your assets into cash, also known as *liquidating* your assets). Although you may think that you are worth only the $7,000 you have in the bank as cash, your true value (or net worth) is $36,500.

Personal Balance Sheet As at December 31, 2018			
Assets		**Liabilities**	
Cash	$7,000	Unpaid Accounts	$500
Contents of Home	5,000	Mortgage	100,000
Automobile	10,000	Bank Loan	5,000
House	120,000	Total Liabilities	105,500
		Net Worth	36,500
Total Assets	$142,000	Total Liabilities + Net Worth	$142,000

FIGURE 1.4

Net worth is equal to assets minus liabilities. This relationship is discussed later in the chapter.

In Figure 1.5, despite the fact that your cash balance is lower than the scenario in Figure 1.4, your net worth is higher.

Personal Balance Sheet As at December 31, 2018			
Assets		**Liabilities**	
Cash	$1,000	Unpaid Accounts	$5,000
Investments	18,000	Mortgage	100,000
Contents of Home	4,500		
Automobile	10,000	Total Liabilities	105,000
House	120,000	Net Worth	48,500
Total Assets	$153,500	Total Liabilities + Net Worth	$153,500

FIGURE 1.5

In Figure 1.6, you have a negative bank balance, meaning that you have withdrawn more money than you have in your bank account. Note that in accounting, negative numbers are expressed in parentheses. For example, –$2,000 is shown as ($2,000). This is a bank overdraft, which means you owe the bank money and will have to repay the amount with interest. However, your net worth is significantly higher than in Figures 1.4 and 1.5.

Personal Balance Sheet As at December 31, 2018			
Assets		**Liabilities**	
Cash	($2,000)	Unpaid Accounts	$10,000
Investments	30,000	Mortgage	80,000
Contents of Home	5,000	Bank Loan	7,000
Automobile	10,000	Car Loan	6,000
House	180,000	Total Liabilities	103,000
		Net Worth	120,000
Total Assets	$223,000	Total Liabilities + Net Worth	$223,000

FIGURE 1.6

In Figure 1.7, you have a large amount of cash, a valuable home and an expensive car. However, your net worth is lower than the previous three scenarios. This is because you borrowed a large amount from the bank for your house and car, which increased your liabilities.

The net worth reflected in Figure 1.6 (with the negative cash balance) is actually greater than the net worth shown in the other figures.

Personal Balance Sheet As at December 31, 2018			
Assets		**Liabilities**	
Cash	$50,000	Unpaid Accounts	$15,000
Investments	8,000	Mortgage	220,000
Contents of Home	12,000	Bank Loan	60,000
Automobile	50,000	Car Loan	40,000
House	250,000	Total Liabilities	335,000
		Net Worth	35,000
Total Assets	$370,000	Total Liabilities + Net Worth	$370,000

FIGURE 1.7

The Income Statement

The **income statement** is a temporary record used to show and summarize revenue and expenses. **Revenue** is an increase to net worth caused by providing goods or services in exchange for an asset, usually cash. In your personal life, revenue is usually earned by working and earning a salary. **Expenses** are a decrease to net worth caused by day-to-day activities. These costs are incurred and will be paid later or use up an asset, usually cash. In your personal life, expenses can include items such as rent or food.

The purpose of the income statement is to determine the *change* in net worth over a specific period of time. The date of the income statement is presented as "For the Period Ended..." since the statement covers a period of time. For example, an income statement prepared on December 31, 2018 covering a year would have the date "For the Year Ended December 31, 2018."

If you did not want to use an income statement, you could record every transaction in the net worth section on the balance sheet. A **transaction** is a trade or exchange with someone else in order to receive something of value. Since revenue increases net worth and expenses decrease net worth, you could record every revenue and expense amount directly into net worth on the balance sheet. However, this method would not keep track of the specific type of revenue or expense you had. Instead, you could note revenue and expenses on a separate document, the income statement. A difference between revenue and expenses is the change in net worth.

Figure 1.8 illustrates a sample personal income statement. This shows that $36,000 was earned during the year and expenses amounted to $29,500. The difference between revenue and expenses is a surplus of $6,500, which is added to the person's net worth. If expenses are more than revenue, a deficit is recorded and subtracted from the person's net worth.

Personal Income Statement For the Year Ended December 31, 2018		
Revenue		$36,000
Expenses		
Food Expense	$12,000	
Insurance Expense	1,000	
Maintenance Expense	800	
Rent Expense	15,000	
Utilities Expense	700	
Total Expenses		29,500
Surplus (Deficit)		**$6,500**

FIGURE 1.8

A CLOSER LOOK

Imagine playing a sport without a scorecard. It would be difficult to play the game effectively without knowing the score during the game. Your economic life is no different. It is crucial to monitor how your day-to-day activities impact your net worth on a monthly basis so you can change your spending behaviors in a timely manner to fit within your income. Remember that there is a difference between cash and your net worth.

Accounting Periods

LO 4

You can keep recording and calculating changes to net worth continuously; however, for accounting purposes, it is more convenient to record changes to net worth in separate periods. You can use any period you choose as an accounting period. An **accounting period** is the time frame in which the financial statements are prepared and can be one year, six months or one month, as shown in Figure 1.9.

If you use one month as your accounting period, you can look back at previous months (periods) and estimate what your expenses and income will be in

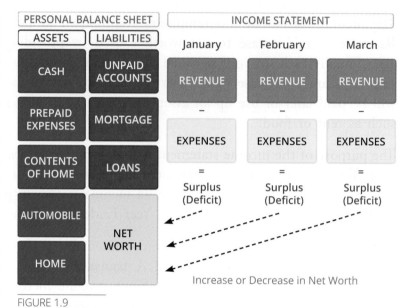

FIGURE 1.9

the coming months. You can also estimate the surplus or deficit you will generate each month. If you are saving for a major purchase, such as a car, computer or entertainment system, you can determine when you will have enough money to buy the desired item or provide a down payment.

Some advantages of using monthly accounting periods for your personal financial statements include

- tracking regular monthly living expenses (e.g. rent, cell phone);
- frequently assessing realistic expectations; and
- controlling errors effectively.

The Accounting Equation

LO 5

Just as Newton's Third Law applies to science (for every action there is an equal and opposite reaction), the same concept can be applied to the logic of the accounting equation: For every transaction, there is an equal financial consequence. In accounting terms, each transaction has at least two entries of the same value, called a **double entry**. The logic of the double entry is based on the **accounting equation**, shown in Figure 1.10.

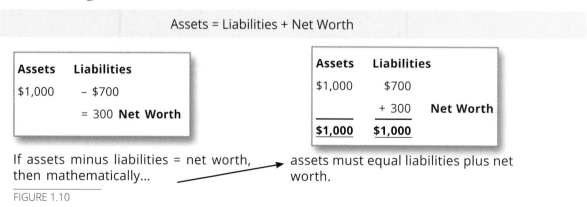

FIGURE 1.10

Imagine the accounting equation as a scale; the left side of the scale includes assets and the right side includes liabilities and net worth. The scale must always be in balance, as shown in Figure 1.11.

Assets   Liabilities + Net Worth
1,000   700 + 300

Assets = Liabilities + Net Worth
$1,000 = $700 + $300

FIGURE 1.11

If you receive $500 cash, it increases your assets. Recording only the increase in cash causes the scale to go out of balance, as shown in Figure 1.12.

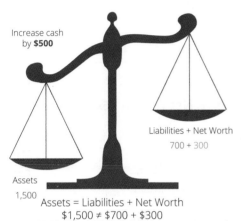

Increase cash by **$500**

Liabilities + Net Worth
700 + 300

Assets
1,500

Assets = Liabilities + Net Worth
$1,500 ≠ $700 + $300

FIGURE 1.12

To balance the scale, you must ask yourself why you received the cash. If you earned it at your job, then the $500 must also increase net worth. This is recorded as revenue and brings the scale back into balance, as shown in Figure 1.13.

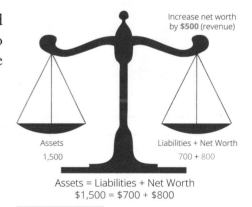

Increase net worth by **$500** (revenue)

Assets   Liabilities + Net Worth
1,500   700 + 800

Assets = Liabilities + Net Worth
$1,500 = $700 + $800

FIGURE 1.13

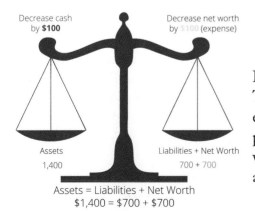

Decrease cash by **$100**

Decrease net worth by $100 (expense)

Assets   Liabilities + Net Worth
1,400   700 + 700

Assets = Liabilities + Net Worth
$1,400 = $700 + $700

FIGURE 1.14

If you make a cash payment of $100, your assets decrease in value. The scale will only balance if you record the $100 somewhere else. Ask yourself why you made a $100 payment. If it was a rent payment for the month, then the $100 must also decrease net worth. This is recorded as an expense and the scale is balanced, as shown in Figure 1.14.

As these examples demonstrate, we can see that without a logical opposite entry, the balance sheet does not balance. Figure 1.15 shows how the transactions are analyzed using an accounting equation. The only way to keep it in balance is to impact at least two accounts. The first two transactions were illustrated in Figures 1.13 and 1.14 in terms of balancing the scale. The Explanation column in Figure 1.15 provides more details on why net worth changes.

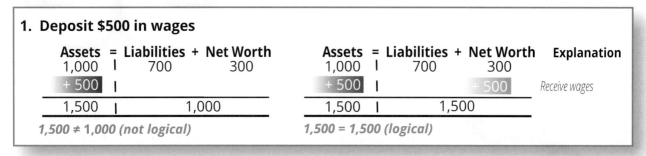

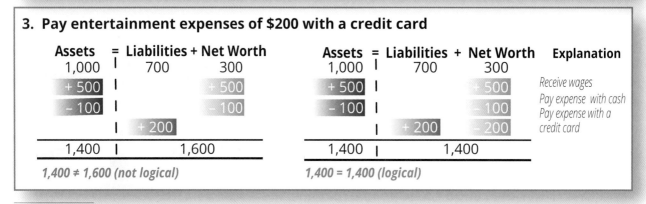

FIGURE 1.15

In the third transaction from Figure 1.15, $200 of expenses were paid with a credit card. The amount owed on the card represents an additional liability, so we increase liabilities by $200. Because the charge was for an expense, we must also decrease net worth by $200 so the accounting equation remains balanced.

Introduction to T-Accounts

An **account** allows us to track detailed information about the values of individual items, such as cash and unpaid accounts. A tool used to record transactions and to keep the accounting equation balanced is a **T-account**, named as such because it looks like a capital T, as shown in Figure 1.16.

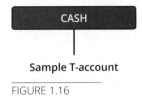

Sample T-account

FIGURE 1.16

Every item has its own T-account, with increases recorded on one side and decreases recorded on the other. The category of the account (asset, liability, net worth, revenue or expense) determines which side of the T-account is the increase and which side is the decrease.

Figure 1.17 shows how the T-accounts behave in each category. The following diagram can be used to help memorize which side is an increase and which side is a decrease for T-accounts.

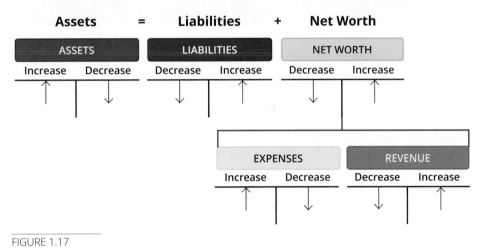

FIGURE 1.17

All assets, such as cash, use the left side of the T-account for increases and the right side for decreases. You can remember this by referring to the accounting equation. Assets are on the left of the accounting equation and assets use the left side of the T-account for increases.

All liabilities, such as unpaid accounts, use the right side of the T-account for increases and the left side for decreases. Again, refer to the accounting equation. Liabilities are on the right side of the accounting equation and liabilities use the right side of the T-account for increases.

Net worth also uses the right side of the T-account for increases and the left side for decreases since it is also on the right side of the accounting equation.

Revenue increases net worth and expenses decrease net worth. The more revenue earned, the more should be added to net worth. Therefore, the revenue T-account increases on the right side and decreases on the left side. The more expenses incurred, the more should be subtracted from net worth. Therefore, the expense T-accounts increase on the left side and decrease on the right side.

Figure 1.18 shows an example of the cash T-account.

Since cash is an asset, the left side of the T-account is for increases and the right side is for decreases. The first thing to enter into a T-account is the **opening balance**, or *beginning balance*, which is the amount left over from the last period carried over to the beginning of the current period. Cash has an opening balance of $1,000, shown at the top of the increase side of the T-account. After all transactions have been recorded, we total both sides of the T-account, shown in red. The increase side

INCREASE			DECREASE
+	CASH		**–**
Opening Balance	$1,000		
	1. 2,000	2. 1,500	
	4. 4,000	3. 1,000	
	5. 500	6. 600	
Subtotal	7,500	3,100	
Closing Balance	$4,400		

FIGURE 1.18

includes the opening balance in addition to the transactions. The difference between the increase and decrease sides is $4,400, which is the closing balance of cash. The **closing balance**, or *ending balance*, is the amount remaining in an account at the end of the period. It becomes the opening balance of the account in the next period. The difference is placed on the side that has the larger subtotal, which is the increase side in this example.

Pause & Reflect

Exercise 1-1

a) Use the accounting equation to calculate your net worth if you have $1,500 in assets and $300 in liabilities at the beginning of the month. Fill your answer in the Beginning Balances row of Table 1 below.

b) Assume that the three transactions listed in Table 1 happened during the current month. Analyze how each transaction affects your assets, liabilities and net worth, and fill in your answers. The first transaction has been started for you.

c) Calculate the ending balances for assets, liabilities and net worth after accounting for the three transactions in part b). Fill your answers in the Ending Balances row of Table 1.

Table 1

	Assets	=	Liabilities	+	Net Worth
Beginning Balances	$1,500	=	$300	+	
1. Paid $100 toward credit card balance	–100		–100		
2. Paid $25 for a meal using cash					
3. Deposited $300 in wages					
Ending Balances		=		+	

d) The cash T-account below shows this month's transactions. Calculate the closing balance of cash and fill in your answer at the bottom of the T-account.

INCREASE			DECREASE
+	CASH		**–**
Opening Balance	$200		
3. 300		1. 100	
		2. 25	
Closing Balance			

See Appendix I for solutions.

Accrual-Based Accounting

A typical reason for personal financial failure (and small business failure) is not understanding accruals. People tend to think intuitively that an increase in cash represents an increase in wealth, and vice versa. The notion of the accrual is recognizing how much you are worth at a point in time.

Accrual-based accounting means that revenue (an increase to net worth) and expenses (a decrease to net worth) are recorded in the period in which they occur, regardless of when cash payment is received or paid.

So far we have assumed that every expense is paid when it is incurred. In reality, many expenses are not paid until a later date.

Assume that you have $1,000 of cash and a net worth of $1,000. If you pay for a $300 expense with cash, your cash and net worth both decrease by $300, as shown in Figure 1.19.

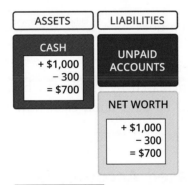

FIGURE 1.19

If, instead, you receive a phone bill for $300 to be paid next month, there is no change in cash in the current month. However, the phone debt (or unpaid accounts) increases by $300 and net worth decreases by $300, as shown in Figure 1.20. You recognize the expense that decreases net worth even if the expense is not paid until a later date.

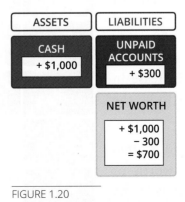

FIGURE 1.20

In general, keep in mind that the word "expense" relates to a decrease in net worth, which does not necessarily relate to cash.

Cash Flow vs. Accruals

There are two key points to understand when discussing cash flow and accruals. Refer to Figure 1.21, which illustrates the difference between these two key points.

ⓐ Cash flow relates to cash flowing into and out of the bank account. In this instance, you paid $500 for a food expense, which did decrease your net worth. However, if the $500 was to purchase another asset, your net worth would not change because you are simply exchanging one asset (cash) for another asset (computer). Therefore, cash flow does not necessarily connect to net worth.

ⓐ Accruals relate to net worth, which does not necessarily connect to cash flow. In this instance, you received a bill and decided to pay it later. Your unpaid accounts increased by $500, which caused your net worth to decrease by $500. However, because the bill will be paid later, cash flow is not affected.

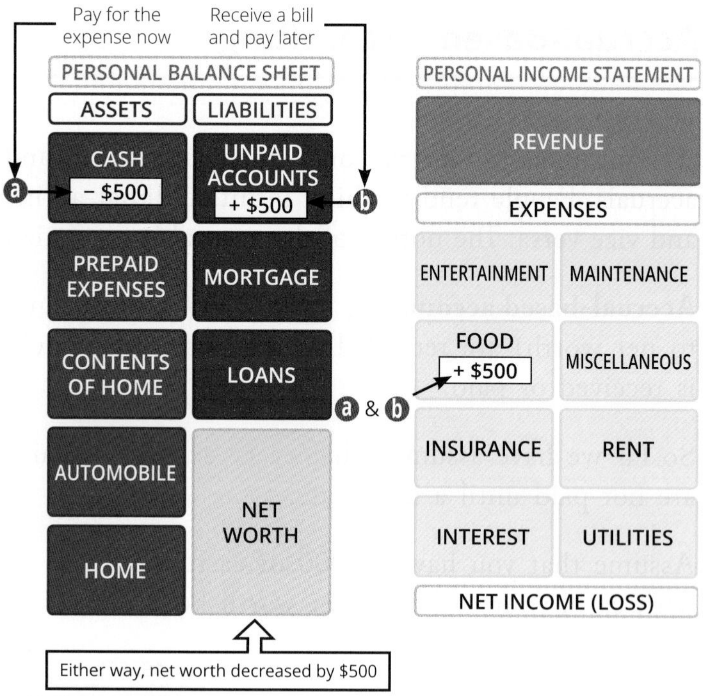

Both points are important and distinct.

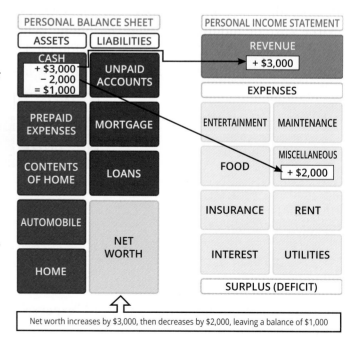

FIGURE 1.21

Cash-Based vs. Accrual-Based Accounting

In **cash-based accounting**, revenue and expenses are recorded only when the cash is received or paid. Since it is more straightforward than accrual-based accounting, individuals tend to use this method of accounting.

As illustrated in Figure 1.22, at the end of January you deposit $3,000 in salary earned that month and pay expenses of $2,000 using cash from the bank. The difference between revenue and expenses results in an increase in net worth of $1,000, which happens to be the same as the increase in cash.

Suppose that you deposit a salary of $3,000 in January, but charge all $2,000 worth of expenses to your credit card, which is to be paid in February. When you use cash-based accounting, your net worth appears to be $3,000 in January, since no cash is used to pay your expenses.

FIGURE 1.22

If, on the other hand, you are using accrual-based accounting, you need to recognize the expense in January, the month in which it was actually incurred. This textbook focuses on accrual-based accounting, since businesses are required to use this method.

In Figure 1.23, the income statement for the month of January shows that you have matched the revenue of $3,000 (an increase in net worth) to the expenses in January of $2,000 (a decrease in net worth), resulting in an overall increase in net worth of $1,000. Cash remains at $3,000 because you have not yet paid any of the expenses incurred.

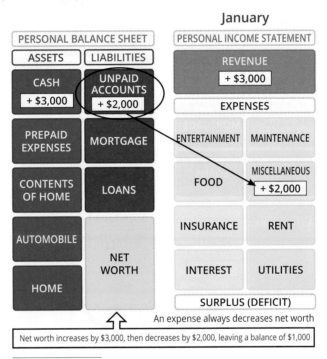

FIGURE 1.23

The accrual system of accounting recognizes the change in net worth even though payment is not necessarily received or paid.

Four transactions that occurred in January are presented below. Their impact on the balance sheet and income statement are shown in Figure 1.24. Keep in mind that the accounting equation must always stay in balance.

1. Earn and deposit $5,000 in salary. Cash increases by $5,000, which increases the total assets in the accounting equation. Why did cash increase? Because you deposited your salary. Net worth increases, which is shown as revenue on the income statement.

2. Pay $1,000 in cash for food expenses. Cash decreases by $1,000, which decreases the total assets in the accounting equation. Why did cash decrease? Because you bought some food. Thus, net worth decreases, which is shown as food expense on the income statement.

3. Record a $500 credit card bill for gasoline expenses (due in one month). Cash is not affected; however, you have a debt that must be paid next month. Debt increases, which increases the total liabilities in the accounting equation. Why did your debt increase? Because you have to pay

for the gasoline at some point in the future. Net worth decreases, which is shown as gasoline expense on the income statement.

4. Record a $1,500 credit card bill for entertainment expenses. Debt increases, which increases the liabilities in the accounting equation. Why did your debt increase? Because you have to pay for the entertainment at some point in the future. Net worth decreases, which is shown as entertainment expense on the income statement.

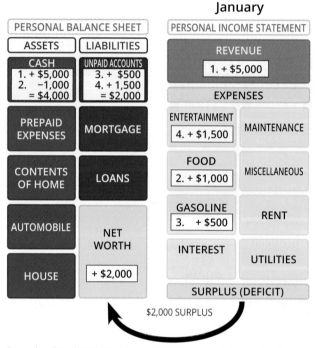

Remember: Everything that is shown on the income statement impacts net worth.

FIGURE 1.24

We can also illustrate these transactions with the accounting equation to ensure that assets equal liabilities plus net worth. This is shown in Figure 1.25.

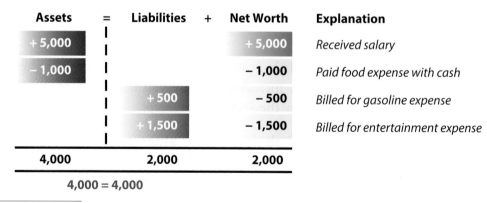

FIGURE 1.25

The accounting equation is balanced.

Assets	=	Liabilities	+	Net Worth
$4,000	=	$2,000	+	$2,000

As the examples in Figures 1.24 and 1.25 illustrate, you need to record your expenses for the month even though cash has not been paid for them in the same month. According to the concept of accruals, the credit card expenses are recognized in January when they were incurred, not in February when they are paid.

It is easy to mistakenly think that since cash increased by $4,000, net worth also increased by the same amount. This is not the case. It is important to understand that net worth is affected by revenue and expenses, regardless of when cash changes hands.

It is important to stress that the accounting equation must be in balance after every transaction. Many transactions affect the net worth of an individual; however, the net worth account itself is rarely directly changed by a transaction. Most changes to net worth are actually recorded in the income statement as either revenue or expenses. Thus, when you analyze transactions and determine that net worth is affected, you must then ask if this change to net worth should be recorded on the income statement as revenue or an expense.

Borrowing Money and Repaying Debt   LO 7

Other than cash in your bank account, every other financial aspect of your life relates to values—not to cash. Your assets have value, but only become cash if you sell them. Your liabilities represent an obligation you have, but they do not affect your cash until you actually pay them.

When you borrow money, you increase your assets and your debts. Net worth is not affected. When you pay your debts (principal), you decrease your assets and your debts. Again, net worth is not affected. To keep track of your assets and liabilities, you can record these transactions on the balance sheet. However, remember that the income statement is used to track the reasons for a change to net worth. Since net worth is not affected, there is nothing to record on the income statement.

For example, assume you borrow money from a friend and then repay the money, as shown in Figure 1.26.

1. Borrow $100 from a friend: You have more cash, but your net worth does not change because you incurred $100 in liabilities.

PERSONAL BALANCE SHEET

ASSETS	LIABILITIES
CASH 1. + $100 2. – $100	UNPAID ACCOUNTS
PREPAID EXPENSES	MORTGAGE
CONTENTS OF HOME	LOANS 1. + $100 2. – $100
AUTOMOBILE	NET WORTH
HOUSE	

No change in net worth

FIGURE 1.26

2. Repay your friend: You have less cash, but your net worth still does not change because you reduced your liabilities by $100.

The T-account entries related to these two transactions are shown in Figure 1.27.

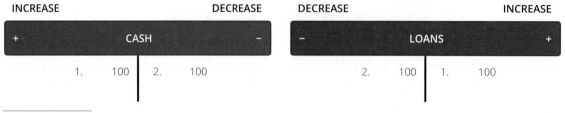

INCREASE		DECREASE		DECREASE		INCREASE
+	CASH	–		–	LOANS	+
	1. 100	2. 100			2. 100	1. 100

FIGURE 1.27

Only assets and liabilities are affected, so there is no entry on the income statement. There is no change to net worth.

Figure 1.28 demonstrates that not all the cash you spend is used to pay expenses. For example, you arrange for a loan of $15,000 and your loan repayments are $500 each month ($100 toward the principal and $400 in interest). There are three transactions to consider.

1. Receive the loan. Both cash and loans liability are increased. There is no impact to net worth.

2. Pay the interest portion of $400. Net worth has decreased and an expense is recognized.

3. Pay the principal of $100, reducing the amount owing to the loan company. Your net worth does not change and there is no need to record this transaction on the income statement.

The transactions would appear on the T-accounts, as in Figure 1.29.

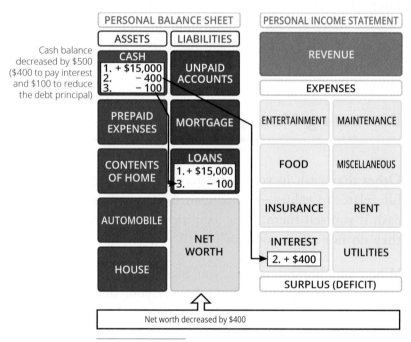

FIGURE 1.28

INCREASE		DECREASE		DECREASE		INCREASE		INCREASE		DECREASE
+	CASH	–		–	LOANS	+		+	INTEREST EXPENSE	–
	1. 15,000	2. 400			3. 100	1. 15,000			2. 400	
		3. 100								

FIGURE 1.29

Even though your cash decreased by $500 when you made a payment to reduce the loan, your net worth decreased by $400 as a result of the interest expense.

Buying and Selling Assets

Buying or selling assets (according to the value stated in the balance sheet) has no impact on net worth. For example, imagine you purchase a new car for $10,000 by paying $3,000 in cash and taking a loan from the bank for the remaining $7,000.

The cash used to purchase the car is just an exchange of one asset for another (cash for the car), so there is no change in net worth. The loan is borrowed to pay for the car, so the liability increases as does the asset (car). Again there is no change in net worth.

FIGURE 1.30

The effect on the accounts is shown in Figure 1.30. Although you now own a $10,000 car, there has been no change in your net worth.

The transactions appear on the T-accounts as shown in Figure 1.31. Cash decreases by $3,000 and your loan increases by $7,000. You have an increase to your automobile account of $10,000.

If you exchange cash for an item, how do you know whether the item should be considered an asset or an expense? Typically, it is a question of how long it will provide a benefit to you and the cost of the item. The $10,000 car that was just purchased is an asset because it will benefit you for several years. On the other hand, spending $200 on food or entertainment is an expense since they only benefit you for a short period of time.

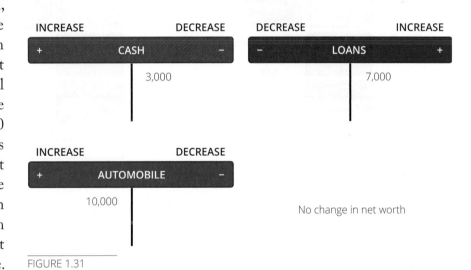

FIGURE 1.31

A CLOSER LOOK

Over time, the assets you own change in value based on usage and changes in the market. The car you purchased for $10,000 will not always be worth that amount. After several years of use, it is worth less than what you paid for it. Your house, however, may increase in value if you maintain it and the area you live in is desirable. On personal financial statements, there are no rules preventing you from changing the values of these assets as the market values change. In business, though, there are strict rules on how values of assets are recorded. This will be covered in later chapters.

So, borrowing and repaying debt principal does not impact net worth, and neither does buying or selling assets for the value stated on the balance sheet. The primary way you can change your net worth is to have revenue exceed expenses (net worth increases) or have expenses exceed revenue (net worth decreases).

Prepaid Expenses

It is a common practice to pay for various expenses in advance, for example, insurance and rent. These prepayments are not considered an expense at the time they are paid because the services have not yet been provided.

Prepaid Insurance

The example illustrated in Figure 1.32 explains the prepayment of $1,200 for one year of insurance.

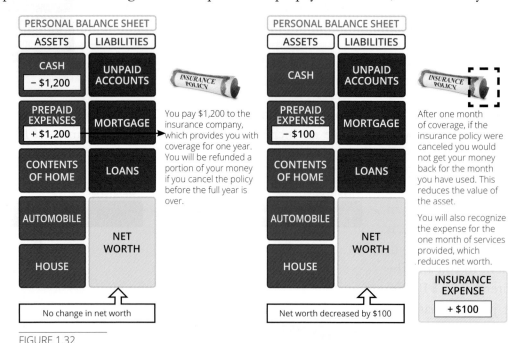

FIGURE 1.32

When you prepay your insurance, you might think that your net worth decreased because the cash is no longer in your bank account. However, what you have really done is purchase a one-year insurance policy, which you now own. Anything you own and will benefit you in the future is considered an asset and recorded as such on the balance sheet. In this case, the amount paid for the insurance policy is considered a prepaid expense. A **prepaid expense** occurs when you pay cash for an expense (like insurance) before you use it. You own the policy for one year and the insurance company must provide you with coverage for that period of time. If you cancel the insurance policy before the year is up, the company has to refund your money for the amount of the policy that you did not use.

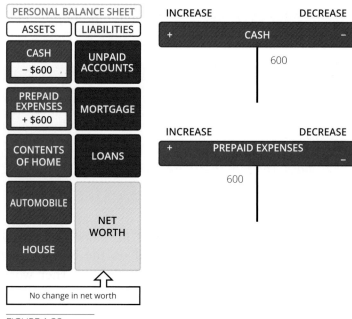

FIGURE 1.33

Prepaid Maintenance

Figure 1.33 illustrates another example of a prepaid expense. Assume that you hire a gardening service that costs $600 per year ($50 per month). The service provider requests that you prepay the full $600 in January. Ideally, if you were to cancel the contract with the company the next morning, you would receive all the money back because the company has not yet provided the service. In effect, you have simply given the company an interest-free loan. If you were to cancel the contract in three months, you would get back $450 [$600 – ($50 per month × 3 months)]; if it were canceled in six months, you would get back $300; and so on.

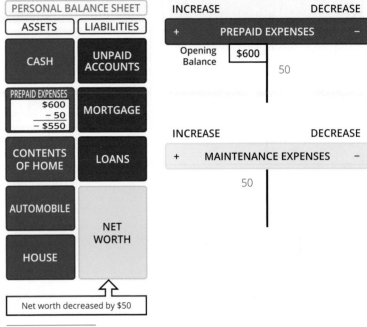

When you pay the $600 in advance the service provider owes you the service. As a result, this payment is considered an asset (which is a prepaid expense). There is no expense (i.e. a decrease in net worth) until the service is provided.

As each month goes by, the value of the prepaid expense decreases together with your net worth. You are *recognizing* the expense in the month in which it is used—not when it is paid.

FIGURE 1.34

As Figure 1.34 shows, after the first month of service is provided, you record $50 as an expense for that month, which decreases net worth. The remaining prepaid portion is $550. You will recognize $50 as an expense for each of the next 11 months as the supplier provides the service.

An increase in expenses relates to a decrease in net worth. Cash does not have to be involved to increase an expense and decrease net worth.

According to accrual-based accounting, expenses are always recorded when they are incurred. This has nothing to do with when the cash payment is made. If we assume an expense is $100, there are three possible timings the payment can be made in relation to the expense being incurred (see Figure 1.35).

1. Pay before and recognize the expense when it is incurred (prepaid expense)

2. Pay as the expense is incurred (cash)

3. Pay after the expense is incurred (unpaid account)

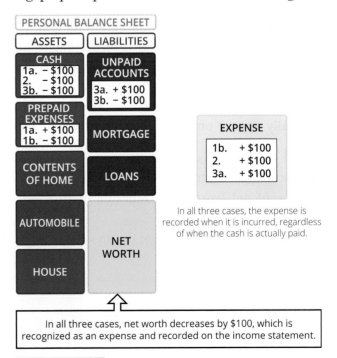

FIGURE 1.35

Figure 1.36 shows how to record each possible timing of payment in the relevant T-accounts.

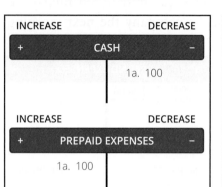

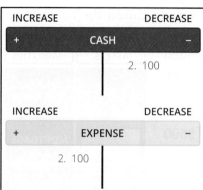

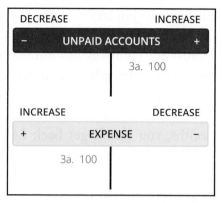

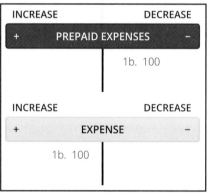

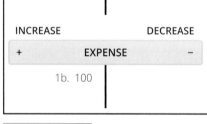

FIGURE 1.36

T-Account Transactions

To demonstrate how T-accounts are used to record financial transactions during a period, and how the income statement is linked to the balance sheet, we will examine several transactions. We begin the month with opening balances for assets, liabilities and net worth, which are the ending balances from the previous month. The opening balances of the asset accounts normally appear on the left side of the T-accounts (increase side), and the opening balances of the liabilities and net worth normally appear on the right side of the T-accounts (increase side).

Recall that the change in net worth is calculated by deducting expenses from revenue as reported on the income statement. The formula in Figure 1.37 shows how to calculate the ending or closing balance of net worth over a period of time.

Ending Net Worth = Beginning Net Worth + Capital + Surplus (Deficit)

FIGURE 1.37

The transactions are numbered in the list and in the T-accounts. Recall that the accounting equation must balance, so every transaction has a double entry that affects at least two accounts. To demonstrate how to record transactions in T-accounts, the information in Figure 1.39 will be used.

Opening Balances as at April 1, 2018			
Cash	$1,000	Unpaid Accounts	$1,500
Prepaid Insurance	0	Mortgage	90,000
Contents of Home	6,000	Bank Loan	0
House	150,000	Net Worth	65,500

FIGURE 1.38

The following transactions occurred during the month.
1. Earned and deposited a salary of $2,500
2. Paid $1,200 cash for a one-year insurance policy
3. Paid for $150 of entertainment with a credit card
4. Received a $4,000 loan from the bank
5. Paid $1,000 toward a mortgage; interest is $100 and the remainder is the principal
6. Purchased new furniture worth $1,400 with a credit card
7. Bought food with $400 cash

The transactions are recorded in T-accounts by using the following steps, illustrated in Figure 1.40.

ⓐ If applicable, enter the opening balances in the appropriate T-account. Then check that the accounting equation is in balance before you begin entering transactions.

ⓑ Enter both sides of the transaction in the correct account on the balance sheet and/or income statement. Be sure to record the transaction number so that you may check your work.

ⓒ Calculate the totals of the T-accounts on the income statement and the surplus or deficit.

ⓓ Calculate the totals of the T-accounts on the balance sheet and complete the accounting equation at the bottom of the balance sheet to check that it balances.

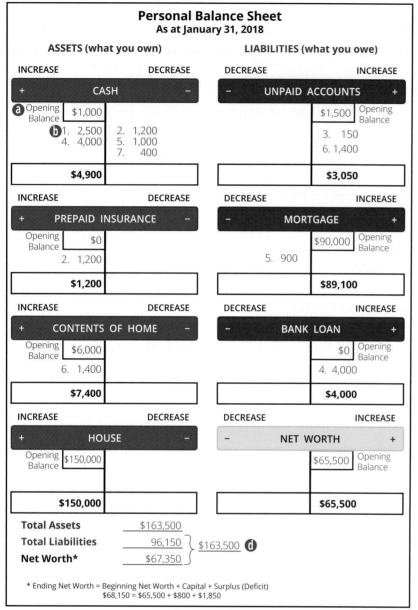

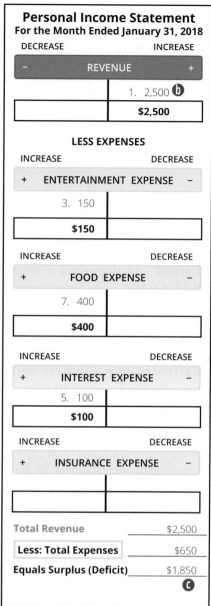

FIGURE 1.39

To calculate net worth, start with the the opening net worth of $65,500 and add the surplus of $1,850 from the income statement. This gives a closing net worth balance of $67,350. Note that if there was a deficit on the income statement, this would be subtracted from net worth.

Ethics and Internal Controls Related to Personal Accounting

LO 11

Throughout this accounting course, we will consider the concepts of ethics and internal controls. Any consideration of ethics begins with a look at ourselves. Businesses do not commit fraud as impersonal entities. It is the employees of those organizations who struggle with ethical lapses and may commit fraud. While ethics in all areas of an organization are important, it is critical that the accounting department and the management team exhibit high ethical standards.

Personal Ethics

Personal ethics include making moral and value-based decisions between right and wrong; sometimes referred to as having a conscience. Our actions and decisions affect everything and everyone around us. Personal ethics govern how we interact with other people and the goal is to have a positive impact on others. Over time, personal ethics have become the basis for business and legal ethics.

An individual faces countless ethical decisions over the course of a lifetime. Some decisions may be more obvious or easier to make than others. Some may be difficult and painful. There are many websites and even apps dedicated to helping people break down the steps required to make a thoughtful and responsible decision. Many of them follow a similar framework, which we will discuss here.

1. Identify the issue

The first step is to determine if this is an ethical dilemma. An ethical dilemma is when there is a choice between two or more options, none of which will resolve the situation without compromising some ethical principle. A situation is not an ethical dilemma if you have no choice in your course of action, perhaps because you are legally required to do something.

2. Get the facts

The second step is to determine the relevant facts of the case. You may need to do more research or investigation to collect all the facts. It also helps to consult with relevant persons or groups and come up with creative options together. Identify the individuals and groups that have an important stake in the outcome.

3. Evaluate alternative actions

Understanding the outcome of each course of action will help you determine the best way to proceed. For example, there may be an option that produces the most good and does the least harm. Or an option that best respects the rights of all who have a stake. Perhaps one option treats people equally or proportionately. Assess which option most closely aligns with your personal ethics, or the ethics of the organization you are representing.

4. Make a decision

Once you have considered all of the options, ask yourself which one best addresses the situation. Consult those involved who can help you make a decision and support your course of action. Ask yourself how your decision can be implemented with care and attention to the concerns of all stakeholders.

5. Act and reflect on the outcome

It is important once you have acted to evaluate the results and ask yourself what you have learned from the situation. These self-reflections help you learn from both your mistakes and success and make you a more effective decision-maker when faced with future problems.

Internal Controls

Internal controls are another issue to consider. Companies will have many internal controls to protect and manage the business. On a more personal level, internal controls for individuals are needed to:

- protect assets and accounts;
- ensure accurate financial records; and
- protect identity.

There are variety of things we can all do to protect ourselves, our accounts and to retain strong control over our money and assets.

- change passwords
- maintain identity theft protection
- check bank accounts regularly (at least once per week)
- change bank debit card PINs regularly
- use locks on doors and windows in your home
- use password protection on your computers, credit cards, accounts and websites
- monitor and review your bank statement for all the deposits and withdrawals

We need these personal internal controls to protect the things we own and make sure that our accounts are accurate and safe.

In Summary

LO 1 Describe the purpose of accounting

▸ Accounting identifies, measures and communicates financial activities. This can be done for an individual or a business.

LO 2 Describe the balance sheet

▸ The balance sheet is a permanent record that records what you own (assets), what you owe (liabilities) and your net worth.

LO 3 Describe the income statement

▸ The income statement is a temporary record used to determine the change in net worth (revenue minus expenses) over a period of time.

LO 4 Define an accounting period

▸ An accounting period is the time frame in which the financial statements are prepared.

LO 5 Explain how the accounting equation works

▸ The accounting equation is Assets = Liabilities + Net Worth. All transactions must be recorded in a way to ensure the accounting equation is always balanced.

LO 6 Explain accrual-based accounting

▸ Accrual-based accounting recognizes revenue and expenses in the time period in which they occur, regardless of when the payment is received or made.

▸ The change in net worth is recognized when the activity occurs, not when cash is transferred.

LO 7 Explain how to account for debt

▸ Borrowing money and repaying debt only affect assets and liabilities. The income statement and net worth are not affected.

LO 8 Explain how to account for assets

▸ Buying assets or selling them for the value shown on the balance sheet does not affect net worth. It is simply an exchange of one asset for another.

LO 9 Explain how to account for prepaid expenses

▸ Prepaid expenses are expenses paid for before the expense is incurred. Initially, they are recorded as an asset on the balance sheet. Once the expense has been incurred, the asset is reduced and an expense is recorded on the income statement.

LO 10 **Demonstrate how double entries are recorded in T-accounts**

▶ T-accounts are used to track the increases and decreases in the values of assets, liabilities, net worth, revenue and expenses. Double entries are used to keep the accounting equation balanced.

LO 11 **Describe ethics and internal controls related to personal accounting**

▶ Personal ethics govern how we interact with others and dictate our social behavior.

▶ Internal controls, such as locks and passwords, protect our assets, money and identity.

AMEENGAGE™ *Access **ameengage.com** for integrated resources including tutorials, practice exercises, the digital textbook and more.*

Review Exercise 1-1

When you woke up in the early morning of January 1, 2018, the opening balances in your personal accounting records appeared as follows.

Cash	$3,000
Contents of Home	3,000
House	100,000
Mortgage	70,000
Net Worth	36,000

The following transactions occurred during the month of January.

1. Earned and deposited $2,000 from salary
2. Earned and deposited $300 from providing tutoring services
3. Paid $300 cash for food
4. Went out for dinner and a show and spent $200 cash
5. Purchased new clothes with $100 cash
6. Paid $500 cash for maintenance on the house
7. Paid $100 cash for utilities

Complete the T-account worksheet for the January transactions and calculate ending net worth.

Personal Balance Sheet
As at January 31, 2018

ASSETS (what you own)

INCREASE   DECREASE
+ CASH −
Opening Balance

INCREASE   DECREASE
+ CONTENTS OF HOME −
Opening Balance

INCREASE   DECREASE
+ HOUSE −
Opening Balance

LIABILITIES (what you owe)

DECREASE   INCREASE
− UNPAID ACCOUNTS +
Opening Balance

DECREASE   INCREASE
− MORTGAGE +
Opening Balance

DECREASE   INCREASE
− NET WORTH +
Opening Balance

Total Assets _____
Total Liabilities _____
Net Worth* _____

* Ending Net Worth = Beginning Net Worth + Capital + Surplus (Deficit)

Personal Income Statement
For the Month Ended January 31, 2018

DECREASE   INCREASE
− REVENUE +

LESS EXPENSES

INCREASE   DECREASE
+ CLOTHING EXPENSE −

INCREASE   DECREASE
+ ENTERTAINMENT EXPENSE −

INCREASE   DECREASE
+ FOOD EXPENSE −

INCREASE   DECREASE
+ MAINTENANCE EXPENSE −

INCREASE   DECREASE
+ UTILITIES EXPENSE −

Total Revenue _____
Less: Total Expenses _____
Equals Surplus (Deficit) _____

See Appendix I for solutions.

Chapter 2
Linking Personal Accounting To Business Accounting

Learning Objectives

LO 1 List the differences between personal accounts and business accounts

- Equity vs. Net Worth

LO 2 Describe the three main types of businesses

- Service Business
- Merchandising Business
- Manufacturing Business

LO 3 Record revenue based on the concept of accruals

- Cash Received Before the Service is Performed
- Cash Received When the Service is Performed
- Cash Received After the Service is Performed

LO 4 Record expenses based on the concept of accruals

- Cash Paid Before the Expense is Incurred

- Cash Paid When the Expense is Incurred
- Cash Paid After the Expense is Incurred

LO 5 Record business transactions in T-accounts

LO 6 Identify the four required financial statements and prepare three financial statements

- Income Statement
- Statement of Owner's Equity
- Balance Sheet
- Statement of Cash Flows

LO 7 Describe ethics related to financial statement reporting

- Fraud Triangle

 *Access **ameengage.com** for integrated resources including tutorials, practice exercises, the digital textbook and more.*

MAKING IT REAL TO YOU

Starting today, notice where you go and how you do business. In other words, become aware of your financial transactions. If you were to record all of your transactions for a few months, you would quickly see where your money comes from and where it goes. You would also see the different types of businesses that you buy from—some are *service* businesses, like your internet service provider; others are retail (*merchandising*) businesses, like an office supplies store; or maybe you need to order a replacement part for your home coffee maker directly from the manufacturer (a *manufacturing* business). Also note *how* you pay for these things. Does the supplier require a deposit, or payment in full, before it provides the goods or services? Perhaps payment can be made after the goods or services are provided? How does the business account for receiving your cash or credit card payment? How does the business handle debit and credit card transactions? Let us begin by taking a closer look at the business side of things and how accounting works.

Business Accounts

Most of what you have learned about accounting in the personal context is similar to accounting in a business context. However, business accounting is more complex than personal accounting. To begin examining the differences, we will look at how terminology differs in business accounting.

1. The personal balance sheet and the personal income statement are called the balance sheet and the income statement, respectively.

2. Cash in a business is like cash in personal accounting. However, businesses may have several different bank accounts and all of these amounts are reported and known as cash.

3. Accounts receivable is a new business asset account. This is used when the business sells services or products to a customer and allows the customer to pay later. **Accounts receivable** is the amount owed to the business by its customers.

4. Merchandise inventory is an asset account used when a business sells products to customers. This account is discussed in detail in later chapters.

5. Equipment, buildings, land and other similar assets that provide the business with benefits for a long period of time are called **property, plant and equipment** or noncurrent assets. These items are not intended to be sold to customers.

6. Unpaid accounts in the personal context are called accounts payable in a business. **Accounts payable** is the obligation the business owes to others.

7. **Unearned revenue** is an obligation the business has to provide products or services to a customer. It is used when a customer prepays the business for products or services.

8. Just as a person may have loans or mortgages, a business may also have long-term debt. Notes payable is a business liability account used when a business signs a written document, such as a bank loan agreement, to borrow money. This account is discussed in detail in later chapters.

9. The category of net worth is referred to as **equity**. The equity may belong to the business owner, the partners, or stockholders, depending on the organization of the business. Business organization is discussed later.

10. Revenue is called either service revenue or sales revenue. If a business provides services to its customers, it uses **service revenue**, a broad term to include various types of revenue, such as interest or fees earned. If it sells products to its customers, it uses **sales revenue**. Some businesses provide both and use both accounts on the income statement.

11. Although there are some similarities in the expense items on the income statement, a business usually has more types of expenses. We will discuss these new expenses as they appear in the textbook. A business typically lists its expenses on the income statement in alphabetical order.

12. Surplus (deficit) on the personal income statement is now called net income (loss). **Net income** occurs when revenue exceeds expenses for the period, which causes equity to increase. A **net loss** occurs when expenses exceed revenue for the period, which causes equity to decrease.

Figure 2.1 shows the comparison between the personal balance sheet and the business balance sheet, and between the personal income statement and the business income statement.

PERSONAL		BUSINESS		PERSONAL		BUSINESS	
PERSONAL BALANCE SHEET		**BALANCE SHEET**		**PERSONAL INCOME STATEMENT**		**INCOME STATEMENT**	
ASSETS	LIABILITIES	ASSETS	LIABILITIES	REVENUE		SERVICE REVENUE	
CASH	UNPAID ACCOUNTS	CASH	ACCOUNTS PAYABLE	EXPENSES		EXPENSES	
PREPAID EXPENSES	MORTGAGE	ACCOUNTS RECEIVABLE	UNEARNED REVENUE	ENTERTAINMENT	INTEREST	DEPRECIATION	RENT
CONTENTS OF HOME	LOANS	MERCHANDISE INVENTORY	NOTES PAYABLE	FOOD	MAINTENANCE	INSURANCE	SUPPLIES
AUTOMOBILE	NET WORTH	PREPAID EXPENSES	EQUITY	INSURANCE	UTILITIES	INTEREST	UTILITIES
HOUSE		PROPERTY, PLANT & EQUIPMENT		SURPLUS (DEFICIT)		NET INCOME (LOSS)	

FIGURE 2.1

A CLOSER LOOK

The list of accounts shown here is a small sample of common accounts used. Large companies usually have dozens of asset and liability accounts to track these items. The income statement usually has multiple types of revenue accounts and hundreds of different expense accounts. As we progress through this textbook, we will introduce more accounts as needed, indicating whether they are asset, liability, equity, revenue or expense accounts.

Equity vs. Net Worth

Equity is the net worth of a business. Similar to net worth introduced in personal accounting, a business' equity is the leftover value after all assets have been sold and all liabilities have been paid.

WORTH REPEATING

The accounting equation is now
Assets = Liabilities + Owner's Equity

There are a few different forms of organizations, and equity has different names based on which form an organization takes. You will learn about different forms of organizations and different names of equity in Chapter 3. In this chapter, we will focus on the sole proprietorship form of business, which is a business owned by a single person. The term "owner's equity" is used to describe the equity of the business. At the end of the accounting period, the ending owner's equity balance can be calculated as shown in Figure 2.2.

Ending Owner's Equity = Beginning Owner's Equity + Owner's Contributions
+ Net Income (Loss) – Owner's Withdrawals

FIGURE 2.2

Owner's contributions is the amount of cash or assets invested in the business by the owner. **Owner's withdrawals** is the amount of cash or assets taken by the owner for personal use. If a company is brand new and has just started operations, then beginning owner's equity will be $0. If a company has been established for at least one accounting period, then the beginning owner's equity is equal to the previous period's ending owner's equity.

In business accounting, owner's equity is a category on the balance sheet but not an account. Separate accounts are required to record transactions such as owner's contributions and owner's withdrawals.

The **owner's capital account** is used to record the amount of the owner's equity including owner's contributions. Owner's contributions are added directly into owner's capital. The owner can also withdraw cash from the business to pay for personal items. These withdrawals are recorded in the **owner's withdrawals account** (or owner's drawings account) and decrease the business' assets and the value of owner's equity. Owner's withdrawals are never an expense and never appear on the income statement. Owner's withdrawals, although a part of equity, do not appear on the balance sheet. Instead, they appear on the statement of owner's equity, which will be introduced later in the chapter.

In the personal T-account worksheet from Chapter 1, we used a single T-account to track the net worth transactions of an individual. In the context of a business, this single T-account is now represented by owner's capital. A separate T-account is used for owner's withdrawals to track the amount removed from the business for personal use. The two T-accounts in Figure 2.3 are the generic capital and withdrawals accounts. In an actual sole proprietary business, these accounts typically have the owner's name attached to them. For example, if John Smith was the owner, the accounts are called "Smith, Capital" and "Smith, Withdrawals."

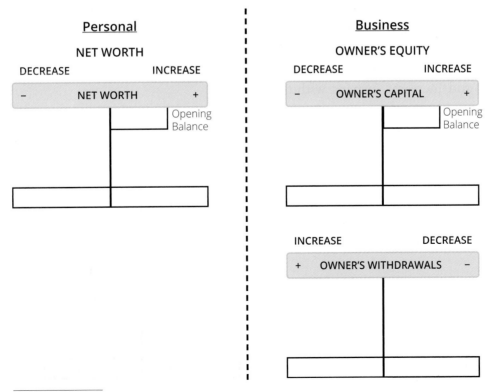

FIGURE 2.3

The T-account increase and decrease map introduced in Chapter 1 needs to be modified to accommodate the new T-accounts that make up owner's equity: capital and withdrawals. Figure 2.4 shows the new T-account map that will be followed throughout the chapter. Notice that owner's withdrawals increases on the left side of the T-account, like an expense, and owner's capital increases on the right side of the T-account, like revenue.

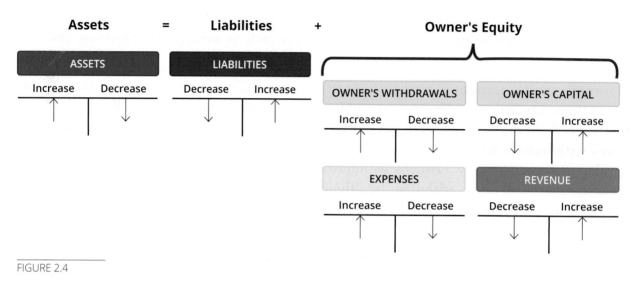

FIGURE 2.4

Figure 2.5 illustrates how T-account entries relate to the owner's capital and owner's withdrawals. Suppose that the owner of a new company invested $10,000 in cash into the company (transaction 1). This increases owner's capital and increases cash. Because this is a newly formed company, all opening account balances are $0.

Also, suppose that the owner withdrew $1,000 from the company for personal use (transaction 2). In this transaction, the capital of the business is distributed to the owner for personal use and not for generating revenue; therefore, owner's withdrawal is different from incurring expenses. It is the reverse of what happens when the owner invests some assets into the business. This transaction decreases cash and increases owner's withdrawals:

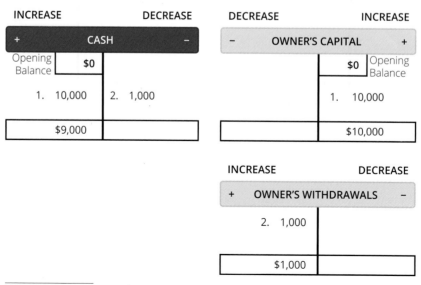

FIGURE 2.5

Financial Statements of Different Types of Businesses

Different types of businesses use different financial statement layouts: a small consulting firm uses a very simple income statement and balance sheet compared to a complex manufacturing company that produces goods. A manufacturing company requires a more detailed set of financial statements, which provides the information a manager needs to operate the business effectively.

The following examples display financial statements for three main types of businesses: service, merchandising, and manufacturing.

Service Business

The financial statements shown in Figure 2.6 represent a simple service business. Examples of services include accounting, consulting, lawn maintenance or general contracting. A few new items are presented on the income statement and balance sheet: cost of sales, gross profit and work in progress.

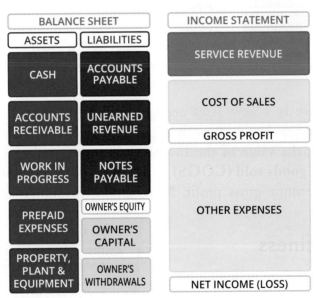

FIGURE 2.6

Cost of sales are the expenses directly tied to the service revenue earned; for example, in a consulting firm, this would be the salary of the consultants. All other expenses are part of the operating expenses (i.e. rent, insurance, depreciation, etc.). The difference between service revenue and cost of sales is called **gross profit**. Gross profit is used to pay for all other expenses and is discussed in detail later in the text. Some service businesses do not separate cost of sales from other expenses, in which case gross profit is not reported.

On the balance sheet, there may be an asset account called Work in Progress. This represents jobs that are currently being worked on but are not yet complete. An example is a training company in the middle of developing a training program. This partially completed work is eventually recognized as cost of sales and matched to revenue when the service is delivered to the client.

Merchandising Business

The financial statements shown in Figure 2.7 represent a merchandising business. Any company that buys goods to resell to customers is considered a merchandising business. A common example is a retail store, such as a hardware, clothing, toy or convenience store.

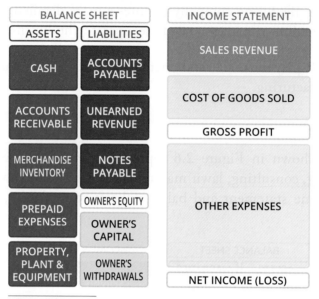

FIGURE 2.7

On the balance sheet, there is a new asset account called Merchandise Inventory. This account tracks the value of all the goods the store has purchased and intends to sell to its customers. Once these items are sold, the value of the inventory is transferred to cost of goods sold on the income statement. **Cost of goods sold (COGS)** is the value of all the goods sold and is subtracted from sales revenue to determine gross profit. Merchandise inventory and COGS are covered in later chapters.

Manufacturing Business

The financial statements of a manufacturing company are shown in Figure 2.8. A manufacturing company makes the products that it sells. Examples of manufacturers include auto makers, steel mills and furniture makers.

The balance sheet has an asset account called Inventory, similar to a retail store. However, a manufacturer has different types of inventory at various stages of production. Raw materials represent items that will be transformed into the product that can be sold (e.g. lumber used to make furniture). Work in progress represents partially completed products, and finished goods represent

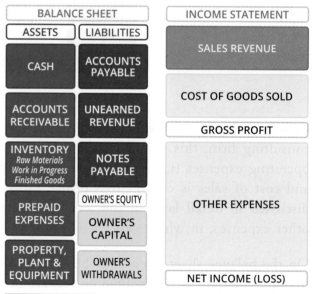

FIGURE 2.8

products that can be sold to customers. Once the items are sold, they are recorded in COGS.

IN THE REAL WORLD

 It is simple to grasp the nature of a particular business by labeling it as either a service, merchandising or manufacturing business. However, some companies operate as a combination of two or more of these types of businesses.

Consider Apple Inc., which is a well-known manufacturer of breakthrough technology, such as the Macintosh operating system, iPod, iPhone and iPad. The company also has a merchandising segment; it operates online and retail stores. These stores sell Apple manufactured products, as well as complementary products from other manufacturers, such as security software and computer speakers.

Apple is also a service business because it provides online support as well as warranty and repair services for its products. It also provides online services such as iCloud, a cloud storage and computing service that allows users to store personal data on remote servers, synchronize data, back up key files and so on.

Therefore, Apple is a hybrid of a service, merchandising and manufacturing business. However, it is reasonable to deem the company as primarily a manufacturing business since sales of its own products represent the majority of its total revenue.

Recording Revenue   LO 3

In business accounting, as in personal accounting, accrual-based accounting is used to record transactions. Revenues are recorded or recognized when they are earned regardless of when cash is received from customers. Cash payment for products or services can be received from customers at three different times.

1. Received before services are performed or products are sold
2. Received when services are performed or products are sold
3. Received after services are performed or products are sold

Revenue transactions are recorded differently depending on whether cash is received before, when, or after services are performed or products are sold. This section illustrates how revenue transactions are recorded for each of the above three scenarios. While a service business is used in our examples, the same concept also applies to merchandising and manufacturing businesses. In all cases, *equity increases when revenue is recognized.*

Cash Received Before the Service is Performed

When a customer pays a business for services before they are performed, it is known as a **customer deposit**. A number of different types of businesses require deposits or prepayments for their services. Examples include banquet halls (hall rental fees), health clubs (memberships), magazine publishers (subscription dues) and insurance companies (insurance premiums). In each case, the business receives cash up front and provides a service at a later date.

Since services have not been performed at the time the cash is received, service revenue cannot be recognized at this time. Instead, the business has an obligation to provide services in the future. You will recall that an obligation of a business is a liability. Thus, a new liability account known as Unearned Revenue must be used.

Suppose a business receives a deposit of $1,100 from a customer one month before services must be provided. Figure 2.9 illustrates the impact on the business accounts at the time the customer paid for the services. The prepayment by the customer is a liability for the business (unearned revenue) because the business now has an obligation to provide services to the customer. The payment is essentially held in trust on behalf of the customer. In this scenario, both cash and unearned revenue are increased by $1,100, meaning that assets and liabilities are both increased by the same amount. At this point, there is no impact on equity because even though cash is received, revenue is not recognized since no work has been completed. If the business fails to provide the services, they must return the deposit to the customer.

It is only when work is completed in the next month that revenue can be recognized. The transaction to record this is covered in a later chapter.

FIGURE 2.9

Cash Received When the Service is Performed

When a company performs a service and the customer pays for it immediately, the transaction is fairly straightforward. From the service provider's perspective, cash increases and equity increases. The increase in equity is recognized as revenue and increases net income.

In this example, a client purchases a service from a business for $1,100. If the client pays cash immediately when the business provides the service, then cash and service revenue are both increased by $1,100. Owner's equity increases by $1,100 as a result of the increase in service revenue. The impact on cash and service revenue is shown in Figure 2.10. Remember that recognizing revenue results in an increase to equity.

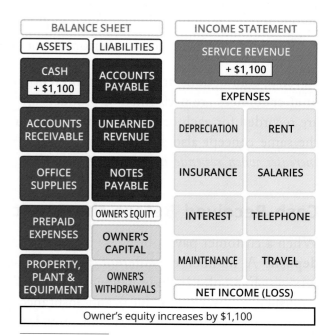

FIGURE 2.10

Cash Received After the Service is Performed

Most businesses provide customers with payment terms, allowing them to pay after they have received the product or service (e.g. 30 days to pay the balance owing). This is sometimes referred to as "selling on account." It may seem that the value of equity would not change when selling with payment terms because cash has not been received from the sale. However, revenue must be recorded at the time the product is sold or the service is delivered, regardless of when the payment is received.

When a company provides payment terms to sell its products or services, the money owed by its customers is recorded as an asset, called Accounts Receivable. After a service is provided, the seller issues an invoice to the buyer. The **invoice** includes the details of the service rendered, the amount owing, and the terms of payment. From the seller's perspective, this is an increase in accounts receivable (an asset) and an increase in equity (recognized as revenue). Later, when the customer actually pays the outstanding amount, the issuing company increases cash and decreases accounts receivable. The decrease in accounts receivable shows that the service provider received cash and is no longer owed any amount from the customer (i.e. nothing is "receivable").

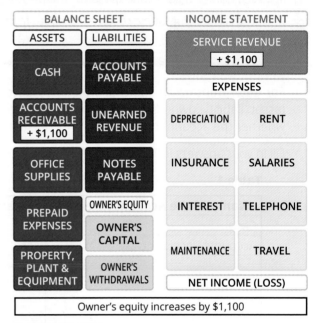

FIGURE 2.11

For example, suppose a business provides services valued at $1,100 and sends an invoice to the client. The client has promised to pay in one month. Even though this client is not paying for the services immediately, equity increases and is recognized as service revenue on the income statement. This causes net income to increase. The amount is also recorded in accounts receivable, an asset indicating the business expects to receive cash from the client in the future. This is illustrated in Figure 2.11. Remember that recognizing revenue results in an increase to equity.

Now assume that one month has passed and the business receives a payment of $1,100 from the client. Figure 2.12 illustrates the accounting impact of this transaction. This transaction is often referred to as "receipt of account." It increases cash by $1,100 and reduces accounts receivable by the same amount. Equity does not change since one asset is exchanged for another.

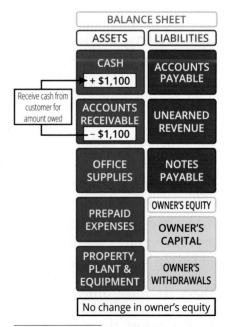

FIGURE 2.12

Pause & Reflect

Exercise 2-1

Felix Graham owns and operates a photography business called Eternity Photography, which is a sole proprietorship. The following transactions occurred this month.

1. A customer paid $3,000 owed for the photographs that Felix had already provided last month.
2. Eternity Photography received $4,000 from a couple immediately after the wedding had been photographed.
3. A customer paid a $1,000 deposit for Eternity Photography to photograph her wedding next year.

For each transaction, indicate which two accounts are affected and the category of each account (asset, liability, owner's capital, owner's withdrawal, revenue or expense). In the final column, indicate whether the account balance would increase or decrease as a result of each transaction.

Fill in your answers in Table 1. The first transaction has been completed as an example.

Table 1

	Name of the Account Affected	Category of Account	Increase or Decrease
1.	Cash	Asset	Increase
	Accounts Receivable	Asset	Decrease
2.			
3.			

See Appendix I for solutions.

Recording Expenses

LO 4

Expenses, similar to revenues, are recorded when they are incurred, not necessarily when they are paid.

An expense is incurred by a company if the activities related to the expense have been used or consumed. You may also see the term "recognized" when it comes to expenses and revenue. **Recognizing** an expense or revenue means recording it on the income statement. For example, if a company has hired a lawn care service company to water the grass on August 16, the expense is incurred once the grass has been watered; the expense is recognized at that time. If a company pays for internet services, the internet expense for a given month is incurred once that month has ended. In all cases, *equity decreases when an expense is recognized.*

There are three different timings of the cash payments for expenses.

1. Pay before the expense is incurred
2. Pay when the expense is incurred
3. Pay after the expense is incurred

This section illustrates how expense transactions are recorded for each of the above three scenarios.

Cash Paid Before the Expense is Incurred

When a company pays before the expense has been incurred, it is a supplier prepayment. This requires increasing an asset account called Prepaid Expense, which was discussed in the context of personal accounting. These prepayments are not considered an expense at the time they are paid because the service or the product has not been used. Some common examples of prepaid expenses are rent and office supplies.

Another example is purchasing an insurance policy. Assume, a business paid cash ahead of time to an insurance company for one year of insurance coverage. At the time of the payment, cash decreases and a prepaid expense called prepaid insurance increases. This prepaid expense is considered an asset because it could be turned back into cash if the entire year of insurance is not used up (e.g. the policy is canceled).

The business paid $3,600 on January 1, 2018 for insurance coverage throughout 2018. On January 1, 2018, when the payment is made, the business' cash (an asset) decreases by $3,600 and prepaid insurance (another asset) increases by $3,600. At this point, equity is not affected. One asset was exchanged for another asset. This is shown in Figure 2.13.

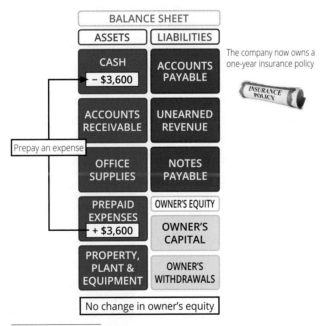

FIGURE 2.13

Notice that expenses, and thus equity, have not been affected yet. Only as the asset is used up is the expense recorded. If the insurance company fails to provide the services, or the business cancels the policy, the insurance company has to return cash to the business for the unused portion of the policy. In this example, a portion of the prepaid insurance becomes an expense as each month passes. The details for this transaction are covered in a later chapter.

Cash Paid When the Expense is Incurred

When a company incurs an expense and pays for it immediately, the transaction is fairly straightforward. From the company's perspective, cash decreases and equity decreases. The decrease in equity is recorded as an expense on the income statement, which reduces net income. Suppose a business paid $800 cash for a salesperson to travel to a client's head office. Figure 2.14 illustrates the accounting treatment when paying immediately in cash for travel expenses. Remember that recognizing an expense results in a decrease to equity. This transaction reduces cash by $800 and increases travel expense by the same amount. The $800 increase in expenses decreases equity by $800.

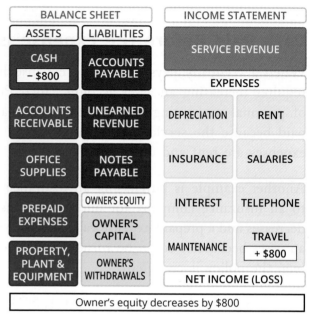

FIGURE 2.14

Cash Paid After the Expense is Incurred

Many expenses are paid after they have been incurred. This form of paying expenses is sometimes referred to as "paying on account" or "on credit." You may think that the value of equity would not change until the expense is paid for. However, accounting standards require expenses to be recorded at the time they are incurred, *regardless of when the payment is made.*

A business that provides products or services to another business is known as a supplier. When a company owes a supplier for a product or service, the money owed is recorded as a liability called Accounts Payable. When an invoice is issued to the company by the supplier (after the expense has been incurred), the value of the invoice is recorded as an increase to the accounts payable account and an increase to the appropriate expense account. Later, when the company actually pays the outstanding amount, the transaction is recorded as a decrease to cash and a decrease to accounts payable. The company used cash to pay and it no longer owes any amount to the supplier (i.e. nothing is "payable").

Suppose a business will pay for a maintenance expense two months after it has been incurred. Even though the business is not paying for the services immediately, the supplier issues an invoice as soon as the maintenance work is done. Assume that the supplier is charging $700 for its maintenance services. Figure 2.15 shows the impact on the

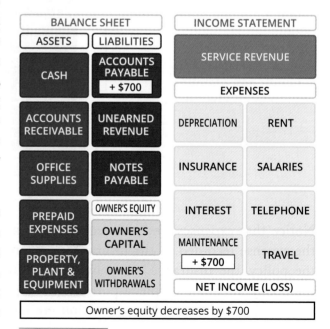

FIGURE 2.15

applicable accounts of the business when the invoice is received from the supplier. Remember that recognizing an expense results in a decrease to equity. This transaction increases both accounts payable and maintenance expenses by $700. The $700 increase in expenses means there is a $700 decrease in equity.

Now assume that two months have passed and the business pays the $700 owed to the maintenance supplier. Figure 2.16 illustrates the accounting impact of this transaction. This transaction is often referred to as a "payment of account." Both cash and accounts payable decrease by $700. Equity does not change. Only an asset (cash) and a liability (accounts payable) are affected.

FIGURE 2.16

Pause & Reflect

Exercise 2-2

Eternity Photography had the following transactions occur during the current month.

1. Eternity Photography paid $50 cash for gas to travel to a client's wedding venue.
2. Eternity Photography received a telephone bill for $120, which will be paid next month.
3. Eternity Photography purchased a one-year insurance policy for $1,400 cash, to insure its photography equipment.

For each transaction, indicate which two accounts are affected and the category of the account (asset, liability, owner's capital, owner's withdrawal, revenue or expense). In the final column, indicate whether the account balance would increase or decrease as a result of the transaction.

Fill in your answers in Table 1. The first transaction has been completed as an example.

Table 1

	Name of the Account Affected	Category of Account	Increase or Decrease
1.	Travel Expense	Expense	Increase
	Cash	Asset	Decrease
2.			
3.			

See Appendix I for solutions.

Business Transactions

The ultimate goal of recording business transactions is to be able to create financial statements and assess how well the business is performing. A transaction occurs when the business trades something of value with another person or business and this causes a change in assets, liabilities or equity. This could include services, products, cash, a promise to pay money or the right to collect money.

However, not everything the business does will be recorded in the T-accounts and appear on the financial statements. An **event** does not involve trading something of value. Since assets, liabilities and equity are not affected by an event, nothing is recorded in the T-accounts. An event can lead to a transaction at a later date, but it is only then that the transaction is recorded in the T-accounts. For example, signing a contract with a customer to provide service in two months' time is an event. At the signing, nothing of value has been traded; therefore, nothing is recorded in the T-accounts. However, two months later after the services have been provided, a transaction has occurred and is recorded in the T-accounts.

The following pages examine several business transactions made by Ace Bookkeepers, a sole proprietorship owned by John Smith, during the month of March 2018. For each transaction that follows, we will show how it is recorded in the T-accounts, how the accounting equation remains in balance, and explain any impact on owner's equity. Keep in mind that every transaction must leave the accounting equation in balance, so every transaction must be recorded in at least two accounts.

1. The owner deposited $30,000 cash into the new business' bank account

When an owner invests his or her own cash into a sole proprietorship, the cash is recorded directly in the owner's capital and regarded as owner's equity. This transaction increases cash by $30,000 (impacting the left side of its T-account), and increases owner's capital by $30,000 (impacting the right side of its T-account). An increase in cash increases assets and an increase in the capital increases owner's equity, balancing the accounting equation, as shown in Figure 2.17.

Record the transaction in the T-accounts

FIGURE 2.17

2. Ace Bookkeepers borrowed $10,000 from the bank

The business has increased its debt by getting a loan from the bank. As shown in Figure 2.18, this transaction increases cash by $10,000 (impacting the left side of its T-account), and increases the value of notes payable by $10,000 (impacting the right side of its T-account). An increase in cash increases assets and the receipt of the

WORTH REPEATING

A bank loan increases an asset and a liability without affecting the balance of owner's equity.

bank loan increases liabilities. The transaction has no impact on owner's equity; therefore nothing is recorded on the income statement. The accounting equation is balanced.

Record the transaction in the T-accounts

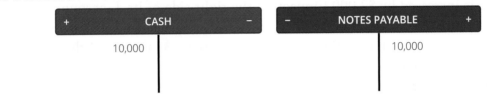

+	CASH	−		−	NOTES PAYABLE	+
	10,000				10,000	

Analyze the accounting equation and impact on owner's equity

Assets	=	**Liabilities**	+ **Owner's Equity**	**Impact on Owner's Equity**
+ 10,000		+ 10,000		None

FIGURE 2.18

3. Ace Bookkeepers bought $8,000 worth of furniture with cash

Furniture, computers, cars and other similar items are considered to be property, plant and equipment and are noncurrent assets. These assets are used to run the business and generate sales and should not be sold to customers or to raise cash for day-to-day expenses. Each type of property, plant and equipment is given its own T-account. Cash payment for furniture means that cash is decreased by $8,000 (impacting the right side of its T-account) and furniture is increased by $8,000 (impacting the left side of its T-account). This transaction is simply an exchange of one asset for another with no impact on the owner's equity, as shown in Figure 2.19.

Record the transaction in the T-accounts

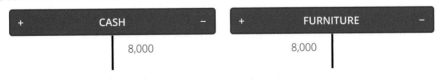

+	CASH	−		+	FURNITURE	−
		8,000			8,000	

Analyze the accounting equation and impact on owner's equity

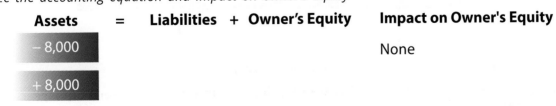

Assets	=	**Liabilities**	+ **Owner's Equity**	**Impact on Owner's Equity**
− 8,000				None
+ 8,000				

FIGURE 2.19

4. A customer paid $2,000 cash for bookkeeping services to be provided next month

One way to receive payment for services is for the customer to pay before the services are performed. In this case, when the customer pays cash, the services will not be provided until next month. This means that service revenue cannot be recognized when cash is received. Ace Bookkeepers has accepted an obligation to provide services in one month. An obligation is a liability, meaning the amount received is recorded as an increase to cash and an increase to a liability account called unearned revenue. Unearned revenue represents the obligation the business has to provide services or products to customers in the future. If services are not performed by the business, the cash must be returned to the customer.

In this transaction, cash is increased by $2,000 (impacting the left side of its T-account) and unearned revenue is increased by $2,000 (impacting the right side of its T-account). The transaction is illustrated in Figure 2.20. An increase in cash increases assets and an increase in unearned revenue increases liabilities, balancing the accounting equation. At this time, there is no impact on owner's equity as revenue has not been earned. The transaction to turn this liability into revenue is covered in a later chapter.

Record the transaction in the T-accounts

Analyze the accounting equation and impact on owner's equity

FIGURE 2.20

5. Ace Bookkeepers provided services to customers and received $15,000 cash

The sale of services is called revenue and is the primary way a service business increases owner's equity. As shown in Figure 2.21, this transaction is recorded by increasing cash by $15,000 (impacting the left side of its T-account), and increasing service revenue by $15,000 (impacting the right side of its T-account). An increase in cash increases assets and an increase in service revenue increases owner's equity. The accounting equation is balanced.

Record the transaction in the T-accounts

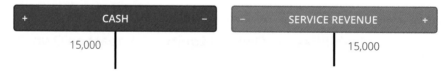

Analyze the accounting equation and impact on owner's equity

FIGURE 2.21

6. Ace Bookkeepers provided services for $4,000 on account

Another way to receive payment for services provided is to allow a customer to pay at a later date. Services have been provided, so revenue must be recognized. However, cash is not affected since there has been no payment. Instead, another asset called accounts receivable increases. Recall that accounts receivable is the amount owing to the business from its customers. Since accounts receivable will eventually be collected and become cash, it is regarded as an asset. In this transaction, as shown in Figure 2.22, accounts receivable is increased by $4,000 (impacting the left side of its T-account) and service revenue is increased by $4,000 (impacting the right side of its T-account). The increase in service revenue is also an increase in owner's equity. The accounting equation is balanced.

Record the transaction in the T-accounts

Analyze the accounting equation and impact on owner's equity

FIGURE 2.22

7. Ace Bookkeepers paid $6,000 cash for a one-year insurance policy, which starts on the first of next month

It is common for a business to prepay various expenses such as insurance, web-hosting fees, consulting fees and legal fees. Recall from Chapter 1 how prepaid expenses are recorded. The same concept is practiced in business. The item that is prepaid is initially recorded as an asset on the balance sheet. In this transaction, cash is decreased by $6,000 (impacting the right side of its T-account) and prepaid insurance is increased by $6,000 (impacting the left side of its T-account). Figure 2.23 shows how the prepayment for insurance is recorded by decreasing one type of asset (cash) and increasing another type of asset (prepaid insurance) with no impact on the owner's equity. The accounting equation is balanced. The transaction to convert prepaid insurance (an asset) to an expense is covered in a later chapter.

Record the transaction in the T-accounts

Analyze the accounting equation and impact on owner's equity

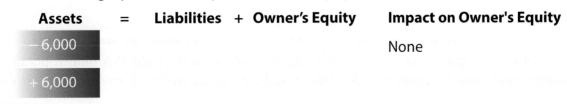

FIGURE 2.23

8. Ace Bookkeepers paid $1,100 cash for rent for the month

9. Ace Bookkeepers paid $6,000 cash to employees for salaries

10. Ace Bookkeepers paid $200 cash for interest on the note payable

All of these transactions relate to cash expenses. As illustrated in Figure 2.24, the transactions are recorded by decreasing the value of the cash account and increasing the value of the appropriate expense accounts. In these transactions, cash is decreased by a total of $7,300 (impacting the right side of its T-account) and the appropriate expense accounts are increased by a total of $7,300 (impacting the left side of their T-accounts). These expenses were incurred by the business in order to run the business and help generate revenue. Remember, the equity in the business decreases and is recorded as an increase to expenses while assets are reduced as cash decreases. The accounting equation is balanced.

Record the transactions in the T-accounts

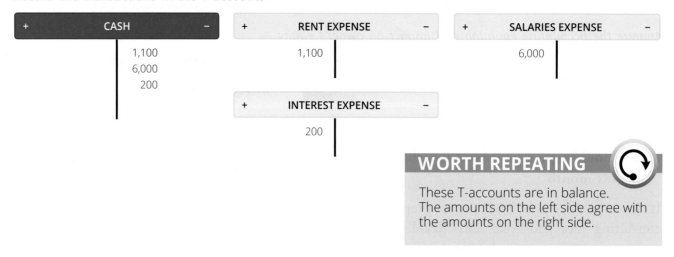

Analyze the accounting equation and impact on owner's equity

Assets	=	Liabilities	+	Owner's Equity	Impact on Owner's Equity
− 1,100				− 1,100	Decreased because of rent expense
− 6,000				− 6,000	Decreased because of salaries expense
− 200				− 200	Decreased because of interest expense

FIGURE 2.24

11. Ace Bookkeepers received a telephone bill for $300, which will be paid later

12. Ace Bookkeepers paid travel expenses of $2,000 with a credit card, which will be paid next month

The telephone expense is due to be paid next month and travel expenses were billed to a credit card that is also to be paid next month. These expenses must be recorded this month because they were incurred and used to generate sales this month; expenses incurred are matched to revenue earned in the same period. In these transactions, accounts payable is increased by $2,300 (impacting the right side of its T-account) and the appropriate expense accounts are increased by a total of $2,300 (impacting the left side of their T-accounts). This transaction is recorded by increasing both liabilities and the appropriate expense accounts, as illustrated in Figure 2.25. The equity in the business decreases and is recorded as an increase to expenses. The accounting equation is balanced.

Record the transactions in the T-accounts

Analyze the accounting equation and impact on owner's equity

FIGURE 2.25

13. Ace Bookkeeping repaid $3,000 toward the note payable

This transaction is the opposite of transaction 2. To pay back part of the note payable principal, cash (an asset) and notes payable (a liability) are both decreased, with no impact on the owner's equity. As illustrated in Figure 2.26, cash is decreased by $3,000 (impacting the right side of its T-account) and the notes payable is decreased by $3,000 (impacting the left side of its T-account). The accounting equation is balanced. Repaying any debt, including accounts payable, is recorded in a similar manner. It is important to be able to pay back loans when they are due. Failure to pay loans on time is called defaulting on the loan and can make it more difficult to borrow in the future. In some cases, defaulting may also cause the business to close down.

Record the transaction in the T-accounts

Analyze the accounting equation and impact on owner's equity

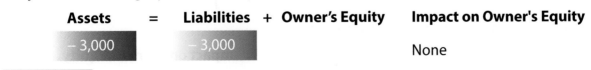

FIGURE 2.26

14. The owner withdrew $2,000 cash for personal use

In a sole proprietorship, the owner is not an employee and does not receive a salary the way that other employees do. Instead, the owner can be compensated in the form of cash withdrawal from the business. As discussed earlier, owner's withdrawals are a direct decrease to owner's equity and are not recorded as expenses. This transaction is recorded by decreasing cash by $2,000 (impacting the right side of its T-account) and increasing owner's withdrawals by $2,000 (impacting the left side of its T-account), as shown in Figure 2.27. The decrease in equity is recorded as an increase to owner's withdrawals and a decrease in cash reduces assets. The accounting equation is balanced.

Record the transaction in the T-accounts

Analyze the accounting equation and impact on owner's equity

FIGURE 2.27

15. A customer paid $500 cash for the amount owing for services provided earlier in the month

In transaction 6, Ace Bookkeepers provided services to a customer and allowed them to pay later. Cash only increases when payment is received. Since amounts owed by customers are recorded in the asset account called accounts receivable, this account decreases when a customer pays the bill. In this transaction, cash is increased by $500 (impacting the left side of its T-account) and accounts receivable is decreased by $500 (impacting the right side of its T-account). An increase in cash increases assets, while a decrease in accounts receivable decreases assets. Notice that service revenue is not affected by this transaction, so owner's equity is not impacted. Service revenue increased in transaction 6 when the service was performed. This transaction is just an exchange of one asset for another, as shown in Figure 2.28. The accounting equation is balanced.

Record the transaction in the T-accounts

Analyze the accounting equation and impact on owner's equity

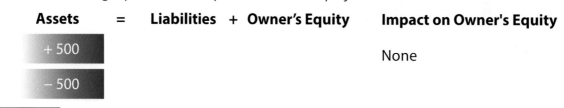

FIGURE 2.28

16. Ace Bookkeepers paid the telephone bill received earlier in the month

In transaction 11, a telephone bill was received but not paid immediately. Cash only decreases when the payment is made. Recall that amounts owed to suppliers are recorded in the liability account called accounts payable. Thus, when Ace Bookkeepers pays the bill, accounts payable decreases. In this transaction, cash decreases by $300 (impacting the right side of its T-account) and accounts payable decreases by $300 (impacting the left side of its T-account). A decrease in cash decreases assets, while a decrease in accounts payable decreases liabilities. Notice that telephone expense is not affected by this transaction. Telephone expense increased in transaction 11 when the bill was received. This transaction is just paying off debt, as shown in Figure 2.29. The accounting equation is balanced.

Record the transaction in the T-accounts

Analyze the accounting equation and impact on owner's equity

FIGURE 2.29

All the transactions have been compiled in the T-account worksheet shown in Figure 2.30. Notice that the net income from the income statement is calculated first so it can be added to owner's equity. The owner's equity calculation is at the bottom of the balance sheet and shows an ending balance of $37,400. This calculation is discussed in more detail in the next section.

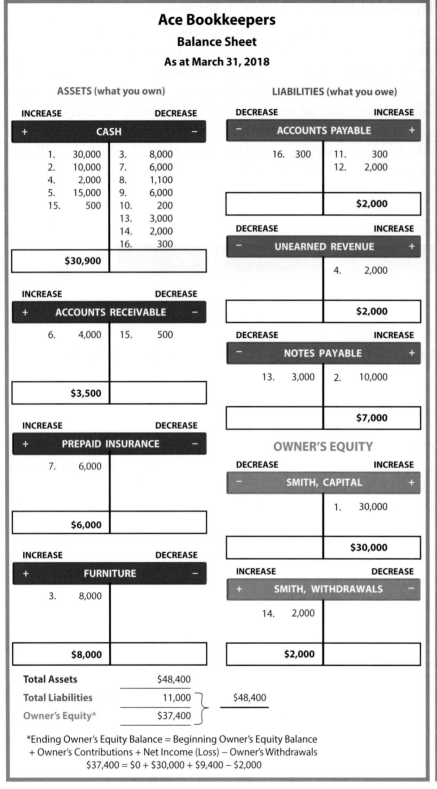

Ace Bookkeepers
Balance Sheet
As at March 31, 2018

ASSETS (what you own)

INCREASE		DECREASE
+	CASH	−
1. 30,000	3.	8,000
2. 10,000	7.	6,000
4. 2,000	8.	1,100
5. 15,000	9.	6,000
15. 500	10.	200
	13.	3,000
	14.	2,000
	16.	300
$30,900		

INCREASE		DECREASE
+	ACCOUNTS RECEIVABLE	−
6. 4,000	15.	500
$3,500		

INCREASE		DECREASE
+	PREPAID INSURANCE	−
7. 6,000		
$6,000		

INCREASE		DECREASE
+	FURNITURE	−
3. 8,000		
$8,000		

LIABILITIES (what you owe)

DECREASE		INCREASE
−	ACCOUNTS PAYABLE	+
16. 300	11.	300
	12.	2,000
	$2,000	

DECREASE		INCREASE
−	UNEARNED REVENUE	+
	4.	2,000
	$2,000	

DECREASE		INCREASE
−	NOTES PAYABLE	+
13. 3,000	2.	10,000
	$7,000	

OWNER'S EQUITY

DECREASE		INCREASE
−	SMITH, CAPITAL	+
	1.	30,000
	$30,000	

INCREASE		DECREASE
+	SMITH, WITHDRAWALS	−
14. 2,000		
$2,000		

Total Assets	$48,400	
Total Liabilities	11,000	$48,400
Owner's Equity*	37,400	

*Ending Owner's Equity Balance = Beginning Owner's Equity Balance
+ Owner's Contributions + Net Income (Loss) − Owner's Withdrawals
$37,400 = $0 + $30,000 + $9,400 − $2,000

Ace Bookkeepers
Income Statement
For the Month Ended March 31, 2018

DECREASE		INCREASE
−	SERVICE REVENUE	+
	5.	15,000
	6.	4,000
	$19,000	

LESS EXPENSES

INCREASE		DECREASE
+	INTEREST EXPENSE	−
10. 200		
$200		

INCREASE		DECREASE
+	RENT EXPENSE	−
8. 1,100		
$1,100		

INCREASE		DECREASE
+	SALARIES EXPENSE	−
9. 6,000		
$6,000		

INCREASE		DECREASE
+	TELEPHONE EXPENSE	−
11. 300		
$300		

INCREASE		DECREASE
+	TRAVEL EXPENSE	−
12. 2,000		
$2,000		

Total Revenue	$19,000
Less: Total Expenses	9,600
Net Income (Loss)	$9,400

FIGURE 2.30

Pause & Reflect

Exercise 2-3

The following transactions occurred this month at Eternity Photography.

1. Eternity Photography paid last month's telephone bill of $140.
2. Felix Graham deposited an additional $50,000 cash into the business' bank account.
3. Furniture that cost $6,000 was purchased using the business' credit card, which will be paid later.
4. Eternity Photography borrowed $20,000 cash from the bank.
5. Felix Graham withdrew $8,000 cash for personal use.

For each transaction, indicate which two accounts are affected and the category of the account (asset, liability, owner's capital, owner's withdrawal, revenue or expense). In the last column, indicate whether the account balance would increase or decrease as a result of the transaction.

Fill in your answers in Table 1. The first transaction has been completed as an example.

Table 1

	Name of the Account Affected	Category of Account	Increase or Decrease
1.	Cash	Asset	Decrease
	Accounts Payale	Liability	Decrease
2.			
3.			
4.			
5.			

See Appendix I for solutions.

Financial Statements

Now that the T-account worksheet for Ace Bookkeepers is complete, we can prepare formal financial statements. All financial statements follow certain formatting standards when being created.

- Each statement has three lines at the top to identify the company (e.g. Ace Bookkeepers), the type of financial statement (e.g. Income Statement) and the time period or date the statement covers (e.g. For the Month Ended March 31, 2018).

- The first number in each column has a dollar sign to indicate the currency of values presented in the statement.

- The last number in a calculated column has a single underline to indicate a total or subtotal is being calculated.

- The final number on the financial statement, or in the case of the balance sheet the total assets and the total liabilities plus the owner's equity figures, has a dollar sign and is double underlined.

Figure 2.31 on the next page shows the four financial statements discussed in this section: the income statement, the statement of owner's equity, the balance sheet, and the statement of cash flows. All of the statements were prepared based on the transactions completed by Ace Bookkeepers during the month of March 2018. The labeled arrows show you how one statement relates to the next, and each statement is discussed in detail in its relevant section. Please refer back to Figure 2.31 as you read each section, to better understand both the individual statements and how they are connected.

Income Statement

The first statement to complete is the income statement, shown in Figure 2.31. The income statement reports revenue earned and expenses incurred during the period. For Ace Bookkeepers, this income statement is for the month ended March 31, 2018 and shows a net income of $9,400.

Statement of Owner's Equity

The **statement of owner's equity** shows how an owner's equity changed during the month. It covers the same reporting period as the income statement, so Ace Bookkeepers prepares the statement of owner's equity for the month ended March 31, 2018. The basic calculation for the change in equity was shown at the bottom of the T-account worksheet in Figure 2.30. The statement of owner's equity is the formal presentation of this calculation and is the second financial statement shown in Figure 2.31.

Since the business is brand new, the balance of the owner's capital account was $0 at the beginning of the month. The investment made in transaction 1 is added, as is the net income that was calculated from the income statement (indicated by arrow ❶). The amount of withdrawals by the owner is subtracted to give the final balance of the owner's capital of $37,400. The closing balance for March will be the opening balance shown on April's statement of owner's equity.

Balance Sheet

After the statement of owner's equity is prepared, the balance sheet can be created to report on the balances of assets, liabilities and owner's equity on March 31, 2018. The balance sheet is shown as the third financial statement in Figure 2.31. Notice how the value of the owner's capital is taken from the statement of owner's equity (indicated by arrow ❷). Also, the total of the assets is equal to the total of liabilities plus owner's equity. These totals must be the same, otherwise, the accounting equation is not balanced and there is an error either in recording the transactions in the T-accounts or in the calculation of the financial statements.

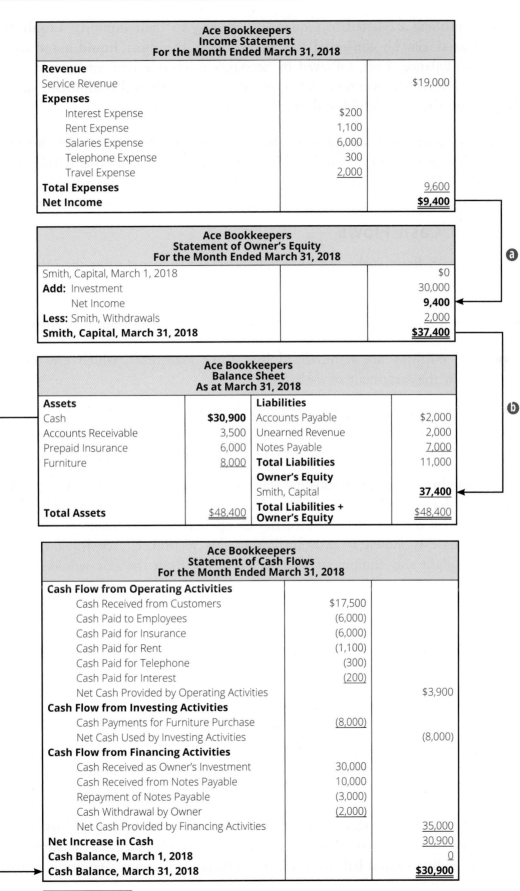

Ace Bookkeepers
Income Statement
For the Month Ended March 31, 2018

Revenue		
Service Revenue		$19,000
Expenses		
Interest Expense	$200	
Rent Expense	1,100	
Salaries Expense	6,000	
Telephone Expense	300	
Travel Expense	2,000	
Total Expenses		9,600
Net Income		**$9,400**

Ace Bookkeepers
Statement of Owner's Equity
For the Month Ended March 31, 2018

Smith, Capital, March 1, 2018		$0
Add: Investment		30,000
Net Income		**9,400**
Less: Smith, Withdrawals		2,000
Smith, Capital, March 31, 2018		**$37,400**

a

Ace Bookkeepers
Balance Sheet
As at March 31, 2018

Assets		Liabilities	
Cash	**$30,900**	Accounts Payable	$2,000
Accounts Receivable	3,500	Unearned Revenue	2,000
Prepaid Insurance	6,000	Notes Payable	7,000
Furniture	8,000	**Total Liabilities**	11,000
		Owner's Equity	
		Smith, Capital	**37,400**
Total Assets	$48,400	**Total Liabilities + Owner's Equity**	$48,400

b

Ace Bookkeepers
Statement of Cash Flows
For the Month Ended March 31, 2018

Cash Flow from Operating Activities		
Cash Received from Customers	$17,500	
Cash Paid to Employees	(6,000)	
Cash Paid for Insurance	(6,000)	
Cash Paid for Rent	(1,100)	
Cash Paid for Telephone	(300)	
Cash Paid for Interest	(200)	
Net Cash Provided by Operating Activities		$3,900
Cash Flow from Investing Activities		
Cash Payments for Furniture Purchase	(8,000)	
Net Cash Used by Investing Activities		(8,000)
Cash Flow from Financing Activities		
Cash Received as Owner's Investment	30,000	
Cash Received from Notes Payable	10,000	
Repayment of Notes Payable	(3,000)	
Cash Withdrawal by Owner	(2,000)	
Net Cash Provided by Financing Activities		35,000
Net Increase in Cash		30,900
Cash Balance, March 1, 2018		0
Cash Balance, March 31, 2018		**$30,900**

c

FIGURE 2.31

The assets of a business are listed in sequence according to their liquidity. **Liquidity** is the ease with which an asset can be converted to cash. Cash is the most **liquid asset** and is therefore listed first on the balance sheet, followed by accounts receivable (the amount of money owed by customers to the business), inventory and so on. Property, plant and equipment, such as buildings and machinery, are the least liquid and are therefore listed last.

Liabilities are also listed in a similar way. Those that are payable within the shortest amount of time are listed first (e.g. accounts payable). These amounts are usually due within one year of the balance sheet date. Debts that will last longer, such as long-term notes payable, are listed last.

Statement of Cash Flows

The statement of cash flows is the last financial statement prepared after the other three financial statements are created. It summarizes the movement of cash during the same reporting period as the income statement and the statement of owner's equity. Ace Bookkeepers' statement of cash flows for the month ended March 31, 2018 is presented at the bottom of Figure 2.31.

Cash inflows and outflows are summarized into three categories, which are reported in three separate sections in the statement of cash flows.

1. **Cash flow from operating activities** shows cash inflows and outflows that are related to the company's primary business operations. Cash received from customers is reported as cash inflow, while cash paid for expenses such as insurance, rent and interest are reported as cash outflow.

2. **Cash flow from investing activities** shows cash inflows and outflows that are related to long-term investments in the company's infrastructure. Cash paid to purchase property, plant and equipment is reported as cash outflow. Because Ace Bookkeepers purchased furniture in transaction 3, the furniture purchase is shown as cash outflow in this section. If Ace Bookkeepers had instead sold property, plant and equipment, the cash received from the sale would be shown as cash inflow.

3. **Cash flow from financing activities** shows cash inflows and outflows that are related to investments by owners and borrowing from lenders. If owners invest cash into the business or if cash is borrowed from a financial institution, the cash inflow is shown in this section. On the other hand, if the owners withdraw cash from the business or if the business pays off its loan to the bank, the cash outflow is shown here.

As noted by arrow **C**, the value of the ending cash balance at March 31, 2018 on the statement of cash flows must be the same as the cash balance on the balance sheet. Preparing the statement of cash flows is beyond the scope of this course. It is only presented here to illustrate a full set of financial statements.

In conclusion, all four financial statements are connected. The net income (or loss) from the income statement is added to (or deducted from) the opening capital balance on the statement of owner's equity. Then, the ending capital balance from the statement of owner's equity is transferred to the capital balance on the balance sheet. Lastly, the cash balance from the balance sheet is shown on the statement of cash flows.

IN THE REAL WORLD

Public US companies are required to periodically file their financial statements with the US Securities and Exchange Commission (SEC). The annual and quarterly report filings are known as Forms 10-K and 10-Q, respectively. These filings are accessible to the public through SEC's online database called EDGAR (www. sec.gov/edgar.shtml). Most large companies also publish their financial statements on their websites.

Ethics   LO 7

Ethics are a set of guidelines that define if a behavior is moral or not. Sometimes it is hard to make an ethical decision if the path is not clear-cut. An ethical dilemma can occur when a decision may positively affect a group of individuals while negatively affecting another group at the same time. In this type of situation, one should evaluate all possible consequences before making a decision, and then choose the course of action that results in an optimal outcome for the most people involved.

When it comes to ethics in accounting, owners and managers of businesses have some level of control over how revenue and expenses are recorded and reported on the income statement. The owners and managers have an ethical responsibility to record and report revenue and expenses in a way that best represents economic reality, even if doing so means the company reports an unfavorable result. Reporting not "what is," but "what the owners and managers want it to be," is an accounting fraud.

Perhaps the most infamous example of accounting fraud that involves misrepresenting revenue comes from Enron, a large energy company in the United States. Over a period of five years, Enron reported an increase in revenue of more than 750%. This massive increase in revenue was partly due to counting the full amount of trading contracts, instead of just brokerage fees, as revenue.

Another example of corporate fraud was committed by WorldCom, a telecommunications company. In addition to misrepresenting revenue, it took certain expenses and recorded them as assets on the balance sheet. Thus, by increasing revenue and eliminating certain expenses, WorldCom was able to show very large profits. In both the Enron and WorldCom cases, executives were charged and went to jail for their involvement in fraud.

Fraud Triangle

As depicted in Figure 2.32, fraud is caused when three factors are present, including pressure, rationalization and opportunity. To illustrate the three factors, consider this example. The owner of a banquet hall receives deposits from customers to book the hall months in advance. As we learned, customer deposits must be treated as a liability (unearned revenue) until the service is actually performed.

FIGURE 2.32

Fraud Scenario 1

Suppose the owner requires additional financing from the bank to help pay for an expansion to the hall and feels her income may not be enough to get the loan (pressure). While the owner knows that she's not supposed to manipulate the numbers, she believes that doing so is necessary not only for herself, but also for her employees, who need their jobs at the banquet hall to make their living (rationalization). To make her net income appear higher, the owner records the customer deposits as revenue instead of a liability. Because the owner also acts as the company's accountant, and there's no one else to double check the accuracy of the financial statements (opportunity), she feels that manipulating the numbers is easy to do. By inflating her revenue and profits, she hopes the bank will grant her the loan she needs. This action is unethical.

Fraud Scenario 2

Consider a sole proprietor who is attempting to minimize the amount of taxes he must pay to the government on his business income. He needs money to pay for his house mortgage (pressure). He argues with himself that he needs to do this so his family has a place to live (rationalization). He has a significant amount of prepaid expenses recorded as assets, and can easily manipulate the numbers (opportunity), and so he reports those assets as expenses. He also overstates the expenses by including personal expenses in his business records. All of these actions reduce his net income and the amount of taxes to be paid. Including personal expenses in business records is illegal, and can lead to charges and penalties imposed by the government.

In Summary

LO 1 **List the differences between personal accounts and business accounts**

- ▶ Some differences include surplus (deficit) is called net income (loss); revenue is classified as sales revenue or service revenue; and the net worth section is replaced with the owner's equity section.

LO 2 **Describe the three main types of businesses**

- ▶ A service business provides services to clients.
- ▶ A merchandising business buys inventory and resells it to customers.
- ▶ A manufacturing business makes its own products and sells them to customers.

LO 3 **Record revenue based on the concept of accruals**

- ▶ Revenue is recorded when services have been provided to customers, regardless of when cash is received.
- ▶ Unearned revenue is used to record cash receipts before services are performed and accounts receivable is used when a customer will pay after services are performed.

LO 4 **Record expenses based on the concept of accruals**

- ▶ Expenses are recorded when they are incurred, regardless of when cash is paid.
- ▶ Prepaid expenses are used to record cash payments before expenses are incurred and accounts payable is used when suppliers will be paid after expenses are incurred.

LO 5 **Record business transactions in T-accounts**

- ▶ When recording transactions in T-accounts, every transaction must be recorded in at least two accounts and the accounting equation must always be balanced.
- ▶ Revenues and expenses must be recorded when they are incurred, not necessarily when cash is transferred. This creates a need for additional accounts such as accounts receivable, prepaid expenses, accounts payable, and unearned revenue.

LO 6 **Identify the four required financial statements and prepare three financial statements**

- ▶ The income statement reports the revenue earned and expenses incurred during the period.

- ▶ The statement of owner's equity shows the changes in owner's equity during the period.

- ▶ The balance sheet reports the balances of assets, liabilities and owner's equity at the end of the period.

- ▶ On the balance sheet, assets are listed in order from most to least liquid. Liabilities are listed in order from shortest to longest maturity.

- ▶ The statement of cash flows reports cash inflows and outflows from operating, investing and financing activities during the period.

LO 7 **Describe ethics related to financial statement reporting**

- ▶ A business should report its financial statements in a way that reflects the true substance of business transactions and economic reality. It is unethical to misrepresent financial information.

Review Exercise 2-1

Miranda Jones owns a salon called Style House. Below are the balances of the accounts on March 1, 2018.

Cash	$3,000
Equipment	12,000
Accounts Payable	5,000
Jones, Capital	10,000

The following transactions for Style House occurred during the month of March 2018.

1. Borrowed $12,000 from the bank
2. Purchased chairs and dryers with $8,000 cash
3. Paid $333 cash toward the principal of the note payable
4. Paid $50 cash for interest on the note payable
5. Prepaid $600 cash for a monthly maintenance contract that will last six months
6. Provided services to customers and received $8,000 cash
7. Paid $4,000 cash to employees for salaries for the month
8. Received a telephone bill for $250, which will be paid next month
9. Received a bill for $300 for advertising and a bill for $500 for travel, both of which will be paid later
10. Paid monthly rent with $2,000 cash
11. Paid $1,000 owing to a supplier
12. Withdrew $3,000 cash from the business for personal use
13. Provided $400 worth of services to customers on account
14. Received $100 cash from a customer for services to be provided next month

Required

a) Record the March transactions for Miranda's business on the following T-account worksheet.

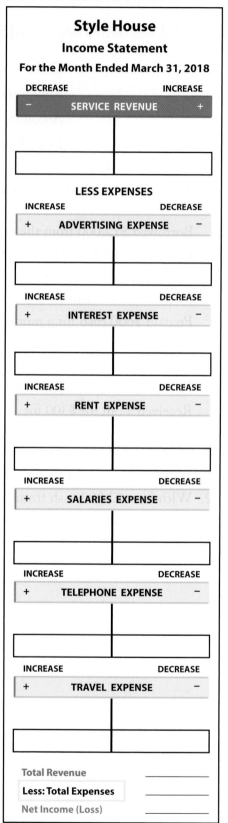

Style House

Balance Sheet

As at March 31, 2018

ASSETS (what you own)

INCREASE			DECREASE
+	CASH		−

Opening Balance

LIABILITIES (what you owe)

DECREASE			INCREASE
−	ACCOUNTS PAYABLE		+

Opening Balance

INCREASE			DECREASE
+	ACCOUNTS RECEIVABLE		−

Opening Balance

DECREASE			INCREASE
−	UNEARNED REVENUE		+

Opening Balance

DECREASE			INCREASE
−	NOTES PAYABLE		+

Opening Balance

INCREASE			DECREASE
+	PREPAID MAINTENANCE		−

Opening Balance

OWNER'S EQUITY

DECREASE			INCREASE
−	JONES, CAPITAL		+

Opening Balance

INCREASE			DECREASE
+	EQUIPMENT		−

Opening Balance

INCREASE			DECREASE
+	JONES, WITHDRAWALS		−

Total Assets _____

Total Liabilities _____ ⎫
                                    ⎬ _____
Owner's Equity* _____ ⎭

*Ending Owner's Equity Balance = Beginning Owner's Equity Balance + Owner's Contributions + Net Income (Loss) − Owner's Withdrawals

Style House

Income Statement

For the Month Ended March 31, 2018

DECREASE			INCREASE
−	SERVICE REVENUE		+

LESS EXPENSES

INCREASE			DECREASE
+	ADVERTISING EXPENSE		−

INCREASE			DECREASE
+	INTEREST EXPENSE		−

INCREASE			DECREASE
+	RENT EXPENSE		−

INCREASE			DECREASE
+	SALARIES EXPENSE		−

INCREASE			DECREASE
+	TELEPHONE EXPENSE		−

INCREASE			DECREASE
+	TRAVEL EXPENSE		−

Total Revenue _____

Less: Total Expenses _____

Net Income (Loss) _____

b) Complete the income statement for Style House.

Style House Income Statement For the Month Ended March 31, 2018		

c) Complete the statement of owner's equity for Style House.

Style House Statement of Owner's Equity For the Month Ended March 31, 2018	

d) Complete the balance sheet for Style House.

Style House Balance Sheet As at March 31, 2018			

e) The table below lists transactions for Style House. Complete the table to identify which section of the statement of cash flows (operating, investing or financing) each one belongs to.

Transaction	Cash Flow Section
Borrowed $12,000 from the bank	
Purchased chairs and dryers with $8,000 cash	
Paid $333 cash toward the principal of the bank loan	
Paid $50 cash for interest on the bank loan	
Prepaid $600 cash for a six-month maintenance contract	
Provided services to customers and received $8,000	
Paid $4,000 cash to employees for salaries	
Paid monthly rent with $2,000 cash	
Paid $1,000 owing to a supplier	
Miranda withdrew $3,000 cash from the business	

See Appendix I for solutions.

Chapter 3
The Accounting Framework

Learning Objectives

LO 1 **Describe the users of accounting information**

LO 2 **Describe the fields of accounting**
- Financial Accounting
- Managerial Accounting
- Accounting Credentials

LO 3 **Compare the different forms of business organization**
- Sole Proprietorship
- Partnership
- Corporation
- Nonprofit Organizations

LO 4 **Identify the objective, constraints and qualitative characteristics of financial information**
- Objective and Constraints of Financial Information
- Qualitative Characteristics of Financial Information
- Trade-Offs of Qualitative Characteristics

LO 5 **List and apply basic accounting assumptions and principles**
- Assumptions
- Principles

LO 6 **Explain the importance of ethics in accounting**

MAKING IT REAL TO YOU

At the beginning of the previous chapter, we suggested that if you recorded all of your transactions for a few months, you could track where your money comes from and where it goes. In other words, you would get a picture of your income and expenses, as well as your current financial position. This information would likely be very useful to you, the *user* of the financial information, to help you control your finances and monitor your success in achieving your personal goals. Just as you use this information for personal purposes, businesses have users that depend on such information to make important decisions about their business. Depending on the form of the business, there are different types of users. A one-person business has different users of its information than a large corporation with many managers and owners (known as shareholders). In this chapter we take a look at the different types of businesses and the specific needs of their users. You will also learn what users' expectations are, and how they are protected by a framework of accounting principles and practices.

Users of Accounting Information

The fundamental objective of accounting is to prepare financial statements to help a wide variety of users make decisions. Users of accounting information can be divided into two categories.

1. **Internal users**, people who own the business and/or work in the business
2. **External users**, people or organizations outside the business, such as suppliers, banks and external accountants

Internal users rely on financial statements to manage the business efficiently. They assess the business by examining the financial results on a regular basis. To an internal user, financial statements serve the same purpose as a scoreboard does to a sports team; the statements give internal users a snapshot of how the business is performing and what needs to be done going forward so the business is successful.

Typically, external users need financial statements to ensure that their investment in the business is protected, whether they provide loans or supply products or services on credit. If a business is poorly managed or not operating profitably, external users can decide whether or not to associate themselves with the business. They want assurance that their loans can be repaid or that they receive a sufficient return on their investment.

There are also indirect external users of financial statements. For example, tax authorities look at the financial statements to confirm that the business is paying the appropriate amount of taxes. Indirect external users also include customers and trade unions.

Fields of Accounting

Accountants measure, record and report on an individual's or a business' financial activities. Businesses large and small need accountants to ensure that internal and external users have the information they need to make informed decisions. There are two general fields of accounting that focus on the needs of different users: financial accounting and managerial accounting.

Financial Accounting

Financial accounting is concerned with keeping records of the business and preparing the financial statements, similar to what has been discussed so far. Financial accounting serves the external users of the business, such as investors, suppliers, customers and lenders, who use financial accounting information to make decisions. For example, an investor may decide to invest more money into a business that reports growing profits, or a supplier may decide to cut ties with a business that reports low cash flows.

Financial accountants make certain that the information in financial statements (income statement, balance sheet, etc.) is accurate and up-to-date so that users can make informed decisions. Financial accountants may be employees of the business, or may work for an accounting firm that services many businesses.

Managerial Accounting

Managerial accounting serves the internal users of the accounting information by preparing specialized reports to assist in decision-making inside the business. Managerial accountants track and classify costs, prepare and analyze budgets, and assist with strategic decision-making. Managers and executives use cost reports and budgets generated by managerial accountants to determine whether certain products, services or business functions are still profitable and how to improve them if necessary. Managerial accountants are often employees of the business.

Accounting Credentials

An accounting-related education is required to work in the accounting field. Becoming an accounting clerk requires a college diploma, but many accounting positions (financial or managerial) require further specialized education to obtain an accounting certification. The most common examples of accounting certifications recognized in the US include the following.

- Certified Public Accountant (CPA)
- Certified Internal Auditor (CIA)
- Certified Management Accountant (CMA)
- Certified Payroll Professional (CPP)
- Certified Bookkeeper (CB)
- Certified Fraud Examiner (CFE)

These certifications are each governed by separate profesional organizations. For instance, the CPA certification is governed by the American Institute of Certified Public Accountants (AICPA). Obtaining a CPA designation requires an individual to complete the required educational and practical experience and pass the AICPA's Uniform Certified Public Accountant Examination. Another example of an accounting professional organization is the Institute of Management Accountants (IMA), which governs the CMA certification.

Accountants may work for a single organization, or they may work in a firm that provides accounting services for many other organizations or individuals. The practice of accounting for a single organization is referred to as **private accounting**. A company's bookkeeping is an example of private accounting. A company's bookkeeper is responsible for recording accounting transactions and compiling accounting information into financial statements, and works only for that company. **Public accounting** involves providing services, such as auditing and tax advice, to different companies or individuals. The CPA designation is generally required for an individual to work in the public accounting field.

Forms of Business Organization

So far we have dealt with accounting for sole proprietorships. However, a business could also be organized as a partnership, corporation, or nonprofit organization. The form of organization is important because it determines the laws and accounting standards that must be adhered to. This section discusses each form of organization in detail.

Sole Proprietorship

A **sole proprietorship** is owned and generally operated by one owner. A proprietorship is usually a small business, and could provide products or services, such as bookkeeping, gardening or general contracting. Many proprietorships have only a small amount of money invested by the owner. Starting a sole proprietorship can be an easy process; often it is enough to register a business name and obtain a business license. The proprietorship lasts as long as the owner runs the business, or as long as the owner is alive. Sole proprietorships are examples of private enterprises because ownership of the business is restricted to one person. A **private enterprise** is any business or organization in which ownership is restricted to a select group of people; the general public cannot acquire ownership of the business.

From an accounting perspective, the financial affairs of the business must be separate from the financial affairs of the owner. For example, the proprietor cannot list personal assets, such as home contents, on the same statement as the business' assets. From a legal perspective, however, a sole proprietorship is *not* a separate entity from its owner. This means that the assets and liabilities of the business legally belong to the owner, even though the financial activities are recorded separately. If the business is unable to pay its debts, business creditors can force the owner to sell personal assets to pay the business debts. This is called **unlimited liability**; the owner will receive all the net income, suffer any net loss and be personally liable for all financial obligations of the business.

We will be using a sole proprietorship to illustrate various transactions. Figure 3.1 shows the names of some typical accounts used in a service business in the form of a sole proprietorship.

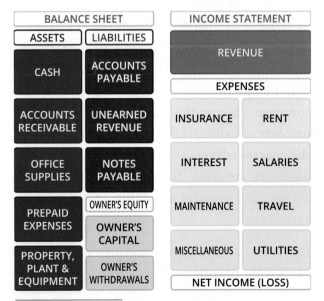

FIGURE 3.1

A CLOSER LOOK

Often, the owner of a sole proprietorship incorrectly records business transactions in the same set of records as his personal records. This makes it almost impossible to monitor the activities of the business to evaluate its performance.

Consider this scenario. Emilio operates a gardening service and combines all his business and personal records. He also has a job at night for extra income. The gardening business has become very busy and he needs to arrange a bank loan to buy more equipment and supplies. By maintaining personal and business records together, Emilio faces the following challenges.

1. He does not know how much the night job and the gardening business are each contributing toward his income.

2. By not separating business and personal expenses, he does not know which expenses are being used to generate sales. This is important because business expenses can be tax deductible.

3. He does not know the expenses of each gardening job, such as insurance and gas, to help identify the profitability of the business.

Before lending money to Emilio, the bank will want to see financial statements to assess if the business is capable of servicing the loan. This will be a problem for Emilio in the current situation.

Partnership

A **partnership** is a business owned by two or more people, called partners. As in a sole proprietorship, the only legal requirements that must be met to start a partnership are registering the business name and obtaining a business license. To manage a business together, the partners need an oral or written partnership agreement that states how to share profits and losses. Partnerships use the term "partners' equity" as the title of the equity section on the balance sheet, as shown in Figure 3.2. The partnership lasts as long as the partners continue to run the business, or as long as all partners are alive. If the partners end the business, the partnership's assets are sold and existing liabilities are paid. The remaining cash is divided among the partners according to the partnership agreement.

Partnerships are private enterprises. A partnership, like a sole proprietorship, is not legally separated from its owners. Depending on the type of partnership, partners may be subject to unlimited liability, which means that the partners are jointly

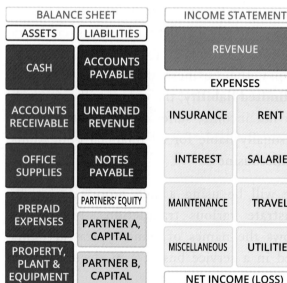

FIGURE 3.2

responsible for all the debts of the partnership. In a partnership, **mutual agency** exists, which means each partner is able to speak for the other partners and bind them to business contracts.

Corporation

A **corporation** is a business that is registered with the state government as a separate legal entity from its owners. The corporation has all the rights of a person and is responsible for its own activities and liable for its own debts. It can enter into contracts and buy and sell products or assets. It can also sue others and be sued.

A **stockholder** (or shareholder) is an owner of the business through ownership of **stocks** (or shares). Each share provides partial ownership of the business. For example, if a person owns one share and there are 100 shares available, the person owns 1/100th of the corporation. A stockholder who owns more than 50% of all the stock of a corporation can control the business. Stockholders are legally distinct from the business and their financial risk is limited to the amount they have invested in the form of stock. Thus, owners or stockholders have **limited liability**.

The life of a corporation is indefinite and independent of the lives of the stockholders. The corporation's operations are not directly managed by its stockholders, but by an elected board of directors to oversee the corporation. Members of the board of directors and senior management can be financially and legally accountable for the actions of the corporation. The behavior of officers of the corporation is governed by a number of rules, including those relating to responsible accounting and cash management.

As shown in Figure 3.3, the balance sheet of a corporation uses the term "stockholders' equity" for the equity section, and it is equal to the difference between assets and liabilities, just like a sole proprietorship or partnership. For example, a company has assets worth $100,000 and liabilities worth $60,000. If the corporation sells all its assets and pays the liabilities, the remaining $40,000 cash is the stockholders' equity and belongs to the stockholders. The stockholders' equity is divided among the stockholders in proportion to the number of shares that they own. If there are two equal stockholders, each one is paid $20,000. If there are 20 equal stockholders, each one is paid $2,000.

Corporations can be set up as either public or private enterprises. A **public corporation** allows its stock to be sold to anyone in the general public. This gives the public corporation access to a large amount of cash to help grow the business. Typically, a public corporation has thousands of

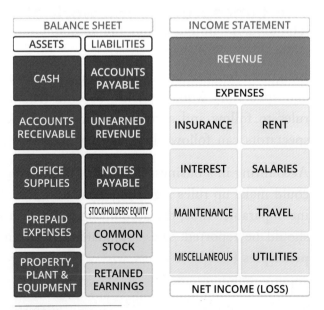

FIGURE 3.3

individual stockholders. Stock exchanges, such as the NASDAQ Stock Market or the New York Stock Exchange, allow buyers and sellers to trade stock of public corporations.

A **private corporation** does not allow its stock to be sold to just anyone, and often the stock is held by a few individuals. Private corporations are generally subject to less stringent reporting requirements than public corporations.

The major differences between the three forms of organization are summarized in Figure 3.4.

	Sole Proprietorship	Partnership	Corporation
Title of Owners	Proprietor (One)	Partners (Two or More)	Stockholders (One or More)
Public or Private	Private	Private	Public or Private
Equity Section	Owner's Equity	Partners' Equity	Stockholders' Equity
Owner's Liability	Unlimited	Limited or Unlimited	Limited

FIGURE 3.4

Nonprofit Organizations

As you have learned, the primary objective of a for-profit business is to maximize profits for the business' owner(s). **Nonprofit organizations** aim to improve or benefit communities by taking profits and redistributing them as services or products. They usually obtain funding from donations and government grants. Nonprofit organizations include religious organizations, community care centers and charitable organizations. They do not have an identifiable owner but require financial statements because they are accountable to donors, sponsors, lenders, tax authorities and so on.

Accounting records provide key information pertaining to the activities of nonprofit organizations, enabling them to operate as permitted. This textbook does not focus on nonprofit organizations.

The Conceptual Framework of Accounting

Imagine a football or baseball game with no rules or consistent method to keep score. The players and spectators would quickly become frustrated because of the lack of consistency. By having rules to follow and a consistent method to keep score, players know how to play the game and spectators can follow along as they watch.

Accounting in a business is similar. If there were no rules to follow, business owners and accountants could make up rules regarding what to report. External users would find the reports unreliable and incomparable. Thus, the accounting profession has created standards for how financial information should be reported. These standards are commonly referred to as **generally accepted accounting principles (GAAP)**.

A CLOSER LOOK

Consider the origins of the human race. Our ancestors led challenging lives and worked hard to provide safe shelter and nourishment for themselves and their families. Part of this lifestyle likely included storing food and supplies for future use. Ancient cave paintings indicate simple pictorial record keeping of all sorts including systematic markings and illustrations of animals and humans. Jumping ahead to Egyptian hieroglyphics in B.C.E., these tomb illustrations show precise, detailed record keeping. Further ahead, a simple Franciscan monk and scholar, Luca Pacioli, made the accounting system famous in 1494 with his Italian publication *Summa de Arithmetica*. While this was a sort of math textbook, it included a wide range of topics including a section on "The Rules of Double-Entry Bookkeeping" for business accounting. Pacioli documented the accounting system, which had been in use for some time. The key was Guttenberg, the printing press of 1440, the educational system for male scholars in the late 15th century Italy and Pacioli himself. The result was the distribution and implementation of the accounting system on a universal scale. While the accounting system has evolved and expanded tremendously in the ensuing generations, the one in use today is substantially the accounting system as it has always been.

In the United States, the development of GAAP is under the legal authority of the **Securities and Exchange Commission (SEC)**, a federal government agency whose mission is to protect investors. The SEC has mostly delegated the writing of GAAP to a private, nonprofit organization called the **Financial Accounting Standards Board (FASB)**. Specifically, the FASB is designated to develop guidelines that all public US companies are required to use in reporting their financial statements according to GAAP. The guidelines developed by the FASB, which are referred to as "US GAAP," encompass both broad and specific accounting issues, and are constantly updated. However, sometimes there are accounting issues that have not been adequately addressed by the FASB, in which case the SEC can step in and issue interpretations and policies to supplement the FASB standards.

In addition to establishing the local accounting standards, the FASB also participates in the development of the **International Financial Reporting Standards (IFRS)** in conjunction with the **International Accounting Standards Board (IASB)**. As the global trend has been intensifying in the business world, the IFRS is designed as the unified set of global accounting standards so that the financial statements of companies from different countries are comparable. IFRS are very well received and widely used around the world. Over 100 governments have required public companies in their countries to adopt IFRS. Figure 3.5 illustrates the various organizations involved with financial accounting standards.

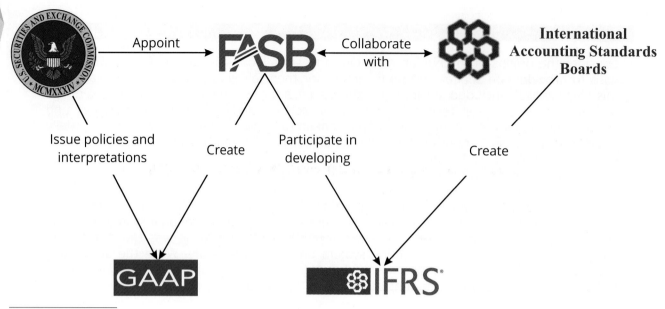

FIGURE 3.5

In the US, private US companies and foreign companies that sell their shares in the US stock markets are permitted to adopt IFRS if they do not want to use US GAAP. However, public US companies are not allowed to adopt the IFRS standards and must use US GAAP. The differences between IFRS and US GAAP will likely have to be reconciled before public US companies are allowed to use IFRS the way public companies in many other countries have already been permitted or required to do.

In 2010, in an attempt to bridge the differences between US GAAP and IFRS, the SEC announced its commitment to one global set of accounting standards. The SEC has also encouraged the FASB to pursue a convergence process with the IASB by incorporating IFRS into US GAAP. Some of the convergence projects between the FASB and the IASB have been completed. However, some important differences between US GAAP and IFRS remain, and it is unclear whether and when the remaining convergence projects will go forward and whether public companies in the US will be permitted or required to use IFRS in the future.

One of the projects that the FASB and the IASB worked on together until 2014 is the Conceptual Framework project. In 2014, the FASB and the IASB decided to continue this project separately (i.e. it's no longer a joint project). However, both US GAAP and IFRS conform to a similar underlying conceptual framework. This **conceptual framework** forms the basis to determine how business transactions should be measured and reported. It ensures external users (e.g. stockholders) have the most consistent, reliable and useful information when reviewing companies' financial reports. US GAAP follows rules-based accounting, meaning the accounting standards are stated as a list of specific, detailed rules that must be followed when preparing financial information. To apply these rules, accountants have little room to make their own judgments. This ensures that accounting standards are applied consistently by all companies.

On the other hand, IFRS is principles-based accounting, meaning IFRS is designed as guidelines and accountants are allowed flexibility to apply these standards when preparing financial information. This removes long lists of detailed rules but requires accountants to use their own judgment on how to apply them.

Next, we will examine the important characteristics, assumptions and principles of GAAP that form the conceptual framework of accounting. Figure 3.6 illustrates the framework.

The Conceptual Framework of Accounting

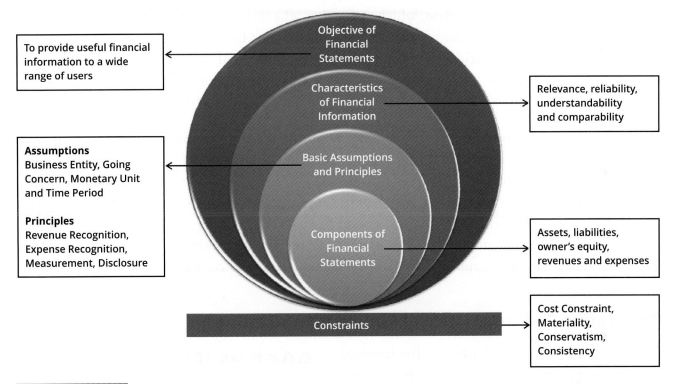

FIGURE 3.6

Objective and Constraints of Financial Information

The fundamental objective of financial reporting is to provide useful and complete information to the users. However, there are four major constraints, or restrictions, for a business to consider when trying to achieve this objective. The first underlying constraint in the accounting framework is the cost constraint. The **cost constraint** ensures that the value of reported financial information outweighs the costs incurred to report it, even if the information would improve the accuracy and completeness of the financial statements. For example, a company may find some information that is not required by accounting standards to be somewhat useful but costly to prepare. If the value of this information does not outweigh the costs, the company should not prepare it.

The second constraint in the accounting framework is materiality. **Materiality** refers to the significance of information to users. A piece of information is considered material if it could influence or change a user's decision. Material amounts must be recorded correctly on financial statements. For example, suppose a company paid $100 cash for office supplies. The supplies could be recorded as an asset and expensed as they are used, or they can simply be expensed immediately. While recording them as an asset is more accurate, it is also more complex and more costly to account for. Is this $100 a material amount? It depends on the size of the company. If the company typically lists more than $100,000 in assets, the $100 is not likely to affect any user's decision and is therefore immaterial. On the other hand, if the company typically lists assets totaling $1,000, the treatment of $100 in office supplies may impact the decision of an investor.

The third constraint is **conservatism**, which states that whenever an accountant has several options in applying an accounting standard, the least optimistic or least favorable option should be selected. This means choosing the option that results in a lower balance of assets, lower net income or a higher balance of debt; the accountant should have a *conservative* mindset when making estimates to avoid overstating assets, overstating net income or understating debt.

The last constraint is **consistency**, which prevents businesses from changing accounting methods for the sole purpose of manipulating figures on the financial statements. Accountants must apply the same methods and policies from period to period. For example, a merchandising business must have a method to assign value to its merchandise inventory and use the same method from year to year. When a method changes from one period to another, the change must be clearly explained in notes to the financial statements. The users of financial statements have the right to assume that consistency has been applied if there is no statement to the contrary.

Qualitative Characteristics of Financial Information

Accounting standards are based on fundamental characteristics in the accounting framework. These characteristics form the foundation of the conceptual framework and define how information should be presented in financial statements. For financial statements to be effective, financial information must be relevant, reliable, understandable and comparable.

GAAP vs IFRS

GAAP is more "rules-based" in contrast to IFRS, which is more "principles-based." It could be argued that the strong regulations-based system in the US is a main contributor to all the industry-specific rules enforced by GAAP. The nature of IFRS allows users to have more room for interpretation and judgment, whereas GAAP is stricter and more detailed about proper accounting practices.

Relevance

Relevance means that all information useful for decision-making is present in the financial statements. Information is relevant if it helps users predict future performance or confirms previous predictions. For example, if an investor wants to predict the future cash flows of a company, and the company deliberately avoided reporting a bank loan, the investor cannot understand the company's debt correctly. Therefore, the investor cannot accurately predict the company's interest expenses and available cash flow. In this scenario, the balance of the bank loan would be considered relevant financial information.

A component of relevance is **timeliness**. Information is timely if there is no delay in reporting crucial information. To be useful to a decision maker, information must be received before it is no longer able to influence decisions. For example, if a business only prepares annual statements, the information may be available too late to correct problems with the company. Therefore, a business owner may prefer to have monthly statements prepared to help monitor the company's performance.

Reliability

Reliability means that information is free from significant error and bias, which means different independent people looking at the evidence will arrive at the same values. The activities that a business records must be based on objective evidence. A component of reliability is **verifiability**, which means the ability to see how a company arrived at a certain result. For example, if a company records an expense transaction in its financial records, an invoice must be provided to back it up (i.e. the expense can be verified).

Reliability also depends on the **faithful representation** of the information. This means that transactions must be presented as their true economic substance rather than their legal form. For example, a company that leases a machine for its entire useful life may list the machine as an asset even though it does not legally own the machine.

In order to be reliable, the information must be neutral. The concept of **neutrality** means that financial information must be free from bias. Bias occurs when the information is influenced by the interests of particular users. For example, managers may be tempted to report higher sales and profit figures if they are paid a bonus based on the success of their department.

Understandability

Understandability means that the financial information can be reasonably understood by its users if the users have knowledge of the business and a basic knowledge of accounting. To be understandable, companies include notes in the financial statements to explain the numbers, especially those that are based on company policy. For example, details of long-term debt such as the principal, interest and term would be outlined in the notes.

Comparability

Comparability means that the financial statements of a company must be prepared in a similar way year after year. The accounting policies used should be consistent to prevent misconceptions. This allows a comparison of the current year's performance to past years. By comparing yearly statements, users can identify trends in the company's financial position and performance. For example, an investor may compare a company's debt balance from one year to the next to see if the company incurred additional debt or was able to pay off its creditors. The financial information should also be comparable between companies.

Trade-Offs of Qualitative Characteristics

As discussed, accounting standards dictate that financial information should be relevant, reliable, understandable and comparable. However, sometimes it is difficult to fully represent all of these characteristics. There could be a trade-off among some of the characteristics. A trade-off is an exchange of part of one characteristic for part of another.

A frequently discussed trade-off is the one between relevance and reliability, as shown in Figure 3.7. For information to be relevant, it needs to be timely. For example, presenting information that is a few years old on today's financial statements is likely not very relevant. However, reliable information often requires time to gather.

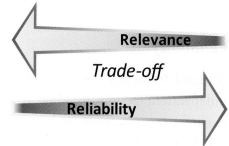

FIGURE 3.7

Suppose that a company chooses to prepare financial statements on a monthly basis instead of a quarterly or semi-annual basis. In this case, the financial statements are very timely and relevant. However, some reliability may be sacrificed since there is less time for the accounting staff to scrutinize and make necessary adjustments to the monthly financial figures. If the financial statements are less frequent (such as quarterly or semi-annually), the accounting staff can allocate more time to verify the accuracy of the statements, but some relevance might be lost since statements are prepared less frequently.

Basic Assumptions and Principles

 LO 5

The conceptual framework of accounting also includes several basic accounting assumptions and principles. Accountants must ensure that these assumptions and principles are met by all of the financial information presented by the business.

Assumptions

There are four basic assumptions underlying all accounting information that is prepared in accordance with US GAAP. These assumptions are necessary for users to rely on the information presented.

The **business entity assumption** states that accounting for a business must be kept separate from the personal affairs of its owner or any other businesses. The owner of a business cannot record personal transactions on the income statement or balance sheet of the business. Any personal expenses are charged to the owner and are not allowed to affect the operating results of the business. Financial statements of a business can be assumed to only contain items that pertain to the business and, therefore, reflect the financial position of the business alone.

The **going concern assumption** assumes that a business will continue to operate into the foreseeable future. Determining the value of the assets belonging to a business that is alive and well is not complicated. For example, items such as property, plant and equipment are listed on the balance sheet at their cost, or original purchase price. However, if an accountant deems that the business is unable to continue operating into the foreseeable future, the balance sheet must instead show the value for which the property, plant and equipment could realistically be sold. When a company is going out of business, the value of the assets usually suffers because they have to be sold under unfavorable circumstances. Companies at risk of going out of business must include this information in the notes to their financial statements.

The **monetary unit assumption** requires that accounting records are expressed in terms of money. Accounting records should all be reported in a single currency, such as US dollars or euros. This allows accountants to assign monetary values to business events. For instance, suppose that a company hires a salesperson. The event of officially hiring the employee is not reflected in the company's accounting records since a value cannot be easily assigned to the event (i.e. expressed in terms of money). However, over time, the financial impact of the hiring will be evident (e.g. recognizing the salary expense for the salesperson and realizing an increase in sales). Furthermore, it is also assumed that the unit of measure used in the accounting records remains fairly constant over time and that transactions can be measured relevantly in current monetary units. That is, inflation (a rise in prices) or deflation (a drop in prices) is ignored when comparing dollars of different years.

The **time period assumption** requires that accounting takes place over specific time periods known as fiscal periods. These fiscal periods are of equal length, and are used when measuring the financial progress of a business.

Principles

The following section discusses some of the basic accounting principles and concepts outlined by the conceptual framework of accounting.

Measurement is the process of determining the amount at which an item is recorded in the financial statements. Primarily, items must be recorded at their historical cost. This is sometimes referred to as the *cost principle*. In almost all cases, the historical cost is the amount that appears on the source document for the transaction. If the owner purchased $7,000 worth of office furniture on sale for $5,000, the furniture is recorded as $5,000, as shown on the receipt. There are times when the historical cost of an item is not appropriate. For example, a building could be received as a gift. In such a case, the transaction would be recorded at fair market value, which must be determined by independent appraisals.

Revenue recognition states that revenue can only be recorded (recognized) when goods are sold or services are performed. This means that the item sold must be transferred to the buyer and the buyer has agreed to pay, or has already paid, for the item. If the transaction involves a large project, such as building a dam, it may take a construction company a number of years to complete.

The construction company does not usually wait until the project is entirely completed before it recognizes the revenue. Periodically, it bills for work completed and recognizes this as revenue.

Expense recognition states that an expense must be recorded in the same accounting period in which it is used to generate revenue. For example, suppose a manufacturing business spent $20,000 to produce 1,000 units of inventory in the current accounting period. If 500 units are sold in each of the following two accounting periods, $10,000 would be expensed in each period. This concept is commonly referred to as the *matching principle* because expenses must be matched to the same period as the revenue that they helped to generate. If an expense cannot be tied to revenue, then it should be recorded in the period that it occurs.

Disclosure states that any and all information that affects the full understanding of a company's financial statements must be included with the financial statements. Some items may not affect the accounting records directly. According to the full disclosure principle, these items would be included in the notes accompanying the statements. Examples of such items are outstanding lawsuits, tax disputes and company takeovers.

Pause & Reflect

Exercise 3-1

a) Identify the terminology that matches each description provided in Table 1.

b) Identify each description as characteristic, assumption, principle or constraint.

The first line has been filled in as an example.

Table 1

Description	Terminology	Characteristic, Assumption, Principle or Constraint
1. A piece of information is considered significant if it could influence or change a user's decision.	Materiality	Constraint
2. A company is believed to stay in business for the foreseeable future and not go bankrupt any time soon.		
3. Revenue must be recorded or recognized when goods are sold or when services are performed.		
4. The financial statements of a company must be prepared in a similar way year after year.		
5. Information is free from significant error and bias.		
6. The value of reported financial information outweighs the costs incurred to report it.		
7. An expense must be recorded in the same accounting period in which it was used to produce revenue.		
8. Accounting records are expressed in a single currency, such as US dollars.		

See Appendix I for solutions.

Ethics in Accounting

Users place significant trust in the accuracy of financial records so they can make informed decisions regarding a business. It is an accountant's responsibility to ensure that the financial status of the business is accurately reported. The standards by which these actions are judged as being honest or dishonest, right or wrong, fair or unfair, are also known as **accounting ethics**.

Professional accounting bodies have strict rules governing the behavior of their members. For example, members of the American Institute of Certified Public Accountants (AICPA) must follow the AICPA Code of Professional Conduct. The violation of these rules has resulted in jail sentences in some cases. Two of the most infamous examples are Enron and Worldcom. The senior executives of these companies were found guilty of various offences, including using company funds for personal use and covering up negative financial information.

Typical ethical standards for accountants state the following.

- Members shall act with trustworthiness, integrity and objectivity.

- Members shall not participate in any activity or provide services to any company that the member, or a reasonably prudent person, would believe to be unlawful.

- Members shall not engage in a discriminatory practice prohibited by any antidiscrimination laws.

- Members shall not criticize another professional colleague without first submitting this criticism to the colleague for explanation.

- Members shall act in the interest of their clients, employers and interested third parties, and shall be prepared to sacrifice their self-interest to do so.

- Members shall honor the trust bestowed upon them by others, and shall not use their privileged position without their principal's knowledge and consent.

- Members shall avoid conflicts of interest.

- Members shall not disclose or use any confidential information concerning the affairs of any client, former client, employer or former employer.

- Members shall, when engaged to audit or review financial statements or other information, be free of any influence, interest or relationship with respect to the client's affairs, which impairs the member's professional judgment or objectivity, or which, in the view of a reasonable observer, may have that effect.

- Members shall not, without an employer's or client's consent, use confidential information relating to the business of the member's employer or client to directly or indirectly obtain a personal advantage.

- Members shall not take any action, such as acquiring any interest, property or benefit, that is for unauthorized use, or is confidential relating to an employer's or client's affairs, based on information obtained in the course of his or her duties.

- Members shall strive to continually upgrade and develop their technical knowledge and skills in the areas in which they practice as professionals. This technical expertise shall be employed with due professional care and judgment.

- Members shall adhere to acknowledged principles and standards of professional practice.

- Members shall not be associated with any information that the member knows, or ought to know, to be false or misleading, whether by statement or omission.

- Members shall always act in accordance with the duties and responsibilities associated with being members of the profession, and shall work in a manner that will enhance the image of the profession and the association.

Some of the common concerns about ethics in a business are issues related to the following.

- cash discounts

- operation of a petty cash fund

- manipulation of expenses to manage earnings

- trading a company's shares based on insider information (insider trading)

In 2002, to prevent accounting practices from committing fraudulent activities, the United States Congress passed the **Sarbanes-Oxley Act (SOX)** to be enforced upon all public companies. SOX created an independent oversight body called the Public Company Accounting Oversight Board (PCAOB) to be in charge of ensuring the compliance of all public companies with the specific mandates of SOX. The law requires more stringent policies over codes of conduct, financial disclosure, corporate governance and effectiveness of internal controls. Executive members, such as CEOs and CFOs, along with auditors, could be criminally convicted if the internal control procedures are determined to be ineffective.

There is often a fine line between the law and ethics. A behavior can be quite legal, but unethical. For example, a manager may employ his nephew in the company where he is working. He decides to pay his nephew a higher salary than others in a similar position in the business. While this practice may not be illegal, it could be considered unethical. Many organizations create their own set of rules pertaining to ethics and morals.

In Summary

LO 1 **Describe the users of accounting information**

▶ Internal users include owners and employees of the business. They use accounting information to make internal strategic decisions regarding products, services and business departments.

▶ External users include investors, suppliers, lenders and customers of the business. Financial statements help these users make informed business decisions.

LO 2 **Describe the fields of accounting**

▶ Financial accounting serves the needs of external users by preparing financial statements.

▶ Managerial accounting provides valuable information to internal users to make decisions regarding the future of the business.

LO 3 **Compare the different forms of business organization**

▶ A small business that is owned by one person is generally structured in the form of a sole proprietorship. Sole proprietorships are private enterprises.

▶ A partnership is a business owned by two or more persons operating under a partnership agreement. Partnerships are private enterprises.

▶ A corporation is a business that is registered with the state government and sells ownership of the company to individuals in the form of stock. Corporations may be private or public.

▶ Sole proprietorships and partnerships, excluding LLCs, are subject to unlimited liability, which means that one or more owners are personally and legally accountable for the liabilities of the business.

▶ Corporations (both private and public) are subject to limited liability, which means that their risk is limited to their monetary investment in the business.

▶ Unlike other businesses, profits made by nonprofit organizations are redistributed to the community by providing services or products.

LO 4 **Identify the objective, constraints and qualitative characteristics of financial information**

▶ The objective of financial reporting is to provide useful financial information to both internal and external users.

▶ The four constraints are cost constraint, materiality, conservatism and consistency.

▶ The four qualitative characteristics of financial information are relevance, reliability, understandability and comparability.

▶ Accountants may face a trade-off between two or more characteristics (e.g. relevance and reliability).

LO 5 List and apply basic accounting assumptions and principles

▶ The assumptions of the accounting framework are the business entity, going concern, monetary unit and time period assumptions.

▶ The basic principles of the accounting framework are measurement, revenue recognition, expense recognition and disclosure.

LO 6 Explain the importance of ethics in accounting

▶ Accountants must adhere to a high standard of ethics to ensure that the financial information of a business is accurately reported.

▶ All of a business' users rely on this information to make decisions.

AMEENGAGE™ *Access **ameengage.com** for integrated resources including tutorials, practice exercises, the digital textbook and more.*

Review Exercise 3-1

Hollinger Runners Inc. (HRI) is a publicly traded manufacturer of high-quality, stylish sneakers with hundreds of stockholders. The company has been in business for more than 20 years and has experienced good and bad economic times. The company's financial performance has usually been aligned with the state of the economy. Lately, the economy has been booming.

The company has a year end of April 30. It is now May 31, 2018. Hollinger produces financial statements on an annual basis. The company's accountant has prepared the balance sheet as at April 30, 2018, using GAAP. The assets portion of this balance sheet is shown below.

Hollinger Runners Inc.
Balance Sheet
As at April 30, 2018

	2018	2017
Assets	(in thousands)	
Current Assets		
Cash	$10	$500
Accounts Receivable	10	140
Merchandise Inventory	5	120
Other Current Assets	60	70
Total Current Assets	85	830
Noncurrent Assets		
Available-for-Sale Investments	60	65
Property, Plant and Equipment	1,210	2,120
Goodwill	40	50
Total Noncurrent Assets	1,310	2,235
Total Assets	$1,395	$3,065

On May 1, 2017, the company changed the location of its headquarters from Europe to the United States. Therefore, the 2017 column in the balance sheet is presented in the currency unit of euros and the 2018 column is presented in US dollars. The company did not disclose this information in the notes to the financial statements. The euro was stronger than the US dollar during 2017 and 2018.

Additional information regarding HRI's financial statements and accounting records is shown below.

- HRI indicated in the notes to the financial statements that in 2018 it changed the accounting policy it used for depreciating assets. It did not justify its reason for doing so.

- The cash account is comprised of two sub-accounts: cash related to the business and personal cash savings of a few of the stockholders.

- All assets purchased during the year have been valued at fair market value at the year-end date, which is higher than the amount of money that HRI paid for the purchases.

- Regarding expenses, there are numerous invoices that did not match the cost amounts reported in the accounting records. The amounts on the invoices are significantly greater than the amounts in the accounting records.

- The company's income statement has shown a significant net loss for the past three years.

Required

a) Which of the four qualitative characteristics of financial information has HRI failed to apply? Explain.

_____

_____

_____

_____

_____

_____

_____

_____

_____

_____

_____

_____

_____

_____

_____

b) Which of the basic accounting principles and/or assumptions has HRI violated? Explain.

_____

_____

_____

_____

_____

_____

_____

_____

_____

_____

_____

_____

_____

_____

_____

_____

_____

_____

_____

_____

_____

_____

See Appendix I for solutions.

Notes

Chapter 4
The Accounting Cycle: Journals and Ledgers

Learning Objectives

LO 1 Distinguish between debits and credits
- Debit and Credit Reference Guide
- Double-Entry Sample Transactions

LO 2 Describe the accounting cycle

LO 3 Explain how to analyze a transaction

LO 4 Record transactions in the general journal
- Compound Journal Entries

LO 5 Post journal entries to the general ledger
- Establishing a Chart of Accounts

LO 6 Prepare a trial balance
- Correcting Entries

LO 7 Describe ethics and internal controls related to recording and posting transactions

AMEENGAGE Access **ameengage.com** for integrated resources including tutorials, practice exercises, the digital textbook and more.

MAKING IT REAL TO YOU

If you were to keep a record of all your financial transactions for a few months, pretty soon you would likely want to organize them into more meaningful collections. For example, if you had simply recorded all transactions in one big list, you could start to arrange the data for each month (or *accounting period*) so you could easily compare one month to another. You could further categorize each transaction according to the goods or services it applies to; for example, all purchases of office supplies could be listed under an appropriate heading for that category or *account* (e.g. Office Supplies). Your food purchases could be listed under another heading (e.g. Food), and so on. You could further arrange each category's transactions under two separate columns: one for increases to that account, and the other for decreases. At the end of the month, you could total each column and calculate the difference between the two, to arrive at a final balance for the account for that period. This is a very simple example of how accounting records are kept, yet it will help you as you learn about the accounting cycle, journals and ledgers.

Transition to Debits and Credits

We have been using the terms "increase" and "decrease" to record transactions in T-accounts, but formal accounting requires the use of debits and credits. In the debit and credit system (unlike increases and decreases), a **debit** is always recorded on the left-hand side of an account and a **credit** is always recorded on the right-hand side, as illustrated in Figure 4.1. Debits are represented by DR, and credits are represented by CR.

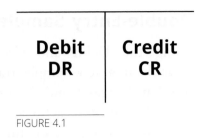

FIGURE 4.1

Debit and Credit Reference Guide

Remember that debit does not always mean decrease and credit does not always mean increase. A credit means an entry on the right side of the account, which may cause the account to increase or decrease, depending on its type. Similarly, a debit means an entry on the left side of the account, which may cause the account to increase or decrease, depending on its type. Recall that the accounting equation is

Assets = Liabilities + Owner's Equity

For the accounting equation to stay in balance, the total value of the debits must always equal the total value of the credits. Throughout this textbook, you may use the Debit and Credit Reference Guide shown in Figure 4.2 to help when analyzing transactions.

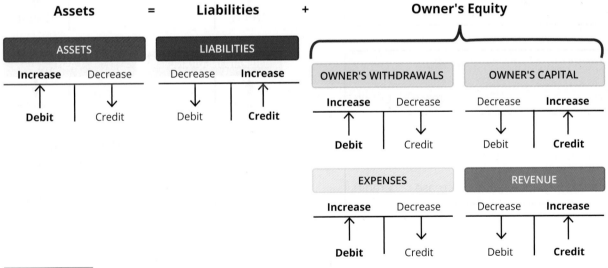

FIGURE 4.2

Every transaction has at least one debit and one credit, referred to as a double entry. The total of all debits in a transaction must equal the total of all credits. If debits do not equal credits, the accounting equation is not balanced.

Each type of account also has a normal balance. A **normal balance** corresponds to the side of the T-account that records the increase and is shown in bold in Figure 4.2. A normal balance indicates a positive balance for the account. For instance, the cash account (an asset) has a debit normal balance.

Double-Entry Sample Transactions

Using the Debit and Credit Reference Guide, let us look at a few sample transactions and see how to translate increases and decreases into debits and credits. The following transactions were completed by Hoffman Company during the month of June 2018.

1. Provided services to a customer who paid cash
2. Paid cash to reduce the principal of the bank loan
3. Paid cash for a one-year insurance policy
4. Recorded maintenance expense, which will be paid later

These transactions are summarized in a table and illustrated in T-accounts in Figure 4.3.

WORTH REPEATING
In accounting, there are always at least two parts to a transaction. For each transaction, the total value of debits equals the total value of credits. This is known as double entry.

1.	Cash	Increase	Debit
	Service Revenue	Increase	Credit
2.	Notes Payable	Decrease	Debit
	Cash	Decrease	Credit
3.	Prepaid Insurance	Increase	Debit
	Cash	Decrease	Credit
4.	Maintenance Expense	Increase	Debit
	Accounts Payable	Increase	Credit

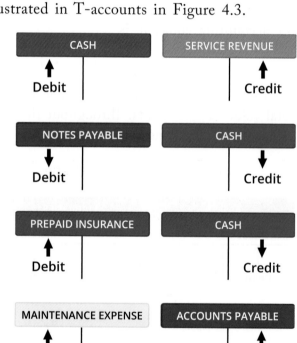

FIGURE 4.3

The Accounting Cycle

[LO 2]

As discussed in Chapter 3, the purpose of accounting is to prepare financial statements to help users make informed decisions. There are many transactions during an accounting period and it is important to summarize them all within the financial statements.

Take note of the photo on the first page of Chapter 4. It shows a group of cyclists in a race around a track. The cyclists must go around the track with no break in between each lap (i.e. the end of the first lap is the beginning of the second lap, the end of the second lap is the beginning of the third lap, etc.), and must follow the rules of the race. Similarly, accountants use something called the **accounting cycle,** which is a series of steps required to complete the financial statements. In accounting, the end of the first cycle (the first period's closing balances) is the beginning of the second cycle (the second period's opening balances). Also, accountants have to follow the rules according to GAAP, Generally Accepted Accounting Principles, from Chapter 3. Businesses prepare financial statements at the end of each accounting period, whether it is a month, quarter, year, or other period of time. Every period, the cycle repeats. Over the next three chapters, the accounting cycle will be illustrated using a monthly period for a sample company.

Figure 4.4 shows the steps required to generate a formal set of financial statements for a given period. A computerized system either performs most of these steps automatically or has them available immediately, while a manual system requires each step to be completed by hand. The first three steps are performed repeatedly during the accounting period while the remaining steps are all completed at the end of the current period and prepare the accounts for the next period. This chapter covers the first four steps of the accounting cycle (shown in blue).

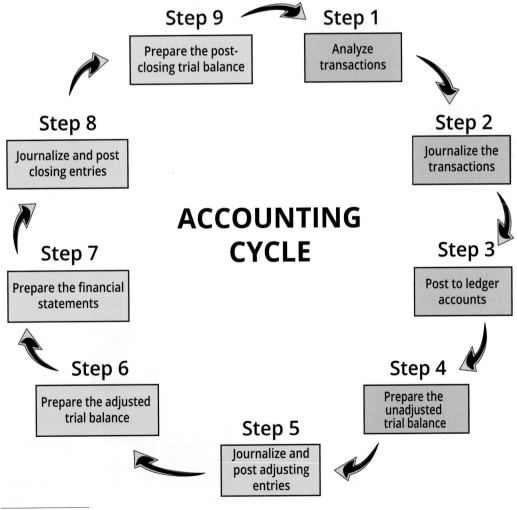

FIGURE 4.4

Analyze Transactions

The first step of the accounting cycle is to gather and analyze what must be recorded as transactions. All transactions must have **source documents**, or evidence that they actually happened. Source documents can include sales receipts, bills, checks, bank statements, and so on.

As discussed earlier, we must determine which accounts are affected, which parts of the accounting equation the accounts belong to and identify whether these accounts will increase or decrease as a result of this transaction. The extra step now is to match the increase or decrease of each account with a debit or credit entry to the account. Use the Debit and Credit Reference Guide in Figure 4.2 to help with this.

For example, suppose you pay a $100 utility bill with cash. To analyze this, first determine which accounts are affected (utilities expense and cash). Now, for each account, answer the following questions.

- Which category does the account belong to?
- Is the account increasing or decreasing?
- Is the increase or decrease a debit or a credit?

The full analysis for the transaction is shown in Figure 4.5. It is important to note that the analysis is just to determine whether the account will be debited or credited. At this point, which account is analyzed first is irrelevant. Later, in step two of the accounting cycle, we will record the accounts in a standardized format.

Which accounts are affected?	Utilities Expense	Cash
What category does the account belong to?	Expense	Asset
Is the account increasing or decreasing?	Increasing	Decreasing
Is the increase or decrease a debit or a credit? (Use the Debit and Credit Reference Guide)	Debit	Credit

FIGURE 4.5

From this analysis, we can illustrate how the accounts are affected. Notice in Figure 4.6 that utilities expense increases with a debit and cash decreases with a credit.

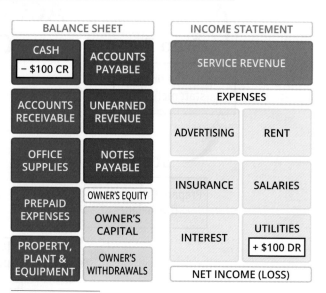

FIGURE 4.6

This type of analysis can be done for any transaction. Keep this in mind as you progress through

the textbook and come across new accounts and new types of transactions. To help you analyze how increases and decreases translate into debits and credits, consider these common transactions.

1. Provided consulting services to a customer for cash
2. Received a bill for advertising, which will be paid later
3. Received cash from a customer for work to be completed next month
4. Paid cash toward the principal of a bank loan
5. Prepaid cash for four months' rent
6. Purchased office furniture with cash
7. Provided consulting services to a customer on account
8. Paid cash toward the advertising bill received in transaction 2
9. A customer paid an amount they owed

Using the steps illustrated above on these transactions, we can create a table to determine which accounts will be debited and credited. The table for the nine transactions is shown in Figure 4.7.

	Account Name	Category	Increase or Decrease	Debit or Credit
1	Cash	Asset	Increase	Debit
	Service Revenue	Revenue	Increase	Credit
2	Advertising Expense	Expense	Increase	Debit
	Accounts Payable	Liability	Increase	Credit
3	Cash	Asset	Increase	Debit
	Unearned Revenue	Liability	Increase	Credit
4	Notes Payable	Liability	Decrease	Debit
	Cash	Asset	Decrease	Credit
5	Prepaid Rent	Asset	Increase	Debit
	Cash	Asset	Decrease	Credit
6	Furniture	Asset	Increase	Debit
	Cash	Asset	Decrease	Credit
7	Accounts Receivable	Asset	Increase	Debit
	Service Revenue	Revenue	Increase	Credit
8	Accounts Payable	Liability	Decrease	Debit
	Cash	Asset	Decrease	Credit
9	Cash	Asset	Increase	Debit
	Accounts Receivable	Asset	Decrease	Credit

FIGURE 4.7

Pause & Reflect

Exercise 4-1

Victor Lee owns and operates a personal training business, which is a sole proprietorship.

a) For each of the following transactions that occurred this month, indicate in Table 1 which two accounts are affected and their category (asset, liability, owner's capital, owner's withdrawal, revenue or expense).

b) Indicate whether the account balance would increase or decrease and whether the account needs to be debited or credited as a result of the transaction. Refer to Figure 4.7 for help, if necessary.

1. Victor invested $10,000 cash in the business.

2. Victor trained a customer for one hour and immediately received a $50 payment.

3. Furniture worth $3,000 was purchased using the business' credit card and will be paid later.

4. A customer was trained for a total of eight sessions this month, and promised to pay Victor $400 next month.

5. Victor paid $5,000 to advertise his business on a billboard.

6. Victor prepaid $2,000 for two months worth of rent.

Table 1

	Name of the Account Affected	Category	Increase or Decrease	Debit or Credit
1.				
2.				
3.				
4.				
5.				
6.				

See Appendix I for solutions.

Journalize the Transaction

Once the analysis is complete, the transaction must be recorded. The transaction is recorded in a **journal**, which is referred to as a book of original entry. The act of recording in the journal is called **journalizing**. There are various journals available for a company to use, but at this point we will focus solely on the general journal.

The **general journal** lists all the transactions of the business in one place and in chronological order. Keeping all transactions in one place makes them easier to follow and makes it easier to trace any mistakes, compared to only recording them in T-accounts.

As an example, consider a business called MP Consulting, owned by Mark Parish. Mark runs the business as a sole proprietorship and provides financial consulting to his clients. On January 2, 2018, he completed some work for a client who paid $1,500 cash. Our analysis indicates that cash should be debited and service revenue should be credited. Figure 4.8 shows how this is recorded in the journal. The circled letters explain how to properly create a journal entry.

JOURNAL				Page 1
ⓐ Date	**Account Title and Explanation ⓑ**	**PR ⓒ**	**Debit ⓓ**	**Credit**
2018				
Jan 2	Cash ⓑ1		1,500	
	Service Revenue ⓑ2			1,500
	Completed work for client ⓑ3			
	ⓔ			

FIGURE 4.8

ⓐ **Date**

The date column includes the current year at the top of the column, followed by the month and day of the transaction. The journal entries are entered in chronological order.

ⓑ **Account Title and Explanation**

This column indicates the names of the accounts being affected. The logic used to indicate which account is affected has not changed. For example, if revenue is earned and cash is received, cash increases (debit) and service revenue increases (credit). The journal places this information in a standard order to keep the information organized.

ⓑ1   Any accounts that are debited in the transaction are listed first.

ⓑ Any accounts that are credited in the transaction are listed after the debited accounts and indented slightly. This is a formatting standard that makes it easier to read long lists of transactions.

ⓒ A brief explanation is listed immediately after the transaction.

If you are given a list of accounts to choose from, use accounts from that list. If you are not provided with a list, use an appropriate name that accurately describes what the account is tracking. For example, repairs performed in the office may be called Repairs Expense, Maintenance Expense or Repairs & Maintenance Expense. Once an account name has been used, the same name should be used for all similar transactions.

ⓒ PR (Posting Reference)

The posting reference column is initially left blank when the journal entry is prepared. We will use this column when we start the third step of the accounting cycle, posting to the ledger accounts.

ⓓ Debit or Credit

These two columns are used to record the amount of the transaction in the appropriate side—debit or credit.

ⓔ Leave a space between journal entries to make it easier to read and separate them.

Compound Journal Entries

If a journal entry only affects two accounts, one account is debited and one account is credited. This type of entry is fairly straightforward to complete. However, some journal entries may affect three or more accounts. These entries are called **compound journal entries** and have multiple debits or multiple credits.

To illustrate a compound journal entry, suppose you purchase equipment for $5,000 on May 25, 2018. You pay $1,000 cash at the time of the purchase, but will not pay the remainder until some time later (accounts payable). This transaction affects the following accounts: equipment is increased with a debit for the full amount, $5,000; accounts payable is increased with a credit for $4,000; and cash is decreased with a credit for $1,000. The journal entry is illustrated in Figure 4.9.

JOURNAL				Page 1
Date 2018	**Account Title and Explanation**	**PR**	**Debit**	**Credit**
May 25	Equipment		5,000	
	Accounts Payable			4,000
	Cash			1,000
	Purchased equipment			

FIGURE 4.9

Pause & Reflect

Exercise 4-2

Prepare a compound journal entry for the $1,000 service completed for a client on April 18, 2018. Cash was received in the amount of $600 and the remainder was put on account.

JOURNAL				Page 1
Date	**Account Title and Explanation**	**PR**	**Debit**	**Credit**

See Appendix I for solutions.

Post to Ledger Accounts

Although all the activities for the month have been recorded in the general journal, the ending balance for each account has not yet been determined. For example, there may have been several transactions relating to cash. To calculate the closing cash balance, the accounts need to be sorted into a manageable format where all transactions affecting that account are included and summarized.

The **general ledger** records and organizes the accounts used by the business. Each account is given a unique number to help identify it and is assigned a separate page to track the balance of the account. The list of all the accounts in the general ledger is called a **chart of accounts**. Combined with the journal introduced in the previous section, the journal and ledger can be referred to as the books of the business.

Establishing a Chart of Accounts

To set up a chart of accounts, first define the various accounts used by the business and then give each account an identifying number. For small businesses, three-digit account numbers may be sufficient, although more digits allow for new accounts to be added as the business grows. Large organizations may have thousands of accounts and require longer account numbers. It is important to assign account numbers in a logical manner and to follow specific industry standards. One example of a numbering system is shown in Figure 4.10.

Account Numbering

100–199: **Asset** accounts	400–499: **Revenue** accounts
200–299: **Liability** accounts	500–599: Expense accounts
300–399: **Equity** accounts	

FIGURE 4.10

Separating each account by several numbers allows new accounts to be added while maintaining the same logical order. Note that the account numbering follows the order of the financial statements: balance sheet (assets, liabilities and equity) and income statement (revenue and expenses).

Different types of businesses use different types of accounts. For example, a manufacturing business requires various accounts for reporting manufacturing costs. A retail business, however, has accounts for the purchase of inventory. Figure 4.11 shows how a service company may set up its accounts. Other accounts can be set up as needed. For example, if the business requires a new expense account, the new account is added to the chart of accounts.

Account Description	Account #	Account Description	Account #
ASSETS		**REVENUE**	
Cash	101	Service Revenue	400
Accounts Receivable	105		
Prepaid Insurance	110	**EXPENSES**	
Office Supplies	115	Advertising Expense	500
Equipment	120	Bad Debt Expense	505
Accumulated Depreciation—Equipment	125	Insurance Expense	510
		Interest Expense	515
LIABILITIES		Maintenance Expense	520
Accounts Payable	200	Miscellaneous Expense	525
Interest Payable	205	Office Supplies Expense	530
Unearned Revenue	210	Professional Fees Expense	535
Notes Payable	215	Rent Expense	540
		Salaries Expense	545
OWNER'S EQUITY		Telephone Expense	550
Owner's Capital	300	Travel Expense	555
Owner's Withdrawals	310		
Income Summary	315		

FIGURE 4.11

Each of the accounts listed in Figure 4.11 has its own ledger account. Think of the ledger as an expanded T-account. In Figure 4.12, notice the red "T" under the debit and credit columns. This is shown to illustrate its similarity to the T-accounts you have been working with.

Account: Cash					GL No: 101
Date	Description	PR	DR	CR	Balance

FIGURE 4.12

Each entry in the journal must be posted to the appropriate ledger account. To maintain up-to-date records, posting should be completed regularly, whether daily, weekly or monthly. The posting of the first journal entry to the general ledger is completed in Figure 4.13. The cash account has an opening balance of $3,000.

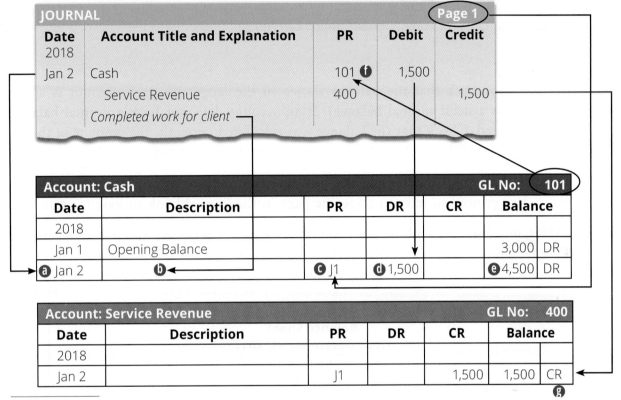

FIGURE 4.13

There are a number of steps to complete when posting items from the journal to the general ledger.

ⓐ Transfer the date of the transaction.

ⓑ The description in the ledger does not have to be completed for every transaction, provided you have a description already recorded in the journal.

ⓒ Transfer the page number of the journal to the posting reference column (PR) in the ledger.

ⓓ Enter the transaction amount into the appropriate debit or credit column.

ⓔ Calculate the new account balance (i.e. the ending, or closing balance). Increase and decrease the previous balance according to the debit and credit rules in Figure 4.1.

ⓕ Enter the ledger number into the posting reference column in the journal as a checking process once the amount has been posted.

ⓖ Repeat the steps for all lines in the journal entry.

IN THE REAL WORLD

Accounting software, such as QuickBooks and Sage, automatically perform the functions of double entries. For example, assume that cash is received by the company and the user identifies the receipt as payment from a customer for services or goods provided. The user is usually the company's bookkeeper or accountant. The software automatically debits the correct asset account and credits the revenue account. After the entry is journalized by the software, the amounts are automatically posted to the general ledger and the trial balance. There is a significant level of automation provided by accounting software, which can reduce the number of accounting errors and misstatements if used correctly.

It is good practice to check that the balance shown in the ledger for each account is a normal balance (e.g. cash has a debit normal balance). If an account does not have a normal balance, an error has likely occurred. Check that the balance was calculated correctly, the amount in the ledger was correctly copied from the journal and the journal entry was created correctly.

In the modern accounting system, the posting process is automatically done by a computer system. Accountants no longer need to refer to a specific page in the journal book to look for transactions.

Return to MP Consulting to see how a full set of journals are prepared and posted to the ledger accounts. First, examine the opening balances from the previous period's balance sheet in Figure 4.14.

MP Consulting Balance Sheet As at December 31, 2017			
Assets		**Liabilities**	
Cash	$3,000	Accounts Payable	$1,000
Accounts Receivable	1,200	Unearned Revenue	900
Equipment	6,000	Notes Payable	3,000
		Total Liabilities	4,900
		Owner's Equity	
		Parish, Capital	5,300
Total Assets	$10,200	**Total Liabilities + Equity**	$10,200

FIGURE 4.14

Note that the balance sheet is dated December 31, 2017. It shows the ending account balances for December 2017, which are the beginning balances for January 2018. These opening balances are already recorded in the ledger accounts. In general, a balance sheet account's ending balance for a given accounting period is the beginning balance of the next period. In this textbook, the term "opening balance" is used synonymously with "beginning balance," and "closing balance" is synonymous with "ending balance."

The income statement is only prepared for the period (the month or year) and always starts the new period with no balances in the accounts. This idea is explained in a later chapter.

MP Consulting had the following transactions for the month of January 2018. The transactions have been entered in the journal in Figure 4.15.

Jan 2   Completed work for a client and the client paid $1,500 cash
Jan 3   Paid $800 cash for January's rent
Jan 4   Prepaid $1,200 cash for a one-year insurance policy
Jan 5   Mark invested $5,000 cash into the business
Jan 7   Paid $2,300 cash for equipment
Jan 10   Completed work for a client, who will pay $1,800 next month
Jan 16   Paid $500 toward the principal of the bank loan
Jan 19   Received $1,100 cash from a client for work to be completed next month
Jan 20   Received a telephone bill for $250 to be paid next month
Jan 30   Mark withdrew $2,000 cash for personal use

JOURNAL				Page 1
Date	**Account Title and Explanation**	**PR**	**Debit**	**Credit**
2018				
Jan 2	Cash	101	1,500	
	Service Revenue	400		1,500
	Completed work for client			
Jan 3	Rent Expense	540	800	
	Cash	101		800
	Paid rent for month of January			
Jan 4	Prepaid Insurance	110	1,200	
	Cash	101		1,200
	Prepaid annual insurance policy			
Jan 5	Cash	101	5,000	
	Parish, Capital	300		5,000
	Owner invested cash			
Jan 7	Equipment	120	2,300	
	Cash	101		2,300
	Bought equipment			
Jan 10	Accounts Receivable	105	1,800	
	Service Revenue	400		1,800
	Completed work on account			
Jan 16	Notes Payable	215	500	
	Cash	101		500
	Paid bank loan principal			
Jan 19	Cash	101	1,100	
	Unearned Revenue	210		1,100
	Received customer deposit			
Jan 20	Telephone Expense	550	250	
	Accounts Payable	200		250
	Received telephone bill			
Jan 30	Parish, Withdrawals	310	2,000	
	Cash	101		2,000
	Owner took cash for personal use			

FIGURE 4.15

Figure 4.16 shows how the general ledger would look after posting all the journal entries from Figure 4.15.

GENERAL LEDGER

Account: Cash					GL No:	101
Date	**Description**	**PR**	**DR**	**CR**	**Balance**	
2018						
Jan 1	Opening Balance				3,000	DR
Jan 2		J1	1,500		4,500	DR
Jan 3		J1		800	3,700	DR
Jan 4		J1		1,200	2,500	DR
Jan 5		J1	5,000		7,500	DR
Jan 7		J1		2,300	5,200	DR
Jan 16		J1		500	4,700	DR
Jan 19		J1	1,100		5,800	DR
Jan 30		J1		2,000	3,800	DR

Account: Accounts Receivable					GL No:	105
Date	**Description**	**PR**	**DR**	**CR**	**Balance**	
2018						
Jan 1	Opening Balance				1,200	DR
Jan 10		J1	1,800		3,000	DR

Account: Prepaid Insurance					GL No:	110
Date	**Description**	**PR**	**DR**	**CR**	**Balance**	
2018						
Jan 1	Opening Balance				0	DR
Jan 4		J1	1,200		1,200	DR

Account: Equipment					GL No:	120
Date	**Description**	**PR**	**DR**	**CR**	**Balance**	
2018						
Jan 1	Opening Balance				6,000	DR
Jan 7		J1	2,300		8,300	DR

Account: Accounts Payable					GL No:	200
Date	**Description**	**PR**	**DR**	**CR**	**Balance**	
2018						
Jan 1	Opening Balance				1,000	CR
Jan 20		J1		250	1,250	CR

Account: Unearned Revenue — GL No: 210

Date	Description	PR	DR	CR	Balance	
2018						
Jan 1	Opening Balance				900	CR
Jan 19		J1		1,100	2,000	CR

Account: Notes Payable — GL No: 215

Date	Description	PR	DR	CR	Balance	
2018						
Jan 1	Opening Balance				3,000	CR
Jan 16		J1	500		2,500	CR

Account: Parish, Capital — GL No: 300

Date	Description	PR	DR	CR	Balance	
2018						
Jan 1	Opening Balance				5,300	CR
Jan 5		J1		5,000	10,300	CR

Account: Parish, Withdrawals — GL No: 310

Date	Description	PR	DR	CR	Balance	
2018						
Jan 30		J1	2,000		2,000	DR

Account: Service Revenue — GL No: 400

Date	Description	PR	DR	CR	Balance	
2018						
Jan 2		J1		1,500	1,500	CR
Jan 10		J1		1,800	3,300	CR

Account: Rent Expense — GL No: 540

Date	Description	PR	DR	CR	Balance	
2018						
Jan 3		J1	800		800	DR

Account: Telephone Expense — GL No: 550

Date	Description	PR	DR	CR	Balance	
2018						
Jan 20		J1	250		250	DR

FIGURE 4.16

To summarize, the first three steps of the accounting cycle (analyze transactions, journalize transactions and post to the general ledger) are done repeatedly during the period. There may be hundreds of journal entries each period, depending on the size of the business. Once the period ends, the accountant moves on to the rest of the accounting cycle, starting with step 4.

Prepare the Trial Balance   LO 6

Remember that in every journal entry, the total value of the debits must equal the total value of the credits at *all* times. To ensure that this rule has been adhered to, we need to create a trial balance. A **trial balance** lists all accounts in the general ledger and their balances at a specific date. If the total debits equals total credits, then the trial balance is balanced. The trial balance is created at the end of the accounting cycle and is used as an internal report for the preparation of financial statements. Some accountants choose to total the debit and credit columns in journals as an added control.

The trial balance has a title that indicates the company name, the name of the report (Trial Balance) and the date the trial balance was prepared. It then lists each account in the order they appear in the general ledger and their final balances in the debit or credit column. The trial balance in Figure 4.17 is based on the accounts and balances from Figure 4.16. Only accounts that have a balance are listed in the trial balance.

If the trial balance does not balance, the financial statements cannot be prepared because there is an error somewhere in the accounts. Double check the following items to identify the error.

MP Consulting Trial Balance January 31, 2018		
Account	DR	CR
Cash	$3,800	
Accounts Receivable	3,000	
Prepaid Insurance	1,200	
Equipment	8,300	
Accounts Payable		$1,250
Unearned Revenue		2,000
Notes Payable		2,500
Parish, Capital		10,300
Parish, Withdrawals	2,000	
Service Revenue		3,300
Rent Expense	800	
Telephone Expense	250	
Total	**$19,350**	**$19,350**

1. Do all accounts on the trial balance show a normal balance?

2. Were the balances on the trial balance copied correctly from the ledger accounts?

3. Was the calculation of the ledger account balances done correctly?

4. Were the amounts in the ledger accounts copied correctly from the journal?

5. Were the journal entries created correctly?

FIGURE 4.17

The fact that a trial balance is balanced does not necessarily mean that all transactions were correctly recorded. For example, the following errors can be made but still leave the trial balance in balance.

- The wrong account was used. For example, debiting an asset instead of debiting an expense.

- An entire journal entry was omitted.

- An entire journal entry was recorded or posted twice.

- Incorrect amounts were used for the journal entry.

- Debits and credits were placed on the wrong side of the entry. For example, instead of debiting cash and crediting revenue, the entry may have debited revenue and credited cash.

Locating errors can be a frustrating experience, so it is important to do your best to ensure that entries are made correctly the first time.

A CLOSER LOOK

A common error that leaves the trial balance unbalanced is transposition. A transposition error occurs when two numbers are switched (e.g. 530 is written as 350). If the difference between the total debits and total credits is evenly divisible by 9, then it is likely a transposition error has been made. Another common error is a slide error, where the decimal point is slid to the left or right of its correct position (e.g. $1,011.10 is written as $10,111.00).

Correcting Entries

During the process of preparing a trial balance or at any time during the accounting cycle, errors in a journal entry may be discovered in the accounting records. The error could be for the incorrect amount, or the wrong account may have been used. In either case, a correction must be made.

In accounting systems, there must always be a paper trail to document what has happened to affect the ledger balances. Errors cannot be simply erased to be corrected. Instead, a correcting journal entry should be made to reverse the error. Correcting entries can be made at any time during the accounting cycle and are meant to fix an error in a previous journal entry.

For example, suppose an entry was made on March 1, 2018 to prepay a one-year insurance policy for $1,800. Instead of debiting the prepaid insurance account, the prepaid rent account was debited. The incorrect journal entry is shown in Figure 4.18.

JOURNAL				Page 1
Date 2018	Account Title and Explanation	PR	Debit	Credit
Mar 1	Prepaid Rent		1,800	
	Cash			1,800
	Pay for one-year insurance policy			

FIGURE 4.18

This journal entry overstates prepaid rent and understates prepaid insurance. The error is discovered on March 8, 2018 and must be corrected. First, a reversing entry is prepared to reverse the original transaction from March 1, and then the correct journal entry is prepared. This is shown in Figure 4.19.

JOURNAL				Page 2
Date 2018	**Account Title and Explanation**	**PR**	**Debit**	**Credit**
Mar 8	Cash		1,800	
	Prepaid Rent			1,800
	To reverse incorrect entry			
Mar 8	Prepaid Insurance		1,800	
	Cash			1,800
	To correctly pay for one-year insurance policy			

FIGURE 4.19

After the correcting entries are made, they are posted to the appropriate general ledger accounts, the balances of which are subsequently transferred to the trial balance. At this point, the ledger account balances and the trial balance is correct.

Pause & Reflect

Exercise 4-3

On September 5, a company paid $5,000 to reduce the principal of the bank loan. The transaction was recorded as a debit to interest expense by mistake. Prepare the correcting entries on September 28, when the error was discovered.

JOURNAL				Page 2
Date	**Account Title and Explanation**	**PR**	**Debit**	**Credit**

See Appendix I for solutions.

Ethics and Internal Controls

Regardless of whether a company uses accounting software or records transactions manually, there is ample opportunity to manipulate the books. Computerized accounting information is only as reliable and accurate as the information that goes into the system. Most of the time, the accounting system used by a company is not fully automated. This means that the user must input information into the system or interact directly with the software at one point or another, which provides opportunity for inaccurate reporting.

For instance, some types of accounting software allow automated recurring entries; they can be set up to repeat the same entry at various time intervals. Some examples of companies that have recurring entries include a rental property company that receives rent from tenants on a monthly basis, an Internet provider that receives subscription payments on a monthly basis, or a bank that receives mortgage payments on a bi-weekly basis.

Consider GG Property Management, which manages and rents out offices in high-rise buildings. Since the company receives rent from its tenants on a monthly basis, it set up its accounting software to record rent revenue automatically at the beginning of each month.

Suppose that a tenant moves out and stops paying rent to GG. However, GG's accounting system continues to record the rent revenue for every subsequent month after the office has been vacated. Allowing the entries to continue being recorded automatically is inaccurate. The additional entries for rent revenue will automatically flow to the general ledger, the trial balance, the income statement and ultimately the balance sheet. Earnings for the period will be inflated. The financial statements will be misstated and this significant error will mislead the users of the financial statements if it goes undetected.

If the above behavior is intentional and management conceals the misstatement, then it is considered highly unethical and fraudulent. However, assume the error was unintentional and the business wants to ensure it does not happen again. A possible control that may detect the error is to compare the current list of tenants to the transaction details in the journal at regular intervals (such as month end). Another method of preventing this error is to program the software to automatically prompt the software administrator to authorize each entry or avoid using automated recurring entries entirely.

Such internal control procedures among US companies have been strengthened as a result of the passage of the Sarbanes-Oxley Act (SOX), which requires statements from every public company's management and external auditor regarding the effectiveness of internal controls.

In Summary

LO 1 **Distinguish between debits and credits**

► Debits are recorded on the left side of an account and credits are recorded on the right side. For the accounting equation to stay in balance, the total value of the debits must equal the total value of the credits.

► Assets, expenses and owner's withdrawals increase with debits and decrease with credits. Liabilities, revenues and owner's capital increase with credits and decrease with debits.

LO 2 **Describe the accounting cycle**

► The accounting cycle consists of the steps required to record financial transactions into the accounting records and ultimately prepare financial statements. The cycle repeats each month or every accounting period.

LO 3 **Explain how to analyze a transaction**

► Analysis of a transaction begins with source documents, which indicate that a transaction has occurred. The analysis helps to determine which accounts are affected, whether they are increasing or decreasing and whether they are debited or credited.

LO 4 **Record transactions in the general journal**

► A journal is a record in which transactions are recorded before they are posted. Journals are known as books of original entry.

► Double-entry transactions are called journal entries. Every journal entry must have at least one debit and one credit entry so that the total of the debits equals the total of the credits.

► Journal entries are dated and listed in chronological order. Accounts that are debited in a journal entry are listed first, followed by the accounts that are credited (indented). A short explanation is included for every journal entry.

LO 5 **Post journal entries to the general ledger**

► The general ledger is a record of all accounts and balances of the business. These accounts represent the complete financial position of the business. They also make up the accounting data from which all reports are generated.

► The listing of all the accounts being used by a business is called a chart of accounts.

► The general ledger is similar to a collection of T-accounts. The debits and credits of each account are shown along with the current balance of the account.

LO 6 **Prepare a trial balance**

► The trial balance lists all accounts in the general ledger and their balances. If the total debits equals total credits, then the trial balance is balanced.

► If the trial balance is not balanced, an error has occurred and must be fixed before continuing with the accounting cycle.

► Correcting entries are made to fix journal entry errors due to wrong accounts or incorrect amounts.

LO 7 **Describe ethics and internal controls related to recording and posting transactions**

► Accountants should record and post transactions truthfully without manipulating the numbers.

► Internal controls, such as double checking and authorization procedures, should be put in place to detect and avoid errors in recording and posting transactions.

 *Access **ameengage.com** for integrated resources including tutorials, practice exercises, the digital textbook and more.*

Review Exercise 4-1

Catherine Gordon is running her own sole proprietary business called CG Accounting. CG Accounting provides bookkeeping services to small and mid-sized companies. The company prepares financial statements on a monthly basis and had the following closing balances at the end of May 2018.

CG Accounting Balance Sheet As at May 31, 2018			
Assets		**Liabilities**	
Cash	$4,200	Accounts Payable	$2,300
Accounts Receivable	3,100	Unearned Revenue	600
Equipment	6,000	Notes Payable	4,000
		Total Liabilities	6,900
		Owner's Equity	
		Gordon, Capital	6,400
Total Assets	$13,300	**Total Liabilities + Owner's Equity**	$13,300

CG Accounting uses a variety of accounts and account numbers in its accounting records.

Account Description	Account #
ASSETS	
Cash	101
Accounts Receivable	105
Prepaid Insurance	110
Equipment	120
Accumulated Depreciation—Equipment	125
LIABILITIES	
Accounts Payable	200
Interest Payable	205
Unearned Revenue	210
Notes Payable	215
OWNER'S EQUITY	
Gordon, Capital	300
Gordon, Withdrawals	310
Income Summary	315

Account Description	Account #
REVENUE	
Service Revenue	400
EXPENSES	
Advertising Expense	500
Bad Debt Expense	505
Insurance Expense	510
Interest Expense	515
Maintenance Expense	520
Miscellaneous Expense	525
Office Supplies Expense	530
Professional Fees Expense	535
Rent Expense	540
Salaries Expense	545
Telephone Expense	550
Travel Expense	555

During the month of June 2018, CG Accounting made the following transactions.

Jun 1	Paid $900 cash for rent incurred
Jun 3	Prepaid $1,200 cash for a one-year insurance policy
Jun 6	Completed work for a client who immediately paid $2,100 cash
Jun 11	Received a bill for advertising for $450, which will be paid next month
Jun 13	Catherine contributed an extra $3,000 cash to the business
Jun 16	Received $300 from a client for work to be completed in July
Jun 18	Completed work for a client who will pay $1,500 next month
Jun 23	Paid $950 cash toward the principal portion of the bank loan
Jun 30	Catherine withdrew $1,000 cash for personal use

Required

a) Complete the journal entries for each transaction.

JOURNAL					Page 1
Date	Account Title and Explanation	PR	Debit	Credit	

JOURNAL				Page 1
Date	**Account Title and Explanation**	**PR**	**Debit**	**Credit**

b) Post the journal entries to the general ledger.

GENERAL LEDGER

Account: Cash						GL No: 101	
Date	**Description**	**PR**	**DR**	**CR**	**Balance**	

Account: Accounts Receivable						GL No: 105	
Date	**Description**	**PR**	**DR**	**CR**	**Balance**	

Account: Prepaid Insurance						GL No: 110	
Date	**Description**	**PR**	**DR**	**CR**	**Balance**	

Account: Equipment					GL No:	120
Date	Description	PR	DR	CR	Balance	

Account: Accounts Payable					GL No:	200
Date	Description	PR	DR	CR	Balance	

Account: Unearned Revenue					GL No:	210
Date	Description	PR	DR	CR	Balance	

Account: Notes Payable					GL No:	215
Date	Description	PR	DR	CR	Balance	

Account: Gordon, Capital					GL No:	300
Date	Description	PR	DR	CR	Balance	

Account: Gordon, Withdrawals					GL No:	310
Date	Description	PR	DR	CR	Balance	

Account: Service Revenue					GL No:	400
Date	Description	PR	DR	CR	Balance	

Account: Advertising Expense					GL No: 500	
Date	Description	PR	DR	CR	Balance	

Account: Rent Expense					GL No: 540	
Date	Description	PR	DR	CR	Balance	

c) Prepare a trial balance.

Account Title	DR	CR

See Appendix I for solutions.

Review Exercise 4-2

On June 28, Jeremy Preston reviewed the transactions that were made for the month. During his review, he came across two errors in the journals.

1. A cash payment of $400 for minor repairs on the company vehicle was debited to the automobile asset account instead of the maintenance expense account.

2. A cash payment of $200 for office supplies was debited to the equipment asset account instead of the office supplies asset account.

Prepare the journal entries to correct the two errors on June 28.

JOURNAL					Page 2
Date	Account Title and Explanation	PR	Debit	Credit	

See Appendix I for solutions.

Notes

Chapter 5
The Accounting Cycle: Adjustments

Learning Objectives

LO 1 **Describe the purpose of adjustments**

LO 2 **Prepare adjusting entries for accrued revenue**

LO 3 **Prepare adjusting entries for accrued expenses**
- Salaries Expense
- Interest Expense

LO 4 **Prepare adjusting entries for unearned revenue**

LO 5 **Prepare adjusting entries for prepaid expenses**
- Prepaid Rent
- Office Supplies

LO 6 **Prepare adjusting entries for depreciation**
- Contra Account
- Calculation of Depreciation
- Summary of Adjusting Journal Entries

LO 7 **Prepare an adjusted trial balance**

LO 8 **Describe ethics and internal controls related to adjusting entries**

AMEENGAGE *Access **ameengage.com** for integrated resources including tutorials, practice exercises, the digital textbook and more.*

121

MAKING IT REAL TO YOU

Businesses of all sizes will frequently get to the end of an accounting period—whether it is a month, a quarter (3 months), or a year (12 months)—and still have transactions that have not been recorded. This regularly occurs with certain types of transactions, such as those where the business pays for goods or services in advance, or where the business owes its employees for work performed for a period, but it actually pays out the salaries in the next period. What happens when the business purchases office supplies on account, so that it owes the supplier for goods but doesn't actually have to pay the supplier for 30 days? It may seem that situations like these, which occur all the time, could make it nearly impossible to get an accurate picture of how the business is doing from one period to the next. Fortunately, accounting principles and practices provide a consistent and reliable way of including the required information in the proper accounting period through the use of adjusting entries, or adjustments.

Introduction to Adjustments

As shown in the Chapter Opener photo, when pilots are in flight, they are constantly assessing information from the instruments and gauges and making adjustments to keep the plane on course. Similarly, accountants must regularly analyze transactions, and make adjustments to reflect what is happening before the financial statements can be prepared.

Accrual-based accounting records revenues when they are earned and expenses when they are incurred. However, cash payments and receipts do not always coincide with the recording of revenues and expenses. Thus, cash can change hands in a period before or after recording revenues or expenses.

For example, suppose you prepay $3,000 for a one-year insurance policy in January. In July, the true value of the insurance has decreased by six months and is now worth only $1,500. The value of the prepaid asset must be adjusted to reflect its true value. The decrease in value of the asset decreases equity, which is recorded as an expense on the income statement.

There are a number of adjustments that need to be made to update the values of assets and liabilities. The process to ensure that all accounts are reported accurately at the end of the period is called the adjusting process. This chapter explains the adjusting process and the preparation of an adjusted trial balance. These are the fifth and sixth steps in the accounting cycle, which are shown in blue in Figure 5.1.

*The first three steps are performed repeatedly during an accounting period, while the remaining steps are performed only at the end of the period.

FIGURE 5.1

An accounting period is the period of time covered by the financial statements. A company has a **fiscal year**, which is a consecutive 12-month period that a company chooses for its financial reporting. A company's fiscal year may cover the same time as the calendar year from January 1 to December 31. However, some companies may choose a **natural business year**, which means the fiscal year ends during a slow time of the year. For example, some retail companies, such as Target and Lowe's, have their fiscal year end at the end of January, after the holiday rush is finished. In this case, the fiscal year is from February 1 to January 31.

A company usually prepares a set of financial statements at the end of each fiscal year, although some prepare the statements more frequently to meet statutory requirements or better manage the business. Remember that accrual-based accounting states that revenue and expenses should be recognized in the accounting period when they occur, regardless of when the cash payment is received or made.

Adjusting entries are made at the end of the accounting period to record assets, liabilities, equity, revenue and expenses according to revenue and expense recognition principles. Do not confuse adjusting entries with correcting entries, which you learned about in Chapter 4. A correcting entry is only made when an error is discovered and needs to be corrected. Adjusting entries are prepared at the end of every fiscal period, regardless of whether any errors were made, to update

> ## WORTH REPEATING
>
> Revenue recognition states that revenue must be recorded when services are performed, regardless of when cash is received. Expense recognition requires that expenses must be recorded in the same period in which they were used to generate revenue.

account balances accurately as at the last day of the period. Every adjustment affects both a balance sheet account and an income statement account. Adjusting entries typically fall under five broad categories.

1. Accrued revenue
2. Accrued expenses
3. Unearned revenue
4. Prepaid expenses
5. Depreciation

Each category will be examined in detail along with examples of adjustments. It is important to note that all adjustments presented in this chapter are just changes made to the recorded values in the books. At no time will cash be received from customers or paid to suppliers. Therefore, adjusting entries never involve the cash account.

Accrued Revenue

LO 2

Accrued revenue is revenue that has been earned but not yet recorded. There is nothing in the ledger accounts to show for this yet. Revenue can accrue or accumulate over a period of time, such as interest on a loan or collecting rent. Other examples of accrued revenue are where completed services have not been billed or there is a contract for work to be performed over a long period of time. Accrued revenue always increases a receivable asset account and increases a revenue account.

Suppose you have a contract with a client stating you will provide them with services for 30 days. At the end of the contract, you will bill the client and they will pay you. The contract starts on September 21 and is worth $6,000. You will not make a journal entry on September 21, since you have not yet completed any work and no cash has been paid to you.

At the end of September, you want to prepare your financial statements. At this point, there is nothing in the books to indicate that you have done work for this client and that the client owes you money for the work completed so far. As stated by the revenue recognition principle under GAAP, revenue must be recognized (recorded) when goods are sold or services are performed. This means that the portion of the services performed in September must be recognized in September. Between September 21 and September 30, 10 out of 30 days of the services, which are equivalent to one-third of the contract, have been performed. Therefore, an adjusting entry is required on September 30 to accrue the revenue equal to one-third of the $6,000 contract, which is $2,000. Accounts receivable is used to record the amount owing because this is a binding contract and the customer is obligated to pay in the future. Figure 5.2 illustrates the adjusting entry that must be made. Without this adjusting entry, service revenue and accounts receivable would be understated by $2,000 in September. Consequently, both assets and owner's equity would be understated.

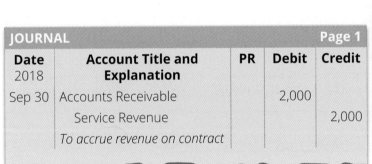
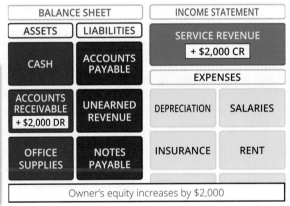

FIGURE 5.2

Once the contract is completed on October 20, you can bill the client. If they pay you immediately, you receive the full $6,000 cash; however, you only record $4,000 worth of revenue earned for the month of October since the other $2,000 was recorded on September 30. There is also a $2,000 decrease to accounts receivable to indicate that the client has now paid you the amount owed. This is illustrated in Figure 5.3.

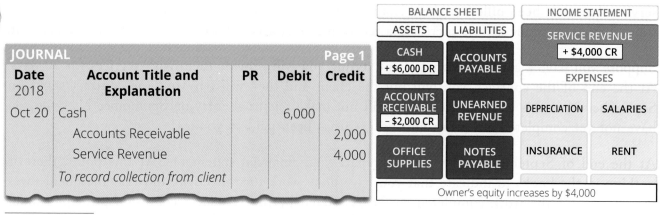

FIGURE 5.3

IN THE REAL WORLD

In most cases, sales are entered from a sales invoice directly into the accounting records, without looking back to see if there were any adjustments made in the previous period. Thus, the transaction on October 20 could be recorded incorrectly if the adjusted amount in accounts receivable is forgotten and not applied to the transaction. If accounts receivable is not applied, $6,000 would be recorded as service revenue for October instead of $4,000. To eliminate the risk of forgetting about the adjustment for accrued revenue and making an error, an optional step is to record a reversing entry. This is done on the first day of the new accounting period; in this example it would be made on October 1, 2018 so it would not affect the reporting in September. The reversing entry is the opposite of the adjustment on September 30, 2018.

| Oct 1 | Service Revenue | 2,000 | |
| | Accounts Receivable | | 2,000 |

By creating this reversing entry, the effect of the adjustment of the previous month is undone for the current month and leaves the service revenue account with a negative (debit) balance of $2,000. On October 20, the full amount of the contract of $6,000 can be recorded, but since service revenue already has a negative balance of $2,000, only $4,000 of revenue is recognized in the month of October.

| Oct 20 | Cash | 6,000 | |
| | Service Revenue | | 6,000 |

It is important to note that a reversing entry is just an option businesses can use to make their bookkeeping easier. It does not change anything about the accrual-based accounting and it typically occurs only at the beginning of an accounting period.

Pause & Reflect

Exercise 5-1

Diane Winston owns and operates a pet-sitting business, which is a sole proprietorship. She was hired to care for Angus' dog for 10 days from December 24, 2018 to January 2, 2019, while Angus is away on vacation. Angus signed a contract to pay Diane $600 on January 2. Prepare journal entries for Diane on December 31, 2018 to record revenue accrual, and on January 2, 2019 to record the cash receipt.

JOURNAL					Page 2
Date	Account Title and Explanation	PR	Debit	Credit

See Appendix I for solutions.

Accrued Expenses

Similar to accrued revenue, **accrued expenses** are expenses that have been incurred but have not yet been recorded. Examples of expenses that may accrue at month end include property taxes, salaries, interest on a loan, and rent. Sometimes, a business has to estimate the accrued expense because the bill is not received until later the following month, such as an electricity or water bill. An accrued expense always increases a liability and increases an expense account.

For accrued expenses, the end of the period will report an understated amount of expenses on the income statement without an adjustment. Also, since this expense represents an amount owed, liabilities on the balance sheet will also be understated. The adjusting entry for an accrued expense corrects this. We will examine two examples of accrued expenses: salaries and interest.

Salaries Expense

Salaries to employees are paid after the work has been completed. If the work and the payment for the work occur within the same period, no adjustment has to be made. However, if the work done by the employee occurs in a different period than the payment, an adjustment must be made at the end of the period.

For example, suppose an employee is paid every two weeks. From the calendar in Figure 5.4, we see the first pay period starts on November 12 and ends on November 23, when the employee gets paid. Since the payment on November 23 is for work done in the same month, this is a transaction similar to what you have learned to pay salaries expense with cash.

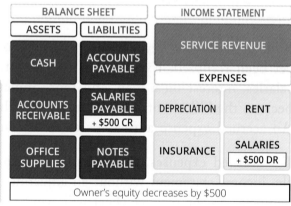

November

Sun	Mon	Tue	Wed	Thu	Fri	Sat
				1	2	3
4	5	6	7	8	9	10
	Start of pay period					
11	(12)	13	14	15	16	17
					Pay Date	
18	19	20	21	22	(23)	24
25	26	27	28	29	30	
	Days worked but not yet paid					

2018

December

Sun	Mon	Tue	Wed	Thu	Fri	Sat
						1
					Pay Date	
2	3	4	5	6	(7)	8
9	10	11	12	13	14	15
16	17	18	19	20	21	22
23	24	25	26	27	28	29
30	31					

2018

FIGURE 5.4

The employee then works the last week of November but the next pay date is not until December 7. The business accrues a salary expense for the employee for the week worked in November. This expense must be recorded in November, even though the employee is not paid until December.

If the employee earns $1,000 every two weeks, he earns $100 per day ($1,000 ÷ 10 working days). Thus, the business must create an adjusting entry for salaries expense for $500 ($100 per day × 5 days). Figure 5.5 illustrates the adjusting entry. Although the $500 has not been paid to the employee, it has to be accrued. Remember, expenses should be recorded when they are incurred, not necessarily when payments are made. This adjustment is recorded as a salary expense, which decreases equity. Since the salary payment is owed to the employee, a liability account called Salaries Payable tracks the amount owing.

JOURNAL   Page 1

Date 2018	Account Title and Explanation	PR	Debit	Credit
Nov 30	Salaries Expense		500	
	Salaries Payable			500
	To accrue salaries owing			

BALANCE SHEET

ASSETS	LIABILITIES
CASH	ACCOUNTS PAYABLE
ACCOUNTS RECEIVABLE	SALARIES PAYABLE + $500 CR
OFFICE SUPPLIES	NOTES PAYABLE

INCOME STATEMENT

SERVICE REVENUE

EXPENSES

DEPRECIATION	RENT
INSURANCE	SALARIES + $500 DR

Owner's equity decreases by $500

FIGURE 5.5

On December 7, the business pays the salary of $1,000. The accrued amount of $500 in the liability account is cleared out since the business is paying the debt to the employee. Only $500 is recorded as an expense, since we only need to record the salary expense for the time worked in December. The journal entry for this transaction is shown in Figure 5.6.

JOURNAL				Page 1
Date 2018	Account Title and Explanation	PR	Debit	Credit
Dec 7	Salaries Expense		500	
	Salaries Payable		500	
	Cash			1,000
	To record payment of salaries owing			

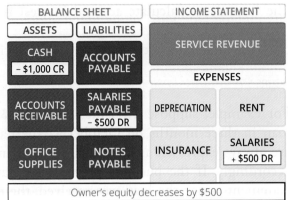

FIGURE 5.6

IN THE REAL WORLD

In most cases, expenses are entered from a purchase invoice or other source documents directly into the accounting records, without checking if any adjustments were made in the previous period. Thus, the transaction on December 7 could be recorded incorrectly if the adjusted amount in salaries payable is forgotten and not applied to the transaction. If salaries payable is not applied, $1,000 would be recorded as salaries expense for December instead of $500. To eliminate the possibility of forgetting about the adjustment for accrued expenses and making an error, an optional step is to record a reversing entry. This is done on the first day of the new accounting period; in this example it would be made on December 1, 2018 so it would not affect the reporting in November. The reversing entry is the opposite of the adjustment on November 30, 2018.

Dec 1	Salaries Payable	500	
	Salaries Expense		500

By creating this reversing entry, the effect of the adjustments of the previous month is undone for the current month and leaves the salaries expense account with a negative (credit) balance of $500. On December 7, the salary payment is made as usual for $1,000, but since salaries expense already has a negative balance of $500, only $500 of salaries expense is recognized in the month of December.

Dec 7	Salaries Expense	1,000	
	Cash		1,000

Some accounting software can create reversing entries for accrued revenue and accrued expenses, thus removing the possibility of double counting revenue and expenses that have already been accrued.

Interest Expense

When borrowing cash, the lender charges interest on the amount borrowed and expects payment at regular intervals. Interest accumulates, or accrues, during the interval before the payment is made. At the end of an accounting period, the borrower must calculate and record the amount of interest that has accumulated to date as an accrued expense. Since it is owed to the lender, it is recorded in a liability account as well.

To calculate interest, three pieces of information must be known.

1. The principal amount (the amount that was originally borrowed)
2. The interest rate (an annual percentage of interest charged on the principal)
3. The term of the loan (how long the debt will last)

The formula to calculate accrued interest is shown in Figure 5.7.

Accrued Interest = Principal × Interest Rate × Time in Years

FIGURE 5.7

For example, suppose a business borrows $10,000 from the bank on July 1 and must repay the loan in three months on October 1. The bank is charging 5% interest on the loan. Interest rates are always expressed as an annual rate, so any duration that is less than one year must be adjusted accordingly. If the business prepares its statements on September 30, and has not prepared any statements since the loan was received, the entire amount of interest that has accrued in the three months from July 1 to September 30 must be recorded. Using the formula from Figure 5.7, the calculation is shown here.

$$\text{Accrued Interest} = \$10,000 \times 5\% \times {}^{3}/_{12}$$
$$= \$125$$

This means that a $125 interest expense has been incurred between July 1 and September 30 as a result of the $10,000 loan. Because this loan is used to fund the company's revenue-generating operations during the period ending September 30, the interest expense must be accrued in this accounting period. Accruing the interest expense in the same period that the loan is used to generate revenue follows the expense recognition principle under the accrual basis of accounting. The expense recognition principle states that an expense must be recognized in the same accounting period in which it is used to generate revenue. Thus, an adjusting entry to record the accrual of interest of $125 must be made by debiting interest expense and crediting the liability account called interest payable. This account tracks all the interest owed. The adjusting entry is shown in Figure 5.8.

JOURNAL				Page 1
Date 2018	Account Title and Explanation	PR	Debit	Credit
Sep 30	Interest Expense		125	
	Interest Payable			125
	To accrue interest owing			

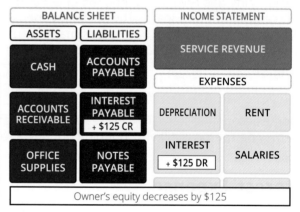

FIGURE 5.8

After the accrued interest for the loan is recorded, the statements are up-to-date and accurate. When the loan is paid back with interest on October 1, there is no interest expense to record. The payment is a reduction of the bank loan and the interest payable, as shown in Figure 5.9.

JOURNAL				Page 1
Date 2018	Account Title and Explanation	PR	Debit	Credit
Oct 1	Notes Payable		10,000	
	Interest Payable		125	
	Cash			10,125
	To pay loan and interest			

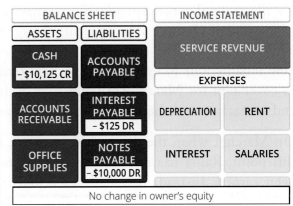

FIGURE 5.9

Pause & Reflect

Exercise 5-2

Confident Walk Shoe Repair has one employee who works five days a week from Monday to Friday and receives a weekly salary of $550 every Friday. The company borrowed a nine-month bank loan of $8,000 on January 1, 2018. The bank charges an annual interest rate of 6%. The loan interest and principal will be repaid altogether on October 1, 2018. Prepare journal entries on Wednesday, January 31, 2018 to accrue salaries and interest expenses.

JOURNAL				Page 1
Date	Account Title and Explanation	PR	Debit	Credit

See Appendix I for solutions.

Unearned Revenue

Unearned revenue is a liability that arises when a customer pays for services or products in advance. For example, when a company sells a gift card, the company receives cash in advance, which increases the cash account. The company also incurs an obligation to later provide products or services to the gift card holder. The amount of this obligation is recorded in unearned revenue, a liability account, until the product or service is provided to the customer. The adjustment to unearned revenue is to account for the earning of revenue for the products or services that were paid for in advance. This adjustment always decreases unearned revenue and increases revenue.

To illustrate the concept of adjustments related to unearned revenue, consider Raina Property Management (Raina). Raina recently bought a large office building and rents out office space for $2,200 a month. The company's policy is to collect the first three months' rent in advance from new tenants. On March 1, 2018, a new tenant moved in and paid $6,600 immediately to Raina to cover rent for March, April and May. Raina makes adjustments to its accounting records at the end of each month because it produces financial statements internally on a monthly basis.

On March 1 when the payment is received, Raina cannot record the $6,600 as revenue because at this point, Raina has not provided any rental service yet. Therefore, on March 1, revenue has not been earned. Instead, Raina makes a journal entry that increases cash (an asset) by $6,600 and increases unearned revenue (a liability) by $6,600. This is shown in Figure 5.10.

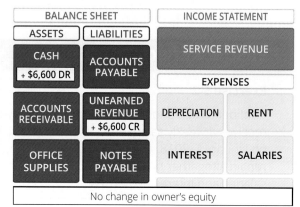

JOURNAL				Page 1
Date 2018	**Account Title and Explanation**	**PR**	**Debit**	**Credit**
Mar 1	Cash		6,600	
	Unearned Revenue			6,600
	Receive cash for three months' rent			

FIGURE 5.10

As of March 31, Raina has earned one month of revenue. On this date, the company decreases unearned revenue (a liability) by $2,200 and increases rent revenue (an income statement account) by $2,200. Waiting until March 31 to recognize the $2,200 rent revenue follows the accrual basis of accounting. Under the accrual basis of accounting, revenue is recognized when it is earned, not when cash is received. After this adjustment is made on March 31, Raina still owes $4,400 worth of rented office space to the tenant, as shown in Figure 5.11.

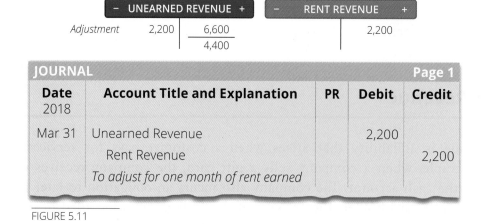

JOURNAL				Page 1
Date 2018	**Account Title and Explanation**	**PR**	**Debit**	**Credit**
Mar 31	Unearned Revenue		2,200	
	Rent Revenue			2,200
	To adjust for one month of rent earned			

FIGURE 5.11

The same adjustment will be made on April 30 (to recognize April's rent revenue) and May 31 (to recognize May's rent revenue). Figure 5.12 shows the timing of the transactions related to unearned revenue from Raina's perspective.

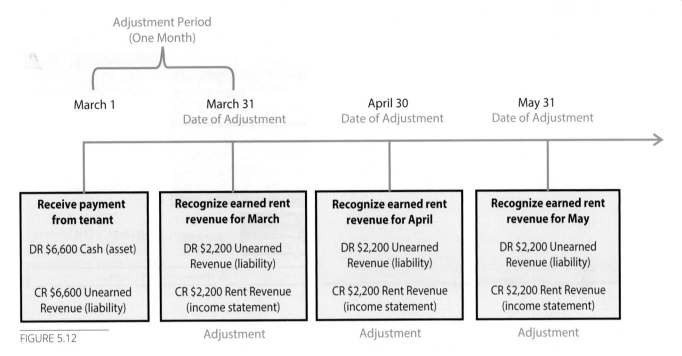

Adjustment Period (One Month)

March 1 — **March 31** Date of Adjustment — **April 30** Date of Adjustment — **May 31** Date of Adjustment

Receive payment from tenant	**Recognize earned rent revenue for March**	**Recognize earned rent revenue for April**	**Recognize earned rent revenue for May**
DR $6,600 Cash (asset)	DR $2,200 Unearned Revenue (liability)	DR $2,200 Unearned Revenue (liability)	DR $2,200 Unearned Revenue (liability)
CR $6,600 Unearned Revenue (liability)	CR $2,200 Rent Revenue (income statement)	CR $2,200 Rent Revenue (income statement)	CR $2,200 Rent Revenue (income statement)
	Adjustment	Adjustment	Adjustment

FIGURE 5.12

As shown in Figure 5.12, even though Raina received cash on March 1, the recognition of revenue is deferred to the end of March, April and May, when the revenue has been earned. For this reason, unearned revenue is sometimes referred to as deferred revenue. To "defer" means to put off or delay to a future period. Unearned revenue is different from accrued revenue, which is revenue that is recorded right away when revenue is earned, even though cash has not been received.

Prepaid Expenses

Similar to unearned revenue, accounting for prepaid expenses requires making adjustments as amounts are used. Recall that when a prepaid expense is recognized as an actual expense, prepaid expenses (an asset) decreases and the expense (an income statement account) increases. This is the adjusting entry for prepaid expenses.

Prepaid Rent

We can apply this to the example of Raina Property Management, which was illustrated in the unearned revenue section. Now examine the financial impact of the transactions from the perspective of the tenant who paid Raina three months of rent in advance at $2,200 per month. On March 1, the tenant records a cash payment to Raina for $6,600 as a prepayment for rent, as shown in Figure 5.13. Even though the tenant paid $6,600 cash on March 1, the tenant does not record the transaction as an expense on this date. Under the accrual basis of accounting, expenses are recorded as they are incurred, not when cash is paid. Because rent expense has not been incurred as of March 1, the owner's equity has not decreased on this date. Paying cash for prepaid rent is similar to using cash to purchase another asset. It is simply an exchange of one asset (cash) for another (prepaid rent).

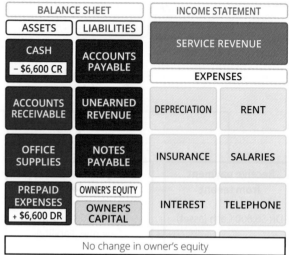

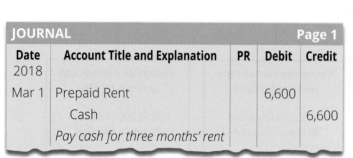

JOURNAL				Page 1
Date 2018	**Account Title and Explanation**	**PR**	**Debit**	**Credit**
Mar 1	Prepaid Rent		6,600	
	Cash			6,600
	Pay cash for three months' rent			

FIGURE 5.13

If the tenant also uses a monthly accounting period, then the prepaid rent is adjusted at the end of each month. In this case, the tenant is adjusting based on what has been used (one month) on March 31. The adjustment decreases the prepaid rent account and increases rent expense on the income statement. As Figure 5.14 shows, after the adjustment on March 31 the prepaid rent account is left with a balance of $4,400, which means two months are still prepaid.

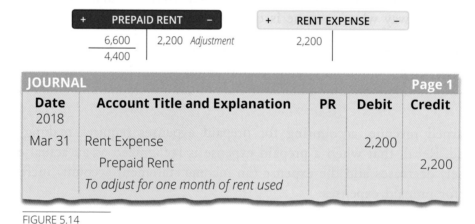

JOURNAL				Page 1
Date 2018	**Account Title and Explanation**	**PR**	**Debit**	**Credit**
Mar 31	Rent Expense		2,200	
	Prepaid Rent			2,200
	To adjust for one month of rent used			

FIGURE 5.14

The same adjustment is made on April 30 (to recognize April's rent expense) and May 31 (to recognize May's rent expense). Figure 5.15 shows the timing of the transactions related to the prepaid rent from the perspective of the tenant.

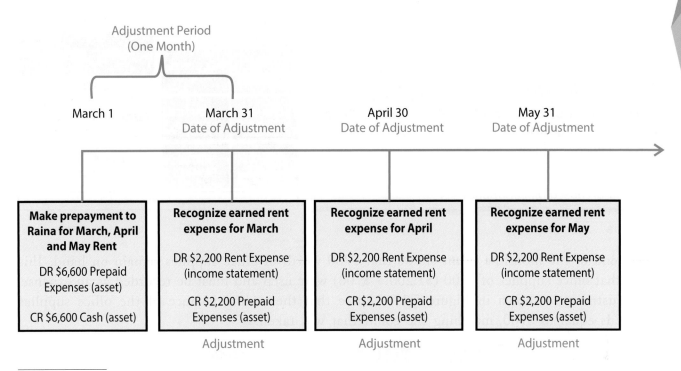

FIGURE 5.15

Prepaid expenses and unearned revenue are opposites. Usually, as in this example, the prepaid expense of one company (the tenant) is the unearned revenue of another company (Raina). The above example illustrated prepaid rent, however the same idea and transactions apply for items such as prepaid insurance or prepaid property taxes.

Office Supplies

Another type of prepaid expense is office supplies. Office supplies are the physical items used to run the office of a business and include paper, photocopy toner, printer toner, pens and so on. When they are initially purchased, these items are recorded as assets on the balance sheet. Instead of recording each item as an expense when it is used, a single adjusting entry is made for the total office supplies used. At the end of the period, a count is made to determine the value of the remaining office supplies and an adjusting entry is created to record the amount of office supplies used as an expense.

To illustrate, suppose a business paid $1,200 cash for office supplies on September 4. This initial purchase of office supplies is just a transfer of one asset (cash) for another (office supplies) and is shown in Figure 5.16.

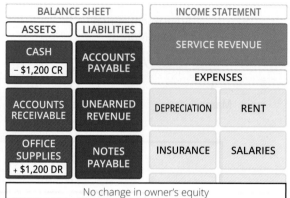

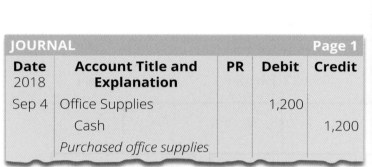

FIGURE 5.16

At the end of the month, a count shows that $700 worth of office supplies remain on hand. This means that office supplies of $500 ($1,200 – $700) were used and must be recorded as an expense. The adjustment is shown in Figure 5.17. Notice that the ending balance of the office supplies account is equal to $700, matching the count that was taken.

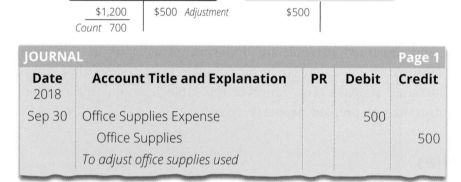

FIGURE 5.17

IN THE REAL WORLD

Office supplies are often low-value items, such as paper and pens. In many businesses, keeping track of these small amounts as an asset, then counting them to see what was used, is not viewed as an important procedure. The materiality constraint introduced earlier indicates that if a piece of information could influence a user's decision, it is material and must be accounted for properly according to GAAP. For many businesses, it is easier to simply record office supplies as an expense immediately instead of an asset first. This is done when the amount is not material, since the extra work and detail would not affect users' decisions.

Pause & Reflect

Exercise 5-3

On August 1, Armadillo Property Management collected $36,000 from Beaver Company for 12 months' rent in advance. Beaver Company started its occupancy on August 1. Prepare journal entries for both Armadillo and Beaver on August 1, when cash is received or paid, and on December 31 to recognize rent revenue or expense for the year. Assume no adjusting entries have been made between August 1 and December 31.

Armadillo Property Management's Journal Entries

JOURNAL					Page 1
Date	**Account Title and Explanation**	**PR**	**Debit**	**Credit**	

Beaver Company's Journal Entries

JOURNAL					Page 1
Date	**Account Title and Explanation**	**PR**	**Debit**	**Credit**	

See Appendix I for solutions.

Depreciation

We learned that items such as land, furniture, computers and automobiles fall under the property, plant and equipment category. These assets are used to run the business and generate sales. However, with the exception of land, these assets eventually become obsolete, unusable or broken.

This may not happen for several years, but however long it is, the length of time the asset can be used is called the **useful life**.

These noncurrent assets are like prepaid expenses since the asset is purchased and then used up over time. **Depreciation** is how accountants allocate the cost of a noncurrent asset over its useful life. The reason that land does not depreciate is that land has an unlimited useful life. Depreciation matches the expense of the noncurrent asset to the period in which it generates revenue for the business.

Different types of assets depreciate at different rates. For example, the value of a car tends to depreciate much faster than the value of a desk. For this reason, accountants have come up with multiple depreciation methods that reflect different patterns of depreciation. Examples of depreciation methods include the straight-line method, units-of-production method and double-declining-balance method. For simplicity, only the straight-line method, which assumes that an asset depreciates equally throughout its useful life, will be used during this course.

For example, suppose a machine, which is expected to last for five years and then be thrown out, was purchased for $10,000 one year ago. After one year, a depreciation of $2,000 ($10,000 ÷ 5 years) must be recorded. The $2,000 of depreciation reduces the value of the machine and gives its net book value. The **net book value** of the asset is its original value less the total depreciation that has been recognized. This does not represent what it could be sold for; net book value is just the accounting value of the asset. Thus, the net book value of the machine after recording depreciation is $8,000. However, GAAP requires companies to keep information about the amount assets originally cost and how much they have depreciated so far. Therefore, accounting for depreciation requires a special account called a contra account.

Contra Account

Contra means opposite. A **contra account** is linked to another account and records decreases in the value of that account. This is done so that the original value of the related account remains unchanged. The value of the contra account is subtracted from the related account to arrive at a net book value for the item. In the case of property, plant and equipment (PPE), the contra account is called **accumulated depreciation**. This contra asset account reflects the decrease in the net book value of PPE without changing the original cost of the asset.

With the exception of land, every asset that is considered part of property, plant and equipment has its own separate accumulated depreciation account to track the decrease in net book value.

Suppose an asset was purchased for $10,000 and has accumulated $2,000 worth of depreciation. To preserve the original amount of $10,000, the asset account under PPE is not directly adjusted. Instead, as illustrated in Figure 5.18, accumulated depreciation records the total decrease in net book value of the asset. The contra asset account is called accumulated depreciation because the depreciation accumulates as the asset's cost is allocated to each period. This is different from depreciation expense, an income statement account which only shows the depreciation for the current period.

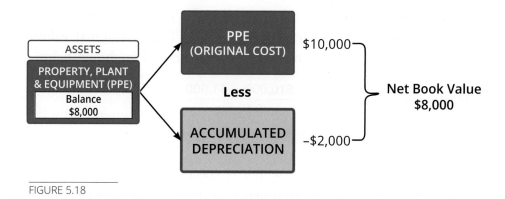

FIGURE 5.18

The contra asset account behaves in a manner opposite to the way a regular asset account behaves. Recall that an asset account increases with a debit and decreases with a credit. The contra asset account (accumulated depreciation) increases with a credit and decreases with a debit. Figure 5.19 illustrates the T-accounts for property, plant and equipment and accumulated depreciation.

FIGURE 5.19

Calculation of Depreciation

As mentioned earlier, we are going to use a simple method called straight-line depreciation. Straight-line depreciation is a method to allocate the cost of the asset evenly over the life of the asset. The calculation for straight-line depreciation is shown in Figure 5.20.

$$\text{Straight-Line Depreciation Rate} = \frac{\text{Cost of Asset} - \text{Residual Value}}{\text{Useful Life}}$$

FIGURE 5.20

There are three parts of this calculation that must be explained.

1. The cost of the asset is the original purchase price of the asset. This is the value shown on the balance sheet in the asset account.
2. Residual value is the estimated value of the asset at the end of its useful life. By subtracting the residual value from the original cost of the asset, we determine the cost that is allocated over the life of the asset. It is possible for an asset to have a residual value of $0, meaning the asset will be fully depreciated and worthless at the end of its useful life.
3. The useful life is how long the asset is expected to be used by the business. Like residual value, this is also an estimate. The useful life can be expressed in years or months, depending on how often depreciation is recorded.

For example, suppose a machine was purchased on January 1, 2018 for $10,000. The machine is expected to last for five years, after which it is expected to have a residual value of $1,000. The calculation for yearly depreciation under the straight-line method is shown below.

$$\text{Straight-Line Depreciation} = \frac{\$10,000 - \$1,000}{5 \text{ Years}}$$

$$= \$1,800/\text{year}$$

The cost allocated over five years is $9,000, which is the original purchase price minus the estimated residual value. Each year, $1,800 is recorded as a depreciation expense and $1,800 is added to accumulated depreciation. The journal entry is shown in Figure 5.21.

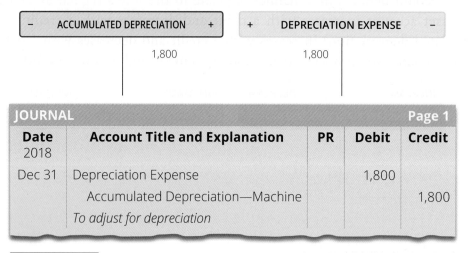

JOURNAL					Page 1
Date 2018	**Account Title and Explanation**	**PR**	**Debit**	**Credit**	
Dec 31	Depreciation Expense		1,800		
	Accumulated Depreciation—Machine			1,800	
	To adjust for depreciation				

FIGURE 5.21

Since the income statement resets and starts from scratch each year, a depreciation expense of $1,800 is recorded each year. The accumulated depreciation account, on the other hand, increases by $1,800 each year. As the accumulated depreciation account increases, the net book value of the machine decreases. Net book value is the original cost of the asset less accumulated depreciation. The transaction in Figure 5.19 is recorded at the end of each year. The amount of accumulated depreciation and the net book value of the machine over the five-year useful life are shown in Figure 5.22.

Year	Original Cost of Machine	Depreciation Expense	Accumulated Depreciation	Net Book Value
2018	10,000	1,800	1,800	8,200
2019	10,000	1,800	3,600	6,400
2020	10,000	1,800	5,400	4,600
2021	10,000	1,800	7,200	2,800
2022	10,000	1,800	9,000	1,000
Total	$10,000	$9,000	$9,000	$1,000

FIGURE 5.22

The net book value at the end of 2022 is equal to $1,000, which is the estimated residual value of the machine. This means that $9,000 of the cost of the machine was allocated over five years.

It is possible that depreciation may be recorded for periods of time that are less than one year. For example, suppose the machine was purchased on September 1, 2018 and the business records adjustments at year end, December 31, 2018. In this case, depreciation should only be recorded for four months. The calculation of depreciation is shown below.

$$\text{Straight-Line Depreciation} = \frac{\$10,000 - \$1,000}{5 \text{ Years}} \times \frac{4}{12}$$

$$= \$600 \text{ for 4 months}$$

The same accounts would be used as the ones in the journal entry in Figure 5.21, but the amount of depreciation would only be $600.

Summary of Adjusting Journal Entries

The five categories of adjustment are summarized in Figure 5.23. This shows which account categories are increased or decreased as a result of the adjustment. Each category of adjustment affects both income statement and balance sheet accounts (but never the cash account). Therefore, if adjusting entries are not prepared, some accounts in the income statement and the balance sheet will be either overstated or understated.

Category	Adjusting Entry		Impact of Omitting Adjusting Entry	
	Account Category	Increase/ Decrease	Income Statement	Balance Sheet
Accrued Revenue	DR Asset	Increase	Revenue understated	Asset understated
	CR Revenue	Increase	Net income understated	Equity understated
Accrued Expenses	DR Expense	Increase	Expense understated	Liability understated
	CR Liability	Increase	Net income overstated	Equity overstated
Unearned Revenue	DR Liability	Decrease	Revenue understated	Liability overstated
	CR Revenue	Increase	Net income understated	Equity understated
Prepaid Expenses	DR Expense	Increase	Expense understated	Asset overstated
	CR Asset	Decrease	Net income overstated	Equity overstated
Depreciation	DR Expense	Increase	Expense understated	Asset overstated
	CR Contra Asset	Increase	Net income overstated	Equity overstated

FIGURE 5.23

Pause & Reflect

Exercise 5-4

Seel Inc. purchased a piece of equipment on January 1, 2018, for $20,000. The useful life of the equipment is estimated to be eight years, after which the company expects to sell it for $4,000. Prepare the adjusting entry on December 31, 2018, to record the equipment's depreciation using the straight-line depreciation method.

JOURNAL					Page 2
Date	Account Title and Explanation	PR	Debit	Credit	

See Appendix I for solutions.

Adjusted Trial Balance

The sixth step of the accounting cycle is to prepare the adjusted trial balance. To help illustrate this step, return to the sample company MP Consulting introduced in Chapter 4. At the end of the fourth step of the accounting cycle, we had prepared the unadjusted trial balance for the business, shown in Figure 5.24.

MP Consulting Trial Balance January 31, 2018		
Account Titles	DR	CR
Cash	$3,800	
Accounts Receivable	3,000	
Prepaid Insurance	1,200	
Equipment	8,300	
Accounts Payable		$1,250
Unearned Revenue		2,000
Notes Payable		2,500
Parish, Capital		10,300
Parish, Withdrawals	2,000	
Service Revenue		3,300
Rent Expense	800	
Telephone Expense	250	
Total	$19,350	$19,350

FIGURE 5.24

This unadjusted trial balance is the balance of the general ledger accounts after all the regular day-to-day transactions have been recorded in the general journal and posted to the general ledger. It is from these balances that MP Consulting will make adjusting entries. Suppose the company has the following adjustments to make at the end of the month. The five adjustments are lettered here and in Figure 5.25 to illustrate how each one is recorded.

ⓐ The company borrowed cash from the bank at a 12% rate of interest. Using the accrued interest calculation from Figure 5.7, accrued interest for the month is calculated as

$$\text{Accrued Interest} = \$2{,}500 \times 12\% \times \frac{1}{12}$$

$$= \$25 \text{ per month}$$

ⓑ One month of the prepaid insurance has been used. Since the balance of $1,200 represents a one-year policy, $100 ($1,200 ÷ 12 months) must be adjusted as an expense.

ⓒ Based on the records of MP Consulting, $200 worth of unearned revenue had been earned by the end of the month. This amount must be recognized as revenue.

ⓓ All the equipment that MP Consulting owns has an estimated useful life of four years and an estimated residual value of $1,100. Using the depreciation calculation from Figure 5.20, depreciation for the month is calculated as

$$\text{Depreciation} = \frac{\$8{,}300 - \$1{,}100}{4 \text{ Years}} \times \frac{1}{12}$$

$$= \$150 \text{ per month}$$

ⓔ On January 2, MP Consulting began a two-month contract with a client. The contract covers work for the months of January and February. On February 28, 2018, the contract will be completed and MP Consulting will bill the client $2,000. An adjusting entry must be made on January 31 to accrue the revenue earned during the month of January. MP Consulting will create an adjusting entry showing revenue of $1,000 earned during the month.

Before recording the adjustments in the general journal, it is helpful to see the impact of the adjustments and to ensure that the accounts will balance after the adjustments are made. To assist in this process, a **spreadsheet**, which is a work sheet prepared using programs like Excel, can be used to display the trial balances before and after the adjustments are made. The trial balance before adjustments are made is called the **unadjusted trial balance**. The trial balance after the adjustments are made is called the **adjusted trial balance**.

The spreadsheet shown in Figure 5.25 shows the unadjusted trial balance at the end of January. Beside this trial balance is a set of debit and credit columns for the adjustments. It is important to ensure the debit and credit columns of the adjustments column balance, otherwise the adjusted trial balance will not balance.

The last set of debit and credit columns is the adjusted trial balance. The amounts in the adjustment columns are added or subtracted from the original balances and placed in the adjusted trial balance columns. This shows what the ledger balances will be after the adjustments are made. If the debit and credit columns balance, then the financial statements can be prepared.

	MP Consulting Spreadsheet January 31, 2018					
	Unadjusted Trial Balance		Adjustments		Adjusted Trial Balance	
Account Title	**DR**	**CR**	**DR**	**CR**	**DR**	**CR**
Cash	$3,800				$3,800	
Accounts Receivable	3,000		ⓔ $1,000		4,000	
Prepaid Insurance	1,200			ⓑ $100	1,100	
Equipment	8,300				8,300	
Accumulated Depreciation—Equipment		$0		ⓓ 150		$150
Accounts Payable		1,250				1,250
Interest Payable		0		ⓐ 25		25
Unearned Revenue		2,000	ⓒ 200			1,800
Notes Payable		2,500				2,500
Parish, Capital		10,300				10,300
Parish, Withdrawals	2,000				2,000	
Service Revenue		3,300		ⓒ ⓔ 1,200		4,500
Depreciation Expense	0		ⓓ 150		150	
Insurance Expense	0		ⓑ 100		100	
Interest Expense	0		ⓐ 25		25	
Rent Expense	800				800	
Telephone Expense	250				250	
Total	**$19,350**	**$19,350**	**$1,475**	**$1,475**	**$20,525**	**$20,525**

FIGURE 5.25

Once the spreadsheet is prepared and the adjusted trial balance is in balance, the journal entries are recorded in the general journal and posted to the general ledger. The journal entries are shown in Figure 5.26. All the postings to general ledger accounts, including these adjustments, are discussed in Chapter 6.

JOURNAL			Page 1	
Date 2018	Account Title and Explanation	PR	Debit	Credit
Jan 31	Interest Expense		25	
	Interest Payable			25
	Record one month of accrued interest			
Jan 31	Insurance Expense		100	
	Prepaid Insurance			100
	Record one month of insurance used			
Jan 31	Unearned Revenue		200	
	Service Revenue			200
	Record revenue now earned			
Jan 31	Depreciation Expense		150	
	Accumulated Depreciation—Equipment			150
	Record depreciation for one month			
Jan 31	Accounts Receivable		1,000	
	Service Revenue			1,000
	Record accrued revenue			

FIGURE 5.26

The preparation of the spreadsheet is optional. It is possible to simply prepare the journal entries as shown in Figure 5.26 and post them to the general ledger, then create the adjusted trial balance without preparing the end-of-period spreadsheet. However, the spreadsheet can be a useful tool to ensure all accounts remain in balance because going back to find errors can be a difficult process.

Ethics and Internal Controls

Reliable and relevant accounting information is important to both internal and external users. Internal users (managers and executives) rely on the information to plan, control and assess business operations. External users (creditors and lenders) rely on accounting information to determine a company is credit-worthy. However, it is possible to intentionally manipulate adjustments to change how the financial performance and position of the company is presented. If the manipulation hides information from users, this is unethical.

Consider the example of a company applying for a bank loan. As a potential lender, the bank's main concern is whether the business generates sufficient cash from its day-to-day operations to repay the loan. Before the bank considers lending to the company it wants to see certain indicators of financial health, such as steady sales, regular collection of accounts receivable, good control over expenses, and the timely payment of debt. If the company's management feels that the company falls short in one or more of these areas, it may be tempted to portray a more favorable picture to the lender by doing one or more of the following.

- adjusting for only accrued revenues and unearned revenues, but not adjusting for depreciation, accrued expenses, or prepaid expenses, which would properly show revenue but understate expenses

- making high estimates of unearned revenue, which would inflate the company's revenues

Unethical practices related to accounting adjustments can take many forms, such as the intentional misstatement of information, abuse in applying accounting principles, underestimation of liabilities and accruals, overstatement of earnings, or the unjustified revision of an asset's estimated useful life in order to alter depreciation figures.

Consider the accrual of interest on a bank loan. Management should not wait until the interest is paid to record interest. Interest should be accrued at the end of an accounting period and thus reflected as interest expense on the income statement. If management fails to accrue interest at the end of an accounting period, the financial statements will understate liabilities (since interest payable is understated) and overstate net income (since interest expense is understated). This will provide investors and creditors an incorrect representation of the company's performance and debt position.

Under the Sarbanes-Oxley Act (SOX), the CEO and CFO of a publicly traded company must certify that the financial statements that are filed with the SEC fairly present the company's operations and financial condition. It is a violation of SOX if management fails to prepare or manipulates the adjusting entries in a way that does not truly present the company's operations and financial condition. Those who violate SOX compliance can be fined or imprisoned.

WORTH REPEATING

The Sarbanes-Oxley Act (SOX) of 2002 was introduced in Chapter 3. It was co-sponsored by Senator Paul Sarbanes and Representative Michael G. Oxley. The bill was passed as a response to major corporate and accounting scandals. SOX requires top levels of management to certify the accuracy of financial information, and has created more severe penalties for committing financial fraud.

Internal control procedures must be in place to ensure that all necessary adjustments are accounted for. For example, the current period's adjusting entries should be compared with the previous period's adjusting entries to check whether any adjusting entries are missing. Any significant deviance from the last period's adjusting entries may need to be investigated. As another example of internal control, management should review the terms of the debt contracts for all outstanding noncurrent liabilities at the end of an accounting period. This provides management with a reasonable idea of what the interest expense should be for the period after including accrued interest as well.

In Summary

LO 1   **Describe the purpose of adjustments**

▶   Adjustments are made to ensure that all accounts are accurately reported at the end of the period.

▶   Adjustments are made before the creation of the financial statements.

LO 2   **Prepare adjusting entries for accrued revenue**

▶   Accrued revenue is revenue that has been earned but has not yet been recorded. The adjustment is made by debiting (increasing) accounts receivable and crediting (increasing) service revenue.

LO 3   **Prepare adjusting entries for accrued expenses**

▶   Accrued expenses are expenses that have been incurred but have not yet been recorded. The adjustment is made by debiting (increasing) an expense and crediting (increasing) a liability.

LO 4   **Prepare adjusting entries for unearned revenue**

▶   Adjustments to unearned revenue is to account for revenue that has now been earned. The adjustment is made by debiting (decreasing) unearned revenue and crediting (increasing) service revenue.

LO 5   **Prepare adjusting entries for prepaid expenses**

▶   Adjustments to prepaid expenses is to account for expenses that have now been incurred. The adjustment is made by debiting (increasing) an expense and crediting (decreasing) the prepaid expense.

LO 6   **Prepare adjusting entries for depreciation**

▶   Adjustments for depreciation is to allocate the cost of a noncurrent asset over its useful life. The adjustment is made by debiting (increasing) depreciation expense and crediting (increasing) the contra account called accumulated depreciation.

LO 7   **Prepare an adjusted trial balance**

▶   The adjusted trial balance is prepared after the adjusting entries have been made. This is to ensure the accounts are still in balance and the financial statements can be prepared.

LO 8   **Describe ethics and internal controls related to adjusting entries**

▶   Adjusting entries must be prepared in a way that fairly present the company's operations and financial condition.

▶   An internal control system must be in place to ensure that all necessary adjustments are accounted for.

 *Access **ameengage.com** for integrated resources including tutorials, practice exercises, the digital textbook and more.*

Review Exercise 5-1

Catherine Gordon is running her own proprietary business called CG Accounting. CG Accounting provides bookkeeping services to small and mid-sized companies. The company prepares financial statements on a monthly basis and was previously introduced. Before you begin this exercise, familiarize yourself with the review exercise in Chapter 4.

The journal entries for the month of June have already been entered in the journal and posted to the ledger. The trial balance, before adjustments, is presented below.

CG Accounting Trial Balance June 30, 2018		
Account Title	**DR**	**CR**
Cash	$5,550	
Accounts Receivable	4,600	
Prepaid Insurance	1,200	
Equipment	6,000	
Accounts Payable		$2,750
Unearned Revenue		900
Notes Payable		3,050
Gordon, Capital		9,400
Gordon, Withdrawals	1,000	
Service Revenue		3,600
Advertising Expense	450	
Professional Fees Expense	900	
Total	**$19,700**	**$19,700**

CG Accounting uses the following accounts and accounting numbers in its accounting records.

Account Description	Account #
ASSETS	
Cash	101
Accounts Receivable	105
Prepaid Insurance	110
Equipment	120
Accumulated Depreciation—Equipment	125
LIABILITIES	
Accounts Payable	200
Interest Payable	205
Unearned Revenue	210
Notes Payable	215
OWNER'S EQUITY	
Gordon, Capital	300
Gordon, Withdrawals	310
Income Summary	315

Account Description	Account #
REVENUE	
Service Revenue	400
EXPENSES	
Advertising Expense	500
Bad Debt Expense	505
Depreciation Expense	510
Insurance Expense	515
Interest Expense	520
Maintenance Expense	525
Office Supplies Expense	530
Professional Fees Expense	535
Rent Expense	540
Salaries Expense	545
Telephone Expense	550
Travel Expense	555

At the end of June 2018, CG Accounting had to make the following adjustments.

Jun 30   The prepaid insurance represents a one-year policy that started in June. One month has now been used.

Jun 30   When examining the balance of unearned revenue, Catherine determined that $450 has now been earned.

Jun 30   Interest has accrued on the balance of the bank loan for the month. The loan interest rate is 10%. (For simplicity, round the interest to the nearest whole number.)

Jun 30   Depreciation on the equipment for the month must be recorded. The equipment is depreciated using the straight-line method. The equipment is expected to last five years and will have no residual value

Jun 30   Catherine started an audit for a new client. The contract is for 20 days of work starting June 21. At the end of the contract, the client will pay CG Accounting $1,800. Accrue the revenue earned for June.

Required

a)   Complete the spreadsheet.

	CG Accounting Spreadsheet June 30, 2018					
	Unadjusted Trial Balance		Adjustments		Adjusted Trial Balance	
Account Title	DR	CR	DR	CR	DR	CR
Cash	$5,550					
Accounts Receivable	4,600					
Prepaid Insurance	1,200					
Equipment	6,000					
Accumulated Depreciation—Equipment		$0				
Accounts Payable		2,750				
Interest Payable		0				
Unearned Revenue		900				
Notes Payable		3,050				
Gordon, Capital		9,400				
Gordon, Withdrawals	1,000					
Service Revenue		3,600				
Advertising Expense	450					
Depreciation Expense	0					
Insurance Expense	0					
Interest Expense	0					
Rent Expense	900					
Total	$19,700	$19,700				

b) Prepare the journal entries for the adjusting entries.

JOURNAL				Page 2
Date	Account Title and Explanation	PR	Debit	Credit

c) Post adjusting journal entries from the General Journal to the General Ledger.

GENERAL LEDGER

Account: Cash					GL No: 101	
Date	**Description**	**PR**	**DR**	**CR**	**Balance**	
2018						
Jun 1	Opening Balance				4,200	DR
Jun 1		J1		900	3,300	DR
Jun 3		J1		1,200	2,100	DR
Jun 6		J1	2,100		4,200	DR
Jun 13		J1	3,000		7,200	DR
Jun 16		J1	300		7,500	DR
Jun 23		J1		950	6,550	DR
Jun 30		J1		1,000	5,550	DR

Account: Accounts Receivable					GL No: 105	
Date	**Description**	**PR**	**DR**	**CR**	**Balance**	
2018						
Jun 1	Opening Balance				3,100	DR
Jun 18		J1	1,500		4,600	DR

Account: Prepaid Insurance					GL No: 110	
Date	**Description**	**PR**	**DR**	**CR**	**Balance**	
2018						
Jun 1	Opening Balance				0	DR
Jun 3		J1	1,200		1,200	DR

Account: Equipment					GL No: 120	
Date	**Description**	**PR**	**DR**	**CR**	**Balance**	
2018						
Jun 1	Opening Balance				6,000	DR

Account: Accumulated Depreciation—Equipment					GL No: 125	
Date	**Description**	**PR**	**DR**	**CR**	**Balance**	

Account: Accounts Payable — **GL No: 200**

Date	Description	PR	DR	CR	Balance	
2018						
Jun 1	Opening Balance				2,300	CR
Jun 11		J1		450	2,750	CR

Account: Interest Payable — **GL No: 205**

Date	Description	PR	DR	CR	Balance	

Account: Unearned Revenue — **GL No: 210**

Date	Description	PR	DR	CR	Balance	
2018						
Jun 1	Opening Balance				600	CR
Jun 16		J1		300	900	CR

Account: Notes Payable — **GL No: 215**

Date	Description	PR	DR	CR	Balance	
2018						
Jun 1	Opening Balance				4,000	CR
Jun 23		J1	950		3,050	CR

Account: Gordon, Capital — **GL No: 300**

Date	Description	PR	DR	CR	Balance	
2018						
Jun 1	Opening Balance				6,400	CR
Jun 13		J1		3,000	9,400	CR

Account: Gordon, Withdrawals — **GL No: 310**

Date	Description	PR	DR	CR	Balance	
2018						
Jun 30		J1	1,000		1,000	DR

Account: Service Revenue — **GL No: 400**

Date	Description	PR	DR	CR	Balance	
2018						
Jun 6		J1		2,100	2,100	CR
Jun 18		J1		1,500	3,600	CR

Account: Advertising Expense					GL No: 500	
Date	Description	PR	DR	CR	Balance	
2018						
Jun 11		J1	450		450	DR

Account: Depreciation Expense					GL No: 510	
Date	Description	PR	DR	CR	Balance	

Account: Insurance Expense					GL No: 515	
Date	Description	PR	DR	CR	Balance	

Account: Interest Expense					GL No: 520	
Date	Description	PR	DR	CR	Balance	

Account: Rent Expense					GL No: 540	
Date	Description	PR	DR	CR	Balance	
2018						
Jun 1		J1	900		900	DR

See Appendix I for solutions.

Notes

Chapter 6
The Accounting Cycle: Statements and Closing Entries

Learning Objectives

LO 1 **Prepare financial statements using the adjusted trial balance**
- Income Statement
- Statement of Owner's Equity
- Balance Sheet

LO 2 **Prepare closing journal entries and post them to the general ledger**
- Direct Method: Close Directly to Owner's Capital
- Income Summary Method: Close Using the Income Summary Account

LO 3 **Prepare the post-closing trial balance to complete the accounting cycle**

LO 4 **Prepare the classified balance sheet**
- Current Assets vs. Noncurrent Assets

- Current Liabilities vs. Noncurrent Liabilities

LO 5 **Analyze the financial statements using liquidity measures**
- Working Capital
- Current Ratio
- Quick Ratio

LO 6 **Describe the benefits of a computerized accounting system over a manual system**

Appendix

LO 7 **Prepare a 10-column spreadsheet**

 *Access **ameengage.com** for integrated resources including tutorials, practice exercises, the digital textbook and more.*

155

MAKING IT
REAL TO YOU

The preceding chapters have focused on the importance of providing timely and accurate accounting records from one period to the next. We also know the importance of reliable information to the many users of financial information—from the smallest business to the biggest corporation or even a nonprofit organization. There are many internal and external users of this information—from the owner of a one-person business, to the executives and department managers of the largest organization. All of them are stakeholders in a business in one way or another, and they all depend on meaningful reporting. Was it a good month, quarter or year for the business? Did the company achieve its sales objectives? Are costs increasing, decreasing, under control or getting out of control? Does the company have enough cash to take care of its regular short-term needs? Is the company's debt level manageable and can it cover the regular expenses? Users need the financial statements to tell them that story. As we wrap up the accounting cycle, we move through regular transactions to adjusting entries all the way to closing entries and posting. Our final destination is a meaningful set of financial statements that enables users to analyze the business from many perspectives and make important business decisions.

Preparing the Financial Statements

At this point in the accounting cycle, day-to-day journal entries have been made, adjustments have been recorded, all transactions have been posted to the general ledger and the adjusted trial balance has been completed. It is time to complete the final three steps of the accounting cycle, shown in blue in Figure 6.1, beginning with the preparation of financial statements. Recall that the first three steps of the accounting cycle are repeated many times during the period, while the remaining six steps are only completed at the end of the period.

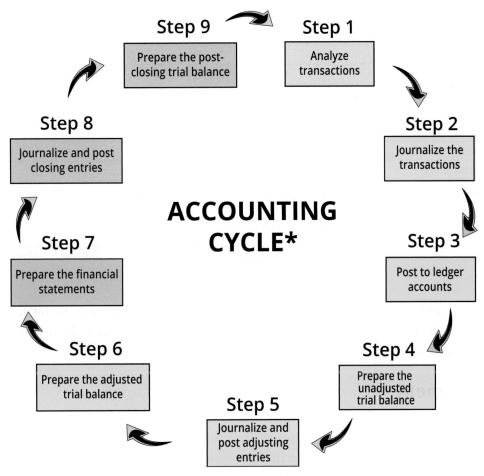

*The first three steps are performed repeatedly during an accounting period, while the remaining steps are performed only at the end of the period.

FIGURE 6.1

The final steps of the accounting cycle are illustrated using the MP Consulting example from Chapter 5. If necessary, refer to Figure 5.25 to recall the steps required to record each adjustment. The spreadsheet has been recreated in Figure 6.2 showing the unadjusted trial balance, adjustments and adjusted trial balance for easy reference. Since the adjusted trial balance is balanced, the accounts are ready to be compiled into the financial statements.

| | MP Consulting Spreadsheet January 31, 2018 | | | | | |
| | Unadjusted Trial Balance | | Adjustments | | Adjusted Trial Balance | |
Account Title	DR	CR	DR	CR	DR	CR
Cash	$3,800				$3,800	
Accounts Receivable	3,000		$1,000		4,000	
Prepaid Insurance	1,200			$100	1,100	
Equipment	8,300				8,300	
Accumulated Depreciation—Equipment		$0		150		$150
Accounts Payable		1,250				1,250
Interest Payable		0		25		25
Unearned Revenue		2,000	200			1,800
Notes Payable		2,500				2,500
Parish, Capital		10,300				10,300
Parish, Withdrawals	2,000				2,000	
Service Revenue		3,300		1,200		4,500
Depreciation Expense	0		150		150	
Insurance Expense	0		100		100	
Interest Expense	0		25		25	
Rent Expense	800				800	
Telephone Expense	250				250	
Total	$19,350	$19,350	$1,475	$1,475	$20,525	$20,525

FIGURE 6.2

The spreadsheet is only a working paper for accountants; it is not meant to be read by external users of financial information. It is therefore important to create formal documents including an income statement, a statement of owner's equity and a balance sheet.

Income Statement

The income statement takes the values from the adjusted trial balance columns of the spreadsheet and organizes them into a format that shows the net income or loss. To illustrate the importance of preparing the adjustments, first look at the income statement in Figure 6.3. This income statement was prepared before any adjustments were made. The net income is reported as $2,250.

MP Consulting Income Statement (Pre-Adjustment) For the Month Ended January 31, 2018		
Service Revenue		$3,300
Expenses		
Rent Expense	$800	
Telephone Expense	250	
Total Expenses		(1,050)
Net Income (Loss)		$2,250

FIGURE 6.3

After the adjustments, the income statement can be prepared properly. In Figure 6.4, net income is accurately reported as $3,175. If no adjustments had been made, net income would have been understated (as it was in Figure 6.3), which would have caused owner's equity to also be understated. The final net income value (marked **ⓐ**) is transferred to the statement of owner's equity.

MP Consulting Income Statement For the Month Ended January 31, 2018		
Service Revenue		$4,500
Expenses		
Depreciation Expense	$150	
Insurance Expense	100	
Interest Expense	25	
Rent Expense	800	
Telephone Expense	250	
Total Expenses		(1,325)
Net Income (Loss)		$3,175 **ⓐ**

adjusted entries { Depreciation Expense, Insurance Expense, Interest Expense }

FIGURE 6.4

Statement of Owner's Equity

The statement of owner's equity reports any changes in equity during the reporting period. It is presented with a date format of an elapsed time period similar to the income statement. The statement of owner's equity for MP Consulting is shown in Figure 6.5.

MP Consulting Statement of Owner's Equity For the Month Ended January 31, 2018		
Parish, Capital at January 1		$5,300
Add:		
Additional Investment	$5,000	
Net Income	**ⓐ** 3,175	8,175
Subtotal		13,475
Less:		
Parish, Withdrawals		2,000
Parish, Capital at January 31		$11,475 **ⓑ**

FIGURE 6.5

WORTH REPEATING

The ending balance of owner's equity for a given period can be calculated as follows.

Ending Owner's Equity = Beginning Owner's Equity + Owner's Contributions + Net Income (Loss) – Owner's Withdrawals

The statement begins with the opening balance of the owner's capital account. In our example, the opening balance was $5,300 on January 1, 2018.

Owner's equity increases if the owner invests more cash or assets into the business, or if the business earns a profit during the period. In our example, the owner invested $5,000 into the business during the month. Notice that the net income (marked **ⓐ**) from the income statement in Figure 6.4 is also added.

Owner's equity decreases if the owner withdraws any capital (cash or assets) from the business for personal use, or if the business suffers a loss during the period. There was no loss in our example, but there was a $2,000 withdrawal, as shown in the spreadsheet under Parish, Withdrawals.

The final closing balance of the capital account (marked **ⓑ**) is transferred to the owner's equity section of the balance sheet.

Balance Sheet

The balance sheet is prepared using the values from the asset and liability accounts from the adjusted trial balance. Previous chapters showed the balance sheet organized horizontally, with assets beside liabilities and owner's equity. This format of the balance sheet presentation is called the account form. An alternate organization, and the way balance sheets are most commonly presented, is vertically, which is known as the report form. Assets are listed above liabilities and owner's equity, as shown in Figure 6.6.

MP Consulting Balance Sheet As at January 31, 2018		
Assets		
Cash		$3,800
Accounts Receivable		4,000
Prepaid Insurance		1,100
Equipment	$8,300	
Accumulated Depreciation	(150)	8,150
Total Assets		$17,050
Liabilities		
Accounts Payable	$1,250	
Interest Payable	25	
Unearned Revenue	1,800	
Notes Payable	2,500	
Total Liabilities		$5,575
Owner's Equity		
Parish, Capital		11,475 **ⓑ**
Total Liabilities and Owner's Equity		$17,050

FIGURE 6.6

Notice that the value of Parish, Capital (marked) comes directly from the statement of owner's equity in Figure 6.5 and not from the spreadsheet. The journal entries used to update the capital account will be demonstrated in the next section.

Notice how equipment is presented. The accumulated depreciation is subtracted from the asset account, giving the net book value of $8,150.

Closing Entries

LO 2

The statement of owner's equity shows the balance of the owner's capital account after it has been updated with the net income or loss from the period and any withdrawals. Although the ending balance of owner's capital is in the financial statements, the actual account in the general ledger does not yet reflect this new balance and must be updated. This process is called closing the books. **Closing the books** updates owner's capital (the equity of the business) and starts a new income statement for the next accounting period.

An income statement reports net income (or net loss) for a specific period of time. For example, if MP Consulting had a net income of $100,000 for a period ended December 31, 2018, this amount is exclusive to the period ended on that date and is not carried over to the next period.

In a manual accounting system, equity (owner's capital) is only updated at the end of the period. This means that all accounts that affect equity must have their balances transferred to owner's capital. Since these accounts are brought back to a zero balance at the end of each period, they are called **temporary accounts**, or nominal accounts. Revenue and expense accounts are classified as temporary accounts. Once the accounts are cleared, a new income statement can be prepared for the next period.

Besides revenue and expenses, owner's withdrawals is also a temporary account that needs to be closed at the end of the period. This is because owner's withdrawals measures the amount the owner takes from the business during a specific accounting period and is used to calculate the value of equity.

Permanent accounts, or real accounts, are balance sheet items that have their balances carried forward from one accounting period to the next, with no need of being closed. Accounts such as cash, accounts receivables or notes payable are examples of permanent accounts. Figure 6.7 illustrates which accounts are temporary and which are permanent.

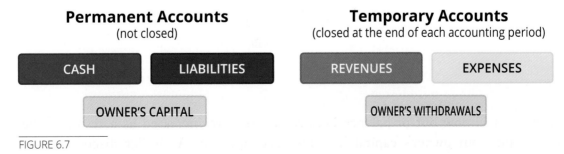

FIGURE 6.7

Closing entries are made to revenue, expenses and owner's withdrawals at the end of an accounting period to close out the accounts. We will illustrate the concept of closing entries by walking you through how MP Consulting closes its temporary accounts at the end of January 2018. First, examine MP Consulting's balance sheet at the beginning of January 2018 (i.e. the end of December 2017). At the beginning of the period, MP Consulting's balance sheet is in balance, as shown in Figure 6.8. The T-accounts are also shown to illustrate the overall values of three categories: assets, liabilities and equity.

MP Consulting Balance Sheet As at December 31, 2017		
Assets		
Cash		$3,000
Accounts Receivable		1,200
Equipment		6,000
Total Assets		$10,200
Liabilities		
Accounts Payable	$1,000	
Unearned Revenue	900	
Notes Payable	3,000	
Total Liabilities		$4,900
Owner's Equity		
Parish, Capital		5,300
Total Liabilities and Owner's Equity		$10,200

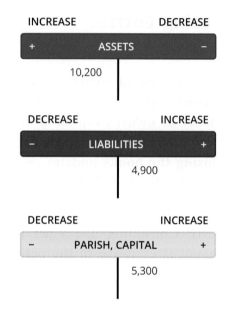

FIGURE 6.8

Notice what happens in Figure 6.9 when services are provided in January to a customer who pays $1,500 in cash.

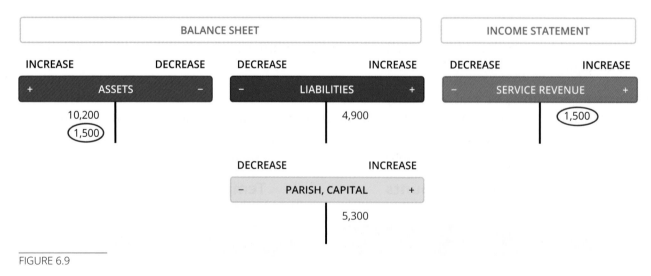

FIGURE 6.9

The balance sheet is now out of balance because assets have increased as a result of the increase in service revenue, but owner's capital has not been updated. A similar discrepancy occurs if a telephone bill is received in January and will be paid later, as shown in Figure 6.10.

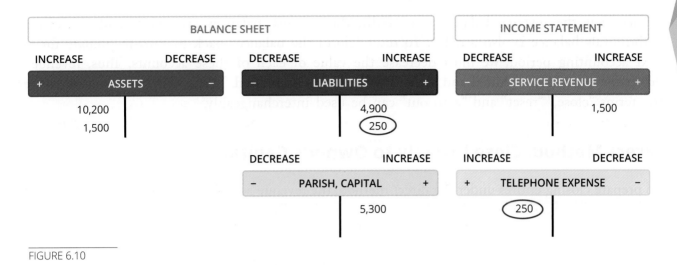

FIGURE 6.10

To get the balance sheet back into balance, owner's capital must be updated with the transactions for revenue and expense. If the owner withdrew cash from the business during the period, owner's capital must be updated with owner's withdrawals as well. In other words, closing entries must be prepared. There are two methods to prepare the closing entries, and MP Consulting will be used to illustrate both methods.

To see how to close the books for MP Consulting, we use the adjusted trial balance from the last column of the spreadsheeet in Figure 6.2. The adjusted trial balance is shown again in Figure 6.11.

Account Title	DR	CR
MP Consulting **Adjusted Trial Balance** **January 31, 2018**		
Cash	$3,800	
Accounts Receivable	4,000	
Prepaid Insurance	1,100	
Equipment	8,300	
Accumulated Depreciation—Equipment		$150
Accounts Payable		1,250
Interest Payable		25
Unearned Revenue		1,800
Notes Payable		2,500
Parish, Capital		10,300
Parish, Withdrawals	2,000	
Service Revenue		4,500
Depreciation Expense	150	
Insurance Expense	100	
Interest Expense	25	
Rent Expense	800	
Telephone Expense	250	
Total	**$20,525**	**$20,525**

FIGURE 6.11

Notice that the revenue balance is a credit, the expense balances are debits and the owner's withdrawals balance is also a debit. To reset (close) the balances back to zero to prepare for the next accounting period, we must decrease the value of each of these accounts. Thus, revenue is debited, expenses are credited and owner's withdrawals is credited. In the context of closing entries, the terms "close," "reset" and "zero out" can be used interchangeably.

Direct Method: Close Directly to Owner's Capital

To prepare closing entires under the direct method, the revenue account must be closed by decreasing revenue and increasing owner's capital, as illustrated in Figure 6.12. The revenue account is now reduced to a zero balance.

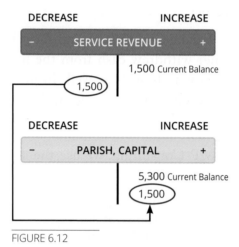

FIGURE 6.12

The telephone expense account must also be closed by decreasing the expense and decreasing owner's capital, as illustrated in Figure 6.13. The expense account is now reduced to zero.

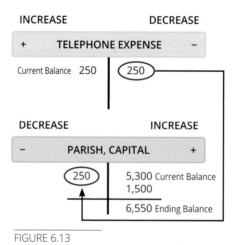

FIGURE 6.13

The end result is that owner's capital has a new balance and assets equal liabilities plus equity.

Returning to the example of MP Consulting, Figure 6.14 illustrates the journal entries to close the accounts directly to the capital account. The steps involved are explained.

JOURNAL					Page 3
	Date	Account Title and Explanation	PR	Debit	Credit
	2018				
a	Jan 31	Service Revenue	400	4,500	
		Parish, Capital	300		4,500
		To close revenue			
b	Jan 31	Parish, Capital	300	1,325	
		Depreciation Expense	510		150
		Insurance Expense	515		100
		Interest Expense	520		25
		Rent Expense	540		800
		Telephone Expense	550		250
		To close expenses			
c	Jan 31	Parish, Capital	300	2,000	
		Parish, Withdrawals	310		2,000
		To close owner's withdrawals			

FIGURE 6.14

a Zero out the revenue account

The transaction is recorded by debiting (decreasing) the current revenue balance with $4,500 and crediting (increasing) owner's capital with the same amount. The revenue account is now reduced to zero.

b Zero out the expense accounts

The transaction is recorded by crediting (decreasing) the current expense balances and debiting (decreasing) owner's capital with the total of all expense amounts. The expense accounts are now reduced to zero. Notice in Figure 6.14 that instead of closing each expense account individually to owner's capital, all expenses were listed in one transaction. This saves time and effort (imagine if the company had 50 or more expense accounts). The debit to owner's capital is the total of all the expenses.

c Zero out the owner's withdrawals account

The transaction is recorded by crediting (decreasing) the current owner's withdrawals balance with $2,000 and debiting (decreasing) owner's capital with the same amount. The owner's withdrawals account is now reduced to zero.

Net Result

Owner's capital has increased by the total revenue and decreased by the total expenses and owner's withdrawals. Figure 6.15 shows the new balance is $11,475. This is the same figure shown as the ending value on the statement of owner's equity from Figure 6.5. Note that the direct method of closing accounts is not commonly used in practice; however, the illustration of this method provides you with a better understanding of the next method—the income summary method.

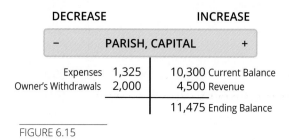

FIGURE 6.15

Income Summary Method: Close Using the Income Summary Account

Instead of debiting and crediting owner's capital directly, it is common to use a temporary holding account called **income summary** to close the revenue and expense accounts. Using our T-account example, in which $1,500 in cash was received for services and a $250 telephone bill was received, Figure 6.16 shows how the income summary account is used.

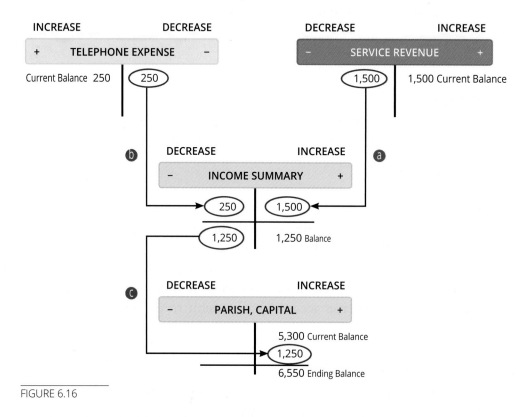

FIGURE 6.16

To close accounts using the income summary method, the following steps are used.

(a) Debit each revenue account to clear it and credit the income summary account for the total amount.

(b) Credit each expense account to clear it and debit the income summary account for the total amount.

(c) Calculate the balance of the income summary account. This is equal to the net income or loss for the period. Credit owner's capital and debit income summary with the net income amount, or debit owner's capital and credit income summary with the net loss amount.

Remember, the income summary account is only used to close the revenue and expense accounts. The owner's withdrawals account is not closed through the income summary account because owner's withdrawals do not affect the amount of net income or net loss. The owner's withdrawals account is closed directly to the owner's capital account.

Using the adjusted trial balance amounts for MP Consulting (Figure 6.11), the closing entries are shown in the journal in Figure 6.17.

	JOURNAL				Page 3
	Date	Account Title and Explanation	PR	Debit	Credit
(a)	Jan 31	Service Revenue	400	4,500	
		Income Summary	315		4,500
		To close revenue			
(b)	Jan 31	Income Summary	315	1,325	
		Depreciation Expense	510		150
		Insurance Expense	515		100
		Interest Expense	520		25
		Rent Expense	540		800
		Telephone Expense	550		250
		To close expenses			
(c)	Jan 31	Income Summary	315	3,175	
		Parish, Capital	300		3,175
		To close income summary			
(d)	Jan 31	Parish, Capital	300	2,000	
		Parish, Withdrawals	310		2,000
		To close owner's withdrawals			

FIGURE 6.17

ⓐ The first transaction is to zero out the revenue account. Similar to what was discussed in the direct method, the transaction is recorded by debiting (decreasing) the current revenue balance with $4,500; however, instead of crediting (increasing) owner's capital, the income summary account is credited. The revenue account is now reduced to zero.

ⓑ The second transaction is to zero out the expense accounts. The transaction is recorded by crediting (decreasing) the current expense balances and debiting (decreasing) the income summary account with the total of all expense amounts. The expense accounts are now reduced to zero. Notice in Figure 6.17 that instead of closing each expense account individually to income summary, all expenses were listed in one transaction to save time and effort. The debit to the income summary account is the total of all the expenses.

ⓒ The third transaction is to close the income summary to the capital account. The value of $3,175 is the difference between the revenue and expense accounts. Note that this value is the same as the net income reported on the income statement in Figure 6.4.

ⓓ The last transaction is identical to the one shown in the direct method (Figure 6.14). The owner's withdrawals account is closed to the owner's capital account. The withdrawals account decreases with a credit and the capital account decreases with a debit.

Figure 6.18 summarizes how the temporary accounts are closed at the end of an accounting period under each method.

Direct Method

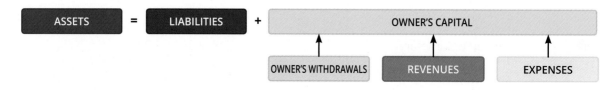

Income Summary Method

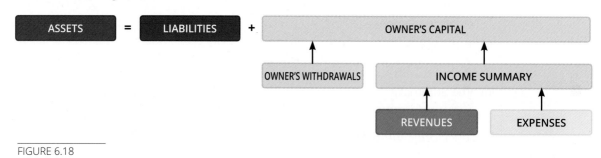

FIGURE 6.18

Remember, all journal entries must be posted to the general ledger. Assuming MP Consulting uses the income summary method to close its books, Figure 6.19 shows how the ledger accounts would look at the end of the period. All journal entries from the two previous chapters and the closing entries from this chapter are reflected here. Notice that adjustments and closing entries include a description to make them stand out in the ledger.

GENERAL LEDGER

Account: Cash — GL No: 101

Date	Description	PR	DR	CR	Balance	
2018						
Jan 1	Opening Balance				3,000	DR
Jan 2		J1	1,500		4,500	DR
Jan 3		J1		800	3,700	DR
Jan 4		J1		1,200	2,500	DR
Jan 5		J1	5,000		7,500	DR
Jan 7		J1		2,300	5,200	DR
Jan 16		J1		500	4,700	DR
Jan 19		J1	1,100		5,800	DR
Jan 30		J1		2,000	3,800	DR

Account: Accounts Receivable — GL No: 105

Date	Description	PR	DR	CR	Balance	
2018						
Jan 1	Opening Balance				1,200	DR
Jan 10		J1	1,800		3,000	DR
Jan 31	Adjustment	J2	1,000		4,000	DR

Account: Prepaid Insurance — GL No: 110

Date	Description	PR	DR	CR	Balance	
2018						
Jan 1	Opening Balance				0	DR
Jan 4		J1	1,200		1,200	DR
Jan 31	Adjustment	J2		100	1,100	DR

Account: Equipment — GL No: 120

Date	Description	PR	DR	CR	Balance	
2018						
Jan 1	Opening Balance				6,000	DR
Jan 7		J1	2,300		8,300	DR

Account: Accumulated Depreciation—Equipment — GL No: 125

Date	Description	PR	DR	CR	Balance	
2018						
Jan 31	Adjustment	J2		150	150	CR

Account: Accounts Payable — GL No: 200

Date	Description	PR	DR	CR	Balance	
2018						
Jan 1	Opening Balance				1,000	CR
Jan 20		J1		250	1,250	CR

Account: Interest Payable					GL No:	205	
Date	**Description**	**PR**	**DR**	**CR**	**Balance**		
2018							
Jan 31	Adjustment	J2		25	25	CR	

Account: Unearned Revenue					GL No:	210	
Date	**Description**	**PR**	**DR**	**CR**	**Balance**		
2018							
Jan 1	Opening Balance				900	CR	
Jan 19		J1		1,100	2,000	CR	
Jan 31	Adjustment	J2	200		1,800	CR	

Account: Notes Payable					GL No:	215	
Date	**Description**	**PR**	**DR**	**CR**	**Balance**		
2018							
Jan 1	Opening Balance				3,000	CR	
Jan 16		J1	500		2,500	CR	

Account: Parish, Capital					GL No:	300	
Date	**Description**	**PR**	**DR**	**CR**	**Balance**		
2018							
Jan 1	Opening Balance				5,300	CR	
Jan 5		J1		5,000	10,300	CR	
Jan 31	Closing Entry	J3		3,175	13,475	CR	
Jan 31	Closing Entry	J3	2,000		11,475	CR	

Account: Parish, Withdrawals					GL No:	310	
Date	**Description**	**PR**	**DR**	**CR**	**Balance**		
2018							
Jan 30		J1	2,000		2,000	DR	
Jan 31	Closing Entry	J3		2,000	0	DR	

Account: Income Summary					GL No:	315	
Date	**Description**	**PR**	**DR**	**CR**	**Balance**		
2018							
Jan 31	Closing Entry	J3		4,500	4,500	CR	
Jan 31	Closing Entry	J3	1,325		3,175	CR	
Jan 31	Closing Entry	J3	3,175		0	CR	

Account: Service Revenue					GL No:	400	
Date	Description	PR	DR	CR	Balance		
2018							
Jan 2		J1		1,500	1,500	CR	
Jan 10		J1		1,800	3,300	CR	
Jan 31	Adjustment	J2		200	3,500	CR	
Jan 31	Adjustment	J2		1,000	4,500	CR	
Jan 31	Closing Entry	J3	4,500		0	CR	

Account: Depreciation Expense					GL No:	510	
Date	Description	PR	DR	CR	Balance		
2018							
Jan 31	Adjustment	J2	150		150	DR	
Jan 31	Closing Entry	J3		150	0	DR	

Account: Insurance Expense					GL No:	515	
Date	Description	PR	DR	CR	Balance		
2018							
Jan 31	Adjustment	J2	100		100	DR	
Jan 31	Closing Entry	J3		100	0	DR	

Account: Interest Expense					GL No:	520	
Date	Description	PR	DR	CR	Balance		
2018							
Jan 31	Adjustment	J2	25		25	DR	
Jan 31	Closing Entry	J3		25	0	DR	

Account: Rent Expense					GL No:	540	
Date	Description	PR	DR	CR	Balance		
2018							
Jan 3		J1	800		800	DR	
Jan 31	Closing Entry	J3		800	0	DR	

Account: Telephone Expense					GL No:	550	
Date	Description	PR	DR	CR	Balance		
2018							
Jan 20		J1	250		250	DR	
Jan 31	Closing Entry	J3		250	0	DR	

FIGURE 6.19

Pause & Reflect

Exercise 6-1

ZooTak Service has journalized its adjusting entries and prepared the adjusted trial balance. Based on the list of accounts, prepare the closing entries using the income summary account for the month of August.

ZooTak Service List of Accounts August 31, 2018		
Account Title	**DR**	**CR**
ZooTak, Capital		25,310
ZooTak, Withdrawals	3,050	
Service Revenue		9,400
Depreciation Expense	290	
Insurance Expense	260	
Interest Expense	70	
Rent Expense	1,870	
Salaries Expense	2,250	
Telephone Expense	250	

JOURNAL				Page 5
Date	**Account Title and Explanation**	**PR**	**Debit**	**Credit**

See Appendix I for solutions.

Post-Closing Trial Balance

Once the closing entries are completed, it is necessary to ensure that the balance sheet still balances. This is done by completing another trial balance called the **post-closing trial balance**.

The post-closing trial balance only lists accounts that have a balance. Since the closing entries have been journalized and posted, only assets, liabilities and owner's capital should have a balance. The post-closing trial balance is shown in Figure 6.20.

MP Consulting Post-Closing Trial Balance January 31, 2018		
Account Title	**DR**	**CR**
Cash	$3,800	
Accounts Receivable	4,000	
Prepaid Insurance	1,100	
Equipment	8,300	
Accumulated Depreciation—Equipment		$150
Accounts Payable		1,250
Interest Payable		25
Unearned Revenue		1,800
Notes Payable		2,500
Parish, Capital		11,475
Total	$17,200	$17,200

FIGURE 6.20

Once the post-closing trial balance is complete, the entire accounting cycle for the period is done. The company is ready to begin the next accounting cycle for the upcoming accounting period.

Classified Balance Sheet

We have learned that the balance sheet lists assets, liabilities and equity, and have studied the unclassified balance sheet so far. However, it is useful to group together similar assets and similar liabilities on the basis of their financial characteristics. Before we go into the details of a classified balance sheet, we will first discuss the groupings of assets (current assets and noncurrent assets) and liabilities (current liabilities and noncurrent liabilities).

Current Assets vs. Noncurrent Assets

Assets are divided into two categories.

1. **Current assets** are those that are likely to be converted into cash or used up through the day-to-day operations of the business within the next 12 months or the operating cycle, whichever is longer. The **operating cycle** is the time between the use of cash and the receipt of cash for the business. Since the majority of businesses have operating cycles of a year or less, one year is most often used as the difference between the two categories of current and noncurrent. Some examples of current assets are cash, inventory (products sold to customers), accounts receivable and prepaid expenses.

2. **Noncurrent assets**, also called *long-term assets*, are used to operate a business and are not expected to turn into cash or be used up within the next 12 months (unless they are sold for reasons other than the day-to-day operations of the business). Any asset that is not included in the current asset category is assumed to be noncurrent.

Therefore, the classified balance sheet includes two sections of assets. Current assets are presented under a current asset heading. Noncurrent assets are presented separately.

Certain types of noncurrent assets must be presented separately on the classified balance sheet. Although not all of the noncurrent assets discussed are covered in detail in this textbook, you may come across these terms if you look at the balance sheet of other companies.

Property, plant and equipment are long-term physical assets used to help run the business. This category, also called **plant assets** or **fixed assets**, contains several types of noncurrent assets such as land, building, equipment and furniture. Each of these items must be presented separately along with any accumulated depreciation to show its net book value. Figure 6.21 shows the groupings of assets and liabilities on the balance sheet.

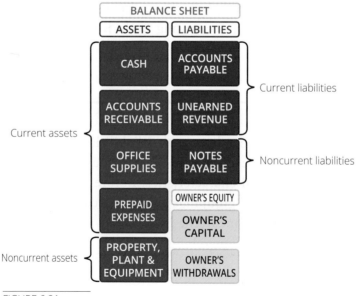

FIGURE 6.21

Current Liabilities vs. Noncurrent Liabilities

Liabilities are divided into two categories.

1. **Current liabilities** are amounts due to be paid within the next 12 months. Examples of current liabilities include accounts payable, interest payable and unearned revenue (assuming the related revenue will be earned within the next 12 months).

2. **Noncurrent liabilities**, also called *long-term liabilities*, are amounts due to be paid after 12 months. Examples of noncurrent liabilities include notes payable and mortgages.

Noncurrent liabilities usually have a portion that is considered current. That is, a portion must be repaid within the next 12 months. To properly plan for cash payments in the upcoming year, accountants will separate the current portion from the noncurrent portion on the classified balance sheet.

For example, if a company has a $50,000 bank loan that is supposed to be paid off in five equal installments, $10,000 ($50,000 ÷ 5 years) is due within one year and is considered current. The rest ($40,000) is due after one year and is considered noncurrent. This separation of current debt from noncurrent debt is done on the date of the balance sheet. Each year, the amount of noncurrent debt decreases because a portion becomes due within one year and is classified as current debt. This is illustrated in Figure 6.22.

Balance Sheet as at December 31, 2017

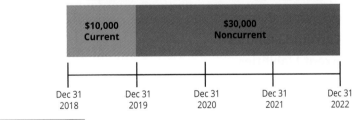

Balance Sheet as at December 31, 2018

FIGURE 6.22

What is the reason for splitting the balance sheet assets and liabilities between current and noncurrent items? Readers of the financial statements are interested in the ability of the business to pay the upcoming debt, and where it will get the money to do so. Current liabilities indicate the upcoming debt, and current assets indicate where the money will come from. The classified balance sheet also indicates how much the company has invested in itself by means of noncurrent assets. The amount of noncurrent liabilities and equity also provide a snapshot of how the company finances its operations.

Now that we have defined current and noncurrent assets, as well as current and noncurrent liabilities, we can demonstrate the difference between the unclassified balance sheet that we have been using so far and a classified balance sheet.

The classified balance sheet for MP Consulting is illustrated in Figure 6.23. The balance sheet for MP Consulting was shown in Figure 6.6. It was not a classified balance sheet, so all assets and liabilities were grouped as one. The company has a $2,500 bank loan, of which $1,000 will be paid off by January 31, 2019 (one year from the balance sheet date).

MP Consulting Classified Balance Sheet As at January 31, 2018		
Assets		
Current Assets		
Cash	$3,800	
Accounts Receivable	4,000	
Prepaid Insurance	1,100	
Total Current Assets		$8,900
Property, Plant & Equipment		
Equipment	8,300	
Accumulated Depreciation	(150)	
Total Property, Plant & Equipment		8,150
Total Assets		$17,050
Liabilities		
Current Liabilities		
Accounts Payable	$1,250	
Interest Payable	25	
Unearned Revenue	1,800	
Notes Payable, Current Portion	1,000	
Total Current Liabilities		$4,075
Noncurrent Liabilities		
Notes Payable, Noncurrent Portion	1,500	
Total Noncurrent Liabilities		1,500
Total Liabilities		5,575
Owner's Equity		
Parish, Capital		11,475
Total Owner's Equity		11,475
Total Liabilities and Owner's Equity		$17,050

FIGURE 6.23

The balance sheet illustrates the categories used to classify the various assets and liabilities of the business. The order of presentation for the current assets is shown as most liquid (cash) to least liquid (prepaid insurance) followed by noncurrent assets. Liabilities are shown in the order of when they are due, with the debts due earlier listed first. Notice that $1,000 of the note payable is classified as current because it will be paid within the next one-year period.

Analyzing the Financial Statements

Financial statements can do more than just tell us how much profit was earned or the total of our assets or liabilities. Financial statement analysis includes calculating ratios between two values to provide insight into the business and how well it is operating. This topic will be covered in more detail later, but for now we will look at a few ratios that indicate how liquid the business is. Liquidity is the ability of the business to convert current assets to cash to pay its debts as they come due.

This presentation of the classified balance sheet, which separates current from noncurrent items, allows for the easy calculation of working capital, the current ratio and the quick ratio. Each of these looks at how well the company can pay its debts with its liquid, or current, assets.

Working Capital

Working capital is the difference between current assets and current liabilities. This provides a dollar figure, which, if positive, means the business has more current assets than current liabilities and should be able to pay its current debt. If current liabilities are greater than current assets, the business may have difficulty paying its debt as it comes due. The formula to calculate working capital is shown in Figure 6.24.

Working Capital = Current Assets – Current Liabilities

FIGURE 6.24

Using the values from the balance sheet in Figure 6.23, the working capital for MP Consulting is

Working Capital = $8,900 – $4,075

= $4,825

MP Consulting has more than enough current assets to pay for the current liabilities and should have no trouble paying the debts as they come due.

Current Ratio

The **current ratio** measures a company's ability to pay off short-term debt. The higher the current ratio, the more current assets the company has to pay off debt that is due within one year. The formula to calculate the current ratio is shown in Figure 6.25.

$$\text{Current Ratio} = \frac{\text{Current Assets}}{\text{Current Liabilities}}$$

FIGURE 6.25

From the balance sheet in Figure 6.23, the current ratio is calculated as

$$\text{Current Ratio} = \frac{\$8,900}{\$4,075}$$
$$= 2.18$$

This indicates that the company has $2.18 in current assets for every $1.00 in current liabilities. MP Consulting is doing well, since it has enough current assets to cover its upcoming debt payments.

Quick Ratio

The **quick ratio** is similar to the current ratio, but only counts assets that can easily be turned into cash. Thus, assets such as prepaid items are omitted and only cash, accounts receivable and short-term investments are included. The formula to calculate the quick ratio is shown in Figure 6.26.

$$\text{Quick Ratio} = \frac{\text{Cash} + \text{Accounts Receivable} + \text{Short-Term Investments}}{\text{Current Liabilities}}$$

FIGURE 6.26

From the balance sheet in Figure 6.23, the quick ratio is calculated as

$$\text{Quick Ratio} = \frac{\$3,800 + \$4,000 + 0}{\$4,075}$$
$$= 1.91$$

This shows that the company has $1.91 of very liquid current assets for every $1.00 of current liabilities. Again, MP Consulting is doing well. If the quick ratio were to drop below 1.00, it could indicate problems with paying back debts.

Pause & Reflect

Exercise 6-2

Health Services has provided you with the financial information in Table 1. Calculate the required ratios. Round your final answers to two decimal places.

Table 1

Account	Balance
Cash	$120,000
Accounts Receivable	90,000
Prepaid Rent	65,000
Equipment	150,000
Accounts Payable	101,000
Unearned Revenue	80,000
Notes Payable, Noncurrent	70,000
Health, Capital	45,000

Working Capital	
Current Ratio	
Quick Ratio	

See Appendix I for solutions.

The Evolution from Manual to Computerized Accounting LO 6

One of the challenges in teaching a modern accounting course is the need to combine traditional concepts and methods with modern technology. However, the reality is that today's accounting students may never see or use a set of paper-based accounting journals and ledgers, such as the ledger shown in Figure 6.27.

Although computerized systems are now quite common, and while they make gathering and analyzing information easier for the accountant, having a sound knowledge of traditional paper-based systems provides a foundation for understanding what accounting is all about. It also allows for an understanding of how the computerized system stores the information and how to look for errors or anomalies in the data.

FIGURE 6.27

Before computers, bookkeepers used various types of journals to maintain company financial records. Special journals were used to track similar types of transactions, such as sales and purchases. The general journal was used for infrequent transactions, such as adjustments. All of these journals were used to update the general ledger and other accounts.

In manual systems, recording procedures often provide the analytical structure for the accountant. If accounts receivable needs analyzing, the accountant refers to all related journals and ledgers for accounts receivable. If, on the other hand, inventory is being analyzed, the paper trail from receipt to shipping is tracked accordingly.

Similar to the manual system, a computerized system typically has special sections or journals to enter similar types of transactions, such as sales and purchases. There is also a general journal for adjusting entries and other specific types of transactions. All of these journals update the general ledger and other accounts and this information is kept in a database for easy storage and retrieval.

In effect, accountants analyze and create the journal entries for the day-to-day transactions, and journalize the adjusting entries at the end of the period. The day-to-day transactions do not have to be entered in chronological order since the software automatically orders them when reports are prepared. All the postings to the general ledger, preparing the various reports, and even preparing the closing entries are done automatically by the computer.

It is the responsibility of management and the accounting department to work with information technology personnel to buy or design a system that meets organizational objectives. Manual systems help accountants learn the basics of their profession; however, in today's business world, a properly designed computer system, tailored to the needs of a specific company, can make accounting more efficient.

Pause & Reflect

Exercise 6-3

a) List the similarities and differences between a manual accounting system and a computerized accounting system.

_____

_____

_____

b) What are some of the benefits of using a computerized system rather than a manual system?

_____

_____

_____

See Appendix I for solutions.

In Summary

LO 1 Prepare financial statements using the adjusted trial balance

▶ The adjusted trial balance provides the updated balances that are used to create the financial statements.

▶ The income statement shows the net income or loss for the period.

▶ The statement of owner's equity shows the change in equity for the period.

▶ The balance sheet shows the financial standing of the business at the period end date.

LO 2 Prepare closing journal entries and post them to the general ledger

▶ Closing journal entries zero out the income statement accounts and the owner's withdrawals account. The entries are then posted to the general ledger. After closing these accounts, a new income statement can be started for the next accounting period.

▶ There are two ways to close the income statement accounts: close directly to owner's capital or close to an intermediary income summary account.

LO 3 Prepare the post-closing trial balance to complete the accounting cycle

▶ A post-closing trial balance is created after the books are closed. It will only show accounts with a balance, which are assets, liabilities and owner's capital.

LO 4 Prepare the classified balance sheet

▶ The classified balance sheet presents assets and liabilities separated into current and noncurrent items.

▶ Current assets are assets that will be converted to cash or used up within one year. Noncurrent assets are typically used to run the business and will not be used up within one year.

▶ Current liabilities are liabilities that are due within one year. Noncurrent liabilities are due beyond one year.

LO 5 Analyze the financial statements using liquidity measures

▶ Working capital is the difference between current assets and current liabilities.

▶ The current ratio is calculated as current assets divided by current liabilities.

▶ The quick ratio is calculated as liquid assets (cash and accounts receivable) divided by current liabilities.

LO 6 Describe the benefits of a computerized accounting system over a manual system

▶ A computerized system automates many of the steps of the accounting cycle, such as posting to the general ledger and preparing reports. It also allows for easy retrieval of the data.

 *Access **ameengage.com** for integrated resources including tutorials, practice exercises, the digital textbook and more.*

Review Exercise 6-1

Catherine Gordon is running her own sole proprietary business called CG Accounting. CG Accounting provides bookkeeping services to small and mid-sized companies. The company was introduced in the review exercises from Chapters 4 and 5. Before you begin this exercise, familiarize yourself with the review exercise in Chapter 5 because this is a continuation.

Journal entries for the month have already been completed, as have the adjustments at month end. The adjusted trial balance is presented below.

CG Accounting Trial Balance June 30, 2018		
Account Title	DR	CR
Cash	$5,550	
Accounts Receivable	5,500	
Prepaid Insurance	1,100	
Equipment	6,000	
Accumulated Depreciation—Equipment		$100
Accounts Payable		2,750
Interest Payable		25
Unearned Revenue		450
Notes Payable		3,050
Gordon, Capital		9,400
Gordon, Withdrawals	1,000	
Service Revenue		4,950
Advertising Expense	450	
Depreciation Expense	100	
Insurance Expense	100	
Interest Expense	25	
Rent Expense	900	
Total	**$20,725**	**$20,725**

The balance of owner's equity as at May 31, 2018 was $6,400. Also, recall from the Chapter 4 review exercise that during June the owner contributed $3,000 cash to the business and withdrew $1,000 cash for personal use. Assume that $800 of the note payable must be paid by June 30, 2019.

CG Accounting uses the following accounts and accounting numbers in its accounting records.

Account Description	Account #
ASSETS	
Cash	101
Accounts Receivable	105
Prepaid Insurance	110
Equipment	120
Accumulated Depreciation—Equipment	125
LIABILITIES	
Accounts Payable	200
Interest Payable	205
Unearned Revenue	210
Notes Payable	215
OWNER'S EQUITY	
Gordon, Capital	300
Gordon, Withdrawals	310
Income Summary	315

Account Description	Account #
REVENUE	
Service Revenue	400
EXPENSES	
Advertising Expense	500
Bad Debt Expense	505
Depreciation Expense	510
Insurance Expense	515
Interest Expense	520
Maintenance Expense	525
Office Supplies Expense	530
Professional Fees Expense	535
Rent Expense	540
Salaries Expense	545
Telephone Expense	550
Travel Expense	555

Required

a) Prepare the income statement, statement of owner's equity and the classified balance sheet.

b) Complete the closing entries using the income summary method and post them to the general ledger.

JOURNAL				Page 3
Date	Account Title and Explanation	PR	Debit	Credit

GENERAL LEDGER

Account: Cash					GL No:	101
Date	**Description**	**PR**	**DR**	**CR**	**Balance**	
2018						
Jun 1	Opening Balance				4,200	DR
Jun 1		J1		900	3,300	DR
Jun 3		J1		1,200	2,100	DR
Jun 6		J1	2,100		4,200	DR
Jun 13		J1	3,000		7,200	DR
Jun 16		J1	300		7,500	DR
Jun 23		J1		950	6,550	DR
Jun 30		J1		1,000	5,550	DR

Account: Accounts Receivable					GL No:	105
Date	**Description**	**PR**	**DR**	**CR**	**Balance**	
2018						
Jun 1	Opening Balance				3,100	DR
Jun 18		J1	1,500		4,600	DR
Jun 30	Adjusting Entry	J2	900		5,500	DR

Account: Prepaid Insurance					GL No:	110
Date	**Description**	**PR**	**DR**	**CR**	**Balance**	
2018						
Jun 1	Opening Balance				0	DR
Jun 3		J1	1,200		1,200	DR
Jun 30	Adjusting Entry	J2		100	1,100	DR

Account: Equipment					GL No:	120
Date	**Description**	**PR**	**DR**	**CR**	**Balance**	
2018						
Jun 1	Opening Balance				6,000	DR

Account: Accumulated Depreciation—Equipment					GL No:	125
Date	**Description**	**PR**	**DR**	**CR**	**Balance**	
2018						
Jun 30	Adjusting Entry	J2		100	100	CR

Account: Accounts Payable					GL No:	200
Date	**Description**	**PR**	**DR**	**CR**	**Balance**	
2018						
Jun 1	Opening Balance				2,300	CR
Jun 11		J1		450	2,750	CR

Account: Interest Payable				GL No:	205	
Date	**Description**	**PR**	**DR**	**CR**	**Balance**	
2018						
Jun 30	Adjusting Entry	J2		25	25	CR

Account: Unearned Revenue				GL No:	210	
Date	**Description**	**PR**	**DR**	**CR**	**Balance**	
2018						
Jun 1	Opening Balance				600	CR
Jun 16		J1		300	900	CR
Jun 30	Adjusting Entry	J2	450		450	CR

Account: Notes Payable				GL No:	215	
Date	**Description**	**PR**	**DR**	**CR**	**Balance**	
2018						
Jun 1	Opening Balance				4,000	CR
Jun 23		J1	950		3,050	CR

Account: Gordon, Capital				GL No:	300	
Date	**Description**	**PR**	**DR**	**CR**	**Balance**	
2018						
Jun 1	Opening Balance				6,400	CR
Jun 13		J1		3,000	9,400	CR

Account: Gordon, Withdrawals				GL No:	310	
Date	**Description**	**PR**	**DR**	**CR**	**Balance**	
2018						
Jun 30		J1	1,000		1,000	DR

Account: Income Summary				GL No:	315	
Date	**Description**	**PR**	**DR**	**CR**	**Balance**	

Account: Service Revenue — GL No: 400

Date	Description	PR	DR	CR	Balance	
2018						
Jun 6		J1		2,100	2,100	CR
Jun 18		J1		1,500	3,600	CR
Jun 30	Adjusting Entry	J2		450	4,050	CR
Jun 30	Adjusting Entry	J2		900	4,950	CR

Account: Advertising Expense — GL No: 500

Date	Description	PR	DR	CR	Balance	
2018						
Jun 11		J1	450		450	DR

Account: Depreciation Expense — GL No: 510

Date	Description	PR	DR	CR	Balance	
2018						
Jun 30	Adjusting Entry	J2	100		100	DR

Account: Insurance Expense — GL No: 515

Date	Description	PR	DR	CR	Balance	
2018						
Jun 30	Adjusting Entry	J2	100		100	DR

Account: Interest Expense — GL No: 520

Date	Description	PR	DR	CR	Balance	
2018						
Jun 30	Adjusting Entry	J2	25		25	DR

Account: Rent Expense — GL No: 540

Date	Description	PR	DR	CR	Balance	
2018						
Jun 1		J1	900		900	DR

c) Prepare the post-closing trial balance.

Account Title	DR	CR

See Appendix I for solutions.

Appendix 6A: The 10-Column Spreadsheet

In Chapter 5, the six-column spreadsheet was introduced to help track the changes in account balances due to adjustments. Although this spreadsheet is optional, it shows the unadjusted trial balance, the adjustments and the adjusted trial balance all in one place. An extension of this is the optional 10-column spreadsheet. In this spreadsheet, the first six columns are identical to those in the six-column spreadsheet. The extra columns are to show the accounts and balances that will appear on the financial statements. One set of columns is for the income statement accounts and the other set is for the balance sheet and owner's equity accounts. The values shown in these columns are copied directly from the adjusted trial balance columns.

The 10-column spreadsheet is shown in Figure 6A.1, with the new columns shown in red.

Account Title	Unadjusted Trial Balance		Adjustments		Adjusted Trial Balance		Income Statement		Balance Sheet & Equity	
	DR	CR	DR	CR	DR	CR	DR	CR	DR	CR
Cash										
Accounts Receivable										
Prepaid Insurance										
Equipment										

FIGURE 6A.1

In Figure 6A.2, the income statement accounts are separated from the balance sheet and equity accounts. Notice that the initial debit and credit totals of the income statement accounts do not balance. This is expected because the company should report an income or a loss. In this case, MP Consulting shows a greater credit balance (see letters ⓐ and ⓑ). Since the credit total is higher, MP Consulting generated an income. Find the difference between the two figures and add the difference to the smaller total. In the case of MP Consulting, the difference is $3,175 (see letter ⓒ) and is added to the smaller debit total to get $4,500. This ensures the income statement columns balance. If the company had a net loss, the difference would be added to the credit column to ensure the income statement columns balance.

A similar process is completed for the balance sheet and equity columns. The difference is calculated and added to the smaller total (see letter ⓓ) to ensure the balance sheet and equity columns balance. Notice that the difference between the income statement columns and the difference between the balance sheet and equity columns are identical. This should always be the case. A net income increases the capital account; therefore it is always a credit to the balance sheet and equity accounts. Conversely, a net loss decreases equity and is placed on the debit side of the balance sheet and equity accounts.

MP Consulting
Spreadsheet
January 31, 2018

Account Title	Unadjusted Trial Balance		Adjustments		Adjusted Trial Balance		Income Statement		Balance Sheet & Equity	
	DR	CR	DR	CR	DR	CR	DR	CR	DR	CR
Cash	$3,800				$3,800				$3,800	
Accounts Receivable	3,000		$1,000		4,000				4,000	
Prepaid Insurance	1,200			$100	1,100				1,100	
Equipment	8,300				8,300				8,300	
Accumulated Depreciation—Equipment		$0		150		$150				$150
Accounts Payable		1,250				1,250				1,250
Interest Payable		0		25		25				25
Unearned Revenue		2,000	200			1,800				1,800
Notes Payable		2,500				2,500				2,500
Parish, Capital		10,300				10,300				10,300
Parish, Withdrawals	2,000				2,000				2,000	
Service Revenue		3,300		1,200		4,500		$4,500		
Depreciation Expense	0		150		150		$150			
Insurance Expense	0		100		100		100			
Interest Expense	0		25		25		25			
Rent Expense	800				800		800			
Telephone Expense	250				250		250			
Total	$19,350	$19,350	$1,475	$1,475	$20,525	$20,525	ⓑ $1,325	ⓐ $4,500	$19,200	$16,025
Net Income (Loss)							ⓒ 3,175			ⓓ 3,175
Total							$4,500	$4,500	$19,200	$19,200

In Summary

 Prepare a 10-column spreadsheet

- ▶ A 10-column spreadsheet is an extension of a six-column spreadsheet where the four additional columns are for the income statement, balance sheet and owner's equity accounts.

- ▶ For the income statement columns, the difference between the initial debit and credit totals is equal to the company's reported income or loss.

- ▶ The debit and credit columns of the balance sheet and equity should have the exact same difference as the income statement columns.

 *Access **ameengage.com** for integrated resources including tutorials, practice exercises, the digital textbook and more.*

Review Exercise 6A-1

Catherine Gordon is running her own proprietary business called CG Accounting. CG Accounting provides bookkeeping services to small and mid-sized companies. The company prepares financial statements on a monthly basis.

The journal entries for the month of June have already been entered in the journal and posted to the ledger.

At the end of June 2018, CG Accounting had to make the following adjustments.

Jun 30 The prepaid insurance represents a one-year policy that started in June. One month has now been used.

Jun 30 When examining the balance of unearned revenue, Catherine determined that $450 has now been earned.

Jun 30 Interest has accrued on the balance of the bank loan for the month. The loan interest rate is 10%. (For simplicity, round the interest to the nearest whole number.)

Jun 30 Depreciation on the equipment for the month must be recorded. The equipment is depreciated using the straight-line method. The equipment is expected to last five years and will have no residual value

Jun 30 Catherine started an audit for a new client. The contract is for 20 days of work starting June 21. At the end of the contract, the client will pay CG Accounting $1,800. Accrue the revenue earned for June.

Complete the spreadsheet.

CG Accounting Spreadsheet June 30, 2018

Account Title	Unadjusted Trial Balance DR	Unadjusted Trial Balance CR	Adjustments DR	Adjustments CR	Adjusted Trial Balance DR	Adjusted Trial Balance CR	Income Statement DR	Income Statement CR	Balance Sheet & Equity DR	Balance Sheet & Equity CR
Cash	$5,550									
Accounts Receivable	4,600									
Prepaid Insurance	1,200									
Equipment	6,000									
Accumulated Depreciation—Equipment		$0								
Accounts Payable		2,750								
Interest Payable		0								
Unearned Revenue		900								
Notes Payable		3,050								
Gordon, Capital		9,400								
Gordon, Withdrawals	1,000									
Service Revenue		3,600								
Advertising Expense	450									
Depreciation Expense	0									
Insurance Expense	0									
Interest Expense	0									
Rent Expense	900									
Total	$19,700	$19,700								
Net Income (Loss)										
Total										

See Appendix I for solutions.

Chapter 7
Accounting for Cash: Internal Controls and Fraud Prevention

Learning Objectives

LO 1 **Apply internal controls for the business organization**
- Definition of Internal Controls
- Implementing Internal Controls

LO 2 **Apply internal controls for cash**
- Internal Controls for Cash Receipts
- Cash Over and Short
- Internal Controls for Cash Payments

LO 3 **Prepare a bank reconciliation and related journal entries**
- Unrecorded Deposits from the Bank Statement
- Unrecorded Charges from the Bank Statement

- Outstanding Deposits
- Outstanding Checks
- Bank Errors
- Ledger Errors
- Bank Reconciliation Summary

LO 4 **Prepare a petty cash fund and record related journal entries**
- Setting Up a Petty Cash Fund
- Posting Petty Cash to the General Ledger
- Petty Cash Controls

 *Access **ameengage.com** for integrated resources including tutorials, practice exercises, the digital textbook and more.*

195

MAKING IT REAL TO YOU

Cash is the lifeblood of a business. The business needs cash to pay suppliers and vendors. The business needs cash to pay contractors and employees. Since cash is so important, cash management is a critical element of sound business management. Cash is the most likely area for fraud, embezzlement and misappropriation in a business. Think for a moment about any recent purchases you have made with cash. Depending on how the business operates, it could be very easy or very difficult for the employees of the company to take the cash for themselves. Internal controls, such as bank reconciliations, are the forces preventing, and hopefully stopping, fraud and embezzlement. We will take a closer look at the cash accountand how businesses can protect this valuable asset.

Internal Controls

While internal controls over cash are extremely important for any business, there are many internal control aspects that relate to the business overall, including cash. Figure 7.1 shows examples of some controls you likely have in your personal life. You have locks on the doors and windows to your house or apartment. You have a PIN on your bank card or credit card. You have access to a bank statement that allows you to monitor all the deposits and withdrawals from your bank account. The locks, PIN and bank statement are all considered controls. Why do you have controls? You want to protect the things you own and make sure that all payments and transactions are authorized. Businesses also implement controls to protect what they have.

FIGURE 7.1

Definition of Internal Controls

Internal controls are the policies and procedures that a business uses to

- protect its assets
- encourage effectiveness and efficiency of operations
- ensure that the accounting records are accurate
- ensure adherence to company practices as well as compliance to laws and regulations

Internal controls are designed to

- align managers and employees with the objectives of the business
- safeguard assets against loss, misuse and theft
- prevent and detect fraud and error
- encourage good management
- allow appropriate action to be taken
- reduce exposure to risks
- ensure compliance with financial reporting standards, such as generally accepted accounting principles (GAAP)
- ensure accuracy and validity of the accounting records

Internal controls can include, but are not limited to, the following measures.

- cash controls
- budgetary controls
- credit controls
- working procedures
- inventory controls
- production processes
- hiring policies
- safety standards
- environmental regulations

The Sarbanes–Oxley Act

Chapter 3 discussed how, as a result of the financial scandals in the early 2000s, the US Congress passed the Sarbanes–Oxley Act (SOX) in 2002. SOX outlines specific requirements for the managers and auditors of any company whose stocks are publicly traded on a stock exchange. Its purpose is to maintain public confidence in the accounting practices and financial reporting of public companies by improving financial disclosure. However, it also emphasizes the importance of effective internal controls in all companies, regardless of their size.

Section 404 of SOX is a key mandate that requires a company's senior management and auditors to establish internal controls. Furthermore, the managers and auditors must assess and certify to the effectiveness of the internal controls, as well as the record-keeping and reporting practices based on those controls.

The following specific requirements are included under SOX.

- Auditors are subject to independent oversight by the Public Company Accounting Oversight Board (PCAOB).
- Auditors (i.e. auditing companies) must be external to, and independent from, the client (the audited company) in order to limit any conflict of interest.
- Auditors are restricted from providing other consulting services to the client company.
- A company's senior management (its corporate officers) must take responsibility for the accuracy and completeness of the financial reports.
- Severe penalties exist for non-compliance with SOX. Non-compliance includes the destruction, alteration or manipulation of financial records.

The requirements under SOX are very costly for a company to implement and maintain; however, the benefits are greater public confidence in the company's financial accounting and reporting. It is also worthwhile to note that while SOX requirements affect only large publicly traded companies, nearly all companies, large and small, are influenced by SOX, including attention to the development of a strong internal control system.

Figure 7.2 shows a portion of Apple's SOX internal control report from management, taken from its 2017 annual report to stockholders. This report must be included with the company's annual 10-K report that is filed with the Securities and Exchange Commission (SEC). In addition, the Apple CEO and CFO both personally signed Form 10-K and take responsibility for the information reported.

Management's Annual Report on Internal Control Over Financial Reporting

The Company's management is responsible for establishing and maintaining adequate internal control over financial reporting (as defined in Rule 13a-15(f) under the Exchange Act). Management conducted an assessment of the effectiveness of the Company's internal control over financial reporting based on the criteria set forth in Internal Control – Integrated Framework issued by the Committee of Sponsoring Organizations of the Treadway Commission (2013 framework). Based on the Company's assessment, management has concluded that its internal control over financial reporting was effective as of September 30, 2017 to provide reasonable assurance regarding the reliability of financial reporting and the preparation of financial statements in accordance with GAAP. The Company's independent registered public accounting firm, Ernst & Young LLP, has issued an audit report on the Company's internal control over financial reporting, which appears in Part II, Item 8 of this Form 10-K.

FIGURE 7.2

Elements of Internal Control

The Sarbanes–Oxley Act emphasizes the need for internal controls to promote the accuracy and reliability of financial reports.

The **Committee of Sponsoring Organizations (COSO)** of the Treadway Commission (www.coso.org) provides a framework to help companies design and implement internal controls. This framework, known as the *Internal Control—Integrated Framework (2013)* provides tools and guidance on the five key **elements of internal control**, which are as follows.

- Control Environment—This refers to corporate management's overall attitude toward the importance of internal controls. The control environment takes into account the company's structural organization, its human resources policies and its management style.
- Risk Assessment—This refers to assessing the common risks that businesses encounter in day-to-day operations, such as competition, regulatory changes, changes in the economy and changing customer trends.
- Control Procedures—These are the activities that help the company stay on track to meet its goals and to safeguard its assets. Control procedures are a key element of internal control. They include such practices as
  - hiring competent and properly trained staff;

- rotating staff duties, and ensuring that all employees take regular vacations (it is during such changes that any fraudulent behavior can often become evident);
- separating responsibilities so that no single employee handles all related activities (e.g. one person receives the checks in the mail, another person records the payments in the accounting records, and another person deposits the checks in the bank, so that three checkpoints exist in the system);
- implementing and maintaining effective security measures; and
- separating the custody of assets from responsibilities for recordkeeping (e.g. an employee that handles cash should not also be responsible for the bookkeeping activities).

- Monitoring Activities—This refers to management's regular evaluation of business operations to identify any weaknesses and to improve the company's internal controls. It includes measures such as observing staff behavior, having internal auditors monitor day-to-day operations and using external auditors to perform regular reviews and audits of the financial records.
- Information and Communication—This is a key element that encompasses the other four key elements of internal control. Within the organization, management uses information about the control environment, risk assessment, control procedures and monitoring activities to guide the company's operations and ensure adherence and compliance to standards, laws and regulations. Management also evaluates external information such as economic conditions, competition, industry trends and other factors that could affect reporting and decision-making.

Limitations of Internal Control

The objectives of internal controls are to safeguard assets, encourage efficiency in operations, ensure accuracy of accounting records and encourage companies to comply with laws and regulations. Still, internal controls are not a guarantee against errors, omissions or intentional misuse of company resources. As you learned earlier in this section, there is a cost-benefit element since it can be very expensive to implement and maintain internal controls, and the costs may outweigh the expected benefits.

Policies and procedures are devised and applied by humans, and so there are potential limitations to internal control. The human element of internal control takes into account that errors can occur from things such as fatigue, carelessness, insufficient training or misjudgment. The human element also takes into account intentional breaches of procedure, or fraud. **Fraud** is defined as any illegal intentional act of deception that results in a financial benefit or gain. Fraud may not always be easy to identify because the intention is to hide the fraudulent act within normal business activities.

Fraudulent behavior can arise from opportunity (insufficient controls that enable someone to easily carry out fraud), from an attitude of rationalization (the perpetrator feels justified in carrying out fraud), or from personal stressors such as financial difficulties, family pressure or social pressure. One individual may carry out fraud or there may be collusion between two or more employees who agree to override the internal controls.

Warning Signs of Internal Control Problems

One of the key elements of internal control is the monitoring of activities, which refers to management's regular evaluation of business operations to identify any weaknesses in internal controls. Warning signs of internal control problems often become evident from several sources.

- by observing staff behavior—behaviors such as excessive alcohol or drug use, resistance to taking vacation, overly-close relationships with suppliers or service providers, a sudden change in lifestyle, or constantly borrowing money from fellow employees can be signs of potential internal control problems
- by detecting changes within the company's accounting system—behaviors such as slow or missing payments to suppliers, frequent or regular discrepancies in cash receipt records and bank deposits, missing documents, gaps or backlogs in the financial records, or a sudden increase in refunds to customers can all be signs of possible internal control problems

A properly designed internal control system can reduce the potential for loss due to fraud as well as help detect problems in their earliest stages, when corrective actions can be taken.

IN THE REAL WORLD

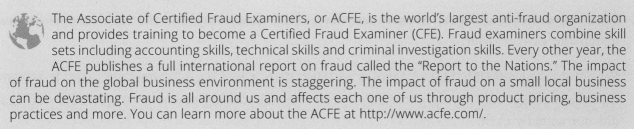

The Associate of Certified Fraud Examiners, or ACFE, is the world's largest anti-fraud organization and provides training to become a Certified Fraud Examiner (CFE). Fraud examiners combine skill sets including accounting skills, technical skills and criminal investigation skills. Every other year, the ACFE publishes a full international report on fraud called the "Report to the Nations." The impact of fraud on the global business environment is staggering. The impact of fraud on a small local business can be devastating. Fraud is all around us and affects each one of us through product pricing, business practices and more. You can learn more about the ACFE at http://www.acfe.com/.

Implementing Internal Controls

Under an adequate system of internal controls, each business transaction is complete, accurate, authorized, real (i.e. it exists) and valid. In addition, when internal controls are present, errors in the system are automatically identified and corrected, duties are segregated and financial reports are timely.

Generally, internal controls can be classified as preventive (i.e. to stop an incident before it happens), or detective (i.e. to discover an incident after it happens). Obviously, it is better to prevent incidents than to discover them after they occur.

Fraud Case: Michael's Family Restaurant

Consider the following situation. Michael purchased a family restaurant, which he managed himself. He bought supplies, paid bills, and opened and closed the restaurant himself each day. He was doing so well that he decided to open a second location. He promoted an employee, who had worked with him for the past three years, to manage the old location while he focused on setting up the new location.

Michael disliked anything to do with accounting. He operated a simple hands-on business and his bookkeeper updated the books each month to ensure that sales taxes and payroll were paid in full and on time. Other than these two functions, the bookkeeper relied on the accountant to complete the financial statements at the end of each year and complete Michael's annual tax return.

Michael's business was performing well, so Michael and his wife decided to take a vacation. Not long after they returned, Michael discovered that a payment he had issued a few days before he left to his supplier was returned by the bank because of insufficient funds in the business account. Michael was not only frustrated but also extremely embarrassed. He had to transfer money from his personal savings account to cover the shortfall in his business account and immediately started looking into what happened.

Since Michael knew very little about accounting, he contacted his accountant to investigate. An entire year had passed since the accountant had worked with Michael's financial statements, so the investigation was no easy task. The following issues were discovered.

1. Cash was only being deposited every few days, rather than daily, and the cash receipts did not match the cash register.

2. Payroll was considerably higher, relative to sales, than it had been in previous years. It appears that the manager was paying ghost employees—he was making payments to contract staff that did not actually exist.

3. His trusted manager was stealing food supplies and selling them for cash. This increased the food costs and decreased profits.

4. Some of the servers were "sweet-hearting" customers—meaning that friends and family were being given free meals or extras at no charge.

As a result of a lack of controls, poor bookkeeper oversight and his employees' fraudulent behavior, Michael nearly went bankrupt. He hired a new manager, and with the help of his accountant he implemented the following controls to prevent problems from happening again.

1. The new manager does not handle any sales and deposits the cash every day. Any discrepancies between the cash receipts and the register are investigated by the manager immediately.

2. The new manager is responsible for scheduling and keeping payroll costs to a certain percentage of sales.

3. The head chef at the restaurant counts food supplies at the beginning of each day and is responsible for ordering replacement food. The manager compares the daily inventory counts to the inventory used in the daily sales to ensure there are no anomalies.

4. A hiring package was created to collect personal information on new employees (such as name, address, SIN, bank account number). Michael has to approve all new hires and payroll is deposited directly into employees' bank accounts.

5. A computerized system is now used to record sales. All servers have their own pass code to record sales. Discounts or free meals must be approved by the manager, who then has to enter a special code to allow the discount or free meal.

6. Overall, the bookkeeper still updates the books every month, but also prepares financial statements on a monthly basis for Michael to examine.

As this example shows, when controls are not in place, organizations are vulnerable to fraudulent or harmful activities. Once Michael uncovered how theft and fraud were taking place, he was able to implement controls and policies to better monitor business activities and identify problems before they caused financial harm.

Cash Controls

LO 2

We will now turn our attention to internal controls specifically designed for cash. As illustrated in Figure 7.3, the current assets section of the balance sheet starts with cash because it is the most liquid asset. **Cash** is defined as currency (paper money), coins, checks, money orders, and money on deposit in a bank account. Cash is essentially anything that a bank or other financial institution will accept for deposit in an account. A business receives cash for providing services or selling products to customers and uses that cash to purchase assets and pay for expenses. Without cash, a business will likely fail. Thus, it is important for a business to ensure that controls are in place to protect this valuable asset.

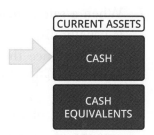

FIGURE 7.3

While it is important to have sufficient cash on hand, if a business earns more cash than it currently needs, leaving it in a checking account earns little return. Instead of having the cash sitting idle, some companies choose to invest their excess cash into highly liquid investments, known as **cash equivalents**, which are expected to generate a higher return. Cash equivalents are considered a short-term investment, usually shorter than three months (or 90 days). They are highly liquid and can be quickly converted into cash when needed. Therefore, they get recorded under cash in the current assets section of the balance sheet. Some examples of cash equivalents are treasury bills, money market funds, CDs (certificates of deposit), commercial paper and short-term government bonds.

Alternatively, a business may have less cash than it currently needs. This can create a negative balance in the bank account, which is known as a bank overdraft.

Internal Controls for Cash Receipts

Businesses usually receive cash from customers in two different ways.

- from cash sales—at the cash counter when the products or services are sold
- from credit sales—when a customer pays on account after an invoice has been issued for products or services; payment may be made by sending it in the mail, or by sending it electronically

We will look at each of these types of payment in more detail.

Cash Received from Cash Sales

In a retail sales environment where a cash register is used, proper internal controls should be used to safeguard cash and prevent its misuse.

1. At the beginning of a work shift, provide each cash register clerk with his or her own cash drawer with a predetermined amount of cash. This cash amount, known as a cash float, is used to make change for customers. The cash float normally consists of a range of bills and coins.

2. When a sale is made, the clerk keys the amount of the sale into the cash register. The amount is usually displayed so the customer can see it, to ensure that the clerk has entered the correct amount. Once the sales clerk has received the payment, the customer receives a printed cash register receipt showing the date, amount and method of payment.

3. At the end of the work shift, the cash register clerk and the manager or supervisor count the amount of cash in the cash drawer to verify that it equals the amount of the original cash float plus the cash sales for that shift.

4. The cash is taken to the cashier's department by the supervisor, and is placed in a safe. The manager or supervisor then sends the cash register receipts to the accounting department.

5. The cashier prepares a bank deposit slip in duplicate and sends (or takes) it, along with the cash, to deposit in the bank. In many companies where there is a considerable amount of cash involved, the deposit may be picked up and delivered to the bank by an armored vehicle service.

6. The accounting department uses the cash register receipts to prepare a summary report to record the cash sales for the day.

7. When the bank deposit is made, the bank clerk stamps one copy of the deposit slip to verify that the correct amount of cash has been received. The stamped deposit slip is returned to the company's accounting department, where it is verified against the amount recorded per the cash register receipts. It is at this point that any cash shortages can be immediately detected.

Cash Received in the Mail

Customers sometimes pay their bills by sending cash (usually checks or money orders) by mail. Most companies send an invoice that includes a remittance advice, a detachable part of the invoice that is returned along with the customer's payment. A remittance advice includes details such as the customer's account number, the amount of payment requested and the date the payment is due. The remittance advice is an important part of the internal controls that a business uses as part of the following process.

1. The employee who opens the mail compares the amount of payment with the amount on the remittance advice. If the business does not provide remittance advices with their invoices, the employee prepares one. This ensures that the amount actually received is immediately recorded upon receipt. The employee also stamps the back of the check or money order "For Deposit Only." As extra protection, the stamp often includes the name of the business as well as its bank account number.

2. The checks and money orders are taken to the cashier's department. The remittance advice and a summary report of payments received are delivered to the accounting department.

3. The cashier prepares a bank deposit slip in duplicate and sends (or takes) it, along with the checks and money orders, to deposit in the bank. If there is a considerable amount of money involved, the deposit may be picked up and delivered to the bank by an armored vehicle service.

4. The accounting department records the amount received and posts it to the customer's account.

5. When the bank deposit is made, the bank clerk stamps one copy of the deposit slip to verify that the correct amount of checks and money orders have been received. The stamped deposit slip is returned to the company's accounting department, where it is verified against the amount recorded per the accounting records. It is at this point that any cash shortages can be immediately detected.

As you learned in the section on internal controls, these control procedures reinforce the importance of the separation of duties between those who receive, record and deposit the cash. When these control procedures are consistently enforced it is much easier to detect fraud or misuse as soon as it occurs.

Debit and Credit Card Transactions

In addition to receiving cash from customers for payment, many businesses will also allow customers to pay using debit or credit cards. Debit and credit card customer payments may be received via a card reader alongside a cash register in a store setting or, increasingly, via a mobile square card reader at any possible location, such as a farmer's market or outdoor setting away from a traditional business place. From the business perspective, these payments are like cash since they will be deposited into the business bank account. The business may have the amounts from debit and credit card sales transferred into the bank account each day or less frequently if it does not have many daily sales.

A debit card sale transfers cash from the customer's bank account to the business bank account. This limits the customer to spending only what they have in their account. A credit card sale gives the customer access to credit which usually available through their bank. This is like a loan from the bank to the customer.

In both cases, a sale paid for by credit card or debit card will result in a small transaction fee the business must pay to the bank or processing company. This fee is to cover the bank's cost of providing the equipment and technology to allow these transactions. In the case of credit card fees, it also covers the risk that the customer may not repay the bank the money they borrowed. From the business' perspective, this fee is a cost of processing the sale and is recorded as an expense.

For example, suppose a business made total credit card sales of $2,000 on May 25, 2018. The bank will charge 2.5% of total sales as the transaction fee to the business. Thus, $50 ($2,000 × 2.5%) will be kept by the bank and only $1,950 will be deposited to the business bank account. The transaction is illustrated in Figure 7.4.

JOURNAL			
Date	Account Title and Explanation	Debit	Credit
May 25	Debit/Credit Card Expense	50	
	Cash	1,950	
	Sales Revenue		2,000
	To record credit card sales		

FIGURE 7.4

On the other hand, a bank can charge a fixed percentage of all debit transactions, such as 1% or 2%, or charge a per-transaction fee, such as $0.006 per transaction, depending on the terms of the bank account. This debit card expense is recorded in the journal under the Debit/Credit Card Expense account as shown in Figure 7.4.

Cash Received by Electronic Funds Transfer

Many businesses accept payment on account using **electronic funds transfer (EFT)**, which is a method of sending payment online directly from the customer's bank account into the bank account of the supplier. EFT is a secure, inexpensive and fast method of paying bills for things such as internet services, cell phone plans and utilities. It is also convenient for the customer and the supplier because their respective financial institutions automatically prepare and send all required documentation. The customer can set up and authorize a regular monthly transfer so that the payment is made automatically on a specified date.

EFT provides a reliable internal control over cash payments because transactions are recorded accurately and the receipt is posted directly to the customer's account. It also avoids late payments, and eliminates the need for any intermediaries to handle cash. EFT is also particularly well suited for debit and credit card transactions, because the actual funds from debit or credit card sales are automatically and electronically deposited into the company's bank account.

Remote Deposit

Many financial institutions allow customers to deposit checks directly into their bank accounts remotely (such as from home) without having to physically deposit the check at a bank machine or bank branch. Such a deposit is known as a **remote deposit**. This is different from an online deposit, which requires that the customer later mail or physically deposit the check into the bank.

A remote deposit allows the customer to scan the image of the check, front and back, into a computer or handheld digital device. The images are then electronically transmitted to the bank via a special computer application and deposited directly into the customer's designated account. Both businesses and individuals can use remote deposit.

Remote deposit was introduced in the US in the mid-2000s under the *Check Clearing for the 21st Century Act (the Check 21 Act)*. The act enables the country's financial system to continue operating even if mobility is limited, such as in the case of a catastrophic event. However, it has also become a secure, convenient, time-saving and accurate way to conduct transactions. It reduces paperwork and travel time, and eliminates the risk of losing checks in transit, or having them entered incorrectly into the system. It also eliminates the longer waiting period for a check to clear the issuer's bank, because checks are both cashed and cleared electronically.

Cash Over and Short

Any cash that a business receives must be properly recorded and protected until it is deposited to the business' bank account. Occasionally, a cashier may make an error when making change, causing the count of cash and the actual amount to be different. If the difference is a large amount, the business should investigate the reason for the discrepancy.

For very small differences, the discrepancy is recorded in an account known as **cash over and short**. At the end of the accounting period, a debit balance in this account is reported as part of miscellaneous expenses on the income statement. A credit balance in the account is reported in the other income section of the income statement.

To illustrate how the cash over and short account is used, suppose a store had cash sales on May 25, 2018 of $1,425.56, but counted only $1,425.55 in the cash drawer. In this example, $0.01 is missing and is not worth the effort to track down. The difference is recorded in the cash over and short account, as shown in Figure 7.5.

JOURNAL			
Date	**Account Title and Explanation**	**Debit**	**Credit**
May 25	Cash Over and Short	0.01	
	Cash	1,425.55	
	Sales Revenue		1,425.56
	To record cash sales		

FIGURE 7.5

Internal Controls for Cash Payments

In a small owner-operated business, there may be only one person responsible for all aspects of managing the business, so separation of responsibility is not possible. The owner-operator is intimately involved with the day-to-day operations of the business, from buying and receiving inventory to the payment of suppliers. In larger businesses, however, it is possible that different employees handle these related functions. Internal controls can help a larger business ensure that cash is not misused and payments are properly issued to suppliers and creditors. Good internal controls for cash payments should aim at ensuring the following.

- all transactions that involve cash payments have been authorized
- cash payments take advantage of all allowable discounts (such as discounts for early payment)

Transactions that use the corporate account's debit and credit cards are also considered to be cash payments, and are subject to the same control policies. For example, all purchases using corporate debit and credit cards must be itemized and substantiated by original receipts with a description of the business purpose of each purchase. Similar to cash payments, there must be a segregation of duties. For example, the person who makes a purchase using the company's debit or credit card should be different from the person receiving and inspecting the goods, and there should be a third person approving the purchase.

Voucher System

One common internal control for cash payments is a voucher system. A **voucher system** is a set of control procedures that a business uses to authorize, record and disburse cash payments. The documentation used to authorize and record the cash payment is called a **voucher**. A voucher can be as official as a special form designed by the company to record all the necessary information, or as simple as an invoice that has been approved by a designated employee for payment.

A voucher is normally prepared using the input from a supplier's invoice, as well as any related purchase orders and receiving slips that accompany the goods received. After a voucher has been approved by the designated employee, it is recorded in the books and then eventually paid as a normal account payable. If the voucher system is an electronic one, all required information is entered directly into the system and a payment is issued on the specified due date. For a small business on a manual system, payment may be made by check. Many larger companies now use EFT to make payments. Once the payment has been made, the related voucher is filed in the company's accounts payable system.

Cash Payments by Electronic Funds Transfer

Many businesses opt for the security and convenience of paying vendors and creditors by EFT. You may be familiar with EFT from using an automated teller machine (ATM) to withdraw cash from your bank account. It is also very common for businesses to pay their employees by EFT. When employees hired, they are asked to provide their bank branch and account information. This authorizes the employer to transfer payment directly from the company's system into an employee's designated bank account. Cash payments by EFT are examples of payments made by direct deposit.

Pause & Reflect

Exercise 7-1

Stacy Dixon operates a convenience store and has two employees. One employee is the cashier and the other stocks the shelves with inventory. Stacy orders inventory, manages day-to-day operations, looks after bills and helps elsewhere as the need arises.

Since this is a small business, the cashier looks after most of the paperwork related to creating the float for the cash drawer, totaling the day's sales and preparing the deposit at the end of the day. Stacy will give a quick glance at the deposit slip and bring the deposit to the bank.

Some inventory is delivered and stocked by suppliers, such as soda and chips. These suppliers present an invoice to the cashier and are paid cash upon delivery from the cash drawer by the cashier.

Identify areas that can be improved with better controls.

_____

_____

_____

_____

_____

See Appendix I for solutions.

Bank Reconciliations

A **bank statement** is a record of all activity (the transactions) in a bank account for a given period, usually a month. The bank statement is provided to the account owner (the depositor) by the bank at the end of the period. The format of a bank statement varies by bank, but they all provide the same basic information. The statement shows the beginning balance for the period, all additions and deductions during the period, and the ending balance as of the statement date. A bank reconciliation is a simple internal control that compares, reconciles and explains the difference between a company's bank statement and its own cash accounting records. This is usually done at the end of a statement period.

To understand bank statements and bank reconciliations, we must first look at the records from the different perspectives of the bank and the company (the depositor). Figure 7.6 illustrates the differences. For the bank, the depositor's account balance represents a liability. This is because the money belongs to the depositor and the bank has an obligation to pay the balance to the depositor on demand. Therefore, in the bank's records, the depositor's account shows a credit balance. From the bank's point of view, any increase to the depositor's account requires a credit memo entry. Conversely, any decrease to the depositor's account requires a debit memo entry. From the depositor's perspective, a credit memo from the bank increases the asset cash on the depositor's books, and a debit memo from the bank decreases the asset cash on the depositor's books.

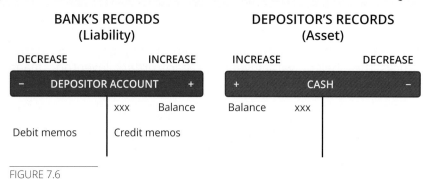

FIGURE 7.6

Typical reasons for the bank making debit entries (issuing debit memos) to the company's cash account include the following.

- loan interest charges
- repayment of a bank loan (note payable)
- bank charges
- payments by electronic funds transfer (EFT)
- automatic cash payments to other accounts
- non-sufficient funds (NSF) checks

Typical reasons for the bank making credit entries (issuing credit memos) to the depositor's cash account include the following.

- interest earned on the depositor's account
- payment from a customer deposited directly into the account

- deposits by electronic funds transfer (EFT)
- automatic cash deposits from other accounts
- proceeds from collection of notes receivable
- corrections of bank errors

The bank statement balance and the cash ledger balance at the end of the month may not be the same. The bank reconciliation is prepared to reconcile these two balances and ensure no errors have been made by either the bank or the company bookkeeper. If an error has been made, it must be corrected.

In the process of comparing the items in your records with the items shown on the bank statement, you may notice that some items shown correctly on the bank statement may not appear in your records. Similarly, some items shown correctly in your records may not appear on the bank statement.

As illustrated in Figure 7.7, a bank reconciliation compares the bank statement balance (shown on the left side of the bank reconciliation) and the company's actual bank account (i.e. cash) balance per its accounting records (shown on the right side of the bank reconciliation). The bank reconciliation adjusts both balances to the correct cash balance based on GAAP principles. To determine the correct cash balance, cash balance per bank statement must be adjusted in the bank reconciliation by adding and deducting transactions that are missing from the bank statement due to timing differences or errors.

Example Bank Reconciliation Month of October, 2018			
Cash balance per bank statement	$1,000	Cash balance per company books	$1,500

Add
   Debits to cash not included on bank statement (e.g. outstanding deposits, errors)
	800	Add
		   Credits to bank account not included in company books (e.g. notes receivable collected by bank)
			400

Deduct
   Credits to cash not included on bank statement (e.g. EFT payments, outstanding checks, errors)
	200	Deduct
		   Debits to bank account not included in company books (e.g. bank charges, NSF checks)
			300

Adjusted bank balance	$1,600	Adjusted book balance	$1,600

Balances must be equal

FIGURE 7.7

For example, if a company deposits checks worth $800 on October 31, the bank processes these checks at the beginning of November, and the deposits appear in the November bank statement, not in the October bank statement. However, because the checks were deposited in October, the $800 balance has to be added to the cash balance per bank statement in the bank reconciliation in October. Likewise, check payments in October that have not been processed by the bank and thus do not appear in the October bank statement have to be deducted from the cash balance per bank statement in the October bank reconciliation.

Conversely, cash balance per company books must be adjusted to reflect the items that appear on the bank statement but have not been recorded in the company's books, such as bank charges. After adjusting both cash balance per bank statement and cash balance per company books, these two adjusted balances must match because there can only be one correct cash balance at a specific point in time.

In the following sections, different scenarios will be presented illustrating how discrepancies in bank reconciliations can occur, and how to correct them. A complete bank reconciliation statement is presented at the end of the discussion.

Unrecorded Deposits from the Bank Statement

From time to time, the bank may automatically record a deposit in the company's bank account. The company would be unaware of the amount until it receives the bank statement. For example, compare HR Clothing Company's cash ledger entries to the company's bank statement, shown in Figure 7.8.

Company's Records

GENERAL LEDGER

Account: Cash				GL No:	101
Date	**Description**	**DR**	**CR**	**Balance**	
Jun 1	Opening Balance			5,000	DR
Jun 2	Check #1		300	4,700	DR
Jun 3	Check #2		500	4,200	DR
Jun 10	Check #3		700	3,500	DR

Bank's Records

Bank Statement			June 1–June 30, 2018	
Date	**Description**	**Withdrawal**	**Deposit**	**Balance**
Jun 1	Opening Balance			5,000
Jun 2	Check #1	300		4,700
Jun 3	Check #2	500		4,200
Jun 10	Check #3	700		3,500
Jun 30	Interest		5	3,505

FIGURE 7.8

All of the checks have been recorded by the bank as well as by the company. However, notice that on June 30 the bank has recorded a $5 deposit to HR Clothing because of interest. Since the interest earned is correctly shown on the bank statement, it should also be recorded in the general ledger by debiting (increasing) cash and crediting (increasing) interest revenue.

Assume that HR Clothing's ledger balance is $3,500, and the bank statement for the month shows a balance of $3,505. The bank reconciliation for this is shown in Figure 7.9.

HR Clothing Company Bank Reconciliation June 30, 2018			
Cash balance per bank statement	$3,505	Cash balance per books	$3,500
		Add unrecorded deposit	
		Interest received June 30	5
Adjusted bank balance	$3,505	Adjusted book balance	$3,505

FIGURE 7.9

Since the adjusting amount is in the cash balance per books, or general ledger column, the general ledger balance must be corrected with an adjusting journal entry. The entry is shown in Figure 7.10. Notice that the journal entry includes interest revenue. On the Accounting Map, interest revenue is listed under other revenue on the income statement.

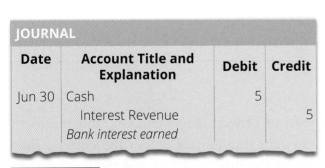

JOURNAL			
Date	Account Title and Explanation	Debit	Credit
Jun 30	Cash	5	
	Interest Revenue		5
	Bank interest earned		

FIGURE 7.10

Another type of deposit occurs when a note receivable is collected on behalf of the depositor. For example, in Figure 7.11, the bank has recorded the proceeds of a $1,000 note receivable from

Models Inc. in HR Clothing's account on June 30. Compare HR Clothing's cash ledger entries to the company's bank statement.

Company's Records

GENERAL LEDGER

Account: Cash				GL No:	101	
Date	Description	DR	CR	Balance		
Jun 1	Opening Balance			5,000	DR	
Jun 2	Check #1		300	4,700	DR	
Jun 3	Check #2		500	4,200	DR	
Jun 10	Check #3		700	3,500	DR	

Bank's Records

Bank Statement			June 1–June 30, 2018	
Date	Description	Withdrawal	Deposit	Balance
Jun 1	Opening Balance			5,000
Jun 2	Check #1	300		4,700
Jun 3	Check #2	500		4,200
Jun 10	Check #3	700		3,500
Jun 30	Proceeds of note receivable—Models Inc.		1,000	4,500

FIGURE 7.11

Assume that HR Clothing's ledger balance is $3,500 and the bank statement for the month shows a balance of $4,500. The bank reconciliation for this is shown in Figure 7.12.

HR Clothing Company Bank Reconciliation June 30, 2018			
Cash balance per bank statement	$4,500	Cash balance per books	$3,500
		Add unrecorded deposits	
		Note receivable collected June 30	1,000
Adjusted bank balance	$4,500	Adjusted book balance	$4,500

FIGURE 7.12

The adjusting amount is in the cash balance per books, or general ledger column. This means that the general ledger balance must be corrected with an adjusting journal entry. The entry is shown in Figure 7.13. The journal entry includes the receipt of the cash (a debit) and the corresponding decrease in notes receivable (a credit). For the sake of simplicity, we will disregard any interest earned on the note receivable as well as any bank charges for collection expense. On the Accounting Map, the transaction is shown in the two related balance sheet accounts.

JOURNAL			
Date	Account Title and Explanation	Debit	Credit
Jun 30	Cash	1,000	
	Note Receivable—Models Inc.		1,000
	Proceeds of note receivable		

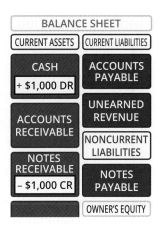

FIGURE 7.13

Unrecorded Charges from the Bank Statement

As with unrecorded deposits, there may be charges shown on the bank statement that are not yet recorded in the general ledger. Typical examples are a monthly bank charge for using account services, such as an ATM withdrawal, or an annual fee for a safe deposit box. Such charges should be adjusted in the ledger.

Figure 7.14 shows that HR Clothing has a cash ledger balance of $3,500. The bank statement shows a balance of $3,450. All checks are recorded in both the bank statement and the general ledger. Upon comparison, the bookkeeper of the company notices that the bank recorded bank charges of $50 on the last day of the month. This change must be updated in the general ledger.

GENERAL LEDGER

Account: Cash				GL No:	101
Date	Description	DR	CR	Balance	
Jun 1	Opening Balance			5,000	DR
Jun 2	Check #1		300	4,700	DR
Jun 3	Check #2		500	4,200	DR
Jun 10	Check #3		700	3,500	DR

Bank Statement				June 1–June 30, 2018
Date	Description	Withdrawal	Deposit	Balance
Jun 1	Opening Balance			5,000
Jun 2	Check #1	300		4,700
Jun 3	Check #2	500		4,200
Jun 10	Check #3	700		3,500
Jun 30	Bank Charges	50		3,450

FIGURE 7.14

The bank reconciliation for this item is shown in Figure 7.15.

HR Clothing Company Bank Reconciliation June 30, 2018			
Cash balance per bank statement	$3,450	Cash balance per books	$3,500
		Deduct unrecorded charges	
		Bank service charge	50
Adjusted bank balance	$3,450	Adjusted book balance	$3,450

FIGURE 7.15

The adjustment is shown in the cash balance per books, or general ledger column, so it must be updated with a journal entry as shown in Figure 7.16. The journal entry includes the account Bank Charges Expense. On the Accounting Map, bank charges are listed under other expenses on the income statement.

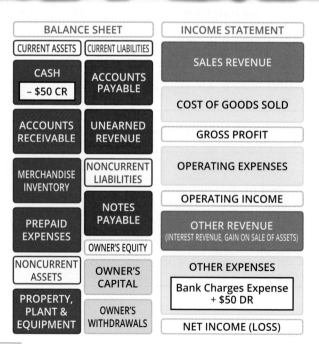

JOURNAL

Date	Account Title and Explanation	Debit	Credit
Jun 30	Bank Charges Expense	50	
	Cash		50
	Record bank service charge		

FIGURE 7.16

The journal entry is recorded by debiting (increasing) bank charges expense and crediting (decreasing) cash (an asset).

Another type of bank charge is for **non-sufficient funds (NSF) checks,** which are payments made to the company by a customer who does not have sufficient funds in his or her bank account to cover the amount of the check. If this is the case, the bank charges the customer an NSF fee. The company's bank also charges the company with an NSF fee. The fee is to cover the bank's administrative costs of dealing with the NSF check.

For example, HR Clothing receives a $400 check from a customer and deposits the check into the company's bank account on June 17. However, the bank cannot successfully collect the $400 from the customer's account because the customer does not have enough money in his account to support this withdrawal. The bank would return the check to the company and charge an additional service fee.

Figure 7.17 shows the deposit of the check in both the general ledger and bank statement, and the two additional transactions (withdrawing the NSF check and the NSF charge) in the bank statement.

GENERAL LEDGER

Account: Cash				GL No:	101	
Date	**Description**	**DR**	**CR**	**Balance**		
Jun 1	Opening Balance			5,000	DR	
Jun 2	Check #1		300	4,700	DR	
Jun 3	Check #2		500	4,200	DR	
Jun 10	Check #3		700	3,500	DR	
Jun 17	Deposit	400		3,900	DR	

Bank Statement			June 1–June 30, 2018	
Date	**Description**	**Withdrawal**	**Deposit**	**Balance**
Jun 1	Opening Balance			5,000
Jun 2	Check #1	300		4,700
Jun 3	Check #2	500		4,200
Jun 10	Check #3	700		3,500
Jun 17	Deposit		400	3,900
Jun 19	NSF Check	400		3,500
Jun 19	NSF Charge	10		3,490

FIGURE 7.17

The bank reconciliation for this item is shown in Figure 7.18.

HR Clothing Company Bank Reconciliation June 30, 2018				
Cash balance per bank statement	$3,490	Cash balance per books		$3,900
		Deduct unrecorded charges		
		Check returned NSF	$400	
		Bank charges for NSF check	10	410
Adjusted bank balance	$3,490	Adjusted book balance		$3,490

FIGURE 7.18

This adjustment should also be recorded in the journal and updated in the ledger. Since an NSF check represents the amount of cash receipts unsuccessfully collected, this amount should be added to the company's Accounts Receivable account. In addition, the bank charge associated with the NSF check should also be recorded. The journal entries are shown in Figure 7.19.

JOURNAL			
Date	Account Title and Explanation	Debit	Credit
Jun 30	Accounts Receivable	400	
	Cash		400
	NSF check returned by bank		
Jun 30	Bank Charges Expense	10	
	Cash		10
	Bank charge for NSF check		

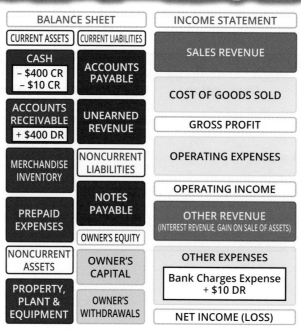

FIGURE 7.19

HR Clothing was charged because the customer was unable to honor the check. The company will not want to pay the extra fee for the customer's error. HR Clothing will create a new invoice charging the customer an extra amount to cover the NSF fee. Some companies charge the exact amount of the bank's NSF fee, in this case $10. Other companies charge the customer a flat fee greater than the NSF charge to cover both the NSF fee and the administrative process of handling the NSF check.

IN THE REAL WORLD

Non-sufficient funds checks are commonly known as bad checks or bounced checks. In our example, it is assumed that NSF checks occur because the issuer of the check does not have enough money in his or her own bank account to support the check. However, NSF checks can result from a variety of reasons including the following.

1. The issuer purposely cancels the check.
2. The account is frozen.
3. The account does not exist (i.e. the issuing party engaged in a fraudulent act).
4. The account is under investigation.

Outstanding Deposits

An outstanding deposit is one that has been recorded in the company's general ledger but not shown on the bank statement. These are also referred to as *deposits in transit*. This can occur when the company makes a deposit in the bank (perhaps using the night deposit box) on the last day of the month, but the bank does not record the deposit until the following business day—in the next month. The bank statement and the company's ledger account may appear as shown in Figure 7.20.

GENERAL LEDGER

Account: Cash					GL No: 101	
Date	**Description**	**DR**	**CR**	**Balance**	
Jun 1	Opening Balance			5,000	DR
Jun 2	Check #1		300	4,700	DR
Jun 3	Check #2		500	4,200	DR
Jun 10	Check #3		700	3,500	DR
Jun 30	Deposit	1,000		4,500	DR

Bank Statement		June 1–June 30, 2018		
Date	**Description**	**Withdrawal**	**Deposit**	**Balance**
Jun 1	Opening Balance			5,000
Jun 2	Check #1	300		4,700
Jun 3	Check #2	500		4,200
Jun 10	Check #3	700		3,500

FIGURE 7.20

The balance on the bank statement is $3,500. The balance in the general ledger is $4,500. There was a deposit of $1,000 on June 30 that was not recorded by the bank. Since the balance is missing from the bank statement, it should be added to the bank balance as shown in Figure 7.21.

HR Clothing Company Bank Reconciliation June 30, 2018			
Cash balance per bank statement	$3,500	Cash balance per books	$4,500
Add outstanding deposit June 30	1,000		
Adjusted bank balance	$4,500	Adjusted book balance	$4,500

FIGURE 7.21

Notice that the reconciled balances are the same for the bank and the cash balance per books, or general ledger columns. There is no adjustment required in the ledger because the entry is only in the bank account column of the bank reconciliation worksheet. The outstanding deposit is a timing difference; it should appear on the bank statement that includes the following business day (in July). If the deposit does not show up within one or two business days, further investigation should be made to rule out theft or fraud.

IN THE REAL WORLD

With banking and cash functions shifting to more digital formats, we see fewer actual checks. A check is a written order to pay. Suppose that check #1025 for $300 from HR Clothing Company represents payment to Fancy Scarves and More, Inc. Here is an example of what a physical paper check looks like.

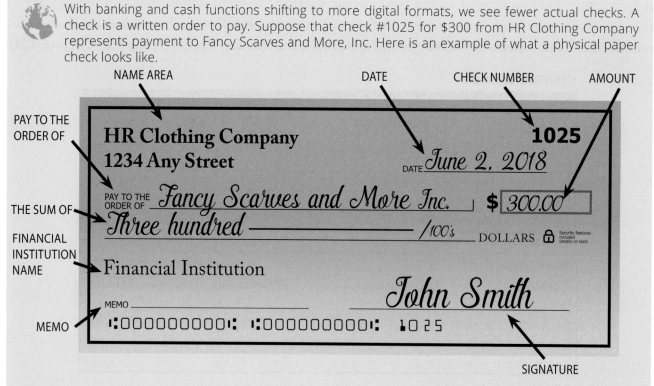

Notice the date, payee, payer and amount. HR Clothing Company is moving cash funds from its business checking account to Fancy Scarves and More, Inc. by writing and sending this check. This type of payment could also be accomplished electronically with the company's checking account number and routing number, or debit card/credit card information completed online with a few clicks.

Outstanding Checks

The next item to consider is outstanding checks. An outstanding check (issued by the company) has been recorded in the general ledger, but has not been recorded on the bank statement. This can happen because after the company records the check, it is mailed to the supplier. The supplier then records it in its books, prepares the deposit and takes it to the bank. The process can take several days, so a check mailed on June 29 may not appear on the bank statement until July 2 or 3.

Consider the following example. Six checks have been recorded in the ledger for the month of June, as shown in Figure 7.22. Three of the checks (Check #1, Check #2 and Check #3) appear on the bank statement. The checks that were written at the end of the month (Check #4, Check #5 and Check #6) have not yet been processed by the bank as of June 30.

GENERAL LEDGER

Account: Cash				GL No:	101	
Date	Description	DR	CR	Balance		
Jun 1	Opening Balance			5,000	DR	
Jun 2	Check #1		300	4,700	DR	
Jun 3	Check #2		500	4,200	DR	
Jun 10	Check #3		700	3,500	DR	
Jun 15	Deposit	1,000		4,500	DR	
Jun 28	Check #4		400	4,100	DR	
Jun 29	Check #5		800	3,300	DR	
Jun 30	Check #6		700	2,600	DR	

Bank Statement			June 1–June 30, 2018	
Date	Description	Withdrawal	Deposit	Balance
Jun 1	Opening Balance			5,000
Jun 2	Check #1	300		4,700
Jun 3	Check #2	500		4,200
Jun 10	Check #3	700		3,500
Jun 15	Deposit		1,000	4,500

FIGURE 7.22

To reconcile the ledger account with the bank statement, we must treat the checks as if the transaction had been completed by the bank (i.e. deduct the amounts from the bank record).

The bank reconciliation for outstanding checks is shown in Figure 7.23.

HR Clothing Company Bank Reconciliation June 30, 2018				
Cash balance per bank statement		$4,500	Cash balance per books	$2,600
Deduct outstanding checks				
Check #4 (June 28)	400			
Check #5 (June 29)	800			
Check #6 (June 30)	700	1,900		
Adjusted bank balance		$2,600	Adjusted book balance	$2,600

FIGURE 7.23

No adjustment is required in the ledger account because the checks are correctly recorded in the general ledger but have not been cashed by the bank. The bank will eventually include them on the bank statement.

Bank Errors

Although rare, it is possible that banks will make errors, such as charging the company incorrectly with a check belonging to another company. In this case, the company's ledger balance is correct and the bank must correct the error.

Consider the following example. When the bookkeeper for HR Clothing Company receives the bank statement and compares it with the company records, she notices that the bank processed a check for $800 on June 8, but the company has no knowledge of the check. This is shown in Figure 7.24.

GENERAL LEDGER

Account: Cash				GL No:	101	
Date	**Description**	**DR**	**CR**	**Balance**		
Jun 1	Opening Balance			5,000	DR	
Jun 2	Check #1		300	4,700	DR	
Jun 3	Check #2		500	4,200	DR	
Jun 10	Check #3		700	3,500	DR	

Bank Statement		June 1–June 30, 2018		
Date	**Description**	**Withdrawal**	**Deposit**	**Balance**
Jun 1	Opening Balance			5,000
Jun 2	Check #1	300		4,700
Jun 3	Check #2	500		4,200
Jun 8	Check #108	800		3,400
Jun 10	Check #3	700		2,700

FIGURE 7.24

At this point, the bookkeeper calls the bank and discovers that the check belongs to another bank client. The bank reconciliation for this item is shown in Figure 7.25.

HR Clothing Company Bank Reconciliation June 30, 2018			
Cash balance per bank statement	$2,700	Cash balance per books	$3,500
Add bank error			
Check incorrectly charged to account on June 8	800		
Adjusted bank balance	$3,500	Adjusted book balance	$3,500

FIGURE 7.25

Since the adjustment is in the bank column, it does not need to be adjusted in the company's books. The amount is the bank's error, not a timing difference, and the bank must correct the error by depositing funds back into HR Clothing Company's account. The company needs to follow up to ensure that the bank corrects the error.

An incorrect deposit may also appear on the bank statement, which would incorrectly overstate the bank balance. In that case, the bank reconciliation would show a deduction from the bank balance to correct the error. The company would follow up to ensure that the amount was deducted from its bank account.

Ledger Errors

It is possible for bookkeepers to make errors that appear in the company's records.

Consider the following example. Upon investigating the difference between the bank statement and the ledger, HR Clothing Company's bookkeeper discovers that Check #2 was recorded as $950 in the ledger and should have been recorded as $590. The bank cashed the correct amount of the check ($590), as shown in Figure 7.26.

GENERAL LEDGER

Account: Cash					GL No: 101	
Date	**Description**	**DR**	**CR**	**Balance**		
Jun 1	Opening Balance			5,000	DR
Jun 2	Check #1		300	4,700	DR
Jun 3	Check #2		950	3,750	DR
Jun 10	Check #3		700	3,050	DR

Bank Statement			June 1–June 30, 2018	
Date	**Description**	**Withdrawal**	**Deposit**	**Balance**
Jun 1	Opening Balance			5,000
Jun 2	Check #1	300		4,700
Jun 3	Check #2	590		4,110
Jun 10	Check #3	700		3,410

FIGURE 7.26

In this situation, the deduction from the general ledger was greater than the amount of the check. To correct this error, the difference between what was recorded and the amount deducted by the bank ($950 – $590 = $360) is added to the general ledger. The bank reconciliation is shown in Figure 7.27.

HR Clothing Company Bank Reconciliation June 30, 2018			
Cash balance per bank statement	$3,410	Cash balance per books	$3,050
		Add recording error on Check #2	360
Adjusted bank balance	$3,410	Adjusted book balance	$3,410

FIGURE 7.27

Because the correcting entry is in the cash balance per books, or general ledger column, an adjusting entry must be recorded in the journal. Assuming the original check was written to purchase inventory by using a perpetual method, the journal entry to correct the ledger is shown in Figure 7.28.

JOURNAL			
Date	Account Title and Explanation	Debit	Credit
Jun 30	Cash	360	
	Merchandise Inventory		360
	Correct error in ledger		

FIGURE 7.28

When an error is made by the bookkeeper, the bookkeeper must go back into the records to determine what the original entry was for. This determines which account will be used to offset the cash account. In our example, the payment was for inventory, so the merchandise inventory account is used. If the payment was to pay off an account, accounts payable would be used; if it was to pay this month's rent, rent expense would be used, and so on.

As with the previous examples, any discrepancy between the bank statement and the ledger record should be examined and then corrected with the appropriate entries.

Incorrect amounts in the ledger can be more or less than the amounts shown on the bank statement. Each error must be analyzed carefully for appropriate adjustments.

A CLOSER LOOK

In a computerized accounting system, errors in the ledger, such as the one described in Figure 7.26, are corrected using two entries instead of one. The first entry is a $950 debit to cash and a $950 credit to merchandise inventory. This entry reverses the original incorrect entry. The second entry is a $590 debit to merchandise inventory and a $590 credit to cash to record the correct amount of the June 3 check. The net result is the same as the single entry in the amount of $360 shown in Figure 7.28. Manual accounting systems may not use this method because it requires more entries, which means more room for error.

Bank Reconciliation Summary

Once all the items on a bank statement and the ledger have been matched up, only a few items should remain that need to be reconciled. Figure 7.29 summarizes how items will be treated on a bank reconciliation. Remember that all items that must be added to or subtracted from the ledger balance must be recorded in a journal entry.

Add to Ledger Balance*	Add to Bank Balance
• Interest earned • Direct deposit from customer • Receipts through EFT • Notes receivable collected • Bookkeeper error	• Outstanding deposits • Bank error
Subtract from Ledger Balance*	**Subtract from Bank Balance**
• Loan interest charges • Repayment of bank loan • Bank service charges • Payments through EFT • NSF checks • Bookkeeper error	• Outstanding checks • Bank error

*Must also create a journal entry to update the ledger balance.

FIGURE 7.29

To illustrate, we will complete a bank reconciliation with journal entries for HR Clothing for the month of October 2018. Before comparing the new items, it is always important to consider the outstanding items from the last period. We need to ensure these items have been cleared. The completed bank reconciliation from September is shown in Figure 7.30. There are three items in the bank column that are outstanding as of September 30, 2018: the deposit for $2,200 and checks #57 and #59. It is likely that these will clear the bank in October and must be compared to the October bank statement. If they appear on the bank statement, we will check the items on the September bank reconciliation and the October bank statement.

HR Clothing Company
Bank Reconciliation
September 30, 2018

Cash balance per bank statement	$4,930		Cash balance per books		$7,360
Add outstanding deposit	✓2,200		Add EFT deposit		250
Deduct outstanding checks			Deduct charges		
Check #57	✓350		EFT—Rent	1,300	
Check #59	✓480	830	Bank service charge	10	1,310
Adjusted bank balance		$6,300	Adjusted book balance		$6,300

FIGURE 7.30

The cash ledger account and the bank statement for October are shown in Figure 7.31.

GENERAL LEDGER

Account: Cash				GL No: 101	
Date	**Description**	**DR**	**CR**	**Balance**	
Oct 1	Opening Balance			6,300	DR
Oct 2	Check #62		✓ 140	6,160	DR
Oct 4	Deposit M. Smith	✓ 200		6,360	DR
Oct 7	Check #63		570	5,790	DR
Oct 15	Check #64		820	4,970	DR
Oct 17	Deposit	✓ 1,200		6,170	DR
Oct 21	Check #65		✓ 540	5,630	DR
Oct 25	Check #66		320	5,310	DR
Oct 29	Check #67		410	4,900	DR
Oct 31	Deposit	900		5,800	DR

Bank Statement			October 1–October 31, 2018	
Date	**Description**	**Withdrawal**	**Deposit**	**Balance**
Oct 1	Opening Balance			4,930
Oct 1	EFT Rent	1,300		3,630
Oct 2	Deposit		✓ 2,200	5,830
Oct 4	Check #57	✓ 350		5,480
Oct 5	Deposit		✓ 200	5,680
Oct 6	NSF Check ⓐ	200		5,480
Oct 6	NSF Fee	15		5,465

Oct 8	Check #62	✓ 140		5,325
Oct 10	Check #59	✓ 480		4,845
Oct 15	EFT Deposit **b**		300	5,145
Oct 18	Deposit	✓ 1,200		6,345
Oct 23	Check #63 **c**	750		5,595
Oct 25	Check #65	✓ 540		5,055
Oct 31	Service Charge	10		5,045

a The NSF Check was from a customer as payment of her account.

b The EFT deposit was a customer paying his account.

c Check #63 was for advertising and was cashed for the correct amount by the bank.

FIGURE 7.31

The October bank statement is compared to the October general ledger and the September bank reconciliation. The green check marks, in Figures 7.30 and 7.31, indicate that the item on the October bank statement matches an item from the ledger or September's bank reconciliation. As shown in Figure 7.32, only the items on the October bank statement without a check mark need to be included on the bank reconciliation for October.

HR Clothing Company Bank Reconciliation October 31, 2018					
Cash balance per bank statement		$5,045	Cash balance per books		$5,800
Add outstanding deposit		900	Add EFT deposit		300
Deduct outstanding checks			Deduct charges		
Check #64	820		EFT—Rent	1,300	
Check #66	320		NSF Check	200	
Check #67	410	1,550	Bank charges for NSF Check	15	
			Bank service charge	10	
			Error on Check #63	180	1,705
Adjusted bank balance		$4,395	Adjusted book balance		$4,395

FIGURE 7.32

Once the bank is reconciled to the ledger, all items that increase or decrease the ledger balance must be recorded in the journal. The journal entries are shown in Figure 7.33.

JOURNAL			
Date	**Account Title and Explanation**	**Debit**	**Credit**
Oct 31	Cash	300	
	Accounts Receivable		300
	Collection from customer		
Oct 31	Rent Expense	1,300	
	Cash		1,300
	Payment for rent		
Oct 31	Accounts Receivable	200	
	Cash		200
	NSF check from customer		
Oct 31	Bank Charges Expense	15	
	Cash		15
	Record NSF fee		
Oct 31	Bank Charges Expense	10	
	Cash		10
	Record bank service charge		
Oct 31	Advertising Expense	180	
	Cash		180
	Correct error on check		

FIGURE 7.33

An alternative way to record the journal entries is to make compound journal entries to combine similar transactions. All transactions that credit cash can be combined into a single transaction. Each debited account is still listed, but there is a single credit to cash for $1,705.

Pause & Reflect

Exercise 7-2

Prescott Marketing received its bank statement for the month of September 2018. The accountant compared the bank statement to the general ledger cash account and made a list of the items that remained unchecked after the comparison. The accountant also included the ending balances of both the bank statement and the cash ledger account.

1. Balance of cash at September 30, 2018 is $9,260

2. Balance of the bank account at September 30, 2018 is $8,570

3. Deposit of $2,480 is unrecorded in the bank statement

4. Checks #287 for $650 and #291 for $870 do not appear on the bank statement

5. The bank showed an EFT deposit from a customer for $1,560

6. There was an NSF check from a customer for $1,240

7. Total service charges were $50

Prepare the bank reconciliation for the month of September 2018.

See Appendix I for solutions.

Petty Cash

At times, a business may require small amounts of cash to pay for petty (small) expenses, such as parking, postage stamps and courier fees. Instead of issuing a check each time, the business will set up a petty cash fund to pay for these small amounts in cash.

Petty cash is usually operated on what is known as an *imprest system.* An imprest system for petty cash ensures that spending is limited to the amount available in the petty cash fund. For example, if a petty cash fund starts with $100, that is the maximum amount that can be spent. When the amount spent approaches the $100 limit, the petty cash fund is replenished up to $100. In any case, the petty cash fund should always be replenished at the end of the accounting year so that expenses paid from petty cash are recorded in the year in which they were incurred.

Setting Up a Petty Cash Fund

1. **Designate one individual as the petty cash custodian.** There are many ways in which petty cash can be mishandled. Having one person responsible for the fund increases transparency and accountability. The petty cash custodian ensures that petty cash is properly safeguarded and disbursed for legitimate reasons and that an accurate record is maintained for all activities related to the fund.

2. **Establish the amount of the fund.** The petty cash custodian needs to determine the amount of the fund as well as the frequency with which it is replenished.

3. **Record the initial petty cash transaction.** The establishment of a petty cash fund requires one initial transaction. The journal entry is shown in Figure 7.34.

JOURNAL			
Date	Account Title and Explanation	Debit	Credit
Dec 10	Petty Cash	100	
	Cash		100
	To set up the petty cash fund		

CURRENT ASSETS

CASH
– $100 CR

PETTY CASH
+ $100 DR

FIGURE 7.34

4. **Require users of petty cash to provide receipts.** Any employee who requires petty cash must provide a receipt from the supplier indicating the amount of money spent and the reason for the purchase. The petty cash custodian will require the person to sign the receipt, indicating that the person has been reimbursed. Figure 7.35 shows a petty cash receipt.

RECEIVED IN PETTY CASH

Date: *December 13, 2018*

Description	Amount
Office supplies	7 00
TOTAL	7 00

Received By

Rebecca McGillivray
Approved By

FIGURE 7.35

5. **Provide a summary of petty cash.** At the end of the period, which in this example is one week, the petty cash custodian prepares a summary that lists the details of the fund before it is reimbursed. The summary sheet is shown in Figure 7.36.

Petty Cash Summary Sheet

Period: Dec 10–Dec 16

Opening Balance		**$100.00**
Parking		
Dec 10	$10.00	
Dec 12	6.00	
Dec 14	5.00	$21.00
Delivery		
Dec 10	$18.00	
Dec 11	6.00	$24.00
Office Supplies		
Dec 13	$7.00	
Dec 16	13.00	$20.00
Gasoline		
Dec 14	$18.00	$18.00
Total Disbursements		**$83.00**
Cash over and short	$2.00	
Total to be reimbursed to Petty Cash		**$85.00**

Opening balance less disbursements

FIGURE 7.36

The petty cash summary should include a list of all the items, in groups, paid with the petty cash fund. Both subtotals and a grand total should be calculated. In this example the grand total comes to $83. The amount of cash remaining in the petty cash box should be equal to the opening balance minus the total spent, which in this case is $17 ($100 − $83).

6. **Reconcile any overage or shortage.** The petty cash custodian must take care of any amounts over or short in the petty cash box. This is done by making additions or subtractions to the account called Cash Over and Short. In our current example, there was only $15 in the petty cash box at the end of the week, meaning there was a $2 shortage. Such discrepancies can result from a miscount of coins or an overpayment during the period. The total disbursements recorded, along with any cash over or short, constitute the total amount to be reimbursed to petty cash to restore it to its original value of $100. In this case, the amount is $85.

7. **Present a summary slip to a supervisor.** The petty cash custodian presents the supervisor with a summary slip and all supporting vouchers. After reviewing these documents, the supervisor provides the petty cash custodian with a check to reimburse the petty cash fund. The receipts are stamped "paid" so that they cannot be reused.

8. **Reimburse the petty cash fund.** The petty cash custodian cashes the check (in this example the check is for $85) and replenishes the fund to its original amount ($100).

Posting Petty Cash to the General Ledger

We have examined the steps that an organization must take when establishing a petty cash fund. Now look at how this process affects the organization's general ledger.

We have already described the transaction that occurs when the petty cash fund is initially established. Cash is credited and petty cash is debited for the same amounts, which was $100 as shown in Figure 7.34. Until now, all the activity has been in the petty cash box itself, with no transactions affecting the ledger.

> **WORTH REPEATING**
>
> Transferring assets from one account (e.g. cash) to another account (e.g. petty cash) has no impact on owner's equity.

When it is time to replenish the fund, we need to increase the amount of petty cash to $100 and allocate the amounts used to the appropriate expense accounts.

The journal entry is recorded with a debit to various expenses (parking, delivery, office supplies, gasoline, cash over and short), and a credit to cash in the amount of $85. Figure 7.37 shows this transaction. On the Accounting Map, the expenses are listed under other expenses on the income statement.

JOURNAL			
Date	**Account Title and Explanation**	**Debit**	**Credit**
Dec 17	Parking Expense	21	
	Delivery Expense	24	
	Office Supplies Expense	20	
	Gasoline Expense	18	
	Cash Over and Short	2	
	Cash		85
	Replenish the petty cash fund		

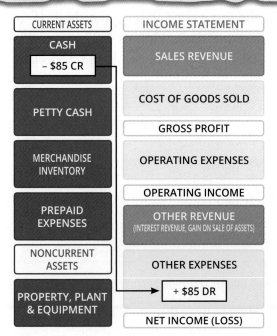

FIGURE 7.37

The cash over and short account behaves like an expense account when there is a shortage. It will be debited in the journal entry. If there is an overage, the cash over and short account behaves like a revenue account. It will be credited in the journal entry.

No change is made to the amount of the petty cash ledger account when the reimbursement check is issued, and the reimbursed cash is placed in the petty cash box. You may think that the transaction should be recorded by debiting expenses and crediting petty cash, followed by a debit to petty cash and a credit to cash. However, in practice, when the bookkeeper records the check there is no change to the petty cash account.

It is important to note that the *only* time the petty cash account in the ledger is debited or credited is when the account is established or when the amount in the petty cash fund is increased or decreased.

Assume that on December 31, the manager decided to increase the petty cash fund to $150. The journal entry to record the $50 increase is shown in Figure 7.38.

JOURNAL			
Date	Account Title and Explanation	Debit	Credit
Dec 31	Petty Cash	50	
	Cash		50
	Increase the petty cash fund		

FIGURE 7.38

When the petty cash fund is increased, the petty cash account should be debited (increased) and the cash account should be credited (decreased).

Petty cash can also increase at the same time it is replenished. If on December 17 petty cash was replenished and increased at the same time, Figures 7.37 and 7.38 would be combined, meaning cash would be credited by a total of $135. The combined transaction is shown in Figure 7.39.

JOURNAL			
Date	Account Title and Explanation	Debit	Credit
Dec 17	Parking Expense	21	
	Delivery Expense	24	
	Office Supplies Expense	20	
	Gasoline Expense	18	
	Cash Over and Short	2	
	Petty Cash	50	
	Cash		135
	Replenish and increase petty cash		

FIGURE 7.39

A spreadsheet may be maintained listing the various expenses so that each month the general ledger can be updated with the correct allocation of expenses. An example is shown in Figure 7.40.

Description	Receipt #	Amount	Office	Travel	Meals	Marketing
HR Clothing **Petty Cash Expenses Paid** **July 2018**						
Photo Developing	1	$8.07				$8.07
Taxis	2	65.00		$65.00		
Meals	3	33.00			$33.00	
Batteries	4	11.00				11.00
Photocopying—brochures	5	23.32				23.32
Photocopying—general	6	3.05	$3.05			
Parking	7	1.87		1.87		
Parking	8	10.26		10.26		
Parking	9	3.00		3.00		
Parking	10	4.00		4.00		
Parking	11	6.50		6.50		
Parking	12	7.00		7.00		
Parking	13	6.00		6.00		
Parking	14	3.94		3.94		
Parking	15	1.00		1.00		
Gas	16	10.00		10.00		
Meals	17	8.10			8.10	
Travel	18	49.01		49.01		
TOTALS		**$254.12**	**$3.05**	**$167.58**	**$41.10**	**$42.39**

Cash will be credited with this amount. (assuming no cash over/short).

= $254.12
Each of these amounts will be debited to the respective GL expense accounts.

FIGURE 7.40

Pause & Reflect

Exercise 7-3

Empire Architects created a petty cash fund on November 1, 2018 with $500. By November 15, there was only $56 left in the petty cash box. The petty cash custodian had the following receipts.

1. Postage, $58

2. Delivery expense, $94

3. Entertainment expense, $242

4. Maintenance, $46

Prepare the journal entry to establish the petty cash fund on November 1 and to replenish the petty cash fund on November 15.

JOURNAL			
Date	Account Title and Explanation	Debit	Credit

See Appendix I for solutions.

Petty Cash Controls

Using petty cash funds can be a convenient way to purchase small items. However, the funds also provide opportunities for abuse. It is therefore important to regulate the use of the petty cash fund to ensure that it is not mishandled. Here are some steps to ensure that petty cash is used appropriately.

1. **Establish guidelines.** The first step in ensuring that petty cash is used properly is to draw up a list of items that can be purchased with petty cash. Determine what purchases may be made with purchase orders, and then make a list of other types of regular purchases. The fund should be reserved strictly for small ("petty") expenses and not for items such as noncurrent assets or inventory, or for paying accounts payable and independent contractors.

2. **Maintain documentation.** It is difficult to keep accurate records unless you have a uniform documentation system. Establish an easy-to-use system and follow it consistently. The easiest way to do this is by keeping track of all receipts, whether they are register receipts or written invoices. Each receipt should have the date of purchase, the name of the vendor, a list of the items or services purchased, the price of each item and the total cost. Accurate recordkeeping also requires the following measures.

   - the person who made the purchase signs the receipt

   - all receipts are filed correctly so they can be checked for discrepancies

3. **Review the rules with employees.** If the regulations are not well known, abuse of the petty cash fund becomes easier. Keep everyone up-to-date and do not allow exceptions to the rules.

4. **One person should be responsible for petty cash—the petty cash custodian.** The appointment of one person to administer and be exclusively responsible for the fund limits the opportunities for mismanagement.

5. **Periodically count the petty cash fund.** Have one person independent from the petty cash custodian, such as a manager, count the fund with the custodian present. This discourages misuse of the funds and can detect shortages early.

This chapter discusses cash equivalents and petty cash as separate functions within a business. At this point, we can look at the impact of these two items and how they affect the balance sheet and its presentation. Figure 7.41 shows a partial balance sheet of Donatello's restaurant.

Donatello's Restaurant Balance Sheet As at December 31, 2018	
Assets	
Current Assets	
Cash and Cash Equivalents	
Bank Account—Checking	$13,220
Bank Account—Savings	4,700
Petty Cash Fund	300
Cash Equivalents	6,500
Total Cash and Cash Equivalents	24,720

FIGURE 7.41

Figure 7.41 shows the presentation of cash items shown in order of liquidity, with actual cash items listed before cash equivalents. Specifically, petty cash and cash equivalents are shown as separate line items.

In Summary

LO 1 Describe and apply internal controls for a business

▶ Controls are procedures and methods used to protect assets, monitor cash payments, ensure transactions are authorized and generally make sure the accounting records are accurate.

▶ Generally, internal controls can be classified as preventive (i.e. to stop an incident before it happens), or detective (i.e. to discover an incident after it happens).

LO 2 Apply cash controls

▶ Cash must be recorded immediately when it is received so it can be tracked from receipt to deposit in the business bank account.

▶ Cash should be stored in a secure place until it can be deposited to the business bank account.

▶ Regular bank deposits should be made to ensure a minimal amount of cash is kept on site.

▶ All payments must have an authorization. This includes checks as well as debit and credit cards.

▶ Cash payments should take advantage of payment discounts if they are offered.

▶ An account to track the cash over and short should be used. Any small discrepancies between expected cash and actual cash is recorded in this account.

LO 3 Prepare a bank reconciliation and related journal entries

▶ A bank reconciliation compares the bank statement to the cash ledger account to ensure no errors have been made.

▶ Amounts added or deducted by the bank that do not appear in the ledger must be added or deducted from the cash ledger balance. These amounts must also be recorded in the journal to update the cash ledger account.

▶ Amounts added or deducted by the business that do not appear in the bank statement must be added or deducted from the bank balance.

LO 4 Prepare a petty cash fund and record related journal entries

▶ A petty cash fund is used to pay for small, incidental expenses. A check is cashed and the money is kept by a petty cashier in a secure location.

▶ As cash is spent, receipts are placed in the petty cash box to explain why the cash was spent.

▶ A comparison of remaining cash and the total receipts may indicate a cash overage or shortage. The receipts and any over or short is recorded in a journal entry.

AMEENGAGE™ *Access **ameengage.com** for integrated resources including tutorials, practice exercises, the digital textbook and more.*

Review Exercise 7-1

JP has been running his dry cleaning business, called Clean 4U, since he purchased it last year. It is a small business with eight employees. He has run into some difficulty with his business. His cash flow has declined every month, but he is as busy as last year.

Every single order has its own multiple-part receipt: the office gets a copy, the cash drawer gets a copy, and customers get a copy when they pay. Customers get a ticket stub as part of the receipt based on their first and last names only. The garments get tagged and matched to the receipt to get processed and returned with the receipt.

The company has only a cash drawer to accept cash payments. The drawer does not lock, and the cash cannot be locked away when the business is closed. Cash is deposited when large quantities of cash are on hand. The company uses a manual point-of-sale terminal to accept debit and credit payments and the counter clerk must enter the dollar amount before the customer can complete the transaction.

Recently, JP discovered a small pile of cash-drawer receipts in the garbage while he was cleaning the storefront. He knows that many of the customers are regulars and always pay cash. JP discovers that the counter clerk has been stealing cash when customers pay and throwing out the cash-drawer receipts. He has been committing fraud.

Required

a) What recommendations should be made with respect to cash controls for a company this size?

_____

_____

_____

_____

_____

_____

_____

_____

_____

_____

b) What is the overall goal for cash controls?

_____

_____

_____

_____

_____

c) What recommendations should be made for Clean 4U in general?

_____

_____

_____

_____

_____

_____

_____

_____

_____

_____

_____

_____

_____

_____

_____

_____

_____

See Appendix I for solutions.

Review Exercise 7-2

The following is the general ledger and bank statement for Martin Furniture.

GENERAL LEDGER

Account: Cash				GL No:	101
Date	**Description**	**DR**	**CR**	**Balance**	
Jun 1	Opening Balance			3,100.50	DR
Jun 6	Check #541		900.50	2,200.00	DR
Jun 9	Reo's Interiors Inc.	1,925.00		4,125.00	DR
Jun 10	Check #543		1,600.00	2,525.00	DR
Jun 16	Check #542		400.00	2,125.00	DR
Jun 16	Check #256	2,000.00		4,125.00	DR
Jun 19	Check #544		110.00	4,015.00	DR
Jun 19	Check #545		500.00	3,515.00	DR
Jun 28	Eric Draven Enterprises	1,300.00		4,815.00	DR
Jun 30	Closing Balance			4,815.00	DR

Reserve Bank 146 Lineage Avenue, Springfield Martin Furniture 234 Lakeview Drive Springfield, Oregon				
Date	**Explanation**	**Withdrawal**	**Deposit**	**Balance**
Jun 1	Balance Forward			3,100.50
Jun 8	Check #541	900.50		2,200.00
Jun 9	Deposit		1,925.00	4,125.00
Jun 10	Check #543	1,600.00		2,525.00
Jun 16	Deposit		2,000.00	4,525.00
Jun 16	Check #542	400.00		4,125.00
Jun 18	NSF Check #256	2,000.00		2,125.00
Jun 18	NSF Charge	6.00		2,119.00
Jun 21	Check #544	110.00		2,009.00
Jun 27	Interest on Bank Account		5.00	2,014.00
Jun 29	Service Charge	14.00		2,000.00
Jun 30	Ending Balance			2,000.00

Required

a) Reconcile the ledger and bank statement.

Martin Furniture **Bank Reconciliation** **June 30, 2018**					

b) Record the relevant transactions in the general journal.

JOURNAL			
Date	**Account Title and Explanation**	**Debit**	**Credit**

See Appendix I for solutions.

Review Exercise 7-3

On April 1, 2018, Clayton Company established a petty cash fund of $200.

During the month, the custodian placed the following receipts in the petty cash box.

Apr 6   Paid $40 for postage
Apr 8   Paid $20 to FedEx for delivery of a package
Apr 10   Paid $25 for travel expenses of employees on company business
Apr 14   Paid $8 for coffee and donuts for a client meeting
Apr 15   Paid $7 for paper for the photocopier

The custodian counted the fund on April 16 and found $95 in the petty cash box.

Required

a) Prepare the journal entry to record the establishment of the fund.

JOURNAL			
Date	Account Title and Explanation	Debit	Credit

b) Prepare the journal entry to record the reimbursement of the fund on April 16.

JOURNAL			
Date	Account Title and Explanation	Debit	Credit

See Appendix I for solutions.

Notes

Chapter 8
Accounting For Receivables

Learning Objectives

 *Access **ameengage.com** for integrated resources including tutorials, practice exercises, the digital textbook and more.*

MAKING IT REAL TO YOU

If cash is the king of business, then sales are the queen. To reflect this, the account right after sales is Accounts Receivable. Receivables represent what will be received in payment from customers. Receivables occur regularly in business. The sale takes place at an earlier date, and then the payment takes place at a later date. While we hope and expect all customers to pay their invoice amount and clear their receivable balance, the truth is that not all customers will pay what they owe. We will use a new account called Allowance for Doubtful Accounts to estimate the amounts that will go unpaid. Tracking and managing product sales and receivables is critical to the cash flow and success of the business. We need those customer payments to reinvest in the business or contribute to profits. Let's get tracking.

Accounts Receivable: An Introduction

You have been introduced to many common assets and liabilities on the balance sheet. You know their definitions and how to record them as debits and credits. However, there are more complex accounts and processes that companies use to account for assets and liabilities. These topics will be covered in depth as we explore the balance sheet in more detail.

Accounts Receivable

On a company's balance sheet, presented below cash, is a category of current assets known as receivables, which are amounts due from other businesses, customers or financial institutions. As with other assets on the balance sheet, receivables are listed in order of liquidity, from most to least liquid. Common types of receivables are notes receivable, interest receivable, taxes receivable and accounts receivable. This chapter focuses on one of the largest of these amounts: accounts receivable.

Accounts receivable are amounts owing from customers for credit sales; that is, sales billed on account for goods and services. You may recall that when a sale is made on account, it is recorded as a debit to accounts receivable and a credit to sales. The debit to accounts receivable increases the asset of the company, while the credit to sales increases equity. When the customer pays the amount owed to the company, the company records the transaction as a debit to cash and a credit to accounts receivable. The remaining amount that has not been received from customers at the end of an accounting period is reported as accounts receivable on the balance sheet. Accounts receivable amounts are normally due to be paid within 30 or 60 days; hence, they are current assets.

When customers purchase a product or service from a company, they are issued an invoice that shows the **payment terms**, which are the conditions by which the vendor expects to be paid by the customer. Also known as credit terms, they specify the payment due date and any other conditions on that payment, such as the discount rate for early payment. For example, the term 2/10, n/30 means that the customer will get a 2% discount if payment is received within 10 days; otherwise, the full amount is due within 30 days. Payment terms ensure that the customer pays the invoice in a reasonable amount of time. They are an example of an internal control that a company uses to manage its assets.

Figure 8.1 highlights a portion of the current assets section of the classified balance sheet. Starting with cash and cash equivalents, as we move down the accounts, there is a decrease in liquidity. Accounts receivable is less liquid than cash because it takes some time for accounts receivable to be converted into cash through collection from customers. In addition, there is some risk that customers will not pay the amount they owe.

FIGURE 8.1

Nevertheless, accounts receivable is an integral part of doing business in a modern economy. Sales may be increased by allowing customers to pay at a later date since some customers may be unable to pay for their purchases immediately. Many businesses have accounts receivable on their books, so it is important to know how to record and manage them. Compared to cash and cash equivalents, accounts receivable requires more hands-on administration, because it involves debt collection and management of debtor information.

IN THE REAL WORLD

 One of the most prominent business trends of the past decade has been outsourcing, whereby one company hires another company to take over a certain business function, whether it is call center duties or specialized manufacturing capabilities.

The accounts receivable department has not escaped this outsourcing trend. Accounts receivable may represent only a small percentage of a company's total assets; yet the administrative burdens associated with this asset can be overwhelming, and a company's resources in dealing with it are often inadequate.

To handle this challenge, companies have the option of hiring firms that specialize in taking over the accounts receivable function. Such specialists possess the technical hardware, expertise and experience to maximize this important asset.

Outsourcing accounts receivable offers certain advantages, especially for companies that have a poor history of managing this asset. Outsourcing can

- improve a company's profitability by having the asset managed and controlled more efficiently;

- make a company's accounts receivable function more consistent, thereby making customers more satisfied;

- ensure financial reporting is more accurate; and

- allow a company to focus on its core business, while leaving some of the administrative duties to specialists.

Accounts receivable is an important asset for most companies. Ensuring they are collected is necessary for business success, whether the company itself handles this, or it is outsourced to a third party.

Administration of accounts receivable requires some basic information to be collected and managed. The information can include a debtor's or customer's company name, full address, contact information, what the company bought, the cost of the item(s) bought, delivery and payment or credit terms.

Each business organization needs to spend a significant amount of time on the day-to-day administration of accounts receivable. Even a business with a relatively small number of customers has many transactions to record and manage on a daily basis. To reduce the amount of time spent on administering accounts receivable, many companies opt for the services of third-party credit card companies, as will be discussed next.

Credit Card Sales

Many businesses offer customers the choice to pay for goods and services using credit cards. Major credit cards such as VISA, MasterCard, and American Express are known as third-party credit cards, because they accept customer payments on behalf of other businesses in return for a service fee. When a customer pays for a purchase using a third-party credit card, the sale is recorded as a cash sale by the vendor. The actual funds from the credit card sale are automatically and electronically deposited into the vendor company's bank account by the third party, so the sale is not a receivable for the vendor. The credit card company bills the customer directly, shifting the risk of uncollectible debt to that credit card issuer. For the vendor, this a good method of internal control because it reduces the overall risk to its cash flow.

Many large retailers, such as Best Buy, Target, IKEA and some department stores, offer their own credit cards. These retailer-specific or store-issued credit cards are for use exclusively at that card issuer's physical and online stores. That is, a Target credit card can only be used at Target and not at any other retailer. However, these cards usually offer benefits, such as rewards points, product discounts and advance sales to cardholders. With store-issued credit cards, the retailer is responsible for approving and issuing credit as well as for collecting the customers' balances. Interest is charged to the customer on any unpaid balance after the payment due date. Store-issued credit cards carry a risk of uncollectible debt for the issuer, but by issuing cards that are specific to its store, the company hopes to promote customer loyalty.

Accounting for Bad Debt

There is an upside and a downside to selling goods and services to customers on credit. The upside is that selling on credit encourages people to buy. For the most part, people pay their bills when they are due. The downside is that there are inevitably customers who delay paying their bills. There are also customers who never pay their bills, resulting in an uncollectible account known as **bad debt**.

Bad debt is considered an operating expense, and must be recorded in a way that is consistent with GAAP principles. Because GAAP's expense recognition principle requires recording expenses during the same period in which the related revenue is generated, bad debt expense must be recorded during the same period in which credit sales are generated. Accurately determining the amount of bad debt in the same period as credit sales can be challenging, because it is sometimes difficult to know if a customer is just late with the payment or is unable to pay. Assumptions and estimates must be made in this regard because the records must reflect the company's current financial position as accurately as possible. GAAP provides two accounting methods for doubtful accounts and bad debt: (1) the allowance method, and (2) the direct write off method. The direct method can only be allowed in very specific circumstances, which is discussed later in this section.

The Allowance Method

To record bad debt in a way that satisfies expense recognition, accountants have created an account called **allowance for doubtful accounts (AFDA)**. It is located directly beneath accounts receivable on the balance sheet and is a contra account. Recall that a contra account is linked directly to another account and is used to decrease the account balance. In this case, the AFDA contra account is linked directly to accounts receivable. The AFDA account has a normal credit balance, unlike accounts receivable, which has a normal debit balance. The use of the AFDA account in recording bad debt is referred to as the allowance method of accounting for bad debt.

The **allowance method** estimates an amount that will be bad debt and records it in the books. Recording bad debt decreases the equity of the company by recognizing an expense on the income statement, and decreases assets by using the AFDA account. Bad debt is recorded in the same period in which revenue is generated in order to adhere to expense recognition.

For example, assume that at the end of 2018, Columbo Company has an outstanding accounts receivable balance of $100,000. After analyzing the existing data and the current economy, it is determined that $5,000 of the accounts receivable may not be collectable. However, since there is still a chance that Columbo will collect, the accounts are not removed from the accounts receivable list. Note that the amount estimated to be uncollectable is not based on one specific customer but is an overall estimate for the entire accounts receivable.

The accounts receivable account of $100,000 does not change. It remains as a debit on the balance sheet. Instead, the AFDA contra account is credited with $5,000, resulting in a net realizable value of $95,000. The **net realizable value** of accounts receivable is the amount of cash that the accounts receivable are likely to turn into; in other words, the accounts receivable balance net of the AFDA. For the debit side of this transaction, bad debt expense is increased by $5,000 and this amount is reported as an expense for the period on the income statement. The journal entry at the end of 2018 for this transaction is shown in Figure 8.2.

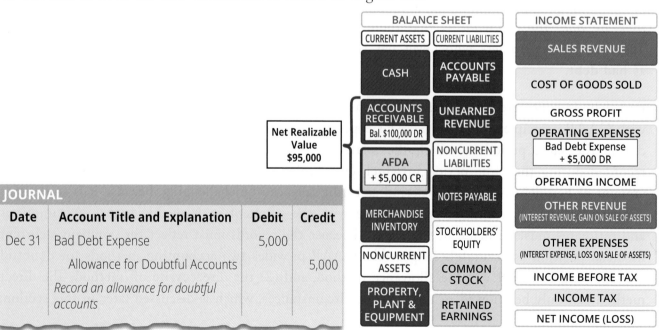

FIGURE 8.2

The net realizable value of accounts receivable is $95,000 and is presented on the balance sheet. The partial balance sheet for Columbo Company is shown in Figure 8.3.

Columbo Company Balance Sheet (partial) As at December 31, 2018		
Current Assets		
Cash		$12,500
Accounts Receivable	$100,000	
Allowance for Doubtful Accounts	(5,000)	
Net Accounts Receivable		95,000
Merchandise Inventory		210,000
Prepaid Insurance		12,000
Total Current Assets		329,500

FIGURE 8.3

The AFDA contra account allows for the possibility that some of the accounts receivable generated in the current period will not be collected. The debit to bad debt expense supports expense recognition since this amount is deducted as an expense in the period when the sale was recorded. Note that the company's equity decreases as a result of recognizing the bad debt expense.

A company must have a good reason to believe that some amounts will not be paid in order to justify the adjustments made to the assets and expenses. There should be some documentation to justify the amount of bad debt estimated. Such measures are warranted because estimates such as AFDA are easy targets for manipulation by management.

After companies anticipate bad debt by setting up the AFDA contra account, several scenarios can exist.

1. A customer is unable or unwilling to pay the debt and the amount is considered uncollectible.
2. After an account is written off as uncollectible, the customer informs the company that he or she will pay the amount.
3. The customer is unable to pay the debt when it is due, but will be able to pay it in the future.

We will examine each scenario as a continuation of the estimation of bad debt from Figure 8.3.

Scenario 1: On February 16, 2019, Jacob Soloman, who owes $250, informs the company that he is unable to pay his account.

The amount is now considered uncollectible and needs to be written off.

Since the allowance method was used, the bad debt expense was previously entered to match prior period revenue, and the AFDA account was established. Now, the AFDA account is debited and the accounts receivable account is credited to remove the amount from the company's records. The entry shown in Figure 8.4 has no impact on the company's equity, since the amount was already accounted for by the original debit to bad debt expense in 2018.

Usually, a company attempts to collect outstanding payments from a customer for many months. If it is unsuccessful, the company writes off that account. The journal entry is shown in Figure 8.4.

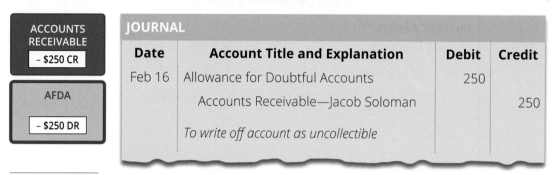

	ACCOUNTS RECEIVABLE		AFDA
	– $250 CR		– $250 DR

JOURNAL

Date	Account Title and Explanation	Debit	Credit
Feb 16	Allowance for Doubtful Accounts	250	
	Accounts Receivable—Jacob Soloman		250
	To write off account as uncollectible		

FIGURE 8.4

Scenario 2: Jacob Soloman is now able to pay his account (which was previously written off as uncollectible). He pays the amount on June 25, 2019.

Two journal entries must be made in this scenario. The first journal entry is to reinstate the customer's account balance (by reversing the entry in Figure 8.4). The second journal entry records the amount being paid. These journal entries are shown in Figures 8.5 and 8.6, respectively.

1. Reinstate the customer's account balance.

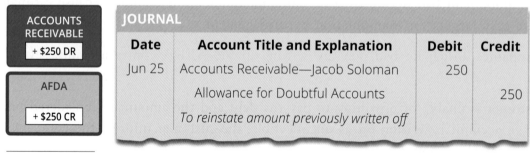

	ACCOUNTS RECEIVABLE		AFDA
	+ $250 DR		+ $250 CR

JOURNAL

Date	Account Title and Explanation	Debit	Credit
Jun 25	Accounts Receivable—Jacob Soloman	250	
	Allowance for Doubtful Accounts		250
	To reinstate amount previously written off		

FIGURE 8.5

2. Record receipt of payment on account.

	CASH		ACCOUNTS RECEIVABLE
	+ $250 DR		– $250 CR

JOURNAL

Date	Account Title and Explanation	Debit	Credit
Jun 25	Cash	250	
	Accounts Receivable—Jacob Soloman		250
	To record receipt of payment from customer		

FIGURE 8.6

Scenario 3: Jacob Soloman is unable to pay the debt by the due date, but will be able to pay in the future.

Even customers with a good credit record sometimes take time to settle their bills. After many months of attempting to collect from a customer, a company faces the decision of writing off the account as uncollectable. If the amount is written off, the transaction in scenario 1 is made. If the customer finally does pay, the two transactions in scenario 2 are made.

However, if it is relatively certain that the customer will pay eventually, the company can decide to take no action, except to periodically issue a reminder to the customer. The original amount in accounts receivable remains on the books and is credited when the account is finally paid. Another alternative is to convert the accounts receivable into a notes receivable, which allows the customer additional time to pay with interest added.

Pause & Reflect

Exercise 8-1

Using the allowance method, Sybil Company estimated $6,500 in bad debt for the year ending December 31, 2018. On March 5, 2019, its customer, Basil's Hotel, declared bankruptcy. Basil's Hotel owed $2,100, which was written off.

Prepare the journal entries for these two events. Assume that before any adjusting entries were made on December 31, 2018, AFDA has a zero balance.

JOURNAL			
Date	Account Title and Explanation	Debit	Credit

See Appendix I for solutions.

The Direct Method

When a sale is made on account, it is recorded as a debit to accounts receivable and a credit to sales revenue. The debit to accounts receivable increases the assets of the company, while the credit to sales increases equity and is recorded as sales revenue.

However, consider this example. A customer informs you on March 3 that her company, Sweet Treats, has filed for bankruptcy and is unable to pay its outstanding account balance of $5,000.

When it is determined that the bill will not be paid, the direct method requires a journal entry to increase (debit) bad debt expense and decrease (credit) accounts receivable. Note that the AFDA account is never used when the direct method is used, thus it never shows up in the journal entries. Figure 8.7 shows the required journal entry for this transaction.

JOURNAL			
Date	**Account Title and Explanation**	**Debit**	**Credit**
Mar 3	Bad Debt Expense	5,000	
	Accounts Receivable—Sweet Treats		5,000
	Direct write off of bad debt from accounts receivable		

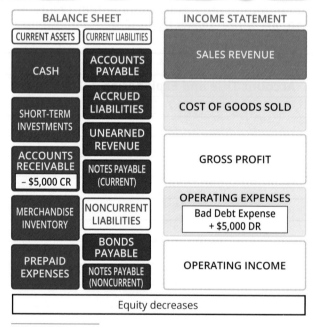

FIGURE 8.7

One drawback of using the direct method to write off bad debt is that it does not always satisfy expense recognition. Recall that expense recognition states that expenses must be recorded during the same period in which the related revenue is generated.

The write off should be made in the same accounting period in which the sale was recorded in order to properly recognize the expense; however, it is more likely to be made in a later period, which violates expense recognition. The write off under the direct method is usually made in later periods because it takes time to determine whether or not a customer will pay. For businesses that experience very few bad debts or if the dollar amount involved is considered immaterial to the business, the direct method may be used. In the above example, assume that the year-end balance of accounts receivable was $50 million and credit sales for the year were $650 million. The company experiences very few write offs and management considers $5,000 immaterial. In this case, using the direct method is acceptable.

The second drawback to using this method arises if the customer is able to repay the account *after* the account has been written off. For example, suppose the owner of Sweet Treats is able to pay her account of $5,000 on August 7, after the account has already been written off. Figure 8.8 shows the journal entries that are recorded if this occurs.

JOURNAL			
Date	**Account Title and Explanation**	**Debit**	**Credit**
Aug 7	Accounts Receivable—Sweet Treats	5,000	
	Bad Debt Expense		5,000
	To reinstate the customer's account		
Aug 7	Cash	5,000	
	Accounts Receivable—Sweet Treats		5,000
	To record receipt of payment on account		

FIGURE 8.8

The amount needs to be reinstated into the customer's account. This requires a journal entry to increase (debit) accounts receivable and decrease (credit) bad debt expense, which causes a reduction in expenses and an overstatement of net income for the current period. Unless the write off and the subsequent reinstatement occur in the same period, the expense recognition is violated.

After the amount is reinstated, a second journal entry is required to record the receipt of the payment from the customer.

Approaches to Estimate Bad Debt

Managing accounts receivable includes assessing how much of it will end up as bad debt. This has an impact on how a company reflects its financial position on a timely basis, and also has implications for meeting GAAP requirements. Business should always have good reasons for their treatment of bad debt and must maintain the necessary documentation to justify it.

We will examine two approaches for estimating bad debt under the allowance method: the income statement approach and the balance sheet approach.

The Income Statement Approach

The **income statement approach**, or the percentage of sales method, uses credit sales from the income statement as a basis to predict future bad debt. More specifically, the current year's bad debt expense is calculated by multiplying credit sales by a percentage. Different companies use different percentages based on their own collection history and credit policy.

For example, if the collection history of a company suggests that 1% of credit sales will result in bad debt, that rate is used to estimate the portion of each period's sales that will not be collectible.

Total credit sales for Columbo Company in 2018 amounted to $1,000,000, of which $200,000 is currently owed by customers. On the basis of historical sales, 1% of credit sales is expected to be uncollectible, which is $10,000 ($1,000,000 × 1%). The bad debt expense for the period is shown in Figure 8.9.

JOURNAL			
Date	**Account Title and Explanation**	**Debit**	**Credit**
Dec 31	Bad Debt Expense	10,000	
	Allowance for Doubtful Accounts		10,000
	To record bad debt expense based on percentage of credit sales		

FIGURE 8.9

As previously discussed, the accounts receivable account, or controlling account, maintains the same debit amount, which in this case is $200,000. The $10,000 that is expected to be uncollectible is added to the current balance in the AFDA account. Assuming that the AFDA starts with a zero balance, it now has a $10,000 credit balance. This leaves a net realizable value of $190,000 in accounts receivable. The AFDA credit balance of $10,000 represents a decrease in the company's assets. The income statement includes a debit balance of $10,000 for bad debt expense. This is shown in Figure 8.10.

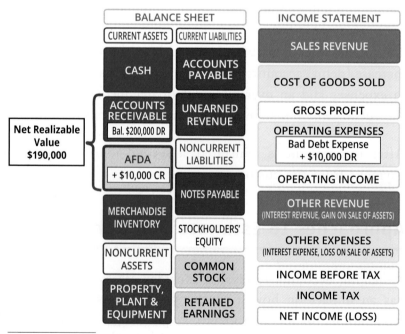

FIGURE 8.10

This approach is called the income statement approach because bad debt expense is calculated based on the credit sales figure from the income statement. Nevertheless, adjustments must be made to both the income statement and the balance sheet accounts when accounting for bad debt expense.

The Balance Sheet Approach

Under the **balance sheet approach**, a company can calculate allowance for bad debt using either the percentage of total accounts receivable method or the aging method. The **percentage of total accounts receivable method**, as the name implies, uses a percentage of receivables to estimate bad debt. The percentage is applied to the ending accounts receivable balance. For example, if the accounts receivable balance at the end of the period is $200,000, and the company estimates, based on its experience, that 4% of total accounts receivable will become uncollectible, the allowance for bad debt in this period is $8,000 ($200,000 × 0.04). Therefore, the AFDA account must be adjusted to have a credit balance of $8,000. We will show entries to adjust the AFDA balance later in this section.

Under the **aging method**, percentages are applied to groupings based on the age of outstanding accounts receivable amounts. We will use an example to illustrate this procedure.

The chart in Figure 8.11 contains three groups of customers and their outstanding balances on December 31, 2018.

1. Those who have not paid within 30 days
2. Those who have not paid for 31 to 60 days
3. Those who have not paid for more than 60 days

Aging Category	Bad Debt %* (probability of being uncollectible)	Balance of Accounts Receivable
30 days	2%	$80,000
31–60 days	3%	90,000
More than 60 days	5%	30,000
Total		$200,000

*Percentages are based on historical collectability.

FIGURE 8.11

A percentage is applied to each aging category. A 2% rate is applied to the first group, 3% to the second group and 5% to the third group. These percentages are the probability, or likelihood, that these amounts will be uncollectible. The longer that a customer takes to pay, the more likely the account will never be paid; that is why the highest rate is used for the third group.

The Balance of Accounts Receivable column of the chart in Figure 8.12 shows the amount that each group still owes the company. The percentages are applied to these amounts to calculate the expected total bad debt per customer group. These amounts are then added to give the total amount of estimated bad debt.

Aging Category	Bad Debt % (probability of being uncollectible)	Balance of Accounts Receivable	Estimated Bad Debt*
30 days	2%	$80,000	$1,600
31–60 days	3%	90,000	2,700
More than 60 days	5%	30,000	1,500
Total		$200,000	$5,800

*Balance of Accounts Receivable x Bad Debt %

FIGURE 8.12

In this example, $5,800 of the gross accounts receivable balance of $200,000 is estimated to be uncollectible. The $5,800 of estimated bad debt becomes the ending balance of AFDA for the period regardless of AFDA's existing balance or which method was used: the percentage of total accounts receivable method or the aging method. Under the balance sheet approach, the adjustments required could be grouped into three different scenarios based on AFDA having a credit, zero or debit balance. These scenarios are presented through the following examples.

Scenario 1: AFDA has a credit balance of $3,000.

If there is already a credit balance in the AFDA account, it needs to be subtracted from the $5,800 total to give us the bad debt expense for the period. A credit balance indicates the company has overestimated bad debt expense in the past. In this example, the AFDA account already has a credit balance of $3,000. Subtracting that from the calculated amount of $5,800 leaves us with an adjustment in the AFDA account of $2,800. In effect, this "tops up" the AFDA account, because we are adjusting it to reflect the total amount of bad debt expected. Figure 8.13 shows the journal entry for this transaction and Figure 8.14 shows its impact on the balance sheet and income statement.

Scenario 1

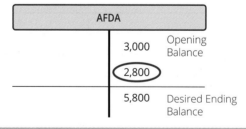

JOURNAL			
Date	**Account Title and Explanation**	**Debit**	**Credit**
Dec 31	Bad Debt Expense	2,800	
	Allowance for Doubtful Accounts		2,800
	To adjust the AFDA account to the correct balance		

FIGURE 8.13

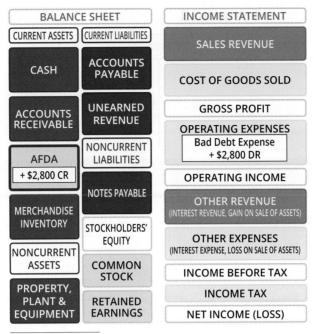

FIGURE 8.14

Scenario 2: AFDA has a balance of zero.

If AFDA has a zero balance, then the amount calculated as uncollectible becomes the amount of the adjustment. In our example, the amount of the credit to the AFDA account is $5,800. Figure 8.15 shows the journal entry for this transaction.

Scenario 2

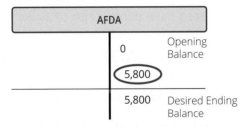

JOURNAL			
Date	**Account Title and Explanation**	**Debit**	**Credit**
Dec 31	Bad Debt Expense	5,800	
	Allowance for Doubtful Accounts		5,800
	To adjust the AFDA account to the correct balance		

FIGURE 8.15

Scenario 3: AFDA has a debit balance of $1,000.

If there is already a debit balance in the AFDA account, it is added to the $5,800 total to give us the bad debt expense for the period. A debit balance indicates the company has underestimated bad debt expense in the past. In this example, the AFDA account already has a debit balance of $1,000. Adding that to the calculated amount of $5,800 leaves us with an adjustment in the AFDA account of $6,800. Figure 8.16 shows the journal entry for this transaction.

Scenario 3

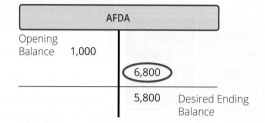

JOURNAL			
Date	**Account Title and Explanation**	**Debit**	**Credit**
Dec 31	Bad Debt Expense	6,800	
	Allowance for Doubtful Accounts		6,800
	To adjust the AFDA account to the correct balance		

FIGURE 8.16

Note that the net adjustment of accounts receivable adheres to conservatism, which requires assets to be valued at the lower amount of possible alternatives and, as a result, reflects a reduced net income for the period. This approach allows the business to make decisions based on figures that do not overstate assets, net income or the financial position of the company.

Rather than using only the income statement approach or only the balance sheet approach, a company can use a mix of procedures. The mix of procedures involves the initial use of the income statement approach and later adjusting AFDA using the balance sheet approach. Specifically, in the initial stage, bad debt is calculated as a percentage of sales while ignoring the existing AFDA balance. At the end of the period, accounts receivable is reviewed to check the appropriateness of the AFDA balance, and adjustments to the AFDA balance are made as required.

A CLOSER LOOK

For the income statement approach, the calculated amount is recorded as the bad debt expense regardless of what the existing balance of AFDA is. The calculated amount for the balance sheet approach is the ending balance of AFDA and not necessarily the amount of adjustment required.

Under the income statement approach, after the amount based on a percentage of credit sales is calculated, it is debited to bad debt expense and credited to AFDA. The expense is based on sales to appropriately match the bad debt expense with the credit sales of the period. The total amount of the allowance is essentially ignored. If the percentage of credit sales used realistically reflects the actual amount of bad debt experienced, the allowance account reflects a reasonable balance.

If the actual bad debt experienced is materially lower than the estimate (based on a percentage of sales), the allowance for doubtful accounts may build to an unrealistically large amount. This would occur because the increase in AFDA based on the estimate of bad debt is not consistent with a reduction from actual bad debt write offs.

If the allowance account is becoming unusually large, you could forego recording additional bad debt expenses (and the corresponding credit to the allowance account), until debits (i.e. actual bad debt write offs) reduce the allowance account to a reasonable balance. What is a reasonable balance? As with many items in accounting, the answer is based on professional judgment.

Pause & Reflect

Exercise 8-2

Manuel Enterprise is preparing its year-end adjustments for bad debt. Accounts receivable has a debit balance of $400,000 and allowance for doubtful accounts has a credit balance of $3,400. The aging breakdown of accounts receivable is shown below.

a) Calculate the esimated bad debt using the aging of account receivable method and complete the final column of the table.

Aging Category	Bad Debt %	Balance of Accounts Receivable	Estimated Bad Debt
30 days	1%	$200,000	
31-60 days	5%	120,000	
More than 60 days	10%	80,000	
Total		$400,000	

b) Prepare the journal entry to record the bad debt expense on December 31, 2018.

JOURNAL			
Date	Account Title and Explanation	Debit	Credit

See Appendix I for solutions.

Managing Accounts Receivable LO 4

Much of our analysis of accounts receivable has involved accounting for receivables in the company's books. This is important because these records give management accurate information with which to make good business decisions. This also allows companies to adhere to external reporting standards and principles.

Another important aspect of accounts receivable is managing or controlling them. It is important for a business to know not only the amount of its accounts receivable but also which policies and procedures will lead to collecting the maximum possible amount.

Having too many customers owing the company too much money on overdue bills restricts cash flow and working capital.

A CLOSER LOOK

A number of strategies ensure that a company effectively manages and controls its accounts receivable. These include the following.

- **Commitment to efficiency**—Management commits to ensuring that accounts receivable are handled efficiently.

- **Measuring results**—After using ratios and reports to manage information, it is essential to determine whether these measures are working.

- **Cutting-edge technology**—Having the company's technology up-to-date to provide accurate and useful information about accounts receivable assists in informed decision-making.

Among other things, it limits the ability of the company to meet its commitments, such as accounts payable and loans.

Since accounts receivable plays such a prominent role in the financial well-being of a company, it is important that information about this asset is efficiently organized.

Computer software is available to collect, organize and process information in different ways. Reports can be produced to give management insight into financial affairs in ways that raw data cannot.

The Accounts Receivable Subledger or Aging Schedule

Accounts receivable is considered a controlling account, since it is the sum total of all amounts owed by customers to the company and controls the accounts receivable subledgers. The subledgers are individual customer accounts to track the amounts each customer owes. The list in Figure 8.17 is a customer-by-customer list of outstanding amounts owing to a company; these amounts represent the total in the accounts receivable controlling account.

Accounts Receivable listing as at July 31					
	Current	31–60 days	61–90 days	91 days +	Total
Archer Limited	1,300	900	1,500		**3,700**
Beta Company	1,200	1,800	1,300	150	**4,450**
Cooper Limited	1,800	150			**1,950**
Dunwoody Company	200	500	200		**900**
Harry's Supplies	4,000	3,000	1,600	1,200	**9,800**
Lino Inc.	400	600	100		**1,100**
Total	**8,900**	**6,950**	**4,700**	**1,350**	**21,900**
	40.64%	31.74%	21.46%	6.16%	

FIGURE 8.17

This kind of accounts receivable listing is sometimes called an **aging schedule**, because we analyze each customer account by how old it is or how aged it is. For example, Archer Limited shows three amounts due for $1,300, $900 and $1,500. For the first amount due, $1,300, the sale and billing took place sometime during July, so the payment is still current because it is due by July 31. The sale and billing for $900 took place during June. Since payment has not been received, it is at least 31 days overdue. Finally, the sale and billing for $1,500 took place during May. Since payment has not been received, it is at least 61 days overdue An aging analysis looks at the age and determines how old each account balance is for the business. The age of the account combined with other factors, such as the relationship with the customer, determine what action the company should take next.

Presenting the data in this form facilitates the analysis of accounts receivable by customer. It also highlights the figures that stand out from the others. In this case, the areas to note are marked in yellow, red and green in the revised chart in Figure 8.18.

Accounts Receivable listing as at July 31					
	Current	31–60 days	61–90 days	91 days +	Total
Archer Limited	1,300	900	1,500		**3,700**
Beta Company	1,200	1,800	1,300	150	**4,450**
Cooper Limited	1,800	150			**1,950**
Dunwoody Company	200	500	200		**900**
Harry's Supplies	4,000	3,000	1,600	1,200	**9,800**
Lino Inc.	400	600	100		**1,100**
Total	**8,900**	**6,950**	**4,700**	**1,350**	**21,900**
	40.64%	31.74%	21.46%	6.16%	

FIGURE 8.18

As the yellow and red areas show, two customers have bills outstanding more than 90 days.

The yellow area shows an amount of $150 from Beta Company that has not been paid for more than 90 days. However, this is a relatively small amount, especially in comparison with Beta's total amount owing. It could be the result of an invoice discrepancy or some other minor issue. Although Beta is one of only two customers with balances owing for more than 90 days, management may not be too concerned about this balance. There should still be controls in place to follow up with the customer either to correct or adjust the amount.

The other customer with a balance exceeding 90 days, Harry's Supplies, is certainly cause for concern. The amount marked in red, $1,200, represents a significant portion of the outstanding balance. Furthermore, the amount might be even more problematic, given that the same customer was given $4,000 in credit in the current month. This account is not being well managed, and management should follow up with the company and reconsider the credit policies that allowed this situation to develop.

The green area of this chart is notable because, unlike all the other customers on the list, Cooper Limited does not have an outstanding balance for the 61–90 day period. Furthermore, it has only $150 outstanding for the 31–60 day period. Therefore the $1,800 credit given to Cooper in the current period appears to be justified; this customer has paid bills promptly, and providing more credit for this customer makes good business sense.

Alternative Presentation Formats

The preceding examples represent just a few ways in which accounts receivable information can be organized and presented. Computer software allows for multiple methods of analysis. Management should tailor computer programs to meet the specific needs and objectives of the company with regard to information about accounts receivable, bad debt, internal controls and all other related issues.

The reports that can be generated involving accounts receivable include the following.

* Current active customers

- Past customers not active for the last 12 months
- Customer activities listing value of sales per month
- Customer activities listing value of sales per product
- Categorization of customers according to sales representative or geographic location
- Overdue accounts

Analyzing Accounts Receivable with Ratios

Another approach to measuring the effectiveness of the company's collection efforts is financial ratios. This section examines two types of ratios: accounts receivable turnover and days' sales outstanding.

Accounts Receivable Turnover Ratio

The **accounts receivable turnover ratio (ART)** measures how often during the year a company collects its entire accounts receivable amount. This is done by using two basic figures from the financial records: average net accounts receivable and net credit sales for the past 12 months. Recall that the net accounts receivable is equal to the gross accounts receivable less allowance for doubtful accounts. The net credit sales is equal to the total of credit sales less sales discounts, returns and allowances. The formula to calculate ART is shown in Figure 8.19.

$$\text{Accounts Receivable Turnover (ART)} = \frac{\text{Net Credit Sales}}{\text{Average Net Accounts Receivable}}$$

FIGURE 8.19

The following two examples illustrate the use and function of this particular ratio.

Example 1: Juniper Company

Assume that Juniper Company has an average net accounts receivable of $200,000 and net credit sales of $1,200,000. The accounts receivable turnover is calculated as shown.

$$\text{ART} = \frac{\$1,200,000}{\$200,000}$$

$$= 6 \text{ times}$$

The turnover of six times per year means Juniper Company collects the entire amount of accounts receivable six times a year, or approximately every two months.

Example 2: Willow Company

Assume that Willow Company has an average net accounts receivable of $135,000 and net credit sales of $1,650,000. The accounts receivable turnover is calculated as shown.

$$\text{ART} = \frac{\$1,650,000}{\$135,000}$$

$$= 12.2 \text{ times}$$

The turnover of 12 times per year means Willow Company collects the entire amount of accounts receivable 12 times a year, or every month.

Days' Sales Outstanding

Another way of organizing accounts receivable information is to use days' sales outstanding. **Days' sales outstanding (DSO)** tracks how long customers take to pay their bills. The formula is shown in Figure 8.20.

$$\text{Days' Sales Outstanding (DSO)} = \frac{\text{Average Net Accounts Receivable}}{\text{Net Credit Sales}} \times 365$$

FIGURE 8.20

As shown in the formula, the average net accounts receivable figure is divided by the net credit sales of the past 12 months. The result is then multiplied by 365 (days in the year). The result provides the company with the average number of days that customers take to pay their bills.

Example 1: Juniper Company

From the previous example, the total average net accounts receivable amount for Juniper Company is $200,000, and the total net credit sales amount for the past year is $1,200,000. The DSO ratio is calculated as shown.

$$\text{DSO} = \frac{\$200,000}{\$1,200,000} \times 365$$

$$= 61 \text{ days}$$

Juniper Company collects amounts outstanding in an average of 61 days, or approximately two months.

Example 2: Willow Company

From the previous example, the total average net accounts receivable amount for Willow Company is $135,000, and the total net credit sales for the past year was $1,650,000. The DSO ratio is calculated as shown.

$$\text{DSO} = \frac{\$135,000}{\$1,650,000} \times 365$$

$$= 30 \text{ days}$$

Willow Company collects amounts oustanding in an average of 30 days, or approximately one month. On the basis of these calculations, Willow Company is collecting its accounts receivable from customers twice as fast as Juniper Company. Because of the importance of cash in operating a business, it is in the company's best interest to collect outstanding accounts receivable as quickly as possible. By quickly turning sales into cash, a company can effectively use the cash for reinvestment and to produce more revenue. One of the most important factors that affect both ART and DSO is a company's credit terms.

If both companies allow customers 30 days to pay for their purchases on account, Willow Company is doing well in terms of collection whereas Juniper Company is doing poorly.

Pause & Reflect

Exercise 8-3

The Practical Company obtained the following information from its financial records for 2018.

Net Credit Sales	$278,000
Average Net Accounts Receivable	$23,000

a) Calculate the accounts receivable turnover ratio. Explain what this result means.

b) Calculate the days' sales outstanding. Explain what this result means.

See Appendix I for solutions.

Internal Controls and Ethical Considerations for Accounts Receivable LO 6

Now that we have examined various ways of organizing, presenting and managing accounts receivable information, the information can be used to implement sound control policies. There is no value in collecting all that data unless it is used to better manage a company's accounts receivable.

This is the purpose of accounts receivable internal controls—to help a company get the most out of one of its largest and most crucial assets. We will look specifically at how a credit policy can serve as a control mechanism to ensure that the accounts receivable asset is managed, protected and maximized in value.

Credit Approval

Providing payment terms to customers involves making unsecured loans to the customers so that they can buy the company's product or service. Instead of automatically offering these terms, a company can implement various measures to better understand its customers and follow up when necessary. This is the essence of credit approval. The company can have the customer complete a credit application and update the information regularly. It can also request a customer's financial statements to ensure the customer is in a position to pay the bills.

Credit Information

Of course, customers may not always be completely open about their financial health or ability to pay their bills. Companies, therefore, get independent credit information about customers from credit reporting agencies, financial institutions or other vendors.

Credit agency reports can be very useful in getting up-to-date information on current and potential customers. They can provide payment history, claims against the customer, banking information, existing credit granted, a record of recent inquiries as well as any credit ratings.

Credit Terms

One of the first decisions a company should make when establishing a credit policy is whether to adopt a lenient or restrictive approach to providing credit. This is an important decision because the company's credit policy can have a significant impact on sales volume. The more lenient a company's credit policy, the more likely it is to generate additional sales. A lenient credit policy provides potential customers with the incentive to buy goods without having to pay for them immediately. However, it also increases the risk of bad debt for the company. In order to make credit policy decisions effectively, a company should take the following factors into consideration.

Firstly, the company should consider its own financial situation. The stronger its financial situation is, the better the company can afford to make sales on credit. If a company is financially constrained, it probably cannot risk extending credit to customers. Similarly, low sales volumes for custom-made products leave a company with less room to extend generous credit terms.

Secondly, a company should consider its competitive situation. The more competition the company has, the greater the pressure to extend credit in order to increase sales. A company with little or no competition does not need to increase market share, and has little incentive to adopt lenient credit policies.

In conclusion, a competitive market environment, homogeneous products and high sales volumes are greater incentives for a company to extend more lenient credit terms to customers.

After analyzing the factors above, the company can set its credit terms, which are often an integral component of credit control. A certain period, such as 30 days, can be used and enforced with all approved customers.

A company should try to assess whether its collection period is stringent enough. Accounts receivable should not remain uncollected for more than 10 or 15 days beyond the credit terms. Industry standards differ, so assessing what the competition is doing, then setting a benchmark to meet or surpass those expectations, may be a wise business strategy. Setting a high standard and routinely enforcing it might improve the collection of accounts.

Credit Collection

Finally, deciding on the methods of collecting from customers is another control in credit policy. The invoice is always the first tool of collection. If a customer is overdue with payment, the company can send a copy of the invoice as a reminder. If that is unsuccessful, other measures such as letters, phone calls and even personal visits can be used to put pressure on the customer. If all else fails, a collection agency can be hired to enforce payment, especially when the account is long overdue.

Other controls for accounts receivable that may be implemented include the following.

- Keeping individual records for each customer.

- Following up on large accounts that are overdue.

- Writing off a bad debt when all reasonable measures have been exhausted to collect the debt.

- Ensuring that the original write off is reversed when payments are received for a previously written off account.

> ## A CLOSER LOOK
>
> An important objective for any successful business is to maximize its control and management of accounts receivable. To that end, a company can establish a checklist of items to monitor how well it is doing in meeting this objective. Such a checklist may include the following items.
>
> - Is the staff fully trained to handle accounts receivable issues?
> - Is all sensitive accounts receivable information adequately secured?
> - Are invoices being processed accurately?
> - Are customers informed quickly enough of credit decisions made by the company?
> - Are third-party collection agencies being properly monitored?

An Ethical Approach to Managing Accounts Receivable

The company and its accounting department are responsible for managing accounts receivable accurately and ethically. This includes properly recording credit sales and receipt of cash, as well as properly estimating bad debt. Accounts receivable is an important asset on the balance sheet and managing and accounting for this asset is open to manipulation.

Various ethical principles and standards have been established to prevent or detect manipulation of accounts receivable. The following case study illustrates unethical behavior, which violates the full disclosure principle.

Case Study 8-1

Charles owns a manufacturing business, which has been growing steadily. His bank wants to examine his financial statements before approving his loan to finance his increasing need for capital. His records show a total of $250,000 in accounts receivable, and he has earned a net income of $80,000 for the current year. Charles is also aware that there is an amount of $50,000 that is likely to be uncollectible; however, he knows that if he allows for the bad debt in his statements, he may not be successful in securing the loan. Charles justifies his non-disclosure by committing himself to allowing for the bad debt the following year because there is a slight chance that he may still get paid.

What Charles did was unethical. He deliberately overstated the value of his assets to try to secure the loan. He believed that the debt was not going to be paid, but he represented it otherwise to distort the current value of the accounts receivable.

Charles consciously violated the full disclosure principle by withholding information relevant to the valuation of these assets.

Consider another example of unethical behavior. This time we will examine the importance of maintaining the integrity of the accounts receivable information that a company collects and manages. Failure to do so can put into doubt the accuracy of the company's books, and the ethics of the people in charge.

Case Study 8-2

Sophie is hired by the controller, Rick, to manage the company's accounts receivable. Upon assuming the job, Sophie notices that the company's accounts receivable has been poorly managed. The computer system was old and the invoices were not detailed enough, thus leading to customers questioning their invoices. Furthermore, the company would increase prices on the date of shipment instead of using the prices on the date the order was placed. Customers complained and did not want to pay invoices showing prices they had not agreed to.

Sophie brings her concerns to Rick, who asks her to keep quiet and do the best she can. Rick is afraid that he will be held accountable if upper management finds out, so he has tried to hide the problems. Sophie does not know what to do about the unethical accounting practices. If she remains silent, the integrity of the company's accounts receivable is in serious jeopardy.

An accountant is responsible for maintaining the integrity of the information in the books. Rick should have dealt with these problems as soon as he became aware of them. Instead, when these problems were identified, he tried to hide them and absolve himself of any responsibility. The company's customers are being treated unfairly, the integrity of the financial information of the company is compromised and the tactics used in response to the problems are ethical violations. Furthermore, Rick has imposed an unacceptable dilemma on his employee, Sophie, requiring her to choose between her job and the proper management of the company's assets. Unless Rick accepts responsibility for the problems and corrects them, he puts both himself and his company in a vulnerable position both financially and ethically.

In Summary

LO 1 Explain the importance of accounts receivable

- ► Accounts receivable often represents a significant percentage of a company's assets.

- ► Allowing the existence of accounts receivable is instrumental in increasing sales in a modern economy. This includes allowing customers to buy on credit or make purchases using credit cards.

- ► While most companies find day-to-day administration of accounts receivable burdensome, effective and efficient management of accounts receivable by factoring (selling) them can help improve cash flows and customer satisfaction.

LO 2 Account for bad debt using the allowance method and the direct write off method

- ► When accounts receivable are deemed uncollectible, they can be accounted for as bad debt using two different methods: the allowance method, and the direct write off method.

- ► The expense recognition principle requires bad debt expense to be estimated and accounted for in the same period that sales are recorded.

- ► The allowance method satisfies expense recognition through the use of an allowance for doubtful accounts (AFDA), which is a contra account attached to the accounts receivable account.

- ► Under the direct write off method, as soon as a receivable is determined to be uncollectible, it is written off by a debit (increase) to bad debt expense and a credit (decrease) to accounts receivable.

LO 3 Estimate bad debt using the income statement and balance sheet approaches

- ► The income statement approach estimates bad debt based on credit sales of the year.

- ► The balance sheet approach estimates bad debt based on the balance of accounts receivable or on the aging of accounts receivable at year end.

LO 4 Manage accounts receivable

- ► The accounts receivable subledger shows accounts receivable balances by customer and by the length of time the debt has been outstanding. Detailed examination of the accounts receivable subledger can help the company highlight important areas that require management focus or changes in credit policies.

- ► Using computer software, a company can generate various accounts receivable reports that are tailored to management's needs.

LO 5 Analyze accounts receivable with ratios

- ► The effectiveness of accounts receivable collections can be gauged with the use of two ratios: accounts receivable turnover (ART) and days' sales outstanding (DSO).

LO 6 **Apply internal controls and ethics related to accounts receivable**

▶ Credit controls and policies are necessary to manage and protect the accounts receivable asset.

▶ Examples of controls related to accounts receivable include setting competitive yet firm credit terms and getting independent credit information about customers before approving their credit.

▶ Management must ensure that accounts receivable is properly managed and any estimates for bad debt are recorded as accurately as possible.

Review Exercise 8-1

ABC Company uses the allowance method to account for bad debt. During 2018, the company had $350,000 in sales, of which 80% were on account and 20% were cash sales. During the year, the company received $250,000 from customers as payment on their accounts. In June, it wrote off $1,500 for a customer who filed for bankruptcy and would not pay. However, some time after the account was written off, the customer notified ABC Company that she would to pay the account early in the new year. The company expects that $5,000 of the accounts receivable balance at the end of the year may be uncollectible.

Note: Do not consider cost of goods sold in any of the transactions.

Required

a) Using the general journal and December 31 as the date for all transactions, record the sales, collections for customers on account, write off of accounts and bad debt expense for 2018. You may omit explanations for each entry. Assume accounts receivable had a debit balance of $35,000 and that the AFDA had a credit balance of $2,500 at the beginning of the year (January 1, 2018).

JOURNAL			
Date	Account Title and Explanation	Debit	Credit

b) Show how the transactions from part a) are posted in the related T-accounts.

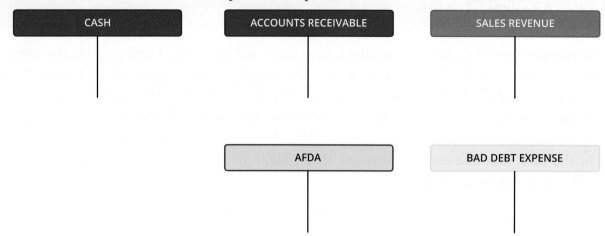

c) Show how accounts receivable is reported on the December 31, 2018 balance sheet after the entries from part a) are posted.

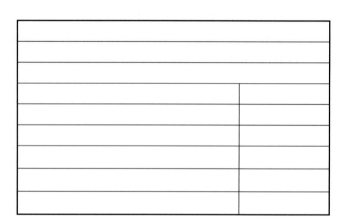

d) Assume that instead of using the balance sheet approach, the company uses the income statement approach and expects that 1% of credit sales may be uncollectible. Record the journal entry to estimate bad debt on December 31. Assume that AFDA has a credit balance of $2,500 at the beginning of the year.

JOURNAL			
Date	**Account Title and Explanation**	**Debit**	**Credit**

See Appendix I for solutions.

Chapter 9
Accounting for Inventory

Learning Objectives

LO 1   **Define a merchandising business**

LO 2   **Differentiate between the perpetual and the periodic inventory systems**

LO 3   **Record journal entries under the perpetual inventory system**
- Purchase of Inventory
- Sale of Inventory

LO 4   **Calculate gross profit and gross profit margin percentages**

LO 5   **Prepare the income statement under the perpetual inventory system**
- Single-Step Income Statement
- Multiple-Step Income Statement

LO 6   **Prepare closing entries for a merchandising business under the perpetual inventory system**

LO 7   **Identify inventory controls**
- Compliance with Plans, Policies, Procedures, Regulations and Laws
- Safeguarding Inventory
- The Economical and Efficient Use of Resources
- Inventory Objectives

LO 8   **Measure inventory using inventory ratios**
- Inventory Turnover Ratio
- Days' Sales in Inventory

 *Access **ameengage.com** for integrated resources including tutorials, practice exercises, the digital textbook and more.*

MAKING IT REAL TO YOU

Companies that sell products—whether they are large corporations like Apple, or small proprietorships like a local coffee shop—have a business that revolves around selling those products. If you have ever worked for a business that sells a product, you have probably experienced some of the concerns that business has. What were the sales yesterday, last month or last year? What is our sales goal for today, this month, this year and next year? What do our customers want? Do we know what our customers want before they know what they want? How do we keep inventory moving from order to a sale to a customer? How can we negotiate better and lower inventory costs to maximize gross profit? How should we record and manage inventory? Do we have too much inventory on hand, not enough, or is it just right? Depending on the business, tracking inventory and inventory costs is a critical concern that demands a lot of attention.

Merchandising Businesses

So far, you have learned the complete accounting cycle of service companies. In reality, many companies not only provide services, but also sell products. A **merchandiser,** or merchandising business, is any business that buys and sells products, referred to as *merchandise* or *goods*, to make a profit. A merchandiser is an intermediary between the manufacturer and the end consumer. Two main categories of merchandisers are wholesalers and retailers. A **wholesaler** buys mostly bulk merchandise from a manufacturer for reselling to retailers, other wholesalers or end consumers. A **retailer** buys merchandise from a wholesaler or manufacturer to sell to end consumers.

There are a number of similarities between a merchandiser and a service provider. Both of them incur expenses to market and sell their products or services. If they hire any employees, both incur salaries expense. In addition, both a merchandiser and a service provider buy items that are classified as property, plant and equipment, and likely incur debt and pay it off. Thus, most of the accounting transactions for service providers that you learned in previous chapters are still applicable to merchandisers.

The main difference between a merchandising business and a service company is that the merchandising business holds an asset called merchandise inventory for sale. **Merchandise inventory,** or simply *inventory,* is a collection of physical goods that a company has purchased or manufactured to sell to its customers. Merchandisers usually have to invest their own cash to buy merchandise inventory, and it may take some time before they are able to resell the inventory and receive cash from customers. Once merchandisers receive cash from customers, the cash can be used to buy more inventory for resale. This cycle of merchandiser's operations is called the operating cycle. As shown in Figure 9.1, the operating cycle involves purchasing inventory and selling it for cash or on account. If merchandise inventory is sold on account, cash collection from the owing customer becomes an additional step in the cycle. The length of the whole cycle depends on the type of merchandise inventory. Merchandisers of perishable items, such as grocery stores, tend to have short operating cycles (usually a few weeks) compared to merchandisers of expensive items, such as jewelry stores, which tend to have a long operating cycle (multiple months or sometimes over a year).

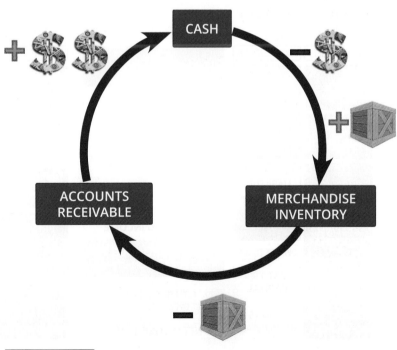

FIGURE 9.1

Carrying inventory presents operational and financial risks for a merchandiser. Inventory value fluctuates based on market demands and the conditions of the goods. Some inventory, such as jewelry, increases in value over time; some inventory, such as technology, decreases over time. In all cases, a merchandiser must sell inventory for more than its cost to make a profit. Senior management and accountants ensure controls are in place to accurately track the value of inventory from the point of purchase to the point of sale. Methods to track the value of inventory are discussed in Chapter 8.

Because merchandisers sell products instead of services, their revenue is called sales revenue, or simply *sales*. An expense account called cost of goods sold (COGS) is used to track the cost of the inventory that was sold during a particular period. For example, if a company purchased a television from a supplier for $200 and sold it for $500, it would have sales revenue of $500 and COGS of $200. The difference between sales revenue and COGS is called gross profit. Figure 9.2 shows the formula to calculate gross profit.

Gross Profit = Sales Revenue – Cost of Goods Sold

FIGURE 9.2

Gross profit is used to pay for all other expenses in the business. The television sale generated $300 ($500 – $200) of gross profit, which can be used to pay for expenses such as rent, salaries and advertising. After all expenses are deducted, the remaining amount is net income.

Figure 9.3 illustrates the difference in the configuration of the accounts of a merchandising business and a service company. Notice that merchandise inventory is listed as a current asset on the balance sheet right below accounts receivable because it is generally a fairly liquid asset. Cost of goods sold and gross profit are listed on the income statement of the merchandising company. Other income and other expenses will be covered later in this chapter.

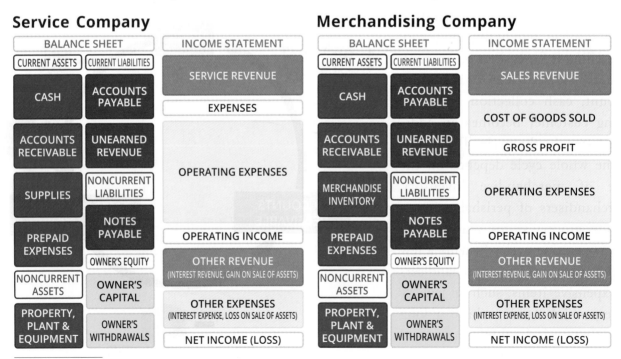

FIGURE 9.3

To see how sales, COGS, gross profit and operating expenses interact, consider the following example. A business purchases T-shirts for $5.00 each and plans to sell them for $7.00 each. The business also incurs a variety of operating expenses, including business travel, printing up business cards, printing up flyers for advertising, and renting office space, which total $700.

Figure 9.4 shows how to calculate net income (loss) if the business sells 200 T-shirts.

Operating expenses of the business

1. Travel	$100
2. Business cards	100
3. Flyers for advertising	300
4. Temporary rental space	200
Total Operating Expenses	**$700**

Every business has various monthly operating expenses that occur regardless of services or products sold. The sale of merchandise, less merchandise cost, contributes toward paying these expenses.

Sell 200 T-shirts

Sales Revenue (200 × $7.00)	**$1,400**
Less COGS	1,000
= Gross Profit	**400**
Less Operating Expenses	700
= Net Income (Loss)	**($300)**

These T-shirts may have been purchased several months earlier. The business is now recognizing (matching) the cost of the shirts against the value of the sale. The COGS for 200 T-shirts is $1,000 (200 x $5.00). To determine gross profit, COGS is subtracted from sales revenue, for a total of $400.

FIGURE 9.4

The business sold 200 T-shirts for a gross profit of $400 ($1,400 – $1,000). However, the business requires $700 to pay for its operating expenses. Selling 200 T-shirts means the company incurs a net loss of $300 ($400 – $700). The business needs to sell more T-shirts to provide enough gross profit to pay for operating expenses. Figure 9.5 shows the results of selling 350 T-shirts and 500 T-shirts.

Sell 350 T-shirts

Sales Revenue (350 x $7.00)	**$2,450**
Less COGS	1,750
= Gross Profit	**700**
Less Operating Expenses	700
= Net Income (Loss)	**$0**

Sell 500 T-shirts

Sales Revenue (500 x $7.00)	**$3,500**
Less COGS	2,500
= Gross Profit	**1,000**
Less Operating Expenses	700
= Net Income (Loss)	**$300**

FIGURE 9.5

If the business sells 350 T-shirts (shown on the left in Figure 9.5), COGS is $1,750 (350 × $5.00). This means the gross profit is $700 ($2,450 – $1,750), which exactly covers the operating expenses. The business did not produce a net income or suffer a net loss, which is known as breaking even.

If the business sells 500 T-shirts (shown on the right in Figure 9.5), COGS is $2,500 (500 × $5.00). This means the gross profit is $1,000 ($3,500 – $2,500), which is more than enough to cover operating expenses. The business produced a net income of $300 ($1,000 – $700).

Pause & Reflect

Exercise 9-1

OnTime Company purchases wall clocks from a supplier for $14 per unit and resells them for $35 each. Calculate this month's sales revenue, COGS, gross profit and net income if OnTime Company sells 300 clocks and incurs $5,000 in operating expenses. Fill in your answers in Table 1.

Table 1

Sales Revenue	
COGS	
Gross Profit	
Net Income	

See Appendix I for solutions.

Perpetual vs. Periodic Inventory Systems

Imagine you are shopping for a particular item at a department store. You cannot find it on the shelf, so you ask an employee if there are any left. The employee checks the computer, which says there is one left. The employee finds it in the storage room, gives it to you and you go to the cashier. The cashier scans the item, you pay the bill and you leave the store. If another customer asked for that same item after you bought it, the computer would show that there are none in stock.

This example illustrates the perpetual inventory system. The **perpetual inventory system** updates inventory levels after every purchase and sale. Most merchandising companies use technology, such as scanners, to update their records for inventory, as well as COGS. All the updates happen automatically when the item is scanned.

On the other hand, some small merchandising companies, such as a small convenience store, may not have scanning technology in place. Without the scanning technology, the business can track its sales, but inventory and COGS are not updated automatically. The **periodic inventory system** only updates the inventory and COGS values after physically counting the items on hand. These inventory counts occur periodically, usually at the end of the month or year.

Figure 9.6 highlights the difference between the perpetual and periodic inventory systems. It shows sample revenue and COGS amounts for a company under both systems over a period of three months. Notice that the perpetual system updates COGS continuously while the periodic system updates COGS only when a physical inventory count is performed (at the end of March).

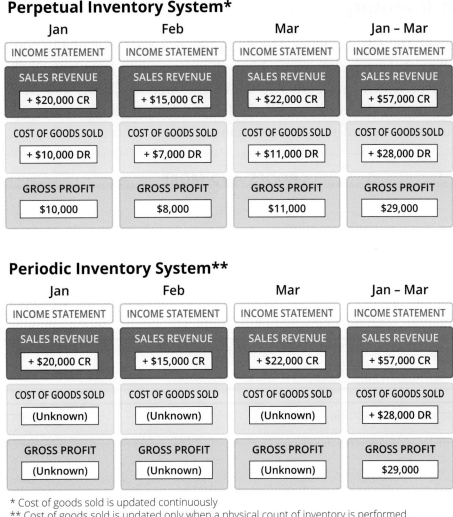

Perpetual Inventory System*

	Jan	Feb	Mar	Jan – Mar
INCOME STATEMENT				
SALES REVENUE	+ $20,000 CR	+ $15,000 CR	+ $22,000 CR	+ $57,000 CR
COST OF GOODS SOLD	+ $10,000 DR	+ $7,000 DR	+ $11,000 DR	+ $28,000 DR
GROSS PROFIT	$10,000	$8,000	$11,000	$29,000

Periodic Inventory System**

	Jan	Feb	Mar	Jan – Mar
INCOME STATEMENT				
SALES REVENUE	+ $20,000 CR	+ $15,000 CR	+ $22,000 CR	+ $57,000 CR
COST OF GOODS SOLD	(Unknown)	(Unknown)	(Unknown)	+ $28,000 DR
GROSS PROFIT	(Unknown)	(Unknown)	(Unknown)	$29,000

* Cost of goods sold is updated continuously
** Cost of goods sold is updated only when a physical count of inventory is performed.

FIGURE 9.6

Perpetual inventory systems are more commonly used in today's computerized environment. In this textbook, unless otherwise stated, assume the perpetual inventory system is used. We will now examine how to record various transactions regarding the purchase and sale of merchandise inventory under the perpetual inventory system.

The Perpetual Inventory System

A perpetual inventory system involves recording all transactions affecting the balance of merchandise inventory on hand, as they occur. In reality, most businesses have separate, detailed records for each type of product they sell. For simplicity, our examples will focus on one type of product, where all transactions affect a single merchandise inventory account directly.

We will demonstrate various inventory-related transactions using an example of a retail store called Tools 4U, which buys and sells tools. Tools 4U is a sole proprietorship owned by Wayne Sanders.

Purchase of Inventory

Tools 4U purchased 100 fall protection kits for resale at a total cost of $10,000 from Roofs and More, which delivered the merchandise and issued an invoice on January 1, 2018. The invoice for this transaction is presented in Figure 9.7. While the supplier (Roofs and More) refers to this invoice as a sales invoice, the customer (Tools 4U) refers to it as a purchase invoice and uses it as a source document to record the purchase transaction.

ROOFS AND MORE
121 Main Street
Paterson NJ 07501

INVOICE

SOLD TO

Tools 4U
1818 1st Avenue
Dallas, TX 75210

Invoice #	876-1
Invoice Date	1/1/2018
Customer ID	905

ORDER DATE	YOUR ORDER #	SALES REP.	F.O.B.	SHIP VIA	TERMS
12/29/17	2017122908	52	Destination	ShipPlus	2/10, n/30

QTY.	MODEL NO.	DESCRIPTION	UNIT PRICE	TOTAL
100	DK771R	Fall Protection Kit	100	$10,000

	Subtotal	$10,000
	Tax	-
	Shipping	-
	Miscellaneous	-
	BALANCE DUE	$10,000

FIGURE 9.7

When merchandise inventory and a purchase invoice are received under the perpetual inventory system, the merchandise inventory account is debited and the cash or accounts payable account is credited. Assume all purchases and sales are made on account. Figure 9.8 shows how this purchase is journalized.

JOURNAL			
Date	**Account Title and Explanation**	**Debit**	**Credit**
2018			
Jan 1	Merchandise Inventory	10,000	
	Accounts Payable		10,000
	Purchased inventory on account		

FIGURE 9.8

Purchase Returns

Sometimes, goods are returned for reasons such as incorrect product, over-shipments or inferior product quality.

When the manager of Tools 4U examined the new shipment of inventory from the company's supplier, Roofs and More, he noticed that there were some damaged goods in the shipment. The damaged goods cost $500. The goods were returned and a journal entry for $500 was recorded to reverse part of the original purchase transaction, as shown in Figure 9.9.

JOURNAL			
Date	**Account Title and Explanation**	**Debit**	**Credit**
2018			
Jan 2	Accounts Payable	500	
	Merchandise Inventory		500
	Goods returned to Roofs and More		

BALANCE SHEET	
CURRENT ASSETS	CURRENT LIABILITIES
CASH	ACCOUNTS PAYABLE − $500 DR
ACCOUNTS RECEIVABLE	UNEARNED REVENUE
MERCHANDISE INVENTORY − $500 CR	NONCURRENT LIABILITIES
PREPAID EXPENSES	NOTES PAYABLE
	OWNER'S EQUITY
NONCURRENT ASSETS	OWNER'S CAPITAL
PROPERTY, PLANT & EQUIPMENT	OWNER'S WITHDRAWALS
No change in owner's equity	

FIGURE 9.9

Purchase Allowances

Purchase allowances occur when the buyer agrees to keep the undesirable goods at a reduced cost. When a buyer encounters undesirable goods, the buyer issues a **debit memorandum**, or a *debit memo* in short, to inform the seller about the purchase returns or allowances. The document is called a debit memorandum because accounts payable is debited in the buyer's books, meaning that the buyer's liabilities decrease. Assume Tools 4U found another $500 worth of unsatisfactory goods and the supplier offered a 20% allowance for the company to keep the goods, rather than returning them. The journal entry is recorded by debiting accounts payable and crediting merchandise inventory as shown in Figure 9.10. The transaction amount is $100 ($500 × 20%).

A balance of $9,400 ($10,000 – $500 – $100) is still owing to Roofs and More.

JOURNAL			
Date	**Account Title and Explanation**	**Debit**	**Credit**
2018			
Jan 4	Accounts Payable	100	
	Merchandise Inventory		100
	Allowance from Roofs and More		

FIGURE 9.10

Purchase Discounts

Various types of discounts exist when purchasing products or services. Sellers often give discounts to encourage customers to purchase more and to encourage early payments.

Two types of common discounts given are trade discounts and cash discounts.

Trade discounts represent the discount from the *manufacturer's suggested retail price* that is usually given by manufacturers to merchandisers in order to resell their products. The manufacturer's suggested retail price is usually printed in a catalog, so it is sometimes called a *catalog price* or a *list price*. Merchandisers, who act as intermediaries between manufacturers and end consumers, make a profit by paying less than the list price. The difference between the list price and the price that the merchandiser has to pay for the product is the trade discount.

For example, suppose the list price of the fall protection kit, according to Roofs and More's catalog, is $250. Roofs and More gives a 60% trade discount to Tools 4U. The purchase price that Tools 4U has to pay is $100 [$250 - ($250 × 60%)]. The buyer records the price net of trade discount in its inventory purchase journal entry. In this example, if Tools 4U purchased one fall protection kit on account, it records a debit to merchandise inventory and a credit to accounts payable of $100.

Merchandisers sometimes encourage prompt payment from customers by offering a **cash discount**, which is a percentage off the final bill if it is paid in a specified amount of time. **Credit terms** are the terms indicating when a buyer has to pay for the merchandise and whether there are any discounts for paying early. The **credit period** is the maximum number of days that the buyer can wait before paying the full amount due. The **discount period** is the number of days within which the buyer has to pay to receive the cash discount.

In our example, the invoice in Figure 9.7 has a "Terms" field, which shows 2/10, n/30 (read as "two-ten, net thirty," the credit terms). This means that Roofs and More will apply a 2% discount if payment is received within 10 days (the discount period); otherwise the net amount of $10,000 is due within 30 days (the credit period).

Another example is 3/15, n/30, which means a 3% discount is applied if payment is received within 15 days, otherwise the net amount owing is payable within 30 days. While sellers refer to these discounts as **sales discounts**, buyers refer to them as **purchase discounts**. The following example illustrates how to record a purchase discount.

Tools 4U made the original purchase from Roofs and More on January 1, 2018 for $10,000. The amount Tools 4U owes has been reduced by $600 due to returns and allowances, so only $9,400 remains to be paid. The supplier (Roofs and More) allows 2/10, n/30 on all invoices. The discount period and credit period for this transaction are shown in Figure 9.11. The amount owing during the discount period is $9,212 ($9,400 – [$9,400 × 2%]). The amount owing after the discount period (10 days), is the full amount of $9,400. Since Tools 4U has excess cash at this time, the manager decides to take advantage of the cash discount by paying the invoice within 10 days.

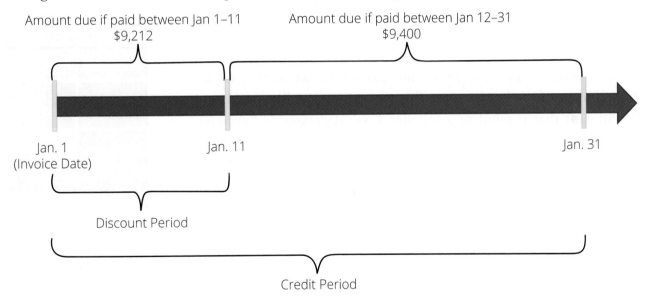

FIGURE 9.11

A CLOSER LOOK

Some credit terms contain EOM, which stands for end of month. For example, if the credit term is n/EOM or "net EOM", it means that the buyer has to pay the full amount by the last day of the same month as the invoice date. If the credit term is n/10 EOM or "net 10 EOM", it means that the buyer has to pay the full amount within 10 days after the end of the month that is written on the invoice.

Since Tools 4U makes the payment on January 11, the amount for the bill is $9,400 less the $188 discount ($9,400 × 2%). Since the business is paying less for the inventory, the value of the inventory needs to decrease by the value of the discount. The entry to record the payment is shown in Figure 9.12.

JOURNAL

Date	Account Title and Explanation	Debit	Credit
2018			
Jan 11	Accounts Payable	9,400	
	Cash		9,212
	Merchandise Inventory		188
	Paid invoice and took purchase discount		

FIGURE 9.12

BALANCE SHEET

CURRENT ASSETS | CURRENT LIABILITIES
CASH − $9,212 CR | ACCOUNTS PAYABLE − $9,400 DR
ACCOUNTS RECEIVABLE | UNEARNED REVENUE
MERCHANDISE INVENTORY − $188 CR | NONCURRENT LIABILITIES
PREPAID EXPENSES | NOTES PAYABLE
NONCURRENT ASSETS | OWNER'S EQUITY
PROPERTY, PLANT & EQUIPMENT | OWNER'S CAPITAL / OWNER'S WITHDRAWALS

No change in owner's equity

The discount of $188 is credited to merchandise inventory because the adjustment is made to reflect the true cost of the goods.

If Tools 4U decides not to pay the amount owing within 10 days, then it is not entitled to the discount. It must pay the full amount of $9,400 within 30 days of the invoice date. This payment is just like paying any other amount that is owed to a supplier. Cash decreases and accounts payable decreases by the amount owed. The entry is shown in Figure 9.13. Notice the date is more than 10 days past the invoice date.

JOURNAL

Date	Account Title and Explanation	Debit	Credit
2018			
Jan 31	Accounts Payable	9,400	
	Cash		9,400
	Paid amount owing to Roofs and More		

FIGURE 9.13

BALANCE SHEET

CURRENT ASSETS | CURRENT LIABILITIES
CASH − $9,400 CR | ACCOUNTS PAYABLE − $9,400 DR
ACCOUNTS RECEIVABLE | UNEARNED REVENUE
MERCHANDISE INVENTORY | NONCURRENT LIABILITIES
PREPAID EXPENSES | NOTES PAYABLE
NONCURRENT ASSETS | OWNER'S EQUITY
PROPERTY, PLANT & EQUIPMENT | OWNER'S CAPITAL / OWNER'S WITHDRAWALS

No change in owner's equity

A buyer's failure to take advantage of a purchase discount is often very costly. On the surface, the 2% discount that Tools 4U must forfeit if it pays on January 31 instead of January 11 may seem insignificant. However, the 2% discount for 20 days can be converted to a very high annual percentage. Specifically, the annual interest rate for the 2% higher price in order to pay 20 days later is 36.5% [(365 days ÷ 20 days) × 2%]. Because a commercial bank usually charges much lower interest than 36.5% annually for a loan, it is in the buyer's best interest to pay within the discount period, even if a bank loan has to be taken out to do so.

A CLOSER LOOK

Realistically, most buyers take advantage of all available purchase discounts to avoid paying an interest rate that is much higher than a bank loan. Buyers that do this may use an alternative accounting method to record the inventory purchase and cash payment transactions called the *net method*, instead of the *gross method* shown in Figure 9.12.

Under the net method, inventory purchase and cash payment transactions are always recorded at the amount that is net of purchase discount. To illustrate, if Tools 4U had made a purchase from Roofs and More on January 1 for $9,400 under the credit term of 2/10, n/30, and if it had paid $9,212 for the purchase on January 11, the transactions are recorded as shown here.

Jan 1	Merchandise Inventory	9,212	
	Accounts Payable		9,212
	Purchased inventory on account		
Jan 11	Accounts Payable	9,212	
	Cash		9,212
	Paid invoice and took purchase discount		

Regardless of which method is use, account balances are the same. In Tools 4U's case, merchandise inventory increases by $9,212 and cash decreases by $9,212 under both methods when the payment is made during the discount period.

Freight Cost

When one company purchases goods from another, the items must be transported from the seller's place of business to the buyer's place of business. There are a number of ways to transport goods (sea, rail, truck, etc.). The selling company may have its own fleet of vehicles to deliver goods to customers, or it may use a common carrier. A common carrier in this context is a company that provides shipping services to the general public. Examples include railroad companies, trucking companies, local couriers, or the postal service.

In addition to arranging transport of the goods, ownership of the goods must be legally transferred from the seller to the buyer. The term used to determine when ownership of the goods changes hands is called the FOB point. "FOB" stands for Free On Board. There are two possible FOB points. FOB shipping point and FOB destination. Each of these points have implications regarding who pays for shipping, when ownership passes from the buyer to the seller and who bears the risk for the goods during transport.

FOB Shipping Point

FOB shipping point indicates that ownership of the purchased items changes as soon as the goods leave the seller's place of business (i.e. when shipping begins). In this case, a common carrier is often used to deliver the items to the buyer. The buyer pays for shipping and is responsible to insure the items while they are in transport. If anything happens to the items while they are being transported, the buyer bears the risk of loss.

The seller records revenue earned and the buyer records an increase to merchandise inventory as soon as the goods are loaded on the truck (or other transport). Under FOB shipping point, the delivery expense that the buyer pays is often referred to as *freight-in* or *transportation-in*, and it increases the cost of merchandise inventory on the buyer's balance sheet. The reason the buyer includes shipping costs in merchandise inventory is that the value of the goods must include all costs that are incurred to get the goods ready to sell, such as transportation. Figure 9.14 illustrates who pays the shipping costs for FOB shipping point.

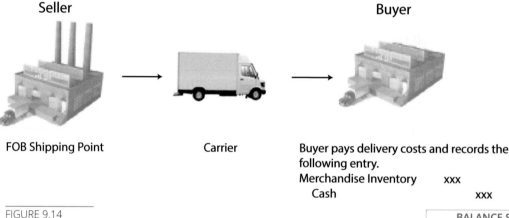

Seller

Buyer

FOB Shipping Point   Carrier   Buyer pays delivery costs and records the following entry.
Merchandise Inventory   xxx
Cash   xxx

FIGURE 9.14

Assume that Tools 4U had inventory shipped FOB shipping point. This means that Tools 4U must pay the cost of shipping. Suppose the shipping charge totaled $100 and was paid in cash on January 2. This amount must be included in the merchandise inventory account. The journal entry is shown in Figure 9.15.

JOURNAL			
Date	**Account Title and Explanation**	**Debit**	**Credit**
2018			
Jan 2	Merchandise Inventory	100	
	Cash		100
	Paid for freight costs		

BALANCE SHEET	
CURRENT ASSETS	CURRENT LIABILITIES
CASH − $100 CR	ACCOUNTS PAYABLE
ACCOUNTS RECEIVABLE	UNEARNED REVENUE
MERCHANDISE INVENTORY + $100 DR	NONCURRENT LIABILITIES
PREPAID EXPENSES	NOTES PAYABLE
	OWNER'S EQUITY
NONCURRENT ASSETS	OWNER'S CAPITAL
PROPERTY, PLANT & EQUIPMENT	OWNER'S WITHDRAWALS
	No change in owner's equity

FIGURE 9.15

FOB Destination

FOB destination indicates that ownership of the purchased items changes when the goods arrive at the buyer's place of business. In other words, ownership changes at the point of destination. In this case, the seller may have a fleet of vehicles and use them to deliver goods to its customers. Thus, the seller pays for the shipping and is responsible for the items while they are in transport. If anything happens to the items while they are being transported, the seller bears the risk of loss.

The seller records revenue earned and the buyer records an increase to merchandise inventory once the goods reach their destination (the buyer's place of business). Under FOB destination, the delivery expense that is paid by the seller is often referred to as *freight-out* or *transportation-out*, and it is recorded as a selling expense on the seller's income statement. Figure 9.16 illustrates who pays the shipping cost for FOB destination.

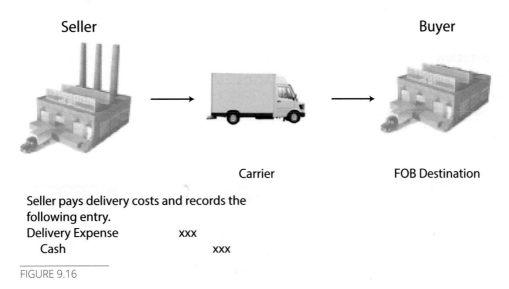

Seller | Buyer

Carrier | FOB Destination

Seller pays delivery costs and records the following entry.
Delivery Expense   xxx
      Cash   xxx

FIGURE 9.16

Suppose that Tools 4U shipped inventory to a customer FOB destination on January 3. Tools 4U must pay the cost of shipping because it is the selling company. The shipping cost is a delivery expense. Suppose that it costs Tools 4U $120 to ship the order and this amount was paid in cash. The journal entry for this transaction is shown in Figure 9.17.

JOURNAL			
Date	**Account Title and Explanation**	**Debit**	**Credit**
2018			
Jan 3	Delivery Expense	120	
	Cash		120
	To record shipping expenses on a customer order		

FIGURE 9.17

Sometimes the party that is not responsible for paying the delivery cost may prepay it and then charge it back to the responsible party later. To illustrate, assume that Tools 4U purchases $10,000 worth of merchandise from Roofs and More under FOB shipping point, which means that Tools 4U is responsible for paying the delivery cost. If Roofs and More prepays the $100 delivery cost, this is added to the invoice. The prepaid delivery portion of the invoice is not covered in the discount terms. For example, if the terms are 2/10, n/30 and if Tools 4U pays within 10 days, it receives a $200 discount ($10,000 x 2%) and has to pay a total of $9,900 ($10,000 merchandise inventory − $200 discount + $100 prepaid delivery cost) to Roofs and More.

A summary of FOB shipping point and FOB destination is presented in Figure 9.18.

	FOB Shipping Point	**FOB Destination**
Ownership Change	When goods leave the seller on a common carrier	When goods arrive at the buyer's place of business
Transportation Costs	Paid by the buyer and recorded in merchandise inventory	Paid by the seller and recorded as an expense
Risk of Loss	Buyer bears risk of loss during transport	Seller bears risk of loss during transport

FIGURE 9.18

Sale of Inventory

WORTH REPEATING

When goods are shipped from the selling company to the buyer's company, whoever pays for shipping owns the goods while they are being transported. They also bear the risk of loss during transport.

Suppose on January 15, Tools 4U sells $7,200 worth of inventory for $15,000 on account. The sale of inventory is recorded by using two journal entries.

1. Accounts receivable is debited and sales revenue is credited for $15,000 to show the sale on account. This records the proceeds from the sale. If the sale was made for cash, then the cash account is debited instead of accounts receivable.

2. COGS is debited and merchandise inventory is credited for $7,200 to show that inventory has been reduced. This entry is necessary because it removes the inventory sold from the balance sheet and records its cost on the income statement as a cost of doing business for the period.

These transactions are shown in Figure 9.19. Note that the gross profit generated by this sale is equal to $7,800 ($15,000 − $7,200).

JOURNAL			
Date	**Account Title and Explanation**	**Debit**	**Credit**
2018			
Jan 15	Accounts Receivable	15,000	
	Sales Revenue		15,000
	To record product sales on account		
Jan 15	Cost of Goods Sold	7,200	
	Merchandise Inventory		7,200
	Sold inventory to a customer		

FIGURE 9.19

When inventory is sold by a merchandiser, it is no longer an asset of the company because it is owned by the customer. This is the reason for the second journal entry in Figure 9.19. In a service company, this entry is not recorded because assets are not sold in the ordinary course of business.

Sales Returns

Goods are sometimes returned to a merchandiser for any number of reasons: excess quantity ordered, defective goods received, goods arrived too late, product specifications were incorrect, and so on. A merchandiser must track returns over a period of time. High return levels may indicate serious problems with the products being sold. Therefore, instead of reversing the revenue account with a debit when recording returns, a contra-revenue account called **sales returns and allowances** is used to track the number of returns. Recall that "contra" means opposite and a contra account holds an opposite normal balance of its related account.

Sales returns and allowances is a contra-revenue account with a normal debit balance. It is generally used to record both sales returns and sales allowances. **Sales returns** occur when undesirable products are returned to the seller. **Sales allowances** occur when the customer decides to keep such undesirable products at a reduced price. When sales returns and allowances occur, a seller issues a **credit memorandum**, or a *credit memo* in short, to inform the buyer that the accounts receivable balance has been credited (or decreased) in the seller's books.

Continuing with our example, suppose that a customer returned $4,000 worth of undesirable goods to Tools 4U (the original cost of the inventory was $3,000). There is nothing wrong with the goods and they can be resold. The journal entries to record this return, using the contra-revenue account, are shown in Figure 9.20. Note that two entries are required: one to record the reduction in sales and accounts receivable (or cash, if applicable) and one to reverse the reduction of merchandise inventory.

JOURNAL			
Date 2018	**Account Title and Explanation**	**Debit**	**Credit**
Jan 18	Sales Returns & Allowances	4,000	
	Accounts Receivable		4,000
	Customer returned items		
Jan 18	Merchandise Inventory	3,000	
	Cost of Goods Sold		3,000
	Restock returned inventory		

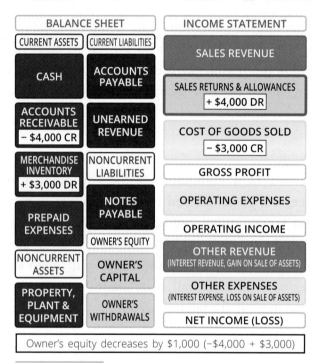

FIGURE 9.20

There is a $4,000 increase in the sales returns and allowances account. This amount decreases revenue since the contra-revenue account has the opposite effect than the revenue account.

In the example in Figure 9.20, the inventory that was returned was not what the customer wanted. There was nothing wrong with the product in terms of quality, so it was placed back on the shelf to be sold again. If the items returned by the customer were damaged, then the inventory cannot be sold again. In that case, Tools 4U would not record the second journal entry from Figure 9.20 because the damaged inventory is worthless.

Sales Allowances

There are circumstances where a reduction to the original selling price is given to a customer.

Assume the customer from January 15 discovered that some goods were damaged during shipping. Instead of returning the items, the customer agreed to accept an allowance of 5% on the price of the goods kept. The customer kept $11,000 worth of goods ($15,000 original sale – $4,000 return), so there is a $550 reduction ($11,000 × 5%) on what is owed to Tools 4U.

The journal entry is shown in Figure 9.21. The amount is recorded as a debit to sales returns and allowances and a credit to accounts receivable. The transaction decreases equity by $550.

A balance of $10,450 ($15,000 – $4,000 – $550) is still owed by Tools 4U's customer.

JOURNAL			
Date	**Account Title and Explanation**	**Debit**	**Credit**
2018			
Jan 18	Sales Returns & Allowances	550	
	Accounts Receivable		550
	Sale allowance for damaged goods		

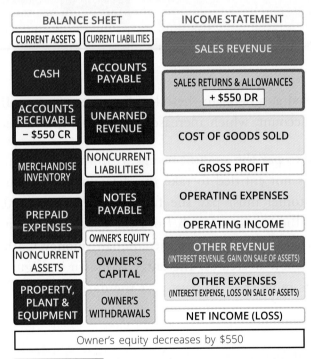

FIGURE 9.21

Sales Discounts

When selling products or services, it is common to offer sales discounts to customers for early payment. The concept works in the same way as the purchase discount. Assume that Tools 4U offered its customer from January 15 terms of 2/10, n/30 on the invoice. If the customer pays by January 25, a 2% discount is applied to the amount owing of $10,450.

Assume the customer made the payment on January 20; the amount is $10,241 ($10,450 less the 2% discount). The journal entry to record this transaction is shown in Figure 9.22.

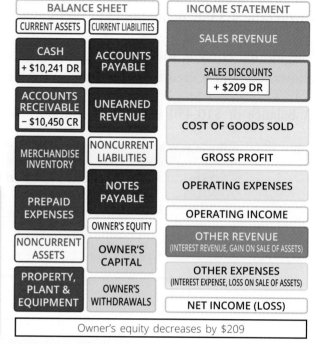

JOURNAL			
Date	**Account Title and Explanation**	**Debit**	**Credit**
2018			
Jan 20	Cash	10,241	
	Sales Discounts	209	
	Accounts Receivable		10,450
	Payments received from customer less discount		

FIGURE 9.22

The $209 discount is recorded as a debit to the sales discounts account. The **sales discount account** is another contra-revenue account, which increases with a debit and decreases with a credit.

If the customer decides not to pay the amount owing within the discount period, then the customer is not entitled to take the discount that Tools 4U offers. Instead, the customer must pay the full amount of $10,450 within 30 days of the sale. The receipt of cash from the customer is just like receiving cash from any customer that owes the company money. Cash increases and accounts receivable decreases. The entry is shown in Figure 9.23. Notice that the date is more than 10 days past the date of the sale.

JOURNAL			
Date	**Account Title and Explanation**	**Debit**	**Credit**
2018			
Feb 2	Cash	10,450	
	Accounts Receivable		10,450
	Payment received from customer		

FIGURE 9.23

A CLOSER LOOK

Because a sales discount normally represents a very high annual percentage, as shown in the purchase discount calculation, it is in the buyer's best interest to take advantage of the discount. Therefore, it is reasonable for a seller to expect that the buyer will pay within the discount period and that the seller will receive the amount net of sales discount. One of the options under GAAP is for the seller to record the sale transaction at the most likely amount to be collected, or the amount net of the sales discount in this case, rather than the total amount of the goods sold.

To illustrate, assume that on January 15, Tools 4U sells $15,000 worth of merchandise inventory under the terms 2/10, n/30. If Tools 4U expects the customer to pay within the discount period, and if the customer in fact pays on January 25, Tools 4U can record the sale and the cash receipt transactions at $14,700, which is the amount net of the $300 ($15,000 x 2%) sales discount as shown here. (The COGS transaction is omitted for simplification.)

Jan 15	Accounts Receivable	14,700	
	Sales Revenue		14,700
	To record product sales on account		
Jan 25	Cash	14,700	
	Accounts Receivable		14,700
	Payment received from customer		

Figure 9.24 summarizes the required journal entries in the buyer's and the seller's books for the merchandising transactions covered in this chapter so far. Every merchandising transaction affects both the buyer and the seller, except for the freight transaction, which affects only the party that is responsible for paying the freight cost.

Transactions	Seller's Journal Entries	Buyer's Journal Entries

Sale/purchase of merchandise on account	Accounts Receivable
	   Sales Revenue
	Cost of Goods Sold
	   Merchandise Inventory
		Merchandise Inventory
		   Accounts Payable

Sale/purchase returns	Sales Returns & Allowances
	   Accounts Receivable
	Merchandise Inventory
	   Cost of Goods Sold
		Accounts Payable
		   Merchandise Inventory

Sale/purchase allowance	Sales Returns & Allowances
	   Accounts Receivable
		Accounts Payable
		   Merchandise Inventory

Cash receipt/payment with sale/purchase discount	Cash
	Sales Discounts
	   Accounts Receivable
		Accounts Payable
		   Cash
		   Merchandise Inventory

Cash receipt/payment without sales discount	Cash
	   Accounts Receivable
		Accounts Payable
		   Cash

Freight cost: FOB shipping point	No entry	Merchandise Inventory Cash
Freight cost: FOB destination	Delivery Expense Cash	No entry

FIGURE 9.24

Pause & Reflect

Exercise 9-2

On May 10, 2018, Caterpy Company sold merchandise that originally cost the company $3,000 to Weezle Company for $5,000 cash. The delivery term was FOB shipping point, and the freight cost was $130. Journalize the necessary transactions for both Caterpy and Weezle.

Caterpy Company

JOURNAL			
Date	Account Title and Explanation	Debit	Credit

Weezle Company

JOURNAL			
Date	Account Title and Explanation	Debit	Credit

See Appendix I for solutions.

Gross Profit Margin: A Profitability Ratio

Recall that net sales is equal to the difference between sales revenue and any sales returns, allowances and discounts. Gross profit is the difference between sales revenue and COGS. Gross profit expressed as a percentage of sales is called **gross profit margin**, or simply gross margin. The gross profit margin represents the percentage of sales left over to pay for all the operating expenses.

When gross profit is expressed as a percentage, it is calculated as shown in Figure 9.25.

$$\text{Gross Profit Margin (\%)} = \frac{\text{Gross Profit}}{\text{Net Sales}}$$

FIGURE 9.25

Gross profit margin is more meaningful when comparing the results from one period to another or between different companies. For example, suppose Company A has sales revenue of $100,000 and its COGS is $60,000, which means it has a gross profit of $40,000. It does not have any sales returns, allowances or discounts, so its sales revenue is equal to its net sales. If Company B has sales of $500,000, with a gross profit of $175,000, which of the two companies is performing better? You may think that Company B is performing better because a gross profit of $175,000 is greater than a gross profit of $40,000. However, to assess the results properly, it is important to compare the two percentages.

Company A: $\dfrac{\$40,000 \text{ Gross Profit}}{\$100,000 \text{ Sales}}$ = 0.40 or 40%

Company B: $\dfrac{\$175,000 \text{ Gross Profit}}{\$500,000 \text{ Sales}}$ = 0.35 or 35%

The results show that Company A is more efficient because it used only 60% of revenue to cover the cost of the product, leaving $0.40 of every dollar to contribute toward its operating expenses. Company B, on the other hand, used 65% of its revenue to cover the COGS, leaving only $0.35 of each dollar to contribute toward its operating expenses.

Keep in mind that ratios should be compared within industry groups, taking industry norms into account. Suppose Company A and Company B are both hardware stores and other hardware stores have a gross profit margin of 38%. In this situation, Company A is doing better than the industry average and Company B is doing worse than the industry average.

Pause & Reflect

Exercise 9-3

a) In 2018, Cochran Company has net sales of $400,000 and its COGS is $220,000. What is the company's gross profit margin?

_____

_____

b) If Cochran expects its net sales to increase to $500,000 in 2019, what is the maximum COGS required to maintain the same gross profit margin as in 2018?

_____

_____

See Appendix I for solutions.

Income Statement

Single-Step Income Statement

The income statement of a merchandising business follows the same principles as those of a service business. Until now, we have been grouping revenue accounts together and listing all expenses together, without further categorizing. The income statement that is presented in this format is referred to as the **single-step income statement**. This is shown in Figure 9.26. This format of the income statement classifies expenses by their nature, which means that expenses are presented based on their purposes, without further categorizing them by function.

Tools 4U Income Statement For the Year Ended December 31, 2018		
Revenues		
Net Sales		$194,000
Interest Revenue		8,000
Total Revenues		202,000
Expenses		
Cost of Goods Sold	$100,000	
Depreciation Expense	8,000	
Interest Expense	4,000	
Rent Expense	10,000	
Salaries Expense	40,000	
Office Supplies Expense	4,000	
Advertising Expense	3,500	
Delivery Expense	1,300	
Insurance Expense	1,200	
Total Expenses		(172,000)
Net Income		$30,000

FIGURE 9.26

Multiple-Step Income Statement

A **multiple-step income statement** is an income statement that further divides specific revenues and expenses to show subtotals like gross profit, operating expenses and income from operations (also referred to as operating income). This format classifies **expenses by function**, which means that related expenses are grouped together. Also, important measures, such as gross profit, are clearly shown. A multiple-step income statement is illustrated in Figure 9.27.

Tools 4U Income Statement For the Year Ended December 31, 2018			
Sales Revenue			$200,000
Less: Sales Returns & Allowances		$4,000	
Sales Discounts		2,000	(6,000)
Net Sales			194,000
Cost of Goods Sold			(100,000)
Gross Profit			94,000
Operating Expenses			
Selling Expenses			
Depreciation Expense—Store Equipment	$5,000		
Rent Expense—Retail Space	8,000		
Salaries Expense—Sales	32,000		
Advertising Expense	3,500		
Delivery Expense	1,300		
Total Selling Expenses		49,800	
Administrative Expenses			
Depreciation Expense—Office Equipment	3,000		
Rent Expense—Office Space	2,000		
Salaries Expense—Office	8,000		
Supplies Expense	4,000		
Insurance Expense	1,200		
Total Administrative Expenses		18,200	
Total Operating Expenses			(68,000)
Income from Operations			26,000
Other Income and Expenses			
Interest Revenue		8,000	
Interest Expense		(4,000)	4,000
Net Income			$30,000

Labels in the left margin:

1. Calculate Net Sales and Gross Profit
2. Calculate Selling Expenses
3. Calculate Administrative Expenses and Income from Operations
4. Calculate Non-Operating Activities and Net Income

FIGURE 9.27

The multiple-step income statement further groups the revenues and expenses that are not part of the main operations of the business, such as interest expense, interest revenue or loss from a lawsuit, under a separate category called Other Income and Expenses or Other Revenues and Expenses.

The expenses incurred as part of the main operations of the business that are beyond the cost of goods sold are referred to as **operating expenses**. Operating expenses can be further divided by function into selling and administrative expenses. **Selling expenses** are those related to actually selling inventory. Examples include sales salaries, rent for retail space, and advertising. **Administrative expenses**, sometimes referred to as *general expenses* or *general and administrative expenses*, are those related to running the business, which are not directly tied to selling inventory. Examples include office salaries, office supplies and depreciation of office equipment.

The multiple-step income statement is particularly useful for the company's internal analysis. It allows managers and executives to clearly see a detailed breakdown of costs by function and compare performance in different areas against competitors and its own financial history.

GAAP vs IFRS

GAAP provides no guidance on whether a company has to present its expenses on an income statement by nature or by function. However, the SEC requires its registrants to present the expenses by function.

Under IFRS, expenses can be classified either by nature or by function on an income statement. Using a mixture of nature and function is prohibited.

IN THE REAL WORLD

An actual company's income statement usually looks similar to what we have seen up to this point. However, it will also have additional columns to show amounts from the previous fiscal years, as required by GAAP. For instance, a company reporting for the 2018 fiscal year will have a column with the header "2018" in its income statement to report revenue and expense information for the most recent fiscal year. There would also be additional columns with the headers "2017" and "2016" to show amounts from the previous fiscal years. This form of financial reports is referred to as comparative financial statements. This allows users to easily compare the financial performance and position of a company to that of the previous years.

Closing Entries

When using a perpetual inventory system, merchandise inventory is immediately updated after each purchase and sale transaction. However, the value of merchandise inventory on the balance sheet may not accurately represent the value of inventory actually on hand. To verify the accuracy of the accounting records, a physical inventory count should be performed at the end of the reporting period. If the count does not match the records, an adjustment must be made to bring the merchandise inventory to its correct balance. A physical inventory count that is lower than the recorded amount in the merchandise inventory account is often referred to as **inventory shrinkage**, resulting either from an error in recording transactions, theft or breakage. The journal entry to adjust for inventory shrinkage of $200 is shown in Figure 9.28.

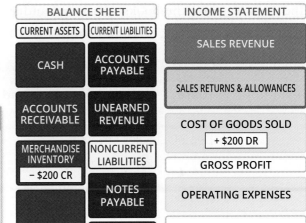

JOURNAL			
Date	Account Title and Explanation	Debit	Credit
2018			
Dec 31	Cost of Goods Sold	200	
	Merchandise Inventory		200
	Adjust inventory to physical count		

FIGURE 9.28

After this adjustment and all other adjustments have been made, assume Tools 4U has the adjusted trial balance shown in Figure 9.29.

Tools 4U Adjusted Trial Balance December 31, 2018		
Account Title	**DR**	**CR**
Cash	$25,000	
Accounts Receivable	18,000	
Merchandise Inventory	45,000	
Prepaid Expenses	12,000	
Equipment	180,000	
Accumulated Depreciation—Equipment		$60,000
Accounts Payable		34,000
Unearned Revenue		8,000
Notes Payable		100,000
Sanders, Capital		48,000
Sales Revenue		200,000
Interest Revenue		8,000
Sales Returns & Allowances	4,000	
Sales Discounts	2,000	
Cost of Goods Sold	100,000	
Depreciation Expense	5,000	
Interest Expense	4,000	
Rent Expense	10,000	
Salaries Expense	40,000	
Supplies Expense	7,000	
Utilities Expense	6,000	
Total	**$458,000**	**$458,000**

FIGURE 9.29

The steps to close the books of a merchandising company are similar to closing a service company. Step 1 is to close the revenue account, as shown in Figure 9.30.

JOURNAL			
Date	**Account Title and Explanation**	**Debit**	**Credit**
2018			
Dec 31	Sales Revenue	200,000	
	Interest Revenue	8,000	
	Income Summary		208,000
	Close revenue accounts		

FIGURE 9.30

Step 2 is to close expenses. In this step, shown in Figure 9.31, the two contra-revenue accounts (sales returns and allowances and sales discounts) are also closed because they have debit balances like the rest of the expense accounts.

JOURNAL			
Date	**Account Title and Explanation**	**Debit**	**Credit**
2018			
Dec 31	Income Summary	178,000	
	Sales Returns & Allowances		4,000
	Sales Discounts		2,000
	Cost of Goods Sold		100,000
	Depreciation Expense		5,000
	Interest Expense		4,000
	Rent Expense		10,000
	Salaries Expense		40,000
	Supplies Expense		7,000
	Utilities Expense		6,000
	Close expense and contra-revenue accounts		

FIGURE 9.31

Step 3 closes the income summary account. Recall from Chapter 6 that the income summary account is closed to owner's capital, as shown in Figure 9.32.

JOURNAL			
Date	**Account Title and Explanation**	**Debit**	**Credit**
2018			
Dec 31	Income Summary	30,000	
	Sanders, Capital		30,000
	Close income summary		

FIGURE 9.32

The end result, just as in a service company, is that the equity in the business is updated with the net income as shown in Figure 9.33.

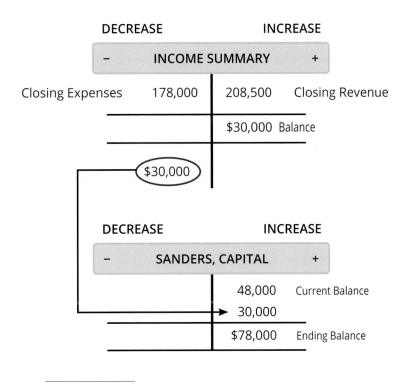

FIGURE 9.33

Similar to a service company, if the owner of a merchandising company withdraws money from the business during the year, the owner's withdrawals account also has to be closed. In Tools 4U's case, the owner's withdrawals account does not have to be closed because the owner did not withdraw any money during the year, and it has a zero balance.

Pause & Reflect

Exercise 9-4

During the year-end physical inventory count, Squaker Company realized that a portion of its merchandise must have been stolen. Squaker Company used the perpetual inventory system and its accounting records showed the merchandise inventory balance of $53,000 as at December 31. However, the actual value of the physical inventory in the warehouse on December 31 was only $50,000. Prepare the journal entry to record the inventory shrinkage.

JOURNAL			
Date	Account Title and Explanation	Debit	Credit

See Appendix I for solutions.

Controls Related to Inventory

The way a company handles its inventory can have a major impact on the state of the business. After all, basic economic theory is about supply and demand. If customers demand goods or services, the goal of a business is to meet that demand. In essence, this is what inventory management is about—to manage supply in order to meet demand.

A company with too much inventory on hand risks tying up resources that could be used productively in other areas. A company with too little inventory on hand risks not having enough supply to meet customer demand. There is a delicate balance that must be maintained by a company. Perpetual inventory systems help companies maintain such a balance.

Keeping track of a company's inventory can be a challenge, but computer software can help. However, every accountant should have an understanding of how merchandise inventory is tracked and recorded manually.

First, even with the use of technology, errors can be made. It is the responsibility of the accounting department and management to ensure that inventory information is accurate and reliable.

Second, a thorough knowledge of manual accounting procedures helps the accountant develop the necessary controls to ensure that this type of asset is managed responsibly and with integrity.

We will provide examples to show how an accountant can develop a personal method of controlling inventory manually. We will then take a closer look at the kinds of controls needed when dealing with the merchandise inventory section of the balance sheet.

Compliance with Plans, Policies, Procedures, Regulations and Laws

All aspects of doing business should be governed by the appropriate plans, policies, procedures, regulations and laws. This is certainly true regarding a company's handling and control of inventory.

All businesses should have plans that are formalized through general policies that lead to specific procedures. These should all comply with the regulations and laws in place within the jurisdiction of the business.

For example, a company can have a plan to train all inventory personnel. This plan can include detection controls to identify instances of procedures not being followed. An example of such a procedure could be to have all items tagged and scanned at the checkout. If this procedure is not followed, then a backup measure could be implemented, such as alarms going off at the exit.

All plans, policies and procedures must adhere to relevant regulations and laws, as illustrated in Figure 9.34. For example, customers cannot be strip-searched because the alarm goes off as they are leaving the store because this would be a violation of their rights. In addition to the human rights law, there are laws and regulations specific to inventory, especially for the industries whose inventory is potentially harmful. For example, companies in the chemical industry must comply with the Toxic Substances Control Act, which regulates distribution and use of chemicals. The companies in food, medical and cosmetic industries must comply with the Federal Food, Drug, and Cosmetic Act. Each company is responsible for observing and complying with the industry-specific laws and continually keeping up-to-date with any amendments.

FIGURE 9.34

All employees should be trained in the inventory procedures that are in place. For example, the receiver should count all goods that enter the premises and match the count with the one initially written on the purchase order. The supervisor should ensure that this procedure is followed. Internal auditors can conduct field visits to ensure that both the supervisor and the receiver are implementing procedures according to plans and policies.

Safeguarding Inventory

All company assets must be physically protected. Cash is generally deposited in a bank; securities can be kept with the brokerage house. Inventory, on the other hand, is often located on company premises in a warehouse or onsite storage facility. The location needs to be easily accessible for receiving or shipping, but it also needs to be protected from the possibility of theft; at the most basic level of safeguarding, inventory facilities are locked up after closing. The more valuable the inventory, the more elaborate the security measures needed to protect it. Examples of the measures to safeguard inventory include inspecting the inventory and comparing it against the company's purchase order and the supplier's invoice when the inventory is received, building fences, and installing alarm systems and video cameras. Other measures can include hiring security guards, guard dogs and inventory custodians, who are charged specifically with protecting the inventory.

The Economical and Efficient Use of Resources

The concept that resources should be used economically and efficiently is especially applicable to inventory. First, financial ratios—which are examined later in this textbook—can be used to determine if there is too much or too little inventory on hand. If there is too much inventory, then money is tied up that could be used more efficiently elsewhere. If there is too little inventory, then customer demand will not be met.

Second, the physical condition of the inventory should be checked regularly. This can be done visually or through inventory reports. Any inventory items that are old or in disrepair, and therefore difficult to sell at market value, can be sold at reduced prices or disposed of so that valuable storage space can be maximized.

Inventory Objectives

All aspects of a business should be guided by the objectives set by management. This not only allows for the accomplishment of specific objectives, but allows all organizational objectives to be properly coordinated. For example, sales objectives can be tied to inventory objectives, and profit objectives can be tied to those set by the marketing department.

All employees should be aware of stated objectives. For example, if a company wishes to keep items in inventory for only a short period of time before being shipped out, then both the receiver and shipper should be aware of this. This objective would guide much of their short-term and long-term activities.

Meeting inventory objectives must be a total team effort. If inventory levels are not maintained close to management's objectives, then initiatives should be implemented to ensure that objectives are reassessed or changed. For example, if inventory levels are higher than expected, the sales department can view it as a challenge to get items moving out faster. The more sales increase, the less inventory builds up in the warehouse.

Measuring Inventory Using Inventory Ratios

LO 8

Generally speaking, a business wants to be as precise as possible when buying inventory for resale. Ideally, inventory should be sold as soon as it is bought; the less time that an item spends in inventory, while still meeting customer demand, the better.

A company can measure the extent to which it is moving inventory through the use of two ratios: inventory turnover and days' sales in inventory.

Inventory Turnover Ratio

The extent to which an organization can quickly sell inventory on hand is known as inventory turnover. Specifically, the **inventory turnover ratio** estimates how many times a year a company is buying inventory. The more often a company buys inventory, the less likely it is that the inventory sits for extended periods of time, and the more likely it is that the turnover is high.

The inventory turnover ratio is calculated by taking COGS for a year and dividing it by average inventory, as shown in Figure 9.35.

$$\text{Inventory Turnover Ratio} = \frac{\text{Cost of Goods Sold}}{\text{Average Inventory}}$$

FIGURE 9.35

Average inventory is calculated by adding the opening and closing inventory numbers and dividing the total by 2.

New Tech Mobile makes mobile devices. Its merchandise inventory and COGS are shown in Figure 9.36 (numbers are in the millions). For 2018, it had an inventory turnover of 6.2. This means the company bought and sold its entire inventory just over six times during the year.

Merchandise Inventory—December 31, 2017	$501.5
Merchandise Inventory—December 31, 2018	$428.3
Cost of Goods Sold	$2,882.8
Average Inventory ($501.5 + $428.3) ÷ 2 = $464.9	
Turnover $2,882.8 ÷ $464.9 = 6.2	

FIGURE 9.36

Inventory turnover is useful when it is compared to another company within the same industry. Suppose a competitor has an inventory turnover of 9.0. This is higher than that of New Tech Mobile and more desirable. The higher turnover indicates that inventory is moving faster at the competitor than at New Tech Mobile. Inventory that moves fast is less likely to become outdated.

Days' Sales in Inventory

There is another way of looking at inventory turnover. Instead of estimating how often a company sells and replaces inventory over a period of time (as indicated by the inventory turnover ratio), turnover can be calculated by estimating how many days it takes to move items out of inventory. **Days' sales in inventory**, sometimes called *inventory days on hand*, is a calculation of how many days inventory will last given the current rate of sales.

The number of days in a year (365) is divided by the inventory turnover ratio, resulting in the days' sales in inventory, as shown in Figure 9.37.

$$\text{Days' Sales in Inventory} = \frac{365}{\text{Inventory Turnover Ratio}}$$

FIGURE 9.37

The days' sales in inventory divides the calendar year into equal-sized portions. The number of portions equals the inventory turnover ratio. The size of the portions translates into the days' sales in inventory.

For example, if a company's inventory turnover ratio is 10, then inventory is completely purchased and sold 10 times throughout the year. Since there are 365 days in the year, each portion is 36.5 days long (365 ÷ 10).

Therefore, the days' sales in inventory is 36.5 days. This means that, on average, it takes 36.5 days to "turn over" inventory. This is shown in Figure 9.38.

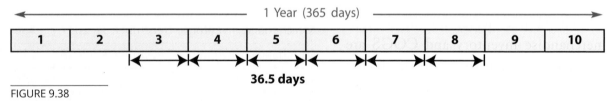

FIGURE 9.38

Returning to the example, New Tech Mobile calculates its days' sales in inventory to be 58.9 days (365 ÷ 6.2). Since its competitor had an inventory turnover of 9.0, the competitor's days' sales in inventory is 40.6 days (365 ÷ 9.0). The competitor's lower ratio means it has a better rate of inventory turnover; it takes less time for the company to move its inventory.

Another way of calculating days' sales in inventory is shown in Figure 9.39.

$$\text{Days' Sales in Inventory} = \frac{\text{Average Inventory}}{\text{Cost of Goods Sold}} \times 365$$

FIGURE 9.39

The relationship (ratio) is between how much inventory is in stock and the amount of inventory used for the year (which is COGS). Dividing the average inventory by how much was used and multiplying this number by 365 (number of days in the year) converts the ratio to the number of days on hand based on how much was used.

Using the values for New Tech Mobile, we can calculate days' sales in inventory using the formula in Figure 9.39.

$$\text{Days' Sales in Inventory} = \frac{\$464.9}{\$2,4882.8} \times 365$$

$$= 58.9$$

Management should not make decisions regarding inventory based on ratios alone. There could be many factors that affect such numbers. For example, some industries might require companies to wait longer periods of time to have goods shipped to them. High turnover in these instances may lead to empty warehouses and customer demands not being met.

As an example, a grocery store will have higher inventory turnover than an appliance store. Car engines will move out of an auto plant warehouse much slower than light bulbs in a hardware store.

It is the responsibility of accountants and management to know what inventory levels are best for business. Ratios can help but they are only one of many tools that can be used.

Pause & Reflect

Exercise 9-5

The data in Table 1 was extracted from the financial statements of Nado Company and Vaporen Company. These two companies are competitors in the same industry.

a) Calculate average inventory, inventory turnover and days' sales in inventory for both companies and fill in your answers in Table 1. Round your answers to whole numbers.

Table 1

	Nado	Vaporen
Cost of Goods Sold	$600,000	$960,000
Opening Merchandise Inventory	100,000	270,000
Closing Merchandise Inventory	140,000	210,000
Average Inventory		
Inventory Turnover		
Days' Sales in Inventory		

b) Which company has more favorable ratios? _____

See Appendix I for solutions.

In Summary

LO 1 **Define a merchandising business**

▶ A merchandising business, or merchandiser, is any business that buys and sells products for the purpose of making a profit.

LO 2 **Differentiate between the perpetual and the periodic inventory systems**

▶ The perpetual inventory system constantly updates merchandise inventory whenever a purchase or sale is made.

▶ The periodic inventory system only updates merchandise inventory when a physical count of the inventory is taken, usually at the end of a period.

LO 3 **Record journal entries under the perpetual inventory system**

▶ Purchase returns and allowances cause accounts payable and merchandise inventory to decrease.

▶ Purchase discounts allow the buyer to save money by paying early. Merchandise inventory value is reduced by the amount of the discount to reflect the actual cost of the inventory.

▶ Goods shipped FOB shipping point are owned by the buyer as soon as they are loaded onto the carrier. The buyer pays for shipping costs and records them in merchandise inventory.

▶ Goods shipped FOB destination are owned by the seller until they arrive at the buyer's destination. The seller pays for shipping costs and records them as a delivery expense.

▶ Inventory sales require two journal entries: one to record the sales revenue and one to remove the merchandise inventory from the balance sheet.

▶ Sales returns and allowances cause an increase to a contra-revenue account called sales returns and allowances. If returned merchandise can be resold, an additional entry must be recorded to increase merchandise inventory and decrease COGS.

▶ Sales discounts allow customers to save money by paying early. Another contra-revenue account called sales discounts is used to track the amount of discounts taken by customers.

LO 4 **Calculate gross profit and gross profit margin percentages**

▶ Gross profit is the amount of profit remaining after the COGS is deducted from revenue. Gross profit is used to cover operating expenses.

▶ Gross profit margin is the gross profit as a percentage of sales. It is calculated by dividing gross profit by sales revenue.

LO 5 **Prepare the income statement under the perpetual inventory system**

▶ A single-step income statement reports all revenues together, followed by all expenses.

▶ A multiple-step income statement further categorizes revenues and expenses to show subtotals, such as gross profit and income from operations. Expenses are categorized into selling expenses and administrative expenses. Other income and expenses that are not part of regular operations are presented separately.

LO 6 **Prepare closing entries for a merchandising business under the perpetual inventory system**

▶ If there is inventory shrinkage, an adjusting entry must be made by debiting COGS and crediting merchandise inventory.

▶ All revenue accounts are closed to the income summary account.

▶ All expense accounts and contra-revenue accounts are closed to the income summary account.

▶ The income summary account is closed to the owner's capital account.

▶ If there are owner's withdrawals, they are closed directly to the owner's capital account.

LO 7 **Identify inventory controls**

▶ All aspects of doing business should be governed by the appropriate plans, policies, procedures, regulations and laws.

▶ All businesses should have plans that are formalized through general policies that lead to specific procedures.

▶ All company assets must be physically protected.

▶ The concept that resources should be used economically and efficiently is especially applicable to inventory.

LO 8 **Measure inventory using inventory ratios**

▶ The inventory turnover ratio is calculated by dividing COGS by the average value of inventory over the period. This ratio is equal to the number of times inventory was completely purchased and sold (turned over) during the period.

▶ A higher inventory turnover ratio means that inventory is less likely to become obsolete because it is sold more quickly.

▶ The days' sales in inventory is calculated by dividing 365 by the inventory turnover ratio. This figure is equal to the number of days on average it takes to sell inventory.

▶ A lower days' sales in inventory means that inventory is less likely to become obsolete because it is sold in fewer days.

 *Access **ameengage.com** for integrated resources including tutorials, practice exercises, the digital textbook and more.*

Review Exercise 9-1

Part 1

The following transactions occurred between George's Gardening Supplies, owned by George Gregg, and Michael's Distributing, owned by Michael Aberdeen, during the month of December 2018.

Dec 3   George's Gardening Supplies purchased $50,000 worth of inventory on account from Michael's Distributing. The purchase terms were 2/10, n/30. The cost of the goods to Michael's Distributing was $35,000.

Dec 6   Freight charges of $200 were paid in cash by the company that incurred them.

Dec 8   George's Gardening Supplies returned $2,000 of incorrect merchandise from the purchase on December 3. Michael's Distributing put the merchandise back into inventory. The cost of the goods to Michael's Distributing was originally $700.

Dec 11   George's Gardening Supplies paid the balance owing to Michael's Distributing.

Assume that both companies use the perpetual inventory system.

Required

a) Journalize the December transactions for George's Gardening Supplies. Assume the goods from December 3 were shipped FOB shipping point.

JOURNAL			
Date	**Account Title and Explanation**	**Debit**	**Credit**

b) Journalize the December transactions for Michael's Distributing. Assume the goods from December 3 were shipped FOB destination.

JOURNAL			
Date	**Account Title and Explanation**	**Debit**	**Credit**

See Appendix I for solutions.

Part 2

Below is the adjusted trial balance for George's Gardening Supplies at the end of the year.

George's Gardening Supplies Adjusted Trial Balance December 31, 2018		
Account Title	**DR**	**CR**
Cash	$54,830	
Accounts Receivable	33,500	
Merchandise Inventory	33,440	
Prepaid Insurance	3,600	
Equipment	45,000	
Accumulated Depreciation—Equipment		$5,000
Accounts Payable		10,000
Notes Payable		30,000
Gregg, Capital		90,000
Gregg, Withdrawals	5,000	
Sales Revenue		113,500
Interest Revenue		6,500
Sales Returns & Allowances	1,000	
Sales Discounts	1,580	
Cost of Goods Sold	44,700	
Depreciation Expense	5,000	
Insurance Expense	2,500	
Interest Expense	2,600	
Rent Expense	6,000	
Salaries Expense	11,000	
Supplies Expense	4,500	
Utilities Expense	750	
Total	**$255,000**	**$255,000**

Note: $10,000 of the notes payable will be paid by December 31, 2019.

Required

a) Prepare a single-step income statement for George's Gardening Supplies for the year ended December 31, 2018.

b) Calculate the gross profit margin.

Gross Profit Margin = _____

c) Prepare a multiple-step income statement for George's Gardening Supplies for the year ended December 31, 2018 using the following information.

- The equipment is used solely for selling purposes.

- Supplies are used for administrative purposes only.

- Insurance, salaries, rent and utilities are allocated 70% to selling and 30% to administration.

d) Journalize the closing entries for George's Gardening Supplies for 2018 using the income summary method.

JOURNAL			
Date	**Account Title and Explanation**	**Debit**	**Credit**

See Appendix I for solutions.

Chapter 10
Accounting Information Systems

Learning Objectives

LO 1 **Explain the flow of accounting information through the accounting paper trail**
- Special Journals
- Subsidiary Ledgers

LO 2 **Describe and record transactions in special journals and subsidiary ledgers**
- The Sales Journal
- The Cash Receipts Journal
- The Purchases Journal

- The Cash Payments Journal
- Reconciling the Controlling Account
- Returns

LO 3 **Identify features of a computerized accounting system**
- QuickBooks Illustration
- Cloud Accounting

LO 4 **Apply internal controls related to the accounting system**

*Access **ameengage.com** for integrated resources including tutorials, practice exercises, the digital textbook and more.*

AMEENGAGE

319

MAKING IT
REAL TO YOU

While this textbook shows the mechanics and concepts of how accounting works, you will most likely encounter a computerized accounting environment in the workplace. Depending on the size and type of the business organization, there are a variety of choices for accounting software. Within each software environment, there are choices for customizing accounts and customizing reports. Despite all of the choices and variations, however, you will find the same foundational architecture of the accounting system: debits and credits, journal entries and trial balance reports. No matter the presentation, it remains the universal double entry accounting system. Another variation is the use of special journals to organize transactions with similar accounts captured in the same location, and subsidiary ledgers to provide details for receivable and payable accounts. We will now explore the variations and features of an expanded accounting system.

The Accounting Paper Trail

Throughout this textbook we have learned how the accounting cycle behaves. We have followed the values from source documents to journals and ledgers, then to trial balances and financial statements. This is the paper trail accountants create to ensure all values are stated correctly. Together, the documents and procedures that are used to collect, classify, summarize and report on a business' transactions and operations all make up an **accounting system**.

Source documents, which provide evidence that a business transaction has occurred, come in many different forms. The most common examples of source documentation are usually associated with accounts payable and accounts receivable. Source documents includes purchase orders, sales invoices, cash receipts and contracts.

Accountants use source documents (in addition to other sources of information) to update the accounting records of an organization. For example, when the accounting department issues a sales invoice, the corresponding journal entry should be made. The procedures to make this entry differ slightly between manual and computerized accounting systems. Our focus in this section is on manual accounting systems; computerized accounting systems are discussed later in the chapter.

Figure 10.1 outlines the traditional accounting paper trail. Once source documentation is received, the accountant updates the journal. At specified times, this information is transferred to the general ledger. At the end of the accounting period, a trial balance is produced. A trial balance lists all the company's accounts and their corresponding balances. The main purpose of a trial balance is to ensure that all debits equal all credits. The trial balance may need to be adjusted (e.g. to take into account recognition of prepaid expenses, depreciation of assets, etc.) before the financial statements are produced. The financial statements are then organized into a financial report for management to review.

The Traditional Accounting Paper Trail

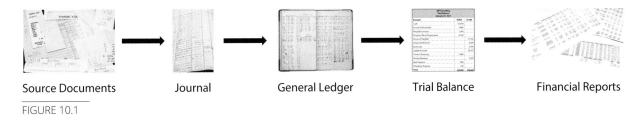

Source Documents   Journal   General Ledger   Trial Balance   Financial Reports

FIGURE 10.1

Regardless of whether one is dealing with a manual or a computerized system, an effective accounting system should ensure

*   adequate internal controls to prevent misuse of assets;
*   accurate information is provided on a timely basis;
*   effective communication across the various components of the system;
*   flexibility to allow for changes as the organization grows and evolves; and
*   maximum benefits at a reasonable cost.

In this section, we will focus on two components of the traditional accounting information system: special journals and subsidiary ledgers.

Special Journals

If we follow the manual accounting paper trail, after the source documentation has been received the next step for the accountant is to record the transaction in journal format.

In a traditional accounting system, recording all business transactions in one journal can be very time consuming, especially when there are lots of activities concerning specific transactions. For transactions that occur regularly, it is wise to maintain a separate book called a **special journal**. Examples of regular transactions include sales, purchases, cash payments, cash receipts and payroll. These journal entries are essentially the same entries already covered, except we will sort them by type and condense the amount of information to be recorded.

WORTH REPEATING

All transactions must be recorded in a journal before being posted to the ledgers, regardless of whether special journals are used or not.

Maintaining these events in a separate set of books organizes accounting information in separate categories, allowing users easy access to specific information. For example, if a sales manager wants to see the amount of credit sales generated in May, she could examine the sales journal and add up all the sales for that month. Examples of special journals include the following.

- **Sales Journal**—This journal is used to record all sales made on account.

- **Cash Receipts Journal**—This journal is used to record all cash deposits (e.g. cash sales) and collections from outstanding accounts receivable.

- **Purchases Journal**—This journal is used to record all purchases (products or services) made on account.

- **Cash Payments Journal**—This journal is used to record all cash payments made by the business (e.g. rent and wages) including payments made to suppliers.

The general journal is the journal that has been used throughout the textbook up until this point. It is used to record any entry that does not belong in one of the special journals. Typical entries recorded in the general journal include the following.

- purchase and sales returns

- adjustments

- correcting entries

Subsidiary Ledgers

The general ledger was first introduced in Chapter 4. It records and organizes the accounts used by a business, which are then used to create the financial statements. However, the general ledger does not list specific information, such as details about individual suppliers or customers, since too much information would clutter up the general ledger accounts. **Subsidiary ledgers** (also called **subledgers**) are a group of similar accounts used to keep track of specific information related to the general ledger account.

For example, subsidiary ledgers for accounts receivable contain all of the information on credit sales to each customer, such as the date of the sale, invoice number, amount of the sale, terms of the sale, and so on. This information can help a company better control its financial information and help with decision-making.

The related account in the general ledger acts as a **controlling account** (sometimes referred to as a *control account*) for the subledgers. It summarizes the information and reports the combined balance of every related subsidiary ledger. For example, the accounts receivable general ledger is the controlling account for all of the accounts receivable subsidiary ledgers.

Transactions are initially recorded in one of the five journals—general, sales, purchases, cash payments, or cash receipts—and are then posted to the general ledger or the subledgers as needed. Examples of transactions that are first posted to subledgers are accounts receivable, accounts payable and merchandise inventory. Examples of transactions that are posted directly to the general ledger are increases or decreases to a company's assets, liabilities or owner equity accounts.

The subledgers are usually updated after each transaction, while the general ledger is usually updated at the end of the period, such as the end of the month. Since subledger accounts only contain details about specific customers or suppliers, and are not used in preparing financial statements, they are not assigned account numbers.

For example, suppose a company has the following list of customers who each owe a certain amount:

- Customer A owes $4,600;

- Customer B owes $500; and

- Customer C owes $300.

The subsidiary ledger tracks each customer and the amount owing, while the accounts receivable controlling account shows the total amount of $5,400, as shown in Figure 10.2.

Subsidiary Ledgers

Accounts Receivable Subsidiary Ledgers

Account: Customer A

Date	PR	DR	CR	Balance (DR or CR)	
O/B				2,400	DR
Apr 1			2,400	0	
Apr 12		4,600		4,600	DR

Account: Customer B

Date	PR	DR	CR	Balance (DR or CR)	
Apr 12		500		500	DR

Account: Customer C

Date	PR	DR	CR	Balance (DR or CR)	
Apr 8		400		400	DR
Apr 12			100	300	DR

FIGURE 10.2

Controlling Account

General Ledger

Account: Accounts Receivable				GL No: 110	
Date	PR	DR	CR	Balance	
Apr 12		5,400		5,400	DR

Customer A	$4,600
Customer B	$500
Customer C	$300
Accounts Receivable	$5,400

A **subsidiary ledger** is a group of accounts.

The total of the subsidiary ledger accounts is equal to the **controlling account**.

It is important to note that amounts are not posted from the subledger to the general ledger. Subledgers simply keep a record of detailed information about specific general ledger accounts. All amounts in the general ledger are posted from either the special journal or the general journal.

At the end of a period, the total of the subledger accounts is compared with the respective controlling account balance. If the sum of the subsidiary ledger accounts is not equal to the controlling account, an error has occurred and must be identified and corrected.

Just as the accounts receivable subsidiary ledger ensures customer amounts to collect are properly recorded, the accounts payable subsidiary ledger ensures supplier amounts owed are properly recorded. For example, a manager may want to know how much product was purchased from a particular supplier, over which time period, when it was paid for, what discounts were allowed for early payment, and so on. To have easy access to this information, an individual subsidiary ledger is maintained for each supplier. The ledger, which records the activities for each individual supplier, is called the accounts payable subsidiary ledger. The total of all the closing balances for the accounts payable subsidiary ledger must be equal to the accounts payable general ledger balance, which is the controlling account.

There are different subsidiary ledgers to control various assets or liabilities (e.g. inventory, noncurrent assets, accounts receivable). Figure 10.3 illustrates how the accounts payable, accounts receivable and merchandise inventory subsidiary ledgers are totaled and reconciled to their corresponding controlling accounts in the general ledger.

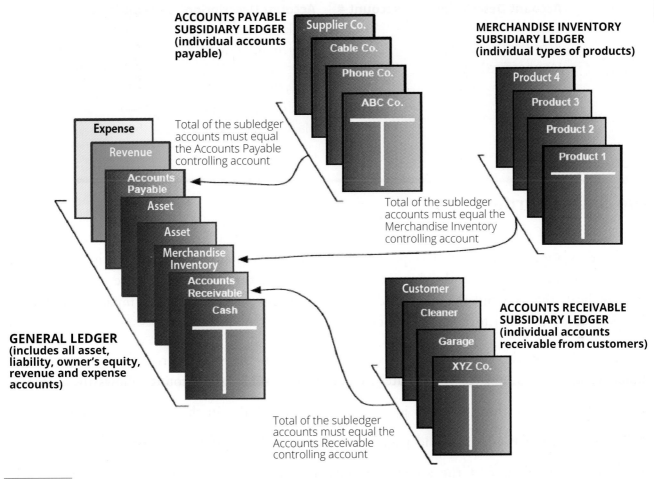

FIGURE 10.3

Once the subledgers have been reconciled to the controlling accounts in the general ledger, a trial balance can be created with the general ledger accounts and balances. The rest of the accounting cycle continues as previously described.

Using Special Journals and Subsidiary Ledgers

It is important to emphasize that the special journals are used to group similar transactions that would normally appear in the general journal. Transactions are entered into the appropriate journal when they occur. For the most part, the subledgers are immediately updated from the special journals while the general ledger is updated at the end of the accounting period. The details of posting from the special journals to the ledgers will be discussed with each journal.

To help with the posting to the general ledger as we discuss the special journals, we will use the selected accounts from Jill Hanlon Retailer, shown in Figure 10.4. You will notice these account numbers being used as we progress through the special journal examples.

Account Description	Account #	Account Description	Account #
Cash	101	Hanlon, Capital	300
Accounts Receivable	110	Hanlon, Withdrawals	310
Merchandise Inventory	120	Sales Revenue	400
Accounts Payable	200	Sales Discount	405
Notes Payable	220	Cost of Goods Sold	500
		Maintenance Expense	525

FIGURE 10.4

The Sales Journal

The sales journal records all the details of sales on account. (Cash sales are not included in this journal; they appear in the cash receipts journal, which records all cash received). The sales journal includes information such as the date of the sale, name of the customer, invoice number and the value of both the sale and the merchandise inventory. Let us look at an example of Jill Hanlon Retailer selling a couch to a customer, Joe Blog.

When a sale is made, the transaction is first recorded in the sales journal. Then, the customer subledger account is updated immediately. Updating the subledger account follows these steps.

ⓐ Transfer the date from the sales journal to the date column in the subledger account.

ⓑ Make a note of the journal and page number in the PR column of the subledger.

ⓒ Transfer the amount of the accounts receivable column from the sales journal to the debit column in the subledger.

ⓓ Indicate the posting is complete by entering a check mark in the PR column of the sales journal.

The steps are illustrated and labeled with the corresponding letters in Figure 10.5.

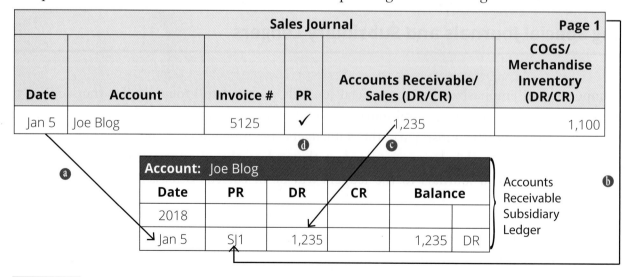

FIGURE 10.5

Note that companies often offer sales discounts to their customers (i.e. 2/10, n/30). The terms of each sale should be recorded in the sales journal. However, if a company provides the same sales terms to all its customers, there is no need to record the terms in the sales journal.

At the end of the month, the totals of all the columns in the sales journal are posted to the appropriate general ledger accounts. The numbers in brackets under the totals represent the ledger numbers of the accounts used. In this example, we are focusing on accounts receivable, account number 110. The posting to the accounts receivable controlling account in Figure 10.6 follows these steps.

ⓐ Transfer the date from the sales journal to the date column in the general ledger account.

ⓑ Make a note of the journal and page number in the PR column of the general ledger.

ⓒ Transfer the total of the accounts receivable column from the sales journal to the debit column in the general ledger account.

ⓓ Indicate the posting is complete by writing the general ledger number(s) under the total in the sales journal.

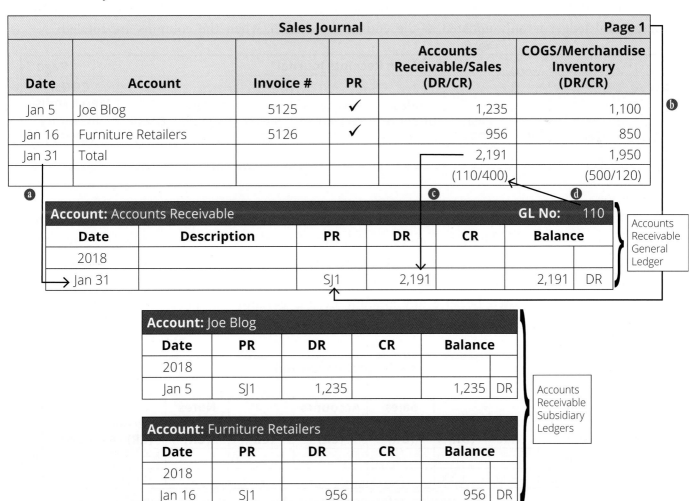

FIGURE 10.6

The total for Accounts Receivable/Sales from the sales journal ($2,191) is posted to the accounts receivable controlling account, and to the sales revenue account (not shown). The total for COGS/ Merchandise Inventory ($1,950) is posted to both the cost of goods sold and merchandise inventory accounts (not shown). Note that the total of the two customer subsidiary ledgers ($1,235 + $956) equals the balance of the accounts receivable controlling account ($2,191).

The Cash Receipts Journal

The cash receipts journal records all receipts of cash. Typical reasons for the receipt of cash are listed in the column headings (e.g. Accounts Receivable, Sales, Notes Payable), which vary depending on the company. A column titled Other is used to record cash receipts that do not fall under one of the frequently used categories. Any amount recorded in the Other column is immediately posted to the appropriate general ledger account. The Sales Discount column is used if customers make a payment within the discount period specified by the company.

Cash sales are first recorded in the cash receipts journal, as shown in Figure 10.7. Because accounts receivable is not affected, nothing is posted to the subledger accounts. Because the Other column was not used, no entry is posted to the general ledger at this time. For the remaining columns, the general ledger is only updated at the end of the month, when the columns are totaled.

Cash Receipts Journal									Page 3
Date	Account	PR	Cash (DR)	Sales Discount (DR)	Accounts Receivable (CR)	Sales (CR)	Notes Payable (CR)	Other (CR)	COGS/ Merchandise Inventory (DR/CR)
Jan 2	Cash Sale		350			350			280

FIGURE 10.7

The transaction on January 4 in Figure 10.8 is an investment into the company by the owner. There is no column with Hanlon, Capital as a heading, so the amount is recorded in the Other column. The post reference (300) indicates that the amount of the investment shown is immediately updated to owner's capital in the general ledger. At the end of the month, the total of the Other column will not be posted because any amount in this column was posted immediately to the appropriate general ledger account.

Cash Receipts Journal									Page 3
Date	Account	PR	Cash (DR)	Sales Discount (DR)	Accounts Receivable (CR)	Sales (CR)	Notes Payable (CR)	Other (CR)	COGS/ Merchandise Inventory (DR/CR)
Jan 2	Cash Sale		350			350			280
Jan 4	Hanlon, Capital	300	4,000					4,000	

This posting reference means the amount in the Other column has been immediately updated in the general ledger.

FIGURE 10.8

Let us look at another type of transaction posted to the cash receipts journal. When a payment is made from a customer who made a purchase on credit, the subledger account is immediately updated because the payment affects the accounts receivable account. Updating the subledger account follows these steps.

ⓐ Transfer the date from the cash receipts journal to the date column in the subledger account.

ⓑ Make a note of the journal and page number in the PR column of the subledger.

ⓒ Transfer the amount of the accounts receivable column from the cash receipts journal to the credit column in the subledger.

ⓓ Indicate the posting is complete by entering a check mark in the PR column of the cash receipts journal.

For example, suppose Joe Blog makes a partial payment on January 10. Since the payment is made within 10 days of the original sale, Joe receives a 2% discount on the amount paid. The discount therefore reduces the amount of cash received, but does not reduce the amount of accounts receivable that is paid off. The steps required to post from the cash receipts journal to the subledger accounts are shown in Figure 10.9.

Cash Receipts Journal									Page 3
Date	Account	PR	Cash (DR)	Sales Discount (DR)	Accounts Receivable (CR)	Sales (CR)	Notes Payable (CR)	Other (CR)	COGS/ Merchandise Inventory (DR/CR)
Jan 2	Cash Sale		350			350			280
Jan 4	Hanlon, Capital	300	4,000					4,000	
Jan 10	Joe Blog	✓	588	12	600				

Account: Joe Blog					
Date	PR	DR	CR	Balance	
2018					
Jan 5	SJ1	1,235		1,235	DR
Jan 10	CR3		600	635	DR

FIGURE 10.9

At the end of the month, when all transactions have been recorded, all columns in the cash receipts journal are totaled and posted to the appropriate general ledger accounts. The posting to the accounts receivable controlling account follows these steps.

ⓐ Transfer the date from the cash receipts journal to the date column in the general ledger account.

ⓑ Make a note of the journal and page number in the PR column of the general ledger.

ⓒ Transfer the total of the accounts receivable column from the cash receipts journal to the credit column in the general ledger account.

ⓓ Indicate the posting is complete by writing the general ledger number under the total in the cash receipts journal.

These steps are illustrated and labeled in Figure 10.10.

Cash Receipts Journal								Page 3
Date	Account	PR	Cash (DR)	Sales Discount (DR)	Accounts Receivable (CR)	Sales (CR)	Notes Payable (CR)	Other (CR)	COGS/ Merchandise Inventory (DR/CR)
Jan 2	Cash Sale		350			350			280
Jan 4	Hanlon, Capital	300	4,000					4,000	
Jan 10	Joe Blog	✓	588	12	600				
Jan 22	Granger Bank		2,000				2,000		
Jan 31	Total		6,938	12	600	350	2,000	4,000	280
			(101)	(405)	(110)	(400)	(220)	(X)	(500/120)

Account: Accounts Receivable   **GL No:** 110

Date	Description	PR	DR	CR	Balance	
2018						
Jan 31		SJ1	2,191		2,191	DR
Jan 31		CR3		600	1,591	DR

Account: Joe Blog

Date	PR	DR	CR	Balance	
2018					
Jan 5	SJ1	1,235		1,235	DR
Jan 10	CR3		600	635	DR

Account: Furniture Retailers

Date	PR	DR	CR	Balance	
2018					
Jan 16	SJ1	956		956	DR

FIGURE 10.10

In this example, $600 is posted as a credit to accounts receivable, $6,938 is posted as a debit to cash (not shown), $12 is posted as a debit to sales discounts (not shown), and so on. Since the entry in the Other column—the investment made by the owner—was immediately posted to the general ledger when the transaction was recorded, an (X) is used to indicate that no posting is required.

The Purchases Journal

The purchases journal records all purchases on account. Several columns are provided to keep track of common items that the company purchases on account (e.g., merchandise inventory and office supplies). If anything else is purchased, it is recorded in the Other column.

When a purchase is made, the supplier subledger account must be updated immediately. Notice that the purchases journal has a column for terms, which is used to keep track of any terms offered by each supplier. Updating the subledger account with the transactions posted to the purchases journal follows these steps.

ⓐ Transfer the date from the purchases journal to the date column in the subledger account.

ⓑ Make a note of the journal and page number in the PR column of the subledger.

ⓒ Transfer the amount of the accounts payable column from the purchases journal to the credit column in the subledger.

ⓓ Indicate the posting is complete by entering a check mark in the PR column of the purchases journal.

Figure 10.11 shows the steps to update the subledger account when a purchase is made.

Purchases Journal									Page 6
Date	Account	Invoice #	Terms	PR	Merchandise Inventory (DR)	Office Supplies (DR)	Other (DR)	Accounts Payable (CR)	
Jan 3	Antonio's Electric	2089	3/15, n 30	✓	4,200			4,200	

Account: Antonio's Electric

Date	PR	DR	CR	Balance	
2018					
Jan 3	PJ6		4,200	4,200	CR

FIGURE 10.11

At the end of the month, after all transactions have been posted, the totals of the columns from the purchases journal are posted to the general ledger accounts. The totals of the individual subledger accounts must equal the balance of the accounts payable controlling account. The posting to the accounts payable controlling account follows these steps.

ⓐ Transfer the date from the purchases journal to the date column in the general ledger account.

ⓑ Make a note of the journal and page number in the PR column of the general ledger.

ⓒ Transfer the total of the accounts payable column from the purchases journal to the credit column in the general ledger account.

ⓓ Indicate the posting is complete by writing the general ledger number under the total in the purchases journal.

The posting of the transactions from the purchases journal to the accounts payable general ledger account is shown in Figure 10.12.

Purchases Journal								Page 6
Date	Account	Invoice #	Terms	PR	Merchandise Inventory (DR)	Office Supplies (DR)	Other (DR)	Accounts Payable (CR)
Jan 3	Antonio's Electric	2089	3/15, n 30	✓	4,200			4,200
Jan 19	Maintenance Expense/Doug's Maintenance	6091		525/✓			80	80
Jan 31	Total				4,200		80	4,280
					(120)		(X)	(200)

Account: Accounts Payable · **GL No:** 200

Date	Description	PR	DR	CR	Balance	
2018						
Jan 31		PJ6		4,280	4,280	CR

Account: Antonio's Electric

Date	PR	DR	CR	Balance	
2018					
Jan 3	PJ6		4,200	4,200	CR

Account: Doug's Maintenance

Date	PR	DR	CR	Balance	
2018					
Jan 19	PJ6		80	80	CR

FIGURE 10.12

Note that if an item is purchased that does not have a heading in the journal, it is placed in the Other column. Suppose the company had maintenance repairs done for the office, and received an invoice for $80. The $80 is placed in both the Other column and the Accounts Payable column of the purchases journal. Since the amount in the Other column must be posted immediately to the general ledger for the maintenance expense account, the GL number (525) is placed in the PR column. Additionally, since the $80 must also be posted to the relevant accounts payable subledger, a check mark is placed in the PR column of the purchases journal.

The Cash Payments Journal

The cash payments journal records all cash payments made by the company. There is a column to record the check number, since a good control is to have all payments made by check. Various columns are provided for the most common reasons for paying with cash, and an Other column is used to record cash payments for items that do not fall under one of the given columns. Merchandise Inventory includes both debit and credit columns. The debit side is used if merchandise inventory is purchased with cash (check) and the credit side is used if the company pays a supplier of merchandise inventory early and receives a discount.

Cash purchases are recorded in the cash payments journal, as shown in Figure 10.13. Since accounts payable is not affected, no entry should be posted to the subledger accounts. The Other column was not used, so no entry should be posted to the general ledger at this time. The general ledger is only updated at the end of the month when the columns are totaled.

Cash Payments Journal								Page 4
				Accounts Payable	**Other**	**Merchandise Inventory**		**Cash**
Date	**Account**	**Check #**	**PR**	**(DR)**	**(DR)**	**(DR)**	**(CR)**	**(CR)**
Jan 6	Electro Parts	748				1,500		1,500

FIGURE 10.13

The transaction on January 15 in Figure 10.14 is a withdrawal from the company by the owner. Since there is no column with Hanlon, Withdrawals as a heading, the amount is recorded in the Other column. The post reference (310) indicates that the amount of the withdrawal shown is immediately updated to owner's withdrawals in the general ledger. At the end of the month, the total of the Other column will not be posted because any amount in this column is posted immediately to the appropriate general ledger account.

Cash Payments Journal								Page 4
				Accounts Payable	**Other**	**Merchandise Inventory**		**Cash**
Date	**Account**	**Check #**	**PR**	**(DR)**	**(DR)**	**(DR)**	**(CR)**	**(CR)**
Jan 6	Electro Parts	748				1,500		1,500
Jan 15	Hanlon, Withdrawals	749	310		500			500

FIGURE 10.14

Updating the transactions posted in the cash payments journal to the relevant subledger account in Figure 10.15 follows these steps.

ⓐ Transfer the date from the cash payments journal to the date column in the subledger account.

ⓑ Make a note of the journal and page number in the PR column of the subledger.

c Transfer the amount of the accounts payable column from the cash payments journal to the debit column in the subledger.

d Indicate the posting is complete by entering a check mark in the PR column of the cash payments journal.

Cash Payments Journal						Merchandise Inventory		Page 4
Date	Account	Check #	PR	Accounts Payable (DR)	Other (DR)	(DR)	(CR)	Cash (CR)
Jan 6	Electro Parts	748				1,500		1,500
Jan 15	Hanlon, Withdrawals	749	310		500			500
Jan 18	Antonio's Electric	750	✓	4,200			126	4,074

Account: Antonio's Electric

Date	PR	DR	CR	Balance	
2018					
Jan 3	PJ6		4,200	4,200	CR
Jan 18	CP4	4,200		0	CR

FIGURE 10.15

Note that the payment to Antonio's Electric (a supplier) on January 18 immediately updates the subledger account since it affects accounts payable. Similar to the other journals, a check mark is placed in the PR column of the cash payments journal to show the transaction has been posted to the subledger account. Since the original purchase was on January 3, and the terms of the purchase were 3/15, n/30, the company can take a 3% discount on the payment. The discount amount is recorded as a credit to merchandise inventory and reduces the amount of cash that must be paid to the supplier.

At the end of the month, all columns from the cash payments journal are totaled and the amounts are posted to the appropriate general ledger accounts. The posting to the accounts payable controlling account follows these steps.

a Transfer the date from the cash payments journal to the date column in the general ledger account.

b Make a note of the journal and page number in the PR column of the general ledger.

c Transfer the total of the accounts payable column from the cash payments journal to the debit column in the general ledger account.

d Indicate the posting is complete by writing the general ledger number under the total in the cash payments journal.

Figure 10.16 illustrates the steps required to post from the cash payments journal to the accounts payable controlling account.

Cash Payments Journal							Page 4
				Accounts Payable (DR)	Other (DR)	Merchandise Inventory		Cash (CR)
Date	Account	Check #	PR			(DR)	(CR)	
Jan 6	Electro Parts	748				1,500		1,500
Jan 15	Hanlon, Withdrawals	749	310		500			500
Jan 18	Antonio's Electric	750	✓	4,200			126	4,074
Jan 31	Total			4,200	500	1,500	126	6,074
				(200)	(X)	(120)	(120)	(101)

ⓐ

Account: Accounts Payable					GL No: 200	
Date	Description	PR	DR	CR	Balance	
2018						
Jan 31		PJ6	ⓒ	4,280	4,280	CR
Jan 31		CP4	→4,200		80	CR

ⓑ

ⓓ

Account: Antonio's Electric					
Date	PR	DR	CR	Balance	
2018					
Jan 3	PJ6		4,200	4,200	CR
Jan 18	CP4	4,200		0	CR

Account: Doug's Maintenance					
Date	PR	DR	CR	Balance	
2018					
Jan 19	PJ6		80	80	CR

FIGURE 10.16

In this example, $4,200 is posted as a debit to accounts payable, $1,500 is posted as a debit to merchandise inventory (not shown), and so on. Since the transaction in the Other column was immediately posted to the general ledger, an (X) indicates that no posting is required.

Figure 10.17 summarizes the types of special journals.

Type of Special Journal	Purpose	Examples of Related General Ledger Accounts
Sales Journal	to record all sales made on account	Accounts Receivable, COGS, Merchandise Inventory
Cash Receipts Journal	to record all cash deposits and collections from outstanding accounts receivable	Accounts Receivable, Cash, Sales Discounts
Purchases Journal	to record all purchases made on account	Accounts Payable, Office Supplies, Merchandise Inventory
Cash Payments Journal	to record all cash payments made by the business	Accounts Payable, Cash, Merchandise Inventory

FIGURE 10.17

A CLOSER LOOK

At times, a transaction recorded in the special journal may require two amounts to be placed in the Other column. When this happens, it is acceptable to use two rows of the special journal to record the transaction. For example, suppose a company makes a $1,050 payment to its bank to pay back a note payable that includes $50 in interest. If the cash payments journal does not have a column for notes payable or for interest expense, both amounts must be recorded in the Other column. The journal below shows how this is recorded.

| Cash Payments Journal | | | | | | | | Page 4 |
Date	Account	Check #	PR	Accounts Payable (DR)	Other (DR)	Merchandise Inventory (DR)	(CR)	Cash (CR)
Aug 31	Notes Payable	263	210		1,000			1,050
	Interest Expense		530		50			

Notice that cash is credited for the total amount of the payment on the first line. The amount of the notes payable principal and interest are listed on two separate lines and the PR column indicates that both amounts were updated in the appropriate general ledger accounts.

Reconciling the Controlling Account

Remember that at the end of the month, when the general ledger is updated by the journals, the total of all the subledger accounts must equal the balance of the appropriate controlling account (e.g. accounts receivable or accounts payable).

To confirm that the total of the individual subledger accounts is equal to the respective controlling account balance in the general ledger, a reconciliation is prepared. From Figure 10.10, the balance of accounts receivable was $1,591. By finding the total of the accounts receivable subsidiary ledger, called a schedule of accounts receivable, we can confirm that the controlling account and subledger balance, as shown in Figure 10.18.

Jill Hanlon Retailer
January 31, 2018
General Ledger

Accounts Receivable	$1,591

Controlling account in the general ledger

Jill Hanlon Retailer
Schedule of Accounts Receivable
January 31, 2018

Joe Blog	$635
Furniture Retailers	956
Total Accounts Receivable	$1,591

The total of all subledger accounts

FIGURE 10.18

A similar schedule can be done for the accounts payable subsidiary ledger. From Figure 10.16, the balance of accounts payable was $80. The total of the accounts payable subledger is shown in Figure 10.19.

Jill Hanlon Retailer
Schedule of Accounts Payable
January 31, 2018

Antonio's Electric	$0
Doug's Maintenance	80
Total Accounts Payable	$80

Jill Hanlon Retailer
January 31, 2018
General Ledger

Accounts Payable	$80

Controlling account in the general ledger   The total of all subledger accounts

FIGURE 10.19

If the comparison of the general ledger controlling account and the total of the subledger accounts shows that they do not balance, the difference must be investigated and resolved before the trial balance can be completed.

Returns

The special journals are designed to record specific types of transactions, but some transactions that must be recorded do not fit into these special journals. In this case, the transaction must be recorded in the general journal. For example, sales and purchase returns do not fit into the special journals and must be recorded in the general journal. The only change to the way these transactions are recorded from what was learned earlier is how the posting is processed for accounts receivable or accounts payable.

Suppose Furniture Retailers, a customer from the example in Figure 10.6, returned $300 worth of items on January 18 that cost $170. The general journal entry is shown in Figure 10.20. The PR for accounts receivable updates the general ledger (shown by the account number 110) and the subsidiary ledger for the customer (shown by the check mark).

JOURNAL				Page 5
Date 2018	**Account Title and Explanation**	**PR**	**Debit**	**Credit**
Jan 18	Sales Returns & Allowances	410	300	
	Accounts Receivable	110/✓		300
	Customer returned items			
	Merchandise Inventory	120	170	
	Cost of Goods Sold	500		170
	Returned items to supplier			

FIGURE 10.20

Also, suppose Jill Hanlon Retailer returned $500 of the merchandise inventory it purchased from Antonio's Electric on January 10 (from the example in Figure 10.12). This purchase return is completed in the general journal, as shown in Figure 10.21. The PR for accounts payable updates the general ledger (shown by the account number 200) and the subsidiary ledger for the supplier (shown by the check mark).

JOURNAL				Page 5
Date 2018	**Account Title and Explanation**	**PR**	**Debit**	**Credit**
Jan 10	Accounts Payable	200/✔	500	
	Merchandise Inventory	120		500
	Returned items to supplier			

FIGURE 10.21

Pause & Reflect

Exercise 10-1

Simmons Inc., a small consulting business, recorded the following transactions for June 2018.

Jun 4	Issued Invoice #325 for $1,200 to Derek Smith for consulting services
Jun 8	Purchased $75 worth of office supplies on account from Supply Depot
Jun 10	Issued Invoice #326 for $800 to Soft Cell Enterprises for consulting services
Jun 15	Paid in full the June 8th invoice from Supply Depot
Jun 20	Purchased a printer for $140 on account from Buzz Electronics
Jun 22	Received $800 cash from Soft Cell Enterprises for payment of Invoice #326
Jun 26	Issued Invoice #327 for $525 to Bill Waites for consulting services
Jun 30	Received $700 cash from Derek Smith for partial payment of Invoice #325

Reconcile that the totals of the individual subledger accounts (Accounts Receivable, Accounts Payable) are equal to their respective account balances in the controlling accounts in the general ledger. Enter the appropriate information in the general ledgers and the schedules below.

Simmons Inc. June 30, 2018 General Ledger	
Accounts Receivable	

Simmons Inc. Schedule of Accounts Receivable June 30, 2018	

Simmons Inc. June 30, 2018 General Ledger	
Accounts Payable	

Simmons Inc. Schedule of Accounts Payable June 30, 2018	

See Appendix I for solutions.

Computerized Accounting

So far in this chapter, all journals, ledgers and subledgers have been illustrated using a manual accounting system. For a small business with a small number of transactions, a manual system may be adequate. However, as the number of transactions increases, so does the amount of information that is kept. In a manual accounting system, storing, tracking and finding information can become tedious and difficult.

These days, even the smallest businesses are opting to use computerized accounting systems. Computerized accounting systems offer numerous benefits, including the following.

- automating and simplifying the record-keeping and posting processes
- providing an intuitive and user-friendly interface for entering and extracting information
- providing current account balances and account activity
- producing timely financial statements and management reports
- allowing the user to customize and format financial statements and reports
- providing features for budgeting and data analysis
- enabling users to account for multiple companies, as well as multiple currencies

Many computerized accounting systems can be tailored to the size of a business, its particular industry, and its specific accounting and reporting requirements, such as payroll or inventory control. Accounting systems are also available for different platforms, or operating environments, such as desktop accounting software installed directly on the user's computer hard drive; desktop software with mobile capabilities so it can be accessed via a wireless portable device; or cloud-based systems that provide access to accounting applications on a subscription basis. (Cloud accounting is discussed later in this section.)

A computerized system is typically set up in a similar manner to the special journals just described. Sales are entered in one section of the software, while receipts are entered in another. Purchases and payments are also separated into different sections. The general journal is available for any transaction that does not fit into any of the special journals.

Although entries can be recorded in different sections, the system updates the appropriate subledgers and the general ledger accounts at the time they are posted. By updating all appropriate ledgers after every posting, reports can be viewed or printed at any time and be up-to-date.

Details about customers and suppliers are available from the subledgers. Contact information and billing information can be stored. Reports on each customer or supplier can be easily generated to show all transactions and any amounts outstanding.

A computerized system keeps track of the terms of a purchase and indicates to the user when a payment should be made to take advantage of discounts. If no discounts are available, the system indicates when the bill should be paid so it is not late. For sales, the system can indicate when a customer is overdue for payment so a letter or email can be sent to remind the customer that payment is required.

Many accounting system vendors offer different levels of their software so that a business can upgrade an application as the business evolves. One of the most popular accounting software programs that offer this capability is QuickBooks®. Intuit and QuickBooks are trademarks and service marks of Intuit Inc., registered in the United States and other countries. We will use QuickBooks to demonstrate the typical functions of a computerized accounting system.

QuickBooks Illustration

We will illustrate how QuickBooks works using the example of Jill Hanlon Retailer from our discussion of manual accounting systems. To simplify things, we will limit our illustration to transactions involving invoicing, cash sales, and customer payments. As you follow the figures in this example, note that the screen titles and the function names (for example, "Create Invoices") may differ depending on the particular accounting program used. However, the accounting principles and procedures are common across all accounting software programs. For our example, we are using the desktop version of the QuickBooks Premier Edition for multiple users. There is also a QuickBooks online version that uses cloud technology, which is discussed later.

The following steps are involved when using a computerized accounting system.

1. Record a sale.

2. Record a payment received by a customer.

3. Print reports.

The first step is to record a sale. Many small businesses offer their customers different methods of making a purchase: by the business invoicing the customer on account (1a.), or by the customer paying cash for goods or services (1b.). We will look at both methods.

1a. Record a sale on account by creating an invoice

From the QuickBooks "Create Invoices" screen, the user selects a customer job from the customer records using a pull-down list. The customer job is usually the customer's name. The program fills in the customer's name and address from the information entered when the customer account was set up. Similarly, the remaining fields of the invoice are completed by using pull-down menus and (for some fields) entering the information manually.

To demonstrate, recall from Figure 10.5 that on January 5, Jill Hanlon sold a couch on account to Joe Blog and issued Invoice #5125 for the value of the sale, $1,235. Figure 10.22 shows how the transaction is recorded in QuickBooks.

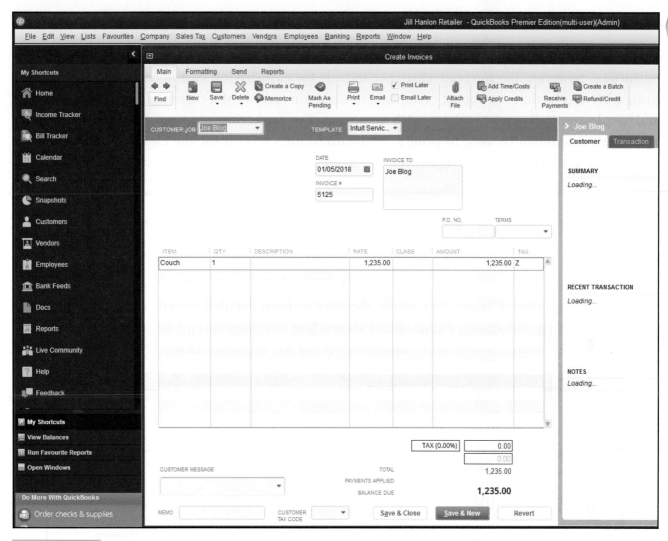

FIGURE 10.22

When the entry is saved and closed, the transaction is automatically posted as a debit to the accounts receivable customer account for Joe Blog, and a credit to the sales revenue account. The equivalent journal entry is shown in Figure 10.23.

JOURNAL				Page 5
Date 2018	**Account Title and Explanation**	**PR**	**Debit**	**Credit**
Jan 5	Accounts Receivable—Joe Blog		1,235	
	Sales Revenue			1,235

FIGURE 10.23

The invoice can then be printed and mailed to the customer, or saved in an electronic form (such as a PDF file) and emailed to the customer.

1b. Record a cash sale

When a customer pays in full for a product or service, accounts receivable is not affected. Most businesses, however, like to create customer records for cash-paying customers for several reasons: to simplify transactions for repeat customers, to maintain records of a customer's previous purchases, and to electronically communicate with customers for marketing purposes. Most importantly, a customer's record can be used to print a personalized sales receipt for the customer. Details of the transaction are entered in the QuickBooks "Sales Receipt" screen using a combination of pull-down menus and manual entries.

To demonstrate, recall from Figure 10.7 that on January 2, Jill Hanlon sold a product to a customer and received $350 in cash. The item was a small table sold to "Customer A," since Jill does not maintain individual customer records for cash sales. Because this is a sale of a product (as opposed to a service), the item must also be accounted for in Jill's merchandise inventory. QuickBooks includes an "Inventory Center" that allows the user to keep detailed records on each item that is purchased, tracked and resold. Figure 10.24 shows how the sales receipt is generated, and Figure 10.25 shows the related merchandise inventory record for the small table.

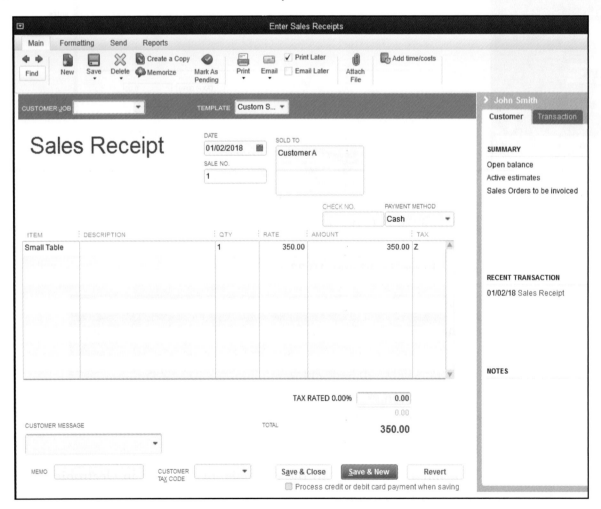

FIGURE 10.24

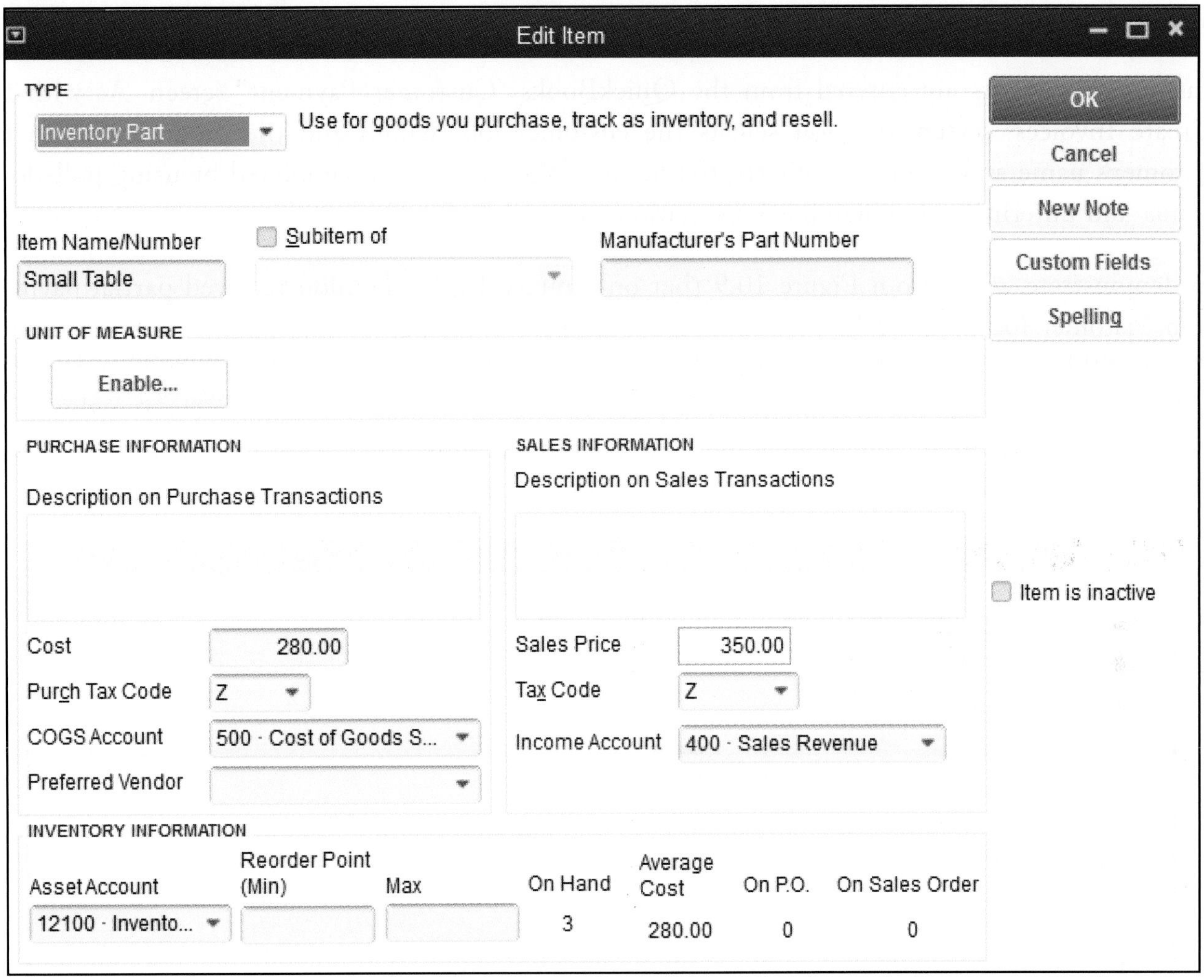

FIGURE 10.25

When the sales receipt entry is saved and closed, the total of $350 is debited to the cash account and credited to the sales revenue account. As well, the $280 cost of the small table is automatically posted as a debit to cost of goods sold, and a credit to merchandise inventory. The journal entries are shown in Figure 10.26.

JOURNAL					Page 5
Date 2018	**Account Title and Explanation**	**PR**	**Debit**	**Credit**	
Jan 2	Cash		350		
	Sales Revenue			350	
Jan 2	Cost of Goods Sold		280		
	Merchandise Inventory			280	

FIGURE 10.26

2. Record a payment received from a customer

Customer payments are entered from the QuickBooks "Customer Payment" screen. As with the "Create Invoices" screen, the user selects the customer job (name) and the program fills in the customer's name and address. Similarly, the fields of the invoice are completed by using pull-down menus and entering any remaining information manually.

To demonstrate, recall from Figure 10.9 that on January 10, Jill Hanlon received partial payment from customer Joe Blog for Invoice #5125. Of the $1,235 owing, Joe can pay $600. Because he is paying within the 10-day discount period, he receives a 2% discount on the amount paid, or $12 ($600 × 0.02). So he will actually pay $588 ($600 − $12). Recall that the discount reduces the amount of cash received, but it does not reduce the amount of accounts receivable that is paid off. Figure 10.27 shows how the transaction is recorded in QuickBooks.

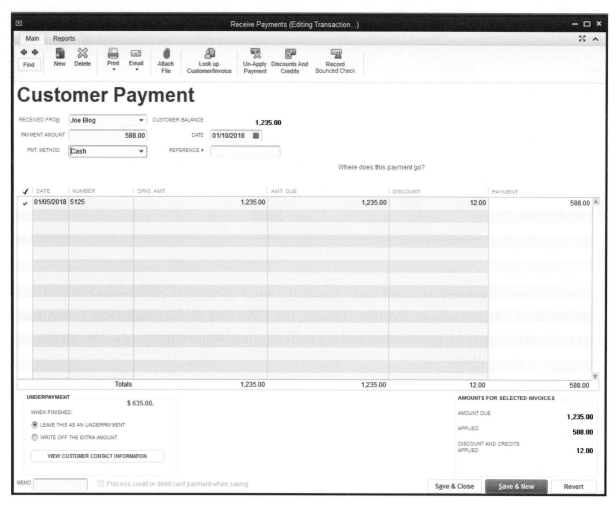

FIGURE 10.27

When the customer payment entry is saved and closed, the payment of $588 is debited to the cash account, the discount of $12 is posted to the sales discounts account, and $600 is credited to accounts receivable. The equivalent journal entry is shown in Figure 10.28.

JOURNAL				Page 5
Date 2018	**Account Title and Explanation**	**PR**	**Debit**	**Credit**
Jan 10	Cash		588	
	Sales Discounts		12	
	Accounts Receivable—Joe Blog			600

FIGURE 10.28

After the partial payment, Joe Blog's accounts receivables will have a balance of $635.

3. Print reports

Computerized accounting systems provide numerous options to print reports, ranging from standard financial statements to user-customized accounting and management reports. Most of these reports can be easily generated using the provided templates and customized depending on the users' needs.

Figure 10.29 shows the Sales by Item Detail report, showing the number of units and the dollar amount sold by item in January by Jill Hanlon Retailer. Note that this report includes both sales on account and cash sales. It also shows the sale that was made to Furniture Retailers in January.

	Type	Date	Num	Memo	Name	Qty	Sales Price	Amount	Balance
Inventory									
Couch									
	Invoice	01/05/2018	5125		Joe Blog	1	1,235.00	1,235.00	1,235.00
	Total Couch					1		1,235.00	1,235.00
Electric Fireplace									
	Invoice	01/16/2018	5126		Furniture Retailers	1	956.00	956.00	956.00
	Total Electric Fireplace					1		956.00	956.00
Small Table									
	Sales Receipt	01/02/2018	1		Customer A	1	350.00	350.00	350.00
	Total Small Table					1		350.00	350.00
Total Inventory						3		2,541.00	2,541.00
TOTAL						3		**2,541.00**	**2,541.00**

Jill Hanlon Retailer
Sales by Item Detail
March 17, 2017 through January 31, 2018

1:18 PM
03/17/17
Accrual Basis

FIGURE 10.29

Figure 10.30 shows the Open Invoices report, listing the customers who still owe money to the company as at the end of January, including the dollar amount that each customer owes. Note that the line item for Joe Blog shows his outstanding balance at January 31 (i.e. after he made his partial payment).

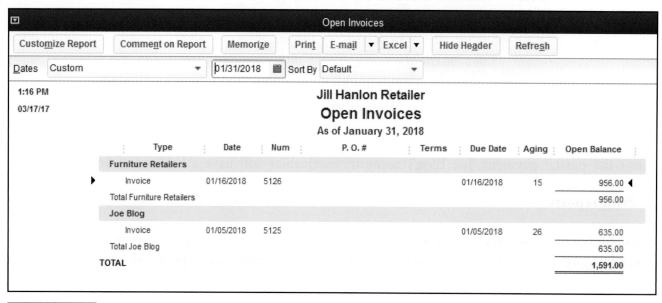

FIGURE 10.30

Figure 10.31 shows the Transactions by Account report, listing all cash transactions, including cash receipts and cash payments, during the month of January. Note that the investment made by the owner is also listed here, since it was a cash investment.

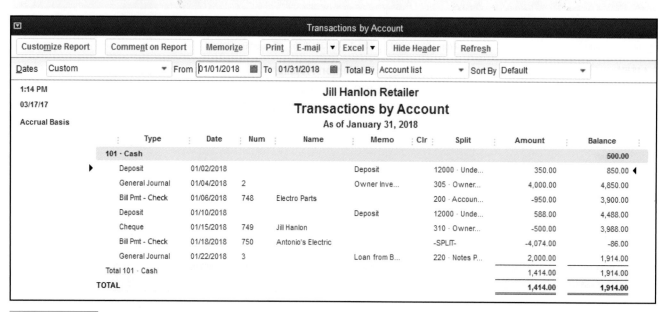

FIGURE 10.31

Transactions by Account reports can be made for any account in the company, allowing users to see transactions related to expenses, merchandise inventory, accounts receivable, and so on. These reports can also be customized, for example, to show only transactions that occurred between specific dates, or transactions related to a specific customer.

General Journal Entries in QuickBooks

Earlier in the chapter, in the example shown in Figure 10.8, Jill Hanlon made an investment into the company as the owner. On January 4, a journal entry was made for the cash receipt of $4,000, and the Hanlon, Capital account was immediately updated for the same amount in the general ledger. Figure 10.32 shows how this transaction is entered in QuickBooks using the "Make General Journal Entries" screen.

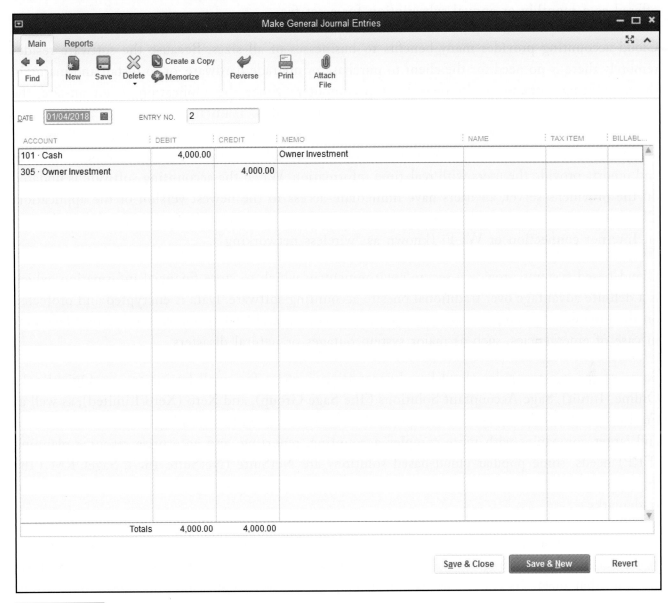

FIGURE 10.32

Also, note that this general journal entry relating to Jill's $4,000 cash investment into the company is included in the Transactions by Account report in Figure 10.31.

Cloud Accounting

Cloud accounting, also known as cloud-based accounting, refers to accounting software that is hosted remotely on the vendor's computer servers and accessed by users through the cloud. Data is entered via a user interface on the client's desktop, and then sent through the cloud (via the Internet or a large computer network) to be processed on the vendor's server. The information is then returned to the client by the same method. Cloud accounting is a service that is usually offered as a monthly or annual subscription for a set fee.

Cloud accounting provides many benefits to businesses of all sizes. Because the software resides remotely there is no need for the client to purchase or upgrade hardware, or to install and maintain the accounting software on its own desktop computers. Since the application is not on-site, the client company does not require specially trained IT staff to maintain it. All users at the client site have access to the same version of the software and can retrieve current financial information and produce customized reports. Accounting data is updated automatically so that account balances and reports provide the users with real-time information. When the accounting software is updated on the provider's server, all users have immediate access to the newest version of the application. Cloud accounting also enables users to access the software via mobile devices anywhere there is an Internet connection or Wi-Fi (known as "wireless networking").

Cloud-based systems provide a secure environment in which to store financial information, which is a definite advantage over traditional on-site accounting software. Data is encrypted and protected on the provider's system, and most providers maintain several backup servers in different locations in case of emergencies, such as major system outages or natural disasters.

Some of the most popular cloud-based accounting services for small businesses are QuickBooks Online (Intuit), Sage Accountant Solutions (The Sage Group), and Xero (Xero Limited), as well as FreshBooks (for self-employed service professionals, such as consultants and agencies). For mid-sized and larger companies with more complex accounting, reporting, and enterprise resource planning (ERP) needs, some popular cloud-based solutions are NetSuite (NetSuite Inc.), SageCRM (The Sage Group), and Oracle Cloud (Oracle). All of the accounting services listed here are registered trademarks.

There are a number of accounting software vendors that provide cloud accounting as part of their entire range of accounting software solutions. This enables a company to start with accounting software that meets its current needs and to upgrade to the vendor's more advanced applications as its business evolves.

Internal Control Aspects of Accounting Information Systems

One of the most basic concepts of internal control is that of a sound accounting system, including policies and procedures that encourage good management and ensure accuracy and validity of the accounting records. As we have seen with this chapter, special journals and subsidiary ledgers accomplish just that.

Special journals are used to track similar types of transactions, such as sales and purchases, or cash receipts and cash disbursements. Cash deposits can be reconciled and traced directly back and forth between the bank statement record and the cash receipt journal. Likewise, checks can be reconciled between the bank statement record and the cash disbursements journal. Special journals facilitate account reconciliation and accurate accounts.

Control accounts, such as accounts receivable subsidiary ledgers, are used to monitor and track all activity with customers through the receivable accounts. If accounts receivable needs analyzing, the accountant refers to all the related journals, control account and subsidiary ledgers for accounts receivable. Likewise, accounts payable can be analyzed and reconciled between the purchases journal, accounts payable control account and accounts payable subsidiary ledgers.

Whether manual or computerized, the organization's use and reconciliation of special journals and ledgers will create strong controls and accurate accounts.

In Summary

LO 1 **Explain the flow of accounting information through the accounting paper trail**

▶ Source documents provide evidence for journal entries, which are then posted to the general ledger accounts. The values from the general ledger accounts are used to create a trial balance and the financial statements.

LO 2 **Describe and record transactions in special journals and subsidiary ledgers**

▶ The sales journal is used to record all sales on account.

▶ The cash receipts journal is used to record all cash received.

▶ The purchases journal is used to record all purchases on account.

▶ The cash payments journal is used to record all cash paid.

▶ The general journal is used to record all transactions that do not fit into the other special journals.

▶ Subsidiary ledgers are used to track details that would clutter the general ledgers.

▶ All special journals are totaled at the end of the month and the totals are posted to the general ledger accounts.

▶ If a transaction in the sales journal or cash receipts journal affects accounts receivable, the accounts receivable subledger for that customer is updated immediately.

▶ If a transaction in the purchases journal or cash payments journal affects accounts payable, the accounts payable subledger for that supplier is updated immediately.

LO 3 **Identify features of a computerized accounting system**

▶ Computerized accounting systems have many benefits, including simplifying record-keeping and posting, providing a user-friendly interface for entering and extracting information, allowing the user to customize and format financial statements and reports, and producing timely financial statements and reports.

▶ Computerized accounting systems are available for different platforms such as desktop, desktop with mobile capabilities, and cloud-based applications on a subscription basis.

▶ A computerized accounting system has sections like the special journals to enter transactions. Transactions automatically update general and subsidiary ledgers.

▶ Subsidiary ledgers keep information about suppliers and customers and can be used to generate reports.

LO 4 **Apply internal controls related to the accounting system**

▶ The proper use of control accounts and subsidiary ledgers can help create strong controls in an organization.

 *Access **ameengage.com** for integrated resources including tutorials, practice exercises, the digital textbook and more.*

Review Exercise 10-1

Lin-Z is an owner-operated office furniture retailer. Lin-Z uses the perpetual inventory system. The following is a list of transactions for the month of June.

Jun 4   Received $4,000 from a cash sale to Gus Van Sand (sold office furniture costing $2,015)

Jun 5   Lin-Z received Invoice #4053 for $100 worth of supplies from Stapl-EZ Inc.

Jun 6   Received $480 from Bo Didley regarding outstanding accounts receivable

Jun 9   Received $2,160 for the cash sale of a lounge suite (costing $1,050) to Rita Patterson

Jun 9   Lin-Z received a bill from Building Services Inc. (Invoice #124) for $350 for repairs and maintenance of the office building

Jun 10   Received $25 in interest from a loan to Kurt Domino

Jun 12   Paid amount owing (Invoice #4053) to Stapl-EZ Inc. (Check #465)

Jun 15   Received a loan of $2,400 from the bank

Jun 18   Sold goods on account (Invoice #10022) to Richard Starkey, for office furniture for $3,000 (costing $2,000)

Jun 21   Purchased $4,000 worth of inventory from Noel's Inc. using Check #466

Jun 22   Paid amount owing (Invoice #124) to Building Services Inc. for repairs (Check #467)

Jun 25   Paid $175 to SKG Inc., for general expenses (Check #468)

Jun 26   Received a bill from Brick & Mortar Inc. (Invoice #404241) for $3,500 worth of inventory

Jun 28   Sold $5,000 worth of inventory (costing $3,700) on account to Pete Best (Invoice #10023)

Required

a) Record the transactions in the relevant cash receipts, sales, purchases, and cash payments journals.

Cash Receipts Journal									Page 1
Date	Account	PR	Cash (DR)	Sales (CR)	Accounts Receivable (CR)	Interest Revenue (CR)	Notes Payable (CR)	Other (CR)	COGS/ Merchandise Inventory (DR/CR)
	Total								

Sales Journal					Page 1
Date	Account	Invoice #	PR	Accounts Receivable/Sales (DR/CR)	COGS/ Merchandise Inventory (DR/CR)
	Total				

Purchases Journal							Page 1
Date	Account	Invoice #	PR	Repairs Expense (DR)	Office Supplies (DR)	Purchases (DR)	Accounts Payable (CR)
	Total						

Cash Payments Journal							Page 1
Date	Account	Check #	PR	Other (DR)	Purchases (DR)	Accounts Payable (DR)	Cash (CR)
	Total						

b) Post from the special journals to the accounts receivable subledger. At the end of the month, post the following opening subledger balances from the special journals to the general ledger controlling account.

- Bo Didley: $2,000 (DR)
- Richard Starkey: $1,000 (DR)
- Pete Best: $1,500 (DR)

Note that Lin-Z's accounts receivable records consist of only these three subledgers. Assume no entries were made directly to accounts receivable through the general journal. Reconcile the subledger to the controlling account at the end of the month.

Accounts Receivable Subsidiary Ledger Bo Didley				
Date	PR	DR	CR	Balance

Accounts Receivable Subsidiary Ledger Richard Starkey				
Date	PR	DR	CR	Balance

Accounts Receivable Subsidiary Ledger Pete Best				
Date	PR	DR	CR	Balance

Post to the general ledger.

Account: Accounts Receivable					GL No: 110
Date	Description	PR	DR	CR	Balance

Lin-Z June 30, 2018 General Ledger	

Lin-Z Schedule of Accounts Receivable June 30, 2018	

c) Post from the special journals to the accounts payable subledger and then to the general ledger controlling account at the end of the month. Assume the following opening subledger balances.

- Stapl-EZ: $500 (CR)
- Building Services Inc: $750 (CR)
- Brick & Mortar Inc: $2,500 (CR)

Note that Lin-Z's accounts payable records consist of only these three subledgers. Assume no entries were made directly to accounts payable through the general journal. Reconcile the subledger to the controlling account at the end of the month.

Accounts Payable Subsidiary Ledger Stapl-EZ Inc.					
Date	PR	DR	CR	Balance	

Accounts Payable Subsidiary Ledger Building Services Inc.					
Date	PR	DR	CR	Balance	

Accounts Payable Subsidiary Ledger Brick & Mortar Inc.					
Date	PR	DR	CR	Balance	

Post to the general ledger.

Account: Accounts Payable					GL No: 200	
Date	Description	PR	DR	CR	Balance	

Lin-Z June 30, 2018 General Ledger	

Lin-Z Schedule of Accounts Payable June 30, 2018	

See Appendix I for solutions.

Chapter 11
Accounting for Noncurrent Assets

Learning Objectives

 Access **ameengage.com** *for integrated resources including tutorials, practice exercises, the digital textbook and more.*

355

MAKING IT REAL TO YOU

Machines and equipment are required to run a business. It could be work trucks to run a construction business, or it could be office equipment and computers to run a graphic design shop. These machines and equipment are noncurrent, or long-term, assets. We record the purchase price of the asset, and then we regularly and systematically record an estimate of the use of that asset. Recording the use of a noncurrent asset is called depreciation. Depreciation can be a very large expense for a business, and it is one of a few non-cash businesses expenses. There are many different ways to record depreciation for financial reporting and tax reporting purposes. We will work with the basic straight-line method for depreciation including account analysis over the life of the asset.

Noncurrent Assets

LO 1

Current assets are defined as those owned for the short term. Noncurrent assets are those that are owned and used by a company as part of normal operations for the long term. Specifically, noncurrent assets must possess the following three characteristics.

1. They provide the infrastructure necessary for operating the business.
2. They are expected to be used on an ongoing basis. Typically, this means longer than the business' operating cycle or one year.
3. They are not intended to be sold to customers.

Noncurrent assets are also commonly referred to as *long-term assets*, *long-lived assets*, *fixed assets* or *capital assets*.

Noncurrent assets can be either tangible or intangible by nature. Tangible assets have physical substance, which can be perceived with our senses, especially by touch. Intangible assets have no physical substance and can only be perceived by the mind or imagination. The noncurrent assets section of the Accounting Map is divided into separate parts containing tangible and intangible assets. As shown in Figure 11.1, Property, Plant & Equipment, which are also called *plant assets*, pertains to a company's noncurrent tangible assets, such as buildings, machinery, vehicles and computer equipment. The intangible part is labeled Intangible Assets and includes items such as patents and trademarks. Goodwill is also intangible by nature, but it has distinctive characteristics deserving of its own section. Each group of assets is covered in this chapter.

A company must have noncurrent tangible assets to accomplish physical tasks. Examples include machines that package bottles, trucks that deliver products and computers that scan and calculate inventory data. Noncurrent tangible assets often form the physical backbone of a company. Without them, a business will not have the property, buildings and machinery it needs to deliver goods and services to its customers. This is particularly true for manufacturers or companies involved in the transportation industry, whose noncurrent assets are often the largest group of assets on the balance sheet.

FIGURE 11.1

For example, Figure 11.2 shows an excerpt of a balance sheet for Amtrak—an American passenger railroad company. The balance sheet shows values for the years ended September 30, 2016 and September 30, 2015.

National Railroad Passenger Corporation and Subsidiaries (Amtrak) Consolidated Balance Sheet (partial) For the Year Ended September 30 (In Thousands of Dollars)		
ASSETS	**2016**	**2015**
Current Assets		
Cash and cash equivalents	$752,488	$523,028
Restricted cash and cash equivalents	7,966	4,978
Accounts receivable, net of allowances of $5,352 and $5,067 as of September 30, 2016 and 2015, respectively	294,548	308,875
Materials and supplies, net of allowances of $27,653 and $27,782 at September 30, 2016 and 2015, respectively	255,095	272,689
Prepaid expenses	37,730	27,721
Other current assets	306,342	36,653
Total Current Assets	**1,654,169**	**1,173,944**
Property and Equipment		
Locomotives	2,127,329	1,944,706
Passenger cars and other rolling stock	3,247,105	3,168,946
Right-of-way and other properties	12,694,726	12,124,468
Construction-in-progress	1,713,510	1,410,974
Leasehold improvements	572,610	556,327
Property and equipment, gross	20,355,280	19,205,421
Less: Accumulated depreciation and amortization	(8,026,218)	(7,502,347)
Total Property and Equipment, Net	**12,329,062**	**11,703,074**
Other Assets, Deposits and Deferred Charges		
Notes receivable on sale-leasebacks	55,833	55,210
Deferred charges, deposits and other	45,160	362,356
Total Other Assets, Deposits and Deferred Charges	**100,993**	**417,566**
Total Assets	**$14,084,224**	**$13,294,584**

FIGURE 11.2

For both fiscal years 2016 and 2015, the company's largest assets were its property, plant and equipment. Figure 11.3 illustrates this important relationship for some other American companies. As you can see, noncurrent assets often make up a large percentage of many companies' total assets. These are important investments for the business and need to be properly managed to achieve success. Because noncurrent assets tend to be worth large amounts of money and constitute major items on a company's balance sheet, it is tremendously important for accountants to properly classify, record and monitor the value of noncurrent assets. This chapter will discuss in detail how accountants perform these tasks.

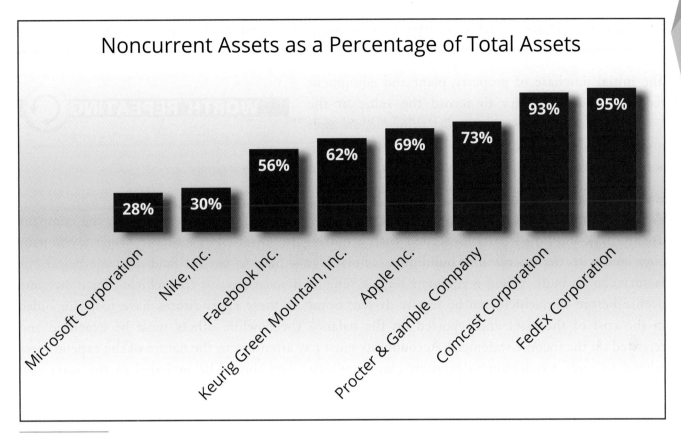

Noncurrent Assets as a Percentage of Total Assets

FIGURE 11.3

Tangible assets that last longer than one year and are used in normal operations are classified as part of property, plant and equipment. Items that are still used, even if only some of the time (e.g. equipment at peak periods of activity), are also reported as property, plant and equipment. However, there are instances of tangible assets that last longer than one year but are not reported in the same way on the balance sheet. Specifically, tangible assets that are not used at all for operations are not reported as property, plant and equipment; for example, old equipment that was once used for manufacturing but is now sitting unused waiting to be sold as scrap metal.

Long-lived assets that are held for sale to customers but not used in normal operations are classified as merchandise inventory. For example, vehicles held in merchandise inventory by an automotive dealership are intended for sale and therefore not considered as noncurrent assets of the dealership. Conversely, a delivery truck that is used in the daily operations of the dealership is classified as a noncurrent asset.

Land that is not used for daily operations but is held for resale or future expansion is classified on the balance sheet as a long-term investment. However, if the land holds a building that is used in normal operations, then that land is classified as a plant asset and is reported as part of property, plant and equipment on the balance sheet.

The Acquisition and Changes in Value of Noncurrent Assets   LO 2

The initial purchase of property, plant and equipment requires a journal entry to record the value of the asset purchased. Following the cost principle, an asset must be recorded at its actual cost. The first step in accounting for the acquisition of property, plant and equipment is to determine the cost of the acquired item.

WORTH REPEATING

Buying assets as well as selling assets at book value has no impact on the value of equity.

When a company purchases physical items, such as land, buildings and equipment, the company usually pays additional costs associated with acquiring the assets. For example, when a company buys land with the intention of building a factory, it may have to pay for land drainage before the factory can be built. When a company buys a vehicle, it must pay for the vehicle's insurance and license before the vehicle can be legally driven. Some of these expenditures have to be included in the cost of the asset and reported on the balance sheet, while others must be expensed and reported on the income statement. Accountants must pay attention to the nature of the expenditures related to asset acquisition to properly classify which costs should be included in the asset cost and which costs should be expensed.

The costs necessary for getting the asset ready for use are those directly related to having the asset set up at its intended location and in a ready-to-use condition. These expenditures benefit the company not only in the current period, but also in future periods as long as the noncurrent asset is still being used. Figure 11.4 lists the items that are usually included in the costs of acquiring the following classifications of noncurrent assets: (1) buildings, (2) machinery and equipment, and (3) land and land improvements.

Buildings	Machinery and Equipment	Land and Land Improvements
• Purchase price • Sales taxes • Brokerage fees • Legal fees • Title fees • Design fees • Building permits • Betterments and extraordinary repairs of existing buildings • Insurance while under construction • Finance costs related to construction • Electrical system • Lighting fixtures • Plumbing • Flooring • Painting and wall coverings • Materials, labor and overhead costs of new building construction	• Purchase price • Sales taxes • Freight and delivery charges • Government permits • Insurance while in transit • Betterments and extraordinary repairs of existing machinery and equipment • Installation • Assembly • Testing prior to use	• Purchase price • Sales taxes • Brokerage fees • Delinquent property taxes • Legal fees • Title insurance • Government permits • Reclamation or remediation of land (if contaminated) to make it suitable for use • Removal of any existing structures • Land surveying fees • Preparation of land, such as clearing, grading, leveling, drainage, government assessments, installing sewers • Land improvements, such as driveways, walkways, paving, fences, landscaping, sprinkler systems, outdoor lighting

FIGURE 11.4

Since these expenditures are directly related to the asset itself, they are not treated as expenses but as part of the cost of the asset. This cost is then recorded on the company's balance sheet. Other costs that are not directly attributable to getting the asset ready for use, such as the costs of advertising products that a recently acquired machine will be producing, or unnecessary costs such as errors or damage in the installation of machinery, are expensed rather than capitalized. Recurring costs that benefit the company only in the current period (without providing long-term benefits, such as the costs of a vehicle's license and insurance) are also expensed.

The value of a noncurrent asset also dictates whether its purchase should be capitalized or expensed. The materiality constraint allows the company to expense low-cost, noncurrent assets that are below the company's materiality threshold; an item can be considered an expense on the income statement instead of a noncurrent asset on the balance sheet if it has no material value relative to the size of the business.

Recording the Acquisition of Property, Plant and Equipment

The asset's purchase price and the costs necessary for getting the asset ready for use are combined into a single amount representing the cost of the asset. The amount is then debited to the appropriate asset account.

For example, the Sunshine Juice Company has purchased a new bottling machine for its orange juice line on February 1, 2018. It was purchased for $120,000, shipped at a cost of $5,000, and had installation costs of $2,000. Assuming one invoice for all these costs, Figure 11.5 shows the journal entry for the acquisition of this noncurrent asset.

JOURNAL			
Date	Account Title and Explanation	Debit	Credit
Feb 1	Machine	127,000	
	Accounts Payable		127,000
	Record the purchase of a machine for $120,000 plus $2,000 for installation and $5,000 for shipping		

FIGURE 11.5

When totaled, the costs amount to $127,000. This is debited to an account that is part of property, plant and equipment and credited to accounts payable, since the company was invoiced and owes this amount to the bottling machine manufacturer. Of course, once the bill is paid, accounts payable is debited and cash is credited.

Although some prepared financial statements may show a single property, plant and equipment line item, there are actually separate accounts for each noncurrent asset within that category.

Lump Sum Purchases of Property, Plant and Equipment

Companies sometimes purchase property, plant and equipment in bundles, or what is known as a "basket of assets." Instead of buying property, plant and equipment individually from different vendors, a company may get a good price for a basket of assets by buying them from the same vendor in one transaction, called a **lump sum purchase** or a **basket purchase**.

The accounting challenge with this type of transaction is that by paying a lower price for the assets, the buyer acquires them for less than their appraised value. In this case, the lump sum paid for all the assets is divided and allocated to each item according to percentages based on the appraised values or fair values. For example, on August 1, 2018, the Huge Bargain Store purchased land, a building and a parking lot to open a new store. It bought the assets in a bundle for the lump sum payment of $800,000. However, each asset has its own appraised value, as listed in Figure 11.6.

Item	Appraised Value
Land	$600,000
Building	300,000
Parking Lot	100,000
Total	**$1,000,000**

FIGURE 11.6

The total of all the appraised values is $1,000,000, which is $200,000 more than the purchase price. The first step is to take each item's appraised value and divide it by the total appraised value. This produces a percentage that should be allocated to each asset and is shown in Figure 11.7.

Land	$600,000 \div 1,000,000 \times 100\%$	60%
Building	$300,000 \div 1,000,000 \times 100\%$	30%
Parking Lot	$100,000 \div 1,000,000 \times 100\%$	10%

FIGURE 11.7

These percentages are now allocated to the amount actually paid, which was $800,000. For example, land made up 60% of the total appraised value, so it makes up 60% of the price paid, which is $480,000. The allocated amounts for the land, building and parking lot are shown in Figure 11.8.

Land	$800,000 \times 60\%$	$480,000
Building	$800,000 \times 30\%$	240,000
Parking Lot	$800,000 \times 10\%$	80,000
Total		**$800,000**

FIGURE 11.8

Figure 11.9 shows the journal entry after calculating the actual value applied to the assets. Each asset is debited by the value calculated and cash is credited by the purchase price of $800,000.

JOURNAL			
Date	Account Title and Explanation	Debit	Credit
Aug 1	Land	480,000	
	Building	240,000	
	Parking Lot	80,000	
	Cash		800,000
	Record the purchase of land, building and parking lot		

FIGURE 11.9

Pause & Reflect

Exercise 11-1

On May 1, 2018, Bristol Holding Company purchased land valued at $600,000, a building valued at $1,000,000 and a parking lot valued at $400,000. Bristol Holding paid $1,800,000 cash for these three assets.

a) Calculate the book value that should be recorded for these assets.

Asset	Appraised Value	Percentage	Book Value
Building	$1,000,000		
Land	600,000		
Parking Lot	400,000		
Total	$2,000,000		

b) Prepare the journal entry for this purchase.

JOURNAL			
Date	Account Title and Explanation	Debit	Credit

See Appendix I for solutions.

Changes in Property, Plant and Equipment

Property, plant and equipment can change in value as a result of two factors: depreciation, which will be examined shortly, and changes made to the asset itself. One challenge with property, plant and equipment is determining whether an item should be classified as a noncurrent asset or simply recorded as an expense in the current year. This challenge is even more difficult when there is a change to the asset. If the change results in beneficial consequences to the asset that extend beyond the current period, the expenses paid for the change are classified as a **capital expenditure**. Two types of capital expenditures are betterments and extraordinary repairs. Capital expenditures increase the net book value of the related asset accounts and are reported on the balance sheet. On the other hand, an expense that benefits the current period is known as a **revenue expenditure**. Revenue expenditures include ordinary repairs and maintenance, and are reported on the income statement.

We will look at the different types of both capital expenditures and revenue expenditures in this section, starting with betterments.

Betterments

A betterment is an improvement that increases an asset's efficiency or effectiveness without necessarily increasing the asset's useful life. Some examples of betterments are plant expansions or major upgrades to equipment or vehicles used in the business. Betterments are capital expenditures and benefit future periods, so they are debited to the asset account (capitalized) and depreciated over the asset's remaining useful life. To illustrate, suppose a company replaces the engine in its existing equipment with a more powerful engine that will improve its efficiency. The new engine, including installation, costs $6,000. The journal entry is shown in Figure 11.10.

JOURNAL			
Date	**Account Title and Explanation**	**Debit**	**Credit**
Oct 1	Equipment	6,000	
	Cash		6,000
	To record installation of upgraded engine to equipment		

FIGURE 11.10

Extraordinary Repairs

Extraordinary repairs, unlike asset betterments, are costs incurred to extend an asset's useful life past the original estimate. Some examples are replacing the existing roof of a building or repaving a parking lot. Extraordinary repairs are capital expenditures and benefit future periods, so they are recorded as a debit to the accumulated depreciation account for that asset. To illustrate, suppose a company overhauls the engine in its 10-year-old delivery van and now expects to get another four years of use from it. The overhaul, including materials and labor, costs $5,000. The journal entry is shown in Figure 11.11.

JOURNAL			
Date	**Account Title and Explanation**	**Debit**	**Credit**
Oct 1	Accumulated Depreciation—Delivery Van	5,000	
	Cash		5,000
	To record cost of engine overhaul for delivery van		

FIGURE 11.11

Because this journal entry changes the value of the delivery van's accumulated depreciation, the depreciation charge needs to be recalculated and adjusted for the delivery van's remaining useful life. The concept of depreciation is explained later in the chapter.

Ordinary Repairs and Maintenance

Ordinary repairs and maintenance are expenditures made for the upkeep of existing assets, but they do not materially improve an asset's efficiency or effectiveness, nor do they extend the asset's useful life. Some examples are painting, minor wall and floor repairs, cleaning, and minor adjustments to equipment and machinery. Ordinary repairs and maintenance are revenue expenditures and benefit the current period, so they are debited to the related expense account. To illustrate, suppose a company pays for repairs to a hole in the drywall in one of its offices. The repairs, including materials and labor, cost $325. The journal entry is shown in Figure 11.12.

GAAP vs IFRS

Under GAAP, accounting treatments are different for ordinary repairs, extraordinary repairs and betterments. Under IFRS, the cost is typically capitalized as part of the cost of the asset if future economic benefit is probable and can be reliably measured.

365

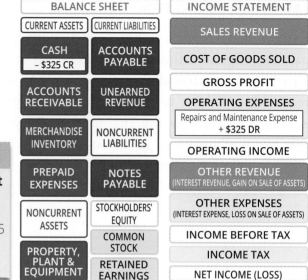

JOURNAL			
Date	**Account Title and Explanation**	**Debit**	**Credit**
Oct 1	Repairs and Maintenance Expense	325	
	Cash		325
	To record repairs to drywall in office		

FIGURE 11.12

The Concept of Depreciation

In any discussion of expenses arising from assets, expense recognition must be considered. Expenses associated with assets need to be matched with associated revenues. Property, plant and equipment are typically used for long periods of time. Depreciation is the allocation of an asset's cost over its life span. We will examine various aspects of depreciation and how noncurrent assets on the balance sheet are affected.

Residual Value

Before discussing specific methods of depreciation, we should first examine what an asset's residual value is and how it affects depreciation calculations. **Residual value** is the estimated value of an asset at the end of its useful life. An asset may still have some value, even if it is no longer useful to the company, or it may have a residual value of $0. Residual value is also referred to as *salvage value* or *scrap value*.

For example, a company has a delivery truck that has been on the road for many years and can no longer be fixed to continue running. A buyer might see some residual value in the truck, buy it, and sell its spare parts or scrap metal. Sometimes, a noncurrent asset carries a residual value even after it is unable to do what it was designed for.

The total amount depreciated for a noncurrent asset is affected by the residual value that is expected to remain at the end of the asset's useful life. An asset's residual value is not depreciated. For example, if a company purchases an item of property, plant and equipment for $5,000, and estimates its residual value as $1,000, the amount depreciated over the useful life of the asset is $4,000. Even though the asset can no longer be used for business after its useful life expires, the company may be able to get some money for it and this price should be subtracted from the depreciation calculations made by the company.

The *actual* residual value of an asset, defined as the proceeds from selling the asset at the end of its useful life less its disposal cost, may turn out to be different from the *estimated* residual value. One of the realities confronting accountants is that depreciation is a theoretical concept. The market value of a noncurrent asset may not decrease at the same rate as its depreciation schedule. The decrease in the market value of an item of property, plant and equipment over time depends on the supply and demand mechanism of the market, which has nothing to do with how much the item has been depreciated in the books. Depreciation involves an accountant's best estimate, which requires justified calculations of a noncurrent asset's value over its useful life with the company. Depreciation does not dictate an asset's market value.

For example, Skyscape Company purchased a noncurrent asset at an initial cost of $100,000. The accountant will examine the asset, study its potential worth over time, and make an educated guess at what someone might be willing to pay to salvage it. This is not an easy task. At the end of the asset's life, if the actual residual value is different from the accountant's original estimate, a gain (or loss) on asset disposal is recorded.

Assume that the accountant estimates an item's residual value to be $10,000. Ten years later, the item is sold for $6,000. Since the selling price was lower than the estimated residual value, the accountant records a loss of $4,000. The overestimation is not an issue as long as the accountant was justified in making the initial estimate and adjusts for a loss once the asset is sold. Similarly, if the asset is sold for more than its estimated residual value, the difference is recorded as a gain.

In addition to estimating the residual value, an accountant must also decide which depreciation method to use. The accountant should try to choose the depreciation method that best reflects the pattern in which the asset will be used by the company in practice. The same depreciation method should be used throughout the life of the asset. However, there are times when an accountant may change the method used, which is acceptable as long as there is justification in doing so.

We will now examine three methods of depreciation related to noncurrent assets. The three methods and their assumptions are listed in Figure 11.13.

Depreciation Method	Assumption
Straight-Line Method	Asset depreciates equally every year
Declining-Balance and Double-Declining-Balance Method	Asset depreciates faster at the beginning
Units-of-Production Method	Asset depreciates based on activity level

FIGURE 11.13

The Straight-Line Method

The straight-line method of depreciation was first introduced in Chapter 5. The **straight-line method of depreciation** produces an average depreciation expense, which is applied each year until the asset is sold or reaches the end of its useful life. Figure 11.14 shows the formula to calculate the amount of depreciation under the straight-line method.

$$\text{Straight-Line Depreciation} = \frac{\text{Cost of Asset} - \text{Residual Value}}{\text{Useful Life}}$$

FIGURE 11.14

There are three components of the calculation.

1. The total cost of the asset is the original purchase price of the asset and any additional costs required to get it in a ready-to-use condition.

2. The residual value is the estimated value of the asset at the end of its useful life. Since the residual value is not depreciated, it is subtracted from the total cost of the asset.

3. The useful life is an estimate of how long the asset is expected to be used by the business. Useful life is usually expressed in years.

For example, Smith Tools buys a machine for $5,000. The machine is expected to have a useful life of five years and its residual value is estimated to be $1,000. The calculation to determine the amount of depreciation applied annually for the machine is shown below.

$$\text{Straight-Line Depreciation} = \frac{\$5,000 - \$1,000}{5 \text{ years}}$$

$$= \$800/\text{year}$$

If the machine was purchased on January 1, 2018, the annual depreciation is applied to the machine as shown in Figure 11.15.

Year	Cost of Machine	Depreciation Expense	Accumulated Depreciation	Net Book Value
2018	$5,000	$800	$800	$4,200
2019	5,000	800	1,600	3,400
2020	5,000	800	2,400	2,600
2021	5,000	800	3,200	1,800
2022	5,000	800	4,000	**1,000**

FIGURE 11.15

A depreciation of $800 is accumulated each year until the end of the asset's useful life. At that time, all that is left of the asset's book value is its residual value. In this case, the amount is $1,000, the final net book value (shown in green in Figure 11.15).

Now, assume that the asset has no residual value at the end of its useful life. This means that the total amount to be depreciated is $5,000, which was the original cost of the asset. The annual depreciation amount is calculated as $1,000 ($5,000 ÷ 5).

As is common in accounting, the calculations are only part of the process. The next step is to record the results of those calculations in the financial statements.

Accountants want to see the original value of the asset on the balance sheet and the net book value change over time. Contra accounts allow both values to be reflected on the balance sheet. Remember, a contra-asset account is linked to another asset account to reduce the value of the asset. The contra account for a noncurrent asset is called accumulated depreciation. It reflects the decrease in value of the noncurrent asset over time. The original cost of the noncurrent asset account remains constant.

Figure 11.16 shows the corresponding journal entry for recording $1,000 of depreciation expense of the machine on December 31, 2018.

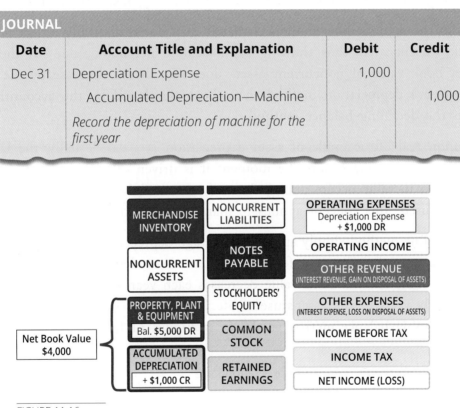

FIGURE 11.16

The initial purchase of the asset on January 1 is shown as a $5,000 debit balance in property, plant and equipment. The entry for depreciation on December 31 is recorded as a $1,000 credit to accumulated depreciation. This reduces the net book value of the machine to $4,000. Equity decreases with the depreciation expense that is recorded on the income statement under operating expenses.

Each year depreciation is recorded, the amount of accumulated depreciation increases and the net book value of the noncurrent asset decreases. This is illustrated in Figure 11.17. Notice that as accumulated depreciation increases by $1,000 each year, the net book value decreases by $1,000.

Year	Cost of Noncurrent Asset	Depreciation Expense	Accumulated Depreciation	Net Book Value
2018	$5,000	$1,000	$1,000	$4,000
2019	5,000	1,000	2,000	3,000
2020	5,000	1,000	3,000	2,000
2021	5,000	1,000	4,000	1,000
2022	5,000	1,000	5,000	0

FIGURE 11.17

The Declining-Balance and Double-Declining-Balance Methods

One drawback to the straight-line method is that it may not realistically reflect how the cost of the asset should be allocated, thus showing an inaccurate net book value for the asset. This is because the net book value of noncurrent assets does not always decrease by the same amount each year. Alternative depreciation methods have been developed by the accounting profession. One of them is the declining-balance method.

The most common real-life example of asset depreciation is a car. Usually, the largest decrease in the net book value of a car occurs the moment it is driven off the dealership's lot. Since the greatest depreciation in value occurs during the early years of the car's useful life, the declining-balance method is used. This concept applies to many noncurrent assets.

While the straight-line method simply applies an average depreciation rate, the **declining-balance method** applies an annual percentage for the calculation of depreciation against the net book value of the asset. Since the net book value decreases each year, a higher level of depreciation is recorded in the early years of the asset's useful life. The formula to calculate annual depreciation rate under the declining-balance method is shown in Figure 11.18.

$$\text{Declining-Balance Depreciation Rate} = \frac{100\%}{\text{Years of Useful Life}}$$

FIGURE 11.18

Consider the purchase of equipment worth $10,000 that has a useful life of five years with no residual value. The percentage for the declining-balance method is calculated as shown below.

$$\text{Declining-Balance Depreciation Rate} = \frac{100\%}{5}$$
$$= 20\%$$

An annual depreciation rate of 20% is applied to the net book value of the asset to calculate depreciation for each year. In the first year, depreciation can be calculated by multiplying the depreciation rate of 20% with the asset's original cost of $10,000. Therefore, the first year's depreciation is equal to $2,000. The net book value of the asset after deducting the first year's depreciation is $8000 ($10,000 – $2,000). In the second year, depreciation is equal to $1,600 (20% × net book value of $8,000). As the asset's net book value decreases, the depreciation amount also gradually decreases from year to year.

Unlike the straight-line method, which applies the same dollar amount of depreciation every year, the declining-balance method applies the same depreciation *percentage rate* to the net book value every year. If the useful life of the asset is 10 years instead of the 5 years shown in the above example, the depreciation rate applied each year is 10% (100% ÷ 10); if the useful life is 20 years, the depreciation rate applied each year is 5% (100% ÷ 20); and so on.

The depreciation rate can be multiplied based on the accountant's estimation of how fast the asset's value will depreciate. One of the most commonly used depreciation rates is the **double-declining-balance method**, which doubles the declining-balance rate of depreciation. For example, a double-declining depreciation rate of 40% (20% × 2) is used when the useful life of an asset is five years. When the useful life is 10 years, a double-declining depreciation rate of 20% is used (10% × 2). For a useful life of 20 years, an annual rate of 10% is used (5% × 2).

The formula for calculating the double-declining depreciation rate is shown in Figure 11.19.

Double-Declining Depreciation Rate = Declining-Balance Depreciation Rate × 2

FIGURE 11.19

Using a double-declining rate exaggerates the declining effect by two. This ensures that much of the depreciation occurs during the early years of an asset's life span.

In the example of the $10,000 piece of equipment with a useful life of five years, assume the company uses the double-declining-balance method. The depreciation for the first year is calculated as follows.

$$\$10,000 \times 40\% = \$4,000$$

The net book value for the beginning of the second year is calculated as follows.

$$\$10,000 - \$4,000 = \$6,000$$

The double-declining depreciation rate of 40% is applied to this new balance to determine the depreciation amount for the second year.

$$\$6,000 \times 40\% = \$2,400$$

The same double-declining rate is applied to a decreasing net book value on an annual basis. This means that over the years, the depreciation amounts are reduced substantially, which generally reflects the way noncurrent assets decline in value.

The rest of the depreciation amounts in the example are shown in Figure 11.20.

Year	Beginning of Year Book Value	@ 40% Double-Declining Depreciation Rate	Remaining Book Value
1	$10,000	minus $4,000 equals	$6,000
2	6,000	2,400	3,600
3	3,600	1,440	2,160
4	2,160	864	1,296
5	1,296	518.40	777.60

FIGURE 11.20

Applying a percentage rate to a balance every year means there will always be a remaining balance when the declining-balance or double-declining-balance methods are used. In this example, the remaining book value at the end of five years under the double-declining-balance method is $777.60 despite the asset having a zero estimated residual value. Because a noncurrent asset is not fully depreciated by the end of its useful life under the double-declining-balance method, companies usually switch from the double-declining-balance method to the straight-line method when the asset reaches half of its useful life so the asset will be fully depreciated. If the asset has a residual value when the declining-balance (or double-declining-balance) method is used, the asset should not be depreciated below the residual value. For example, if the residual value is $1,000 for the example shown above, Figure 11.21 shows the depreciation amounts. Notice that in the last year, depreciation can only be $296 to drop the net book value to the residual amount of $1,000.

WORTH REPEATING

The straight-line method applies the same depreciation amount to the net book value of a noncurrent asset for each year of its useful life.

The declining-balance and double-declining-balance methods apply a depreciation percentage to the net book value of a noncurrent asset. Therefore, a larger amount of depreciation is applied in the early years of the asset's useful life. For many assets, this is a more realistic estimation of how the asset will depreciate each year.

Year	Beginning of Year Book Value	@ 40% Double-Declining Depreciation Rate	Remaining Book Value
1	$10,000	$4,000	$6,000
2	6,000	2,400	3,600
3	3,600	1,440	2,160
4	2,160	864	1,296
5	1,296	296*	1,000

*Only $296, instead of $518.40, is subtracted from the beginning of the year book value to avoid having the remaining book value drop below a residual value of $1,000.

FIGURE 11.21

Pause & Reflect

Exercise 11-2

On January 1, 2018, London Bridge Company purchased a hydraulic stamping machine for $5,000,000. It is expected to last five years and estimated to have a residual value of $400,000 at the end of the five years. London Bridge Company will depreciate the machine using the double-declining-balance method. Prepare the following chart to calculate the depreciation for each year.

Year	Beginning of Year Book Value	Depreciation	Remaining Book Value
2018			
2019			
2020			
2021			
2022			

See Appendix I for solutions.

The Units-of-Production Method

The **units-of-production method** involves a different procedure for depreciating property, plant and equipment. The level of asset usage is the basis for calculating depreciation. The methods studied so far use a predetermined formula that is not based on usage.

The following steps are involved when using the units-of-production method.

1. Choose a unit for measuring the usage of the noncurrent asset. For example, if the asset is a vehicle, the unit can be the number of miles driven. If the asset is a machine, the unit can be the number of hours operated. These measures are known as units-of-production, hence the name of this method.

2. Estimate the number of units used for the entire life of the asset. For example, an estimate for a vehicle may be 200,000 miles, or for a machine may be 600,000 hours.

3. Divide the total cost of the asset by the estimated number of units from step 2. This gives the cost per unit.

4. The cost per unit determined in step 3 is multiplied by the number of units produced in a year to determine that year's depreciation amount.

Step 4 is repeated each year until the end of the asset's estimated useful life. Figure 11.22 shows how to calculate the cost per unit amount.

$$\text{Cost per Unit Amount} = \frac{\text{Cost} - \text{Residual Value}}{\text{Total Units of Production}}$$

FIGURE 11.22

Here is an example to illustrate how the units-of-production method is applied in the depreciation of property, plant and equipment.

Fenway Delivery bought a delivery truck for $110,000. The truck has an estimated residual value of $10,000. The company chooses a mile (mi) as the unit for measuring usage (step 1). The company wants its trucks to be in top condition, so it retires them after 200,000 miles of usage (step 2). The calculation for the per unit amount (step 3) is shown here.

$$\text{Cost per Unit Amount} = \frac{\$110,000 - \$10,000}{200,000 \text{ mi}}$$

$$= \$0.50/\text{mi}$$

Using the cost per unit amount, the amount of depreciation applied for that period is shown in Figure 11.23

Units-of-Production Depreciation = Units of Production Used for Year x Cost per Unit Amount

FIGURE 11.23

If the truck is driven 30,000 miles for the first year, the depreciation for that year (step 4) is calculated as shown here.

$$\text{Units-of-Production Depreciation} = 30,000 \text{ mi} \times \$0.50/\text{mi}$$

$$= \$15,000$$

The amount of depreciation for a year is entirely dependent on the asset's usage. For example, if the truck was driven for 25,000 miles in the second year, the depreciation for that year is calculated as follows.

$$25,000 \text{ mi} \times \$0.50/\text{mi} = \$12,500$$

If the truck was driven for 35,000 miles in the third year, the depreciation for that year is calculated as follows.

$$35,000 \text{ mi} \times \$0.50/\text{mi} = \$17,500$$

This depreciation procedure is applied annually until the truck has been driven for 200,000 miles, the initial estimation for the life of the truck. Once the usage exceeds the estimated units of production, no additional depreciation expense should be allocated to the units produced.

Choosing a Depreciation Method

As is common in accounting, no single method of calculating a balance sheet item is necessarily better than or preferable to another. The challenge for the accountant is to choose a method that best reflects the nature of the asset involved. For example, a company might use the straight-line method to depreciate an advertising sign, but use the declining-balance method to depreciate a company-owned vehicle, since the value of cars and trucks decreases most during their early years.

A Comparison of Depreciation Methods

Figure 11.24 compares depreciation expense under the three different depreciation methods. Using numbers from our previous examples, although the depreciation expense for each period is different, the total over the asset's useful life remains the same under all methods.

Refer to the example of Fenway Delivery, who bought a delivery truck for $110,000. The truck's estimated residual value is $10,000. The company retires all of its trucks after 200,000 miles of use. The cost per unit of production (in which "production" was stated in miles of usage) was calculated as $0.50/mi. For our example, the number of miles the truck was driven per year is shown in brackets under the units-of-production method. Assume that the 200,000 miles occur during a five-year period. This allows a comparison of all the depreciation methods based on an estimated useful life of five years.

	Depreciation Expense		
Year	Straight-Line Method $20,000/year[1]	Double-Declining-Balance Method 40%/year[2]	Units-of-Production Method
2018	$20,000	$44,000 ($110,000 x 40%)	$15,000 ($0.50 x 30,000 mi)
2019	20,000	26,400 ($66,000 x 40%)	12,500 ($0.50 x 25,000 mi)
2020	20,000	15,840 ($39,600 x 40%)	17,500 ($0.50 x 35,000 mi)
2021	20,000	9,504 ($23,760 x 40%)	30,000 ($0.50 x 60,000 mi)
2022	20,000	4,256[3]	25,000 ($0.50 x 50,000 mi)
Total	$100,000	$100,000	$100,000

[1] ($110,000 − $10,000)/5
[2] 100%/5 years x 2
[3] The net book value of $14,256 x 40% gives a depreciation of $5,702; however, only $4,256 is applied because the truck cannot be depreciated beyond a residual value of $10,000.

FIGURE 11.24

Depreciation for Partial Years

Our examination of depreciation has been based on the assumption that property, plant and equipment are purchased on the first day of a year and sold on the last day of another year. Of course, depreciation methods do not dictate when assets are bought and sold. Various tactics can be employed to accommodate the realities of the calendar year when depreciating a company's noncurrent assets. Once a noncurrent asset has been purchased, the accountant must choose a depreciation schedule that accommodates the timing of asset ownership.

A number of possible combinations are available to the accountant to depreciate during the year (or month) of purchase or sale. One common approach, illustrated below, is to calculate the depreciation of the asset purchased between the first and 15th day of a month for the full month of purchase, as if the asset was purchased on the first day of the month, and to not apply any depreciation in the month of purchase if the asset is purchased between the 16th day and the last day of the month, as if the asset was purchased on the first day of the next month. These combinations provide the accountant with the flexibility to develop a depreciation schedule that best reflects the business reality of the company.

Examine the situation that arises from the purchase of a $120,000 packaging machine by the Jones Cookie Factory on March 27, 2011. The company determines that the packager has a useful life of 10 years, after which it will not be salvageable; thus no residual value needs to be estimated. The machine will be depreciated by $12,000 annually, which is equivalent to $1,000 monthly. The machine is eventually sold on October 19, 2018 for $32,000. The fiscal year end for the Jones Cookie Factory is November 30.

The company decides to use the following depreciation rules: the asset is depreciated for a whole month of purchase if it is purchased by the 15th day of the month, and not depreciated in the month of purchase if it is purchased after the 15th day of the month. If the asset is sold by the 15th day of the month, it is not depreciated in the month of sale. If the asset is sold after the 15th day of the month, it is depreciated for a whole month of sale.

Figure 11.25 displays the annual depreciation calculated after the application of the chosen schedule. For fiscal years 2012 to 2017, each year includes 12 full months and has $12,000 of annual depreciation at $1,000 per month. That is the easy part. The challenge is dealing with the partial years of 2011 (year of purchase) and 2018 (year of sale).

In fiscal year 2011, although the actual month of purchase was March, it is assumed that the machine was purchased on April 1. The chosen schedule dictates that there is no depreciation in the month of purchase if the asset is purchased after the 15th day of the month, as illustrated in Figure 11.26. That leaves eight months of depreciation in the fiscal year, or $8,000.

	Months	Depreciation
2011	8	$8,000
2012	12	12,000
2013	12	12,000
2014	12	12,000
2015	12	12,000
2016	12	12,000
2017	12	12,000
2018	11	11,000
	Total	$91,000

FIGURE 11.25

Fiscal Year 2011

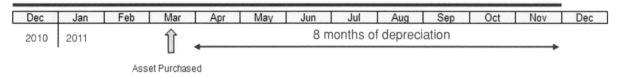

FIGURE 11.26

In fiscal year 2018, the month of sale was October. The chosen schedule dictates that since the sale occurred within the second half of the month, depreciation for the entire month is calculated, as shown in Figure 11.27. This means there are 11 months of depreciation for the fiscal year, for a total of $11,000.

Fiscal Year 2018

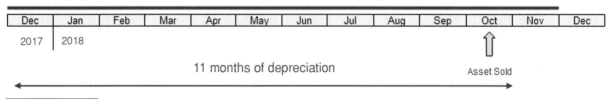

FIGURE 11.27

As Figure 11.28 shows, the total amount depreciated for the packaging machine is $91,000. Subtracting this amount from the original purchase price of $120,000 produces a net book value of $29,000. If the machine is sold for $32,000, it generates a gain of $3,000 on the sale. A different depreciation method would likely result in a different amount for the gain, or even a loss on the sale.

Packaging Machine

Original Purchase Price $120,000

Depreciated $91,000

Net Book Value at Disposal $29,000

$32,000 Sale Price – $29,000 Book Value = $3,000 Gain

FIGURE 11.28

Another common practice of the partial depreciation is a half-year of depreciation in the year of acquisition and a half-year of depreciation in the year of sale. If the company chooses to use this method, the gain or loss on the sale will likely change. Although depreciation is an estimate, the accountant should try to make the estimate as accurate as possible.

Depreciation for Federal Income Tax Purposes

In the US, businesses usually keep separate depreciation records for financial accounting purposes versus tax accounting purposes. Simply put, "book depreciation" is different from "tax depreciation." This is because the purpose of financial accounting is to report a company's financial position and performance, while tax accounting is intended to adhere to the federal Internal Revenue Code. The depreciation rules under US federal income tax law are known as the **Modified Accelerated Cost Recovery System (MACRS)**. MACRS specifies both the method of depreciation to be used (declining-balance methods or the straight-line method) and the lives of the different asset classes. (The units-of-production method is not allowed under MACRS.)

For instance, two of the most commonly used asset classes are the 5-year class (which covers lighter vehicles, such as cars and trucks) and the 7-year class (for heavier machinery and equipment). Both of these classes must be depreciated using a declining-balance method, as shown in Figure 11.29. Note that the 5-year class is depreciated over six years, and the 7-year class is depreciated over eight years. This is because under MACRS, all fixed assets are considered to be entered into service, and removed from service, in the middle of the year.

	Depreciation rate for recovery period	
Year	5-Year	7-Year
1	20.00%	14.29%
2	32.00%	24.49%
3	19.20%	17.49%
4	11.52%	12.49%
5	11.52%	8.93%
6	5.76%	8.92%
7		8.93%
8		4.46%
	100.00%	100.00%

FIGURE 11.29

Because MACRS allocates costs over an arbitrary useful life that is often less than the asset's useful life, it is not considered suitable for financial accounting purposes. It also does not take into account an asset's residual value when computing depreciation. Details of depreciation under MACRS are beyond the scope of this course.

Disposal of Assets

When a noncurrent asset is disposed of, a gain or loss is usually generated from the disposal of the asset. The accountant must remove all the accumulated depreciation for the asset from the books, since the company no longer owns the item. The first step of disposal is to record the depreciation expense for the current year.

For example, a company has equipment that costs $5,000, with a useful life of five years and a residual value of $1,000. Assume that the company has not yet recorded depreciation expense for the year ended December 31, 2018. The first step is to update the depreciation as at the disposal date. For this scenario, we will assume an annual straight-line depreciation of $800 ([$5,000 – $1,000] ÷ 5). The journal entry to update the depreciation before disposal is shown in Figure 11.30. This entry brings the balance in the accumulated depreciation account to $4,000.

JOURNAL			
Date	Account Title and Explanation	Debit	Credit
Dec 31	Depreciation Expense	800	
	Accumulated Depreciation—Equipment		800
	To record current period depreciation on equipment for disposal		

FIGURE 11.30

The asset is eventually sold after five years on December 31, 2018 for $1,000. When the asset is sold, the journal entry to record the transaction is shown in Figure 11.31.

JOURNAL			
Date	**Account Title and Explanation**	**Debit**	**Credit**
Dec 31	Cash	1,000	
	Accumulated Depreciation—Equipment	4,000	
	Equipment		5,000
	To record the sale of used asset for $1,000		

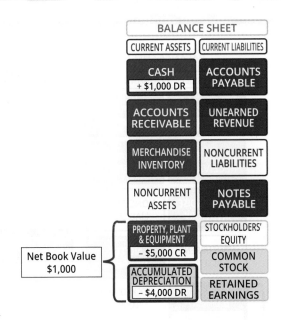

FIGURE 11.31

The amount of $1,000 is received for the asset and debited to cash. An amount of $4,000 is debited to the accumulated depreciation account, which initially had a credit balance of $4,000 due to adjusting entries made over the years. This amount is now cleared. Lastly, $5,000 is credited to the property, plant and equipment account to clear the value of the asset since the company no longer owns it.

Now assume that the equipment was sold for $500, half the estimated residual value. As shown before, depreciation is first updated as at the disposal date. The $4,000 in accumulated depreciation is debited to that account, and the initial cost of $5,000 is credited to the property, plant and equipment asset account. Since only $500 was received for the asset, this amount is debited to cash and the $500 loss is recorded as an other expense on the income statement. The transaction is shown in Figure 11.32.

JOURNAL			
Date	**Account Title and Explanation**	**Debit**	**Credit**
Dec 31	Cash	500	
	Accumulated Depreciation—Equipment	4,000	
	Loss on Disposal of Asset	500	
	Equipment		5,000
	To record the sale of used asset for $500		

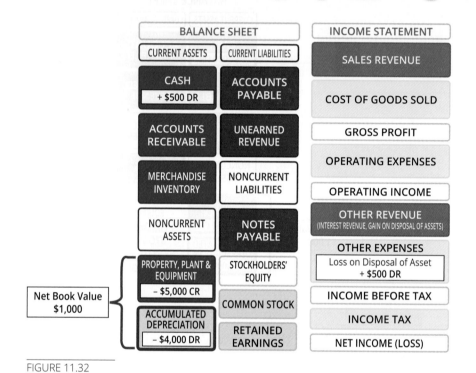

FIGURE 11.32

If the equipment was sold for $1,500, then a $500 gain is recorded under other revenue, since it was sold for more than the net book value. This is shown in Figure 11.33.

JOURNAL			
Date	**Account Title and Explanation**	**Debit**	**Credit**
Dec 31	Cash	1,500	
	Accumulated Depreciation—Equipment	4,000	
	Gain on Disposal of Asset		500
	Equipment		5,000
	To record the sale of used asset for $1,500		

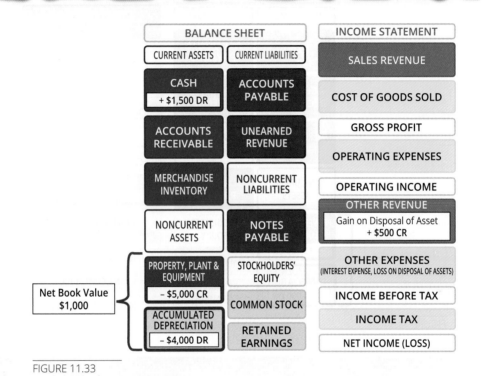

FIGURE 11.33

Instead of trying to sell the noncurrent asset, a company may decide to donate it to charity. The transaction involves a loss for the company and is recorded as a donation expense under other expenses on the income statement.

Assume the company donated the equipment from the previous example to a local charity. The first step, as in the other examples, is to update the depreciation for the period prior to disposal of the asset. This brings the balance in the accumulated depreciation account to $4,000. The journal entry to record the donation is shown in Figure 11.34.

JOURNAL			
Date	**Account Title and Explanation**	**Debit**	**Credit**
Dec 31	Accumulated Depreciation—Equipment	4,000	
	Donation Expense	1,000	
	Equipment		5,000
	To record the donation of used asset		

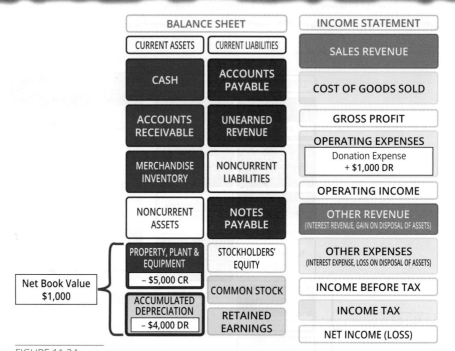

FIGURE 11.34

Pause & Reflect

Exercise 11-3

Whitechapel Manufacturing sold an old piece of equipment on December 31, 2018 for $360,000. The company purchased it on January 1, 2010 for $3,000,000. It was estimated to last 10 years and have a residual value of $400,000. The depreciation for 2018 has not yet been recorded. Prepare the journal entries to record the yearly depreciation and the disposal of the asset on December 31, 2018.

JOURNAL			
Date	**Account Title and Explanation**	**Debit**	**Credit**

See Appendix I for solutions.

Natural Resources

Natural resources have a physical nature, but are different from the nature of property, plant and equipment. In fact, some companies place natural resources in a separate asset category on the balance sheet. **Natural resources** include things such as metal ores, minerals, timber, petroleum and natural gas. We will examine these types of assets in our broader discussion of noncurrent assets and how we account for natural resources in the company's books.

First, natural resources come at a cost. This includes any expenditures to acquire the asset, such as preparing resources for extraction. It also includes any expenditure for restoring the land upon completion of use. The total cost is recorded in the appropriate asset account on the balance sheet.

Second, the value of natural resources decreases over time as more natural resources are extracted from the ground or harvested from the land. As the resources are collected and sold, they must be allocated, or expensed, to the period in which they are consumed. This is called **depletion**, and needs to be accounted for in the books just as depreciation is with property, plant and equipment. The resources must also be reported on the balance sheet at cost less accumulated depletion.

A CLOSER LOOK

Some companies still use the terms *amortization* or *depreciation* instead of *depletion*.

Not all companies use the accumulated depreciation or depletion account. Instead, they credit the natural resource account directly and debit the expense account.

We can use the example of a mining company to illustrate how the natural resource itself is recorded, how depletion is recorded and how both are reported on the balance sheet. Depletion for natural resources is usually calculated using the units-of-production method. The company has bought land containing an estimated 8,000,000 tons of ore (rock from which minerals can be extracted), at a total cost of $10 million. It estimates that once all the ore has been extracted, the land will have zero residual value. In the first year, 2,000,000 tons were mined and sold and depletion expense for the year is $2,500,000. Figure 11.35 shows the journal entry for the purchase of the natural resource and the depletion at the end of the first year.

JOURNAL			
Date	**Account Title and Explanation**	**Debit**	**Credit**
Jan 1	Mineral Deposit	10,000,000	
	Cash		10,000,000
	To record purchase of resource		
Dec 31	Depletions Expense—Mineral Deposit	2,500,000	
	Accumulated Depletion—Mineral Deposit		2,500,000
	To record depletion of mineral deposit for year		

FIGURE 11.35

At the end of the year, the natural resource would be presented in the balance sheet as shown in Figure 11.36.

Mineral Deposit	10,000,000	
Less: Accumulated Depreciation—Mineral Deposit	2,500,000	
Net Book Value		7,500,000

FIGURE 11.36

Intangible Assets and Goodwill

The previous discussion of noncurrent assets covered tangible assets, which are physical in nature and can be touched or sensed. In contrast, **intangible assets** are conceptual in nature. They are *identifiable* assets that have no physical form and largely constitute intellectual property, such as patents and trademarks. An asset is considered to be identifiable if it

1. is separable, meaning it is capable of being separated from the company and sold; or

2. emerges from contractual or legal rights, regardless of whether it is separable or transferable from the company.

An asset that is not identifiable does not count as an intangible asset. Goodwill, for example, is not identifiable, since it does not fit either of the above two criteria. Therefore, it is accounted for differently and reported separately from other intangible assets. Goodwill is discussed at the end of this section.

Different intangible assets differ in their lengths of useful life. Some intangible assets benefit the company for a finite number of years, while others benefit the company indefinitely. Just as property, plant and equipment need to be depreciated, intangible assets with finite useful lives need to go through a similar process. However, the process of allocating the cost of intangible assets over their useful lives is usually called **amortization** instead of depreciation. In addition to amortization, the value of intangible assets (including both those with finite useful lives and those with infinite useful lives) may also decrease due to impairment, which is similar to the impairment of property, plant and equipment discussed earlier.

Intangible Assets with Finite Useful Lives

Patents and copyrights are the most obvious examples of intangible assets that have limited useful lives.

Patents

Individuals and companies invent and develop innovative products, usually at an enormous cost of both money and time. Inventors need to protect their intellectual property and this is achieved through patenting.

A **patent** grants the patentee the exclusive right, for a set period of time, to prevent others from making, using, selling or distributing the patented invention without permission. In most international jurisdictions, a patent term lasts for 20 years, but the duration can differ according to the type of patent. This gives the inventor or inventing company the right to enjoy the rewards of creating a new and successful product.

A patent can be purchased from another party or filed by the company. If the company purchases the patent from another party, the cost of the patent is equal to the purchase price plus any legal costs involved. If the company files its own patent, the application process typically requires the use of patent lawyers (as does the defense and management of a patent). All legal and associated costs in acquiring and defending a patent are capitalized in the noncurrent assets section of the balance sheet. The value of the patent is then amortized for the amount of time left in the patent's legal term or its estimated useful life, whichever is shorter.

This example illustrates how to record journal entries for patent acquisition and amortization. Assume Henry's Lights purchases a patent from Pixie Light Bulbs for $28,000 on January 1, 2018. The patent has seven years remaining in its term and is expected to bring in revenues to the company for the whole seven years. The entries to record the purchase on January 1, 2018, as well as one year's amortization for the year ending December 31, 2018, are recorded as shown in Figure 11.37.

JOURNAL			
Date	**Account Title and Explanation**	**Debit**	**Credit**
Jan 1	Patents	28,000	
	Cash		28,000
	To record purchase of patent with seven years remaining		
Dec 31	Amortization Expense—Patents	4,000	
	Accumulated Amortization—Patents		4,000
	To record amortization expense for one year		

FIGURE 11.37

The $4,000 annual amortization amount is calculated using the straight-line method. The straight-line method divides the amortizable amount ($28,000 less a residual value of zero) by the number of years remaining (7 years). This method is often used for amortizing patents and other intangible assets.

Copyright

Copyright is similar to a patent in that it gives exclusive rights of ownership to a person or group that has created something. The difference with copyright is that it applies to artistic work, such as music and literature, and can exist even if the work has not been registered. For example, it is automatically assumed that an article or photo posted on the Internet is protected by copyright. A person cannot simply assume that he has unlimited rights to use or copy a work from the Internet. Registration with the US Copyright Office, however, puts a copyright holder in a stronger position if litigation arises over the copyright. In the United States, the laws regarding copyrights are governed by the *Copyright Act*, which states that, generally, the life of a copyright lasts throughout the life of the author plus 70 years from the end of the calendar year of his or her death. This means that estimates of a copyright's legal life depend on when the work was first created and how long the author lived. The copyright's useful life, however, is usually shorter than its legal life in practice.

Overall, copyright is treated in much the same way as a patent. The costs may include the purchase price in obtaining the copyright from someone else, legal fees paid to register and defend the copyright, and any other fees involved in its acquisition and defense. The cost of the copyright is amortized over the number of years of its legal term, or its estimated useful life, whichever is shorter.

GAAP vs IFRS

 Under GAAP, research and development costs are always expensed as they are incurred.

Under IFRS, research costs are expensed and development costs are capitalized once technical and economic feasibility is attained.

Intangible Assets with Infinite Useful Lives

Some intangible assets do not have an expiry date, and will keep generating economic benefits for the company as long as the company still owns them. Some examples of these assets include trademarks, trade names, franchises and licenses.

Trademark and Trade Name

A **trademark** is similar to a patent and copyright except that it grants ownership rights for a recognizable symbol or logo. A **trade name** grants exclusive rights to a name under which a company or product trades for commercial purposes, even though its legal or technical name might differ. Some corporations have numerous trademarks and trade names that they protect on a continuing basis. For example, McDonald's is not only a trade name that the company protects, but it serves as an umbrella brand for numerous other trademarks, such as the Golden Arches, the Extra Value Meal and Hamburger University.

Any internal costs incurred for developing and maintaining a trademark or trade name, such as those involved with advertising, are considered indistinguishable from other costs of developing the company's business, and are expensed during the year they are incurred. However, just as with patents and copyrights, legal fees for registering the name or logo are capitalized. Alternatively, trademarks and trade names can be purchased from someone else. Because these can be separately measured, they are capitalized as intangible assets on the balance sheet.

Franchises and Licenses

A **franchise** is a contract that allows the franchisee to operate a branch using the franchisor's brand name and business model. For example, one can buy a franchise to run a KFC branch, Learning Express Toys store, or Midas service station. The franchisee receives operating support from the franchisor, such as marketing and training, while the franchisor maintains some control of how the franchisee operates the branch.

A **license** is a contract that permits the licensee to use the licensor's product or brand name under specified terms and conditions. For example, one can buy a license from Marvel to sell T-shirts with Iron Man printed on them. A license usually does not come with an ongoing formal support from the licensor, and the licensor usually does not have much control over how the licensee operates the business.

The franchisee usually has to pay initial fees when acquiring the franchise. These initial fees are capitalized as noncurrent assets on the balance sheet. Normally, there is no expiry date on the franchise, meaning the franchisee can keep operating the branch under the contract, as long as annual payments called royalties are made. Because there is no expiry date, if the franchisee plans to operate the franchise indefinitely, the initial fees are not amortized. Royalties that are paid annually are expensed. The same principles described here also apply to a licensee obtaining and using a license.

Goodwill

Goodwill arises when a company purchases another company at a cost that is greater than the market value of that company's net assets. The excess of the cost of the company over the total market value of its assets, less its total liabilities, is recorded as goodwill.

Goodwill can be attributed to factors such as a recognizable brand name, experienced management, a skilled workforce or a unique product. Unlike other assets, items representing goodwill do not come with an easily determinable market price to be amortized over time. Nevertheless, businesses are willing to pay for goodwill, and it increases equity on the balance sheet. We will use an example to explain how goodwill works and how accountants should record such items in the company's books.

Vicky's Entrepreneurial Enterprises decides to buy Jack's Sweets, a relatively new but established candy maker on June 1, 2018. The purchase price is $1 million. At the time of purchase, Jack's Sweets has assets with a market value of $1.5 million and liabilities totaling $700,000, giving the purchased company a net asset value of $800,000.

The extra $200,000 in the company's purchase price constitutes goodwill. Vicky is willing to pay for the brand name, because Jack's Sweets is known for great tasting candies. In addition, Jack's Sweets' memorable commercials featured a fictional "Uncle Jack" handing out treats to beloved customers. Vicky considers $200,000 for this brand to be a bargain and is willing to pay this amount for goodwill. However, she also expects a good return on her investment for the premium paid for the business.

To record the purchase of Jack's Sweets, Vicky's accountant adds the value of the assets and liabilities to Vicky's balance sheet. This results in a debit to assets of $1,500,000 and a credit to liabilities of $700,000. The cash payment amount of $1,000,000 is recorded as a credit to cash. The premium paid is recorded as goodwill and increases that asset account by $200,000. Figure 11.38 shows this transaction.

JOURNAL			
Date	Account Title and Explanation	Debit	Credit
Jun 1	Assets	1,500,000	
	Goodwill	200,000	
	Liabilities		700,000
	Cash		1,000,000
	Purchase net assets of Jack's Sweets, including goodwill		

Note: We use the title "Assets" and "Liabilities" in this journal for demonstration purpose. In reality, each asset and liability are recorded in its specific account.

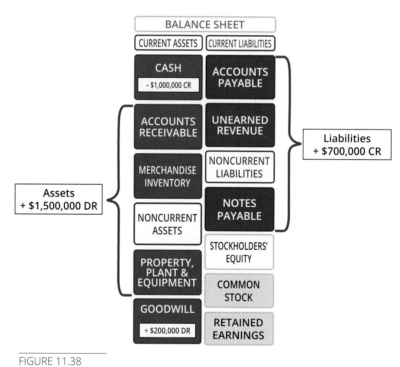

FIGURE 11.38

Unlike other intangible assets with infinite useful lives, items categorized as goodwill do not have their value amortized over time. However, this does not mean that the value of goodwill cannot decrease. Events may occur that impair or reduce the value of goodwill.

Financial Analysis of Noncurrent Assets

The values of the assets on the balance sheet provide an idea of the amount invested in the company to run its operations. However, these values alone do not indicate whether these assets are being used effectively and efficiently. We will examine two ratios that can provide insight on how well assets are being used: asset turnover and return on assets.

Asset Turnover

A turnover ratio measures how rapidly an asset's status changes and becomes productive. Recall that inventory turnover measures how quickly an asset converts from inventory to becoming a sale. **Asset turnover** measures how quickly a company converts its total assets, including noncurrent assets, into revenue.

To calculate asset turnover, we need net sales from the income statement and the average total assets, which is produced by taking the average of beginning and ending total assets. The equations to do this are shown in Figure 11.39.

$$\text{Asset Turnover} = \frac{\text{Net Sales}}{\text{Average Total Assets*}}$$

*Average Total Assets = (Beginning of Year Total Assets + End of Year Total Assets) ÷ 2

FIGURE 11.39

Return on Assets

A company's return on assets is similar to asset turnover except that its focus is on net income instead of revenue. **Return on assets** measures the relationship between net income and assets. In other words, is the company making enough profit from investment in its total assets? Figure 11.40 shows the formula to calculate return on assets.

$$\text{Return on Assets} = \frac{\text{Net Income}}{\text{Average Total Assets}}$$

FIGURE 11.40

Note that the ratios to calculate asset turnover and return on assets both have the same denominator: average total assets. It is the numerators that differ. Asset turnover uses net sales, while return on assets uses net income. Another difference is that asset turnover is expressed as a decimal number, while return on assets is expressed as a percentage.

Using the Ratios

We can calculate and compare these two ratios by using the financial information made available by Amtrak, a US company in the railway transportation industry, and Coastal Rail, a fictitious

US company in the same industry. Using the formulas already outlined, the ratios are calculated in Figure 11.41.

Selected Financial Information (in millions)			
Year 2016		**Amtrak**	**Coastal Rail**
A	Net Sales	$3,241	$21,813
B	Total Assets—Beginning of Year	$13,295	$52,372
C	Total Assets—End of Year	$14,084	$54,600
D = (B+C) ÷ 2	Average Total Assets	$13,690	$53,486
E = A ÷ D	Asset Turnover	0.24	0.41
F	Net Income (Loss)	($1,080)	$4,772
G = F ÷ D	Return on Assets	(7.89%)	8.92%

FIGURE 11.41

For Amtrak and Coastal Rail, both net sales and net income were divided by average total assets to produce the two financial ratios.

With regard to asset turnover, Amtrak has a figure of 0.24 and Coastal Rail has a figure of 0.41. This means that Coastal Rail generated more revenue dollars per investment in assets than Amtrak.

With regard to return on assets, Amtrak has a rate of −7.89% and Coastal Rail's rate is 8.92%. This means that Coastal Rail generated more net income per investment in assets than Amtrak.

All financial ratios represent a simple snapshot of company performance; each ratio tends to focus on one aspect of a business. Calculation and interpretation of multiple ratios can provide a bigger picture of an overall well-being of a company, which will be discussed in a later chapter.

Controls Related To Noncurrent Assets

Tangible assets are purchased by a company, used to earn an income and eventually disposed of. In the meantime, the value of a noncurrent asset depreciates over the period of its estimated useful life. Accounting procedures are used to control and safeguard all tangible assets while the company possesses them. Different companies and industries depend on noncurrent assets to varying degrees. For instance, auto manufacturers General Motors and Ford rely heavily on noncurrent assets, such as machines, robots and factories. It is sometimes possible for people to steal large assets of a company. Security measures, such as physical barriers and security personnel, can protect large items from theft.

Insurance is a more useful measure to protect large noncurrent assets. Insurance can protect not only in the event of theft, but also in the event of catastrophic situations, such as extreme weather or unforeseen breakdowns. It is important for management to make sure that the best possible insurance policies are in place and are updated or adjusted when needed. Some companies may even want to consider some self-insurance options to help protect their noncurrent assets from catastrophic risk.

IN THE REAL WORLD

Although businesses should make certain that all their assets are insured and that potential liabilities are also covered, this does not always mean that an insurance company needs to be involved. Businesses can self-insure to cover various risks. Companies that self-insure are sometimes regarded as being uninsured. In other words, "self-insurance" can be seen as an attempt to avoid paying for insurance. Indeed, this can be true, since some companies fail to adequately self-insure.

Proper self-insurance involves a company setting aside enough capital reserves to cover itself in case of a catastrophic event. If something happens to a company's noncurrent assets, these capital reserves can be used to cover the loss. The advantage of self-insurance is that a company avoids paying premiums that are often very high.

The disadvantage of self-insurance is that a company needs to tie up a certain amount of its capital to cover a disaster, and even that is sometimes insufficient. To minimize this disadvantage, there are alternative self-insurance strategies. For example, a business can still buy some insurance, but add self-insurance. Alternatively, businesses can form collaborative self-insurance groups, whereby a group of companies contributes to a pool of funds that can be used if one or more of them suffer a catastrophic event.

As with most aspects of today's business environment, various innovative solutions can be found to resolve inadequacies in the market. Self-insurance is an example of one of these innovations.

Big or small, expensive or inexpensive, all types of tangible assets should be tracked properly and relevant transactions recorded accurately in the company's books. Experienced accountants should perform these control procedures.

Each noncurrent asset should be tagged in some way, perhaps by a bar code and scanner. The tags should be read and compared with accounting records, and vice versa. Physical audits should be performed on a regular basis to ensure that all assets on the books are on the premises, still in use and accounted for.

For all company assets, paperwork and records should be completed correctly and handled securely. The first priority is to record the correct amount of cost for the noncurrent asset. As always, any costs related to the acquisition of the asset must be included in the total cost. These can include freight, installation and testing costs.

As emphasized throughout our discussion of asset controls, policies, plans and procedures need to be in place, and regulations and laws followed. For example, a large company may have a policy of classifying items as noncurrent assets only if they cost more than $1,000. A smaller company may have a lower threshold for its policy. These policies need to be clearly communicated to the staff responsible for their implementation. Adherence to all related policies, plans, procedures, regulations and laws should be monitored, with audits when necessary.

Economical and efficient use of tangible assets involves purchasing assets at the best possible price. Internal controls should include a bidding process for suppliers, which helps to ensure the best possible price. Financial ratios, discussed earlier in this chapter, can be used on a regular basis to monitor the efficient use of a company's noncurrent assets. If the ratios indicate an inefficient use of these assets, measures can be taken to either dispose of or make better use of them. If sales are slow, this may mean that noncurrent assets are not being used to their full capacity. A business may also find that too much money has been invested in its noncurrent assets. Leasing them could free up some capital. As always, company goals and objectives related to noncurrent assets should be stated, implemented, reviewed and changed when necessary.

Controls related to intangible assets are not very different from those relating to tangible assets. Qualified staff should be available to ensure that transactions are recorded and classified properly in the company's books and all payments are properly documented. Costs should be objectively verified and any supporting documentation should be properly maintained. The procedures involved are similar for both tangible and intangible assets.

However, with intangible assets, the only physical evidence of their existence often comes in the form of contracts, accompanying invoices and supporting cost documentation. That is why it is so important to physically protect such documents. They can be placed in a vault on the premises or a safe deposit box in a bank. These documents can be referenced when changes are made or when the company's books need updating.

Beyond initial registration or purchase, ongoing valuation of intangible assets needs to take place. For example, market conditions may affect the value of goodwill, or competing trademarks may diminish the value of a brand name. Furthermore, companies that own patents, copyright and trademarks should be on the lookout for entities that are using such intellectual property without permission. Any such use diminishes the value of the protected asset. All proper legal avenues should be pursued, including legal action or the threat of legal action, when improper use of protected intellectual assets has taken place.

An Ethical Approach To Noncurrent Assets

Accounting for a firm's noncurrent assets can be manipulated to produce fraudulent figures. Decisions regarding classifying noncurrent assets, depreciating them and estimating residual values can have a significant impact on a company's financial statements. It is important for accountants to understand the ethical principles that help prevent abuse.

When accountants are faced with a decision, they should ask if it should be done because it is an accurate reflection of the business or for some other reason. Other reasons could be to hide one's own incompetence, seek financial gain, succumb to pressure from management or meet public expectation of company performance.

A good accountant always raises a red flag when the answer to the question is anything other than, "This is being done because it is an accurate reflection of the financial condition of the business."

Figures for noncurrent assets can be manipulated to present a financial picture that does not accurately reflect the financial state of the company. One of the first decisions that an accountant must make is whether a noncurrent asset in question is in fact a noncurrent asset. An attempt to falsely classify a noncurrent asset as an expense understates the company's net income in the current period. Conversely, an attempt to classify an expense as a noncurrent asset overstates the company's equity in the current period. Any result that does not reflect the true nature of the asset is an ethical breach and should always be avoided.

IN THE REAL WORLD

The year 2001 saw the beginning of numerous corporate and accounting scandals that breached ethical standards. Authorities began investigating some of America's largest corporations regarding, among other things, accounting fraud. The corporations investigated included three telecommunications companies—Global Crossing, Qwest and WorldCom.

Some of these investigations found a distortion of gains and expenses as a result of misclassifying noncurrent assets. For example, both Global Crossing and Qwest engaged in billions of dollars of what are known as swaps. These companies purchased telecom capacity from customers who then bought it back from the companies. These were falsely treated as noncurrent assets rather than as current operating expenses. The result was that both companies recorded the revenue upfront, then expensed the amount over a period of time. This violates, among other things, the expense recognition principle.

In addition, WorldCom classified billions of dollars of current operating expenses as noncurrent assets. This was done over a period of 15 months. The auditing firm Arthur Andersen failed to raise any red flags over the practice.

Estimating the useful life of a noncurrent asset is also open to manipulation. Intentionally shortening an asset's life span can unduly increase the annual depreciation charges recorded in the company's books. Intentionally increasing a noncurrent asset's residual value decreases the amount to be depreciated and the depreciation charges. An accountant has an ethical obligation to avoid, or detect and correct, these abuses at all times.

Ethical considerations of intangible assets relate mostly to their correct reporting in financial statements. This includes determining the appropriate cost, calculating the correct amortization and impairment and accurately reporting all amounts on the income statement and balance sheet.

Companies should always set up internal controls to ensure that ongoing transactions involving intangible assets are expensed or capitalized properly. Following review procedures ensures that annual amortization is verified and properly reported. Any review procedure should be the joint responsibility of both management and company auditors. Executives and accountants must take responsibility for the company's books; not doing so can lead to serious consequences.

In Summary

LO 1 **Identify the characteristics of noncurrent assets**
- ▶ Noncurrent (long-term) assets provide the infrastructure necessary for operating a business.
- ▶ They are expected to be used on an ongoing basis, typically longer than one year, and are not intended to be sold to customers.

LO 2 **Record the acquisition and changes in the value of property, plant and equipment**
- ▶ Cost of property, plant and equipment includes purchase price and expenditures necessary to get the asset ready for operation. The whole cost is debited to the appropriate noncurrent asset account.
- ▶ In a lump sum purchase, the amount paid for all the assets is divided and allocated to each item according to percentages based on the appraised values or fair values.
- ▶ After acquisition, changes made to property, plant and equipment are classified as a betterment, an extraordinary repair, or ordinary repairs and maintenance.
- ▶ Property, plant and equipment (except land) decrease in value (depreciate) over time. Depreciation is the process of allocating the cost of the asset over its useful life.

LO 3 **Apply and compare the three methods of depreciation of property, plant and equipment**
- ▶ The straight-line method of depreciation uses a simple average, resulting in the same amount of depreciation every year.
- ▶ The declining-balace and double-declining-balance methods apply a depreciation rate to the remaining balance of the book value of the asset.
- ▶ The units-of-production method utilizes the level of asset usage as the basis for calculating depreciation.
- ▶ Accountants choose the depreciation method that best reflects the nature of the asset.
- ▶ "Book depreciation" is different from depreciation for federal income tax purposes. The depreciation rules under US federal income tax law are known as the Modified Accelerated Cost Recovery System (MACRS).

LO 4 **Account for disposal of assets**
- ▶ The disposal of an asset usually involves a gain or loss relative to the item's book value. Gains and losses appear on the income statements.

LO 5 **Account for natural resources**
- ▶ The natural resources that a company owns—such as minerals, oil or timber—are physical in nature, and are capitalized under the noncurrent assets section on the balance sheet. Some companies categorize them separately from other noncurrent assets.
- ▶ A natural resource's value is depleted over time using the units-of-production method.

LO 6 **Define and account for intangible assets and describe the different types of intangible assets**

- Intangible assets are defined as identifiable assets that have no physical form. An asset is considered to be identifiable if it either is separable from the company or emerges from contractual or legal rights.

- The decrease in an intangible asset's value due to amortization is recorded as an expense on the income statement.

- A patent gives the inventor the exclusive right to use a product. The cost of the patent is for legal fees or the purchase of rights from someone else. This cost is amortized over the remaining term of the patent, or its expected useful life, whichever is shorter.

- Copyright gives exclusive rights of a creation to its creator. Copyright is granted automatically to works produced and published.

- A trademark gives exclusive rights to logos and other company symbols. A trade name provides exclusive rights to names of companies and products.

- A franchise is a contract that allows the franchisee to operate a branch using the franchisor's brand name and business model. A license is a contract that permits the licensee to use the licensor's product or brand name under the specified terms and conditions. The initial franchise fees or license fees are capitalized.

- Goodwill arises when a company purchases another company at a cost that is greater than the market value of that company's net assets. Unlike other intangible assets, goodwill is considered to be unidentifiable. Therefore, it is reported separately from other intangible assets.

LO 7 Calculate and interpret asset turnover and return on assets ratios

- Asset turnover measures the revenue a company generates relative to its investment in total assets.

- Return on assets measures the net income a company generates relative to total assets.

LO 8 Describe controls related to noncurrent assets

- Controls to protect a company's noncurrent assets can include accurate recording and tracking procedures, or proper insurance in case of catastrophic events. Qualified accounting personnel should always supervise the policies and measures that a company implements.

LO 9 Describe ethical approaches related to noncurrent assets

- Net income figures and net asset values can be distorted by manipulating decisions regarding the classification of noncurrent assets, the estimation of residual value and useful life, and other aspects of depreciation. Unethical manipulations must always be avoided.

 *Access **ameengage.com** for integrated resources including tutorials, practice exercises, the digital textbook and more.*

Review Exercise 11-1

Nelson Rugasa is an entrepreneur who has just started a consulting business. On December 31, 2018, Nelson used cash to purchase a laptop computer for $3,000 and office equipment for $10,000.

Required

a) Record the purchase of noncurrent assets.

JOURNAL			
Date	Account Title and Explanation	Debit	Credit

Research Component (to be done outside of class time)

b) Research the useful life of noncurrent assets, and suggest the useful life for the computer and office equipment.

_____

_____

_____

_____

_____

_____

_____

_____

c) Research the way in which the value of noncurrent assets decline, and suggest the depreciation method(s) that should be used for the computer and office equipment.

_____

_____

_____

_____

_____

_____

_____

d) Based on your research on useful life, and the ways in which the value of noncurrent assets decline, prepare a table showing the cost, depreciation, accumulated depreciation, and net book value of the computer and office equipment for the first three years.

Year	Cost	Depreciation	Accumulated Depreciation	Net Book Value

Year	Cost	Depreciation	Accumulated Depreciation	Net Book Value

e) Explain how you calculate the profit or loss on the disposal of a noncurrent asset.

_____

_____

_____

_____

_____

_____

_____

_____

_____

_____

_____

_____

_____

_____

_____

_____

_____

_____

_____

_____

See Appendix I for solutions.

Chapter 12
Accounting for Payroll and Current Liabilities

Learning Objectives

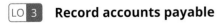

LO 1 **Define and differentiate between determinable and non-determinable liabilities**
- Bank Overdraft and Operating Line of Credit

LO 2 **Record payroll liabilities**
- Payroll as an Accrued Liability
- Gross Pay to Net Pay
- Employee Payroll Deductions—Statutory
- Employee Payroll Deductions—Voluntary
- Employer Payroll Contributions
- Responsibility for Paying Taxes and Benefits
- Payroll Example
- Payroll Register
- Payroll Records
- Paying the Liabilities

LO 3 **Record accounts payable**

LO 4 **Record transactions with sales tax**

LO 5 **Record unearned revenue**

LO 6 **Record short-term notes payable**
- Extending Credit Terms
- Borrowing from a Bank

LO 7 **Record transactions related to the current portion of noncurrent liabilities**

LO 8 **Record estimated liabilities**
- Employee Benefits
- Product Warranties

LO 9 **Apply internal controls relating to current liabilities**
- Controls for Liabilities
- Payroll Controls

*Access **ameengage.com** for integrated resources including tutorials, practice exercises, the digital textbook and more.*

MAKING IT REAL TO YOU

With the exception of inventory, payroll costs are one of the largest business costs and generate a number of liabilities. Payroll costs include hourly wages and salaries. However, payroll costs also include a variety of payroll taxes. Each state and payroll tax requirements are different, but the concepts are similar. The business must consider and carefully plan for salaries and wages, employee payroll taxes that are withheld and employer payroll taxes that are due. As we consider payroll tax amounts due or liable, we can also consider other common types of business debts. Businesses will often borrow to pay for large assets. Just as with personal financial planning, the business needs to consider the total amount of debt, length of the loan, interest rates and payment amounts. Business debt is not necessarily a bad thing, but it needs to be managed and understood.

Current Liabilities

This chapter deals with current liabilities, which are obligations expected to be paid within one year of the balance sheet date or the company's normal operating cycle. Obligations due beyond one year are classified as noncurrent liabilities.

The balance sheet presentation of current liabilities is comparable to the balance sheet presentation of current assets. The main difference is that the order of liabilities is dictated by the timing of settlement, whereas assets are placed in order of liquidity. Figure 12.1 illustrates this difference. Bank overdraft and operating line of credit are listed first among the current liabilities, followed by accounts payable, which is a common type of trade payable. Accrued liabilities include payroll liabilities, sales taxes payable to the government and interest payable on notes and loans. Unearned revenue and the current portion of noncurrent notes payable are also listed as current liabilities.

FIGURE 12.1

A company's liabilities can be divided into two categories: known liabilities and unknown liabilities. These categories are sometimes referred to as *determinable liabilities* and *non-determinable liabilities*, respectively.

Determinable liabilities have a precise value; businesses that have determinable liabilities know exactly who they owe, how much they owe and when they are supposed to pay. Amounts owed to suppliers (trade payables), employees (payroll liabilities) and the government (sales taxes) are determinable liabilities. All determinable liabilities should leave an easily recognizable and traceable paper trail, and may include documents

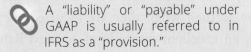

GAAP vs IFRS

A "liability" or "payable" under GAAP is usually referred to in IFRS as a "provision."

such as invoices and contracts. The exact amounts due, and when they are due, should be clearly identified.

A company's unknown or **non-determinable liabilities** include estimated and contingent liabilities. They are non-determinable because the exact amount owing or whether and when they are supposed to be paid is unknown on the date of financial statement issuance. This is similar to a topic that was studied on the assets side of the balance sheet, where the exact amount of bad debt for the year was unknown on the date of financial statement issuance.

We will first discuss each important type of determinable liability, starting with bank overdraft and operating line of credit. Non-determinable liabilities, as well as controls and ethics related to current liabilities, are examined at the end of the chapter.

Bank Overdraft and Operating Line of Credit

A company faced with short-term financial needs can borrow from a financial institution through a bank overdraft or a line of credit. **Bank overdraft** is a financial institution's extension of credit to cover the portion of cash withdrawal that is more than the account's balance. The financial institution will automatically deposit amounts into the company's cash account if it goes into a negative balance up to a pre-specified amount. The negative balance could be due to issues with cash flow or simply timing differences between deposits and withdrawals.

Alternatively, many businesses have an operating line of credit with their financial institution. An **operating line of credit** is the maximum loan balance that a business may draw upon at any time without having to visit or request approval from the bank. The business negotiates a predetermined maximum balance that it is allowed to owe as well as the interest rate charged on the outstanding balance of the account.

If the company's cash account has a negative balance as of the balance sheet date, the bank overdraft is reported as a current liability. Likewise, if the company owes a financial institution on its line of credit as of the balance sheet date, the line of credit is reported as a current liability. Both bank overdraft and line of credit are reported ahead of accounts payable and any other determinable liabilities on the balance sheet.

Payroll Liabilities

Payroll as an Accrued Liability

Payroll is one of the most important business obligations of any organization. Employees are entitled to receive payment for services they have provided to the company. Similar to interest expense, which must be accrued in the same period that it is incurred, payroll expenses must also be accrued when they are incurred even when cash has not yet been paid. In fact, payroll expense is an excellent example of accrued liabilities because payroll journal entries are often recorded in one period, but amounts are not paid until the next period. For example, if an employee works in

December 2018 but will not receive her salary until January 2019, the company still has to accrue December payroll expenses and liabilities in the fiscal year 2018.

The amount of payroll that a company has to accrue is determined partly by employment law and legislation that the company must follow. The law requires not only that a company pay its employees fairly, but also that the employer submit payroll-related taxes to the government. Some taxes are deducted from the employee's paychecks, while others are paid by the employer or are paid jointly by both employee and employer. Therefore, payroll accounting involves three types of payroll liabilities: (1) the net pay owed to an employee, (2) amounts deducted from employee paychecks and owed to the government and other relevant organizations, and (3) employer payroll contributions. Any business that hires people to work on its behalf will incur these liabilities and related expenses.

The net pay owed to an employee amounts to the gross pay minus employee payroll deductions. These deductions can include the following.

- Social Security tax
- Medicare tax
- federal, state and local income taxes
- other voluntary deductions

Gross pay represents the total amount actually earned by the employee, and **net pay** represents the amount after the various deductions have been made.

The amount of gross pay and deductions on each paycheck is affected by the pay period (pay frequency). Pay period refers to the number of times an employee is paid during one year. The table in Figure 12.2 shows how many pay periods there are in a year for the common pay frequencies.

Pay Frequency	Number of Pay Periods in a Year
Weekly	52
Bi-weekly	26
Semi-monthly	24
Monthly	12

FIGURE 12.2

Gross Pay to Net Pay

There are two ways to pay an employee: salaries and wages.

Generally speaking, employees who work full-time in a company, such as in the administrative, sales or management roles, are paid a salary. A salary is a *fixed annual* amount that is divided by the number of pay periods in a calendar year to determine the gross pay for each pay period.

For example, a sales manager who is paid $52,000 per year earns $1,000 per week. If he is paid on a bi-weekly basis, his gross pay is $2,000 for each pay period.

Individuals employed on a part-time basis (e.g. in the retail sector, in factories, or as manual laborers), are more likely to be paid a wage (hourly rate), where the pay for any given pay period is determined by the number of hours worked in that period.

As an example, if a factory worker is paid $17.00 per hour and works for 65 hours in a two-week period, the gross pay is $1,105.00 (65 hours × $17.00 per hour).

Some of the key differences between salaries and wages are payments for overtime and sick pay. In most cases, employees who are paid by salary *do not* receive overtime pay. Salaried employees may continue to receive their pay if they are absent for a few days with legitimate reasons.

Hourly employees are entitled to extra pay when they work on statutory holidays, such as New Year's Day, or if they work overtime. Generally, hourly employees do not receive any pay if they are absent for personal reasons.

The US Department of Labor, under the *Fair Labor Standards Act,* requires employers to pay overtime pay at a rate of at least 1.5 times an employee's regular rate of pay after 40 hours of work in one week. Certain categories of employees are exempt from this stipulation, such as many executive, management and administrative positions.

To illustrate, we can look at the overtime pay calculation for employee Amy Wood of Roofus Construction. Amy normally works a standard 40-hour work week at a rate of $23.75 an hour. During the last week of June, Amy worked a total of 44 hours, which is four hours over her normal work week. Her employer pays 2 times the regular rate (sometimes referred to as "double time") for all hours worked in excess of 40 hours per week. The calculation to determine Amy's gross pay for that week is shown in Figure 12.3.

Earnings at regular rate (40 hrs × $23.75/hr)	$950.00
Earnings at overtime rate* (4 hrs × $47.50)	190.00
Gross pay for last week of June	$1,140.00

*Overtime rate = $47.50 ($23.75 × 2)

FIGURE 12.3

There are at least two different amounts shown on a pay stub. Gross pay is the amount of pay an employee receives before any deductions—statutory or voluntary—are made. The amount remaining after deductions have been made is the net pay, or an employee's "take home pay." Payroll deductions are discussed next.

Employee Payroll Deductions—Statutory

Every business is required to withhold amounts from an employee's gross pay, called statutory deductions. These deductions are eventually paid to the appropriate tax authority in the country. In the Unites States, the tax authorities are the Internal Revenue Service (IRS) for federal income tax purposes and various state authorities for state income tax purposes, such as the California Employment Development Department or the New York State Department of Taxation and Finance. Statutory deductions in the United States include the following.

- federal income tax
- state and local income taxes
- Social Security tax
- Medicare tax

Each of the above statutory deductions is calculated using annual tax tables. The calculated amounts are then subtracted from an employee's pay. The business is responsible for keeping track of payroll and the associated deductions to prepare tax forms for the employee at the end of each calendar year. The tax forms are then used by the employee when preparing a personal tax return for the government.

It is important to note that these deductions are made on the employee's behalf. When the employee files an annual income tax return, the deducted amounts show as payments already made and reduce the final tax amount owed. The system is designed this way to reduce the financial burden on individuals who would otherwise have to pay huge amounts when they file their tax returns every year. As well, businesses withhold and remit these amounts to the tax authorities on behalf of employees to assist in paying for the government services provided all year. Examples of these services include education programs, unemployment programs and transportation funding. Regardless of the level of government that provides or contributes to these services, the majority of the funding comes throughout the year from tax installments.

The amounts withheld are required under law, and failure to withhold the amounts from the employee's pay and remit them to the tax authorities can result in severe penalties. Therefore, payroll liabilities warrant their own account, separate from accounts payable.

Federal Income Taxes

Every business is required to withhold income tax from an employee's gross pay. There is no age limit for paying taxes and no maximum on the total earnings for which taxes must be paid. The more an employee earns, the more tax is deducted from the pay.

Income tax is a major source of revenue for the federal government. The personal income tax rates depend on three factors.

- gross pay
- marital status
- withholding allowances

Every employee must complete an *Employee's Withholding Allowance Certificate*, also known as **Form W-4**, and submit it to the employer. The employer uses the information provided on the W-4, along with the employee's gross salary or gross wages, to calculate the amount of taxes to deduct, or *withhold*, from an employee's earnings.

On a W-4, an employee provides a social security number, marital status, and the withholding allowances to which he or she is entitled. Generally, the more withholding allowances an employee has, the lower the amount of federal income tax withheld. For instance, an employee who is single receives one withholding allowance, whereas a married employee may be entitled to an additional allowance for his or her spouse. Figure 12.4 shows the employee's portion of a W-4.

-------------------------------- **Separate here and give Form W-4 to your employer. Keep the top part for your records.** --------------------------------

Form W-4

Department of the Treasury
Internal Revenue Service

Employee's Withholding Allowance Certificate

▶ Whether you are entitled to claim a certain number of allowances or exemption from withholding is subject to review by the IRS. Your employer may be required to send a copy of this form to the IRS.

OMB No. 1545-0074

2017

1 Your first name and middle initial	Last name	2 Your social security number

Home address (number and street or rural route)	3 ☐ Single ☐ Married ☐ Married, but withhold at higher Single rate.
	Note: If married, but legally separated, or spouse is a nonresident alien, check the "Single" box.
City or town, state, and ZIP code	4 If your last name differs from that shown on your social security card, check here. You must call 1-800-772-1213 for a replacement card. ▶ ☐

5	Total number of allowances you are claiming (from line **H** above **or** from the applicable worksheet on page 2)	**5**
6	Additional amount, if any, you want withheld from each paycheck	**6** $
7	I claim exemption from withholding for 2017, and I certify that I meet **both** of the following conditions for exemption.	
	• Last year I had a right to a refund of **all** federal income tax withheld because I had **no** tax liability, **and**	
	• This year I expect a refund of **all** federal income tax withheld because I expect to have **no** tax liability.	
	If you meet both conditions, write "Exempt" here . . . . ▶	**7**

Under penalties of perjury, I declare that I have examined this certificate and, to the best of my knowledge and belief, it is true, correct, and complete.

Employee's signature
(This form is not valid unless you sign it.) ▶

Date ▶

8 Employer's name and address (Employer: Complete lines 8 and 10 only if sending to the IRS.)	9 Office code (optional)	10 Employer identification number (EIN)

For Privacy Act and Paperwork Reduction Act Notice, see page 2.

Cat. No. 10220Q

Form **W-4** (2017)

FIGURE 12.4

There are various methods for calculating federal income taxes. Each year, the Internal Revenue Service (IRS) issues income tax withholding tables to help employers calculate the amount of federal income tax to withhold, such as the **wage bracket method tables** for income tax withholding (a portion of a table for a single taxpayer is shown in Figure 12.5). This information is annually published by the IRS as the *(Circular E), Employer's Tax Guide.*

Wage Bracket Method Tables for Income Tax Withholding

SINGLE Persons— WEEKLY Payroll Period

(For Wages Paid through December 31, 2017)

And the wages are–		And the number of withholding allowances claimed is—										
At least	But less than	0	1	2	3	4	5	6	7	8	9	10
		The amount of income tax to be withheld is—										
$0	$55	$0	$0	$0	$0	$0	$0	$0	$0	$0	$0	$0
55	60	1	0	0	0	0	0	0	0	0	0	0
60	65	2	0	0	0	0	0	0	0	0	0	0
65	70	2	0	0	0	0	0	0	0	0	0	0
70	75	3	0	0	0	0	0	0	0	0	0	0
75	80	3	0	0	0	0	0	0	0	0	0	0
80	85	4	0	0	0	0	0	0	0	0	0	0
85	90	4	0	0	0	0	0	0	0	0	0	0
90	95	5	0	0	0	0	0	0	0	0	0	0
95	100	5	0	0	0	0	0	0	0	0	0	0
100	105	6	0	0	0	0	0	0	0	0	0	0
105	110	6	0	0	0	0	0	0	0	0	0	0
110	115	7	0	0	0	0	0	0	0	0	0	0
115	120	7	0	0	0	0	0	0	0	0	0	0
120	125	8	0	0	0	0	0	0	0	0	0	0
125	130	8	1	0	0	0	0	0	0	0	0	0
130	135	9	1	0	0	0	0	0	0	0	0	0
135	140	9	2	0	0	0	0	0	0	0	0	0
140	145	10	2	0	0	0	0	0	0	0	0	0
145	150	10	3	0	0	0	0	0	0	0	0	0
150	155	11	3	0	0	0	0	0	0	0	0	0
155	160	11	4	0	0	0	0	0	0	0	0	0
160	165	12	4	0	0	0	0	0	0	0	0	0
165	170	12	5	0	0	0	0	0	0	0	0	0
170	175	13	5	0	0	0	0	0	0	0	0	0

FIGURE 12.5

The withholding table in Figure 12.5 is for single persons, but withholding tables are also issued for married persons, and for different pay periods, such as semi-monthly and monthly. To use the table, the employer locates the employee's wage bracket from the first two columns, and then follows that row across to the column showing the number of withholding allowances claimed by that particular employee. The amount shown in that column is what should be withheld from the employee's gross salary (or wages). For example, if an employee earns a weekly salary of $157, and has claimed one withholding allowance, the employer withholds $4 from the employee's gross salary, as indicated by the highlight in Figure 12.5.

For simplicity in calculating federal income tax deductions, we will use a standard rate. In the real world, withholding tables or accounting software is used to get a precise figure. Figure 12.6 shows the simplified way of calculating how much federal income tax to deduct from an employee's pay.

$$\text{Federal Income Tax Deduction} = \text{Gross Pay} \times \text{Income Tax Rate}$$

FIGURE 12.6

At the end of the year, the employer must complete a *Wage and Tax Statement* for each employee, also known as a **Form W-2**. This form indicates the employees' gross pay and all the statutory deductions taken from the gross pay for the year. This form is given to the employee and sent to the IRS.

State and Local Income Taxes

Like federal income taxes, most states require employers to withhold income taxes from employee earnings. The calculation criterion is similar to that of federal taxes. Each state issues its own tax table similar to *Circular E*.

As with federal income tax, for simplicity in calculating state income tax deductions, we will use a standard rate. In the real world, withholding tables or accounting software is used to get a precise figure. Figure 12.7 shows the simplified way of calculating how much state income tax to deduct from an employee's pay.

$$\text{State Income Tax Deduction} = \text{Gross Pay} \times \text{Income Tax Rate}$$

FIGURE 12.7

Federal Insurance Contributions Act

Every business is required to withhold a portion of an employee's earnings in accordance with the Federal Insurance Contributions Act (FICA) from an employee's gross pay. The amount withheld is known as **FICA tax**. The statutory deduction is to pay for federal Social Security and Medicare benefits programs. The business is also required to match the amount withheld from the employee. For example, if an employee has $50 deducted from gross pay for FICA, the business has to pay an additional $50 towards FICA.

Both Social Security and the Medicare portion have their own rates applied to the gross pay of an employee. The rates usually change annually, but in recent years the typical rate for Social Security is 6.2% and the typical rate for Medicare is 1.45%, for a total FICA deduction of 7.65%. Since the employer must match this amount, the employer pays an additional 7.65% of the employee's gross pay to the federal government for FICA.

FICA Tax Threshold

The amount withheld for an employee is based on the employee's earnings for the calendar year. The amount withheld is also subject to a wage base limit above which additional taxes are withheld. This limit is updated annually. Using 2017 rates and limits, an employee is required to pay FICA taxes (on the calendar year salary/wages) as follows.

- Social Security tax of 6.2% on the first $127,200 of salary/wages, up to a maximum of $7,886.40 ($127,200 × 6.2%)

  plus

- Medicare tax of 1.45% on all earnings with an additional Medicare tax of 0.9% on salary/wages in excess of $200,000

For our examples, we will use the 2017 FICA rates of 6.2% (Social Security tax), and 1.45% (Medicare tax) and assume that all employees are paid wages that fall within the wage base limits. Figure 12.8 shows the formula to calculate the amount of FICA deducted from an employee's pay.

FICA Deduction = Gross Pay × FICA Rate

FIGURE 12.8

Employee Payroll Deductions—Voluntary

An employer may also deduct other amounts from an employee's pay with the employee's permission; these amounts are referred to as voluntary deductions. In each case, the employee is advised of the potential deductions and signs a contract indicating his or her agreement.

While these deductions are generally considered voluntary, they may be required by an employer as part of the employment agreement (typical examples would be union dues, medical and dental coverage).

Unions are organizations that employees can belong to that create better working conditions for the employees. Sometimes belonging to a union is the only way an employee can get a job. Charitable donations can include national and international charities, such as the US Fund for UNICEF, Direct Relief, or a registered local charity to which employees would like to contribute. The donations may be tax deductible.

There are many different types of voluntary deductions, all of which depend on what the business is willing to offer employees. The business deducts these amounts and eventually sends them to the appropriate institution. Examples of other voluntary deductions include the following.

- Accidental death and dismemberment coverage (AD&D)
- Employee Stock Purchase Plan (ESOP and ESPP)
- Roth IRA
- Long-term disability (LTD)
- Medical or dental coverage
- Retirement plan contributions (401K)
- Short-term disability (STD)

Employer Payroll Contributions

Often, the government requires employers to match or contribute to the deductions made from their employee's pay. This amount is an additional expense to the business and is recorded by debiting (increasing) employee benefits expense and crediting (increasing) the related payroll liability account.

Federal Insurance Contributions Act

As mentioned, FICA taxes are mandatory deductions from employees' pay for federal Social Security and Medicare benefits programs. The employer must also match the employee's deduction.

Federal Unemployment and State Unemployment Taxes

The business has to contribute towards federal and state unemployment taxes on behalf of employees. The Federal Unemployment Tax Act (FUTA) rate is 6.0% of gross pay, but only applies to the first $7,000 of gross pay an employee earns in the year.

The State Unemployment Tax (SUTA) rate changes from state to state. The rate fluctuates based on factors such as the number of unemployment claims in the state and the overall "good standing" of the state with the federal government. For this textbook, assume the SUTA rate is 5.4%. The employer is allowed to reduce the federal unemployment tax rate by the state unemployment tax rate. In this example, the FUTA rate of 6.0% is reduced to 0.6% (6.0% - 5.4%).

Figure 12.9 shows the formula to calculate the amount of FUTA that is payable to the government. The formula for SUTA payable is the same, except it uses the SUTA rate.

$$\text{FUTA Payable} = \text{Gross Pay} \times \text{FUTA Rate}$$

FIGURE 12.9

Employee Benefits

Some employers will pay for some or all of the benefits they provide their employees. This is an extra cost to the business. If the employer decides to pay for all of a benefit (for example a health benefit), then the employee would not see any deduction from his or her pay.

Responsibility for Paying Taxes and Benefits

We have just discussed the employee payroll deductions (statutory and voluntary) and the employer payroll contributions. Figure 12.10 summarizes these responsibilities according to who pays them.

Employee Payroll Deductions	Employer Payroll Contributions
• FICA tax—Social security taxes	• FICA tax—Social security taxes
• FICA tax—Medicare taxes	• FICA tax—Medicare taxes
• Federal income taxes	• FUTA tax—Federal unemployment taxes
• State and local income taxes	• SUTA—State unemployment taxes
• Portion of medical coverage (if applicable)	• Portion of medical coverage (if applicable)
• Portion of pension plan (if applicable)	• Portion of pension plan (if applicable)
• Portion of other benefits (if applicable, e.g. insurance)	• Portion of other benefits (if applicable)
• Charitable donations and union dues (if applicable)	

FIGURE 12.10

Payroll Example

Assume that Roofus Construction's gross payroll for the period ending January 31, 2018 is $15,000, consisting of $11,200 in sales salaries and $3,800 in office salaries. Employees are paid every month and have statutory deductions withheld from their pay. In addition, there are voluntary deductions from their gross earnings including union dues, charitable contributions, health insurance plan and retirement savings. As part of their benefits package, Roofus Construction matches employee contributions to health insurance and retirement plans.

Payroll Register

Since businesses usually have multiple employees, a payroll register is often used rather than preparing individual entries. A payroll register lists every employee along with his or her gross pay, deductions and net pay. The bottom of the payroll register calculates totals that can be used to complete the journal entries. Computer accounting software has a similar tool for creating paychecks for multiple employees at one time.

Figure 12.11 shows a sample payroll register. Glen Booth earns $5,000 gross pay per month as a salary. The rest of the employees are paid various hourly wages and work a different number of hours. We will assume all employees must pay monthly union dues of $25 and monthly health insurance of $15. The monthly health insurance premiums are actually $400 per person, but the business pays half. By completing the rest of the payroll information for all the employees, we can use the totals to create the journal entries.

PAYROLL PERIOD JANUARY 1 TO JANUARY 31, 2018			
Name	**Hourly Wage**	**Hours**	**Gross Earnings**
Booth, Glen		160	$5,000.00
Dickens, Charlie	$27.35	100	$2,735.00
Smith, Adam	23.10	150	$3,465.00
Wood, Amy	23.75	160	$3,800.00
Total			$15,000.00

Payroll Register									
	Deductions								
Gross Earnings	**Federal Income Tax**	**State Income Tax**	**FICA Tax**	**Charitable Donations**	**Union Dues**	**Retirement Savings Plan**	**Health Insurance**	**Total Deductions**	**Net Pay**
$5,000.00	$500.00	$250.00	$382.50	$50.00	$25.00	$250.00	$200.00	$1,657.50	$3,342.50
$2,735.00	$273.50	$136.75	$209.23	$50.00	$25.00	$250.00	$200.00	$1,144.48	$1,590.52
$3,465.00	$346.50	$173.25	$265.07	$50.00	$25.00	$250.00	$200.00	$1,309.82	$2,155.18
$3,800.00	$380.00	$190.00	$290.70	$50.00	$25.00	$250.00	$200.00	$1,385.70	$2,414.30
$15,000.00	$1,500.00	$750.00	$1,147.50	$200.00	$100.00	$1,000.00	$800.00	$5,497.50	$9,502.50

FIGURE 12.11

Payroll Records

The business must keep a record of gross pay, deductions, hours worked and a variety of other information about every employee. This information is collected at the time the employee is hired and updated every pay or when any important piece of information relating to payroll changes. A computerized system updates the payroll record automatically after every pay, as shown in Figure 12.12.

Booth, Glen
5234 North Street
Springfield, IL 62704-1234

Single   Number of Withholding Allowances: 1

Phone: (217) 555-1212
Date of Birth: February 16, 1977
Soc. Sec. No.: 123-45-6789
Pay Rate: $5,000.00 per month
Occupation: Sales

Employee No.: 2218

Date of Hire: June 20, 2008

Date of Termination:

			Deductions								
Month Ended	**Hours**	**Gross Earnings**	**Federal Income Tax**	**State Income Tax**	**FICA Tax**	**Charitable Donations**	**Union Dues**	**Retirement Saving Plan**	**Health Insurance**	**Total Deductions**	**Net Pay**
Jan 31, 2018	160	$5,000.00	$500.00	$250.00	$383.50	$50.00	$25.00	$250.00	$200.00	$1,657.50	$3,342.50
Feb 28, 2018	160	$5,000.00	$500.00	$250.00	$383.50	$50.00	$25.00	$250.00	$200.00	$1,657.50	$3,342.50
Mar 31, 2018	160	$5,000.00	$500.00	$250.00	$383.50	$50.00	$25.00	$250.00	$200.00	$1,657.50	$3,342.50
Apr 30, 2018	160	$5,000.00	$500.00	$250.00	$383.50	$50.00	$25.00	$250.00	$200.00	$1,657.50	$3,342.50
May 31, 2018	160	$5,000.00	$500.00	$250.00	$383.50	$50.00	$25.00	$250.00	$200.00	$1,657.50	$3,342.50

FIGURE 12.12

The steps to create the journal entry to record payroll (wages and/or salaries) with deductions are as follows.

- Record gross pay by debiting (increasing) the salaries expense account.

- Record the amounts withheld to various payable accounts by crediting (increasing) each of the payable accounts; these amounts are paid to the IRS and others at a later date.

- Record the net amount actually paid to the employees as a credit (decrease) to cash if the employee is paid immediately. If payment is delayed a few days, post the net amount as a credit (increase) to the salaries payable account for later payment.

The journal entry to record these transactions is shown in Figure 12.13. Note that amounts have been rounded to the nearest dollar for simplicity. The deductions have been calculated based on the gross pay and the calculations presented earlier.

JOURNAL			
Date	Account Title and Explanation	Debit	Credit
Jan 31	Sales Salaries Expense	11,200	
	Office Salaries Expense	3,800	
	Federal Income Tax Payable		1,500
	State Income Tax Payable		750
	FICA Tax Payable		1,148
	Charitable Donations Payable		200
	Union Dues Payable		100
	Retirement Savings Plan Payable		1,000
	Health Insurance Payable		800
	Salaries Payable		9,502
	Record salaries and deductions		

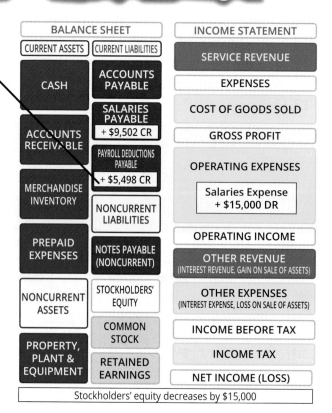

Federal Income Tax Payable $1,500 CR
State Income Tax Payable $750 CR
FICA Tax Payable $1,148 CR
Charitable Donations Payable $200 CR
Union Dues Payable $100 CR
Retirement Savings Plan Payable $1,000 CR
Health Insurance Payable $800 CR
Total Payroll Deductions Payable $5,498 CR

FIGURE 12.13

Net pay is calculated by subtracting all the deductions from the gross pay. The employee's net pay is recorded in salaries payable. This indicates that the business has recorded the payroll journal entry but pays the employee at a later date. If the employee is paid immediately, the employee's net pay is recorded to cash.

The business now has to record its own payroll expenses. In addition to paying for FICA, remember that this business pays for half of the health insurance coverage for its employees.

The steps to record the business expenses as a journal entry are as follows.

- Record total expenses to the business by debiting (increasing) employee benefits expense.
- Record individual amounts by crediting (increasing) the various payable (liability) accounts.

The journal entry to record these transactions is shown in Figure 12.14. The employer amounts have been calculated based on the calculations presented earlier.

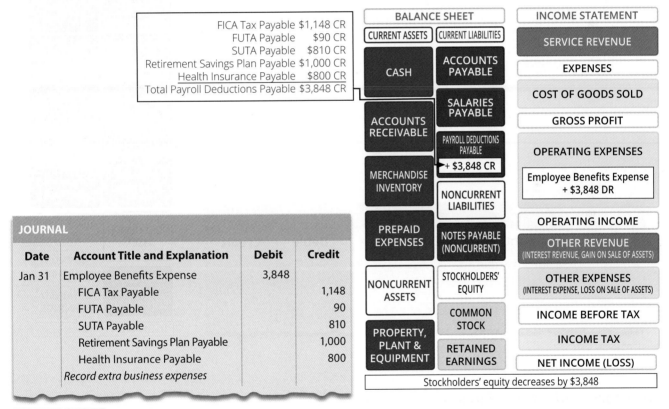

FIGURE 12.14

Paying the Liabilities

The steps to record paying the liabilities as journal entries are as follows.

- Record the reduction of the liabilities by debiting (decreasing) each of the payable accounts.
- Record the payment to the appropriate individual or institution by crediting (decreasing) cash.

Once the journal entries are made and the decreases to the liability accounts are complete, the liability accounts have a zero balance. All the amounts that were payroll debts to the company are completely paid off. Notice that there is no change to the income statement or equity when the liabilities are paid.

Salaries Payable

Employees do not always receive a paycheck on the same day that the payroll entry is recorded. For our example, the journal entry to record salaries and deductions in Figure 12.13 was made on January 31, 2018, and the journal entry to record paying the employee in Figure 12.15 was made on February 1, 2018. When the employees receive their salaries, we can decrease the liability and reduce cash.

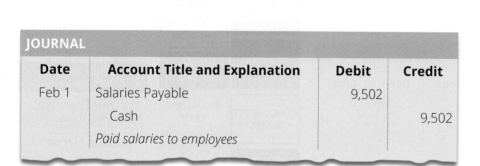

JOURNAL			
Date	**Account Title and Explanation**	**Debit**	**Credit**
Feb 1	Salaries Payable	9,502	
	Cash		9,502
	Paid salaries to employees		

FIGURE 12.15

Statutory Deductions Payable

Figure 12.16 shows the journal entry to record the payment of statuatory deductions payable.

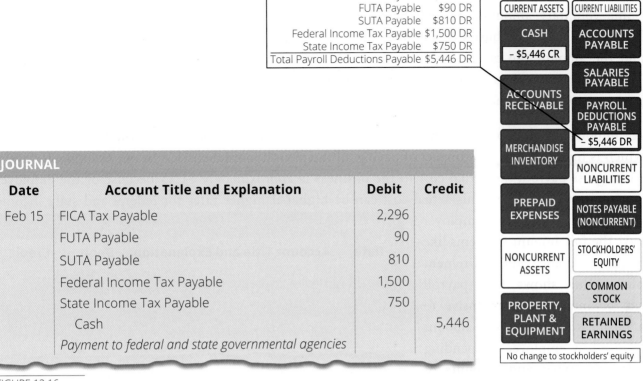

FIGURE 12.16

The government has strict guidelines for when the payroll liabilities are due. Businesses must pay close attention to these dates. If payments are late, the business must pay penalties and interest on top of the amount owed. It is usually best to send payment through the bank. The bank teller's stamp indicates the date the payment was made to record if the payment was made on time or made late. Most moderate size businesses have to pay their statutory deduction liabilities by the 15th of the following month.

In this example, payroll was recorded on January 31, 2018; therefore the government must receive payment by February 15, 2018. Notice that FICA taxes include both the amounts deducted from the employee's pay and the amounts the business had to contribute.

Charitable Donations and Union Dues Payable

Any voluntary amounts deducted from an employee's pay must be sent to the institution to which they are owed. Businesses merely act as an intermediary, taking the money from the employee and sending it to the institution. In this example, union dues must be sent to the union organization by the end of the following month, as indicated by the journal entry in Figure 12.17. Charitable donations are paid in a similar manner to the appropriate charity.

JOURNAL			
Date	**Account Title and Explanation**	**Debit**	**Credit**
Feb 28	Union Dues Payable	50	
	Cash		50
	Payment to union organization		

FIGURE 12.17

Health and Retirement Plan Payable

Some voluntary amounts are split between the employee and the business. In this example for health insurance, the business combines the amount deducted from the employee in Figure 12.13 and the amount the business contributes in Figure 12.14. The journal entry is shown in Figure 12.18. The payment is being made to the health insurance company. The process to record the payment for the retirement plan is similar.

An important point to note is that the $15,000 in gross payroll actually costs the business $18,848, which is the total cash flow impact of paying all the payroll journal entries. In our example, for every $1 of gross payroll, the actual cost to the business is approximately $1.25 because of the employer contributions and taxes. This actual cost can be higher if higher rates for federal and state income taxes are used, or the employer pays the full amount for items like health insurance and retirement plans. This shows that payroll can be much more expensive to a business than just the amount received by employees, depending upon the types and amounts of benefits that a business pays.

JOURNAL

Date	Account Title and Explanation	Debit	Credit
Feb 28	Health Insurance Payable	1,600	
	Cash		1,600
	Payment for health insurance		

FIGURE 12.18

Pause & Reflect

Exercise 12-1

Cranberry Pickers is determining the payroll amounts for the month ending April 30, 2018. Its employees earned a total of $10,000 in gross pay. Assume the following rates.

Federal Income Tax	10%
State Income Tax	5%
FICA	7.65%
FUTA	0.6%
SUTA	5.4%

Calculate the net pay to be paid to the employees, as well as the total employer payroll contributions.

See Appendix I for solutions.

Accounts Payable

Accounts payable is a determinable liability. A company purchases goods or services from a vendor and that vendor issues the company an invoice, which must be paid by a certain date. The terms of the liability are easily recognized and recorded by the company.

In previous chapters, we pointed out that selling an item on account means debiting accounts receivable and crediting sales. With accounts payable, there is a mirror transaction; an asset or expense account is debited and the accounts payable account is credited.

The amount of money owed by customers is controlled by using an accounts receivable subledger (this is further explained in Chapter 10). The same principle applies to the amount of money owed to suppliers, which is controlled by using the accounts payable subledger.

For accounts payable, the controlling account in the general ledger includes the total amount of credit balances in an individual subledger accounts.

Figure 12.9 shows the required journal entry when a company buys a repair service on credit from Plumbers Inc. for $1,000 on September 30, 2018.

BALANCE SHEET	INCOME STATEMENT
CURRENT LIABILITIES	SALES REVENUE
BANK OVERDRAFT & OPERATING LINE OF CREDIT	
ACCOUNTS PAYABLE **+ $1,000 CR**	COST OF GOODS SOLD
ACCRUED LIABILITIES	GROSS PROFIT
	OPERATING EXPENSES
UNEARNED REVENUE	Repairs Expense + $1,000 DR
NOTES PAYABLE (CURRENT)	OPERATING INCOME
NONCURRENT LIABILITIES	OTHER REVENUE (INTEREST REVENUE, GAIN ON SALE OF ASSETS)
NOTES PAYABLE (NONCURRENT)	OTHER EXPENSES (INTEREST EXPENSE, LOSS ON SALE OF ASSETS)
STOCKHOLDERS' EQUITY	
COMMON STOCK	INCOME BEFORE TAX
	INCOME TAX
RETAINED EARNINGS	NET INCOME (LOSS)
	Stockholders' equity decreases by $1,000

JOURNAL			
Date	**Account Title and Explanation**	**Debit**	**Credit**
Sep 30	Repairs Expense	1,000	
	Accounts Payable		1,000
	Record repairs expense owing to Plumbers Inc.		

FIGURE 12.19

Since the purchase was for repairs, the repairs expense account is debited for $1,000 and is listed under operating expenses on the income statement. Accounts payable is credited for the same amount, showing that an invoice was received and must be paid in the future.

Sales Tax

Sales tax is a tax that is applied by the state government to goods or services that are sold. They are calculated as a percentage of a sale, and the percentages can vary from state to state. Figure 12.20 shows some examples of states and the amount of sales tax they charge.

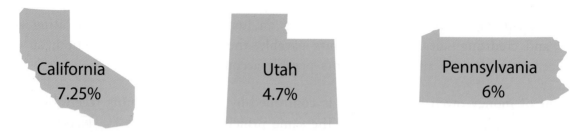

California 7.25%

Utah 4.7%

Pennsylvania 6%

Note: Local sales tax may be added to state sales tax, causing actual sales tax in certain jurisdictions to be higher.

FIGURE 12.20

Although sales tax must be paid to the government, it would be impractical, if not impossible, for individual customers to send the sales tax money to the government every time they bought something. Imagine buying a coffee and having to send the government a few cents in sales tax.

Instead, businesses act as tax collectors for the government by collecting the sales tax from their customers and sending it to the government. For example, imagine a business receives $1,650 from a customer for the purchase of a TV. Of that amount, $1,500 is for the actual TV and $150 is the amount of sales tax. The business has to eventually remit the $150 sales tax to the government. Figure 12.21 demonstrates a simplified version of this process.

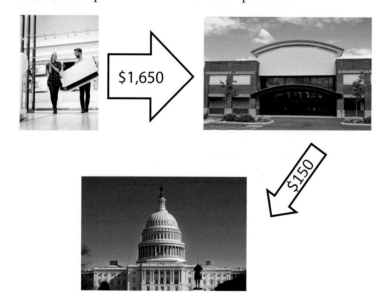

FIGURE 12.21

The retailer is responsible for collecting sales tax from the customer and eventually sending (remitting) the amount collected to the state government. The amount collected does not belong to the company and is considered a liability until it is paid to the government. Therefore, sales tax is recorded in a current liability account until it is remitted.

The range of sales tax varies by each state, from 0% to 7.25%. Some cities and counties impose additional sales tax on top of the state sales tax. The Federal Tax Administration publishes sales tax rates for all states and cities. It is important to note that for certain items that are resold more than once, (e.g. used cars), sales tax can be applied indefinitely. Each state has a list of tax exempt goods and services or items that are taxed at a reduced rate.

The due date to send the collected sales tax to the government varies from business to business. Companies that have a very small amount of sales may be required to send in the sales tax once a year. As the amount of sales increases and the amount of sales tax collected increases, the business may be required to send in the money on a quarterly or monthly basis. The government charges interest and penalties to businesses that fail to send the money or send it late.

As an example, assume Hardware Store Inc. sells inventory to a customer for $1,000 cash on June 15, 2018. The state sales tax rate is 6%. The transaction is shown in Figure 12.22. For this example, ignore cost of goods sold. Notice that while cash increased by $1,060, equity only increased by $1,000.

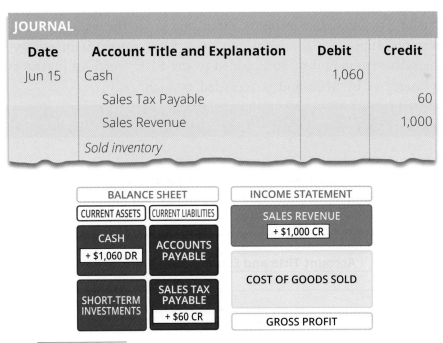

FIGURE 12.22

Each sale gradually increases the amount in the sales tax payable account until it is time for the company to send it to the state government. Assume the payment is made on August 31, 2018 and the account only has a $60 credit balance. Figure 12.23 shows the transaction.

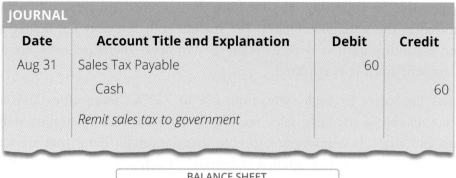

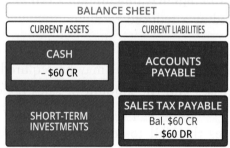

FIGURE 12.23

The sales tax payable account essentially acts as a clearing account. It accumulates the sales tax collected over a period of time, and then is cleared to $0 when a payment is made to send the sales tax to the state government.

Sales tax that is paid on purchased items is often added to the value of the asset or expense purchased. For example, suppose a company purchases $100 worth of inventory in a state where sales tax is 6%. The sales tax amount of $6 is added to the $100 worth of inventory, so merchandise inventory actually increases by $106 and is recorded as such.

Pause & Reflect

Exercise 12-2

On March 13, 2018, Jerrod Furniture Shop sold products for $50,000 cash. The products cost Jerrod $22,000. Jerrod Furniture Shop operates in a state that charges 5% sales tax. Assume Jerrod Furniture Shop uses a perpetual inventory system. Prepare the journal entries for the sale of the products.

JOURNAL			
Date	Account Title and Explanation	Debit	Credit

See Appendix I for solutions.

Unearned Revenue

The accrual basis of accounting applies to both expenses and revenues. As you have learned, expenses are recognized during the period in which they are incurred, and not when they are actually paid. The same applies to unearned revenue: it is recognized in the period in which it was earned, and not when payment was actually received. As shown in Figure 12.24, for both accrued expense and unearned revenue, current liabilities are recorded in the first period. For accrued expense, accounts payable is recorded in the first period because the expense is incurred in the first period, but the company has not yet paid for it. Accounts payable has been covered in a previous section in this chapter. This section focuses on unearned revenue, which is recorded when the company receives cash before rendering goods or services to customers.

Accrued Expense		Unearned Revenue	
Expense Incurred	Expense Paid	Cash Received	Revenue Earned
Period 1	**Period 2**	**Period 1**	**Period 2**

DR Expense
    CR Accounts Payable
	DR Accounts Payable
	    CR Cash
		DR Cash
		    CR Unearned Revenue
			DR Unearned Revenue
			    CR Revenue

FIGURE 12.24

For example, a publishing company might receive payment in advance for a one-year subscription to its magazine. The money is received, but the magazine has not yet been supplied to the customer. Until the product exchanges hands, the amount received in advance cannot be recognized as revenue. The advanced cash receipt is therefore considered unearned revenue, which is a liability.

Business owners sometimes misunderstand how accruals work. This can lead to mistakes and bad decisions. For example, management may be tempted to treat unearned revenue as though it is already earned. Using the example of a magazine subscription again, what would happen if a customer decided to cancel the subscription and the magazine publisher had considered the money as earned? Until the product has been delivered, no transaction has been finalized with the customer. The money should be paid back to the customer when the subscription is canceled.

With a non-refundable subscription, the same principle would apply. It is still the obligation of the company to deliver goods or services that have been paid for and to treat the money as unearned until completion of the transaction.

What happens if a customer voluntarily cancels the rights to the goods or services and notifies the company to that effect? An example of this might be a subscriber moving overseas and informing the publisher that delivery of the magazine is no longer necessary. If the subscription is non-refundable, the customer has no right to request repayment and the company can continue to recognize revenue as it is earned. Of course, if the subscription is refundable, the publisher has to reverse all or part of the initial transaction and refund the subscriber for any remaining unused months of the subscription.

Here is an example to illustrate the concept of accruals and revenue. Tracking Time is the publisher of a magazine with a fiscal year end of December 31. In December, Tracking Time receives $120,000 from subscribers to cover the monthly delivery of magazines for one year, starting on January 1. The transaction is recorded in the company's books as shown in Figure 12.25.

JOURNAL			
Date	**Account Title and Explanation**	**Debit**	**Credit**
Dec 31	Cash	120,000	
	Unearned Revenue		120,000
	Record the deposit of subscription sales		

FIGURE 12.25

The money is received and debited to the cash account in December. However, the revenue is yet to be earned (i.e. it is earned when the magazines are delivered), so the amount is credited to the unearned revenue account. Since revenue is not yet earned, there is no change to the company's equity.

On January 1, the magazine is delivered to customers for that month. This means that Tracking Time's obligation to the customers has been met for the month and the corresponding revenue is now earned. One month of subscriptions equals one-twelfth of the annual subscription; therefore, $10,000 is recognized as revenue for the month of January, as shown in Figure 12.26.

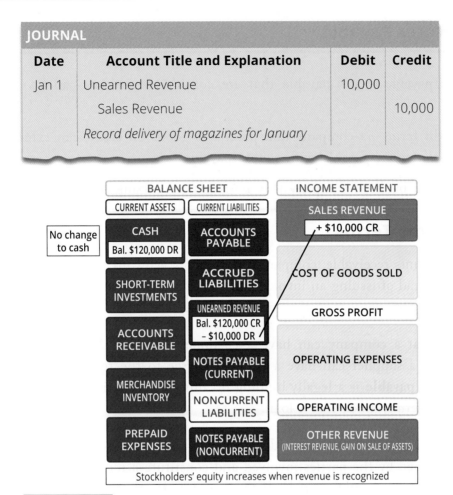

FIGURE 12.26

Unearned revenue originally had a credit balance of $120,000. Of that amount, $10,000 is now debited to the unearned revenue account and credited to the sales revenue account on the income statement. Although cash remains the same, the recognition of the unearned revenue means that equity has increased by $10,000. The obligation that Tracking Time now has to its customers is reduced from $120,000 to $110,000.

Another type of unearned liability gaining popularity in recent years is for gift cards or gift certificates. Similar to the Tracking Time example above, when a business sells a gift card or certificate, it debits the cash account and credits an unearned revenue account. The sales revenue account is only credited, and the unearned revenue account debited, when the gift card or certificate is redeemed for a product or service.

Short-Term Notes Payable

Short-term notes payable (notes payable that are considered current) can be issued for several different reasons.

- To extend credit terms—a company that purchases goods on credit can extend its credit term by replacing an account payable with a note payable

- To borrow from a bank—a company may borrow from a bank by signing a note payable

Extending Credit Terms

With regard to accounts receivable, companies sometimes want greater assurance that a customer will pay the bill. Instead of issuing an invoice and creating an account receivable, a company might make a more formal arrangement in the form of a note receivable.

In the same way that a company can have a customer agree to the terms of a note receivable, a supplier can have a company agree to the terms of a note payable. A **note payable** is a legally binding document that obligates the borrower to certain terms, much like a loan.

Such documents outline the amount owed, when it is due and the interest payable. They are signed by the parties involved and constitute a more formal arrangement than a basic account payable. If the due date is one year or less, the note is reported as a current liability on the balance sheet, as highlighted in Figure 12.27. Figure 12.28 is an example of a note payable.

FIGURE 12.27

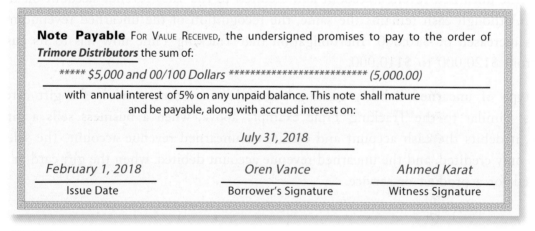

FIGURE 12.28

In the note payable from Figure 12.28, Oren Vance borrowed $5,000 from Trimore Distributors on February 1, 2018. The annual interest rate is 5% and both principal and interest are payable in six months. The journal entry used by the debtor (borrower) to record the extension of the credit term and the conversion of the original account payable to a note payable is shown in Figure 12.29.

JOURNAL

Date	Account Title and Explanation	Debit	Credit
Feb 1	Accounts Payable	5,000	
	Notes Payable		5,000
	Record a six-month, 5% note payable		

FIGURE 12.29

When the note payable is due, Vance pays the principal and interest to Trimore. The journal entry for this transaction is shown in Figure 12.30. Interest is calculated as $125 for six months.

WORTH REPEATING

Recall that the formula to calculate interest is Principal x Interest Rate x Time in Years.

JOURNAL

Date	Account Title and Explanation	Debit	Credit
July 31	Notes Payable	5,000	
	Interest Expense	125	
	Cash		5,125
	Paid $5,000 note payable with interest		

FIGURE 12.30

Borrowing from a Bank

When a company borrows from a bank, the loan is documented with a note payable. To illustrate, suppose that on February 1, 2018, Oren Vance borrows money from Carson Bank to purchase merchandise. A $5,000, six-month, 5% note payable is issued. Note that the 5% is an annual interest rate. The journal entry for this transaction is shown in Figure 12.31.

JOURNAL

Date	Account Title and Explanation	Debit	Credit
Feb 1	Cash	5,000	
	Notes Payable		5,000
	Borrowed $5,000 cash with a six-month, 5% note payable to Carson Bank		

FIGURE 12.31

When the note payable is due, Vance pays the principal and interest to the bank. The journal entry for this transaction is shown in Figure 12.32.

JOURNAL			
Date	**Account Title and Explanation**	**Debit**	**Credit**
July 31	Notes Payable	5,000	
	Interest Expense	125	
	Cash		5,125
	Paid $5,000 note payable with interest		

FIGURE 12.32

Pause & Reflect

Exercise 12-3

Bach Supplies has a short-term cash flow problem. It approaches its bank and receives a $20,000 short-term note payable on April 1, 2018. The note is due in six months on October 1, 2018. The annual interest rate on the note payable is 6%. Record the journal entries for the issuance of the note payable, and the payment of the note when it is due.

JOURNAL			
Date	**Account Title and Explanation**	**Debit**	**Credit**

See Appendix I for solutions.

Current Portion of Noncurrent Liabilities

When the term of a note payable is longer than one year, there will be two components to the note payable. The portion of the loan principal that will be paid within the next 12 months is considered current. This amount must be reported separately when the balance sheet is prepared, in a section under current liabilities called Notes Payable, Current Portion. The remaining amount of the note payable that is due beyond one year is reported on the balance sheet under noncurrent liabilities as Notes Payable, Noncurrent Portion.

For example, a company manufactures a wide range of products for consumers. It wants to purchase a new processing machine to keep up with growing demand for its product. The company has insufficient cash reserves on hand to finance the purchase. Management decides to obtain a loan from a bank to finance an important capital investment.

On January 2, 2018, the company negotiates a loan from the bank of $50,000 with a term of five years, bearing an annual interest rate of 5%. Of that debt, $10,000 plus interest is payable every December 31. The full amount of the loan is recorded as a notes payable in the journal entry. When the balance sheet is prepared, the current portion of $10,000 is presented separately from the noncurrent portion of $40,000. Figure 12.33 shows how the note payable is recorded in the company's books.

JOURNAL			
Date	**Account Title and Explanation**	**Debit**	**Credit**
Jan 2	Cash	50,000	
	Notes Payable		50,000
	Borrowed $50,000 term debt payable over five years		

FIGURE 12.33

On December 31, the first installment plus interest was paid. The transaction is recorded as shown in Figure 12.34.

JOURNAL			
Date	**Account Title and Explanation**	**Debit**	**Credit**
Dec 31	Notes Payable	10,000	
	Interest Expense	2,500	
	Cash		12,500
	Record payment for first notes payable installment plus interest		

FIGURE 12.34

After the first payment, the balance of the note payable decreases to $40,000, $10,000 of which is still considered current. When the balance sheet is prepared at the year end, $10,000 is included as part of current liabilities and $30,000 is included as part of noncurrent liabilities. Figure 12.35 shows how they would be reported on a balance sheet.

Sample Company **Balance Sheet (partial)** **As at December 31, 2018**	
Current Liabilities	
Notes Payable, Current Portion	10,000
Noncurrent Liabilities	
Notes Payable, Noncurrent Portion	30,000

FIGURE 12.35

Estimated Liabilities

 LO 8

We have already discussed various forms of known liabilities, also referred to as determinable liabilities, which are debts taken on by a company for which the terms are readily known. However, some company liabilities exist for which the exact terms are not precisely known and cannot be determined until future events occur. These unknown liabilities are referred to as non-determinable liabilities, and can be divided further into estimated liabilities and contingent liabilities.

Estimated liabilities are financial obligations that a company cannot exactly quantify. Examples include employee benefits and estimated product warranty costs. A company needs to adhere to the expense recognition principle when it makes an estimate of the amount of the upcoming liability.

Employee Benefits

In the section on payroll accounting, we briefly discussed voluntary deductions. These are additional deductions that an employee can authorize the employer to withhold from the employee's gross pay for pensions, medical and dental coverage, and other benefits known as **employee benefits**. Employee benefits are an expense to the employer. According to the matching principle, the cost of these benefits must be estimated and recorded in the period in which they are incurred—that is, in the period in which the employee earns the benefits. Next, we will look at some common employee benefits in more detail: paid vacations, pension benefits, health benefits and employee bonuses.

Vacation Pay

Many employers offer their employees paid vacations, also referred to as *compensated absences*. The employer estimates and records the amount to pay for employee vacations as an accrued liability for the period, either by pay period or at the end of the year. For example, assume that a company's salaried employee has earned an estimated $560 in vacation pay for the month of January. The company accrues its estimated vacation pay liabilities at the end of each month. On January 31, the employer makes the journal entry shown in Figure 12.36.

JOURNAL			
Date	**Account Title and Explanation**	**Debit**	**Credit**
Jan 31	Vacation Pay Expense	560	
	Vacation Pay Payable		560
	To accrue estimated vacation pay payable for the month		

FIGURE 12.36

In many cases, whether by personal choice or by employer policy, the employee uses the vacation entitlement within the year. In this case, any accrued vacation pay at the end of the year is reported on the company's balance sheet as a current liability. Sometimes, employees are allowed to accumulate vacation entitlement and carry it over into another period. If the employee does not take the vacation entitlement within the next year, the estimated vacation pay payable is reported on the company's balance sheet as a noncurrent liability.

When the employee in our example takes her vacation, the employer records a journal entry to debit vacation pay payable and credit cash. The employer must also record the normal entries related to taxes and withholdings in the payroll records.

Pension Benefits

Some employers contribute to *pension plans* for their employees, which allows employees to receive cash payments from the company after they retire. Employee pension rights are accrued during the period of time that the employee works for the company. There are several basic types of pension plans, known as defined contribution and defined benefit plans. Details of these plans are beyond the scope of this textbook. However, in simple terms, the employer accrues employee pensions each period (assume one year) as shown in Figure 12.37.

JOURNAL			
Date	**Account Title and Explanation**	**Debit**	**Credit**
Dec 31	Employee Benefits Expense	5,000	
	Employee Pensions Payable		5,000
	To record accrued pension benefits		

FIGURE 12.37

When the employee retires and the former employer starts paying out the pension benefits, the company records the payments by decreasing (debiting) employee pensions payable and crediting the cash account.

Health Benefits

Some employers provide continuing health benefits to their employees after they retire by paying for their medical and dental insurance coverage. The journal entry to record the accrued benefits for the period is shown in Figure 12.38.

JOURNAL			
Date	**Account Title and Explanation**	**Debit**	**Credit**
Dec 31	Employee Benefits Expense	2,000	
	Employee Medical Insurance Payable		2,000
	To record accrued medical insurance benefits		

FIGURE 12.38

When the medical insurance premiums are paid, the company records the payments by decreasing (debiting) employee medical insurance payable and crediting the cash account.

Employee Bonuses

Some employers offer employee bonuses based on a percentage of the company's net income for a period. Assume an employer plans to pay its staff a bonus equal to 5% of the company's net income. It estimates the total amount of the bonus as $5,000. The company records an accrual with the journal entry shown in Figure 12.39.

JOURNAL			
Date	**Account Title and Explanation**	**Debit**	**Credit**
Dec 31	Employee Bonus Expense	5,000	
	Employee Bonus Payable		5,000
	To record accrued employee bonus payable		

FIGURE 12.39

When the bonuses are paid, the company records the payments by decreasing (debiting) employee bonus payable and crediting the cash account.

Product Warranties

Just as a company needs to estimate how much bad debt it will have in the upcoming period, when a company sells products with warranties it needs to estimate how much warranty liability it will have. Warranties are one way a company reassures customers that its products are free of defects for a certain period of time, and any defects during that period are the responsibility of the company. By estimating the warranty liability, the company can expense this liability in the period in which related revenues are generated. Any errors in estimation can be adjusted once the actual figures are known.

There are two types of product warranties: basic and extended. A basic warranty is included in the price of the product. For example, when you buy a brand new cell phone, the price already includes a one-year warranty. There may be an option to purchase an extended warranty separately. This extended warranty will cover a specific period after the basic warranty expires. Basic warranties and extended warranties are accounted for differently. A basic warranty must be accounted for using the Expense Warranty Approach, which we will now discuss using the example of a company called Star Machines.

Star Machines manufactures industrial labeling machines. A basic warranty of three years is included with the purchase of each machine. If a machine breaks down during this warranty period, Star Machines is obliged to repair it, provide parts and, if necessary, replace the machine.

On the basis of an analysis of historical company trends, the company's accountant determines that an average of $100 per machine is paid out in warranty obligations. The company has sold 50 labeling machines during the 2018 fiscal year; therefore, the journal entry in Figure 12.40 is made to recognize the warranty expense for 2018.

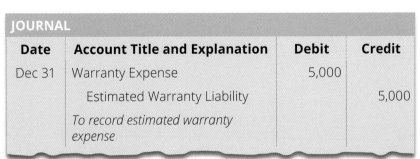

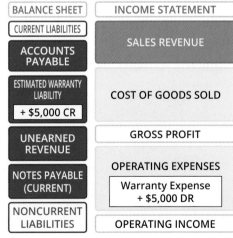

FIGURE 12.40

The $5,000 is expensed for this period on the income statement since this estimate covers expected warranties for the year. The estimated warranty liability of $5,000 is credited to the corresponding liability account.

During the next year, Star Machines receives some warranty claims and has actual expenditures in meeting those claims. Let us assume that Star Machines uses $500 in parts from its own inventory, and maintenance staff reports $1,500 worth of billable hours related to warranty claims. Figure 12.41 illustrates how Star's accountant records these transactions.

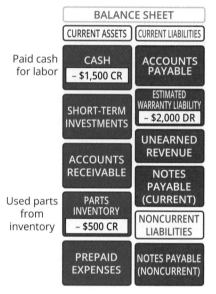

JOURNAL

Date	Account Title and Explanation	Debit	Credit
Jan 31	Estimated Warranty Liability	2,000	
	Parts Inventory		500
	Cash		1,500
	To record inventory and wages for warranty work		

FIGURE 12.41

The estimated warranty liability account is debited with $2,000, leaving a balance of $3,000 to satisfy warranty claims over the remaining two-year period. On the credit side, $500 worth of inventory is taken off the books, and $1,500 is recorded as a decrease to cash.

There is no change to the income statement since the estimated warranty was expensed in the year the machine was sold. The company calculates and records a debit to warranty expense and a credit to estimated warranty liability accounts on the basis of the number of machines sold that year.

Pause & Reflect

Exercise 12-4

Crystal Cleaners sells high-end vacuum cleaners. Every vacuum comes with a two-year warranty on parts and labor. The accountant estimates that an average of $50 worth of warranty work is done on each vacuum sold. During the year ending December 31, 2018, 8,000 vacuums were sold. Prepare the journal entry to record the estimated warranty expense.

JOURNAL			
Date	**Account Title and Explanation**	**Debit**	**Credit**

See Appendix I for solutions.

Internal Controls Relating to Current Liabilities and Payroll

LO 9

Controls for Liabilities

One of the first, basic controls over a company's liabilities involves a simple principle: keep track of company bills and budget well enough to pay them on time. The inability to pay suppliers can cause serious inventory shortages. Even more importantly, not paying suppliers risks a company's reputation and ability to do business with others. Controls are implemented to ensure that the right bills are paid at the right time. To that end, all relevant documents are gathered, such as purchase orders, receipts and original invoices, to verify the legitimacy of the invoices.

After an invoice is paid, it is marked as such and kept on file for verification purposes. A company never wants to pay the wrong bills or pay the same bills more than once. Controls related to invoices should prevent this from happening.

Accounting controls also safeguard that a company's resources are used efficiently and economically. This includes paying bills on time and making use of any payment discounts that are available. Automated systems can alert the appropriate personnel when payments should be made. Manual systems can make use of "tickler files," which allow placement of time-sensitive documents in labeled folders that are quickly and easily accessible.

The amount of current liabilities in a company can play a part in applying for a bank loan. Too many current liabilities compared to current assets may prevent the company from securing a loan. The comparison of current assets to current liabilities is called the current ratio and is an indicator of how liquid the company is. A higher current ratio indicates better liquidity.

WORTH REPEATING

Current ratio was introduced in Chapter 6. If a company has a current ratio of 1.5, this means they have $1.50 in current assets for every $1 in current liabilities.

If the company is showing poor liquidity, this might lead management to either hide current liabilities by not recording them or to reclassify them as noncurrent liabilities. Both actions are unethical and could lead to fines if discovered.

Controls for Payroll

The payroll system must be carefully monitored to prevent abuse. There must be rules established by the business to ensure that an employee actually exists and is getting paid properly.

- Ensure the person hiring employees is not the same person paying employees. An employee start package should be created to collect important information about the employee, including the employee's social security number. This package should be passed to the person who prepares payroll checks. If the person hiring employees also pays them, it is possible to create a phantom employee and collect those paychecks.

- Monitor the hours worked by employees. Management should be responsible for ensuring that employees work the hours they claim they work. A time clock with punch cards or electronic swipe cards can track exactly how much time employees work. It is good practice for managers to physically see the individuals checking in and out to verify that they are actually starting work after checking in and that one person is not checking in many people.

- There should be proper authorization for pay increases or employee termination.

- If manual checks are being created, the person creating them should not be the same person signing them.

- A special payroll bank account could be set up for payroll. This is a separate bank account from the main bank account of the business. All payroll checks are cashed against the special payroll bank account, and only enough cash is available in the special payroll account to cover the payroll checks. This makes reconciliation easier and helps prevent theft through payroll.

In Summary

LO 1 **Define and differentiate between determinable and non-determinable liabilities**

- ► The listing order of liabilities on the balance sheet is dictated by the timing of the amount owed.

- ► A company's known liabilities, or determinable liabilities, are financial obligations with fixed terms that can be traced using documentation (e.g. accounts payable).

- ► Non-determinable liabilities include estimated liabilities for amounts that are not known as of the balance sheet date.

LO 2 **Record payroll liabilities**

- ► An accrued liability is how expenses are reconciled with the expense recognition principle. Even though an expense, such as an employee's salary, may not be paid until the next period, the expense itself must be recognized in the current period with an accrual.

- ► Payroll accounting involves three types of payroll liabilities: (1) the net pay owed to an employee, (2) employee payroll deductions, and (3) employer payroll contributions.

LO 3 **Record accounts payable**

- ► An accounts payable is the flip side of an accounts receivable. Instead of sending a customer a bill, an accounts payable involves receiving an invoice for goods or services received.

LO 4 **Record transactions with sales tax**

- ► Sales taxes are charged on sales. The amount collected by the business must be sent to the government.

LO 5 **Record unearned revenue**

- ► Unearned revenue relates to the way revenues are reconciled with the revenue recognition principle. Even though an amount may have been paid by customers, the revenue itself can only be recognized in a later period when goods or services are delivered.

LO 6 **Record short-term notes payable**

- ► Notes payable represent a more formal contract between a company and a supplier after a sale has been made, as opposed to a standard bill or invoice.

LO 7 **Record transactions related to the current portion of noncurrent liabilities**

- ► If a liability will be paid out over several years, the amount to be paid within 12 months is separated on the balance sheet and called the current portion of noncurrent liabilities.

LO 8 Record estimated liabilities

▸ Estimated liabilities, such as product warranties, represent financial obligations whose specific amount will not be known until some future time.

LO 9 Apply internal controls relating to current liabilities

▸ Controls related to current liabilities should include proper tracking and monitoring of invoices and all related documentation. This ensures that the correct bills are paid on time, which is a crucial part of maintaining the company's finances.

▸ A company should not attempt to understate current liabilities by not recording them or by reclassifying them as noncurrent.

 *Access **ameengage.com** for integrated resources including tutorials, practice exercises, the digital textbook and more.*

Review Exercise 12-1

Elnora Yearby Limited buys and resells machines. During the year, the following transactions took place.

Jan 15   Bought a machine for resale for $105,000 plus 6% sales tax. The amount is payable in 30 days. The company uses a perpetual inventory system.

Jan 30   Sold the machine for $214,000 plus 6% sales tax cash including a five-year warranty. Based on past experience, the accountant determines that an amount of $20,000 will be paid out in warranty obligations.

Jan 30   Paid the sales tax amount owing.

Feb 15   Paid for the machine purchased on Jan 15.

Mar 27   Elnora Yearby must repair the machine under warranty. The company uses $200 in parts from its own inventory.

Record the journal entries for the above transactions.

JOURNAL			
Date	**Account Title and Explanation**	**Debit**	**Credit**

See Appendix I for solutions.

Chapter 13
Decision-Making with Accounting Information

Learning Objectives

LO 1 Describe the importance of managerial accounting
- Financial Accounting vs. Managerial Accounting
- The Importance of Managerial Accounting

LO 2 Make decisions related to business operations
- Understanding Cost Behavior
- Break-Even Analysis as a Management Tool
- Pricing Strategies
- Cash Management
- Balanced Scorecard Analysis

LO 3 Make decisions related to employees
- Hiring
- Healthcare

- Outsourcing
- Re-Structuring

LO 4 Develop management strategies related to compliance
- Tax Issues
- Compliance Issues
- Litigation Issues
- Regulatory Issues
- Union Issues

LO 5 Analyze profitability with ratios
- Gross Profit Margin
- Net Profit Margin
- Return on Equity

LO 6 Ethical considerations for management decisions

 *Access **ameengage.com** for integrated resources including tutorials, practice exercises, the digital textbook and more.*

MAKING IT REAL TO YOU

Beyond the actions and results of the accounting system, we can see how accounting work finds importance in the operations, strategy and success of a business organization. There are decisions to be made: some decisions are urgent and pressing, and other decisions are carefully planned over months and years. We will now take a different perspective on accounting and consider how decision-making issues may affect your professional career, the businesses you create and the businesses that employ you.

A New Perspective on Accounting

Imagine embarking on a mountain climb without mapping out the route, forecasting the weather, or buying the equipment required for summiting the mountain. The climb would not only be dangerous but might also end in tragedy and hardship. Business success is no different. Using historical data, careful planning and good judgment is crucial for business success.

Financial Accounting vs. Managerial Accounting

Chapter 3 introduced you to the two general fields of accounting: financial and managerial. Financial accounting is the branch of accounting concerned with formal financial statement preparation, including classifying, measuring and recording the transactions of a business. The formal financial statements governed by Generally Accepted Accounting Principles (GAAP) include: the balance sheet, the income statement and the statement of cash flows. Both internal stakeholders (e.g. owners and managers) and external stakeholders (e.g. investors and creditors) use the information extracted from these financial statements.

Managerial accounting relies on financial information to help managers and employees make informed business decisions. Reports prepared using managerial accounting principles are used by internal stakeholders and are not usually supplied to external stakeholders.

Cost accounting is an integral part of managerial accounting, which tracks the costs incurred to produce goods or provide services. Imagine quoting a price for a product or service to a customer without even knowing how much it costs to make the product or provide the service. We would take the risk of significant losses because we might underprice our goods or services (sell for less than the costs incurred). The ability to set an appropriate selling price would depend largely on historical cost information that is extracted from the financial reporting system. In short, cost accounting assists management in answering the question, "What does it cost us to produce and sell our products and services?"

Additional differences between financial and managerial accounting are provided in Figure 13.1.

Financial Accounting	Managerial Accounting
Financial accountants follow Generally Accepted Accounting Principles (GAAP) or International Financial Reporting Standards (IFRS) set by professional bodies.	Managerial accountants make use of procedures and processes that are not regulated by standard-setting bodies.
For public companies, financial statements must, by law, be prepared at the end of a fiscal year.	Managerial accounting statements and reports are not a legal requirement.
Financial accounting is concerned with collecting data of a historical nature. The table below shows the important components of a company's income statement. All figures presented here are historical in nature.	Managerial accounting is largely based on forecasting future sales and cash flows, calculating costs and preparing budgets. Below is a simplified budgeted income statement for a company. It is forward-looking in nature as opposed to the formal income statement presented to the left, which is based on historical data.

<table>
<tr><td colspan="2">Excerpt of Income Statement
For the Year Ended December 31, 2017</td><td colspan="2">Excerpt of Budgeted Income Statement
For the Year Ending December 31, 2019</td></tr>
<tr><td>Sales</td><td>$1,000,000</td><td>Budgeted Sales</td><td>$2,000,000</td></tr>
<tr><td>Cost of Goods Sold</td><td>144,500</td><td>Budgeted Cost of Goods Sold</td><td>200,000</td></tr>
<tr><td>Gross Profit</td><td>855,500</td><td>Budgeted Gross Profit</td><td>1,800,000</td></tr>
<tr><td>Operating Expenses</td><td>600,000</td><td>Budgeted Operating Expenses</td><td>500,000</td></tr>
<tr><td>Income from Operations</td><td>$400,000</td><td>Budgeted Income from Operations</td><td>$1,300,000</td></tr>
</table>

Financial Accounting	Managerial Accounting
Financial statements and reports are primarily prepared for external users such as creditors and stockholders so that they can make sound financial or investment decisions.	Managerial reports are primarily prepared for internal use, which will help management make sound operation decisions.
Statements of publicly traded companies must be audited.	Managerial reports do not require independent examination.
Financial reports can be less detailed. Figures are often rounded for reports to stockholders.	Reports are very detailed and provide a wealth of information.

FIGURE 13.1

One of the main differences of financial accounting and managerial accounting is the focus and time dimension of the prepared reports and statements. In financial accounting, the focus is on being reliable and objective about past performance. For example, actual performance recorded in the 2018 income statement is prepared in 2019. In managerial accounting, the focus is on the future and providing relevant financial information to management. For example, the 2018 budget is prepared in 2017. Management may then use the 2018 budget to monitor the company's performance at various intervals in 2018. For instance, if the company has reached the budgeted cost of goods sold for all of 2018 by the third quarter, then it may be that too much is being spent to produce the goods. Costs may have to be reduced significantly.

In addition, regardless of your profession, it is important to understand managerial accounting and cost management. Let us illustrate this principle with a few selected occupations.

Sales Professionals

To sell effectively, it is important to have a solid grasp of the cost of a product or service. For example, if you know that it will cost more than average to service a potential client, you may adjust your sales strategy and sale price to compensate for the increased costs.

Project Managers

If a contractor has no understanding about the costs involved in constructing a building, the company may over- or under-bill homebuyers. Professional project managers, engineers or job supervisors are often responsible for estimating, budgeting and controlling costs to ensure that the job is completed on time, effectively and efficiently.

Entrepreneurs

If an entrepreneur consistently suffers losses or does not manage the cash flow responsibly, there is a possibility that his or her business will fail. Many businesses fail not because the operator is technically incompetent, but because the operator does not understand costing principles and the importance of budgeting.

It is also beneficial to understand costs and budgets in your personal life, as it will help you manage your economic life more effectively. Know that the principles covered in this textbook will be useful regardless of which profession you choose.

The Importance of Managerial Accounting

Managers of a company must constantly make decisions that affect the future direction and financial performance of the business. The decisions made encompass two rather broad stages: planning and controlling. The planning stage involves creating objectives and developing strategies to achieve those objectives. The controlling stage involves implementing the objective, reviewing the results and applying corrective action. Figure 13.2 illustrates how the planning and controlling stages are closely connected. Business will move seamlessly from one stage to the next. Decision-making is involved in all aspects of planning and control, so both stages are included in the decision-making process.

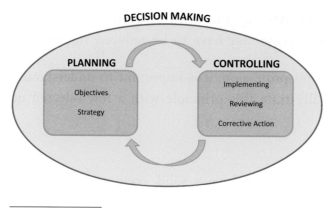

FIGURE 13.2

Setting Objectives

Setting objectives requires looking into the future to desired outcomes and determining how these outcomes can be achieved. An objective is a target that must be measurable in time and value. For example, if a business wants to assemble more computers by the end of May, the objective is not clear. The timeline has been stated (end of May) but not the value (how many computers). Similarly, if a business states it must assemble 20 computers per day, the value is clear, but there is no timeline. Some examples of clearly set objectives include the following.

- Increase sales by 5% by the end of next year

- Achieve a 30% market share in a new state by August of next year

- Sign contracts with three new large clients in the next three months

- Improve customer satisfaction to 85% by the end of July

Formulating Strategy

Once an objective is set, a strategy is then created to reach that objective. Suppose a company called CompuMake assembles computers from components that are purchased from various sources. If the business set an objective to assemble 20 computers per day to meet customer demand, the strategy must answer how the objective will be met. Managers may hire enough employees so 20 computers can be assembled per day, investigate automated systems to assemble computers, or try any other creative ideas that may come to mind.

Implementing Strategies

Controlling work initially begins with implementing the strategies that are created. For CompuMake, managers have decided that hiring enough employees is the ideal strategy. If the assumption is made that each employee can assemble two computers per day, management must hire 10 employees.

Reviewing and Monitoring Results

In a business, reviewing and monitoring results requires the manager to read over many reports, including accounting information. The accounting reports provided are very detailed; more so than what is normally reported on the financial statements prepared for the stockholders of the business. These reports inform on the changes in productivity and profit compared to the costs incurred to make the changes. The reports may also compare the actual financial results with the projected results that were created in the setting objectives stage.

Now that CompuMake has hired 10 employees to assemble computers, the business expects 20 computers to be assembled each day. If only 18 computers are assembled per day, the business must investigate why it did not achieve its objective. The reasons could be numerous, such as underestimating how long it takes to assemble a computer or discovering that employees are not working efficiently. In our example, the manager realizes that the components are not organized properly and employees are spending a lot of time trying to find what they need to build the computers.

Applying Corrective Action

Applying corrective action may be required based on the results of reviewing and monitoring results. CompuMake decides to reorganize the assembly floor to make it more efficient. If the employees are able to build 20 computers per day after the reorganization, then the problem is solved. If the reorganization is still not getting the results, management will have to take other action to solve the problem. This may involve more analysis of the problem and perhaps even setting new objectives that work with the new information that is available.

Managerial accounting provides the necessary financial information which, in conjunction with sound human management principles, can lead managers to make the best decisions for the business. Many companies have set objectives to increase their productivity and managerial accounting can be used to identify potential opportunities and areas for improvements. The planning and controlling principles apply to any industry such as manufacturing, merchandising, services, nonprofit and government.

Decisions Related to Business Operations

Management activities can lead to a variety of tools to help with the decision-making process. Two very important tools that will be examined in this section are cost-volume-profit analysis and the balanced scorecard.

Understanding Cost Behavior

For most businesses, the key objective is to make a profit. Therefore, it is important for managers to ensure that enough revenue is generated to cover all costs of the business. **Cost-volume-profit analysis (CVP)** examines the relationship among the costs of the product or service, the volume sold and the resulting profit.

All costs incurred by a company, including the costs of manufacturing products or providing services, can be broken down into three components: variable costs, fixed costs and mixed costs. Costs that vary with the amount of products manufactured or services provided are called **variable costs**. Costs that remain the same for any given level of activity are called **fixed costs**. Costs that have both a variable cost portion and a fixed cost portion are called **mixed costs**. When managers classify costs based on how they change at different activity levels they are describing their **cost behavior**.

For example, a taxi driver's gas expense is a variable cost because it varies with the total distance driven from day to day. The annual taxi registration, monthly insurance and lease payments for the car are fixed because they do not depend on any other factors, such as total distance driven or number of customers picked up. The repair and maintenance on the taxi may be considered mixed because maintenance must be done, but will likely increase as more distance is driven. It is important to understand that there is a delicate balance between how much a product or service costs to produce, the value for which they are sold, and the resulting profit. To highlight this point, we will now examine a business case for a manufacturing company.

Cost Behavior: StickIt Manufacturing Inc.

StickIt Manufacturing Inc. is a mid-sized company that makes wooden hockey sticks for minor league hockey players. They produce one standard type of hockey stick, which is painted in different colors. The contracts that they have secured with several hockey leagues require them to deliver 10,000 sticks each month.

During May 2018, the company sold 10,000 hockey sticks at a sale price of $200 per stick, resulting in total sales of $2,000,000.

List of Financial Information for May 2018	
Sales	$2,000,000
Manufacturing Costs	
Wood	$800,000
Paint	270,000
Labor	300,000
Rent	15,000
Total Manufacturing Costs	$1,385,000

FIGURE 13.3

The wood and paint are the materials used to manufacture the hockey sticks and labor refers to the workers required to physically cut and assemble the hockey sticks. For simplicity, assume that the hockey sticks are hand-made and each worker is paid based on the number of hockey sticks produced. From these descriptions, it can be concluded that if StickIt Manufacturing has to produce and sell more hockey sticks, then more wood, paint and labor will be needed. Similarly, if fewer hockey sticks are produced, then less wood, paint and labor will be needed. As a result, StickIt Manufacturing classifies these items as variable costs since they vary with the amount of products manufactured.

The manufacturing activities are housed in a small facility for which the company pays a monthly rent. The amount of rent paid every month is the same regardless of how many hockey sticks are manufactured; therefore, it is classified as a fixed cost. Other examples of fixed costs can include depreciation, insurance, administration, leases and so on.

Up to this point in your accounting studies, only the formal income statement has been discussed as a means of presenting a business' financial operations for a specific accounting period. The income statement is prepared using financial reporting standards such as GAAP or IFRS. As a result, costs related to the manufacturing of a product are initially capitalized in inventory and, based on the matching principle, the expense is only recognized (i.e. cost of goods sold) when the corresponding revenue has been earned. See Figure 13.4 for an illustration of the flow of costs related to manufacturing.

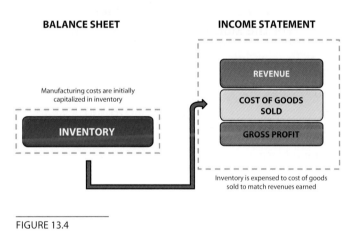

FIGURE 13.4

Figure 13.5 presents StickIt's income statement for May 2018. Cost of goods sold includes the costs of wood, paint, and a portion of the rent expense related to manufacturing process overhead. The income statement also shows the company's gross profit, which identifies what portion of earnings contributes to covering operating expenses.

StickIt Manufacturing Income Statement For the Month Ending May 31, 2018	
Sales	$2,000,000
Less: Cost of Goods Sold	1,377,500
Gross Profit	622,500
Less: Operating Expenses	
Rent	7,500
Net Income	$615,000

FIGURE 13.5

While a formal income statement provides useful information to external users, it may not provide detailed and timely information required by the managers and other internal users. Therefore, to assess operational issues, managerial accountants prepare financial information in the form of a **contribution margin statement**, which is a detailed report that separates variable costs from fixed costs (Figure 13.6). This report contains the same information as a traditional income statement, but reconfigures the details into a different format. Managers use the contribution margin statement as a tool to analyze current operations and to plan future operations.

StickIt Manufacturing Contribution Margin Statement For the Month Ending May 31, 2018		
Sales		$2,000,000
Less Variable Costs:		
Wood	$870,000	
Paint	270,000	
Labor	300,000	1,370,000
Contribution Margin		630,000
Less: Fixed Costs:		
Rent		15,000
Income from Operations		$615,000

FIGURE 13.6

Figure 13.6 shows the current situation of StickIt Manufacturing. They produce and sell exactly 10,000 hockey sticks each month and use a total of $1,370,000 worth of materials and labor to build the hockey sticks. The contribution margin is the amount of revenue left to cover fixed costs, after deducting the variable costs related to the sales. Monthly rent expenses amount to $15,000 per month. For the purpose of this simple example, the only fixed cost we have considered is the rent expense. However, in reality, businesses have other fixed costs, such as salaries paid to administrative staff, telephone and internet connections and so on.

After taking into account all the fixed and variable costs, StickIt Manufacturing has income from operations of $615,000 per month.

The following separate scenarios are examples of the relationship between costs, volume produced and profits.

1. Barry, the manager of StickIt Manufacturing, was able to negotiate a discount on the wood. With all other factors remaining the same, this reduces the costs relating to wood by the total discount and ultimately increases income from operations.

2. Barry decides to reduce the selling price of the hockey sticks to close a deal with a particular house league. This action reduces total revenue while all costs remain the same as before, and therefore decreases income from operations.

3. Barry decides to increase the volume of the number of hockey sticks produced. Assume that StickIt Manufacturing is able to sell all of the hockey sticks it produces in the month. This operational decision increases total sales for the month, and increases the total variable costs since materials and labor costs are directly related to the number of hockey sticks produced. The fixed cost would not change, and if we assume the variable costs remain proportionate to sales, income from operations would increase.

Break-Even Analysis

Being able to determine the break-even point is a critical step in analyzing business operations. The **break-even point** is defined as the level of sales at which the company's operating profit is zero or also described as the point where total sales equal total expenses for no profit. When a company breaks even, there is no profit or no net income. For example, if a company determined that total sales equal total expenses in a period when 10,000 units were sold, then the break-even point for that period was precisely 10,000 units. If more than 10,000 units were sold, the company would have been *above* the break-even point. Or, if less than 10,000 units were sold, the company would have been *below* the break-even point.

Consider the following graph in Figure 13.7 where maximum production is 10,000 units and maximum sales are $120,000. This **cost-volume-profit graph** helps managers understand how costs, sales and operating profit or loss are related.

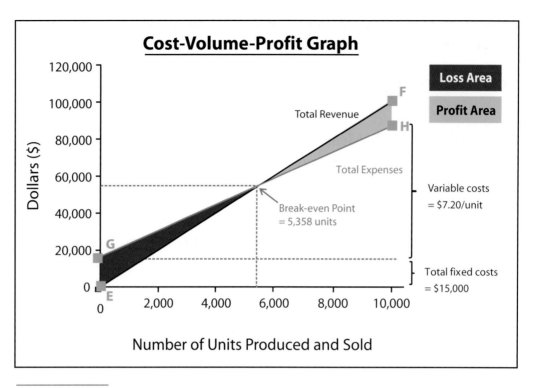

FIGURE 13.7

Understanding the cost-volume-profit graph.

1. The horizontal axis is number of units produced and sold.

2. The vertical axis is dollars as in total fixed costs, total costs and total sales dollars.

3. Line EF represents total revenues at any level of production.

4. Line GH represents total expenses at any level of production.

5. Note that at 0 units, sales are also $0. This simply means that you will generate zero revenue if you do not produce and sell any units.

6. The lower horizontal dotted blue line represents total fixed costs of $15,000. When zero units are produced and sold, total expenses will be equal to fixed costs. Even if no unit is produced and sold, this amount will still have to be paid.

7. The area between the two lines represents the difference between total revenue and total expenses. This area represents profit or loss.

8. To the left of the break-even point, total expenses exceed total revenue. This is the loss area (red shaded triangle).

9. To the right of the break-even point, total revenue exceeds total expenses. This represents the profit area (green shaded triangle).

As you can see, the cost-profit-volume graph can be used to determine the break-even point as well as the number of units required to obtain a certain operating profit.

Break-Even Analysis: A Service Industry Example

Break-even analysis can be used for any industry. Let us use an example of a hair salon called Stylair. The fixed costs incurred by the salon are the rent, depreciation of equipment and staff salaries. The variable costs include hair dye, shampoo, conditioner and other product costs. Stylair charges $50 per haircut and incurs $20 in variable costs for each haircut. This means each haircut has a contribution margin of $30 ($50 - $20). Stylair also has annual fixed costs of $40,000. Figure 13.8 shows the formula to calculate the break-even point.

$$\text{Break-Even Point} = \frac{\text{Fixed Costs}}{\text{Contribution Margin per Unit}}$$

FIGURE 13.8

Using the values for Stylair, the break-even point can be calculated.

$$\text{Break-Even Point} = \frac{\$40,000}{(\$50 - \$20)} = 1,334 \text{ units}$$

The amount of units required to break-even is always rounded up to the nearest whole number. Thus, Stylair must sell 1,334 haircuts in a year to break even.

Break-even is largely about the concept of the relationship between the cost of the product, the volume produced and sold, and the profits generated as a result thereof. By studying the relationships between costs, volume and profit, management can better answer and respond to questions such as:

- How much sales volume is required to break even?

- How far can sales drop before the company starts to lose money?

- How much do sales need to increase to arrive at a specific sales goal?

- How much sales volume is required to earn a desired (target) profit?

- How much profit is expected at a given level of sales volume?

- How would changes in the selling price, variable costs, fixed costs and volume produced affect profits?

Pause & Reflect

Exercise 13-1

O'Sullivan Industries manufactures high-end pool tables. Each table sells for $15,000. The variable cost for the manufacturing of each table is $7,000. Total fixed costs for the year amount to $800,000.

a) What is the contribution margin from each table made?

_____

_____

b) How many tables must O'Sullivan Industries make each year to break-even?

_____

_____

See Appendix I for solutions.

Pricing Strategies

Before establishing a selling price, businesses typically spend a considerable amount of time trying to understand the market for their product. Are identical or similar products available to potential customers from other companies? What is the demand for the product? What are customers willing to spend on the product?

If a business sells raw materials, like precious metals or agricultural items, the business is in competition with other companies that are selling identical commercial products. There will be a market for the product with a set price that all businesses must follow. If one company charges a higher price than the others, customers will simply buy from the lower priced competitors. However, if a company charges too low of a price, it could lose money.

A more common situation is where a business sells a product that is similar to other products that companies sell, but includes additional features to make it stand out. Clothing items, toothpaste and household cleaners are examples where businesses attempt to make their product different from their competitors. In this situation, companies must establish their own selling price for their product. Consider the following business case for an illustration of pricing methods.

Pricing Strategy: A Manufacturing Example

Jamie studied fashion and design in college. In her final year, she created a preliminary business plan for a line of baseball caps as a school project. The line consisted of ten unique designs, all costing approximately the same amount to manufacture. Jamie was able to estimate the cost of sourcing the raw materials for a plain baseball cap as well as the cost of designing and stitching the embroidery on the baseball caps. Jamie wants to implement her business plan and decides that she will perform the embroidery design and stitching processes in-house. She will need to purchase the necessary equipment and hire her friends to help. After reviewing the alternatives for sales channels, Jamie decides to start her business by establishing an online store. She will complete a business plan to apply for a small start-up loan, which will be her only source of start-up financing. To complete her budget, Jamie needs to determine what price she should charge customers for her baseball caps.

Jamie set up social media accounts, which feature her preliminary designs. She has received a number of emails and positive feedback about the unique styles and designs featured in her new line. Jamie needs to determine the price level that her target customers would be willing to pay. If the price is set too high, there may be less interested customers. If it is set too low, the company's costs and required returns may not be covered. Businesses must be aware of the true costs of their products in order to set an appropriate price level. Establishing the right price level is important as businesses strive to maximize revenues and profitability. Understanding these concepts will help Jamie set the appropriate selling price for her baseball caps. In this section, three different pricing methods will be discussed: maximum profit pricing, cost-plus pricing and target costing.

Maximum Profit Pricing

Generally, customers' willingness to buy a product is dependent on its price. Usually, if the price of an item is lower, customers will demand greater quantities. If the price is higher, customers will demand fewer items. You can observe this general rule by watching crowds at a store that has a good sale. This is the foundation of the law of demand from economics. Understanding this relationship between price and quantity demanded means that if a company can accurately forecast the volume of items sold at any particular price, they will be able to set a price that will provide them with the highest operating income possible.

For example, if a company sets a selling price at $1 and three people are willing to purchase at $1 each, then the company generates $3 in profit. If the company sets a selling price at $3 and two people are willing to purchase at $2 each, then the company generates $6 in profit. Finally, if the company sets a selling price at $5 with only one person willing to pay $5 each, then the company generates $5 in profit. This is illustrated in Figure 13.9. In this example, the company should set the selling price at $3 to maximize its profits.

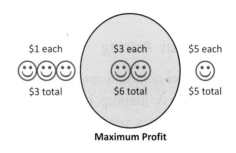

FIGURE 13.9

Returning to the baseball caps example, suppose Jamie has calculated variable costs per baseball cap to be $9. Fixed costs for the year are $9,000. She has estimated the quantity demanded at various selling prices and has created a table illustrating the basic contribution margin statement as shown in Figure 13.10.

Price per Unit	Quantity Demanded	Sales	Variable Costs	Contribution Margin	Fixed Costs	Income from Operations
$16	1,500	$24,000	$13,500	$10,500	$9,000	$1,500
18	1,200	21,600	10,800	10,800	9,000	1,800
20	1,000	20,000	9,000	11,000	9,000	2,000
22	800	17,600	7,200	10,400	9,000	1,400
24	700	16,800	6,300	10,500	9,000	1,500
26	500	13,000	4,500	8,500	9,000	(500)
28	400	11,200	3,600	7,600	9,000	(1,400)

FIGURE 13.10

It is assumed in Figure 13.10 that Jamie can produce and sell (i.e. supply) enough baseball caps to meet any level of demand. Notice that the highest price shown in the table does not generate the highest income from operations. In fact, the highest price would cause an operating loss. The highest income from operations occurs when the selling price is set at $20 per baseball cap.

The challenge with using this pricing scheme is determining an accurate relationship between the price and the quantity demanded. Jamie could use her social media accounts to ask people to indicate how much they would be willing to pay for one of her caps, and count how many people would pay which price. The data collected could then be used to estimate the relationship between the price and demand for her entire market, thus creating the table in Figure 13.10. Jamie could also experiment by selling the baseball caps at various prices to determine the demand. Again, she would have to estimate the relationship between the price and demand for the entire market based on the data she collects. An easier method to set a selling price would be to use the cost-plus pricing method or the target costing method.

Cost-Plus Pricing

The most common method to pricing is applying a markup to cost, which is the **cost-plus pricing method**. A markup is the difference between a product's selling price and its cost, and is often expressed as a percentage of cost. The formula for cost-plus pricing is shown in Figure 13.11.

Selling Price = Cost + (Cost × Markup Percentage)

FIGURE 13.11

For example, if a company's markup is 30%, it adds 30% to the total cost of the product to obtain the selling price. Therefore, for a product that costs $100, the selling price is calculated as shown below.

$$\text{Selling Price} = \$100 + (\$100 \times 30\%) = \$130$$

The formula for cost-plus pricing requires two inputs: cost and mark-up percentage. The key questions for a company are: (1) Which cost amounts should be used?, and (2) What is the appropriate markup percentage? This is illustrated in Figure 13.12.

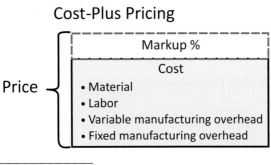

FIGURE 13.12

Variable and fixed manufacturing overhead includes items that are not directly attributed to the manufacturing of a specific item, such as materials and production labor. This can include things such as maintenance on production machines, the supplies and parts used for maintenance on the machines or a production supervisor's salary.

For Jamie's baseball cap business, she has prepared a breakdown of the estimated costs of manufacturing and selling the baseball caps for the upcoming year as shown in Figure 13.13. She has estimated that she will be able to manufacture and sell 1,000 baseball caps during the year.

	Per Unit	Total (1,000 units)
Direct materials	$4	
Direct labor	$3	
Variable manufacturing overhead	$2	
Fixed manufacturing overhead	-	$6,000
General and administrative expenses	-	$3,000

FIGURE 13.13

The cost to manufacture each unit is $15. It is calculated as ($6,000 ÷ 1,000 units) + $4 + $3 + $2.

Now that we have determined a cost on which to apply the markup, the next step is to determine an appropriate markup percentage. Many companies use a markup rate that is deemed as a standard in the industry or one that is determined by the use of professional judgment. Another popular method is to use a calculated markup that is large enough to cover general and administrative expenses and provide a sufficient rate of return. This markup percentage also takes into account unit product cost. If we assume a markup rate of 38%, then the selling price is $20.70 ($15 + [$15 × 38%]).

Target Costing

An alternative to cost-based pricing is target costing. **Target costing** is the process of using the anticipated market price to calculate the maximum costs the business can incur. This means the manufacturing and other costs cannot exceed the maximum allowable cost. The maximum allowable cost is also known as the **target cost**. The target cost is determined using the formula shown in Figure 13.14.

Target Cost = Predetermined Selling Price – Desired Profit

FIGURE 13.14

This formula can also be used to analyze sales and costs and profit on a per unit basis.

Target costing is often used when a company believes it has little or no control over the product's selling price. In these situations, the market determines the selling price based on supply and demand.

For example, suppose a company wishes to introduce a brand new toilet bowl cleaner. There are already a number of different brands available on the market, each with their own twist that makes them different. The prices of these cleaners range from $3.50 to $5.00 per bottle. The company management feels that to keep competitive in this market, they cannot charge more than the high end of $5.00 per bottle. Management may ultimately decide that the selling price should fall midway between the high and low prices, so they set the selling price at $4.25 per bottle.

Another reason some companies use target costing is because they believe a significant portion of the product cost occurs in the design and development stage of a product. The design and development stages can ensure that inexpensive, yet reliable parts are used. Proper design of the production process can be implemented to minimize costs. Also, only the features that customers view as valuable are added. In this scenario, it is believed that once a product has been designed and developed, little can be done to significantly reduce its cost in the production phase. In target costing, the product is designed, developed and produced with the maximum allowable cost kept in mind and not exceeded. An effective implementation of target costing requires a strong understanding of what the customer truly values and encourages the company to avoid spending on activities that add minimal value from the customers' perspective.

Let us return to Jamie's baseball cap business to illustrate target costing. Suppose Jamie knows that similar baseball cap designers are charging $25 per baseball cap. At this selling price, it allows for a suitable premium to be charged for their unique designs and the quality of materials used. Therefore, Jamie sets the unit selling price of her baseball caps at $25. Recall that Jamie projects she can sell 1,000 baseball caps for the upcoming year and that an investment of $13,500 is required to design, develop, and produce the caps. She desires a rate of return of 20% on her investment. The target cost is calculated as follows:

Estimated sales	$25,000	(1,000 units × $25/unit)
Less: Desired profit	2,700	(20% × $13,500)
Target cost (for 1,000 units)	$22,300	
Absorption cost	$15,000	(1,000 units × $15/unit)
Plus: Administrative costs	3,000	General & Administrative
Total cost (for 1,000 units)	$18,000	

FIGURE 13.15

Therefore, the target cost for the 1,000 baseball caps is $22,300. Jamie's total costs amount to $18,000. Therefore, at this target selling price and desired profit, Jamie can easily meet the desired profit of $2,700. In fact, there is a buffer of $4,300 ($22,300 – $18,000) by which her total costs could increase. For example, Jamie can consider increasing the quality of her materials used in the production of his baseball caps to further satisfy her customer base. She could also consider spending more on advertising to try and increase the demand for her product.

An advantage of target costing is that it is a proactive approach to managing costs and helps minimize the use of non-value added activities. It also makes use of information available in the market and allows companies to avoid the burden of determining an acceptable selling price. A key disadvantage is it can reduce the quality of products, since management is pressured to not exceed the maximum allowable cost. This may lead to the use of cheap components in the production phase of the product, which reduces the product's overall quality. In addition, the implementation of target costing requires very detailed cost data.

Once the price is established using a suitable pricing method, Jamie can test her business model by performing cost-volume-profit analysis, discussed earlier in this chapter. These include break-even calculations, determining the volume of baseball caps she must sell before earning a given profit level, and so on.

Pause & Reflect

Exercise 13-2

Linwood Company recently began production of a new navigation device. Linwood is currently considering establishing a selling price for this new device that will provide a 35% markup. The engineering and the sales department compiled the following estimates for producing and selling 80,000 devices.

	Per Unit	Total (80,000 units)
Direct materials	$11	
Direct labor	$24	
Variable manufacturing overhead	$15	
Fixed manufacturing overhead		$240,000
General and administrative expenses		$74,000

a) What is the cost to manufacture each unit?

_____

_____

b) Using the cost-plus pricing method, what selling price should Linwood set?

_____

_____

See Appendix I for solutions.

Cash Management

Managing a successful, sustainable business is a balancing act. A business needs profit to succeed. The right product or service combined with customers promotes a strong business. A business needs cash to operate, including paying its employees, vendors and suppliers. Cash management is a critical aspect of effective management practice.

The Statement of Cash Flows

One way to review the cash account historically and to determine uses of cash and sources of cash is to thoroughly review the statement of cash flows. The **statement of cash flows** indicates how cash was earned and spent during a period. While the statement of cash flows is historical in nature, it is very helpful to cash management because it shows trends in how the company is receiving and using cash.

Operating activities represent activities necessary to run the daily operations of the business. Investing activities represent cash used to purchase noncurrent assets or cash received from selling noncurrent assets such as property, plant and equipment. Financing activities represent cash used or cash received from noncurrent liability and equity transactions, such as payments on noncurrent debt or dividends paid. The statement of cash flows is further explained in Chapter 14.

Figure 13.16 shows the statement of cash flows for Jamie's Baseball Caps. We will analyze the cash account and consider cash management trends and recommendations.

Jamie's Baseball Caps Statement of Cash Flows For the Year Ended December 31, 2018		
Cash Flow from Operating Activities		
Net Income	$2,700	
Add Depreciation Expense	600	
Add (Deduct) Changes to Current Assets and Liabilities		
Increase in Accounts Receivable	(300)	
Increase in Merchandise Inventory	(1,000)	
Increase in Accounts Payable	400	
Total Cash Flow from Operating Activities		$2,400
Cash Flow from Investing Activities		
Cash Used to Purchase Equipment	(10,000)	
Total Cash Flow from Investing Activities		(10,000)
Cash Flow from Financing Activities		
Cash Proceeds from Notes Payable	15,000	
Cash Used to Pay Owner Withdrawals	(5,000)	
Total Cash Flow from Financing Activities		10,000
Net Increase or (Decrease) to Cash		2,400
Cash at the Beginning of the Year		0
Cash at the End of the Year		$2,400

FIGURE 13.16

Take a moment to carefully review Jamie's first statement of cash flows. Notice that operating activities show a positive cash flow of $2,400, indicating the business is self-sufficient in its day-to-day operations. The $15,000 received from the bank was used to pay for the $10,000 piece of equipment needed to run the company, plus $5,000 paid to Jamie as a withdrawal. If this is Jamie's sole source of income for living, $5,000 may not be enough. However, if Jamie has other sources of income, perhaps she could forgo taking any owner withdrawals from the business during the start-up years. Jamie's statement of cash flows indicates a new business in the early growth years. Jamie's Baseball Caps appears to be in very good financial health at the end of the first year with a net income of $2,700 and a cash balance of $2,400.

The Cash Budget

Instead of looking historically at cash with a statement of cash flows, we can look forward with a cash budget. The cash budget considers cash receipts and cash disbursements on a month-by-month basis. The cash budget can be used to forecast, plan and prepare for future business events.

Jamie is wisely considering how to best and most cost effectively promote and market her unique baseball caps. A cash budget will help her determine how much and when she can spend on advertising and web development. Budgeting also shows where there may be cash surpluses, which can be used to enhance the business or invest in cost-saving programs. Perhaps Jamie could stop taking any owner withdrawal funds and use that amount toward advertising and promotion. Or Jamie could take a class in marketing and e-commerce at a local community college and do this work herself instead of paying someone else to do it. Figure 13.17 shows a sample cash budget for Jamie.

Jamie's Baseball Caps Cash Budget For the Quarter Ended March 31, 2019			
	January	February	March
Cash at beginning of month	$2,400	$875	$100
Cash receipts			
Cash sales	1,000	1,000	1,000
Cash collections from receivables	500	500	500
Total cash receipts	1,500	1,500	1,500
Cash disbursements			
Raw material purchases	400	400	400
Overhead and operating costs	1,200	1,200	1,200
Payment on the note payable	175	175	175
Payment for owner withdrawal	0	0	0
Payment for community college course	750	0	0
Payment for advertising and promotion	500	500	500
Total cash disbursements	3,025	2,275	2,275
Cash at end of month	$875	$100	($675)

FIGURE 13.17

The following items will help you analyze this cash budget.

1. January's beginning cash of $2,400 is what the ending cash was from the previous year. During January, Jamie collected a total of $1,500 cash and spent $3,025 in disbursements. At the end of January, cash is $875.

2. January's ending cash of $875 becomes February's beginning cash. Likewise, February's ending cash of $100 becomes March beginning cash.

3. Overall, monthly cash disbursements are consistently larger than monthly cash receipts. This is not sustainable.

4. In the cash receipts section, notice that projected sales are flat and low. One of the goals for the business is to increase sales and increase monthly cash receipts.

5. In the cash disbursements section, notice that Jamie is not taking any owner withdrawals and there is a cash payment for the community college course. Once Jamie completes the course, the cash payment for advertising and promotions can be reduced or eliminated.

Cash budgets are an excellent management tool for forecasting, planning and considering alternatives. Organizations are always thinking of ways to boost sales and cash receipts while minimizing costs and cash disbursements. The cash budget provides a format to view and analyze scenarios to improve the cash flow of the business.

Cash Management Fundamentals

Beyond creating a statement of cash flows to see historical events, or creating a cash budget to plan future cash flow, general cash management on a day-to-day basis is important for any business. There are five main areas of cash management.

1. Manage accounts receivable

Accounts receivable represents products sold or services provided to customers where payment is yet to be made to the company. Collecting accounts receivables equates to receiving cash for the business to operate. Accounts receivable balances are billed to customers via invoices with payments usually due in 30 days. All measures to promote quick customer payment are desirable, such as using an electronic, automated invoicing system, only extending credit to those customers with a history of paying on time, developing firm credit terms such as due dates and discounts for early payment, as well as active communication and fees for those customers paying late. The more steady and robust accounts receivable collections are for a business, the better and stronger the cash position for that business.

2. Manage accounts payable

Accounts payable represents products purchased or services received by the business with payment to be made at a future date. The business will usually receive a bill or invoice due in 30 days. If there is a discount for early payment, the business should carefully evaluate the costs and benefits of paying early. Paying as late as possible while still maintaining a strong relationship with vendors and supplies will allow the business to keep its cash for its own needs as long as possible. However, paying early to get discounts will save the business cash.

3. Manage cash levels

A goal of a business is to both maintain enough cash for current operating needs as well as accumulate enough cash to be able to save for future needs. This accumulated cash presents an opportunity for investment earnings. Cash sitting around in a simple bank account will earn little to no interest. Cash invested carefully in a variety of mid- to long-range investment plans can yield significant investment income. A cash budget is a key tool in helping to determine future needs and investment planning.

4. Manage inventory levels

If the business is a merchandiser or manufacturer, inventory should generally be kept as low as possible while still being able to cover customer demands. For merchandisers, this can be challenging since they want to give the appearance their store is well stocked. Any inventory kept beyond what is needed is costly to secure and store. Determining the optimal level of inventory takes expertise and analysis.

5. Track cash flows

Using the statement of cash flows for a historical view and the cash budget for a forward view, companies can actively review and forecast cash activity. This process can be automated within the company's accounting software for efficiency and ease. The function of cash flow review and forecasting into the regular schedule of management tasks can help the company keep on top of cash flow. By creating and nurturing a culture of cash flow awareness, management decision-making can be greatly enhanced.

Balanced Scorecard Analysis

If you felt ill and went to your doctor, she may take your temperature or measure your blood pressure. If you were running a fever or your blood pressure was too high, your doctor may not know the cause before further examination. After further examination, the doctor may then have enough information to create a strategy to cure your ailment.

Businesses also use the equivalent of a thermometer and blood pressure gauge before implementing a strategy to control or solve a problem. There are various forms of measurements that managers use, including financial ratios and performance metrics. These measurements can be found in the company's **balanced scorecard (BSC)**, which is a strategic performance management framework to help implement the company's strategy. Figure 13.18 shows a typical balanced scorecard.

		Target Performance
Financial Perspective		
Increase stockholder's value	Net profit margin	25%
	Return on equity	10%
	Current ratio	2:1
Customer Perspective		
Increase in customer satisfaction	Customer satisfaction ratings	75%
	Number of complaints received per month	5
Internal Processes Perspective		
Reduce error and defects	Defects per job	5
Reduce delivery time	Time between order and delivery	5 weeks
Increase efficiency	Time required to build a website	7 weeks
Learning and Growth Perspective		
Enhance employee skills	Number of professional development hours	10
	Employee satisfaction rating	7
Empower workforce	Percentage of employees empowered to manage processes	85%

FIGURE 13.18

A typical balanced scorecard includes an integrated set of performance measures that should support the company's strategy by breaking down high-level objectives into specific performance metrics and measures called key performance indicators. Balanced scorecard analysis often involves a chain of cause-and-effect relationships, which will allow management to gain a strong understanding of what particular measures affect the company's strategy.

For instance, hotels often adopt a strategy to increase sales by consistently attracting more and more occupants. A key performance indicator from the customer perspective, for example, can be the customer satisfaction rating for those that have stayed at the hotel. A good satisfaction rating will increase the chances customers will return, which ultimately would contribute to increasing the number of occupants over time. Conversely if the quality of the hotels' service decreases, there would be less satisfied customers resulting in less hotel occupancy. Measuring customer satisfaction in this instance is therefore a crucial measurement for business success.

Decisions Related to Employees

For many organizations, wages and salaries are one of, if not the largest, cost on the income statement. Employees create the product, provide the service and bring the business to life. There are a whole range of issues related to employees that delve into the fields of human resource management, organizational behavior and others. As we consider significant management issues related to finance and accounting, labor and related costs are key.

Hiring

Costs to search, recruit, hire and train can be tremendous. At a minimum, it takes to time to advertise the position, review applicants, interview and train. For more involved positions, there may be signing bonuses, travel costs, recruiter costs and relocation costs for the new hire. The impact of a bad hire on an organization can also be tremendous. Employee turnover is an expensive, undesirable reality for all businesses. Businesses can manage this function with a variety of tactics including careful job descriptions, more time during the interview process and a set process for checking all references.

Figure 13.19 lists some of the costs to hire an employee and the costs of hiring the wrong employee.

Costs of hiring an employee	Costs of hiring the wrong employee
• Advertising	• Lost overall productivity
• In-house recruiter fees/salary	• Time to recruit and train another worker
• External recruiter fees	• Cost to recruit and train another worker
• Sign-on bonuses	• Negative impact on overall employee morale
• Travel expenses for applicants and staff	• Negative impact on clients and customers
• Employee relocation costs	
• Employee referral bonuses	

FIGURE 13.19

Since hiring can be rather costly, it is good to determine how to get the right person for the job. Figure 13.20 lists some way the wrong person may be hired and how the right person can be found.

Why did we hire the wrong person?	How can we hire the right person?
• Searching and advertising in the wrong places	• Start with a strong, clear job description
• Impatience and need to fill the position immediately	• Start early, not late
	• Advertise in the right places
• Indecision on the candidate choice	• Consider soft skills, such as communication and collaboration
• Lack of talent and skill in the candidate pool	• Take time during the interview process to get to know candidates
• Did not check references	• Boost employee referral programs
• Timing is off if there is hiring seasonality in the industry	• Emphasize company culture and organization strengths, look for fit

FIGURE 13.20

Healthcare

The cost of healthcare in the United States is ever changing, complex and expensive to both employers and employees. Organizations must plan and prepare for these costs and organizational changes. Every year, healthcare costs in the US rise at a much higher rate than the corresponding rise in gross domestic product (GDP).

It is understood that both individuals/employees and employers/businesses are paying more every year. Consider the income statement and break-even analysis discussed earlier in this chapter. If business expenses for employee health insurance are increasing, the balance of cost-volume-profit is constantly threatened. Does the rise in health insurance cost require increasing consumer prices to offset those costs? Does the rise in health insurance cost require lowering the cost of materials by using inferior quality materials and thereby decreasing the quality of the product? These are not easy questions without any ready solutions in sight. The issue of US healthcare cost is one of the defining economic issues of our generation.

Outsourcing

There are times it makes sense to shift labor to another location with a focus on both quality and cost. An auto manufacturer may move their plant location from a unionized northern state to a non-unionized southern state. An electronics manufacturer may use an overseas location to lower labor cost, maximize profit and maintain low consumer pricing.

Outsourcing can be both a large international issue or small and local. For example, in the case of Jamie's Baseball Caps, Jamie decided to create her own advertising campaign, or keep it "in-house." Alternatively, Jamie could decide to outsource by paying an advertising firm to handle the campaign. Accounting services are another example. A small business could decide to do their own accounting or select an outside accounting firm.

Some suggestions for management regarding outsourcing include the following.

1. **Quality first.** Always consider quality and product/service reputation first. Consider how your customers will feel about the product and the company.

2. **Cost next.** Consider all costs to outsourcing. Take a close look and estimate initial project outsourcing costs carefully. In the long-term, budget time for more communication as well as additional travel costs.

3. **Screen carefully.** Take time to consider multiple options. Do not always go with the first offer or the lowest bidder. As with any other project, build a collection of information including multiple outsourcing situations leading to a more thoughtful final decision.

4. **Monitor progress.** Set objectives and put your plan to work. Check progress and results and take action to improve and make changes as necessary.

5. Communicate. Throughout the process of outsourcing, keep the lines of communication open with all stakeholders and players. Make time for regular communication and input.

Re-Structuring

There are also times an organization must substantially change to maintain its competitive edge and long-term viability. Product mix may need to be dramatically changed. Automating the manufacturing process may make it possible to significantly increase product quality while reducing employee costs and risk. Pricing in a company's industry may also dictate a difficult shift in budget and staffing. As pricing falls, costs must also fall.

These examples and countless other scenarios lead to significant workplace change and often the loss of positions and layoff of workers. Managing a business re-structure requires management to make difficult decisions. There are issues, communication and sensitivity required for both groups. Employees may very well be our greatest asset and correspondingly our largest cost. Management strives to strike a balance between taking good care of its employees while also being responsible to the bottom line.

Some suggestions for management regarding re-structuring include the following.

1. **Plan thoroughly.** Plan for the short-term as well as the mid-term and long-term. Consider those leaving as well as those staying. Take a long-range view of how the organization will look in several years.

2. **Communication.** Communicate early and often. Do not withhold information and be sure to involve all stakeholders.

3. **Inclusion.** Make every effort to clearly include employees in the decision-making process surrounding the re-structuring. Build consensus and share control.

4. **Emphasize renewal.** A business re-structuring is a business worth keeping and improving. Inspire buy-in and commitment to a new version and a letting go of the past status quo.

Compliance

Many laws and legislations are in place to protect people from harm. Traffic lights are used to control traffic flow and ensure drivers do not hit each other or pedestrians. As long as everyone follows the traffic laws, risk of injury is reduced. Other laws are in place to ensure that common benefits are properly cared for. Thus, taxes are used to pay for infrastructure used by all. Anti-littering laws are in place to protect parkland and waters that can be enjoyed by all. Businesses also have a number of rules and regulations put in place by the government or government agencies that they must adhere to.

Tax Issues

There are quite a few taxes required of businesses in the US today. Tax regulation varies considerably depending on locality while also being consistent for all due to federal tax regulations. As an example, Figure 13.21 lists the taxes for a company located in Detroit, Michigan.

Government Agency	Type of Tax	Filing Requirement	Tax Payment Due
Federal United States	Business income tax • Form 1120 Corporation Income Tax • Form 1120S S-Corporation Income Tax • Form 1065 Partnership Income Tax • Form 1040 Schedule C Self Employment Income	Annual	Quarterly/Annual
	Employee payroll tax (collection & payment of social security tax, Medicare tax and federal income tax) • Form 941	Quarterly	By pay period, monthly or quarterly depending on the size of the payroll
	Employer payroll tax (social security tax and Medicare tax or self- employment tax) • Form 941, or • Form 1040, if self-employed	Quarterly	By pay period, monthly or quarterly depending on the size of the payroll
	Unemployment tax • Form 940	Annual	Determined quarterly depending on the size of the payroll
State of Michigan	Michigan CIT Tax (corporate income tax)	Annual	Quarterly/Annual
	Employee state payroll tax withholdings (collection & payment of state income tax) • Form 5080 • Form 5081	Annual and Quarterly or Monthly	Quarterly/Monthly
	Sales & use tax collection and payment • Form 5080 • Form 5081	Annual and Quarterly or Monthly	Quarterly/Monthly
	Unemployment tax and Obligation Assessment	Quarterly	Quarterly
City of Detroit	Business income tax • Form D-1120	Annual	Quarterly/Annual
	Employee city payroll tax withholdings (collection & payment of city income tax) • Form DW-3	Annual and Quarterly or Monthly	Quarterly/Monthly
City or County	Personal property tax	Annual	Annual
	Property tax (real estate)	Bi-Annual	Bi-Annual

FIGURE 13.21

Not paying taxes, not paying on time and/or not paying the correct amount can all result in a wide range of punitive action on the part of the government. The punitive actions could be as simple as receiving harsh letters and ongoing correspondence to remedy incorrect payment amounts, or could be as severe as seized bank accounts and complete business failure due to repeated failure to pay taxes. A business must have highly qualified individuals monitoring all forms of tax compliance with a goal of absolute compliance and adherence to the law.

Compliance Issues

Numerous regulations and industry standards dictate compliance for business survival. Compliance risk has been defined by Deloitte as "the threat posed to a company's financial, organization, or reputational standing resulting from violations of laws, regulations, codes of conduct, or organizational standards of practice." We will examine a few more commonly applied regulations you may encounter in your business career.

ISO 9000 and ISO 9001

Depending on the industry, ISO 9000 may be critical to a company's reputation and marketability. ISO 9000 are international standards relating to quality issues including quality management, quality assurance and quality systems. Businesses of all sizes and in all industries can achieve ISO 9000 status. The seven ISO 9000 principles of quality management include customer focus; leadership; engagement of people; process approach; improvement; evidence-based decision-making; and relationship management.

ISO 9001 is the certification process available based upon ISO 9000 principles. There are 10 steps to ISO 9001, which include scope, normative references, terms and definitions, context of the organization, leadership, planning, support, operation, performance evaluation, and improvement.

To attain and continue ISO 9001 certification, a company must be audited by an independent accrediting organization. The ultimate goal of ISO 9000 is the development of a process of continual improvement and review leading to effective systems, preventative management and ongoing improvement. Examples of industries with a strong ISO 9000 presence include automotive, aerospace, telecommunications, medical device manufacturers and many others. In these industries, ISO 9000 compliance is essential to industry reputation and competitiveness.

Sarbanes-Oxley Act

In 2002, the Sarbanes-Oxley Act (SOX) became law in the US. This is a federal law affecting public companies, which are companies with stock publicly traded on a stock exchange. While public companies are directly affected, all companies have been indirectly affected by this act including increased attention on internal control systems as well as provisions of the law that make it illegal for any company or employee to willfully destroy evidence in a federal investigation.

While it could be said that SOX is a direct result of the business failure of Enron corporation, that would be an oversimplification. Corporations continue testing legal and ethical boundaries of decency. The goal of SOX is to encourage honest financial disclosure leading to informed decision-making. If the financial statements disclose a profit, then there must really be a profit, not a series of complex irregularities and fraudulent cover-up. The management representing those financial statements must back them up with statements that the financials are legitimate and honest. The auditors that review those financial disclosures must also state that the financials are legitimate and honest. Management and auditors who endorse fraudulent financial statements will be prosecuted and punished. Whistleblowers will be protected and encouraged to come forward. The end goal is a more transparent, honest community of financial reporting.

While many agree that the Sarbanes-Oxley Act is a much-needed collection of far reaching federal regulations on US public corporations, there are others who criticize the act for being redundant of previously existing financial and auditing standards. Additional criticisms center around the labor costs of complying with the act including dedicated staff and time for compliance work and documentation.

Securities and Exchange Commission

The United States Securities and Exchange Commission (SEC) holds primary responsibility for all aspects of regulating the securities industry. Simply put, a security is a trading investment, such as a stock or a bond investment. The SEC, whose mission is to protect investors, run efficient markets and encourage capital formation, such as new investments in equipment and noncurrent assets, enforces various laws and regulations.

Complying with SEC regulations is not an option for a public company—it is the law. One of the more useful tools related to SEC compliance is the annual Form 10-K report required of all public companies. The 10-K is an immensely useful report including detailed written narrative on the company's background and business practices as well as a full set of standard financial statements and all notes to the financial statements. Form 10-K reports can be readily found online for all public companies.

International Financial Reporting Standards

As a global business community, international accounting standards have been developing and progressing throughout the 20th century. For over a decade, International Financial Reporting Standards (IFRS), have been taking shape and making headlines. This began back in 1920 with the creation of what is now known as the International Accounting Standards Board (IASB). The goal of the IASB and resulting IFRS is a universal global business language including accounting practice, accounting language and accounting reporting.

As of January 2018, over 100 countries have adopted IFRS including Canada, Mexico, Brazil, European Union, Japan, India, Russia and Saudi Arabia. Notable exceptions to IFRS include the United States, China, the United Kingdom and Japan.

Reasons for adopting IFRS include a commitment to a universal financial reporting environment. Reasons the US is against adopting IFRS include the following.

- It will be too costly to implement IFRS.

- Financial statements will not be comparable due to the wide breadth of interpretation allowed by IFRS.

- IFRS is inferior to US GAAP, which has had decades of challenge and development.

- IFRS is principles based, whereas GAAP is rules based. There is more room for interpretation and questionable reporting with IFRS.

Litigation Issues

Companies of all sizes and industries have litigation risk. Even a very small business is likely to be involved in at least one lawsuit during the owner's time with the business. A large multi-national corporation may deal with lawsuits and legal issues on an ongoing basis. There are a few general guidelines to help manage this aspect of risk. The overall thing is to be proactive, consider the possibilities and take action before a lawsuit strikes.

Regulatory Issues

There are a tremendous number of legal regulations facing businesses today in the US. Lack of compliance in any of these areas can not only cause headaches and take precious time away from product/service promotion and development; but can derail a business to the point of business failure. While there are too many changing US regulations to count, here are some of the largest and most familiar areas of regulation.

Federal Trade Commission and Advertising

The Federal Trade Commission (FTC) was established in 1914 to protect consumers and prevent anticompetitive business practices, such as industry monopolies. For example, FTC truth-in-advertising laws specify three areas of compliance in advertising. Advertising must be truthful and non-misleading. Advertising claims made in advertisements must be able to be proven at any time. Advertising must be fair to both consumers and competitors. Another FTC law, the Fair Packaging and Labeling Act, is another more familiar FTC regular. This Act requires that many consumer product labels include three categories of consumer information. The label must disclose the identity of the product. The label must disclosed the name and location of the manufacturer or distributor. And finally, the label must disclose the quantity of the contents.

Fair Labor Standards Act and Employment

The Fair Labor Standards Act (FLSA) was established in 1938 to protect employees from unfair labor practices. Provisions and amendments to the Act are numerous and span several decades of revision and enforcement. Foundational elements of the FLSA include:

- Creation and revision of the minimum wage including provisions for tipped employees in the food industry

- Creation of the time-and-a-half standard for overtime pay

- Prohibition of minors working in harsh or dangerous working conditions

- Displaying certain federal labor law posters in the workplace, such as the FLSA employee rights or the equal employment opportunity

Occupational Safety and Health Administration

The Occupational Safety and Health Administration (OSHA) was created in 1970 to ensure safe and healthful working conditions by enforcing standards and providing training opportunities to businesses. Its general goals include creating a workplace free from exposure to toxic chemicals, excessive noise levels, machine and equipment risk, excessive heat, excessive cold or unsanitary conditions. Specific provisions of OSHA include details such as the number of inches between rungs on a work ladder, the requirement for appropriate face and eye protection and detailed regulations when working with chemicals.

Environmental Protection Agency

The Environmental Protection Agency (EPA) was established in 1970 with the goal of protecting human health and the environment. The EPA oversees regulations related to air, water, land, endangered species, and hazardous waste. The EPA is concerned with smoke released out of manufacturing smokestacks and hazardous chemical waste being pumped into rivers and other water sources. They are also concerned with fuel and emissions standards on vehicles and heavy machinery, as well as recycling and composting programs.

Businesses must research and take action regarding compliance with EPA regulations. In many cases, permits must be obtained if a business discharges air or water pollutants, operates near wetlands, affects threatened or endangered species, or produces hazardous waste. Failure to adhere to environmental standards can result in fines or legal battles. A business may also have to consider alternative forms of power or energy-saving measures in order to reduce its emissions, which can be costly and sometimes ineffective. Business owners must stay informed on changing environmental regulations and come up with solutions that protect the environment but still encourage profit and growth.

Union Issues

Unions exist to protect workers. Unions lead to higher wages, better employee benefits, safer work environments, and perhaps most importantly, a clear system of due process for discipline and layoffs. All of these improvements for workers cost a business money. Increased wages and benefits means increased expenses on the income statement and therefore, decreased profit. A careful system of due process takes considerable time and expertise on both sides of the meeting room table. Time equals wages, which means further increased expense and decreased profit. Union contracts can be quite reasonable and agreeable. These contracts can also be a maze of detail, complexity, exceptions, subsections and all form of minutia.

There are many things unions and management can do to thoughtfully, proactively work together.

1. **Communicate.** Formalize a regular, recurring meeting time for a union leadership representative and a management team representative. Consider a fixed weekly or monthly meeting.

2. **Involve and include.** When working through challenging issues, include all stakeholders in the problem-solving process. Always include both union representation and management.

3. **Repeat common goals.** Determine goals that transcend bargaining strategy. Both union and management ultimately want happy customers, strong sales and a reliable, healthy, skilled workforce. Remind one another of agreed upon common goals.

4. **Ask and listen.** Union leadership can ask what management needs. Management can ask what the union needs. Take time to listen, understand and respect one another.

IN THE REAL WORLD

In 2012, Hostess Brands—a large packaged food company—filed for bankruptcy. While consumers lost their sugary goodies, over 18,000 employees lost their jobs. This mature company with over 80 years in business was facing consistent losses with rising expenses due to long-term debt and pension liabilities. The company negotiated with its unions to take concessions to lower costs and save the company. The Teamsters union eventually agreed to concessions. The Bakery, Confectionery, Tobacco Workers, and Grain Millers International union (BCTGM) did not. Hostess filed for full bankruptcy liquidation.

Workers blamed the company for mismanagement stating that the workers had already taken a serious hit in wages, benefits, employee share of health insurance costs and reduced pension benefits. Management blamed the BCTGM union for not taking additional cuts in wages, benefits and pension to bring the company budget in line overall.

The last financial report for Hostess represented the month of September 2012 and showed a $15.1 million loss for that one month alone. This loss included ongoing operating losses combined with final restructuring charges to lay off employees with severance pay and additional costs to close the company. Since that time, the company has undergone several stages of reinvention and reinvestment. The current ownership structure is called Hostess Brands, Inc., which was started in 2013 by Apollo Global Management and C. Dean Metropoulos and Company.

Analyze Profitability with Ratios

Profitability refers to the ability of a company to generate profits. The greater the profitability, the more valuable the company is to stockholders. A consistently unprofitable company is likely to go bankrupt. There are several ratios available to help analyze the profitability of a company. They are calculated using figures from the income statement as opposed to the balance sheet. For our examples, we will use a fictitious company called Big City Cars to analyze profitability.

Gross Profit Margin

Gross profit margin was introduced in Chapter 9 and is gross profit expressed as a percentage of sales. It is calculated by dividing gross profit by net sales.

Figure 13.22 calculates the gross profit margin using figures from Big City Cars' income statement for 2019 and 2018.

	2019	**2018**
Sales	$5,000,000	$4,800,000
Cost of Goods Sold	$4,000,000	$3,700,000
Gross Profit Margin	20%	23%

2019: ($5,000,000 - $4,000,000) ÷ $5,000,000 =.20 or 20%
2018: ($4,800,000 - $3,700,000) ÷ $4,800,000 =.23 or 23%

FIGURE 13.22

A higher gross profit margin means that the company has an easier time covering its expenses and is more likely to be profitable. However, gross profit margins should be compared to an industry average to determine whether a business is healthy or not. Also, a decline in the gross profit margin, such as with Big City Cars, indicates that the company is either not generating enough revenue, has experienced an increase in inventory costs or both.

Net Profit Margin

The **net profit margin** assesses a company's profitability after all expenses have been deducted. This is the amount of net profit or loss per dollar of revenue. The formula is shown in Figure 13.23.

$$\text{Net Profit Margin} = \frac{\text{Net Income}}{\text{Total Revenue}}$$

FIGURE 13.23

As with the gross profit margin, a higher net profit margin is generally considered a better sign than a lower one, although it should be always be compared to an industry average and previous results. Figure 13.24 calculates the net profit margin margins for Big City Cars for both 2018 and 2019.

	2019	2018
Sales	$5,000,000	$4,800,000
Net Income	$75,000	$100,000
Net Profit Margin	1.5%	2%

FIGURE 13.24

Although total revenues have increased from 2018 to 2019, net income has decreased. This is not a good sign for the stockholders because their investments have not earned much of a return for these two years. To perform a complete analysis of net profit margins, comparisons should be made on a monthly and yearly basis to historical company performance, industry averages and direct competitors. Only then will these net income figures be placed in context so that conclusions can be drawn.

Return on Equity

Return on equity (ROE) is a measure of what the owners are getting out of their investment in the company. It is often the most important ratio for investors because it has a large impact on the value of one's investment. This ratio requires information from both the balance sheet and income statement to be calculated. The formula is shown in Figure 13.25.

$$\text{Return on Equity (ROE)} = \frac{\text{Net Income}}{\text{Average Stockholders' Equity}}$$

FIGURE 13.25

For our purposes, the return on equity formula assumes that there is no preferred stock included in stockholders' equity. Notice that the calculation requires average stockholders' equity. Whenever a ratio is calculated that uses some information from the balance sheet and some from the income statement, the balance sheet information is always averaged. This is because the balance sheet represents a snapshot in time while the income statement represents an entire accounting period. By averaging the balance sheet accounts, we are simulating a figure that covers the same time period as the income statement. This makes the ratio more comparable and reliable. Figure 13.26 calculates the 2018 and 2019 return of equity rates for Big City Cars.

	2019	2018	2017
Net Income	$75,000	$100,000	n/a
Stockholder's Equity	$500,000	$475,000	$460,000
Return on Equity	15.4%	21.4%	n/a

2019: $75,000 ÷ (($500,000 + $475,000) ÷ 2) =.154 or 15.4%
2018: $100,000 ÷ (($475,000 + $460,000) ÷ 2) =.214 or 21.4%

FIGURE 13.26

A high ROE is desirable because it means that investors made a good decision by investing in the company. Stockholders like to see a return that is as good as or better than they could have received by investing elsewhere. A negative ROE indicates that stockholders actually lost money on their investments over the year. It also deters investors from investing more money at the risk of losing it. Big City Cars' return on equity has slightly worsened from 21.4% to 15.4%. Net income is decreasing more than stockholder's equity is decreasing over the same period of time.

Ethical Considerations for Management Decision-Making

Many of you will find yourselves working as a part of a management team. You may have a specific role as a manager for an organization, office manager, sales manager or business owner. There are countless ethical decisions facing managers today.

Plant managers in manufacturing environments should consider how their decisions affect customers, employees and suppliers. Perhaps the plant manager convinces a purchasing agent to switch to a lower cost material to bring down overall production costs in order to increase profits. It is then discovered that this lower cost material is also of considerably lower quality and is causing harm to customers. This then affects how customers view the company.

Marketing managers should consider how truthful and reliable their advertising information is to consumers. Advertising messaging should not be misleading and cause harm and distrust with consumers. Aggressive, misleading or false advertising can have long-term negative effects on a company.

Controllers and accounting staff should consider how their decisions affect stockholders, employees and even creditors. Perhaps the company controller decides to shift the timing of certain adjusting entries so that the year-end financial statements look better with less expense and more profit. This will affect how a creditor views the company.

Company officers and those in key management positions should consider how their decisions affect stockholders, customers and employees. Imagine a large corporation in a mature industry, such as the steel industry or the automotive industry. This corporation has crushing levels of debt and is barely surviving with year after year of losses. Layoffs and outsourcing seem inevitable and impossible to avoid. Perhaps there are other options and ways to turn around a struggling corporation.

No matter your role in your professional career, when you are faced with an ethical dilemma, take the time to employ the steps that were discussed in Chapter 1. Decision-making skills are like exercising a muscle: the more you train and adapt to new situations, the stronger your decision-making skills will become.

In Summary

LO 1 **Describe the importance of managerial accounting**

▶ Managerial accounting relies on financial information to help managers and employees make informed decisions.

▶ The primary users of management accounting reports are internal stakeholders (e.g. management) while the primary users of financial accounting statements are external stakeholders (e.g. stockholders).

▶ Cost accounting is an integral part of managerial accounting that analyzes the costs incurred in producing goods and/or providing a service.

LO 2 **Make decisions related to business operations**

▶ Cost behavior is classifying costs based on how they change at different activity levels. Variable costs vary with the amount of products manufactured or services provided. Fixed costs remain relatively the same regardless of the volume produced within the relevant range.

▶ The break-even point is the level of sales at which the company's operating profit is zero.

▶ Maximum profit pricing examines the relationship between price and quantity demanded to find the price that will provide the most income from operations.

▶ A markup is the difference between a product's selling price and its cost.

▶ Target costing is the process of using the anticipated market price to calculate the maximum allowable cost for a product.

▶ Target costing is often used when a company believes it has little or no control over the product's selling price.

▶ The maximum allowable cost is also known as the target cost.

▶ Cash management can be achieved by managing receivables, managing payables, managing inventory levels, managing cash balances with the cash budget and tracking cash with the income statement and statement of cash flows.

▶ Balanced scorecard (BSC) is a strategic performance management framework to help implement the company's strategy.

▶ Key performance indicators are measures that determine a company's ability to meet certain objectives.

LO 3 **Make decisions related to employees**

▶ Hiring costs are large and can be offset by careful job descriptions, more time during the interview process and a set process for checking all references.

▶ Healthcare costs are unpredictable and constantly increasing causing problems with sustaining profits.

▶ Outsourcing shifts business operations from within the organization to outside the organization, which may involve moving operations to another country.

▶ Re-structuring involves major changes to the business in order to renew and sustain operations often including personnel reductions.

▶ Both employees leaving the business and employees staying with the business need consideration and communication throughout the outsourcing and re-structuring events.

LO 4 Develop management strategies related to compliance

▶ There is a wide array of taxes affecting businesses including compulsory filing and payment by pay period, by month, by quarter and annually.

▶ Some compliance issues affecting business include ISO 9000, the Sarbanes-Oxley Act, SEC regulations, and International Financial Reporting Standards.

▶ Litigation risk is always a danger for businesses, requiring forethought and insurance planning.

▶ Governmental regulatory issues include FTC advertising regulations, FLSA employment regulations, OSHA safety regulations, EPA environmental regulations, and many others.

▶ Unions exist to ensure fair wages, compensation, benefits, and so on, are provided to employees. These items often cost a business large amounts of money.

LO 5 Analyze profitability with ratios

▶ A company's profitability can be assessed using gross profit margin, net profit margin and return on equity

▶ Gross profit margin measures the percentage of sales revenue left after deducting cost of goods sold.

▶ Net profit margin assesses a company's profitability after deducting all expenses.

▶ Return on equity is a measure of what the stockholders are getting out of their investment in the company.

LO 6 Ethical considerations for management decisions

▶ As a part of a management team, you will encounter numerous ethical dilemmas throughout the decades of your career. Become familiar with an ethical decision-making model as a regular practice in your professional life.

AMEENGAGE™ *Access **ameengage.com** for integrated resources including tutorials, practice exercises, the digital textbook and more.*

Review Exercise 13-1

Essence Manufacturing has compiled the following information for the production of its beauty product. This information is based on the assumption that 100,000 units will be produced and sold in a year.

	Per Unit	Total (100,000 units)
Direct materials	$5	
Direct labor	$4	
Variable manufacturing overhead	$2	
Fixed manufacturing overhead		$300,000
Fixed general and administrative expenses		$80,000

Required

a) What is the cost to manufacture each unit?

_____

_____

_____

_____

_____

_____

b) Using the cost-plus pricing method, what selling price should Essence Manufacturing set if they want a 50% markup?

_____

_____

_____

_____

_____

_____

c) What is the contribution margin from each unit made?

_____

_____

_____

_____

_____

d) How many units must Essence Manufacturing make each year to break-even?

_____

_____

_____

_____

_____

e) Next year, it is expected that new legislation will be passed that will affect the beauty industry. Manufacturers will be required to meet new strict production standards to minimize the environmental impact of their production process. This will cost Essences Manufacturing an additional $10,000 per year. What will be the impact on the break-even point?

_____

_____

_____

_____

_____

_____

_____

See Appendix I for solutions.

Chapter 14
Analyzing Accounting Information

Learning Objectives

AMEENGAGE Access **ameengage.com** for integrated resources including tutorials, practice exercises, the digital textbook and more.

MAKING IT REAL TO YOU

When you become a professional in the business world, it will be important for you to understand financial statements and what they mean to the success of a business. You already have an understanding and familiarity with account types, such as assets, liabilities, revenues and expenses. However, you must be able to review a set of financial statements and have a good sense of what is happening for the company, what its strengths are and where there may be problems. Studying financial statements is a bit like detective work: you collect data, analyze the data and determine the next course of action. In this chapter, you will learn to calculate, analyze and explain several important financial ratios. These ratios are measurements that are used to get a picture of how a business is doing based on its financial statements.

Reading the Balance Sheet

In this course, you learned that the fundamental objective of accounting is to provide complete and accurate financial information to users for decision-making purposes. But what types of decisions do users need to make and how can they use financial information to make them? This chapter provides details on how the financial statements discussed thus far can be used to make decisions.

Personal financial information helps you make informed financial decisions, such as how to invest money, if you can afford a trip or even when you can retire. Personal financial statements help with these decisions by showing you how much cash you have and how much your net worth has changed over time. Your personal financial information is also used by others that require it to make decisions. For example, when you apply for a mortgage or a credit card, the bank uses your financial information to determine how much to lend you. The government uses your financial information to determine how much tax you owe each year. It is therefore important it is to maintain current and accurate personal financial information.

Business financial statements are useful for both internal and external users. Internal users, such as managers and executives, analyze financial information to correct negative results and take advantage of positive results. External users, such as investors and suppliers, analyze financial information to determine whether to invest money or extend credit terms. First, all users must learn how to properly read and understand financial statements. We will begin with the balance sheet.

The balance sheet is a snapshot of a company's financial position at a single point in time. For example, a company's balance sheet for the year 2018 may show a large increase in assets and liabilities compared to its 2017 balance sheet, due to the purchase of equipment with a large bank loan during 2018. A user of the company's financial statements may see the big increases in the company's loans and equipment in the 2018 balance sheet, and wonder whether the company will be able to make the loan payments or whether the company is using the equipment effectively. There are several analysis tools that can be used to help answer these questions. We will examine these tools later in this chapter.

Up to this point, we have prepared financial statements for sole proprietorships. Sole proprietorships are generally smaller in terms of financing, number of employees and number of locations. Corporations can be large in size with multiple locations and many employees in different cities. Since corporations are a very common form of organization in the United States, it is important to understand how to read the financial statements of a corporation.

For example, Proctor & Gamble Company (P&G) has operating branches on four continents that are responsible for selling approximately 100 brands of consumer products globally. This means that managers of P&G have a lot to track and oversee. Financial statement analysis helps the internal users (management) evaluate their company's operations and explain changes to external users (stockholders/investors).

The presentation of the corporate balance sheet is similar to that of a sole proprietorship's but usually has more details and more accounts. Figure 14.1 shows P&G's consolidated balance sheet from 2017. Its equity section looks different from the equity section in a sole proprietorship's balance sheet that you have seen before. We will look at the highlighted differences in detail. Also note that P&G uses the term "shareholder's equity" in place of "stockholder's equity."

The Procter & Gamble Company Consolidated Balance Sheet Amounts in millions; June 30, 2017	
Assets	
Current Assets	
Cash and cash equivalents	$5,569
Available-for-sale investment securities	9,568
Accounts receivable	4,594
Inventories	
Materials and supplies	1,308
Work in process	529
Finished goods	2,787
Total inventories	4,624
Deferred income taxes	-
Prepaid expenses and other current assets	2,139
Assets held for sale	-
Total Current Assets	26,494
Net Property, Plant and Equipment	19,893
Goodwill	44,699
Trademarks and Other Intangible Assets, Net	24,187
Other Noncurrent Assets	5,133
Total Assets	**$120,406**
Liabilities and Stockholders' Equity	
Current Liabilities	
Accounts payable	$9,632
Accrued and other liabilities	7,024
Liabilities held for sale	-
Debt due within one year	13,554
Total Current Liabilities	30,210
Long-Term Debt	18,038
Deferred Income Taxes	8,126
Other Noncurrent Liabilities	8,254
Total Liabilities	64,628
Stockholders' Equity	
Convertible Class A preferred stock, stated value $1 per share (600 shares authorized)	1,006
Non-Voting Class B preferred stock, stated value $1 per share (200 shares authorized)	–
Common stock, stated value $1 per share (10,000 shares authorized; shares issued 2017—4009.2, 2016—4,009.2	4,009
Additional paid-in capital	63,641
Reserve for ESOP debt retirement	(1,249)
Accumulated other comprehensive income (loss)	(14,632)
Treasury stock, at cost (shares held: 2017—1,455.9, 2016—1,341.2)	(93,715)
Retained earnings	96,124
Non-controlling interest	594
Total Stockholders' Equity	55,778
Total Liabilities and Stockholders' Equity	**$120,406**

FIGURE 14.1

Stockholders' Equity

Owners of a corporation are referred to as stockholders, or shareholders. This is because a corporation can sell a fraction of its ownership to the general public in the form of shares. Corporations use the term "stockholders' equity" instead of "owner's equity" to present the equity section of the balance sheet. The stockholders' equity category includes two subcategories: capital stock and retained earnings.

Capital Stock

Capital stock is a subsection on the balance sheet that includes accounts for a company's equity raised through different types of stock. Corporate stock can be divided into two major types: common stock and preferred stock.

Common stock, also referred to as *common shares*, is sold to investors, known as stockholders, in exchange for an investment (e.g. cash) in the company. Shares that have been sold are called outstanding stock. Common stocks also represent a portion of ownership of the company. This means that common stockholders have the right to vote for the directors and executives of the corporation. The common stock section for P&G is highlighted in Figure 14.1.

Preferred stock, also referred to as *preferred shares*, may also be sold to stockholders in exchange for an investment in the company. However, preferred stockholders do not have any voting rights so they cannot decide on who is in charge of running the company. Instead, preferred stocks offer a higher claim on the assets of the business. This means that in the event of bankruptcy, preferred stockholders are paid before common stockholders. Accordingly, preferred stocks always appear before common stocks in the stockholders' equity section of a corporation's balance sheet. The preferred stock section for P&G is highlighted in Figure 14.1. Proctor & Gamble's outstanding shares of preferred stock are *convertible*, meaning that the preferred stockholders have an option to convert their preferred stock into common stock. Unlike common stocks, preferred stocks may have different features attached to them. Convertibility is only one example of preferred stocks' features.

The common stock and preferred stock accounts separately track the total investments received by the corporation through the sale of those share types. This is in contrast to sole proprietorships, in which additional investments made by the owner are recorded directly in the owner's capital account. Sole proprietorships' net income (loss) and cash withdrawals by the owner are also transferred to the owner's capital account. Corporations, on the other hand, have a separate account for recording their net income (loss) and dividends, which is discussed next.

Retained Earnings

A corporation's net income (or loss) for each period is transferred to the retained earnings account. When the corporation pays dividends to stockholders, the dividends are also deducted from the retained earnings account. Therefore, the **retained earnings** account represents the cumulative net income of a corporation, net of dividends. It is important not to confuse retained earnings with cash or other assets within the business. The retained earnings account is presented in the equity section of the balance sheet. The retained earnings section for P&G is highlighted in Figure 14.1.

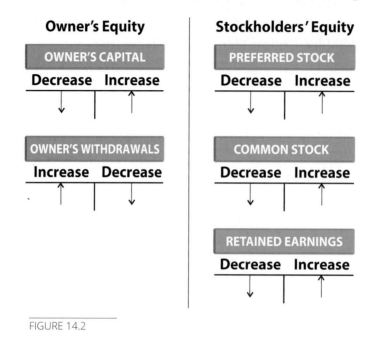

FIGURE 14.2

Figure 14.2 illustrates the primary differences between the equity sections for a sole proprietorship and a corporation. Notice the separation of the stock types for a corporation.

We have identified some key differences between a corporation's and sole proprietorship's respective balance sheets. In addition to capital stock and retained earnings on the balance sheet, there are terms that corporations commonly use on the income statement that are not usually seen in a sole proprietorship's income statement. These are discussed in the following section.

Reading the Income Statement

The income statement is a summary of how profits or losses were generated during an accounting period. Once again, the presentation of a corporation's income statement is similar to that of a sole proprietorships', but there are some new terms. The income statement is also called a statement of income, statement of earnings or statement of operations.

Consider P&G's 2017 consolidated statement of earnings shown in Figure 14.3. This is similar to a sole proprietorship's multiple-step income statement, in which the earnings are subdivided into gross profit, operating income and net income. However, due to the more complicated nature of the corporation's operations, its income statement is more complicated and lists more items. For example, a corporation that has multiple operating segments may decide to discontinue an unprofitable segment. The earnings from this discontinued segment have to be reported as a separate item from the earnings from the continuing segments.

The Procter & Gamble Company Consolidated Statement of Earnings Amounts in millions except per share amounts; Year ended June 30, 2017	
Net Sales	$65,058
Cost of products sold	32,535
Selling, general and administrative expense	18,568
Operating Income	13,955
Interest expense	465
Interest Income	171
Other non-operating income/(expense), net	(404)
Earnings from Continuing Operations Before Income Taxes	13,257
Income taxes on continuing operations	3,063
Net Earnings from Continuing Operations	10,194
Net Earnings from Discontinued Operations	5,217
Net Earnings	15,411
Less: Net earnings attributable to noncontrolling interests	85
Net Earnings Attributable to Procter & Gamble	**$15,326**
Basic Net Earnings Per Common Share:	
Earnings from continuing operations	$3.79
Earnings from discontinued operations	2.01
Basic Net Earnings Per Common Share	**5.8**
Diluted Net Earnings Per Common Share	
Earnings from continuing operations	$3.69
Earnings from discontinued operations	1.90
Diluted Net Earnings Per Common Share	5.59
Dividends Per Common Share	**$2.70**
(1) Basic net earnings per common share and diluted net earnings per common share are calculated on net earnings attributable to Procter & Gamble	

FIGURE 14.3

Discontinued Operations

A **discontinued operation** is a segment of a business that is no longer part of regular operating activities. However, other business segments are still operational. There are a variety of reasons that a corporation may want to discontinue a business segment. For example, the segment may no longer be profitable, so the corporation is shutting it down or selling it. Or management has shifted the corporate mission and the segment no longer fits the company's focus.

Normally, sole proprietorships have only one type of operation, or a single business segment, such as providing a service or selling retail products. Because corporations are usually larger in nature, they tend to be divided into more than one business segment. These segments may operate independently and contribute to the revenues and expenses of the corporation as a whole.

Discontinued operations must be accounted for and presented in the financial statements. The corporation liquidates the net assets of the discontinued business segment. The revenues and expenses generated by discontinued operations, as well as any gains or losses associated with the disposal of net assets, are presented in a separate section called discontinued operations. P&G's net earnings from discontinued operations are highlighted in Figure 14.3.

Other Comprehensive Income

A corporation's income statement, unlike that of a sole proprietorship's, may contain "other comprehensive income." Other comprehensive income can either be shown as a separate section in the income statement, or separated into a stand-alone statement. P&G chose to report its other comprehensive income in a stand-alone statement, called a consolidated statement of comprehensive income, which is shown in Figure 14.4. This statement tracks the value of activities that are not part of the main operations. Other comprehensive income can arise from changes in the value of assets, such as investments, property, plant and equipment, and other items not in the scope of this textbook. The increases or decreases in the value of assets result in gains or losses for a corporation. Such gains and losses are discussed in more details below.

The Procter & Gamble Company Consolidated Statement of Comprehensive Income Amounts in millions; Year ended June 29, 2017	
Net Earnings	**$15,411**
Other Comprehensive Income (Loss), Net of Tax	
Financial statement translation	239
Unrealized gains/(losses) on hedges (net of $(186), $5 and $739 tax, repectively)	(306)
Unrealized gains/(losses) on investment securities (net of ($6), $7 and $0 tax, respectively)	(59)
Defined benefit retirement plans (net of $551, ($621) and $328 tax, respectively)	1,401
Total Other Comprehensive Income (Loss), Net of Tax	1,275
Total Comprehensive Income	16,686
Less Total Comprehensive Income Attributable to Noncontrolling Interests	85
Total Comprehensive Income Attributable to Proctor & Gamble	**$16,601**

FIGURE 14.4

Gains and Losses

Sometimes a corporation may incur gains or losses through transactions or events that are not part of its daily operating activities. In most cases, a **gain** is an increase in the value of noncurrent assets that gives the assets a higher worth than their net book value. A gain increases the value of stockholders' equity. On the other hand, a **loss** is a decrease in the value of noncurrent assets that gives the assets a lower worth than their net book value. A loss decreases the value of stockholders' equity. Gains and losses may result from selling assets, such as equipment, or recording the changes in value of investments. In other cases, gains or losses happen with activities irrelevant from noncurrent assets. For example, the proceeds from winning a lawsuit settlement are considered a gain, while expenditures from losing a lawsuit settlement are considered a loss.

In the case of P&G, the company experienced both gains and losses in 2017. As highlighted in Figure 14.4, the company reported an unrealized loss on investment securities in 2017. The gains and losses are reported on the statement of comprehensive income as being *unrealized* because the investment securities have yet to be sold. The gains and losses are estimated based on available fair market value information. The estimation gives users of the financial statements a clearer idea of how selling assets at the end of the accounting period would affect the company's financial situation. While such gains and losses are not part of the daily operating activities, they still affect the company's comprehensive income. This means they must be presented on the statement of comprehensive income.

We have reviewed the balance sheet and income statement from the perspectives of both a sole proprietorship and a corporation. Now, the financial statements can be analyzed and we can learn more about how accounting information can be used for decision making.

Horizontal and Vertical Analyses

We will inspect the balance sheet of Star Hotel, a fictitious hotel corporation. Suppose this company is planning to renovate to offer more rooms and services. It has contacted the bank to secure a note payable, but the bank must determine whether the company is able to afford the loan and interest payments. The bank has asked for Star Hotel's financial statements for the last three years. Star Hotel's comparative balance sheet is presented in Figure 14.5. A **comparative balance sheet** is simply a balance sheet that shows the balances for multiple years for easy comparison. For readability, a single column is used for each year.

Star Hotel Balance Sheet As at December 31, 2016-2018			
	2018	**2017**	**2016**
Assets			
Current Assets			
Cash	$8,000	$20,000	$32,000
Accounts Receivable	100,000	70,000	40,000
Food Inventory	40,000	28,000	16,000
Prepaid Expenses	12,000	12,000	12,000
Total Current Assets	160,000	130,000	100,000
Property, Plant & Equipment			
Building, Net	390,000	400,000	410,000
Equipment, Net	50,000	55,000	60,000
Total Property, Plant & Equipment	440,000	455,000	470,000
Total Assets	$600,000	$585,000	$570,000
Liabilities			
Current Liabilities			
Accounts Payable	$50,000	$60,000	$80,000
Unearned Revenue	30,000	25,000	20,000
Total Current Liabilities	80,000	85,000	100,000
Total Liabilities	80,000	85,000	100,000
Stockholders' Equity			
Capital Stock			
Common Stock—10,000 outstanding	100,000	100,000	100,000
Preferred Stock—5,000 outstanding	20,000	10,000	10,000
Retained Earnings	400,000	390,000	360,000
Total Stockholders' Equity	520,000	500,000	470,000
Total Liabilities and Stockholders' Equity	$600,000	$585,000	$570,000

FIGURE 14.5

The comparative balance sheet is a tool used to perform **horizontal analysis** because it compares information from one accounting period to another, usually from year to year. This means that you can compare similar line items to see how that item has changed from year to year.

Using the comparative balance sheet, the bank can easily see the increases and decreases in assets and liabilities, and estimate the future trends of the financial information. Specifically, it can quickly see that total assets have increased while total liabilities have decreased, which is a good sign. However, the company's cash balance is dwindling while accounts receivable significantly increased, indicating that there may be some cash or collection issues. To make its decision, the bank needs more in-depth information.

Examining dollar amounts may not reveal trends in the company. Instead we can present the values as percentages. This shows the value of the item compared to a base year. A **base year** is usually the earliest year shown and will be the basis for comparison.

Figure 14.6 shows the formula used to calculate the percentages.

$$\text{Percentage of Base Year} = \frac{\text{New Account Balance}}{\text{Base Year Account Balance}}$$

FIGURE 14.6

In this example, 2016 is the base year. For each line, the 2016 value is the denominator in the calculation. So for cash, we will always divide by $32,000. For 2016, $32,000 divided by $32,000 is 100%. For 2018, the calculation is shown here.

$$\frac{\$8,000}{\$32,000} = 0.25 \text{ or } 25\%$$

A way to describe this trend is that cash in 2018 is at 25% of the balance in 2016. Repeat this calculation for each separate line item across the years. The first table in Figure 14.7 shows the key figures for Star Hotel. The second table shows the percentage of compared to the base year.

Star Hotel Key Figures As at December 31, 2016-2018			
	2018	**2017**	**2016**
Cash	$8,000	$20,000	$32,000
Total Current Assets	160,000	130,000	100,000
Property, Plant & Equipment	440,000	455,000	470,000
Total Assets	600,000	585,000	570,000
Total Current Liabilities	80,000	85,000	100,000
Total Stockholders' Equity	520,000	500,000	470,000

Star Hotel Percentage of 2016 Base Year As at December 31, 2016-2018			
	2018	**2017**	**2016**
Cash	25%*	63%	100%
Total Current Assets	160%	130%	100%
Property, Plant & Equipment	94%	97%	100%
Total Assets	105%	103%	100%
Total Current Liabilities	80%	85%	100%
Total Stockholders' Equity	111%	106%	100%

*$8,000 ÷ $32,000 = 25%

FIGURE 14.7

Using this method, the bank can see trends emerging in the data. Despite cash significantly decreasing over time, total current assets have been steadily increasing. Liabilities have been reduced while stockholders' equity has been increasing since 2016. There are no major concerns with these observations.

There is another way to calculate percentage changes between years for line items. The formula for this method is shown in Figure 14.8.

$$\text{Percentage Changed since Base Year} = \frac{\text{New Account Balance} - \text{Base Year Account Balance}}{\text{Base Year Account Balance}}$$

FIGURE 14.8

As before, 2016 is selected as the base year. For cash, we will always subtract $32,000 from the year we are examining and divide the result by $32,000. For example, the balance of cash in 2018 was $8,000 and the percentage change calculation for 2018 is shown here.

$$\frac{\$8,000 - \$32,000}{\$32,000} = -0.75 \text{ or } 75\%$$

A way to describe this trend is that the cash balance decreased by 75% between 2016 and 2018. This could be the reason why Star Hotel needs a loan, because the company does not have enough cash to pay for renovations. The first table in Figure 14.9 shows key figures for Star Hotel. The second table shows the percentage change compared to the base year.

Star Hotel Key Figures As at December 31, 2016-2018			
	2018	**2017**	**2016**
Cash	$8,000	$20,000	$32,000
Total Current Assets	160,000	130,000	100,000
Property, Plant & Equipment	440,000	455,000	470,000
Total Assets	600,000	585,000	570,000
Total Current Liabilities	80,000	85,000	100,000
Total Stockholders' Equity	520,000	500,000	470,000

Star Hotel Percentage Changed with 2016 Base Year As at December 31, 2016-2018			
	2018	**2017**	**2016**
Cash	-75%*	-38%	0%
Total Current Assets	60%	30%	0%
Property, Plant & Equipment	-6%	-5%	0%
Total Assets	5%	3%	0%
Total Current Liabilities	-20%	-15%	0%
Total Stockholders' Equity	11%	6%	0%

*($8,000 − $32,000) ÷ $32,000 = -75%

FIGURE 14.9

One item to note in Figure 14.9 is that there are 0% changes for 2016. There is no percent change from the base year figure, because they are the same dollar amounts (i.e. $32,000 minus $32,000 equals $0. Next, $0 divided by $32,000 equals 0%).

Instead of comparing the dollars to a base year, the bank could use one of the line items as a base figure known as **vertical analysis**. Usually, the **base figure** is a total dollar amount, such as total assets. Figure 14.10 shows the formula to calculate the percentage of base figure using the data from Figure 14.11.

$$\text{Percentage of Base Figure} = \frac{\text{Line Item Account Balance}}{\text{Base Figure Account Balance}}$$

FIGURE 14.10

To start, a base figure must be selected. In 2018, Star Hotel had a total asset balance of $600,000. Next, divide all line items in the 2018 balance sheet by the base figure selected. For cash, divide the balance of $8,000 by the total assets. The result is 0.01 or 1%.

$$\frac{\$8,000}{\$600,000} = 0.01 \text{ or } 1\%$$

Figure 14.11 shows the key percentages for Star Hotel using vertical analysis.

Star Hotel Key Percentages As at December 31, 2016-2018			
	2018	**2017**	**2016**
Cash	1%*	3%	6%
Total Current Assets	27%	22%	18%
Property, Plant & Equipment	73%	78%	82%
Total Assets	100%	100%	100%
Total Current Liabilities	13%	15%	18%
Total Stockholders' Equity	87%	85%	82%

*$8,000 ÷ $600,000 = 1%

FIGURE 14.11

This type of analysis reveals that cash currently only represents 1% of total assets. Star Hotel should consider holding more cash in case of unexpected events. Fortunately, current assets represent 27% of total assets and have grown to more than double that of current liabilities. Using this information, the bank decides that Star Hotel is in an overall healthy financial position.

The next step is to use the same tools to analyze the company's income statement. Horizontal analysis is done in much the same way on the income statement as it is on the balance sheet. Star Hotel's comparative income statement is shown in Figure 14.12 for the past three years.

Star Hotel Income Statement For the Year Ended December 31, 2016-2018			
	2018	**2017**	**2016**
Revenue			
Service Revenue	$270,000	$200,000	$180,000
Food Sales Revenue	80,000	50,000	40,000
Total Revenue	350,000	250,000	220,000
Cost of Goods Sold	50,000	30,000	25,000
Gross Profit	300,000	220,000	195,000
Operating Expenses			
Advertising Expense	33,000	15,000	5,000
Depreciation Expense	15,000	15,000	15,000
Insurance Expense	12,000	12,000	12,000
Salaries Expense	200,000	150,000	140,000
Supplies Expense	20,000	18,000	15,500
Total Expenses	280,000	210,000	187,500
Net Income	$20,000	$10,000	$7,500

FIGURE 14.12

The comparative income statement allows the bank to quickly see which revenues and expenses have increased or decreased and whether net income is rising or falling. Star Hotel has seen a large increase in revenue, perhaps attributable to an increased advertising budget. The company's net income has doubled since 2017, which is a good sign of profitability. However, if the bank grants a loan, Star Hotel will incur an interest expense, which would reduce the profitability of the company. The bank decides to look at other trends in the company.

Figure 14.13 lists the key figures from the income statement for the previous three years as dollars, percentage of, and percentage changed for the base year of 2016.

Star Hotel Key Figures For the Year Ended December 31, 2016-2018	2018	2017	2016
Total Revenue	$350,000	$250,000	$220,000
Cost of Goods Sold	50,000	30,000	25,000
Gross Profit	300,000	220,000	195,000
Total Expenses	280,000	210,000	187,500
Net Income	20,000	10,000	7,500

Star Hotel Percentage of 2016 Base Year For the Year Ended December 31, 2016-2018	2018	2017	2016
Total Revenue	160%	114%	100%
Cost of Goods Sold	200%	120%	100%
Gross Profit	154%	113%	100%
Total Expenses	150%	112%	100%
Net Income	267%	133%	100%

Star Hotel Percentage Changed with 2016 Base Year For the Year Ended December 31, 2016-2018	2018	2017	2016
Total Revenue	60%	14%	0%
Cost of Goods Sold	100%	20%	0%
Gross Profit	54%	13%	0%
Total Expenses	50%	12%	0%
Net Income	167%	33%	0%

FIGURE 14.13

Star Hotel's sales have been increasing at a faster rate than its expenses, resulting in higher net income. After seeing these trends, the bank decides that the company is likely to continue operating profitably into the future.

Finally, the bank can also use vertical analysis on Star Hotel's income statement by converting everything to a percentage of total revenue for each year, as shown in Figure 14.14.

Star Hotel Percentage of Base Figure Total Revenue For the Year Ended December 31, 2016-2018			
	2018	**2017**	**2016**
Total Revenue	100%	100%	100%
Cost of Goods Sold	14%	12%	11%
Gross Profit	86%	88%	89%
Total Expenses	80%	84%	85%
Net Income	6%	4%	3%

FIGURE 14.14

This analysis reveals that gross profit has remained quite steady, but operating expenses have been gradually falling in relation to total revenue. This indicates that sales have risen without causing as much of an increase to operating expenses, allowing for more net income per dollar of sales.

Considering all of the conclusions, the bank decides to grant the loan to Star Hotel because it has been growing steadily over the past three years and is in a healthy enough financial position to expand operations without much risk.

The Star Hotel example used horizontal and vertical analysis tools to make a decision. While these tools are helpful in providing insight to a company's financial position, there are limitations to what they can actually show. The tools do not consider errors in the figures. Also, the trends may not continue because businesses change and evolve constantly. Fortunately, there are many other analysis tools available to users. These will be discussed next.

Pause & Reflect

Exercise 14-1

Industrial Furnishing's accountant has calculated the trend percentage for each account, using 2015 as the base year.

Industrial Furnishings Percentage of 2015 Base Year For the Year Ended December 31, 2015–2018				
	2018	**2017**	**2016**	**2015**
Total Revenue	122%	120%	105%	100%
Cost of Goods Sold	155%	150%	110%	100%
Gross Profit	114%	113%	104%	100%
Total Operating Expenses	122%	119%	103%	100%
Net Income	82%	88%	106%	100%

Based on the trend percentage calculated in part a), analyze why net income has been decreasing in the past two years.

_____

_____

_____

See Appendix I for solutions.

DUNKIN' BRANDS GROUP, INC. AND SUBSIDIARIES
Consolidated Balance Sheets
(In thousands, except share data)

	December 26, 2015	December 27, 2014
Assets		
Current assets:		
Cash and cash equivalents	$ 260,430	208,080
Restricted cash	71,917	—
Accounts receivable, net	53,142	55,908
Notes and other receivables, net	75,218	49,152
Restricted assets of advertising funds	38,554	34,300
Prepaid income taxes	23,899	24,861
Prepaid expenses and other current assets	34,664	21,101
Total current assets	557,824	393,402
Property and equipment, net	182,614	182,061
Equity method investments	106,878	164,493
Goodwill	889,588	891,370
Other intangible assets, net	1,401,208	1,425,797
Other assets	59,007	67,277
Total assets	$ 3,197,119	3,124,400
Liabilities, Redeemable Noncontrolling Interests, and Stockholders' Equity (Deficit)		
Current liabilities:		
Current portion of long-term debt	$ 25,000	3,852
Capital lease obligations	546	506
Accounts payable	18,663	13,814
Liabilities of advertising funds	50,189	48,081
Deferred income	31,535	30,374
Other current liabilities	292,859	258,892
Total current liabilities	418,792	355,519
Long-term debt, net	2,420,600	1,795,623
Capital lease obligations	7,497	7,575
Unfavorable operating leases acquired	12,975	14,795
Deferred income	15,619	14,935
Deferred income taxes, net	476,510	498,814
Other long-term liabilities	65,869	62,189
Total long-term liabilities	2,999,070	2,393,931
Commitments and contingencies (note 17)		
Redeemable noncontrolling interests	—	6,991
Stockholders' equity (deficit):		
Preferred stock, $0.001 par value; 25,000,000 shares authorized; no shares issued and outstanding	—	—
Common stock, $0.001 par value; 475,000,000 shares authorized; 92,668,211 shares issued and 92,641,044 shares outstanding at December 26, 2015; 104,630,978 shares issued and outstanding at December 27, 2014	92	104
Additional paid-in capital	876,557	1,093,363
Treasury stock, at cost; 27,167 shares at December 26, 2015	(1,075)	—
Accumulated deficit	(1,076,479)	(711,531)
Accumulated other comprehensive loss	(20,046)	(13,977)
Total stockholders' equity (deficit) of Dunkin' Brands	(220,951)	367,959
Noncontrolling interests	208	—
Total stockholders' equity (deficit)	(220,743)	367,959
Total liabilities, redeemable noncontrolling interests, and stockholders' equity (deficit)	$ 3,197,119	3,124,400

FIGURE 14.15

Analyzing the Statements

It is now time to analyze the financial statements. We will use the financial statements of Dunkin' Brands Group, Inc. (Dunkin' Donuts), an American corporation that sells specialty coffee and baked goods. The comparative balance sheet is shown in Figure 14.15. There may be some unfamiliar assets and liabilities listed, but we will focus on the analysis of the statement as a whole rather than on individual accounts. The comparative balance sheet allows us to conduct horizontal and vertical analyses, as well as calculate financial ratios to better understand a company's finances. Ratios are divided into four categories based on what they measure: liquidity, profitability, operations management and leverage.

Liquidity Analysis

Liquidity refers to the ability of a company to convert current assets into cash. This is important because paying off liabilities, purchasing assets and paying for business expenses are generally done using cash. The more liquid a company is, the easier it is to cover obligations such as accounts payable and loan payments. There are several ways to measure liquidity.

Working Capital

Working capital is a measure of liquidity. It can be quickly calculated and easily understood. Figure 14.16 shows the formula to calculate working capital.

Working Capital = Current Assets – Current Liabilities

FIGURE 14.16

Working capital is a dollar figure, not a ratio, so it is difficult to say how much working capital is enough. A positive working capital indicates that the company has enough liquid assets to pay off its upcoming debts. The working capital of Dunkin' Donuts is shown in Figure 14.17 for 2014 and 2015.

Dunkin' Donuts had enough current assets to cover its current liabilities, as evident by its positive working capital in both 2014 and 2015. Its working capital increased from 2014 to 2015, indicating improved liquidity.

	2015	2014
Current Assets	$557,824	$393,402
Current Liabilities	$418,792	$355,519
Working Capital	**$139,032**	**$37,883**

FIGURE 14.17

Current Ratio

The current ratio is a useful ratio assess the extent to which a company's current assets can cover its current debts (those due within one year). Figure 14.18 shows how to calculate current ratio.

$$\text{Current Ratio} \;=\; \frac{\text{Current Assets}}{\text{Current Liabilities}}$$

FIGURE 14.18

No business wants to find itself in a position of having to sell noncurrent assets to pay current bills. A current ratio of 1.0 indicates that the business has just enough current assets to pay for its current liabilities.

Depending on the industry, the higher the current ratio, the more assurance that the business has enough of a cushion that it can afford to have some cash tied up in current assets, such as inventory and accounts receivable. However, a very high current ratio could indicate poor management of current assets. For example, if the current ratio of a business is 5.0, it has $5.00 in current assets for every dollar that it owes in the next 12 months. This indicates that the business may have too much cash. Money in a bank account earning 0.1% interest is not an efficient use of assets, especially if the business can earn a better rate of return elsewhere. Cash should either be invested in new noncurrent assets or perhaps invested in the short term until a better use for the cash can be established.

The table in Figure 14.19 shows the current ratio using the numbers provided in Dunkin' Donuts financial statements.

	2015	2014
Current Assets	$557,824	$393,402
Current Liabilities	$418,792	$355,519
Current Ratio	**1.33**	**1.11**

FIGURE 14.19

In this case, the ratio indicates a healthy situation. Not only is the ratio above 1 for both years, but it has increased from 2014 to 2015.

Quick Ratio

The other liquidity ratio that is relevant to the analysis of a business is the quick ratio (also known as the acid test). This ratio is much like the current ratio, except it excludes some current assets that cannot be quickly converted to cash (i.e. inventory and prepaid expenses). It asses the ability of the business to meet its most immediate debt obligations without relying on the liquidation of inventory. Figure 14.20 shows the formula to calculate the quick ratio.

$$\text{Quick Ratio} = \frac{\text{Cash} + \text{Short-Term Investments} + \text{Accounts Receivable}}{\text{Current Liabilities}}$$

FIGURE 14.20

Short-term investments occur when a company has excess cash and wishes to invest it. This cash can be invested in shares of other companies. The accounting for short-term investments is beyond the scope of this course.

A quick ratio of 1 indicates that the business has just enough liquid assets to pay for its current liabilities. Anything below 1 might mean the business has too much of its money tied up in inventory or other less liquid assets and may be unable to pay its short-term bills.

Quick ratios have been calculated using the numbers from Dunkin' Donuts balance sheet and are shown in Figure 14.21. Note that Dunkin' Donuts does not have any short-term investments.

	2015	**2014**
Cash + Short-Term Investments + Accounts Receivable	$388,790	$313,140
Current Liabilities	$418,792	$355,519
Quick Ratio	**0.93**	**0.88**

FIGURE 14.21

The quick ratio has increased from 0.88 to 0.93. This means that Dunkin' Donuts short-term liquidity has increased to a nearly adequate position and the company should have little problem making payments as they come due.

Profitability Analysis

Profitability refers to the ability of a company to generate profits. The greater the profitability, the more valuable the company is to stockholders. A consistently unprofitable company is likely to go bankrupt. There are several ratios available to help analyze the profitability of a company. They are calculated using figures from the income statement as opposed to the balance sheet. The income statement for Dunkin' Donuts is shown in Figure 14.22. There are several revenues and expenses listed that you may have never seen before, but we will focus on the analysis of the statement as a whole rather than on individual accounts.

DUNKIN' BRANDS GROUP, INC. AND SUBSIDIARIES
Consolidated Statements of Operations
(In thousands, except per share data)

	Fiscal year ended		
	December 26, 2015	December 27, 2014	December 28, 2013
Revenues:			
Franchise fees and royalty income	$ 513,222	482,329	453,976
Rental income	100,422	97,663	96,082
Sales of ice cream and other products	115,252	117,484	112,276
Sales at company-operated restaurants	28,340	22,206	24,976
Other revenues	53,697	29,027	26,530
Total revenues	810,933	748,709	713,840
Operating costs and expenses:			
Occupancy expenses—franchised restaurants	54,611	53,395	52,097
Cost of ice cream and other products	76,877	83,129	79,278
Company-operated restaurant expenses	29,900	22,687	24,480
General and administrative expenses, net	243,796	226,301	230,847
Depreciation	20,556	19,779	22,423
Amortization of other intangible assets	24,688	25,760	26,943
Long-lived asset impairment charges	623	1,484	563
Total operating costs and expenses	451,051	432,535	436,631
Net income (loss) of equity method investments:			
Net income, excluding impairment	12,555	14,846	19,243
Impairment charge	(54,300)	—	(873)
Net income (loss) of equity method investments	(41,745)	14,846	18,370
Other operating income, net	1,430	7,838	9,157
Operating income	319,567	338,858	304,736
Other income (expense), net:			
Interest income	424	274	404
Interest expense	(96,765)	(68,098)	(80,235)
Loss on debt extinguishment and refinancing transactions	(20,554)	(13,735)	(5,018)
Other losses, net	(1,084)	(1,566)	(1,799)
Total other expense, net	(117,979)	(83,125)	(86,648)
Income before income taxes	201,588	255,733	218,088
Provision for income taxes	96,359	80,170	71,784
Net income including noncontrolling interests	105,229	175,563	146,304
Net income (loss) attributable to noncontrolling interests	2	(794)	(599)
Net income attributable to Dunkin' Brands	$ 105,227	176,357	146,903
Earnings per share:			
Common—basic	$ 1.10	1.67	1.38
Common—diluted	1.08	1.65	1.36
Cash dividends declared per common share	1.06	0.92	0.76

FIGURE 14.22

As you can see from Figure 14.22, Dunkin' Donuts' income statement is also shown in horizontal form, allowing users to easily compare the financial results of the company over three years. We can instantly see that Dunkin' Donuts has generated increasing sales for the past two years. We can also see that expenses have correspondingly increased overall, although an impairment charge of $54,300 (primarily due to the termination of leasehold agreements) in 2015 resulted in a drop in operating income to below that of 2014. The impairment charge was an adjustment related to foreign joint ventures, and is not a regular occurrence. In addition to these observations, several more ratios can be calculated to assess profitability.

Gross Profit Margin

Gross profit is the difference between sales revenue and cost of goods sold (COGS). Gross profit expressed as a percentage of sales is called gross profit margin, which represents the percentage of sales left over to pay for all the operating expenses. The formula is shown in Figure 14.23.

$$\text{Gross Profit Margin} \quad = \quad \frac{\text{Gross Profit*}}{\text{Net Sales}}$$

*Gross Profit = Sales Revenue – Cost of Goods Sold

FIGURE 14.23

Figure 14.24 shows the gross profit margin related to the sale and cost of ice cream and other products using figures from Dunkin' Donuts' income statement for 2014 and 2015.

	2015	**2014**
Gross Profit[1]	$38,375	$34,355
Net Sales	$115,252	$117,484
Gross Profit Margin	**0.33 or 33%**	**0.29 or 29%**

(1) Gross Profit for 2014: $117,484 – $83,129 = $34,355
     Gross Profit for 2015: $115,252 – $76,877 = $38,375

FIGURE 14.24

Dunkin' Donuts' low gross profit margin means that the company may have a more difficult time covering its expenses and is less likely to be profitable. A decline in the gross profit margin could indicate that the company is either not generating enough revenue, has experienced an increase in inventory costs or both. However, gross profit margins should be compared to an industry average to determine whether they are healthy or not. An increase in the gross profit is a good sign of increased profitability.

Net Profit Margin

Net profit margin assesses a company's profitability after all expenses have been deducted. This is the amount of net profit or loss per dollar of revenue. The formula is shown in Figure 14.25.

$$\text{Net Profit Margin} \quad = \quad \frac{\text{Net Income}}{\text{Total Revenue}}$$

FIGURE 14.25

As with the gross profit margin, a higher net profit margin is generally considered a better sign than a lower one, although it should be always be compared to an industry average and previous results. Figure 14.26 shows the net profit margin for Dunkin' Donuts for both 2014 and 2015.

	2015	2014
Net Income (Loss)	$105,227	$176,357
Total Revenue	$810,933	$748,709
Net Profit Margin	**0.13 or 13%**	**0.24 or 24%**

FIGURE 14.26

Although total revenue has increased since 2014, net income has dropped since then. This was partially due to the impairment charge of $54,300 in 2015, mentioned earlier. This could be a bad sign for stockholders because earnings on their investments have dropped from 2014 to 2015. To perform a complete analysis of net profit margins, comparisons should be made on a monthly and yearly basis to historical company performance, industry averages and direct competitors. Conclusions can only be drawn when net income figures are placed in context.

Return on Equity (ROE)

Return on equity (ROE) is a measure of what the owners are getting out of their investment in the company. It is often the most important ratio for investors because it has a large impact on the value of one's investment. This ratio requires information from both the balance sheet and income statement to be calculated. Figure 14.27 shows the formula to calculate return on equity.

$$\text{Return on Equity} = \frac{\text{Net Income}}{\text{Average Stockholders' Equity}}$$

FIGURE 14.27

A CLOSER LOOK

The return on equity formula assumes that there is no preferred stock equity included in stockholders' equity. If preferred equity exists, the formula would be as follows:

Return on Equity = (Net Income − Preferred Dividends) ÷ Average Common Stockholders' Equity

Preferred stock is beyond the scope of this course.

Notice that the calculation requires average stockholders' equity. Whenever a ratio is calculated that uses some information from the balance and some from the income statement, the balance sheet information is always averaged. This is because the balance sheet represents a snapshot in time while the income statement represents an entire accounting period. By averaging the balance sheet accounts, we are simulating a figure that covers the same period of time as the income statement. This makes the ratio more comparable and reliable.

We need to know the balance of stockholders' equity at December 28, 2013 to calculate the average stockholders' equity for 2014. Assume that the balance on this date was $407,358. The calculations of ROE for Dunkin' Donuts in 2014 and 2015 are shown in Figure 14.28.

	2015	2014
Net Income (Loss)	$105,227	$176,357
Average Stockholders' Equity[1]	$73,608	$387,659
Return on Equity	**1.43 or 143%**	**0.45 or 45%**
Industry Average	**40%**	**13%**

(1) Average Stockholders' Equity for 2014: ($407,358 + $367,959) ÷ 2 = $387,659
     Average Stockholders' Equity for 2015: ($367,959 + ($220,743)) ÷ 2 = $73,608

FIGURE 14.28

A high ROE is desirable because it means that investors made a good decision by investing in the company. Stockholders like to see a return that is as good or better than they could have received by investing elsewhere. A negative ROE indicates that stockholders actually lost money on their investments over the year. It also deters investors from investing more money at the risk of losing it. Dunkin' Donuts' return on equity has approximately tripled from 2014 to 2015, as has the industry average over that same time period. However, the higher return makes Dunkin' Donuts a more attractive investment.

Return on Assets

Return on assets (ROA) provides an assessment of what the company does with what it has; it measures every dollar earned against each dollar's worth of assets. A business invests in assets for the purpose of generating sales and making a profit. ROA is a measure of how effective the investment in assets is. Although assessing ROA depends on the type of business being analyzed, a higher ROA number is generally considered better than a lower one; it means the business is earning more money on its investment in assets. Figure 14.29 shows the equation to calculate ROA.

$$\text{Return on Assets (ROA)} = \frac{\text{Net Income}}{\text{Average Total Assets}}$$

FIGURE 14.29

Now calculate ROA for Dunkin' Donuts. The net income (loss) comes from the income statement. The total asset figures are found on the balance sheet. Assume that the balance of total assets at the year end in 2013 was $3,177,383. The calculation is shown in Figure 14.30.

	2015	**2014**
Net Income (Loss)	$105,227	$176,357
Average Total Assets[1]	$3,160,760	$3,150,892
Return on Assets	**0.03 or 3%**	**0.06 or 6%**
Industry Average	**7%**	**12%**

[1] Average Total Assets for 2014: ($3,124,400 + $3,177,383) ÷ 2 = $3,150,892
Average Total Assets for 2015: ($3,124,400 + $3,197,119) ÷ 2 = $3,160,760

FIGURE 14.30

There was a slight drop in the ROA in 2015. What the ROA means is that in 2014, Dunkin' Donuts gained $0.06 for every $1 invested in assets. In 2015, the company's returns dropped to $0.03 for every $1 invested in assets. Although in this case it is likely the effect of the impairment charge of $54,300 taken during 2015, there are various other factors that might explain such a drop in ROA. For example, selling noncurrent assets (which would result in a smaller denominator in the ROA formula), or an increase in costs of goods sold or other expenses. Note from the industry averages, however, that the industry appears to have experienced a similar drop from 2014 to 2015, so there could be industry-wide factors affecting the returns. Ultimately, if resources are properly allocated and assets are efficiently used, ROA should increase.

Asset Turnover

Another way to assess how well business assets are being utilized is to calculate the **asset turnover ratio**, which measures a company's ability to generate sales revenue from asset investments. This is calculated by dividing revenue by average total assets, as shown in Figure 14.31.

$$\text{Asset Turnover} = \frac{\text{Total Revenue}}{\text{Average Total Assets}}$$

FIGURE 14.31

Since this is a measurement of generating sales, the higher the number, the better. Figure 14.32 shows the asset turnover for Dunkin' Donuts.

	2015	**2014**
Total Revenue	$810,933	$748,709
Average Total Assets[1]	$3,160,760	3,150,892
Asset Turnover	**0.26 times**	**0.24 times**
Industry Average	**0.80 times**	**0.80 times**

[1] Average Total Assets for 2014: ($3,124,400 + $3,177,383) ÷ 2 = $3,150,892
Average Total Assets for 2015: ($3,197,119 + $3,124,400) ÷ 2 = $3,160,760

FIGURE 14.32

For 2015, an asset turnover of 0.26 means Dunkin' Donuts generated $0.26 of revenue for every dollar tied up in assets. This is a slight increase from the previous year. This indicates the business has become more efficient at generating revenue with its assets. Despite this improvement, Dunkin' Donuts did not perform as well as the industry overall. For both years, its asset turnover fell significantly below the $0.80 per dollar industry average.

IN THE REAL WORLD

 One of the most important assessments that owners of a business can make is to know if they are getting a decent return on their investment. How is this done and how do they know if they are getting their money's worth out of the business?

Any determination of return on investment revolves around stockholders' equity. In other words, how much cash would the owners have left if they sold all the assets of the business and paid off all their debt? Given that this is a hypothetical question, and that the owners do not have to sell everything to assess the return on investment, there are other ways of assessing the value of the investment in the business.

For example, the owners could ask themselves another theoretical question: Should we keep our money in the business, or put it elsewhere? Safe investments, such as fixed deposit accounts, come with relatively lower returns on investment. Investing in a friend's new business comes with a potentially much larger return on investment—but also with greater risk.

In fact, a general rule of thumb can be applied to assessing return on investment associated with certain levels of risk. Generally speaking, investments in publicly traded companies come with the expectation of a return ranging from 15%–25%. Alternatively, the rate of return associated with private companies is expected to be much higher. In fact, it is not unusual to expect a rate of return of 100% or more for an investment in a small private company.

As with most things in life, everything comes at a price. With return on investment, the price can be a matter of risk. If owners want a better return, they must have a greater tolerance for risk.

Operations Management Analysis

Operations management refers to the ability of a company to manage its assets, such as inventory and accounts receivable. Accounts receivable may be a large source of cash for a company, but it is not worth anything if it cannot be collected. As well, inventory is converted into cash by selling it, but it must be managed properly to ensure that it can actually be sold in a timely manner. To determine whether inventory is being managed properly, there are two ratios that can be calculated.

Inventory Turnover Ratio

Management is often concerned with the company's ability to sell, or "turn over," inventory. In industries that deal with food and beverage sales, it is especially important because of the short product life of the inventory. Throwing away expired products is just like throwing away cash. The inventory turnover ratio is calculated as shown in Figure 14.33.

$$\text{Inventory Turnover Ratio} = \frac{\text{Cost of Goods Sold}}{\text{Average Inventory}}$$

FIGURE 14.33

The **inventory turnover ratio** represents the number of times that the company sold its entire inventory. The industry the company is in determines the desirable value for this ratio. For example, hardware stores may only turn over their inventory once or twice per year because the goods do not expire or become obsolete very quickly. The fashion industry may turn over inventory four times per year because fashion trends tend to change quickly and with the seasons. Dunkin' Donuts' inventory turnover ratio is calculated in Figure 14.34. Assume that the inventory balance at December 28, 2013 was $21,409.

	2015	2014
Cost of Goods Sold	$76,877	$83,129
Average Inventory[(1)]	$27,883	$21,255
Inventory Turnover	**2.76 times**	**3.91 times**
Industry Average	**27.49 times**	**27.49 times**

(1)   Average Inventory for 2014: ($21,409 + $21,101) ÷ 2 = $21,255
       Average Inventory for 2015: ($21,101 + $34,664) ÷ 2 = $27,883

FIGURE 14.34

Dunkin' Donuts' very low inventory turnover ratio reflects Dunkin' Brands' accounting practices with regard to reporting inventories, and it also implies a departure from the overall conditions within the industry.

Days' Sales in Inventory

This ratio states the same thing as the inventory turnover ratio but in a different way. **Days' sales in inventory** is equal to the average number of days that it took to turn over inventory during the year. Some users prefer to use this ratio because they are familiar with working in units such as days and months. The formula is shown Figure 14.35.

$$\text{Days' Sales in Inventory} = \frac{365}{\text{Inventory Turnover Ratio}}$$

or

$$\text{Days' Sales in Inventory} = \frac{\text{Average Inventory}}{\text{Cost of Goods Sold}} \times 365$$

FIGURE 14.35

This ratio converts the number of times inventory is turned over into the average number of days it took to turn over inventory. For example, a company that sells its entire inventory twice a year would have an inventory turnover ratio of 2 and an inventory days on hand of 182.5 days. The ratio is calculated for Dunkin' Donuts in Figure 14.36.

	2015	2014
Average Inventory[1]	$27,883	$21,255
Cost of Goods Sold	$76,877	$83,129
Days in a Year	365	365
Days Sales in Inventory	**132.4 days**	**93.3 days**
Industry Average	**14.1 days**	**15.8 days**

(1) Average Inventory for 2014: ($21,409 + $21,101) ÷ 2 = $21,255
    Average Inventory for 2015: ($21,101 + $34,664) ÷ 2 = $27,883

FIGURE 14.36

The lower the result, the faster inventory is sold on average. However, as we saw with industry turnover, Dunkin' Donuts' very high days' sales in inventory for 2014 and 2015 reflect Dunkin' Brands' accounting practices with regard to reporting inventories, and it also implies a departure from the overall conditions within the industry.

Days' Sales Outstanding

Days' sales outstanding (DSO) measures the average number of days that a company takes to collect its receivables. The formula for DSO is shown in Figure 14.37.

$$\text{Days' Sales Outstanding (DSO)} = \frac{\text{Average Net Accounts Receivable}}{\text{Net Credit Sales}} \times 365$$

FIGURE 14.37

Dunkin' Donuts' accounts receivable is primarily comprised of franchise fees, royalty income and rental income owed from franchisees. From an external point of view, we do not know what portion of the total revenue of Dunkin' Donuts is cash versus credit. For our discussion, we will assume that all revenue is on credit except for rental income. The DSO provides an indication of how many days it takes for customers (in this case, franchisees) to pay their bills. This number is important because late payments can cost a business lost interest from cash deposits in a bank, or additional administration costs required to collect payments from customers.

The calculation of DSO for Dunkin' Donuts is shown in Figure 14.38. Assume that the accounts receivable balance at the year end in 2013 was $47,162.

	2015	2014
Average Accounts Receivable[1]	$54,525	$51,535
Net Credit Sales (Total Revenue)[2]	$710,511	$651,046
Number of Days in the Year	365	365
Days' Sales Outstanding	**28 days**	**29 days**
Industry Average	**55 days**	**57 days**

[1] Average Accounts Receivable for 2014: ($47,162 + $55,908) ÷ 2 = $51,535
Average Accounts Receivable for 2015: ($55,908 + $53,142) ÷ 2 = $54,525
[2] Net Credit Sales for 2014: $748,709 – $97,663 = $651,046
Net Credit Sales for 2015: $810,933 – $100,422 = $710,511

FIGURE 14.38

As you can see, the business is improving its ability to collect from customers. The DSO decreased slightly from 29 days in 2014, to 28 days in 2015. This is lower than, but keeping in line with the industry values. If the DSO increased, it might be an indication of disputes with customers, a slowdown in sales resulting in slower payments to the company, or problems in the billing and credit function of the company. None of these reasons would be considered favorably by owners, investors or analysts.

However, there are some cautionary notes to keep in mind related to the DSO. First, the revenue figure used in the ratio should exclude all cash sales, since only sales on account (credit sales) are of concern, relative to collecting customer payments. Second, outliers in sales data, such as sales to a major customer who was given a different credit policy from other customers, should be kept out of the total revenue figure used to calculate DSO, because they can skew the ratio.

Accounts Receivable Turnover

The **accounts receivable turnover ratio (ART)** is similar to DSO. It involves dividing a company's net credit sales by the average amount of accounts receivable. Figure 14.39 shows the formula to calculate accounts receivable turnover.

$$\text{Accounts Receivable Turnover (ART)} = \frac{\text{Net Credit Sales}}{\text{Average Net Accounts Receivable}}$$

FIGURE 14.39

The calculation for Dunkin' Donuts is shown in Figure 14.40.

	2015	2014
Net Credit Sales (Total Revenue)[1]	$710,511	$651,046
Average Accounts Receivable[2]	$54,525	$51,535
Accounts Receivable Turnover	**13.0 times**	**12.6 times**
Industry Average	**21.4 times**	**20.0 times**

[1] Net Credit Sales for 2014: $748,709 – $97,663 = $651,046
Net Credit Sales for 2015: $810,933 – $100,422 = $710,511
[2] Average Accounts Receivable for 2014: ($47,162 + $55,908) ÷ 2 = $51,535
Average Accounts Receivable for 2015: ($55,908 + $53,142) ÷ 2 = $54,525

FIGURE 14.40

Note that the *net credit sales* amount is not usually reported to external users of the financial statements; therefore, external users would simply use the *net sales* figure as the numerator in their ART calculations.

A higher ratio indicates a greater ability to convert accounts receivable into cash. If a business turns over its receivables 12 times per year, it is collecting the average balance of receivables every month. In Dunkin' Donuts' case, an accounts receivable turnover of 12.6 in 2014 means that it collected receivables once every 29 days on average. By 2015, Dunkin's ART had improved to 13.0 times, or nearly once every 28 days.

Leverage Analysis

There are two ways to finance a business: debt and equity. Debts are the liabilities of the business, such as notes payable and accounts payable. Equity is generated by selling stock and generating profits. **Leverage** relates to the amount of debt and risk the company has. Companies often take on debt to finance the purchase of large assets. It then uses these assets to expand operations and generate sales. However, there is usually a high cost of debt in the form of interest expense, which is where the risk comes in. The company must be able to increase profits by more than the interest expense to benefit the stockholders. One measure of leverage is the debt-to-equity ratio.

Debt-to-Equity Ratio

The **debt-to-equity ratio** is used to assess the balance of debt and equity in a business. The debt-to-equity ratio is calculated as shown in Figure 14.41.

$$\text{Debt-to-Equity Ratio} = \frac{\text{Total Liabilities}}{\text{Total Stockholders' Equity}}$$

FIGURE 14.41

It is not healthy for a business to borrow too much relative to what it is worth. This is because there is a cost of debt in the form of interest. The industry the business is in usually influences how much should be borrowed. For example, capital-intensive industries, such as auto manufacturers, have higher debt-to-equity ratios than software developers. The past two debt-to-

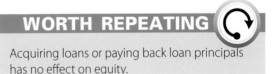

WORTH REPEATING

Acquiring loans or paying back loan principals has no effect on equity.

equity ratios for Dunkin' Donuts are calculated in Figure 14.42. The industry averages are also shown for comparison purposes.

	2015	2014
Total Liabilities	$3,417,862	$2,749,450
Stockholders' Equity	($220,743)	$367,959
Debt-to-Equity Ratio	**−15.5**	**7.5**
Industry Average	**0.06**	**0.85**

FIGURE 14.42

As you can see, the debt-to-equity ratio dropped drastically from 2014 to 2015. By the end of 2015, Dunkin' Donuts had a deficit in stockholders' equity, which significantly affected its D/E ratio. This is due to a deficit accumulated over a period of about four years as the company repurchased its common stock and subsequently retired blocks of its treasury stock. In fact, for 2015, Dunkin' Donuts was reported to have one of the lowest D/E ratios in the industry. Dunkin' Donut's 2014 D/E ratio of 7.5 is significantly higher than the industry average.

There are a few ways a business can improve the debt-to-equity ratio. The first, though not easy, way is making more profit, which directly increases stockholders' equity. Second, the business might consider issuing more stock in exchange for cash.

Figure 14.43 summarizes the formulas used to determine different valuations and indicates whether a higher or lower value is desirable for each ratio.

Ratio	Formula	Is a measure of
Liquidity		
Working Capital	Current Assets − Current Liabilities	Ability to cover current liabilities using current assets
Current Ratio	$\dfrac{\text{Current Assets}}{\text{Current Liabilities}}$	Ability to cover current liabilities using current assets
Quick Ratio	$\dfrac{\text{Cash + Short-Term Investments + Accounts Receivable}}{\text{Current Liabilities}}$	Ability of *highly liquid* assets to cover current liabilities
Profitability		
Gross Profit Margin	$\dfrac{\text{Gross Profit}}{\text{Net Sales}}$	Percentage of profit remaining after deducting cost of goods sold
Net Profit Margin	$\dfrac{\text{Net Income}}{\text{Total Revenue}}$	Percentage of profit remaining after deducting all expenses
Return on Equity	$\dfrac{\text{Net Income}}{\text{Average Stockholders' Equity}}$	Profitability of stockholders' investments
Return on Assets	$\dfrac{\text{Net Income}}{\text{Average Total Assets}}$	Effectiveness of the company's investment in assets
Asset Turnover	$\dfrac{\text{Total Sales}}{\text{Average Total Assets}}$	Ability to generate sales revenue from asset investments
Operations Management		
Inventory Turnover Ratio	$\dfrac{\text{Cost of Goods Sold}}{\text{Average Inventory}}$	Efficiency of inventory management
Days' Sales in Inventory	$\dfrac{\text{Average Inventory}}{\text{Cost of Goods Sold}} \times 365$	Average number of days to turn over inventory during the year
Days' Sales Outstanding	$\dfrac{\text{Average Net Accounts Receivable}}{\text{Net Credit Sales}} \times 365$	Average number of days to collect accounts receivable

Ratio	Formula	Is a measure of
Accounts Receivable Turnover Ratio	$$\dfrac{\text{Net Credit Sales}}{\text{Average Net Accounts Receivable}}$$	Efficiency of accounts receivable collections
Solvency		
Debt-to-Equity Ratio	$$\dfrac{\text{Total Liabilities}}{\text{Total Stockholder's Equity}}$$	Relative amount of debt vs stockholders' equity that is being used to finance a company's assets

FIGURE 14.43

The Statement of Cash Flows

Accountants are required to prepare balance sheets and income statements for the business. These important documents represent the state of company finances and adhere to accounting principles. As such, balance sheets and income statements are filled with promises of an exchange of money that must be recorded in one period, but may take place in another period. Company bills may not get paid for several months. Prepaid expenses can be left unadjusted for a number of periods. A borrower may default on a loan. Depreciation is recorded in the books, but there is no exchange of cash. Because of the way these transactions are accounted for on the balance sheet and income statement, it can be difficult to know where the cash is actually going within the business. As a result, the accounting profession created another financial statement to specifically indicate both the sources of cash and the uses of cash within an organization. This document is known as the statement of cash flows.

The statement of cash flows shows how net income is converted to cash, basically where the cash came from and how cash was used during the financial period. Remember, net income does not necessarily translate into cash in the bank. The way a business is structured—in terms of financing, debt collection, and so on—can have a significant impact on the way net income is turned into cash. It is this aspect of a business that the statement of cash flows reveals to users or readers, who may include management, accountants, potential lenders and investment analysts. Although a statement of cash flows can be of significant help to these financial players, its preparation is also required by GAAP. Knowing what it is and understanding what it presents are essential tasks for an accountant. The statement of cash flows for Dunkin' Donuts is presented in Figure 14.44. Cash inflows are shown as positive numbers and cash outflows are shown in parentheses. Rather than showing how to prepare this statement, this section will explain the three sources and uses of cash in a business in order to further analyze a company's financial information.

DUNKIN' BRANDS GROUP, INC. AND SUBSIDIARIES
Consolidated Statements of Cash Flows
(In thousands)

	Fiscal year ended	
	December 26, 2015	December 27, 2014
Cash flows from operating activities:		
Net income including noncontrolling interests	$ 105,229	175,563
Adjustments to reconcile net income to net cash provided by operating activities:		
Depreciation and amortization	45,244	45,539
Amortization of debt issuance costs and original issue discount	5,969	3,968
Loss on debt extinguishment and refinancing transactions	20,554	13,735
Deferred income taxes	(21,107)	(24,639)
Provision for bad debt	3,343	2,821
Share-based compensation expense	16,092	11,287
Net loss (income) of equity method investments	41,745	(14,846)
Dividends received from equity method investments	6,671	7,427
Gain on sale of joint venture	—	—
Gain on sale of real estate and company-operated restaurants	(1,402)	(7,458)
Other, net	1,083	570
Change in operating assets and liabilities:		
Restricted cash	(65,673)	—
Accounts, notes, and other receivables, net	(26,316)	(27,224)
Prepaid income taxes, net	591	(4,300)
Other current assets	(6,185)	552
Accounts payable	6,514	397
Other current liabilities	40,258	11,876
Liabilities of advertising funds, net	(1,124)	(2,785)
Deferred income	1,866	5,770
Other, net	12,214	1,070
Net cash provided by operating activities	185,566	199,323
Cash flows from investing activities:		
Additions to property and equipment	(30,246)	(23,638)
Proceeds from sale of real estate and company-operated restaurants	2,693	14,361
Proceeds from sale of joint venture, net	—	—
Other, net	(7,914)	(4,827)
Net cash used in investing activities	(35,467)	(14,104)
Cash flows from financing activities:		
Proceeds from issuance of long-term debt	2,500,000	—
Repayment of long-term debt	(1,837,824)	(15,000)
Payment of debt issuance and other debt-related costs	(41,350)	(9,213)
Repurchases of common stock, including accelerated share repurchases	(625,041)	(130,171)
Dividends paid on common stock	(100,516)	(96,775)
Change in restricted cash	(6,770)	—
Exercise of stock options	10,353	5,120
Excess tax benefits from share-based compensation	11,503	10,758
Other, net	(7,211)	1,924
Net cash used in financing activities	(96,856)	(233,357)
Effect of exchange rate changes on cash and cash equivalents	(893)	(715)
Increase (decrease) in cash and cash equivalents	52,350	(48,853)
Cash and cash equivalents, beginning of year	208,080	256,933
Cash and cash equivalents, end of year	$ 260,430	208,080

FIGURE 14.44

Three Sources and Uses of Cash

A business generates and consumes cash in three ways.

- operating activities
- investing activities
- financing activities

As you can see in Figure 14.44, the statement of cash flows is broken into these three sections. At this point, we are not concerned with the individual line items, only the purposes of each section.

Cash Flow from Operating Activities

Operating activities are those necessary to run the daily operations of the business. This section of the statement of cash flows tracks the movement of cash within a business on the basis of day-to-day activities. It is the most important section because the future of a business largely depends on the activities reported here. This section includes items such as the cash regularly received from revenues and collections of receivables throughout the year. It also includes items such as regular payments of cash for expenses, inventory and accounts payable.

Dunkin' Donuts has been able to generate positive cash flow from operating activities in both 2014 and 2015. This is a good sign because it means that the business does not rely on selling capital assets or stock to fund its daily operations.

Cash Flow from Investing Activities

Investing activities include any exchange of cash related to the long-term financial investments or capital assets of the business. Capital assets are noncurrent assets, such as vehicles, equipment, and land. Purchasing these assets can be thought of as the business investing in itself because they usually result in increased operations. For example, if a truck is purchased during the year, cash flow from investing activities decrease. Alternatively, if the business sells land, cash flow increases because the business receives cash in exchange for the land.

It is not necessarily a bad thing to have negative cash flow from investing activities. In fact, positive cash flow from investing activities can be a red flag, especially when cash flow from operations is negative. As shown in the investing activities section of the statement of cash flows, Dunkin' Donuts used a lot of cash to purchase new equipment over the past two years. This is a good sign because it shows that the company is investing in its future by upgrading its capital assets and/ or expanding into new markets.

Cash Flow from Financing Activities

Recall that both debt and equity are used to finance businesses. **Financing activities** are any payments or receipts of cash that relate to changes in either long-term debt or stockholders' equity. This section of the statement of cash flows tracks the movement of cash within a business based on the way a company receives money from those providing financing and pays it back. Companies pay back notes payable with interest to banks and they pay out cash dividends to stockholders. They also receive cash by selling stock and taking out notes payable.

A business that is focused on growth and expansion is likely to be raising money through financing activities such as selling stock or acquiring notes payable. In this case, it would have positive cash flow from financing activities. On the other hand, a well-established business may be attempting to pay back its notes payable and reward stockholders with dividend payments. Therefore it would have negative cash flow from financing activities. For example, Dunkin' Donuts has rolled over some long-term debt, repurchased common stock and paid dividends to its stockholders.

As you can see, there are no hard and fast rules to analyze cash flows. However, it is never a good sign to have consistently overall negative cash flows or to have a dangerously low balance of cash at any point in time. Companies can be quite profitable and have excellent financial ratios, but if they don't have any cash to pay their bills, they will soon be in big trouble. Companies can avoid certain financial issues by always remaining aware of their financial situation.

In Summary

LO 1 **Explain the stockholders' equity section of a corporation's balance sheet**

▶ Corporations use the term "stockholders' equity" instead of "owner's equity" to present the equity section of the balance sheet.

▶ The stockholders' equity category includes two sub-categories, capital stock and retained earnings.

▶ The two types of capital stock, which are preferred stock and common stock, are reported separately in the stockholders' equity section.

LO 2 **Explain the key items in a corporation's income statement**

▶ Unlike sole proprietorships, corporations tend to have multiple operating segments. When some segments are discontinued, the income (or loss) from discontinued operations is reported as a separate line item from the income (or loss) from continuing operations in a corporation's income statement.

▶ Other comprehensive income is reported either as a separate section in a corporation's income statement or in a stand-alone statement.

▶ Gains or losses from the change in value of some assets, such as investments or property, plant and equipment, are not considered to be a part of operating income, but are instead reported as other comprehensive income.

LO 3 **Prepare a horizontal and vertical analysis of financial statements**

▶ The comparative balance sheet is used to perform horizontal analysis because it compares information from one accounting period to another.

▶ One way of conducting horizontal analysis is by calculating the succeeding year's balance sheet items as a percentage of the base year's number.

▶ Another way of conducting horizontal analysis is by calculating the percentage change from a base year to show percentage increase or decrease of each balance sheet item over time.

▶ Vertical analysis is conducted by converting each separate line item in a financial statement into a percentage of the base figure within the specific year.

LO 4 **Assess a company's liquidity, profitability, operations management and leverage using financial ratios**

▶ Ratios measure different aspects of a company's financial situation. They are divided into four categories based on what they measure: liquidity, profitability, operations management and leverage.

▶ A company's liquidity can be assessed using working capital, current ratio and quick ratio.

- A company's profitability can be assessed using gross profit margin, net profit margin, return on equity (ROE), asset turnover and return on assets.
- A company's operations management can be assessed using inventory turnover, days' sales in inventory, accounts receivable turnover and days' sales outstanding.
- A company's leverage can be assessed using debt-to-equity ratio.

LO 5 Analyze the statement of cash flows by interpreting the three sources and uses of cash

- The statement of cash flows reports sources and uses of cash within an organization.
- Cash is generated and consumed by a business through three types of activities, including operating activities, investing activities and financing activities.
- Operating activities are those necessary to run the daily operations of the business.
- Investing activities include any exchange of cash related to the long-term financial investments or capital assets of the business.
- Financing activities are any payments or receipts of cash that relate to changes in either long-term debt or stockholders' equity.

AMEENGAGE™ *Access **ameengage.com** for integrated resources including tutorials, practice exercises, the digital textbook and more.*

Review Exercise 14-1

Use the financial statements for Basil's Bakery to perform a horizontal and vertical analysis and calculate the following financial ratios and figures for 2018.

- Working capital
- Current ratio
- Quick ratio
- Gross profit margin
- Net profit margin
- Return on equity
- Asset turnover
- Return on assets
- Inventory turnover ratio
- Days' sales in inventory
- Accounts receivable turnover ratio
- Days' sales outstanding
- Debt-to-equity ratio

After calculating the ratios, comment on the result for each ratio. In your explanation, state whether or not the result is good along with the possible reasoning behind that determination.

Basil's Bakery Balance Sheet As at December 31, 2018 and 2017		
	2018	**2017**
Assets		
Current Assets		
Cash	$1,605	$987
Accounts receivable	1,175	573
Inventory	396	256
Other current assets	301	103
Total Current Assets	3,477	1,919
Property, plant & equipment	2,034	1,170
Total Assets	$5,511	$3,089
Liabilities and Equity		
Liabilities		
Current liabilities	$1,474	$547
Noncurrent liabilities	104	58
Total Liabilities	1,578	605
Stockholders' Equity	3,933	2,484
Total Liabilities and Equity	$5,511	$3,089

*Note: the numbers in this financial statement is expressed in thousands of dollars.

Basil's Bakery Income Statement For the Year Ended December 31, 2018	
Sales Revenue	$6,009
Cost of goods sold	2,928
Gross Profit	3,081
Operating Expenses	
Depreciation	108
Interest	518
Other operating expenses	723
Total Operating Expenses	1,349
Income from Operations	1,732
Investment income	79
Operating Income Before Tax	1,811
Income tax	516
Net Income	$1,295

*Note: the numbers in this financial statement is expressed in thousands of dollars.

In addition to the financial statements above, the following data is known. The bakery industry average for gross profit margin is 49.47% for 2018, and the industry average for net profit margin is 20.36% of the same time period.

In 2017, Basil's Bakery had a gross profit margin of 52.13% and a net profit margin of 21.95%.

Basil's Bakery				
Balance Sheet				
As at December 31, 2018				
	2018	**2017**	**% Change**	**% of Base Figure 2018**
Cash	$1,650	$987		
Accounts Receivable	1,175	573		
Inventory	396	256		
Other Current Assets	301	103		
Total Current Assets	3,522	1,919		
Property, Plant & Equipment	2,034	1,170		
Total Assets	$5,556	$3,089		
Current Liabilities	$1,474	$547		
Noncurrent liabilities	104	58		
Total Liabilities	1,578	605		
Stockholders' Equity	3,978	2,484		
Total Liabilities and Equity	$5,556	$3,089		

_____

_____

_____

_____

_____

Financial Ratio or Figure	Calculation	Result
Working Capital		
Current Ratio		
Quick Ratio		
Gross Profit Margin		
Net Profit Margin		
Return on Equity		
Asset Turnover		
Return on Assets		
Inventory Turnover Ratio		
Days' Sales in Inventory		
Accounts Receivable Turnover		
Days' Sales Outstanding		
Debt-to-Equity Ratio		

See Appendix I for solutions.

Review Exercise 14-2

Using one or two sentences each, name and describe the three sources and uses of cash based on the statement of cash flows.

_____

_____

_____

_____

_____

_____

_____

_____

_____

_____

_____

_____

_____

_____

_____

_____

_____

See Appendix I for solutions.

Notes

Appendix I

CHAPTER 1 SOLUTIONS

Pause & Reflect Exercise 1-1

a), b) and c)

	Assets	=	Liabilities	+	Net Worth
Beginning Balances	$1,500	=	$300	+	$1,200
1. Paid $100 toward credit card balance	−100		−100		
2. Paid $25 for a meal using cash	−25				−25
3. Deposited $300 in wages	+300			+	+300
Ending Balances	$1,675	=	$200	+	$1,475

d) Closing Balance of Cash = $200 − $100 − $25 + $300 = $375

Review Exercise 1-1

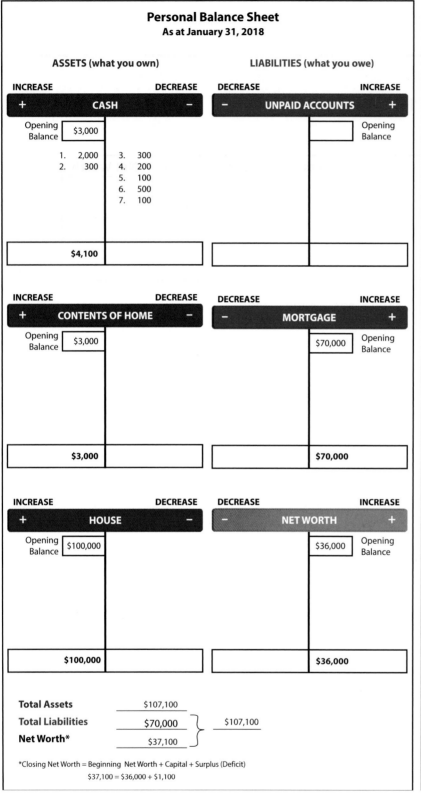

Personal Balance Sheet
As at January 31, 2018

ASSETS (what you own)

INCREASE		DECREASE
+	**CASH**	**−**

Opening Balance | $3,000

		3.	300
1.	2,000	4.	200
2.	300	5.	100
		6.	500
		7.	100

| $4,100 | |

INCREASE		DECREASE
+	**CONTENTS OF HOME**	**−**

Opening Balance | $3,000

| $3,000 | |

INCREASE		DECREASE
+	**HOUSE**	**−**

Opening Balance | $100,000

| $100,000 | |

LIABILITIES (what you owe)

DECREASE		INCREASE
−	**UNPAID ACCOUNTS**	**+**

| | Opening Balance |

| | |

DECREASE		INCREASE
−	**MORTGAGE**	**+**

| | $70,000 | Opening Balance |

| | $70,000 |

DECREASE		INCREASE
−	**NET WORTH**	**+**

| | $36,000 | Opening Balance |

| | $36,000 |

Total Assets	$107,100	
Total Liabilities	$70,000	} $107,100
Net Worth*	$37,100	

*Closing Net Worth = Beginning Net Worth + Capital + Surplus (Deficit)
$37,100 = $36,000 + $1,100

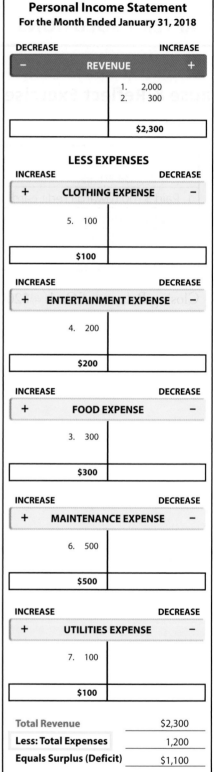

Personal Income Statement
For the Month Ended January 31, 2018

DECREASE		INCREASE
−	**REVENUE**	**+**

| 1. | 2,000 |
| 2. | 300 |

| $2,300 | |

LESS EXPENSES

INCREASE		DECREASE
+	**CLOTHING EXPENSE**	**−**

| 5. | 100 |

| $100 | |

INCREASE		DECREASE
+	**ENTERTAINMENT EXPENSE**	**−**

| 4. | 200 |

| $200 | |

INCREASE		DECREASE
+	**FOOD EXPENSE**	**−**

| 3. | 300 |

| $300 | |

INCREASE		DECREASE
+	**MAINTENANCE EXPENSE**	**−**

| 6. | 500 |

| $500 | |

INCREASE		DECREASE
+	**UTILITIES EXPENSE**	**−**

| 7. | 100 |

| $100 | |

Total Revenue	$2,300
Less: Total Expenses	1,200
Equals Surplus (Deficit)	$1,100

CHAPTER 2 SOLUTIONS

Pause & Reflect Exercise 2-1

	Name of the Account Affected	Category of Account	Increase or Decrease
2.	Cash	Asset	Increase
	Service Revenue	Revenue	Increase
3.	Cash	Asset	Increase
	Unearned Revenue	Liability	Increase

Pause & Reflect Exercise 2-2

	Name of the Account Affected	Category of Account	Increase or Decrease
2.	Telephone Expense	Expense	Increase
	Accounts Payable	Liability	Increase
3.	Prepaid Insurance	Asset	Increase
	Cash	Asset	Decrease

Pause & Reflect Exercise 2-3

	Name of the Account Affected	Category of Account	Increase or Decrease
2.	Cash	Asset	Increase
	Graham, Capital	Owner's Capital	Increase
3.	Furniture (Property, Plant and Equipment)	Asset	Increase
	Accounts Payable	Liability	Increase
4.	Cash	Asset	Increase
	Notes Payable	Liability	Increase
5.	Graham, Withdrawals	Owner's Withdrawal	Increase
	Cash	Asset	Decrease

Review Exercise 2-1

a)

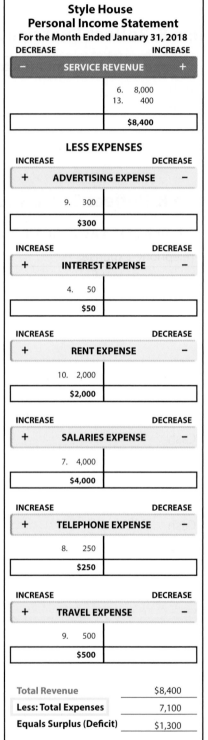

Style House
Balance Sheet
As at January 31, 2018

ASSETS (what you own)

INCREASE		DECREASE
+	**CASH**	**–**

Opening Balance	$3,000	2.	8,000
		3.	333
1.	12,000	4.	50
6.	8,000	5.	600
14.	100	7.	4,000
		10.	2,000
		11.	1,000
		12.	3,000

| $4,117 | |

INCREASE		DECREASE
+	**ACCOUNTS RECEIVABLE**	**–**

| Opening Balance | |
| 13. | 400 |

| $400 | |

INCREASE		DECREASE
+	**PREPAID MAINTENANCE**	**–**

| Opening Balance | |
| 5. | 600 |

| $600 | |

INCREASE		DECREASE
+	**EQUIPMENT**	**–**

| Opening Balance | $12,000 |
| 2. | 8,000 |

| $20,000 | |

Total Assets	$25,117
Total Liabilities	16,817 } $25,117
Owner's Equity*	8,300

*Ending Owner's Equity Balance = Begining Owner's Equity Balance + Owner's Contributions + Net Income (Loss) - Owner's Withdrawals
$8,300 = $10,000 + $0 + $1,300 - $3,000

LIABILITIES (what you owe)

DECREASE		INCREASE
–	**ACCOUNTS PAYBLE**	**+**

	$5,000	Opening Balance
11.	1,000	8.	250
		9.	800

| | $5,050 |

DECREASE		INCREASE
–	**UNEARNED REVENUE**	**+**

| | | Opening Balance |
| | 14. | 100 |

| | $100 |

DECREASE		INCREASE
–	**NOTES PAYABLE**	**+**

| | | Opening Balance |
| 3. | 333 | 1. | 12,000 |

| | $11,667 |

DECREASE		INCREASE
–	**JONES, CAPITAL**	**+**

| | $10,000 | Opening Balance |

| | $10,000 |

DECREASE		INCREASE
–	**JONES, WITHDRAWALS**	**+**

| 12. | 3,000 | |

| $3,000 | |

Style House
Personal Income Statement
For the Month Ended January 31, 2018

DECREASE		INCREASE
–	**SERVICE REVENUE**	**+**

| | 6. | 8,000 |
| | 13. | 400 |

| $8,400 |

LESS EXPENSES

INCREASE		DECREASE
+	**ADVERTISING EXPENSE**	**–**

| 9. | 300 |

| $300 | |

INCREASE		DECREASE
+	**INTEREST EXPENSE**	**–**

| 4. | 50 |

| $50 | |

INCREASE		DECREASE
+	**RENT EXPENSE**	**–**

| 10. | 2,000 |

| $2,000 | |

INCREASE		DECREASE
+	**SALARIES EXPENSE**	**–**

| 7. | 4,000 |

| $4,000 | |

INCREASE		DECREASE
+	**TELEPHONE EXPENSE**	**–**

| 8. | 250 |

| $250 | |

INCREASE		DECREASE
+	**TRAVEL EXPENSE**	**–**

| 9. | 500 |

| $500 | |

Total Revenue	$8,400
Less: Total Expenses	7,100
Equals Surplus (Deficit)	$1,300

b)

Style House Income Statement For the Month Ended March 31, 2018		
Revenue		
Service Revenue		$8,400
Expenses		
Advertising Expense	$300	
Interest Expense	50	
Rent Expense	2,000	
Salaries Expense	4,000	
Telephone Expense	250	
Travel Expense	500	
Total Expenses		7,100
Net Income		$1,300

c)

Style House Statement of Owner's Equity For the Month Ended March 31, 2018	
Jones, Capital, March 1, 2018	$10,000
Add: Net Income	1,300
Less: Withdrawals	3,000
Jones, Capital, March 31, 2018	$8,300

d)

Style House Balance Sheet As at March 31, 2018			
Assets		**Liabilities**	
Cash	$4,117	Accounts Payable	$5,050
Accounts Receivable	400	Unearned Revenue	100
Prepaid Maintenance	600	Notes Payable	11,667
Equipment	20,000	**Total Liabilities**	16,817
		Owner's Equity	
		Jones, Capital	8,300
Total Assets	$25,117	**Total Liabilities and Owner's Equity**	$25,117

e)

Transaction	Cash Flow Section
Borrowed $12,000 from the bank	Financing
Purchased chairs and dryers with $8,000 cash	Investing
Paid $333 cash toward the principal of the bank loan	Financing
Paid $50 cash for interest on the bank loan	Operating
Prepaid $600 cash for a six-month maintenance contract	Operating
Provided services to customers and received $8,000	Operating
Paid $4,000 cash to employees for salaries	Operating
Paid monthly rent with $2,000 cash	Operating
Paid $1,000 owing to a supplier	Operating
Miranda withdrew $3,000 cash from the business	Financing

CHAPTER 3 SOLUTIONS

Pause and Reflect Exercise 3-1

Description	Terminology	Characteristic, Assumption, Principle or Constraint
2. A company is believed to stay in business for the foreseeable future and not go bankrupt any time soon.	Going concern	Assumption
3. Revenue must be recorded or recognized when goods are sold or when services are performed.	Revenue recognition	Principle
4. The financial statements of a company must be prepared in a similar way year after year.	Comparability	Characteristic
5. Information is free from significant error and bias.	Reliability	Characteristic
6. The value of reported financial information outweighs the costs incurred to report it.	Cost constraint	Constraint
7. An expense must be recorded in the same accounting period in which it was used to produce revenue.	Expense recognition	Principle
8. Accounting records are expressed in a single currency, such as US dollars.	Monetary unit	Assumption

Review Exercise 3-1

a) HRI has failed to apply three qualitative characteristics.

Relevance

- A particular piece of information is relevant if its omission may cause the users of the financial information to make decisions differently. In the financial statements, the company did not disclose that two different currencies were used in the comparative balance sheet (one for 2018 and another for 2017). This omission can potentially affect users' (investors') decisions.

- A component of relevance is timeliness. HRI only prepares financial statements on an annual basis. However, the company's hundreds of stockholders would benefit from more timely financial statements (e.g. quarterly or monthly).

Reliability

- A component of reliability is verifiability. Since several invoices did not match the cost amounts listed in HRI's accounting records, the reported costs are not verifiable. Therefore, the amount of total expenses in the company's income statement is not a reliable number.

Comparability

- Even though the company provided balance sheet amounts from the previous year, two different currencies are used from one year to the next. Because one currency is stronger than the other, it is not straightforward to compare the financial information of HRI through time.

b) HRI has violated the following assumptions and principles.

The Business Entity Assumption

- The HRI cash account includes the personal savings of some of the stockholders. This indicates that the accounting for the business was not kept separate from the personal affairs of the owners.

The Monetary Unit Assumption

- HRI has included values in two different currencies on its financial statements.

Measurement

- Except in rare cases, which will be discussed in later chapters, assets must be recorded at their historical cost. However, HRI has valued its purchases at fair market value.

Disclosure

- HRI did not disclose the justification for changing the depreciation method.

- HRI did not disclose the information related to changing the location of the headquarters and the inconsistent measures of currency.

The Going Concern Assumption *(requires critical thinking)*

- There is evidence that the company may not exist and operate in the foreseeable future.

  o HRI has experienced a significant net loss for each of the past three years (even before adjusting for the unverified expense amounts).
  o The cash and merchandise inventory balances are extremely low in 2018.

- o The company's property, plant and equipment balance in 2018 declined significantly from 2017 (even after adjusting for exchange rates). It is possible some of these assets were sold during 2018.
- o The above examples of HRI's poor financial performance occurred during a time when the economy was booming. HRI's performance is normally aligned with the state of economy. This discrepancy should cause stockholders to question the going concern assumption with respect to HRI.

CHAPTER 4 SOLUTIONS

Pause & Reflect Exercise 4-1

	Name of the Account Affected	Category	Increase or Decrease	Debit or Credit
1.	Cash	Asset	Increase	Debit
	Lee, Capital	Owner's Capital	Increase	Credit
2.	Cash	Asset	Increase	Debit
	Service Revenue	Revenue	Increase	Credit
3.	Furniture (Property, Plant and Equipment)	Asset	Increase	Debit
	Accounts Payable	Liability	Increase	Credit
4.	Accounts Receivable	Asset	Increase	Debit
	Service Revenue	Revenue	Increase	Credit
5.	Advertising Expense	Expense	Increase	Debit
	Cash	Asset	Decrease	Credit
6.	Prepaid Rent	Asset	Increase	Debit
	Cash	Asset	Decrease	Credit

Pause & Reflect Exercise 4-2

JOURNAL				Page 1
Date	Account Title and Explanation	PR	Debit	Credit
2018				
Apr 18	Cash		600	
	Accounts Receivable		400	
	Service Revenue			1,000
	Completed work for client			

Pause & Reflect Exercise 4-3

JOURNAL				Page 2
Date	Account Title and Explanation	PR	Debit	Credit
2018				
Sep 28	Cash		5,000	
	Interest Expense			5,000
	To reverse incorrect entry			
Sep 28	Notes Payable		5,000	
	Cash			5,000
	To correctly record bank loan principal repayment			

Review Exercise 4-1

a)

JOURNAL				Page 1
Date	Account Title and Explanation	PR	Debit	Credit
2018				
Jun 1	Rent Expense	540	900	
	Cash	101		900
	Paid cash for month's rent			
Jun 3	Prepaid Insurance	110	1,200	
	Cash	101		1,200
	Prepaid a one-year insurance policy			
Jun 6	Cash	101	2,100	
	Service Revenue	400		2,100
	Received cash for services			
Jun 11	Advertising Expense	500	450	
	Accounts Payable	200		450
	Received invoice for advertising			
Jun 13	Cash	101	3,000	
	Gordon, Capital	300		3,000
	Owner invested cash in business			
Jun 16	Cash	101	300	
	Unearned Revenue	210		300
	Received deposit from customer			

JOURNAL				Page 1
Date	**Account Title and Explanation**	**PR**	**Debit**	**Credit**
Jun 18	Accounts Receivable	105	1,500	
	Service Revenue	400		1,500
	Provided services on account			
Jun 23	Notes Payable	215	950	
	Cash	101		950
	Paid notes payable principal			
Jun 30	Gordon, Withdrawals	310	1,000	
	Cash	101		1,000
	Owner withdrawal for personal use			

b)

GENERAL LEDGER

Account: Cash — GL No: 101

Date	Description	PR	DR	CR	Balance	
2018						
Jun 1	Opening Balance				4,200	DR
Jun 1		J1		900	3,300	DR
Jun 3		J1		1,200	2,100	DR
Jun 6		J1	2,100		4,200	DR
Jun 13		J1	3,000		7,200	DR
Jun 16		J1	300		7,500	DR
Jun 23		J1		950	6,550	DR
Jun 30		J1		1,000	5,550	DR

Account: Accounts Receivable — GL No: 105

Date	Description	PR	DR	CR	Balance	
2018						
Jun 1	Opening Balance				3,100	DR
Jun 18		J1	1,500		4,600	DR

Account: Prepaid Insurance — GL No: 110

Date	Description	PR	DR	CR	Balance	
2018						
Jun 1	Opening Balance				0	DR
Jun 3		J1	1,200		1,200	DR

Account: Equipment — GL No: 120

Date	Description	PR	DR	CR	Balance	
2018						
Jun 1	Opening Balance				6,000	DR

Account: Accounts Payable — GL No: 200

Date	Description	PR	DR	CR	Balance	
2018						
Jun 1	Opening Balance				2,300	CR
Jun 11		J1		450	2,750	CR

Account: Unearned Revenue — GL No: 210

Date	Description	PR	DR	CR	Balance	
2018						
Jun 1	Opening Balance				600	CR
Jun 16		J1		300	900	CR

Account: Notes Payable — GL No: 215

Date	Description	PR	DR	CR	Balance	
2018						
Jun 1	Opening Balance				4,000	CR
Jun 23		J1	950		3,050	CR

Account: Gordon, Capital — GL No: 300

Date	Description	PR	DR	CR	Balance	
2018						
Jun 1	Opening Balance				6,400	CR
Jun 13		J1		3,000	9,400	CR

Account: Gordon, Withdrawals — GL No: 310

Date	Description	PR	DR	CR	Balance	
2018						
Jun 30		J1	1,000		1,000	DR

Account: Service Revenue — GL No: 400

Date	Description	PR	DR	CR	Balance	
2018						
Jun 6		J1		2,100	2,100	CR
Jun 18		J1		1,500	3,600	CR

Account: Advertising Expense — GL No: 500

Date	Description	PR	DR	CR	Balance	
2018						
Jun 11		J1	450		450	DR

Account: Rent Expense — GL No: 540

Date	Description	PR	DR	CR	Balance	
2018						
Jun 1		J1	900		900	DR

c)

CG Accounting		
Trial Balance		
June 30, 2018		
Account Title	**DR**	**CR**
Cash	$5,550	
Accounts Receivable	4,600	
Prepaid Insurance	1,200	
Equipment	6,000	
Accounts Payable		$2,750
Unearned Revenue		900
Notes Payable		3,050
Gordon, Capital		9,400
Gordon, Withdrawals	1,000	
Service Revenue		3,600
Advertising Expense	450	
Rent Expense	900	
Total	**$19,700**	**$19,700**

Review Exercise 4-2

JOURNAL				Page 2
Date	**Account Title and Explanation**	**PR**	**Debit**	**Credit**
2018				
Jun 28	Cash		400	
	Automobile			400
	To reverse incorrect entry			
Jun 28	Maintenance Expense		400	
	Cash			400
	To correctly pay for automobile maintenance			
Jun 28	Cash		200	
	Equipment			200
	To reverse incorrect entry			
Jun 28	Office Supplies		200	
	Cash			200
	To correctly pay for office supplies			

CHAPTER 5 SOLUTIONS

Pause & Reflect Exercise 5-1

JOURNAL				Page 2
Date	Account Title and Explanation	PR	Debit	Credit
2018				
Dec 31	Accounts Receivable		480	
	Service Revenue			480
	To accrue revenue on contract			
	(8 days × $60 per day)			
2019				
Jan 2	Cash		600	
	Accounts Receivable			480
	Service Revenue			120
	To record collection from client			

Pause & Reflect Exercise 5-2

JOURNAL				Page 1
Date	Account Title and Explanation	PR	Debit	Credit
2018				
Jan 31	Salaries Expense		330	
	Salaries Payable			330
	To accrue salaries owing			
	(3 days × $110 per day)			
Jan 31	Interest Expense		40	
	Interest Payable			40
	To accrue interest owing			
	($8,000 × 6% × 1/12)			

Pause & Reflect Exercise 5-3

Armadillo Property Management's Journal Entries

JOURNAL				Page 1
Date	Account Title and Explanation	PR	Debit	Credit
2018				
Aug 1	Cash		36,000	
	Unearned Revenue			36,000
	Receive cash for 12 months' rent			
Dec 31	Unearned Revenue		15,000	
	Rent Revenue			15,000
	To adjust for 5 months rent earned			
	($3,000 per month × 5 months)			

Beaver Company's Journal Entries

JOURNAL					Page 1
Date	Account Title and Explanation	PR	Debit	Credit
2018				
Aug 1	Prepaid Rent		36,000	
	Cash			36,000
	Pay cash for 12 months rent			
Dec 31	Rent Expense		15,000	
	Prepaid Rent			15,000
	To adjust for 5 months rent used			

Pause & Reflect Exercise 5-4

JOURNAL					Page 2
Date	Account Title and Explanation	PR	Debit	Credit
2018				
Dec 31	Depreciation Expense		2,000	
	Accumulated Depreciation—Equipment			2,000
	To adjust for depreciation			
	[($20,000 − $4,000) ÷ 8 years]			

Review Exercise 5-1

a)

CG Accounting Spreadsheet June 30, 2018						
	Unadjusted Trial Balance		Adjustments		Adjusted Trial Balance	
Account Titles	DR	CR	DR	CR	DR	CR
Cash	$5,550				$5,550	
Accounts Receivable	4,600		$900		5,500	
Prepaid Insurance	1,200			$100	1,100	
Equipment	6,000				6,000	
Accumulated Depreciation—Equipment		$0		100		$100
Accounts Payable		2,750				2,750
Interest Payable		0		25		25
Unearned Revenue		900	450			450
Notes Payable		3,050				3,050
Gordon, Capital		9,400				9,400
Gordon, Withdrawals	1,000				1,000	
Service Revenue		3,600		1,350		4,950
Advertising Expense	450				450	
Depreciation Expense	0		100		100	
Insurance Expense	0		100		100	
Interest Expense	0		25		25	
Rent Expense	900				900	
Total	$19,700	$19,700	$1,575	$1,575	$20,725	$20,725

b)

JOURNAL				Page 2	
Date	Account Title and Explanation	PR	Debit	Credit	
2018					
Jun 30	Insurance Expense	515	100		
	Prepaid Insurance	110		100	
	Recognized one month of insurance used				
Jun 30	Unearned Revenue	210	450		
	Service Revenue	400		450	
	Recognized revenue previously unearned				
Jun 30	Interest Expense	520	25		
	Interest Payable	205		25	
	Accrued interest on notes payable				
Jun 30	Depreciation Expense	510	100		
	Accumulated Depreciation—Equipment	125		100	
	Recorded depreciation of equipment				
Jun 30	Accounts Receivable	105	900		
	Service Revenue	400		900	
	Record accrued revenue				

c)

GENERAL LEDGER

Account: Cash				GL No:		101
Date	Description	PR	DR	CR	Balance	
2018						
Jun 1	Opening Balance				4,200	DR
Jun 1		J1		900	3,300	DR
Jun 3		J1		1,200	2,100	DR
Jun 6		J1	2,100		4,200	DR
Jun 13		J1	3,000		7,200	DR
Jun 16		J1	300		7,500	DR
Jun 23		J1		950	6,550	DR
Jun 30		J1		1,000	5,550	DR

Account: Accounts Receivable					GL No:	105
Date	Description	PR	DR	CR	Balance	
2018						
Jun 1	Opening Balance				3,100	DR
Jun 18		J1	1,500		4,600	DR
Jun 30	Adjusting Entry	J2	900		5,500	DR

Account: Prepaid Insurance					GL No:	110
Date	Description	PR	DR	CR	Balance	
2018						
Jun 1	Opening Balance				0	DR
Jun 3		J1	1,200		1,200	DR
Jun 30	Adjusting Entry	J2		100	1,100	DR

Account: Equipment					GL No:	120
Date	Description	PR	DR	CR	Balance	
2018						
Jun 1	Opening Balance				6,000	DR

Account: Accumulated Depreciation—Equipment					GL No:	125
Date	Description	PR	DR	CR	Balance	
2018						
Jun 30	Adjusting Entry	J2		100	100	CR

Account: Accounts Payable					GL No:	200
Date	Description	PR	DR	CR	Balance	
2018						
Jun 1	Opening Balance				2,300	CR
Jun 11		J1		450	2,750	CR

Account: Interest Payable					GL No:	205
Date	Description	PR	DR	CR	Balance	
2018						
Jun 30	Adjusting Entry	J2		25	25	CR

Account: Unearned Revenue					GL No:	210
Date	Description	PR	DR	CR	Balance	
2018						
Jun 1	Opening Balance				600	CR
Jun 16		J1		300	900	CR
Jun 30	Adjusting Entry	J2	450		450	CR

Account: Notes Payable — GL No: 215

Date	Description	PR	DR	CR	Balance	
2018						
Jun 1	Opening Balance				4,000	CR
Jun 23		J1	950		3,050	CR

Account: Gordon, Capital — GL No: 300

Date	Description	PR	DR	CR	Balance	
2018						
Jun 1	Opening Balance				6,400	CR
Jun 13		J1		3,000	9,400	CR

Account: Gordon, Withdrawals — GL No: 310

Date	Description	PR	DR	CR	Balance	
2018						
Jun 30		J1	1,000		1,000	DR

Account: Service Revenue — GL No: 400

Date	Description	PR	DR	CR	Balance	
2018						
Jun 6		J1		2,100	2,100	CR
Jun 18		J1		1,500	3,600	CR
Jun 30	Adjusting Entry	J2		450	4,050	CR
Jun 30	Adjusting Enry	J2		900	4,950	CR

Account: Advertising Expense — GL No: 500

Date	Description	PR	DR	CR	Balance	
2018						
Jun 11		J1	450		450	DR

Account: Depreciation Expense — GL No: 510

Date	Description	PR	DR	CR	Balance	
2018						
Jun 30	Adjusting Entry	J2	100		100	DR

Account: Insurance Expense — GL No: 515

Date	Description	PR	DR	CR	Balance	
2018						
Jun 30	Adjusting Entry	J2	100		100	DR

Account: Interest Expense					GL No:	520
Date	Description	PR	DR	CR	Balance	
2018						
Jun 30	Adjusting Entry	J2	25		25	DR

Account: Rent Expense					GL No:	540
Date	Description	PR	DR	CR	Balance	
2018						
Jun 1		J1	900		900	DR

CHAPTER 6 SOLUTIONS

Pause & Reflect Exercise 6-1

JOURNAL				Page 5
Date	Account Title and Explanation	PR	Debit	Credit
2018				
Aug 31	Service Revenue		9,400	
	Income Summary			9,400
	Close revenue accounts			
Aug 31	Income Summary		4,990	
	Depreciation Expense			290
	Insurance Expense			260
	Interest Expense			70
	Rent Expense			1,870
	Salaries Expense			2,250
	Telephone Expense			250
	Close expense accounts			
Aug 31	Income Summary		4,410	
	ZooTak, Capital			4,410
	Close income summary account			
Aug 31	ZooTak, Capital		3,050	
	ZooTak, Withdrawals			3,050
	Close owner's withdrawals			

Pause & Reflect Exercise 6-2

Working Capital	($120,000 + $90,000 + $65,000) – ($101,000 + $80,000) = $94,000
Current Ratio	($120,000 + $90,000 + $65,000) ÷ ($101,000 + $80,000) = 1.52
Quick Ratio	($120,000 + $90,000) ÷ ($101,000 + $80,000) = 1.16

Pause & Reflect Exercise 6-3

a) Both systems have special sections or journals to enter similar types of transactions. They both have a general journal for adjusting entries and other specific types of transactions. Some differences are that entries for computerized accounting systems do not have to be entered in chronological order.

b) One benefit of a computerized accounting system is that it automatically orders transactions chronologically, so they can be entered in any order. Another benefit is posting to the general ledger, preparing reports, and preparing journal entries are all done automatically.

Review Exercise 6-1

a)

CG Accounting Income Statement For the Month Ended June 30, 2018		
Service Revenue		$4,950
Expenses		
Advertising Expense	$450	
Depreciation Expense	100	
Insurance Expense	100	
Interest Expense	25	
Rent Expense	900	
Total Expenses		1,575
Net Income (Loss)		$3,375

CG Accounting Statement of Owner's Equity For the Month Ended June 30, 2018		
Gordon, Capital at June 1		$6,400
Add:		
Additional Investment	$3,000	
Net Income	3,375	6,375
Subtotal		12,775
Less:		
Gordon, Withdrawals		1,000
Gordon, Capital at June 30		$11,775

CG Accounting Classified Balance Sheet As at June 30, 2018		
Assets		
Current Assets		
Cash	$5,550	
Accounts Receivable	5,500	
Prepaid Insurance	1,100	
Total Current Assets		$12,150
Property, Plant & Equipment		
Equipment	6,000	
Accumulated Depreciation	(100)	
Total Property, Plant & Equipment		5,900
Total Assets		$18,050
Liabilities		
Current Liabilities		
Accounts Payable	$2,750	
Interest Payable	25	
Unearned Revenue	450	
Notes Payable, Current Portion	800	
Total Current Liabilities		$4,025
Noncurrent Liabilities		
Notes Payable, Noncurrent Portion	2,250	
Total Noncurrent Liabilities		2,250
Total Liabilities		6,275
Owner's Equity		
Gordon, Capital		11,775
Total Owner's Equity		11,775
Total Liabilities and Owner's Equity		$18,050

b)

JOURNAL					Page 3
Date	Account Title and Explanation	PR	Debit		Credit
2018					
Jun 30	Service Revenue	400	4,950		
	Income Summary	315			4,950
	Close revenue to income summary				
Jun 30	Income Summary	315	1,575		
	Advertising Expense	500			450
	Depreciation Expense	510			100
	Insurance Expense	515			100
	Interest Expense	520			25
	Rent Expense	540			900
	Close expenses to income summary				
Jun 30	Income Summary	315	3,375		
	Gordon, Capital	300			3,375
	Close income summary to capital				
Jun 30	Gordon, Capital	300	1,000		
	Gordon, Withdrawals	310			1,000
	Close owner withdrawals to capital				

GENERAL LEDGER

Account: Cash					GL No:	101
Date	Description	PR	DR	CR	Balance	
2018						
Jun 1	Opening Balance				4,200	DR
Jun 1		J1		900	3,300	DR
Jun 3		J1		1,200	2,100	DR
Jun 6		J1	2,100		4,200	DR
Jun 13		J1	3,000		7,200	DR
Jun 16		J1	300		7,500	DR
Jun 23		J1		950	6,550	DR
Jun 30		J1		1,000	5,550	DR

Account: Accounts Receivable — GL No: 105

Date	Description	PR	DR	CR	Balance	
2018						
Jun 1	Opening Balance				3,100	DR
Jun 18		J1	1,500		4,600	DR
Jun 30	Adjusting Entry	J2	900		5,500	DR

Account: Prepaid Insurance — GL No: 110

Date	Description	PR	DR	CR	Balance	
2018						
Jun 1	Opening Balance				0	DR
Jun 3		J1	1,200		1,200	DR
Jun 30	Adjusting Entry	J2		100	1,100	DR

Account: Equipment — GL No: 120

Date	Description	PR	DR	CR	Balance	
2018						
Jun 1	Opening Balance				6,000	DR

Account: Accumulated Depreciation—Equipment — GL No: 125

Date	Description	PR	DR	CR	Balance	
2018						
Jun 30	Adjusting Entry	J2		100	100	CR

Account: Accounts Payable — GL No: 200

Date	Description	PR	DR	CR	Balance	
2018						
Jun 1	Opening Balance				2,300	CR
Jun 11		J1		450	2,750	CR

Account: Interest Payable — GL No: 205

Date	Description	PR	DR	CR	Balance	
2018						
Jun 30	Adjusting Entry	J2		25	25	CR

Account: Unearned Revenue — GL No: 210

Date	Description	PR	DR	CR	Balance	
2018						
Jun 1	Opening Balance				600	CR
Jun 16		J1		300	900	CR
Jun 30	Adjusting Entry	J2	450		450	CR

Account: Notes Payable — GL No: 215

Date	Description	PR	DR	CR	Balance	
2018						
Jun 1	Opening Balance				4,000	CR
Jun 23		J1	950		3,050	CR

Account: Gordon, Capital — GL No: 300

Date	Description	PR	DR	CR	Balance	
2018						
Jun 1	Opening Balance				6,400	CR
Jun 13		J1		3,000	9,400	CR
Jun 30	Closing Entry	J3		3,375	12,775	CR
Jun 30	Closing Entry	J3	1,000		11,775	CR

Account: Gordon, Withdrawals — GL No: 310

Date	Description	PR	DR	CR	Balance	
2018						
Jun 30		J1	1,000		1,000	DR
Jun 30	Closing Entry	J3		1,000	0	DR

Account: Income Summary — GL No: 315

Date	Description	PR	DR	CR	Balance	
2018						
Jun 30	Closing Entry	J3		4,950	4,950	CR
Jun 30	Closing Entry	J3	1,575		3,375	CR
Jun 30	Closing Entry	J3	3,375		0	CR

Account: Service Revenue — GL No: 400

Date	Description	PR	DR	CR	Balance	
2018						
Jun 6		J1		2,100	2,100	CR
Jun 18		J1		1,500	3,600	CR
Jun 30	Adjusting Entry	J2		450	4,050	CR
Jun 30	Adjusting Entry	J2		900	4,950	CR
Jun 30	Closing Entry	J3	4,950		0	CR

Account: Advertising Expense — GL No: 500

Date	Description	PR	DR	CR	Balance	
2018						
Jun 11		J1	450		450	DR
Jun 30	Closing Entry	J3		450	0	DR

Account: Depreciation Expense   GL No: 510

Date	Description	PR	DR	CR	Balance	
2018						
Jun 30	Adjusting Entry	J2	100		100	DR
Jun 30	Closing Entry	J3		100	0	DR

Account: Insurance Expense   GL No: 515

Date	Description	PR	DR	CR	Balance	
2018						
Jun 30	Adjusting Entry	J2	100		100	DR
Jun 30	Closing Entry	J3		100	0	DR

Account: Interest Expense   GL No: 520

Date	Description	PR	DR	CR	Balance	
2018						
Jun 30	Adjusting Entry	J2	25		25	DR
Jun 30	Closing Entry	J3		25	0	DR

Account: Rent Expense   GL No: 540

Date	Description	PR	DR	CR	Balance	
2018						
Jun 1		J1	900		900	DR
Jun 30	Closing Entry	J3		900	0	DR

c)

CG Accounting		
Post-Closing Trial Balance		
June 30, 2018		
Account Title	**DR**	**CR**
Cash	$5,550	
Accounts Receivable	5,500	
Prepaid Insurance	1,100	
Equipment	6,000	
Accumulated Depreciation—Equipment		$100
Accounts Payable		2,750
Interest Payable		25
Unearned Revenue		450
Notes Payable		3,050
Gordon, Capital		11,775
Total	$18,150	$18,150

Review Exercise 6A-1

CG Accounting Spreadsheet June 30, 2018

Account Titles	Unadjusted Trial Balance DR	Unadjusted Trial Balance CR	Adjustments DR	Adjustments CR	Adjusted Trial Balance DR	Adjusted Trial Balance CR	Income Statement DR	Income Statement CR	Balance Sheet & Equity DR	Balance Sheet & Equity CR
Cash	$5,550				$5,550				$5,550	
Accounts Receivable	4,600		$900		5,500				5,500	
Prepaid Insurance	1,200			$100	1,100				1,100	
Equipment	6,000				6,000				6,000	
Accumulated Depreciation—Equipment		$0		100		$100				$100
Accounts Payable		2,750				2,750				2,750
Interest Payable		0		25		25				25
Unearned Revenue		900	450			450				450
Notes Payable		3,050				3,050				3,050
Gordon, Capital		9,400				9,400				9,400
Gordon, Withdrawals	1,000				1,000				1,000	
Service Revenue		3,600		1,350		4,950		$4,950		
Advertising Expense	450				450		$450			
Depreciation Expense	0		100		100		100			
Insurance Expense	0		100		100		100			
Interest Expense	0		25		25		25			
Rent Expense	900				900		900			
Total	$19,700	$19,700	$1,575	$1,575	$20,725	$20,725	1,575	4,950	19,150	15,775
Net Income (Loss)							3,375			3,375
Total							$4,950	$4,950	$19,150	$19,150

CHAPTER 7 SOLUTIONS

Pause & Reflect Exercise 7-1

Although this is a small store, Stacy should take a more active role in preparing and recording the cash from sales. She should prepare the float for each day, and compare the day's sales to the actual cash received at the end of the day. She should also count the money for each deposit and compare that to the deposit slip. By getting more involved in the cash sales part of the business, Stacy will have better control over cash receipts.

If cash sales are high during the day, the amount of cash in the cash drawer can become too high. It would be best to periodically take excess cash from the cash drawer and place it in a safe. This would then be deposited at the bank later in the day.

Although the cashier may be authorized to make the cash payments to suppliers that deliver and stock soda and chips, it would be better to pay by means of a check instead of cash. A check ensures that the correct amount is paid (no accidental miscount) and that the supplier company gets paid the full amount (no one is able to take cash for themselves). The invoice and the check would provide a better paper trail if questions of payment were to ever arise.

Pause & Reflect Exercise 7-2

Prescott Marketing					
Bank Reconciliation					
September 30, 2018					
Cash balance per bank statement		$8,570	Cash balance per books		$9,260
Add outstanding deposit		2,480	Add EFT deposit		1,560
Deduct outstanding checks			Deduct		
Check #287	650		Check returned NSF	1,240	
Check #291	870	1,520	Bank service charge	50	1,290
Adjusted bank balance		$9,530	Adjusted book balance		$9,530

Pause & Reflect Exercise 7-3

JOURNAL			
Date	Account Title and Explanation	Debit	Credit
Nov 1	Petty Cash	500	
	Cash		500
	To establish petty cash		
Nov 15	Postage Expense	58	
	Delivery Expense	94	
	Entertainment Expense	242	
	Maintenance Expense	46	
	Cash Over and Short	4	
	Cash		444
	To replenish petty cash		

Review Exercise 7-1

a) ***Record cash immediately when received***

- Use sequential pre-numbered receipts.
- Purchase and use a cash register.
- Compare and reconcile the sum of sales amounts (office copy) to the cash on hand (cash drawer or cash register copy).

Protect cash when it is on the premises

- Lock the cash drawer or cash register when not in use.
- Remove the cash from the cash drawer or cash register at night. Lock it in a safe, or the office.
- Create a customer policy of free cleaning if no receipt is given by the counter clerk. This ensures the customer is always given a receipt when they pay cash.

Remove cash from the premises as soon as possible

- Deposit cash into the bank daily, multiple times if necessary.

b) The overall goal for cash controls is to ensure that the amount of cash received is the amount of cash recorded, which is the amount of cash deposited.

c) Contact authorities to report the counter clerk for fraudulent activities and theft, and provide information for their investigation.

- Terminate the employment of the counter clerk.
- JP can step in as the counter clerk until another employee is found.

Review Exercise 7-2

a)

<table>
<tr><td colspan="5" align="center">**Martin Furniture**
Bank Reconciliation
June 30, 2018</td></tr>
<tr><td>Cash balance per bank statement</td><td>$2,000</td><td>Cash balance per books</td><td></td><td>$4,815</td></tr>
<tr><td>Add outstanding deposit</td><td>1,300</td><td>Add Interest</td><td></td><td>5</td></tr>
<tr><td>Deduct outstanding checks
   Check #545</td><td>500</td><td>Deduct charges</td><td></td><td></td></tr>
<tr><td></td><td></td><td>NSF Check</td><td>2,000</td><td></td></tr>
<tr><td></td><td></td><td>Bank charges for NSF Check</td><td>6</td><td></td></tr>
<tr><td></td><td></td><td>Bank service charge</td><td>14</td><td>2,020</td></tr>
<tr><td>Adjusted bank balance</td><td>$2,800</td><td>Adjusted book balance</td><td></td><td>$2,800</td></tr>
</table>

b)

JOURNAL

Date	Account Title and Explanation	Debit	Credit
2018			
Jun 30	Cash	5	
	Interest Revenue		5
	To record deposit of interest earned		
Jun 30	Accounts Receivable	2,000	
	Cash		2,000
	Reinstate accounts receivable for NSF check		
Jun 30	Bank Charges Expense	6	
	Cash		6
	To record NSF charges		
Jun 30	Bank Charges Expense	14	
	Cash		14
	To record payment of bank service charges		

Review Exercise 7-3

a)

JOURNAL			
Date	**Account Title and Explanation**	**Debit**	**Credit**
2018			
Apr 1	Petty Cash	200	
	Cash		200
	To establish petty cash fund		

b)

JOURNAL			
Date	**Account Title and Explanation**	**Debit**	**Credit**
2018			
Apr 16	Postage Expense	40	
	Delivery Expense	20	
	Travel Expense	25	
	Entertainment Expense	8	
	Office Expenses	7	
	Cash Over and Short	5	
	Cash		105
	To reimburse petty cash fund		

CHAPTER 8 SOLUTIONS

Pause & Reflect Exercise 8-1

JOURNAL			
Date	**Account Title and Explanation**	**Debit**	**Credit**
2018			
Dec 31	Bad Debt Expense	6,500	
	Allowance for Doubtful Accounts		6,500
	To record estimated bad debt		
2019			
Mar 5	Allowance for Doubtful Accounts	2,100	
	Accounts Receivable—Basil's Hotel		2,100
	To write off bad debt		

Pause & Reflect Exercise 8-2

a)

Aging Category	Bad Debt %	Balance of Accounts Receivable	Estimated Bad Debt
30 days	1%	$200,000	$2,000
31-60 days	5%	120,000	6,000
More than 60 days	10%	80,000	8,000
Total		$400,000	$16,000

b)

JOURNAL			
Date	Account Title and Explanation	Debit	Credit
Dec 31	Bad Debt Expense	12,600	
	Allowance for Doubtful Accounts		12,600
	To record bad debt expense		

Pause & Reflect Exercise 8-3

a)

$$\text{Accounts Receivable Turnover Ratio} = \frac{\text{Net Credit Sales}}{\text{Average Net Accounts Receivable}}$$

$$= \frac{\$278,000}{\$23,000}$$

$$= 12 \text{ times}$$

The accounts receivable turnover is 12 times. This means that the company collects the entire amount of accounts receivable about 12 times a year, or approximately once a month.

b) $\text{Days' Sales Outstanding} = \dfrac{\text{Average Net Accounts Receivable}}{\text{Net Credit Sales}} \times 365$

$$= \frac{\$23,000}{\$278,000} \times 365$$

$$= 30 \text{ days}$$

The days' sales outstanding is 30 days. This means that the company collects the entire amount of accounts receivable in an average of 30 days, or approximately one month.

Review Exercise 8-1

a)

JOURNAL			
Date	**Account Title and Explanation**	**Debit**	**Credit**
Dec 31	Cash	70,000	
	Accounts Receivable	280,000	
	Sales Revenue		350,000
Dec 31	Cash	250,000	
	Accounts Receivable		250,000
Dec 31	Allowance for Doubtful Accounts	1,500	
	Accounts Receivable		1,500
Dec 31	Accounts Receivable	1,500	
	Allowance for Doubtful Accounts		1,500
Dec 31	Bad Debt Expense	2,500	
	Allowance for Doubtful Accounts		2,500

b)

Cash

$70,000	
250,000	
$320,000	

Accounts Receivable

Beg. Bal.:	$250,000
$35,000	1,500
280,000	
1,500	
$65,000	

Sales Revenue

	$350,000

AFDA

$1,500	Beg. Bal.:
	$2,500
	1,500
	2,500
	$5,000

Bad Debt Expense

$2,500	

c)

ABC Company Balance Sheet (partial) As at December 31, 2018	
Accounts Receivable	$65,000
Less: Allowance for Doubtful Accounts	5,000
Net Accounts Receivable	$60,000

d)

JOURNAL

Date	Account Title	Debit	Credit
Dec 31	Bad Debt Expense	2,800	
	Allowance for Doubtful Accounts		2,800
	To estimate bad debt for the year		

If the company uses the income statement approach, it does not take the AFDA beginning balance into account when it records the journal entry to estimate bad debt. Simply calculate 1% of credit sales (350,000 × 0.8 = 280,000), which is equal to $2,800, and use this number in the journal entry.

CHAPTER 9 SOLUTIONS

Pause & Reflect Exercise 9-1

Sales Revenue	$10,500	*(300 clocks × $35)*
COGS	$4,200	*(300 clocks × $14)*
Gross Profit	$6,300	*($10,500 − $4,200)*
Net Income	$1,300	*($6,300 − $5,000)*

Pause & Reflect Exercise 9-2

Caterpy Company

JOURNAL

Date	Account Title and Explanation	Debit	Credit
2018			
May 10	Cash	5,000	
	Sales Revenue		5,000
	To record product sales		
May 10	Cost of Goods Sold	3,000	
	Merchandise Inventory		3,000
	Sold inventory to a customer		

Weezle Company

JOURNAL

Date	Account Title and Explanation	Debit	Credit
2018			
May 10	Merchandise Inventory	5,130	
	Cash		5,130
	Purchased inventory and paid freight costs		

Pause & Reflect Exercise 9-3

a) Gross Profit Margin = ($400,000–$220,000)÷ $400,000 = 0.45 or 45%

b) To keep the same level of gross profit margin as in 2018, Cochran's 2019 gross profit will be $225,000 ($500,000 × 45%). This means that its COGS cannot exceed $275,000 ($500,000 net sales – $225,000 gross profit).

Pause & Reflect Exercise 9-4

JOURNAL			
Date	Account Title and Explanation	Debit	Credit
2018			
Dec 31	Cost of Goods Sold	3,000	
	Merchandise Inventory		3,000
	Adjust inventory to physical count		

Pause & Reflect Exercise 9-5

a)

	Nado	Vaporen
Average Inventory	120,000	240,000
Inventory Turnover	5	4
Days' Sales in Inventory	73	91

b) Nado Company has more favorable ratios.

Review Exercise 9-1

Part 1

a)

JOURNAL			
Date	Account Title and Explanation	Debit	Credit
2018			
Dec 3	Merchandise Inventory	50,000	
	Accounts Payable		50,000
	Purchased inventory on account		
Dec 6	Merchandise Inventory	200	
	Cash		200
	Paid freight charges		
Dec 8	Accounts Payable	2,000	
	Merchandise Inventory		2,000
	Purchase return		
Dec 11	Accounts Payable	48,000	
	Merchandise Inventory		960
	Cash		47,040
	Paid supplier and took discount		

b)

JOURNAL			
Date	**Account Title and Explanation**	**Debit**	**Credit**
2018			
Dec 3	Accounts Receivable	50,000	
	Sales Revenue		50,000
	Sold inventory on account		
Dec 3	Cost of Goods Sold	35,000	
	Merchandise Inventory		35,000
	Cost of goods sold for above sale		
Dec 6	Delivery Expense	200	
	Cash		200
	Paid freight charges		
Dec 8	Sales Returns & Allowances	2,000	
	Accounts Receivable		2,000
	Customer returned incorrect merchandise		
Dec 8	Merchandise Inventory	700	
	Cost of Goods Sold		700
	Inventory returned to stock		
Dec 11	Cash	47,040	
	Sales Discounts	960	
	Accounts Receivable		48,000
	Received payment from customer		

Part 2

a)

George's Gardening Supplies		
Income Statement		
For the Year Ended December 31, 2018		
Revenues		
Sales Revenue		$113,500
Less: Sales Returns & Allowances	$1,000	
Sales Discounts	1,580	(2,580)
Interest Revenue		6,500
Total Revenues		117,420
Expenses		
Cost of Goods Sold	44,700	
Depreciation Expense	5,000	
Insurance Expense	2,500	
Interest Expense	2,600	
Rent Expense	6,000	
Salaries Expense	11,000	
Supplies Expense	4,500	
Utilities Expense	750	
Total Expenses		77,050
Net Income		$40,370

b) Gross Profit Margin = $\dfrac{\text{Gross Profit}}{\text{Net Sales}}$

$= \dfrac{\$66,220}{\$110,920}$

= 0.60 or 60%

c)

George's Gardening Supplies			
Income Statement			
For the Year Ended December 31, 2018			
Sales Revenue			$113,500
Less: Sales Returns & Allowances		$1,000	
Sales Discounts		1,580	(2,580)
Net Sales			110,920
Cost of Goods Sold			44,700
Gross Profit			66,220
Operating Expenses			
Selling Expenses			
Depreciation Expense	$5,000		
Insurance Expense—Retail	1,750		
Rent Expense—Retail	4,200		
Salaries Expense—Retail	7,700		
Utilities Expense—Retail	525		
Total Selling Expenses		19,175	
Administrative Expenses			
Insurance Expense—Office	750		
Rent Expense—Office	1,800		
Salaries Expense—Office	3,300		
Supplies Expense	4,500		
Utilities Expense—Office	225		
Total Administrative Expenses		10,575	
Total Operating Expenses			29,750
Income from Operations			36,470
Other Income and Expenses			
Interest Revenue		6,500	
Interest Expense		(2,600)	3,900
Net Income			$40,370

d)

JOURNAL			
Date	**Account Title and Explanation**	**Debit**	**Credit**
2018			
Dec 31	Sales Revenue	113,500	
	Interest Revenue	6,500	
	Income Summary		120,000
	Close revenue accounts		
Dec 31	Income Summary	79,630	
	Sales Returns & Allowances		1,000
	Sales Discounts		1,580
	Cost of Goods Sold		44,700
	Depreciation Expense		5,000
	Insurance Expense		2,500
	Interest Expense		2,600
	Rent Expense		6,000
	Salaries Expense		11,000
	Supplies Expense		4,500
	Utilities Expense		750
	Close expense and debit accounts		
Dec 31	Income Summary	40,370	
	Gregg, Capital		40,370
	Close income summary		
Dec 31	Gregg, Capital	5,000	
	Gregg, Withdrawals		5,000
	Close withdrawals account		

CHAPTER 10 SOLUTIONS

Pause & Reflect Exercise 10-1

Simmons Inc. June 30, 2018 General Ledger	
Accounts Receivable	$1,025

Simmons Inc. Schedule of Accounts Receivable June 30, 2018	
Derek Smith *($1,200 – $700)*	$500
Soft Cell Enterprises *($800 – $800*	0
Bill Waites	525
Total Accounts Receivable	$1,025

Simmons Inc. June 30, 2018 General Ledger	
Accounts Payable	$140

Simmons Inc. Schedule of Accounts Payable June 30, 2018	
Buzz Electronics	$140
Supply Depot ($75 – $75)	0
Total Accounts Payable	$140

Review Exercise 10-1

a)

Cash Receipts Journal								Page 1
Date	Account	PR	Cash (DR)	Sales (CR)	Accounts Receivable (CR)	Interest Revenue (CR)	Notes Payable (CR)	Other (CR)	COGS/ Merchandise Inventory (DR/CR)
Jun 4	Cash Sale		4,000	4,000					2,015
Jun 6	B. Didley	✓	480		480				
Jun 9	Cash Sale		2,160	2,160					1,050
Jun 10	K. Domino		25			25			
Jun 15	Bank Loan		2,400				2,400		
	Total		9,065	6,160	480	25	2,400		3,065

Sales Journal					Page 1
Date	Account	Invoice #	PR	Accounts Receivable/Sales (DR/CR)	COGS/ Merchandise Inventory (DR/CR)
Jun 18	Richard Starkey	10022	✓	3,000	2,000
Jun 28	Pete Best	10023	✓	5,000	3,700
	Total			8,000	5,700

Purchases Journal						Page 1
Date	Account	Invoice #	PR	Repairs Expense (DR)	Office Supplies (DR)	Purchases (DR)	Accounts Payable (CR)
Jun 5	Stapl-EZ	4053	✓		100		100
Jun 9	Building Services Inc.	124	✓	350			350
Jun 26	Brick & Mortar	404241	✓			3,500	3,500
	Total			350	100	3,500	3,950

Cash Payments Journal							Page 1
Date	Account	Chq #	PR	Other (DR)	Purchases (DR)	Accounts Payable (DR)	Cash (CR)
Jun 12	Stapl-EZ Inc.	465	✓			100	100
Jun 21	Noel's Inc.	466			4,000		4,000
Jun 22	Building Services Inc.	467	✓			350	350
Jun 25	SKG Inc.	468		175			175
	Total			175	4,000	450	4,625

b)

Accounts Receivable Subsidiary Ledger Bo Didley					
Date	PR	DR	CR	Balance	
Opening Bal				2,000 DR	DR
Jun 6	CR1		480	1,520 DR	DR

Accounts Receivable Subsidiary Ledger Richard Starkey					
Date	PR	DR	CR	Balance	
Opening Bal				1,000	DR
Jun 18	SJ1	3,000		4,000	DR

Accounts Receivable Subsidiary Ledger Pete Best					
Date	PR	DR	CR	Balance	
Opening Bal				1,500	DR
Jun 28	SJ1	5,000		6,500	DR

Account: Accounts Receivable					GL No: 110	
Date	Description	PR	DR	CR	Balance	
Opening Bal					4,500 DR	DR
Jun 30		CRI		480	4,020 DR	DR
Jun 30		SJ1	8,000		12,020 DR	DR

<table>
<tr><td colspan="2">Lin-Z
June 30, 2018
General Ledger</td></tr>
<tr><td>Accounts Receivable</td><td>$12,020</td></tr>
</table>

<table>
<tr><td colspan="2">Lin-Z
Schedule of Accounts Receivable
June 30, 2018</td></tr>
<tr><td>Bo Didley</td><td>$1,520</td></tr>
<tr><td>Richard Starkey</td><td>4,000</td></tr>
<tr><td>Pete Best</td><td>6,500</td></tr>
<tr><td>Total Accounts Receivable</td><td>$12,020</td></tr>
</table>

c)

Accounts Payable Subsidiary Ledger
Stapl-EZ Inc.

Date	PR	DR	CR	Balance	
Opening Bal				500	CR
Jun 5	PJ1		100	600	CR
Jun 12	CP1	100		500	CR

Accounts Payable Subsidiary Ledger
Building Services Inc.

Date	PR	DR	CR	Balance	
Opening Bal				750	CR
Jun 9	PJ1		350	1,100	CR
Jun 22	CP1	350		750	CR

Accounts Payable Subsidiary Ledger
Brick & Mortar Inc.

Date	PR	DR	CR	Balance	
Opening Bal				2,500	CR
Jun 26	PJ1		3,500	6,000	CR

Account: Accounts Payable					GL No: 200	
Date	Description	PR	DR	CR	Balance	
Opening Bal					3,750	CR
Jun 30		PJ1		3,950	7,700	CR
Jun 30		CP1	450		7,250	CR

Lin-Z June 30, 2018 General Ledger	
Accounts Receivable	$7,250

Lin-Z Schedule of Accounts Payable June 30, 2018	
Stapl-EZ Inc.	$500
Building Services Inc.	750
Brick & Mortar Inc.	6,000
Total Accounts Payable	$7,250

CHAPTER 11 SOLUTIONS

Pause & Reflect Exercise 11-1

a)

Asset	Appraised Value	Percentage	Book Value
Building	$1,000,000	50%	$900,000
Land	600,000	30%	540,000
Parking Lot	400,000	20%	360,000
Total	$2,000,000	100%	$1,800,000

b)

JOURNAL			Page 2
Date	Account Title and Explanation	Debit	Credit
May 1	Building	900,000	
	Land	540,000	
	Parking Lot	360,000	
	Cash		1,800,000
	Purchased assets with cash		

Pause & Reflect Exercise 11-2

Year	Beginning of Year Book Value	Depreciation	Remaining Book Value
2018	$5,000,000	$2,000,000	$3,000,000
2019	$3,000,000	$1,200,000	$1,800,000
2020	$1,800,000	$720,000	$1,080,000
2021	$1,080,000	$432,000	$648,000
2022	$648,000	$248,000	$400,000

Pause & Reflect Exercise 11-3

JOURNAL			
Date	Account Title and Explanation	Debit	Credit
Dec 31	Depreciation Expense	260,000	
	Accumulated Depreciation—Equipment		260,000
	Record annual depreciation		
Dec 31	Cash	360,000	
	Accumulated Depreciation—Equipment	2,340,000	
	Loss on Disposal of Asset	300,000	
	Equipment		3,000,000
	Sold asset for cash		

Review Exercise 11-1

a)

JOURNAL			
Date	Account Title and Explanation	Debit	Credit
Dec 31	Computer	3,000	
	Office Equipment	10,000	
	Cash		13,000
	Purchase of computer and office equipment for cash		

b) A reasonable life for a computer would be three years, and for equipment would be 5–10 years. Students will arrive at various numbers based on their research.

c) Because computers are upgraded quickly, a declining-balance method would be appropriate with large amounts of depreciation early on. For office equipment, straight-line depreciation would be reasonable.

d)

Year	Cost	Depreciation	Accumulated Depreciation	Net Book Value
2017	3,000.00	1,000.00	1,000.00	2,000.00
2018	2,000.00	666.67	1,666.67	1,333.33
2019	1,333.33	444.44	2,111.11	888.89

Year	Cost	Depreciation	Accumulated Depreciation	Net Book Value
2017	10,000	2,000	2,000	8,000
2018	10,000	2,000	4,000	6,000
2019	10,000	2,000	6,000	4,000
2020	10,000	2,000	8,000	2,000
2021	10,000	2,000	10,000	0

e) The profit or loss on disposal of a noncurrent asset is the difference between the amount received, and the net book value of the asset at the time of disposal.

CHAPTER 12 SOLUTIONS

Pause & Reflect Exercise 12-1

			Deductions				
Gross Earnings	Federal Income Tax	State Income Tax	FICA Tax	FUTA	SUTA	Total Contributions	Net Pay
$10,000	$1,000	$500	$765	$60	$540	$1,365	$7,735

The net pay to employees is equal to gross earnings minus employee deductions.

Net Pay = $10,000 – $1,000 – $500 – $765
= $7,735

The employer payroll contributions are equal to adding FICA, FUTA, and SUTA together.

Total Employer Contributions = $765 + $60 + 540
= $1,365

Pause & Reflect Exercise 12-2

JOURNAL			
Date	Account Title and Explanation	Debit	Credit
Mar 13	Cash	52,500	
	Sales Tax Payable		2,500
	Sales Revenue		50,000
	Sold items for cash		
Mar 13	Cost of Goods Sold	22,000	
	Merchandise Inventory		22,000
	Record COGS		

Pause & Reflect Exercise 12-3

JOURNAL			
Date	Account Title and Explanation	Debit	Credit
2018			
Apr 1	Cash	20,000	
	Notes Payable		20,000
	Borrowed cash from the bank, due in six months		
Oct 1	Notes Payable	20,000	
	Interest Expense	600	
	Cash		20,600
	Paid note and interest on due date		

Pause & Reflect Exercise 12-4

JOURNAL			
Date	**Account Title and Explanation**	**Debit**	**Credit**
Dec 31	Warranty Expense	400,000	
	Estimated Warranty Liability		400,000
	Record estimated warranty liability		

Review Exercise 12-1

JOURNAL			
Date	**Account Title and Explanation**	**Debit**	**Credit**
Jan 15	Merchandise Inventory	111,300	
	Accounts Payable		111,300
	Bought machine for resale		
Jan 30	Cash	226,840	
	Sales Tax Payable		12,840
	Sales Revenue		214,000
	Sold machine for cash		
Jan 30	Cost of Goods Sold	111,300	
	Merchandise Inventory		111,300
	Record COGS for above sale		
Jan 30	Warranty Expense	20,000	
	Estimated Warranty Liability		20,000
	Accrued for estimated warranty costs		
Jan 30	Sales Tax Payable	12,840	
	Cash		12,840
	Paid sales tax to the government		
Feb 15	Accounts Payable	111,300	
	Cash		111,300
	Paid for machine bought on account on Jan 15		
Mar 27	Estimated Warranty Liability	200	
	Parts Inventory		200
	To record inventory for warranty work		

CHAPTER 13 SOLUTIONS

Pause & Reflect Exercise 13-1

a) Contribution Margin = Sales Price – Variable Costs
                          = $15,000 – $7,000 = $8,000

b) Break-Even Point   = Fixed Costs ÷ Contribution Margin per Unit
                         = $800,000 ÷ $8,000 = 100 tables

Pause and Reflect Exercise 13-2

a) $11 + $24 + $15 + ($240,000 ÷ 80,000) = $53 per unit

b) Selling Price = $53 + ($53 × 35%) = $71.55

Review Exercise 13-1

a) $5 + $4 + $2 + ($300,000 ÷ 100,000) = $14 per unit

b) Selling Price = $14 + ($14 × 50%) = $21

c) Contribution Margin = Sales Price – Variable Costs
                         = $21 – $11 = $10

d) Break-Even Point   = Fixed Costs ÷ Contribution Margin per Unit
                         = $380,000 ÷ $10 = 38,000 units

e) Break-Even Point   = Fixed Costs ÷ Contribution Margin per Unit
                         = $390,000 ÷ $10 = 39,000 units

Since fixed costs have increased, the company will have to sell more products to break-even.

CHAPTER 14 SOLUTIONS

Pause & Reflect Exercise 14-1

Net income has been decreasing in 2017 and 2018 despite a steady increase in revenue because the expenses have been increasing more than the increase in revenue. While the cost of goods sold increased quite significantly from 110% in 2016 to 150% and 155% in 2017 and 2018, respectively, there was still a modest increase in gross profit year after year. The most important factor causing a decrease in net income is the increase in total expenses, which jumped from 103% in 2016 to 119% and 122% in 2017 and 2018, respectively.

Review Exercise 14-1

a)

Basil's Bakery Percentage Change and Vertical Analysis As at December 31, 2018				
	2018	**2017**	**% Change**	**% of Base-Figure 2018**
Cash	$1,605	$987	62.61%	29.12%
Accounts Receivable	1,175	573	105.06%	21.15%
Merchandise Inventory	396	256	54.69%	7.13%
Other Current Assets	301	103	192.23%	5.42%
Total Current Assets	3,477	1,919	81.19%	63.09%
Property, Plant and Equipment	2,034	1,170	73.85%	36.61%
Total Assets	$5,511	$3,089	78.41%	100.00%
Current Liabilities	$1,474	$547	169.47%	26.53%
Noncurrent Liabilities	104	58	79.31%	1.87%
Total Liabilities	1,578	605	160.83%	28.40%
Stockholders' Equity	3,933	2,484	58.33%	71.36%
Total Liabilities + Equity	$5,511	$3,089	78.41%	100.00%

b)

Financial Ratio or Figure	Calculation	Result
Working Capital	$3,477 – $1,474	$2,003
Current Ratio	$\dfrac{\$3,477}{\$1,474}$	2.36
Quick Ratio	$\dfrac{\$1,605 + \$1,175}{\$1,474}$	1.89
Gross Profit Margin	$\dfrac{\$3,081}{\$6,009}$	0.5127 or 51.27%
Net Profit Margin	$\dfrac{\$1,295}{\$6,009}$	0.2155 or 21.55%
Return on Equity	$\$1,295 \div \dfrac{(\$3,933 + \$2,484)}{2}$	0.4036 or 40.36%
Asset Turnover	$\dfrac{\$6,009}{(\$5,511 + \$3,089) \div 2}$	1.40 times
Return on Assets	$\$1,295 \div \left(\dfrac{(\$5,511 + \$3,089)}{2} \right)$	0.3012 or 30.12%
Inventory Turnover Ratio	$\$2,928 \div \left(\dfrac{(\$396 + \$256)}{2} \right)$	8.98
Days' Sales in Inventory	$\dfrac{(\$396 + \$256) \div 2}{\$2,928} \times 365$	40.64 days

Financial Ratio or Figure	Calculation	Result
Accounts Receivable Turnover	$\$6,009 \div \left(\dfrac{(\$1,175 + \$573)}{2} \right)$	6.88
Days' Sales Outstanding	$\dfrac{(\$1,175 + \$573) \div 2}{\$6,009} \times 365$	53.09 days
Debt-to-Equity Ratio	$\dfrac{\$1,578}{\$3,933}$	0.4012 or 40.12%

c) A positive **working capital** of $2,003 indicates that the company has enough liquid assets to pay off its upcoming short-term debts.

A **current ratio** of 2.36 indicates that the business has a little more than twice the amount of current assets to pay for its current liabilities. It could be argued that the bakery has enough of a cushion that it could afford to have more cash tied up in current assets, such as inventory and accounts receivable. It could also invest a small portion to earn more investment income.

A **quick ratio** of 1.89 which indicates that the business can meet its most immediate debt obligations without relying on the liquidation of inventory. In terms of liquidity as a whole, Basil's Bakery is highly liquid based on the above three financial ratios and figures, indicating a strong financial position in meeting short-term debt obligations.

A **gross profit margin** of 51.27% means that after deducting cost of goods sold from sales revenue, the company still has a little more than half of sales revenue left to cover other expenses. Compared to 2017, the gross profit margin declined, indicating that the company is either generating less revenue, has experienced an increase in inventory costs or both. This should be a point of concern, indicating a downward trend. Comparing 2018's gross profit margin to the industry average of 49.47% shows that the bakery is doing better than the average company in the same industry. It must work to ensure that it remains above this amount by setting appropriate prices and properly managing inventory costs.

A **net profit margin** of 21.55% which means that the company is earning 21 cents of net income for every one dollar of revenue earned. Compared to 2015, the net profit margin declined, indicating that the company's costs have increased. This should be a point of concern, indicating a downward trend. Comparing 2018's net profit margin to the industry average of 20.36% shows that the bakery is doing better than the average company in the same industry. It must work to ensure that it remains above this amount by managing costs and expenses.

Basil's Bakery has a positive 40.36% **return on equity (ROE)**, which is favorable for investors. As always, stockholders can compare the company's ROE with other companies' ROE to see whether the return from investing in Basil's Bakery provides at least as high of a return as they could have received if they had invested elsewhere. In terms of profitability, the company is doing well.

The **asset turnover** is 1.4 times. This means the bakery generates $1.40 of revenue for every one dollar of assets. This is a good indicator that the company is using its assets efficiently.

Basil's Bakery had a **return on assets** of about 30%. This means the company made a profit of $0.30 for every dollar invested in assets in the business. This appears to be a good return, but can be compared to other bakeries for a more thorough assessment.

Basil's Bakery has an **inventory turnover ratio** of 8.98, which represents the number of times that the company sold its entire inventory within the year. Bakeries should have a higher turnover ratio because some of the input products they use can expire, such as milk and eggs. Once items are baked, they have a short shelf life as efficiently.

A **days' sales in inventory ratio** of 40.64 days indicates that the inventory is sold rather slowly. This paired with the inventory turnover ratio, shows that the bakery could be selling inventory faster. This is a point of concern. In terms of operations management, inventory must be addressed immediately. Inventory should be turning over more quickly to ensure that the bakery is not throwing out expired products. A turnaround in operations management could mean more success in profitability and liquidity.

The **days' sales outstanding** and **accounts receivable turnover** ratios indicate the company collects its accounts receivable every 53 days, or turns over it accounts receivable almost seven times a year. This is not a very healthy ratio. Long collection periods can mean that the company's credit policy is too lenient, or that there are billing disputes, resulting in a delay in receivables collection from customers. It can lead to cash flow problems if cash is not being received in a timely manner.

A **debt-to-equity ratio** of 40.12% indicates that the total debt is significantly lower than equity. Having relatively low debt compared to equity is considered low risk because the company has a low cost of debt in the form of interest. Therefore, the company's leverage appears to be at an acceptable level.

Review Exercise 14-2

Operating activities are those necessary to run the daily operations of the business. This section of the statement of cash flows tracks the movement of cash within a business on the basis of day-to-day activities.

Investing activities include any exchange of cash related to the long-term financial investments or capital assets of the business. The purchase of these assets can be thought of as the business investing in itself because the assets usually result in increased operations.

Financing activities are any payments or receipts of cash that relate to changes in either long-term debt or stockholders' equity. This section of the statement of cash flows tracks the movement of cash within a business based on the way a company receives money from those providing financing and pays it back.

GLOSSARY

A

account allows a person to track detailed information about the values of individual items, such as cash and unpaid accounts

accountants people who measure, record and report on an individual's or a business' financial activities

accounting a system to identify, measure and communicate all the financial activities of an individual or a business

accounting cycle a series of steps required to complete the financial statements

accounting equation assets = liabilities + net worth

accounting ethics the standards by which an accountant judges that the financial status of a business is accurately reported

accounting period the time frame in which the financial statements are prepared

accounting system documents and procedures that are used to collect, classify, summarize and report on a business' transactions and operations

accounts payable the obligation a business owes to others

accounts receivable the amount owed to a business by its customers

accounts receivable turnover ratio (ART) measures how often during the year a company collects its entire accounts receivable amount

accrual-based accounting a type of accounting where revenue and expenses are recorded in the period in which they occur, regardless of when cash is received or paid

accruals accruals are related to net worth or equity and not necessarily to cash flow; they help in recognizing how much a person is worth at a point in time

accrued expenses expenses that have been incurred but have not yet been paid

accrued revenue revenue that has been earned but cash has not yet been received

accumulated depreciation the contra asset account for property, plant and equipment (PPE); reflects the decrease in the net book value of PPE without changing the original cost of the asset

adjusted trial balance the trial balance after adjustments are made

adjusting entries made at the end of the accounting period to record assets, liabilities, equity, revenue and expenses according to revenue and expense recognition principles

administrative expenses expenses related to running the business, which are not directly tied to selling inventory; also referred to as *general expenses or general and administrative expenses*

aging method a method to estimate bad debt by which percentages are applied to groupings based on the age of outstanding accounts receivable amounts

aging schedule an account receivable listing that organizes outstanding customer accounts by how old they are

allowance for doubtful accounts (AFDA) a contra asset account that records bad debt in a way that satisfies expense recognition principle

allowance method estimates an amount that will be bad debt and records it in the books

amortization the process of allocating the cost of intangible assets over their useful lives

asset something that you own that will benefit you now and in the future

asset turnover measures how quickly a company converts total assets, including noncurrent assets, into revenue

asset turnover ratio a measure of a company's ability to generate sales revenue from asset investments

B

bad debt an uncollectible account resulting from customers who will never pay their bills

balance sheet a permanent document used to record what you own (assets), what you owe (liabilities) and what you are worth (net worth) on a specific date

balance sheet approach a method by which a company calculates allowance for bad debt using either the percentage of total accounts receivable method or the aging method

balanced scorecard (BSC) a strategic performance management framework including forms of measurement that managers use, including financial ratios and performance metrics

bank overdraft a financial institution's extension of credit to cover the portion of cash withdrawal that is more than the account's balance

bank statement a record of all activities in a bank account for a given period, usually a month

base figure a total dollar amount used to determine the relationship between line items on a financial statement

base year the earliest year shown on a comparative balance sheet; used as a basis for comparison

basket purchase buying property, plant and equipment from the same vendor in one transaction, as opposed to buying them separately from different vendors; also called a *lump sum purchase*

break-even point the level of sales at which the company's operating profit is zero; also described as the point where total sales equal total expenses for no profit

business entity assumption accounting for a business must be kept separate from the personal affairs of its owner or any other businesses

C

capital expenditure expenses paid for a change to an asset resulting in benefits extending beyond the current period

capital stock a subsection of the balance sheet that includes accounts for a company's equity raised through different types of stock

cash currency, coins, checks, money orders and money on deposit in a bank account

cash discount offered by merchandisers to encourage prompt payment from customers, by which a percentage off the final bill is given if it is paid in a specified amount of time

cash equivalents highly liquid investments that can be easily converted into cash

cash flow the amount of cash flowing into and out of a bank account

cash flow from financing activities the movement of cash within a business received from investors and lenders to help run, or finance, a business; also cash paid back to investors and lenders

cash flow from investing activities the movement of cash in a business on the basis of purchases and sales of noncurrent assets

cash flow from operating activities the movement of cash within a business as a result of day-to-day activities

cash over and short the difference between the amount of petty cash on record and the actual amount on hand

cash payments journal a special journal used to record all cash payments made by a business

cash receipts journal a special journal used to record all cash deposits and collections

cash-based accounting a type of accounting in which revenue and expenses are recorded only when cash is received or paid

chart of accounts a list of all the accounts in the general ledger

closing balance the amount remaining in an account at the end of the current accounting period; also called *ending balance*

closing entries entries made to revenue, expenses and owner's withdrawals at the end of an accounting period to close out the accounts

closing the books updates owner's capital (the equity of the business) and starts a new income statement for the next accounting period

cloud accounting accounting software that is hosted remotely on a vendor's computer servers and accessed by users through the cloud; also called *cloud-based accounting*

Committee of Sponsoring Organizations (COSO) part of the Treadway Commission; provides a framework to help companies design and implement internal controls

common stock a type of equity that gives stockholders ownership in a corporation, voting rights to elect a board of directors and potential to receive dividends

comparability financial statements of a company must be prepared in a similar way year after year

comparative balance sheet a balance sheet that shows the balances for multiple years for easy comparison

compound journal entries journal entries that affect three or more accounts

conceptual framework the basis to determine how business transactions should be measured and reported

conservatism states that whenever an accountant has several options in applying an accounting standard, the least optimistic or least favorable option should be selected

consistency prevents businesses from changing accounting methods for the sole purpose of manipulating figures on the financial statements

contra account linked to another account and records decreases in the value of that account

contribution margin statement a detailed report that separates variable costs from fixed costs

controlling account an account in the general ledger that summarizes information and combines the balance of every related subsidiary ledger; also called a *control account*

copyright gives exclusive rights of ownership to a person or group that has created something

corporation a type of business that is a legal entity separate from its owners

cost accounting an integral part of managerial accounting that tracks the costs incurred to produce goods or provide services

cost behaviour a classification of costs based on how they change at different activity levels for manufacturing a product or providing a service

cost constraint ensures that the value of reported financial information outweighs the costs incurred to report it, even if the information would improve the accuracy and completeness of the financial statements

cost of goods sold (COGS) the value of all the goods sold; it is subtracted from sales revenue to determine gross profit

cost plus pricing method the most common method to pricing in which you apply a markup to cost

cost-volume-profit analysis (CVP) examines the relationship among costs, volume and profit

cost-volume-profit graph a graph to help managers understand how costs, sales and operating profit or loss are related

credit a credit is recorded on the right-hand side of a T-account; increases or decreases an account depending on the type of account

credit memorandum issued by the seller to inform the buyer that the accounts receivable balance has been credited in the seller's books; also called a *credit memo*

credit period the maximum number of days that a buyer can wait before paying the full amount of an invoice

credit terms the terms indicating when a buyer has to pay for the merchandise and whether there are any discounts for paying early

current assets assets that are likely to be converted into cash or used up through the day-to-day operations of the business within the next 12 months or the operating cycle, whichever is longer

current liabilities amounts due to be paid within 12 months

current ratio measures a company's ability to pay off short-term debt

customer deposit occurs when a customer pays a business for goods before they are received or for services before they are performed

D

days' sales in inventory calculates how many days inventory will last given the current rate of sales; also called *inventory days on hand*

days' sales outstanding (DSO) tracks how long customers take to pay their bills

debit a debit is recorded on the left-hand side of a T-account; increases or decreases an account depending on the type of account

debit memorandum a notice issued when a buyer encounters undesirable goods and informs the seller about the purchase returns or allowances; also called a *debit memo*

debt-to-equity ratio a measure of how much of a company is being financed by lenders, and how much is being financed by stockholders

declining-balance method applies an annual percentage to calculate depreciation against the net book value of an asset

depreciation allocating the cost of a noncurrent asset over its useful life

determinable liabilities liabilities with a precise value

disclosure states that any necessary information that enables financial statement users to make informed decisions must be included with the financial statements

discontinued operation a business segment that is no longer part of a company's regular operating activities

discount period the number of days within which a buyer has to pay to receive a cash discount

double entry recording the same value on both debit and credit sides for every transaction

double-declining-balance method doubles the declining-balance rate of depreciation

E

electronic funds transfer (EFT) a method of sending payment online directly from a customer's bank account into the bank account of a supplier

elements of internal control items the Internal Control—Integrated Framework provides guidance on, including control environment, risk assessment, control procedures, monitoring activities and information and communication

employee benefits compensation to employees in addition to their normal wages and salaries, such as pensions, medical and dental coverage, and other benefits

equity the net worth of a business, after all assets have been sold and all liabilities have been paid

estimated liabilities financial obligations a company cannot exactly quantify

expense recognition states that an expense must be recorded in the same accounting period in which it is used to generate revenue

expenses a decrease to net worth caused by day-to-day activities; costs that are incurred or use up an asset, usually cash

expenses by function a method of classifying related expenses together, such as selling expenses or administrative expenses, and presenting them as such on the statement of comprehensive income

external users people or organizations outside a business, such as suppliers, banks and external accountants, that use the business' financial statements in making their decisions

F

faithful representation transactions must be presented as their true economic substance rather than their legal form

FICA tax the portion of an employee's earnings deducted in accordance with the Federal Insurance Contributions Act (FICA)

financial accounting a field of accounting concerned with keeping records of a business and preparing the financial statements

Financial Accounting Standards Board (FASB) a private, nonprofit organization designated by the SEC to develop guidelines that all public US companies are required to use in reporting their financial statements according to GAAP

financing activities any payment or receipts of cash that relate to changes in either noncurrent liabilities or stockholders' equity

fiscal year a period of time covered by the financial statements; usually a one-year time frame and not necessarily the same as a calendar year

fixed assets noncurrent assets used to help run the business and not purchased with an intention to resell as inventory

fixed costs costs that remain the same for any given level of activity for manufacturing a product or providing a service

fixed interest rate an interest rate that remains constant for the entire term of a note

FOB destination indicates that ownership of the purchased items changes when the goods arrive at the buyer's place of business

FOB shipping point indicates that ownership of purchased items changes as soon as the goods leave the seller's place of business

Form W-2 a form called the Wage and Tax Statement that states an employee's gross pay and all statutory deductions for the year

Form W-4 a form called the Employee's Withholding Allowance certificate, used to determine the amount of tax a company withholds from an employee's earnings

franchise a contract that allows the franchisee to operate a branch using the franchisor's brand name and business model

fraud any illegal intentional act of deception that results in a financial benefit or gain

G

gain an increase in the value of assets that gives the assets a higher worth than their net book value

general journal a book of original entry used to record transactions; all transactions are listed in one place and in chronological order; used to record any entry that does not belong in one of the special journals

general ledger a book used to record and organize all the accounts and balances of a business

generally accepted accounting principles (GAAP) standards created by the accounting profession, which provide guidance on how financial information should be reported

going concern assumption assumes that a business will continue to operate into the foreseeable future

goodwill arises when a company purchases another company at a cost that is greater than the market value of that company's net assets

gross pay represents the total amount earned by an employee before any deductions

gross profit the difference between sales revenue and cost of goods sold

gross profit margin the difference between sales revenue and COGS expressed as a percentage of sales; also called *gross margin*

H

horizontal analysis a method to compare information from one accounting period to another, usually from year to year

I

income statement a temporary record used to show and summarize revenue and expenses

income statement approach a method that uses credit sales from the income statement as a basis to predict future bad debt

income summary a temporary holding account used to close the revenue and expense accounts, instead of debiting and crediting owner's capital or retained earnings directly

intangible assets conceptual assets that have no physical form and largely constitute intellectual property, such as patents and trademarks

internal users people who own a business and/or work in a business that use the business' financial information in making their decisions

International Accounting Standards Board (IASB) an independent organization that works with the Financial Accounting Standards Board (FASB) to establish the International Financial Reporting Standards (IFRS)

International Financial Reporting Standards (IFRS) standards created by the International Accounting Standards Board (IASB), which provide guidance on how financial information should be reported

inventory shrinkage occurs when there is a difference between accounting records and a physical inventory count

inventory turnover ratio an estimate of how many times a year a company is selling its entire inventory

investing activities any activity involving an exchange of cash related to the long-term financial investments or capital assets of a business

invoice a document issued by a seller to a buyer after a service is provided or a product is sold; includes details of the purchase, the amount owing, and terms of payment

J

journal a book of original entry in which transactions are recorded

journalizing the act of recording in a journal

L

leverage the amount of debt and risk a company has

liabilities something that you owe and considered to be a financial obligation

license a contract that permits the licensee to use the licensor's product or brand name under specified terms and conditions

limited liability a type of liability that extends only to the amount a person has invested in a partnership, limited liability company or a corporation

liquid asset an asset that is cash or easily converted to cash; cash is the most liquid asset and is listed first on the balance sheet, followed by accounts receivable, inventory, and so on

liquidity the ease with which an asset can be converted to cash

loss a decrease in the value of assets that gives the assets a lower worth than their net book value

lump sum purchase buying property, plant and equipment from the same vendor in one transaction, as opposed to buying them separately from different vendors; also called a *basket purchase*

M

managerial accounting a field of accounting that serves the internal users of the accounting information by preparing specialized reports to assist in decision-making inside a business

materiality refers to the significance of information to the users; a piece of information is material if it could influence or change a user's decision

measurement the process of determining the amount at which an item is recorded in the financial statements

merchandise inventory a collection of physical goods that a company has purchased or manufactured to sell to customers; also called *inventory*

merchandiser a business that buys and sells products, referred to as merchandise or goods, to make a profit; also called a *merchandising business*

mixed costs costs associated with manufacturing a product or providing a service that have both a variable cost portion and a fixed cost portion

Modified Accelerated Cost Recovery System (MACRS) depreciation rules under US federal income tax law

monetary unit assumption requires that accounting records are expressed in terms of money and in a single currency

multiple-step income statement an income statement that further divides specific revenues and expenses to show subtotals like gross profit, operating expenses and income from operations

mutual agency in a partnership, each partner is able to speak for the other partner(s) and bind them to business contracts

N

natural business year an accounting period of time in which the fiscal year ends during a slow time of year

natural resources assets with a physical nature that are different from property, plant and equipment, such as metal ores, minerals timber or petroleum

net book value the original value of an asset less the total depreciation that has been recognized

net income occurs when revenue exceeds expenses for the period, which causes equity to increase

net loss occurs when expenses exceed revenue for the period, which causes equity to decrease

net pay the amount an employee is paid after various deductions have been made

net profit margin assesses a company's profitability after all expenses have been deducted

net realizable value the price that a company can realistically expect to sell the item for, less any costs incurred to make the item ready for sale

net worth the amount remaining if you sell all your assets for cash and pay off all your liabilities

neutrality financial information must be free from bias

noncurrent assets used to operate a business and not expected to turn into cash or be used up within the next 12 months; also called long-term assets

noncurrent liabilities amounts due to be paid after 12 months; also called *long-term liabilities*

non-determinable liabilities unknown liabilities including estimated and contingent liabilities

nonprofit organizations formed for the purpose of improving or benefiting communities by taking profits and redistributing them as services or products

non-sufficient funds (NSF) checks payments made to a company by a customer who does not have sufficient funds in his or her bank account to cover the amount of the check

normal balance corresponds to the side of a T-account that records the increase

note payable a legally binding document that obligates the borrower to certain terms, much like a loan

O

opening balance the amount left over from the last accounting period carried over to the beginning of the current accounting period; also called *beginning balance*

operating activities those activities necessary to run the daily operations of a business

operating cycle the time between the use of cash and the receipt of cash for the business

operating expenses expenses incurred as part of the main operations of the business that are beyond the cost of goods sold

operating line of credit the maximum loan balance a business may draw upon at any time without having to visit or request approval from the bank

operations management the ability of a company to manage its assets, such as inventory and accounts receivable

owner's capital account an account used to record the amount of an owner's equity including owner's contributions

owner's contributions the amount of cash or assets invested in a business by the owner

owner's withdrawals account an account used to record owner's withdrawals

owner's withdrawals the amount of cash or assets taken by the owner for personal use

P

partnership an association of two or more people who jointly own a business, its assets and liabilities, and share in its gains or losses

patent grants the patentee the exclusive right, for a set period of time, to prevent others from making, using, selling or distributing the patented invention without permission

payment terms conditions by which a vendor expects to be paid by a customer

percentage of total accounts receivable method a method by which a company uses a percentage of receivables to estimate bad debt

periodic inventory system a method of keeping track of inventory in which the company's record of merchandise inventory is only updated after a physical count, usually at the end of the month or year

permanent accounts balance sheet items that have their balances carried forward from one accounting period to the next with no need of being closed; also called *real accounts*

perpetual inventory system a method of keeping track of inventory in which inventory levels are updated after every purchase and sale

plant assets property, plant and equipment that are long-term physical assets used to help run the business

post-closing trial balance a trial balance that only lists accounts that have a balance after the closing entries are completed

preferred stock a type of equity for which dividends must first be paid before those on common stock

premium when stock is sold for a price more than its par value

prepaid expense occurs when you pay cash for an expense before you use it

private accounting the practice of accounting for a single organization

private corporation one that does not offer its stock to the public

private enterprise any business or organization in which ownership is restricted to a select group of people; the general public cannot acquire ownership of the business

profitability the ability of a company to generate profits

property, plant and equipment equipment, buildings, land and other similar assets that provide a business with benefits for a long period of time

public accounting providing services, such as auditing and tax advice, to different companies or individuals

public corporation one that trades its stock on a stock exchange

purchase discounts cash discounts as referred to by a buyer

purchases journal a special journal used to record all purchases made on account

Q

quick ratio similar to the current ratio, but only counts assets that can easily be turned into cash

R

relevance all information useful for decision-making must be present in the financial statements

reliability information is free from significant error and bias, so different independent people looking at the evidence will arrive at the same values

remote deposit depositing checks directly into a bank account without having to physically deposit the check at a bank machine or bank branch

residual value estimated value of an asset at the end of its useful life

retailer a business that buys merchandise from a wholesaler or manufacturer to sell to end consumers

retained earnings earnings that are kept and accumulated by a company after dividends have been paid to stockholders

return on assets measures the relationship between net income and assets

return on equity (ROE) a measure of what owners are getting out of their investment in a company

revenue an increase to net worth caused by providing goods or services in exchange for an asset, usually cash

revenue expenditure expenses paid for a change to an asset that benefits the current period

revenue recognition states that revenue can only be recorded (recognized) when goods are sold or services are performed

S

sales allowances occur when the customer decides to keep undesirable products at a reduced price

sales discount account a contra-revenue account to record sales discounts offered to customers

sales discounts cash discounts as referred to by a seller

sales journal a special journal used to record all sales made on account

sales returns occur when undesirable products are returned from the buyer to the seller

sales returns and allowances a contra-revenue account used to track the number of returns

sales revenue a type of revenue earned by a business for selling products to customers

sales tax a tax applied by the state government to goods or services that are sold

Sarbanes-Oxley Act (SOX) an act passed by the US Congress to prevent accounting practices from committing fraudulent activities

Section 404 a section of the Sarbanes–Oxley Act that requires a company's senior management and auditors to establish internal controls

Securities and Exchange Commission (SEC) a federal government agency whose mission is to protect investors; the development of GAAP is under its legal authority

selling expenses expenses related to selling inventory

service revenue a type of revenue earned by a business for providing service to customers, such as interest or fees earned

single-step income statement a format of the income statement in which revenue accounts are grouped together and expense accounts are grouped together, with no further categorizing; also called an *income statement*

sole proprietorship a business that is owned and generally operated by one owner

source documents evidence, such as sales receipts, bills, checks, bank statements, and so on, that proves a transaction happened

special journal a separate book to record regular transactions, such as sales, purchases, cash payments, cash receipts, and payroll

spreadsheet a work sheet prepared using programs like Excel, that can be used to display the trial balances before and after the adjustments are made

statement of cash flows a statement that tracks the sources and uses of cash in a business; also called the *cash flow statement*

statement of owner's equity a formal statement that shows how owner's equity changed during the accounting period

stock a unit of equity in a corporation; also called *shares*

stockholders owners of a corporation who own equity in a corporation in the form of stocks; also called *shareholders*

straight-line method of depreciation produces an average depreciation expense, which is applied each year until the asset is sold or reaches the end of its useful life

subledgers a group of similar accounts used to keep track of specific information related to the general ledger account; also called *subsidiary ledgers*

subsidiary ledgers a group of similar accounts used to keep track of specific information related to the general ledger account; also called *subledgers*

T

T-account a tool used to record transactions and keep the accounting equation balanced; it shows increases to the account on one side and decreases on the other

target cost the maximum allowable cost that manufacturing and other costs cannot exceed

target costing the process of using the anticipated market price to calculate the maximum costs the business can incur

temporary accounts accounts that are brought back to a zero balance at the end of each period; also called *nominal accounts*

time period assumption requires that accounting takes place over specific time periods known as fiscal periods

timeliness information is timely if there is no delay in reporting crucial information

trade discounts the discount from the manufacturer's suggested retail price that is usually given by manufacturers to merchandisers to resell their products

trade name grants exclusive rights to a name under which a company or product trades for commercial purposes, even though its legal or technical name might differ

trademark grants ownership rights for a recognizable symbol or logo

transaction a trade or exchange with someone else in order to receive something of value

trial balance lists all the accounts in the general ledger and their balances at a specific date

U

unadjusted trial balance the trial balance before adjusting entries are made

understandability financial information can be reasonably understood by its users if the users have knowledge of the business and a basic knowledge of accounting

unearned revenue an obligation a business has to provide products or services to a customer

unlimited liability if a business is unable to pay its debts, creditors of the business can force the owner to sell personal assets, suffer any net loss and be personally liable for all financial obligations of the business

useful life the length of time an asset can be used

V

variable costs costs that vary with the amount of products manufactured or services provided

verifiability the ability to see how a company arrived at a certain result; a component of reliability

vertical analysis a method to compare a line item to a base figure within the same year

voucher documentation used to authorize and record a cash payment

voucher system a set of control procedures that a business uses to authorize, record and disburse cash payments

W

wage bracket method tables tables to help employers calculate the amount of federal income tax to withhold

wholesaler a business that buys mostly bulk merchandise from a manufacturer for reselling

working capital the difference between current assets and current liabilities

PHOTO AND INFORMATION CREDITS

INDEX

non-determinable liabilities, 402

nonprofit organizations, 74

non-sufficient funds (NSF) checks, 217, 219

normal balance, 93

note payable, 424

O

objectives

    financial reporting, 77–78

    inventory, 306

    setting, 444

Occupational Safety and Health Administration of 1970 (OSHA), 471

office supplies, 135

opening balance, 12

operating activities, 513

operating cycle, 174

operating expenses, 299

operating line of credit, 402

operations management analysis

    accounts receivable turnover ratio, 508–509

    days' sales in inventory ratio, 506–507

    days' sales outstanding ratio, 507–508

    inventory turnover ratio, 505–506

    overview, 505

Oracle Cloud, 348

other comprehensive income, 488

outsourcing, 248, 465–466

outstanding checks, 221–222

outstanding deposits, 219–220

overdraft, bank, 402

owner's accounts, 35

owner's equity, statement of, 56, 159–160

Oxley, Michael G., 146

P

Pacioli, Luca, 75

paper trail, 321–325

partnerships, 72–73

patents, 384–385

payment terms, 247

payroll liabilities

    as accrued liability, 402–403

    employer contributions, 409

    gross pay to net pay, 403–404

    paying the liabilities, 413–416

    payroll register and records, 410–413

    statutory employee deductions, 404–408

    taxes and benefits, responsibility for, 410

    voluntary employee deductions, 408–409

payroll professionals, 70

pension benefits, 429–430

percentage of total accounts receivable method, 257

periodic inventory system, 280–281

permanent accounts, 161

perpetual inventory system

    defined, 280–281

    periodic system vs., 280–281

    periodic versus, 280–281

    purchase of inventory, 282–290

    sale of inventory, 290–296

personal ethics, 24–25

personal financial information, 483

petty cash

    controls, 236–237

    fund set-up, 231–232

    general ledger posting, 233–236

    overview, 230

plant assets. *See* property, plant and equipment

plant managers, 476

post-closing trial balance, 173

preferred stock, 485

prepaid delivery cost, 290

prepaid expenses, 20–22, 133–137

pricing strategies, 452–457

principles, 81

private accounting, 70

private enterprise, 71

procedures controls, 199–200

Notes